EUROPE

From the Renaissance to Waterloo

EMPEROR MAXIMILIAN I

EUROPE

From the Renaissance to Waterloo

BY

ROBERT ERGANG, Ph.D.

New York University

D. C. HEATH AND COMPANY

BOSTON   NEW YORK   CHICAGO   ATLANTA
DALLAS   SAN FRANCISCO   LONDON

TO

M. M. E.

IN GRATITUDE FOR HER DEVOTION,

ENCOURAGEMENT, AND ASSISTANCE

Preface

THE present has been reached not by a succession of abrupt transitions or jerky catastrophes but by a series of gradual and continuous developments. This writer has accordingly regarded history as the study of developments. The word "revolution" has been used sparingly, except to describe the overthrow of one form of government and the substitution of another. Since it suggests cataclysmic change, it may be misleading even when used in such terms as "Commercial Revolution" and "Agrarian Revolution," which have become established from long usage. The changes denoted by these terms were neither sudden nor complete, but gradual and continuous. Many economic historians have of late used the term "Industrial Revolution" with considerable reluctance. George Unwin states that "we may begin to doubt whether the term Industrial Revolution though useful enough when it was first adopted has not by this time served its turn" since "the revolution has been going on for two centuries, and had been in preparation for two centuries before that." [1] J. H. Clapham in his monumental *Economic History of Modern Britain* does not use the term at all. Nevertheless, after attempting to delimit its meaning, the present writer has retained the term because there is no sufficiently virile substitute for it.

It has been the purpose of the author to include in so far as that was possible the latest findings of historical scholarship. The

---

[1] *Studies in Economic History*, edited by R. H. Tawney (1927), p. 15.

new viewpoints, however, have been included not because they were new, but because, in the opinion of this writer, they were supported by sound historical evidence. Furthermore, the author has endeavored to make the great personalities of history more than mere names by including brief characterizations of them. This is not to say that he is of the persuasion which holds that social progress depends most of all on the periodic appearance of eminent personalities. Far be it from him to regard history as a succession of individual portraits or to attribute any great movement to the influence of a single individual. On the other hand, the importance of personality in history must not be overlooked.

Considerable attention has been given to cultural history, but not to the neglect of the political and economic phases, the effort being to present a well-rounded and fairly complete picture. If literature is the reflection of the interests, convictions, and aspirations of an age, this is equally true of art. In harmony with this view considerable attention has also been paid to the development of science. Undoubtedly there will be some difference of opinion on the distribution of the emphasis, but this is inevitable. As Voltaire put it, a historian "must expect to be blamed for everything he has said and everything he has not said."

Others have contributed much to whatever value this volume may possess. Professor Allan Nevins, editor of the Heath New History Series, greatly improved it in many respects through his acute criticism. Professor Joseph Park of New York University was kind enough to read critically the chapters on English history. The chapters on Russia were carefully read by Professor Alexander Baltzly of New York University. Chapters Five and Twenty-six had the benefit of the criticism of Professor Shepard B. Clough of Columbia University. Professor Leo Gershoy of Sarah Lawrence College generously interrupted his own work to read the chapters on the French Revolution and Napoleon, and Professor Homer A. Watt of New York University was good enough to read some of the sections on literature and culture. My colleagues, Dr. Donald O. Wagner and Dr. Stebelton H. Nulle, at all times have been most unselfish in discussing problems and in giving me the benefit of their sound knowledge. To all I extend sincere gratitude for criticisms, suggestions, and emendations. The responsibility for the shortcomings of the book is entirely my own.

R. E.

Contents

List of Maps

List of Illustrations

List of Illustrations

XV

FACING

Basic Factors in Early Modern History

A WIDE divergence of opinion exists as to when the Middle Ages ended and the modern period began. Different dates have been set according to the different points of view taken by historians. Some have declared that modern history begins with the capture of Constantinople by the Turks in 1453 or with the discovery of America by Columbus in 1492. Others have dated the beginning of modern times from the Protestant Reformation early in the sixteenth century. Among more recent scholars there has been a tendency to push the beginning of the modern period further back. Recently an eminent historian stated that the Middle Ages were definitely over by the middle of the thirteenth century. Most writers, however, have drawn the line somewhere near the end of the fifteenth century.

History cannot be sharply divided into periods as a log is cut into lengths of firewood with a saw. Any abrupt line of division between one period and another is necessarily arbitrary and remote from reality, particularly in a movement that is so complex as the development of western civilization. The process of change from one period to another is gradual and continuous. One age or period emerges slowly, almost imperceptibly, from the preceding one. Changes take place at different times in the various spheres of human interest and activity. Therefore, instead of setting a specific date for the end of medieval times, it is perhaps less arbitrary to usher in the modern period with a series of movements, all of which helped to give modern civilization a distinctive character. Some of these movements developed earlier than others, but all were well on their way to maturity by the second half of the fifteenth century.

Moreover, by this time most of the characteristic institutions of the Middle Ages were declining. The two empires which had shared the domination of Europe were both tottering on their foundations. The Eastern Empire was to expire at the hands of the Turks three years after the middle of the century; but the Holy Roman Empire was to linger on until the beginning of the nineteenth century. During the last centuries of its existence, however, it was to carry little weight in international diplomacy as a political unity, for it was actually an assemblage of more or less independent states with the emperor as their nominal head.

Medieval feudalism, which for centuries had imposed some semblance of order on western Europe, was also losing its force. Although feudal standards continued to determine the social order, the military importance of feudalism was being undermined by the rise of mercenary armies and by the invention of more effective weapons than those possessed by the feudal knights. Furthermore, the oath of homage and fealty, the feudal tie which had bound the vassal to his lord, was losing its moral force or was being replaced by an allegiance to the national sovereign. Also in other respects the feudal system was breaking down. The transmuting of feudal services into money payments not only made the vassal less subject to the lord's will and pleasure but also helped to demolish the rigid manorial system. Through the substitution of money rentals for personal labor and payments in kind, the villeins of western Europe were slowly freeing themselves from the shackles of serfdom, and many freedmen were becoming tenant farmers, "sharecroppers" (*métayers*), and peasant proprietors.

Another medieval institution which had outlived much of its usefulness was the craft gild. Instead of changing with the times, the craft gilds had, so to speak, frozen in their molds. Over retail trade they continued to exercise considerable control, but the export trade since the thirteenth century was being absorbed more and more by individual capitalists or by organizations of capitalist merchants. Even in the local trade the influence of the craft gilds was being reduced by associations of journeymen and by capitalist manufacturers.

Furthermore, by the middle of the fifteenth century the Roman Catholic Church, which had so long stood not only for righteousness but also for the solidarity of Latin Christendom, which had civilized the barbarians, imposed restraints on medieval warfare, and maintained a unity of faith, had lost much of its spiritual influence and cosmopolitan character. The papacy, having reached the pinnacle of its power in the thirteenth century, had to submit to a curtailment of its claims by the rising national states in the fourteenth and fifteenth centuries. It also suffered a general loss of prestige. The transfer of the Holy See to Avignon in 1309 for a period of almost seventy years was in itself disastrous to papal influence, for it broke the spell which the name of Rome as a symbol of universal power still exercised over the minds of both the learned and the vulgar. During the Great Schism (1378–1417) the prestige of the papacy suffered still further when first two and then three popes competed with each other for the allegiance of the faithful. Though the schism was ended by the Council of Constance (1414–1418), neither this council nor the others that met in the fifteenth century succeeded in purging the Church of the evils which were afflicting it. Scholasticism, having made its contributions to theology and philosophy, was approaching the point of sterility. The schoolmen still disputed with fervor, but the subjects of dispute were largely of a trivial nature. To quote Francis Bacon, they did little but "spin laborious webs of learning out of no great quantity of matter and infinite agitation of wit."

While the medieval world was disintegrating, new forces, new motives, new factors, were at work producing what we call the modern world. One factor which gave a fresh direction to society was the rise of the middle class. In the Middle Ages society was divided into three main elements: the clergy, the nobility, and the third estate; but before the medieval period ended, the clergy were losing much of their influence, the power of the nobility was declining, and a new social class was rising to importance. Because this class developed, so to speak, between the titled nobility on the one hand and the peasantry and small artisans on the other, it is called the middle class. In France this class was termed *bourgeoisie*, a name which gradually came into use to designate also the middle class of other countries. The lines which separated it from the nobility at one end and from the small shopkeepers at the other were not distinct; yet the members of the middle class, generally speaking, did develop a set of ideals and a way of life which held them apart from the other classes. This new class had originally been composed of those who made the most of the opportunities offered by the revival of commerce during the period of the Crusades. It was, in other words, the money-making class or "that part of the community to which money is the primary condition and the primary instrument of life." [1] As such it included the merchant, in a broad sense of the word, and also the capitalist manufacturer. The early members of this class had risen from the peasantry; but later it received reinforcements from the titled nobility as well—except in Germany and Spain, where it was regarded as dishonorable for a nobleman to be affiliated with commerce. Spurred on by the desire to increase their wealth and improve their social standing, the members of the middle class were ready to make the most of every opportunity for economic or social advancement. Hence the entire economic expansion of the early modern period is in a sense an expression of the development of the middle class. Furthermore, from the middle class came most of the writers who were instrumental in founding the national literatures of the modern period, and many of the scientists responsible for the development of modern science. In time members of the bourgeoisie also obtained positions of political influence and the middle class generally assumed a rôle of increasing importance in political life. In short, it is about the middle class that the forward movement from the Middle Ages into the modern period largely centers.

In the political sphere the factor which helped most to differentiate the modern period from the Middle Ages was the rise of the national state. As the Middle Ages waned the national idea was gradually conquering the idea of the unity of western Christendom. Unified national states, ruled by more or less absolute monarchs, were dividing Europe into sharply separated political groups. Not only were the nobles reduced to impotence in these states, but even the Church tended to split up into national sections. This national consolidation in turn ushered in an age of national and dynastic rivalries. Great or small, each of the states

[1] R. H. Gretton, *The English Middle Class* (1917), p. 8.

of Europe struggled to achieve influence and leadership. Whenever one state showed signs of becoming too powerful, coalitions were formed to preserve the "balance of power." The period of international rivalries and coalitions is generally dated from the expedition of Charles VIII of France into Italy in 1494. No sooner had the French king made himself master of the kingdom of Naples than he found himself confronted by a coalition of powers organized to curb his ambition. In the period which followed, the national rivalries led to a long succession of wars which often involved more than two powers.

The basic economic factor which helped to transform the medieval into the modern world was the expansion of commerce. The later centuries of the Middle Ages had already seen the emergence of large-scale commerce, but during the early modern period not only was the scale of commerce to increase tremendously, but the sphere of commerce was also to expand until it became world-wide. The two events primarily responsible for this commercial expansion were the finding of an all-water route to the East and the discovery of the New World. Both widened immensely the stage upon which modern history was to present its drama. Other results were the change of the center of trade from the Mediterranean to the Atlantic, the scramble for oversea possessions, the foundation of oversea colonies, and the development of sea power as a means of protecting both trade and colonists. Furthermore, capitalism became a factor of increasing importance in commerce, and great trading companies were organized to exploit markets and oversea possessions. Gradually a change also took place in the nature of commerce. Foreign trade in the Middle Ages had been largely a trade in luxuries for the rich, but during the modern period it tended increasingly to include articles of everyday consumption for the common man, with the result that it absorbed the activities of an ever larger proportion of the population.

At the same time that a new world of commerce was being opened, fresh tendencies were becoming manifest in the world of the intellect. Of basic importance in this change was the growth of a secular spirit in contradistinction to the ascetic "otherworldly" temper of the Middle Ages. Life here on earth began to take on a value for itself instead of being only the means of achieving eternal bliss. Nature was no longer regarded as evil and man as essentially sinful. Because the ancients had stressed the importance of this life, the goodness and dignity of man and the joy of living, an intense enthusiasm developed for the civilization of ancient Greece and Rome; more particularly for the literature which mirrored that civilization. These writings in turn gave a further impetus to secularism. Gradually culture became more secular in spirit, secular trends developed in education, and art became more natural. Moreover, the growing interest in nature and in man as a citizen of this world stimulated scientific inquiry. This phase, however, developed more slowly than the others, for the age of experimental science did not really begin until the seventeenth century.

In the field of religion the central factor was the rise of anticlerical sentiment in the fourteenth and fifteenth centuries. In most countries of western Europe protests could be heard against the abuses in the Church and against the exactions of the papal courts—protests which found a wide circulation in popular literature. Familiar examples of such anticlerical literature are Boccaccio's *Decameron* and Chaucer's *Canterbury Tales*. There were also a number of anticlerical movements, of which the Wycliffite movement in England and the Hussite movement in Bohemia are the most outstanding. At the same time, the governments of the rising national states were chafing under the yoke of papal authority. Already in the fourteenth century Parliament passed a series of statutes designed to limit the papal authority in England, and in the following century anticlerical legislation became effective in most other countries of western Europe. In the sixteenth century this anticlerical sentiment was to culminate in a revolt against the Church, and the establishment of the Protestant churches.

All of these factors which ushered in the modern period may be grouped under six headings: the rise of the national state, the intensification of the secular spirit, the expansion of Europe into America and Asia, the rise of modern capitalism, the founding of the Protestant churches, and the rise of modern science. In all these movements an element of major importance was the rise of the middle class.

CHAPTER ONE

The Rise of National States

FROM FEUDALISM TO THE NATIONAL STATE

THE political history of modern Europe deals primarily with the national state. In ancient times the city-state was the predominant type, later to be superseded by the world-state as represented by the Roman Empire. The concept of universal rule which the old Roman Empire had developed was preserved in the Middle Ages by both the Roman Catholic Church and the Holy Roman Empire. Theoretically the whole of Christendom was regarded as one unit ruled jointly by the pope and the emperor. True, the original Roman Empire had been torn in two by the barbaric invasions, so that there was an Eastern Empire besides the Holy Roman Empire, and also a Greek Catholic Church besides the Roman Church. Nevertheless, both the Roman Catholic Church and the Holy Roman Empire clung tenaciously to the idea of universality. The former did not relinquish the idea of an eventual union of the two churches; and the latter, regarding itself as heir of the imperial traditions of ancient Rome, continued to lay claim to world-wide dominion long after it had lost all practical power and influence.

Because of the influence of the Church and the empire the idea of the oneness of Christendom not only was placed in the foreground of ecclesiastical and political theory; it also permeated the other phases of medieval culture and civilization. Learning,

sponsored by the Church, was pervaded by a spirit of universality. With Latin as the common language of learning, medieval
writings could be, and were, read throughout western Europe.
Peter Lombard's *Book of Sentences* and the *Summa Theologica* of
Thomas Aquinas, for example, were the property of all Latin
Christendom. From a social point of view Europe was divided
horizontally into classes rather than vertically into national
groups. The nobles of France had much more in common with
the nobles of Germany than with the lower classes of their own
country. Knighthood rested on a code of honor and on ceremonies observed throughout western Europe. A certain degree of
unity was also to be found in the realm of economics. In all
countries of western Europe the gild system was much the same,
often to minute details. Thus Europe possessed a spiritual unity
that is without counterpart in modern times. National sentiment,
which is a dominating factor in modern Europe, had not yet
sharply separated the national groups.

The practical units of medieval po-
litical life were small, and authority was everywhere divided and
dispersed. Men lived and were governed in princedoms, feudal
states, or communes. It has been estimated that in France alone
the number of political units in the tenth century exceeded ten
thousand. After the collapse of the central government in the
early Middle Ages, the feudal lords had assumed the responsibility of government in their respective feudal states. The emperor's claim to universal rule notwithstanding, each feudal lord
stood at the head of a more or less independent state. Moreover,
the medieval towns were largely independent political and economic units. Each town, like each seigniory, had its laws, its
courts, its local customs, its treasury, and its army. The inhabitant
of one town was regarded as a foreigner in a neighboring town,
and town corporations carried on negotiations with one another
as do the great powers of the present time. A citizen of one town
could sell his merchandise in another only by special permission
and after paying a duty on his goods, like the duty on foreign
imports today. In short, Europe was divided into a large number
of small political units, the inhabitants of which were moved
chiefly by purely local considerations.

The later Middle Ages, however, saw western Europe in the

throes of a great national movement. On the one hand, the national idea was breaking up the theoretical unity of Christendom; on the other, the disjointed political fragments were being fused into more or less homogeneous states. In these new national states the king was the focus of power, for in his person all authority was increasingly concentrating. Slowly, and often painfully, he brought the feudal states under royal control and added their territory to the royal demesnes. The governmental functions which had been exercised by various individuals and groups when the central power was weak were gradually being absorbed by the national authorities; in other words, by the king and his bureaucracy. Thus the national government took over the administration of justice throughout the kingdom, a function which had been exercised largely by the feudal barons. So, too, the national government assumed the regulation of trade, which had formerly been the affair of the chartered towns or the gilds. Furthermore, the organization of military protection, which had been largely a local matter, became more and more the function of the central government, particularly of the monarch. The monarch also gained the right to collect taxes from all the people of his state, and not only from his immediate vassals, though this right was in some instances restricted, as by Parliament in England. In short, national governments under strong monarchs were absorbing the old feudal states both as to territory and as to functions.

In this process of unification the monarch was enabled to overcome the power of the remaining feudal nobles only with the aid of the rising middle class. During the early Middle Ages the feudal nobility, because of their wealth and the military service they rendered, had been the most powerful class in the state. Their wealth consisted of land, and in time of war they fought as armored knights. However, with the rise of money economy and the expansion of trade the middle class had grown to importance through the acquisition of capital, so that the landed property of the feudal nobility was no longer the only source of wealth. Since the middle class found internal peace, security, and the uniform reign of law necessary for the further accumulation of wealth and the further expansion of commerce, it rallied about the king as the only leader able to curb the turbulence of the nobility and secure for the mass of the people an orderly government. The support which the bourgeoisie gave the monarch freed him from his dependence on the feudal noble for both court and military service. With the money he drew from the wealthy middle class in taxes or borrowed from the middle-class bankers the monarch could employ a staff of officials to carry the royal law and the royal administration of justice to every part of his realm, thus allowing him to dispense with the feudal administrative system which had been so essential earlier in the Middle Ages. Moreover, with the hard cash from the royal treasury he was able to maintain a standing army which freed him from dependence upon the military service of the feudal barons.

Another important factor in the rise of strong centralized monarchies, and conversely in the decline of the military prestige of the feudal knight, was the invention of gunpowder and its use in warfare. Just when gunpowder was invented, by whom and under what circumstances, is not known and probably never will be. The Chinese had long known how to make an inflammable or "fiery" powder which they used for pyrotechnical purposes. During the early Middle Ages alchemists or chemists devoted much time to the preparation of what was known as "Greek fire," containing such ingredients as sulphur, pitch, resin, oils, and bituminous earths. The principal purpose of these compounds was incendiary, not the discharge of projectiles. They were employed to ignite wooden buildings and fortifications. As there were many combinations of Greek fire, one or the other probably lacked only saltpeter to make it a detonating powder. Roger Bacon (1214–1294) is by many falsely regarded as the inventor of gunpowder. But gunpowder, it seems, was already known in Bacon's time, for he himself refers to its use as an explosive in children's toys. Such knowledge of it as Bacon had was most likely derived from other sources than personal experiment. Whatever may have been its use in the thirteenth century, there is no doubt that it was used to hurl projectiles in the fourteenth. Metal cannon and iron balls were cast at least as early as 1325 in Italy, and shortly thereafter in the other countries of Europe. As artillery gradually became more effective, the feudal knight lost entirely the military prestige which had already been undermined by the introduction of the long bow into warfare. Resistance to a king who had artillery and a standing army became increasingly difficult, for the feudal castles which had formerly been regarded as impregnable now crumbled under the cannon-shot.

Simultaneously with the growth of the internal organization of the national state and the concentration of power in the royal hands, national feeling became more intense. Some degree of national feeling had already been stimulated during the Crusades when the contact of peoples who spoke different languages gave rise to rivalries and antipathies. During the fourteenth and fifteenth centuries this feeling grew stronger. The Hundred Years' War (1337–1453) in particular did much to excite a national feeling among both the French and the English. On the eve of the sixteenth century national rivalries had become so intense that they ushered in an era of international wars. Diplomatic relations between the states also became more highly organized. Whereas formerly representatives had been sent to other states only on special occasions, they now became permanent residents of foreign states so that they might detect any designs against the state they represented. Thus arose the modern diplomatic system. Moreover, as rules were laid down for the settlement of disputes between nations, international law came into being.

Within a given population national feeling led to the fostering of national customs, tastes, traditions, beliefs, and pastimes. Poets began to exalt patriotism as the supreme virtue. Vernacular languages which had long been spoken were elevated to the position of national languages, replacing Latin as the literary language. In Italy the Florentine dialect, in England Saxon or Old English, in France the Langue d'Oïl of northern France,[1] in Spain the Castilian dialect, and in Germany the dialect of Saxony, finally outstripped the other local or native dialects for the honor of becoming the national literary language. As early as the fourteenth century Dante wrote in Italian and Chaucer in English. Soon great writers were to produce masterpieces in all the national languages of Europe. In short, separate national cultures were forming.

The entire process of national consolidation, which included territorial unification, centralization of governmental functions, growth of national feeling, and rise of separate national cultures,

---

[1] The Langue d'Oïl as distinguished from the Langue d'Oc or Provençal of the south. The terms arose from the two words for "yes," *oc* in the south and *oïl* in the north.

took place in the different states of Europe at different times, in different ways, and with different results. But by the second decade of the fifteenth century the national idea had developed to a point where it was recognized even in the Catholic Church, when the Council of Constance (1414–1418) adopted a method of voting by nations instead of by individuals. In the countries of western Europe the half-century from 1450 to 1500 saw a remarkable growth of national unification and royal absolutism. By 1500 Spain, Portugal, France, and England, it may be said, were full-grown nations in the modern sense. The history of two countries, however, stands in complete contrast to this trend toward consolidation. In Italy and in Germany the many local rulers were strengthening their power; in other words, the medieval political disunion was being established more firmly. While Germany was united in name, Italy had not even a nominal unity. Both were destined to wait until the nineteenth century for the unity which the other states attained by the sixteenth.

SPAIN AND PORTUGAL

Foremost among the "new monarchies" at the end of the fifteenth century was Spain. The history of Spain for centuries preceding the fifteenth was primarily a struggle for supremacy between Christians and Moslems. In 711 the Moslem leader Tarik, at the head of an army, crossed the straits of Africa and landed on the giant rock to which he gave his name (Gibraltar, from Gebel-el-Tarik, the mountain of Tarik). In subsequent decades the Moslems succeeded in conquering most of Spain, but the Christians managed to retain their hold on the northern frontier. After several centuries the Moorish strength began to decline and the Christians started to expand southward. Progress was often slow and at the cost of much blood, but it was on the whole steady. Gradually the Christian rulers of the north and northeast extended their dominion into the central areas and eventually into the southern districts. By the end of the thirteenth century Moslem power was reduced to the kingdom of Granada.

Progress had also been made in the direction of a more unified Spain by the consolidation of the various Christian states into four larger ones: Castile, Aragon, Portugal, and Navarre. The first, embracing about two-thirds of the Peninsula, included within its confines the northwest, the west (except Portugal), and

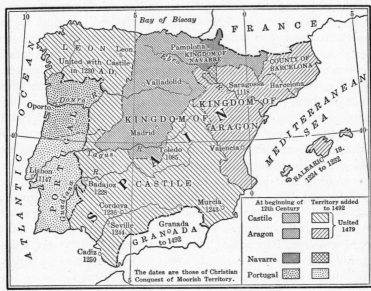

The Unification of Spain

the central portions; Aragon, occupying the northeast and east, extended southward from the Pyrenees almost to Cartagena; Portugal, comprising less than one-fifth of the Peninsula, lay along the western coast; Navarre, a small mountain kingdom, included territory north and south of the Pyrenees, and was controlled by the king of France.

A decisive step toward the political unification of Spain was the marriage in 1469 of Isabella, heiress to the crown of Castile, and Ferdinand, heir to the crown of Aragon. True, this marriage effected a union of the two kingdoms only in the persons of the sovereigns, for the marriage treaty stated that each kingdom was to retain its own laws, institutions, and tariff frontiers. Nevertheless, it established a common policy in the foreign affairs of both states, and to the nations of Europe it signalized the entrance of a new power into European affairs. Thus, for purposes of external policy, Castile and Aragon were Spain. In addition, the marriage made for a common policy in the internal affairs of both states, thereby preparing the way for a more effective union at a later time. Altogether, it ushered in a new era in the history of the Iberian Peninsula.

The object of the internal policy of the new sovereigns [1] was plain enough. They were resolved to centralize all political authority in themselves and bring about religious unity in their dominions. Their first advance in this direction was the restoration of the prestige of the crown. As a result of the laxity of its preceding ruler, Henry IV, Castile was in a state of political confusion which in some parts bordered on anarchy. The nobles, in contempt of existing laws, acted like independent lords, terrorizing the people of their respective districts into submission and collecting the royal taxes for themselves. Lesser subjects, taking the nobles as their example, followed a similar course of lawlessness. The country was infested with bands of robbers who attacked travelers and pillaged entire villages without fear of punishment, making the highways unsafe and interfering with the peaceful development of commerce. The general confusion extended also to the coinage, which had been adulterated by the preceding sovereigns. It has been computed that no fewer than one hundred fifty mints were issuing coins in Castile at the accession of Isabella. Finally much of the currency became so worthless that the peasants refused payment in cash for their products, preferring to carry on trade by the primitive method of barter.

This state of affairs called for vigorous action on the part of the monarchs. For the restoration of law and order an instrument was ready at hand. Since the thirteenth century Castile had possessed an organization called *La Santa Hermandad* (Holy Brotherhood), founded to maintain peace in the various districts and punish all evildoers summarily. It was, in short, a sort of constabulary force, composed principally of those interested in the expansion of trade and industry. This organization was revived and enlarged by Ferdinand and Isabella to serve both as the nucleus of a standing army and as a police force to hunt down bandits and highwaymen. Later a Holy Brotherhood was organized in Aragon also. So well did this organization do its work that within two decades it was no longer needed for the enforcement of law and order.

While they were restoring order, the Spanish rulers also made use of the opportunity to reduce the power of the great nobles.

---

[1] Isabella succeeded to the throne of Castile in 1474, and Ferdinand became king of Aragon in 1479. Though Ferdinand shared the queen's authority in Castile, she did not share his in Aragon.

They revoked the pensions and the extravagant grants of land which the preceding rulers had made to the nobility of Castile. Refractory nobles were forced either to submit or to leave the country. The taxes which had been diverted were restored to the royal treasury, and the castles which had served as strongholds of brigandage and of resistance to the royal authority were demolished. The sovereigns also eliminated many nobles from the administration by filling their places in the councils with members of the middle class. It was through the various councils, centering in the royal council, that the crown exercised its vast powers of administration, legislation, and justice. There were assemblies, both general and local, called cortes, in which sat representatives of the clergy, the nobility, and the cities and towns, but the cortes had no legislative power. Theoretically they were merely consultative organs, except that they had the right to vote taxes and approve subsidies requested by the crown. Since the expanding commerce of Castile multiplied the royal revenue thirtyfold during the three decades after 1474, the Spanish sovereigns found it necessary to summon a general cortes only on rare occasions.

Besides establishing the authority of the crown in their various domains, Ferdinand and Isabella also did much to encourage trade and industry. In Castile, for example, they carried out a much needed reform of the currency. The adulterated coinage which had undermined commercial credit was replaced by coins of a standard value, and the right of coinage was restricted to the five royal mints. Commerce was also aided by the improvement of roads, the construction of bridges, the holding of fairs, and the abolition of some internal customs duties. So great was the immediate expansion of trade in Castile that between the years 1477 and 1482 the royal revenue from customs duties increased nearly sixfold. The discovery of America, which was the most important event of the reign of Ferdinand and Isabella, led to the development in Spain [1] of the national economic policy called mercantilism, which subjected industry, trade, and agriculture to comprehensive regulation. A number of such regulations and prohibitions had been inscribed in the statute books by their predecessors, but Ferdinand and Isabella may be said to have laid the

---

[1] Actually the Spanish colonies in the New World were owned and governed by Castile. For a discussion of mercantilism see pp. 141–145.

broader foundations of Spanish mercantilism. Among other things, they attempted to enforce the laws against the exportation of specie, to limit trade with the colonies to the mother country, to build a strong merchant marine, to discourage colonial industry for the benefit of industry in Spain, and to protect home industries by tariffs on foreign products.

The policy of Ferdinand and Isabella was as firm in religious as in political matters. In questions of orthodoxy they deferred humbly to the pope, and so distinguished themselves as champions of the Catholic faith that Pope Alexander VI bestowed on them the title, "The Catholic Sovereigns." Nevertheless, they firmly circumscribed the pope's power over the Spanish Church. When he endeavored to appoint a foreigner to a Spanish benefice, for example, they opposed him so staunchly that he was forced to give way. Throughout their reign the Catholic Sovereigns jealously guarded the royal prerogative in ecclesiastical preferment. It was their purpose to make the Church a prop for the throne. Both believed, as Ferdinand put it, that religion is to the state what blood is to the human body. Hence they labored zealously to purify "the blood of the state" through the extermination of heresy and through the conversion of non-Christians to the Catholic faith.

An important advance was made toward political and religious unity in Spain when the Moors were brought to complete subjection. Confined to the kingdom of Granada, the Moors at the time of Ferdinand and Isabella were no longer an active menace. They occupied a rich territory, however, which the Catholic Sovereigns desired to add to their domains. The contest between the Spaniards and the Moors for possession of this territory continued ten years before the last Moorish stronghold surrendered, in 1492. This final victory, terminating more than seven centuries of Moslem rule in the Iberian Peninsula, was greeted throughout Christendom with great rejoicing. By many it was hailed as counterbalancing the loss of Constantinople to the Turks in 1453. To the Catholic Sovereigns it meant the annexation to Castile of an extensive territory noted for the fertility of its soil.

By the treaty, Ferdinand and Isabella guaranteed the Moors free exercise of their religion, but the intolerance of the age did not long permit them to enjoy this freedom. Pressure was soon exerted to compel them to embrace Christianity. When those of a certain district in Granada rose against this forced conversion, their action was interpreted as nullifying the terms of the treaty, and in 1502 a royal decree ordered all Moslems of Castile to accept Christianity or leave the country. Many decided to leave, despite the harsh restrictions upon the possessions and destinations of exiles. The greater number, however, remained and outwardly accepted Christianity. Many of these "converted" Moors (called Moriscos) were subsequently arrested on suspicion of heresy and tried by the Inquisition, because it was believed that their conversion was not sincere. In Aragon the Moors were permitted to remain another century.

Meanwhile further progress toward religious unity had been made by the expulsion of the Jews. In the case of the Moors the decree of conversion or expulsion was to some extent the logical outcome of centuries of fighting in the contest for political supremacy; but no similar excuse existed for expelling the Jews. The expulsion of the latter rested more immediately on the desire of Ferdinand and Isabella to establish religious unity. Popular sentiment against the Jew, which had been growing steadily, strengthened their hands. The chief reason for this hostility was probably the obstinacy with which the Jews resisted conversion to Christianity. But there were economic reasons as well. Restrictive laws had compelled large numbers to act as money-lenders, practicing a usury which was condemned by the Church, while others became tax-farmers. Because of these activities, in which many amassed large fortunes, the Jews were bitterly denounced for greed and rapacity. In 1391 popular hostility burst forth in a series of attacks upon the Jewish quarters of many large cities of Castile. Frenzied mobs, their passions whipped up by zealous anti-Semites, massacred thousands of Jews and pillaged their houses. Thousands of other Jews sought safety by submitting to baptism, and were called Conversos, Neo-Christians, or Maranos. Most of these Maranos were, of course, pseudo-converts who outwardly conformed to the practices of the Catholic Church and filled their homes with crucifixes and statues of saints, but secretly observed the Jewish laws and customs.

When this crypto-Judaism became known, zealots for the Catholic faith demanded its extermination. In 1478 a group of Dominican friars attached to the royal court at Seville succeeded in obtaining from Pope Sixtus IV a bull authorizing Ferdinand and Isabella to establish the Inquisition, a tribunal for the detection and punishment of heresy. It remained only to obtain the permission of the Catholic Sovereigns for the establishment of this tribunal. To this end the Dominican group repeatedly represented to Ferdinand how effective the Inquisition would be in purging Spain of the stigma of heresy. An added incentive for its establishment— and this was of no small importance to Ferdinand—was the fact that through it he could lay his hands on the great wealth many Maranos possessed, for two-thirds of the property of a person convicted of heresy was to be confiscated for the royal treasury, the other third going to the inquisitors. Hence the king quickly gave his consent. It was not so easy to gain Isabella's consent for the establishment of a tribunal she knew to be odious to many of her subjects and to a large part of the clergy. But finally she gave way before the solicitations of her avaricious husband and the Dominican group. Thus was established in 1480 the dread Spanish Inquisition, which became an instrument for enforcing civil despotism as well as for exterminating heresy. All its fury was at once directed against the Maranos. So unrestrained was the zeal of the inquisitors that the pope, though he had permitted the establishment of the Inquisition, felt constrained to protest. In a letter to Isabella, dated February 23, 1483, he even hints that the zeal against the Maranos was motivated "by ambition and greed for earthly possessions" rather than by zeal for the faith.

Far from giving heed to the pope's protest, the inquisitors continued their inhuman treatment of "heretics." Moreover, they sought to force the remaining Jews and Moors to accept Christianity. Heresy, they protested to the Catholic Sovereigns, cannot be checked so long as there are unconverted Jews who seduce the Maranos from Christianity. Convinced by these arguments, the Spanish rulers drew up an edict against the Jews but, because they were busy with the conquest of Granada, postponed its execution until the last Moorish stronghold had been taken. Then in March, 1492, they issued the decree that all Jews of whatever age or sex must, within a period of four months, either accept Christianity or leave Spain. The penalty for all who remained in Spain was death and confiscation of property. How many chose exile in preference to conversion it is impossible to state with certainty.[1] Whatever the exact number, Spain could ill afford to lose so many of its most industrious citizens.

In foreign affairs Ferdinand's goal was to make Spain predominant in Europe. To achieve this end he often had recourse to unscrupulous means. So notorious was his duplicity that Machiavelli used him as an example of hypocrisy, stating in *The Prince:* "There is no better instance of a policy of hypocrisy." It is related that when Louis XII of France accused Ferdinand of having deceived him twice, the latter retorted, "The drunkard! He lies! I have cheated him more than ten times." The great obstacle in Spain's path to supremacy was France. Hence Ferdinand used all his skill in diplomacy to isolate France from the other European powers. His first overt move was apparently in the direction of a friendly alliance with France. When Charles VIII was about to embark on his expedition into Italy, Ferdinand agreed not to assist the enemies of France or enter into marriage alliances with the ruling houses of Austria, England, or Naples. Hardly had Charles taken Naples when Ferdinand proceeded to enter into an alliance with the pope, the emperor, Venice, and Milan which forced the French king to cease his conquest. Having succeeded in hindering Charles's designs, Ferdinand came to a secret understanding with him whereby both would share in the division of Naples. After Louis XII ascended the French throne in 1498, war broke out over the division, and when it ended Ferdinand was in possession of the whole of Naples. The agreement concerning the marriage alliances he similarly disregarded. As early as 1496, Juana, daughter of the Catholic Sovereigns, was affianced to Philip the Fair, son of Emperor Maximilian. By another marriage alliance, arranged with England, Catherine of Aragon was first married to Arthur, the eldest son of Henry VII, and when he died to Henry's second son, who later became Henry VIII.

The death of Isabella in 1504 ultimately placed all the states

[1] Whereas the Spanish historian Mariana estimated the number to have been 800,000, Prescott, on the statement of a contemporary Jewish rabbi, gives the number as 160,000. The Spanish historian Altamira calculates the number to have been 165,000, while the Jewish historian Graetz places it at 300,000. Probably the most convincing estimate is that of Isidore Loeb, another Jewish historian, who (in *Revue des Études Juives*, vol. 14, pp. 162–183) attempts to show that the total number of Jews expelled from Spain in 1492 and from Portugal in 1497 was about 165,000. The number of those who remained to be baptized he estimates as 50,000.

of the Iberian Peninsula except Portugal under the rule of Ferdinand. By the terms of Isabella's will her daughter Juana was named as her successor, with the proviso that Ferdinand should govern in case she proved unable. As her increasing mental instability incapacitated Juana for the task of ruling, Ferdinand assumed the rule. For a time it was contested by his son-in-law, Philip the Fair, but Philip's death in 1506 left Ferdinand sole regent. Ferdinand himself died in 1516. Shortly before his demise he took advantage of the difficulties of Louis XII of France, the ally and protector of the king of Navarre, to overrun the part of Navarre which lay south of the Pyrenees, and to add it to the Spanish domains. Thus all of the Iberian Peninsula except Portugal was united under one rule.

The history of Portugal begins during the struggle of the Christian states of the Iberian Peninsula against the Moors. In 1095 Alphonso VI, king of Leon, gave to a certain Count Henry of Lorraine, who had come to aid in the conflict, the western districts of Oporto. The territory was held as a fief of Leon, but the successive counts of Portugal laid down a policy of complete separation from Leon and Castile, and adhered to it with such success that the Portuguese ruler was recognized as king about the middle of the twelfth century by both the ruler of Leon and the pope. During the series of wars which followed to prevent the absorption of Portugal by Castile and to conquer the southern part of Portugal (the ancient Lusitania) from the Moors, a feeling of local patriotism was engendered and the outlines of the nation were definitely fixed. Hemmed in on all sides by the states which later comprised Spain, Portugal turned toward the sea in the fifteenth century. Sea captains sent out by Prince Henry, the son of John I (1382–1433), began that exploration of the west coast of Africa which finally resulted in the discovery of the Cape route to the East and the establishment of the Portuguese Empire. Though national sentiment sharply separated the two states, Portugal followed the lead of Spain in also setting up the Inquisition and expelling the Jews and Moriscos.

FRANCE

Next to Spain, France at the end of the fifteenth century was the most important national state of Europe. The beginnings of the French monarchy had been humble, but through the centuries the king had gradually increased his royal domain and his power by absorbing some of the great feudal lordships of what is now France. During the Hundred Years' War the English had threatened to conquer all France and add it to the English possessions. Ultimately, however, Joan of Arc had inspired the French with a fervid enthusiasm which enabled them to drive back the English until only Calais remained to them of their former French possessions. During this long struggle national sentiment and absolute monarchy were born in France. The presence of the English on French soil, the common hardships, miseries, and victories of the war, intensified national feeling until Frenchmen began to regard themselves as one nation. The new sentiment centered in Charles VII, who while leading his people to victory did not overlook the opportunity to strengthen his own power. In 1439, with the permission of the States-General, he established a national standing army. To finance this force, he was permitted to levy a new national tax, the *taille*.[1] Though meant only as a special war tax, the taille was collected by the king after the war ended in 1453; in fact, it remained the principal source of royal revenue until the French Revolution. Having thus acquired control of the purse, and having gained a standing army, a most effective instrument in the development of royal absolutism, Charles VII was able to lay the foundations upon which his son and successor, Louis XI, reared the structure of absolute monarchy.

During the reign of Louis XI (1461–1483), who possessed considerable practical sagacity, great tenacity of purpose, and a flair for intrigue, the process of French unification was hastened to such an extent that he has been hailed as "the founder of the national state in France." His aims at the time of his accession were to round out his territories and to consolidate his power by centralizing the administration. In both he achieved a large measure of success. When the great nobles of France realized, soon after Louis became king, just what he intended to do, they organized a league in an effort to stop the growth of French unity and the absolute monarchy. It was their desire to remain petty independent sovereigns like the great feudal lords of the Middle Ages.

[1] A tax on landed property from which nobles and clergymen were exempt. Other sources of the royal income were the *aide* (a tax on the price of all merchandise) and the *gabelle du sel*, or monopoly of the sale of salt.

All the powerful houses of France, with few exceptions, joined the league, and it seemed that the country would be overwhelmed by civil dissension. But the fact that the majority of the lesser gentry and of the bourgeoisie lent their support to the king finally enabled him to break up the league.

The most formidable antagonist of Louis XI was his vassal Charles the Bold, who, besides the duchy of Burgundy, possessed Franche-Comté (the county of Burgundy), Flanders, Artois, Picardy, and the Netherlands. To these possessions Charles hoped to add enough territory to form a "middle kingdom" between France and the Holy Roman Empire. His ambitions, however, brought him into conflict with the Swiss, and Charles himself was killed fighting against them in 1477. As the only heir of Charles the Bold was a daughter, Mary of Burgundy, Louis XI made the most of the death of his opponent by seizing Burgundy, Picardy, and Artois. Other provinces which Louis added to the royal domain were Roussillon, Provence, Anjou, and Maine. Of the great feudal lordships only Brittany remained at his death to be absorbed into the royal domain, and that was added by his son, Charles VIII, through marriage to the heiress of Brittany.

As ruler of France, Louis XI was satisfied with nothing less than absolute obedience. He was relentless in weakening or destroying the nobles who would not bow to his will. By the use of craft, force, and tyranny he crushed the remnants of feudal independence so completely that his reign may be said to mark the end of feudal France. After his death France had no princely or vassal house powerful enough to challenge the authority of the king.

While repressing the great nobles, Louis did much to aid the bourgeoisie whose support made his absolutism possible. In return for that support he not only chose his ministers and the general personnel of the administration from the middle class, but he also endeavored to promote the bourgeois interests by fostering industry and commerce. In industry he sought to make France more self-sufficient by encouraging the manufacture of silk and wool. In commerce it was his aim to free French merchants from their subordination to the leaders of the Italian states. To this end he urged his subjects to build ships, and for a time he permitted spices, silks, and other Levantine products to be imported only in the galleys of France. He further aided French commerce by the improvement of harbors and river channels and by the abolition of many toll barriers on the rivers. He also planned to establish a uniform system of weights and measures and a general code of laws, but in this field his hopes failed to materialize. In general, his policies foreshadowed those of the later mercantilists.

So much was Louis XI the "bourgeois king" that he favored the interests of the middle class at the expense of the artisans and peasantry. For the masses his reign was one of oppressive taxation. The cost of the wars and the sums he spent as bribes more than doubled the tax burdens. It is therefore not amazing that the masses hated Louis, regarding him as the principal source of their woes. When he died in 1483, the news was received with open rejoicing.

Nevertheless, the reign of Louis XI marks an epoch in the history of France. He vastly extended the frontiers of the country and made the foundations of absolute monarchy secure. At his death France was a fairly compact kingdom, with its boundaries much as they are today. Yet it is easy to exaggerate the unity of the French nation. The feudal lords, it is true, had been deprived of most of their political independence, but they had not relinquished the idea of regaining it at the first favorable opportunity. Even more antagonistic to national cohesion was the provincial or particularist spirit. The people of the kingdom might call themselves Frenchmen, but most often they were Normans, Bretons, or Provençals first. Each province had its local customs, manners, laws, and traditions—even its peculiar dialect. Centuries were to pass before these local differences were merged in national institutions and customs, and then not entirely.

After Charles VIII (1483–1498), the next French king, had completed the territorial unification of France through the acquisition of Brittany, he opened a new epoch in European politics by embarking on a scheme of national aggrandizement. His immediate purpose was enforcement of the claims on the kingdom of Naples which he had inherited from the house of Anjou. Collecting a large army, Charles crossed the Alps into Italy in 1494. Since the Italian states were wholly unprepared for war, he was able to march from city to city with no resistance worth mentioning. When he reached Naples the people opened the gates and greeted him as if he were a world conqueror. But the capture of Naples fulfilled only a small part of Charles's grandiose plans. He dreamed of crossing to Greece, of driving the Turk out of Constantinople, and of finally recovering the Holy Sepulcher. From these visions he was rudely awakened by news that the pope, Milan, and Venice, alarmed by his speedy and easy success in Naples, had formed a league against him (League of Venice, 1495), and that Spain and the Holy Roman Empire had joined it. As Charles in his eagerness to reach Naples had done nothing to protect his communications, he was now in danger of being cut off from France. Immediately setting out on his return journey, he reached France only after a hard-fought battle against the league's army, which tried to bar his way. Naples did not long remain under French rule. The viceroy whom he had left there with half his army was driven out in 1496, and the kingdom again passed under the house of Aragon. Thus Charles gained from his Italian expedition nothing but "glory and smoke," to use the words of a contemporary writer.

The expedition of Charles VIII into Italy was but the first of a number to be undertaken by French monarchs. With his death, the direct line of Valois became extinct and was replaced by that of Valois-Orléans. The next king, Louis XII (1498–1515), added to the claim upon Naples pretensions to Milan on the basis of his descent, through his grandmother, from the ducal family of the Visconti. The efforts of the Spanish Habsburgs to thwart the ambitions of the French royal house made Italy the battlefield of Europe during the first half of the sixteenth century.

ENGLAND

In England the development of national unity and a national government were further advanced at the end of the fifteenth century than in France or Spain. Not only did physical configuration make for unity, but England had never actually been part of the Holy Roman Empire. Furthermore, the disruptive tendencies which had divided the continent into so many petty principalities had been curbed in England after the Norman Conquest. William the Conqueror (1066–1087) had strongly asserted the royal authority and thenceforth the work of political centralization was more or less steadily carried on by his successors. Gradually the more important political functions were subordinated to the central power, so that when Henry VII (1485–1509), the first of the Tudor sovereigns, became king it remained only for him to establish the work of his predecessors on a firm basis.[1] When he ascended the throne England was thoroughly sick of internal strife. Soon after the English armies had been driven from France during the Hundred Years' War, civil war had broken out between the house of York and the house of Lancaster, rival claimants for the crown. The series of conflicts which followed is known as the Wars of the Roses, from the badges of the two houses, the white rose of York and the red rose of Lancaster. Henry Tudor, earl of Richmond, put an end to the struggle at the battle of Bosworth, in which Richard III lost his life.

On the strength of his decisive victory at Bosworth, Henry was hailed as king by his followers on the field of battle, and soon after was publicly crowned at Westminster. His claim to the crown by descent was of the slightest kind, for he was but remotely descended from the Lancastrian house. Moreover, the Lancastrian line had been set aside as usurpers, and there were two heirs of the Yorkist line who had superior rights to the crown. Nevertheless, Henry called Parliament together and told them that he "had come to the throne by the just title of inheritance and by the judgment of God who had given him victory," and Parliament, tactfully omitting mention of the precise nature of his claims, confirmed him in possession of the crown. Henry further buttressed his position by marrying Elizabeth, heiress of the house of York, a move which united the claims of the two rival houses and silenced all but the most violent of the Yorkists. In the last analysis, however, the Tudor claim to the throne rested on the will of the people. Weary of war and disorder, the English people wanted, above all, a hand strong enough to terminate the futile strife and restore order. They desired peace so that they might pursue their various interests undisturbed. In return for the promise of order and security, they were ready to overlook the fact that other claimants had a better title to the crown.

Only twenty-nine at the time of his accession, Henry was shrewd, patient, and cautious. In keenness of intelligence he had few equals among the statesmen of his time. Always calm and self-possessed, he did not permit passion to dictate his policy;

---

[1] The foundations of strong personal monarchy of the modern type had been laid by Edward IV (1461–1483), but his brother and successor, Richard III, aroused opposition which culminated in the rebellion of Henry Tudor, who was able to carry out Edward's policies with greater success.

once he had deliberately chosen his course, nothing could turn him from it. In a word, he was well fitted for the task at hand, which was by no means easy. The constant wars had not only increased taxes and dislocated trade but had undermined respect for law and order in England. The crown, with its treasury empty and many of the royal jewels in pawn, exercised but little authority. In fact, all the functions of government had been disorganized by the dynastic quarrels. The laws of the land were flouted by both high and low. On the one hand, wealthy landowners bribed or intimidated juries to render verdicts in their favor; on the other, bands of desperadoes and outlaws roamed the country, pillaging and burning with impunity. In the towns and cities crimes of violence were so common, and cutthroats and thieves so numerous, that few respectable citizens ventured out at night. Parliament had repeatedly passed laws to check these evils, but because of the collapse of the royal authority the laws could not be enforced.

Henry VII was not a man to disappoint the expectations of those common English folk who expected him to put down disorder and give them protection. The prime object of his policy, throughout his reign, was the establishment of a strong monarchy, one that could enforce peace and order. In his endeavors to compel obedience and restore stability, Henry had the particular support of two bodies, the lesser nobility and the growing middle class. The former, which had taken little part in the civil strife, desired quietly to cultivate its estates, while the latter wished to make the most of its opportunities for commercial expansion. It was from the middle class that the bulk of his support came. Moreover, his leading ministers and officials were chosen from this class. The chief opposition to the king's ambitions was in the ranks of the barons. True, the Wars of the Roses had weakened the power of the higher nobility. During that long struggle many noblemen had lost their lives and others had lost their property. But it was still necessary to hold the remnants of this turbulent nobility in check to prevent them from creating further disturbances. The great nobles still had in their service a large number of armed retainers, who wore the peculiar badge or livery of their lord, and were ready to fight whenever called upon. Such a group might easily be formed into a small army which would be a definite threat to the king's power, the peace of the country, and the orderly exercise of law.

Against this menace Henry adopted vigorous measures. His object was not so much to enact new laws as to enforce old ones. Since the ordinary courts had shown themselves powerless to enforce the laws in all cases, a special committee of the king's council, by the act of 1487, was granted certain powers long exercised by the council as a whole. This committee appears to have been merely temporary, but the council itself, meeting formally in judicial session, served as an extraordinary court for trying such powerful offenders as might overawe the ordinary tribunals. Known as the Court of Star Chamber, its special characteristic was that it was not bound by common law procedure, and could therefore act with greater speed and efficiency. To procure evidence it could employ torture, but it could not impose the death penalty. Though this court was regarded as an abusive institution under the Stuarts and was abolished in 1641, during Henry's reign it was an effective instrument for correcting irregularities in the administration of justice. Its small size and wide powers enabled it to deal swiftly and efficiently with those offenders who might otherwise have intimidated the regular courts or bribed the juries.

While Henry was restraining the aristocracy, he sought no less to promote the interests of the commercial class. It was but natural that Henry should encourage the development of English trade, for the customs duties on that trade were an important source of royal revenue. His endeavors had a twofold aim: first, to open new markets for English woolen cloth; second, to keep the trade in the hands of English merchants. The former he achieved by means of commercial treaties. In 1496 he signed the agreement later known as the Intercursus Magnus, which, by securing more favorable conditions for English merchants, gave a great impetus to trade with the Low Countries, the chief mart for English cloth and English wool. He also concluded a treaty with the king of Denmark which gave English merchants the right to trade in that country and in Norway, while a treaty with Venice, then the center of commerce in southern Europe, secured them a share in the Mediterranean trade. To protect English shipping against alien competition Henry's government passed the first of the so-called Navigation Acts, restricting the importation of certain goods to English ships.

While English merchants were prospering, English peasants

were not faring so well. The steady demand for wool, both for export and for cloth-making at home, caused many landlords to turn to sheep-farming, which required less labor and brought larger returns than agriculture. For this purpose the lords not only converted their own arable land into sheep runs but also evicted customary tenants to gain more land for pasture. Others appropriated the common lands which had served the peasants as pasture for their cattle and poultry. Although these changes, known in general as "enclosures" from the means taken to prevent the sheep from straying, ultimately contributed greatly to the prosperity of the country at large, they were attended by grave evils. Even those tenants who were not deprived of their arable land frequently were unable to subsist, because the common pasture land had been claimed by the lord. Many peasants, therefore, sold their holdings for a fraction of their worth. Of those who had sold their holdings or been evicted, some went to the towns to increase the number of the poor; others became agricultural laborers or joined the ranks of the vagrants and beggars. In general, the enclosures caused much distress and widespread discontent among the peasantry. A series of enactments were passed by Parliament during the reigns of Henry VII and his successors to restrain the practice of enclosures, but on the whole they proved ineffective. The smoldering resentment of the peasants was to burst forth during the Tudor period in a series of rebellions which were harshly repressed by the government.

Throughout his reign Henry VII assiduously devoted himself to filling his treasury. Always a good business man, he realized that a full money-chest meant power. Besides power to crush rebellion and to resist invasion, it also meant independence from Parliament. The problem of paying the expenses of government from the small amount raised by taxation had been vexing to the medieval kings of England, necessitating the frequent calling of Parliament for additional subsidies. This Henry wished to avoid if possible, lest Parliament curtail his authority. Hence, while practicing the strictest economy in expenditures, he collected his dues to the last penny. But parliamentary taxes were not the only sources of his income. He gathered wealth for the royal exchequer wherever and however he could. Knowing that he would lose the favor of the masses if he increased their tax burden, the king had recourse to various expedients which, while drawing heavily from the nobility and wealthy merchants, spared the pockets of the lower classes. From the supposedly wealthy he collected benevolences or forced loans, on the principle that if they lived handsomely it was plain that they possessed an abundance of wealth, and if they lived frugally they must have saved much. He overlooked no opportunity of exacting immense fines from the nobles for transgressions of the laws, particularly those against livery and maintenance. He even made the most of foreign relations to add to his accumulation of wealth. In 1489, for example, when Parliament granted him a subsidy for war against France, he not only pocketed it but procured a money indemnity from the French as a condition of peace. Thus he managed to fill the royal coffers to overflowing. No previous king of England had possessed so much wealth as he held at the time of his death.

In the intervals of filling the royal treasury and administering the affairs of the realm, Henry VII found time to arrange two marriage alliances which were fraught with tremendous consequences for the future of England. One was the union in 1502 of his daughter Margaret and James IV of Scotland. Only a century elapsed before a descendant of this marriage became king of England, an event later followed by the union of Scotland and England. The other match, concluded in 1501 between Henry's eldest son Arthur and Catherine of Aragon, second daughter of Ferdinand and Isabella, joined the new Tudor dynasty with the royal house of Spain. When Arthur, a youth of fifteen, died less than six months after the marriage, Henry affianced his second son, Henry, now heir to the throne, to Catherine in order to save the Anglo-Spanish alliance and also to make it unnecessary to return the dowry Catherine had brought to England. Since it was contrary to canon law for a man to marry his brother's widow, a special dispensation was obtained from the pope. This marriage, concluded in 1509, was later to become the immediate cause for the break with the Church of Rome and the establishment of the Church of England.

Henry died in 1509 in his fifty-third year, prematurely worn out by incessant toil and anxiety. He had fulfilled the promise of his early years. True, he had reigned with a wisdom rooted in selfishness, but his rule had nevertheless been a great benefit to his people. He had terminated a century of dynastic strife and after a prolonged struggle restored order, security, and public confidence. The years of peace he brought to England allowed the country to develop and its commerce to expand. At his death he left to his son the example of a successful despotism, an undisputed succession, and a full treasury.

GERMANY

The advance toward national unity which marked the development of Spain, Portugal, France, and England had no counterpart in the fortunes of Germany. The tendency here was rather toward disunion. For this the association of the German kingdom with the Holy Roman Empire was largely responsible. By the fifteenth century the empire, which had formerly embraced much of Europe, had dwindled so much that Germany and the Holy Roman Empire were practically synonymous. England, Spain, France, Denmark, Hungary, Poland, Italy, and Burgundy had definitely repudiated the rule of the emperor. Nevertheless, successive Holy Roman Emperors still clung to the idea of universal sovereignty, a pretension which Emperor Frederick III (1440–1493) expressed on his family banner in the device, A.E.I.O.U., which stood for *Austriae est imperare orbi universo* or *Alles Erdreich ist Oesterreich untertan* (Austria's empire is over the universe). This claim proved fatal to the national aspirations of the German people and left the country hopelessly divided into more than three hundred sovereignties, varying from city-states of small area to such large states as the duchy of Saxony and the kingdom of Bohemia.

Not only had the empire lost territory to the new national states by the fifteenth century; the successive emperors had renounced so much of their authority in the lands they still possessed that they had little left. The early Habsburg emperors, instead of confining their attention to Germany, had endeavored to enforce their authority in Italy; and while they were occupied with the wars resulting from their Italian claims, the German princes had seized the opportunity to strengthen their own position at the emperor's expense. Gradually a group of leading princes became so powerful that they usurped the power of electing the emperor, formerly shared by all the great nobles. Disputes followed regarding the right of this or that prince to vote, until finally in 1356 Charles IV issued the famous Golden Bull (so called from the imperial seal or *bulla* attached to the document) which regulated the mode of the imperial election. The number of electors was fixed at seven, and their right was made hereditary. They were the archbishops of Trier (Treves), Mainz, and Cologne, the king of Bohemia, the duke of Saxony, the margrave of Brandenburg, and the count palatine of the Rhine. On the death of an emperor it was the duty of the archbishop of Mainz to summon the electors to Frankfort for the purpose of choosing a new sovereign. Only a majority, not a unanimous vote, was necessary to make the election of a candidate valid. Once they had gained the right of election, the electors resolutely resisted every attempt to make the imperial office hereditary. To obtain their support, candidates for the throne were forced to concede certain powers in advance or promise lands and favors. Thus the elective character of the imperial dignity was the main cause for the decline of the emperor's power.

In exercising what power he still had, the emperor was further limited by the Reichstag or diet, composed of his feudal vassals. The diet was divided into three separate houses, consisting respectively of the electors, the princes (both lay and ecclesiastical), and the representatives of the Free Imperial Cities.[1] Most of the members of the diet, intent only on securing advantages for their respective states, were indifferent to the interests of Germany as a whole. They realized that if the emperor's power were to grow, their own would decrease commensurately. Hence they offered strong opposition to any new pretensions on the part of the emperor. Apart from the income of his own estates, the emperor was dependent on the taxes authorized by the diet; and since these were seldom voted, and less often collected, he was usually in financial straits. In brief, while the rulers of most states of Europe were becoming stronger and stronger, the emperor was falling more and more into weakness. Such powers as he was able to exercise were derived principally from his personal landed possessions. At the end of the fifteenth century the holdings of the Habsburgs, who had occupied the imperial throne intermittently since the election in 1273 of Rudolph, the first emperor of the house, included the archduchy of Austria and several other provinces near that state (Styria, Carinthia, and the Tyrol).

Shortly after the accession of Maximilian I (1493–1519) a

---

[1] The Free Imperial Cities did not secure the right of appearing in all the diets until 1489.

number of princes under the leadership of Berthold, archbishop of Mainz, proposed certain measures of reform to improve the machinery of government. These proposals were designed not to increase the power of the emperor, but to draw the German states into a closer unity on the basis of a federative organization. At the Diet of Worms in 1495, Maximilian, in order to obtain men and money to fight the French and the Turks, conceded the demands of the reforming group. First of all, they strove to put an end to the interminable feuds which had devastated Germany for centuries, by proclaiming a perpetual national peace (*Landfrieden*). Disputes were to be referred to an imperial court of justice (*Reichskammergericht*), composed of sixteen members appointed by the states, and a president chosen by the emperor. Another measure called for annual meetings of the diet to make certain that their decrees would be carried out. Furthermore, an imperial tax known as the common penny was imposed to provide the emperor with funds for the maintenance of the new court. The reformers' efforts were continued at the diet of 1512, which divided the empire into ten districts or "circles" for better administration. Each district was put under a judicial chief and a board of councilors, who were to see that the decrees of the diet and the judgments of the imperial court were carried out.

Actually these reforms accomplished little, for the states of the empire were unwilling to limit their independence for the common good. The imperial court, it is true, met and passed decrees, but there was no force to compel the states to submit to the jurisdiction of this court or to abide by any of its decisions. Neither could the common penny be collected; nor did the division of the empire into circles for purposes of administration reach the point where all the circles functioned as administrative units. These measures having proved inadequate, the disunion of Germany continued for centuries to come.

Though Germany as a whole was making no progress toward national unity, a feeling of nationality was developing in one part of the Holy Roman Empire—the Swiss cantons. As early as 1291 the three Forest Cantons—Uri, Schwyz, and Unterwalden—had allied themselves in a league for mutual defense. After the battle at Morgarten (1315), in which the three cantons decisively defeated the army of the Habsburg prince Frederick of Austria, who claimed the right of sovereignty over them, the league was renewed and during the next half-century was augmented by the admission of neighboring lands and cities. The city of Lucerne joined the confederation in 1332; next came the imperial city of Zurich (1351); then the canton of Glarus and the town of Zug (1352); and finally the great city of Bern (1353). Thus the foundation was laid for the republic of Switzerland. Each canton managed its internal affairs, while a diet composed of representatives of all eight settled questions affecting the confederation as a whole. By a series of victories in the fourteenth century the Swiss succeeded in forcing the Habsburgs to renounce their feudal claims, but the cantons were still a part of the empire and as such subject to its laws. When in 1495 the diet of the empire decreed the collection of the common penny and the establishment of a new imperial court, the Swiss confederation refused to pay the former and to acknowledge the latter. Enraged by this resistance, Maximilian I declared war against the Swiss in 1498. But the attempt to subdue them proved a failure. The half-hearted support of the princes of the empire was not enough to enable the emperor to overcome the sturdy mountaineers. His army was defeated and he was obliged to assent to the treaty of Basel, which made the Swiss cantons practically independent though in name they remained part of the empire until 1648.

The Emperor Maximilian was able to carry out few of the projects he conceived. Some were too fantastic to be executed; for others he lacked the necessary funds or the support of the diet. Thus such schemes as that of uniting the papacy and the emperorship in his own person, the establishment of a permanent imperial army, and his attempted expedition against the Turks all came to naught. However, his efforts to augment the personal fortunes of the house of Habsburg were eminently successful. Through his marriage with Mary of Burgundy he added to his personal possessions the county of Burgundy (Franche-Comté) and twelve provinces of the Netherlands. Another marriage, that of his son Philip to Juana, daughter of Ferdinand and Isabella, laid the foundations for the extensive empire of his grandson, Charles V.

ITALY

Italy, like Germany, was not to be unified until the second half of the nineteenth century. At the opening of the modern period it was a mosaic of independent states of varying sizes and widely different governments. The history of the larger of these is mainly a story of the attempts of each to take as much territory as possible and to keep the others from doing likewise. Consequently some one or other of the states was almost constantly at war with one of its neighbors. For these wars they engaged professional soldiers under the command of *condottieri* or free captains who were ready to hire out their services on any occasion to the highest bidder. Though the mercenaries had a way of preventing the battles from being very bloody, the frequent wars did keep Italy in a state of turmoil. If a state felt itself too weak to oppose its neighbors, it did not hesitate to call in one of the foreign rulers, such as the king of France, the king of Spain, or the emperor of Germany. This resulted not only in making Italy the cockpit of Europe in the first half of the sixteenth century, but also in the subjection of the larger part of the peninsula to European powers. By the middle of the sixteenth century only Venice, the Papal States, and the small duchy of Savoy retained a certain measure of independence.

The five larger states of Italy at the end of the fifteenth century were:

1. *The kingdom of Naples*, which embraced the southernmost parts of Italy and at times included Sicily. Until they were separated by the "Sicilian Vespers" [1] in 1282, Naples and Sicily had been united in one kingdom. Thereafter, for a period of more than a century and a half, Sicily was ruled by the Spanish house of Aragon, while Naples remained under the French house of Anjou. Finally, in 1435 both were again joined under Alphonso V of the Aragon line, who was also ruler of Aragon and Sardinia. As he left no legitimate heirs, Aragon, Sicily, and Sardinia passed to his brother John II, but Naples was given to his natural son Ferdinand, probably better known as Ferrante I. It was during the reign of Ferrante II, grandson of the first of that name, that Charles VIII of France renewed the old claims of the house of Anjou to Naples (1494). Dissatisfied with their Aragonese rulers, the people of Naples received the French king enthusiastically.

---

[1] The revolution called the "Sicilian Vespers"—because it broke out the moment the bells of the churches were ringing for vespers—was directed against the tyranny of the Angevin rule. Originating in Palermo, it quickly spread to the other cities of Sicily, causing the massacre of several thousand Frenchmen. After the forced departure of the French garrisons, the Parliament of Palermo invited Don Pedro of Aragon to assume the rule.

Italy in the Fifteenth Century

But after the departure of Charles VIII for France a few months later, the Aragonese line again resumed its sway in Naples. In civilization and culture this state was far behind the northern states of Italy.

2. *The Papal States* or *States of the Church* in the central part of Italy. These included, besides Rome and the districts about it, the March of Ancona and the whole of Romagna. During the residence of the popes at Avignon (1305–1377) and the Great Schism (1378–1417), the power of the pontiff over these states had been greatly reduced, but Martin V, after his election in 1417, had reëstablished the papal sovereignty. Since any scheme of Italian unity under a secular head was a threat to the sovereign pontiff's temporal power, every aspirant for national sovereignty met his determined opposition.

3. *The duchy of Milan* in northwestern Italy. Originally one of the Lombard communes, Milan under the rule of the Visconti despots had greatly extended its dominion, and in 1395 had been recognized by the emperor as a duchy. When the house of Visconti became extinct in 1447, efforts were made to establish a republican government. At the end of three years, however, the republic failed, and Francesco Sforza, the great condottiere, made himself duke of Milan. For two generations after his death in 1466 the Sforzas ruled Milan, promoting agriculture, commerce, and education.

4. *Venice* in northeastern Italy. Nominally a republic, Venice was actually ruled by a close oligarchy. The doge, who had formerly been elected by the people as a whole, was chosen after the thirteenth century by the Great Council (*Maggiore Consiglio*), membership in which was limited to families previously represented in it. This council gradually curtailed the powers of the doge until he was little more than a figurehead, though a man with a strong personality could still wield considerable influence. The principal occupation of the Venetians was trade. As a result of the Crusades, particularly the fourth (1204), Venice had gained important possessions in the East which greatly increased its trade and its wealth. In the fourteenth century it crushed the sea power of Genoa, its great trade rival, and thereafter held a preëminent position among the states trading with the Levant. But as the Ottoman Turks advanced, the Venetian sphere of trade was gradually narrowed. To make up for these losses, the Venetians

PANORAMA OF FLORENCE IN THE
SIXTEENTH CENTURY

PAGE FROM THE MISSAL OF
ISABELLA OF CASTILE

KING HENRY VII OF ENGLAND

SIR THOMAS MORE   *by Holbein*
By permission of the Frick Collection

ERASMUS   *by Ho[lbein]*

BALDASSARE CASTIGLIONE
by Raphael

LORENZO THE MAGNIFICENT
by Vasari

began to extend their dominion in Italy itself, and by the middle of the fifteenth century had acquired extensive mainland possessions. It was not long, however, before the prosperity of Venice began to decline. The first blow came when the Turks, after the capture of Constantinople, took most of the territories the Venetians held in that vicinity. Just before the end of the fifteenth century an even heavier disaster followed from the discovery of the new route to India around the Cape of Good Hope. The consequent shifting of the highways of trade gradually completed the ruin of Venetian prosperity.

5. *The republic of Florence*, including a large and prosperous area of Tuscany centering in the city of Florence, which exercised a governing authority over the territory. In 1434 Cosimo de Medici, a member of the wealthy banking family, managed to become ruler of Florence and to make his ascendancy a hereditary possession of the family. After his death in 1464 he was succeeded by his son Piero (1416–1469), who in turn was followed by his son Lorenzo the Magnificent (1448–1492). While carefully preserving the forms of republican government, the house of Medici was able, by means of its wealth and the support of the lower classes, to found a party which gave effectual control of the city to Medici rulers for nearly two hundred years. Both Cosimo and his more famous grandson, Lorenzo, used much of their wealth to foster art and learning. The preëminence of Florence in learning and art during the Renaissance was due in no small degree to their munificence.

Among the outstanding figures which the city of Florence produced during this period there were a number of political thinkers, one of whom was Niccolo Machiavelli (1469–1527). *The Prince*, which he wrote in 1513, is one of the most widely read and influential political pamphlets of all time. In it Machiavelli expounded the dogma of the non-moral state, defending the use of force and fraud as proper instruments of statecraft. Others before him had defended terrorism and treachery as political instruments, but Machiavelli was the first to expound this method in detail. In consequence he has been styled by some "the founder of modern political science" and by others "an apostle of duplicity and diabolic cunning." Today the word *Machiavellism* signifies a policy of expediency which subordinates every human and moral consideration to the political needs of the hour. It is from this policy of expediency that the whole moral code of *The Prince* derives. "A prudent lord," Machiavelli wrote, "ought not to keep faith, when keeping faith would make against him. . . . If men were all good this precept would not be good, but as they are bad and would not keep faith with you, you, too, ought not to keep faith with them. . . . A prince cannot do all the things for which men are esteemed good, for, in order to maintain the state, he is often obliged to act contrary to humanity, contrary to charity, contrary to religion." Because it contains such statements as this, both Roman Catholics and Protestants have denounced *The Prince* as subversive of morals and religion, and lovers of liberty have arraigned it as destructive of individual freedom.

Machiavelli's *Prince* cannot be understood except in the light of the time in which the author lived. Its aim was the twofold one of unifying Italy and freeing it from foreign domination. Machiavelli had personally witnessed the invasion of the peninsula by foreign armies. He saw that a disunited Italy was too weak to protect its territories, and that it was further enfeebling itself by internecine warfare. The impotence of his country, in which he saw an unlimited capacity for greatness, grieved him deeply. He longed to see Italy emerge from its chaos, compose its thousand and one conflicting interests, unite in driving out foreign invaders, and rise to a level with the great powers of Europe. In observing the career of Cesare Borgia he had seen what one man can do if he permits nothing to restrict his actions. Hence he prescribed the methods Cesare Borgia had employed for achieving the goal of a strong state in Italy. Machiavelli's ideal of a prince was a patriotic tyrant who could forcibly weld together the Italian states, organize a national army, and permanently expel the foreign powers. So far as the immediate future of Italy was concerned the book was doomed to failure, but outside of Italy *The Prince* was read and reread until its statements became commonplaces. Not only did absolutists of the sixteenth century adopt it as a manual of first principles, but all who have aspired to tyrannical rule since that time have found it a source of inspiration. Louis XIV, for example, studied it assiduously, Frederick the Great wrote a treatise against it before proceeding to apply its principles, and Napoleon, one of the best exemplars of the Machiavellian idea, left a carefully annotated copy of it. Nor has there been a dearth of Machiavellian practitioners in more recent times, for

Machiavelli's *Prince* still remains the Bible of those who believe that politics should not be bound by the rules of morality.

In summary, during the last centuries of the Middle Ages a group of strong centralized national states were emerging in western Europe. Ambitious monarchs, with the help of the middle class, were reducing the great feudal lords to subjection, absorbing their political functions and adding their feudal states to the royal demesnes. This development was dispelling once and for all the noble dream of including the whole civilized world, or at least the whole of Latin Christendom, in one great state under the dual authority of the pope and the Holy Roman Emperor. At the same time that national states were being consolidated politically, a strong nationalist feeling was growing within them, nourished by a common language, a vernacular literature, and common interests and traditions. The states of western Europe in which the process of unification and nationalization had reached a certain maturity by the opening of the sixteenth century were Spain, Portugal, France, and England. In Italy and Germany, however, political unification had not yet taken place. Both remained divided until the nineteenth century. Because of their lack of unity both were to be the battleground of foreign nations, Italy in the sixteenth and Germany in the seventeenth century. Moreover, neither country was to participate in the scramble for oversea possessions.[1] It was the national states that were to play the leading rôles in the drama of modern history.

[1] An exception to this statement was the establishment of a few ports on the west coast of Africa by the Great Elector of Brandenburg. However, the venture soon terminated.

CHAPTER TWO

The Renaissance

THE RENAISSANCE OF SECULARISM

THE word *Renaissance*, used as a historical concept, admits of no simple definition. In its widest sense it is often loosely applied to the entire process of transition in western Europe from the medieval to the modern world, and includes phenomena as diverse as the decay of feudalism; the study of classical literature; the rise of the national state; the beginnings of modern science; the invention of movable type, gunpowder, and the mariner's compass; the opening of new trade routes; the development of early capitalism; and the discovery of America. In a more limited sense the term is used to denote certain cultural changes which took place, broadly speaking, during the centuries from 1300 to 1600. In so far as it is possible to find a common denominator for these changes, it is the intensification of the secular spirit; in other words, an enlargement of interest in the things of this world. Accordingly the word *Renaissance*, as used in the present discussion, signifies the intensification of the secular spirit in the literature, thought, and art of the fourteenth, fifteenth, and sixteenth centuries. Because etymologically it means rebirth, and therefore suggests a cataclysmic conception of historical development, the word *Renaissance* may easily be misleading. What actually took place was no abrupt change, no sudden surge of enthusiasm. It was rather a gradual transformation of values, a progressive accentuation of certain attitudes and interests which had previously been of minor importance, a gradual shift of emphasis from the otherworldliness of the Middle Ages to the secular interests of modern times.

During the earlier centuries of the Middle Ages thought had been dominated by ascetic ideas and ideals. The Catholic Church, whose influence was supreme in the realm of thought, taught men to turn from the realities of this life to the contemplation of God and the hereafter. It impressed upon its members that this life has importance only in so far as it is a prelude to the life hereafter, and that this world, at best a sinful and evil world, has little importance in itself except as the dwelling-place of man for a brief period during which his eternal fate is decided. The message of the Church might be summed up briefly as follows: "Through Christ's redemption man was given the power of saving his soul by the help of God. To achieve salvation, however, man must escape from his senses, renounce this life and its pleasures, and raise himself little by little toward God through the contemplation of higher things and through the communion of the soul with God." Since the general political and economic confusion of the time made life insecure, dull, and miserable, men were inclined to turn their thoughts to, and set their hopes on, a brighter and happier existence. Hence the soul became, at least in theory, the greatest concern, the contemplative life the surest road to salvation, and the world to come the overmastering reality of this life. The secular spirit was not, of course, extinct; neither was this life without its attractions. One need only turn to medieval ecclesiastical literature to see that it was necessary for the clergy to exhort the faithful repeatedly to turn their thoughts away from worldly things. But the Church, aided by political and economic conditions, was able to curb the growth of secularism, even though it could not suppress secularism entirely.

Gradually, however, as conditions of life improved and the influence of the Church declined, a more distinctly secular spirit prevailed. Interest came to be more vitally centered in this world and less vitally in the next. Asceticism, self-abnegation, withdrawal from the world, and mortification of the flesh were no longer regarded as essential. The contemplative life became an active life, and secular human values took on an interest for their own sake. Men grew vividly conscious that this world is after all a glorious and fascinating place, and that life has much to offer. The apostles of secularism started from the same premise as the proponents of mysticism; namely, "Life is short." But whereas the latter proceeded to the conclusion "Let us sacrifice it to the hereafter," the former said, "Let us therefore enjoy it as profoundly as we can." The idea of man's essential sinfulness and guilt gave way to a new appreciation of the dignity of human nature, and Christian humility was replaced by a consciousness of human power. The voice of the Renaissance speaks through Hamlet when he says: "What a piece of work man is! how noble in reason! how infinite in faculty! in form and moving how express and admirable! in action how like an angel! in apprehension how like a god! the beauty of the world! the paragon of animals!"

All this did not, however, involve an open denial of the doctrines of the Catholic Church. The deepening interest in mundane affairs and in man as a citizen of this world was the result of a shift of emphasis rather than of a change in essential ideas. Men were still nominally Christian, but their religion had become a secondary concern. The medieval conceptions of sin, guilt, and redemption still lived in the intellect without exercising a controlling influence on life. Only at a later stage of the Renaissance, and then primarily in Florence, was the medieval Christian view replaced by one that was fundamentally pagan.

The intensified secular spirit which gradually pervaded thought and culture was the product of the new urban society created by the wealth of the bourgeoisie. In this society mundane ideals naturally replaced ascetic. For the wealthy burgher, surrounded by luxuries and intoxicated by pleasures, otherworldliness no longer had any attractions; it was completely alien to his way of life. He still paid a certain lip-service to Christian ethics, but his guiding philosophy was epicurean. His motto, as expressed in the song of Lorenzo the Magnificent, was:

> Let him be happy who wishes to be so,
> For nothing is certain about tomorrow.

Although a direct outgrowth of the expansion of commerce, secularism was not restricted to the middle class; many of the sponsors of the new culture were to be found among the ruling princes of the time and even among the popes. However, it was

by means of wealth acquired through commerce and banking
that some of these, like the Medici, had raised themselves above
the middle class. Nor was the growth of secularism contemporaneous in all parts of Europe. It appeared earliest in those sections
where the development of commerce was most advanced. Of
course it did not express itself everywhere in the same manner.
In various centers it assumed various characteristics, differing
according to local conditions.

One result of the increasing secular-mindedness was the
growth of individualism or individualist assertiveness. There were,
to be sure, striking individualities in the Middle Ages. Certainly
Charlemagne, whose manifold activities included those of soldier,
statesman, monastic and educational reformer, founder of an
academy, collector of folk-songs, agriculturist, and expert swim-
mer, rider, and hunter, must be regarded as such; and numerous
other strong individualities, among them Boethius and Frederick II, could be listed. Nevertheless medieval thought, though it
recognized individual differences, did not encourage or even
sanction self-expression. The Church glorified humility and self-
effacement, teaching that self-realization is to be achieved through
self-surrender. St. Francis was an outstanding individual; yet his
purpose was not self-expression, but self-abnegation. In general,
individuals tended to become submerged in the group, class, corporation, or gild. Medieval man could exercise some choice in selecting his religious order or gild, but once he was a member of a
corporation his identity was stifled by the rigorous system. The
work produced bore a collective rather than an individual stamp.
In sculpture, paintings, and poems there is little that might give a
clue to the personality of the sculptor, artist, or poet. Sculptors
and painters worked silently at their tasks for the greater glory of
God, without inscribing their names on the finished work, and
most of the great epic poems of the Middle Ages are likewise
anonymous.

The Renaissance successors of the anonymous craftsmen,
scholars, and poets of the early Middle Ages were lusty individuals.
They were proud, self-reliant, and eager to attain to the highest
eminence by exploiting their individuality. It was this spirit of
individuality which gave a certain freshness to many of the literary
and artistic works of the Renaissance; and when this spirit was
lost, literature and art degenerated into artificiality and mere

slavish imitation. Few other historical periods present so many men of strong individuality, amazing energy, and astounding versatility. In Italy alone we may name Michelangelo, Raphael, Cellini, the Medicis, the Borgias, Petrarch, Boccaccio, and others. The most striking example of versatility is Leonardo da Vinci, who reached the highest distinction in many phases of human endeavor. And the spirit of individuality was not restricted to the leaders of the time, for the qualities which distinguished them are found in lesser-known contemporaries only in a lesser degree. Self-expression, no longer deemed sinful, became for many the goal of life. The individual consciously strove to leave the indelible impress of his personality on his endeavors, whether in church or state, art or literature. Thus, in contrast to medieval art, which is regarded as corporate or institutional art, as having been done collectively by companies of craftsmen, the work of the Renaissance artist was personal in conception and technique. Similarly, much of the literature of the Renaissance is the peculiar expression of the individuality of the author. Moreover, it is filled with autobiographical material. This is true not only of Italian literature but in greater or lesser degree of the literature of all European countries. In the words of an authority on the French Renaissance: "There is hardly a work of the sixteenth century, however impersonal in form, which is not full of information as to the life and character of the writer." [1]

For the secular-minded individualist the primary purpose of life was the maximum enjoyment of this world and the achievement of personal distinction. In order that a man might enjoy to the fullest the pleasures and beauties of this existence, and also make the most of opportunities to gain fame, emphasis was put on a well-rounded development. It became the highest aim of education to furnish equipment for every situation in life, to make a "complete man." To this end Vittorino of Feltre, one of the great schoolmasters of fifteenth century Italy, introduced a broad and liberal curriculum into his school at Mantua. The old medieval subjects of the trivium (grammar, rhetoric, and dialectic) and the quadrivium (arithmetic, geometry, astronomy, and music) were retained, but they were vitalized with human interest. Besides training his pupils in the so-called seven liberal arts, and requiring them to read widely in Latin and Greek, history and

[1] Arthur Tilley, *The Literature of the French Renaissance*, vol. 2 (1904), p. 315.

literature, Vittorino also provided special tutors to teach them courtly manners, dancing, drawing, and painting. What is more, gymnastic and martial exercises for the purpose of developing hardiness and good health were an important part of the curriculum. Among Vittorino's scholars were some of the most distinguished men of the Italian Renaissance, including the humanist Lorenzo Valla.

To develop all the powers of mind and body harmoniously was the aim of many of Vittorino's contemporaries also. "Man was to train himself like a race-horse, to cultivate himself like a flower, that he might arrive soul and body to such perfection as mortality might covet." [1] In the early sixteenth century Baldassare Castiglione (1478–1529) set up a definitely secular ideal of social and literary accomplishment in his *Book of the Courtier*. Castiglione's model was a perfectly equipped man who was at once a gentleman, a soldier, a man of action, and a man of letters. The perfect gentleman should know not only Latin but also Greek; he should be a good sportsman, skilled in such manly exercises as riding, swimming, jumping, and running, which make the body graceful and agile; he should be adept in such social graces as dancing, jesting, and making light conversation, but should be free of ostentation or affectation; he should have some knowledge of music and painting, and some skill at drawing; his garb must always be neat and dainty, without being eccentric. This ideal gentleman served as a model for contemporaries and for succeeding generations. *The Book of the Courtier*, first published in 1528, was soon translated into Spanish, French, English, and Latin, and before 1600 appeared in no fewer than a hundred editions. All over Europe it was read, applauded, and adopted as the handbook of manners. At both the French and English courts, Castiglione's standards of social and intellectual accomplishment were set up for emulation. His perfect gentleman also became a model for other authors. In England Lyly incorporated the ideal in his *Euphues*, and Spenser in *The Faerie Queene* modeled his Knight of Courtesy after it.

That the secular movement developed earlier in Italy than in the rest of Europe was due to the singularly favorable economic and political conditions existing there. Italy's geographical po-

[1] Walter Raleigh in his essay on Sir Thomas Hoby. Cited by E. F. Jacob, *The Renaissance*, p. 11.

sition on the Mediterranean, then the center of the world's commerce, had enabled merchants to make the most of the commercial opportunities offered by the revival of trade with the Levant, and consequently urban life flourished earlier in Italy than in northern Europe. Politically most of the Italian cities, or rather city-states, enjoyed a large degree of autonomy, having become virtually independent of the empire in the thirteenth century. In these independent city-states, which had grown rich from the trade that flowed through them, a many-sided, self-reliant secular life found adequate nourishment.

Another factor which favored the rise of secularism in Italy was the existence of a strong secular tradition. The break between the pagan civilization of ancient times and the culture of the Middle Ages had not been so complete as in the other countries of western Europe. Such characteristic forms of medieval civilization as feudalism, chivalry, and Gothic architecture had not taken so firm a hold. Furthermore, not only did Roman law and Latin as a living language keep alive the memories of Roman civilization, but the ruins of ancient Rome and the remains of antique sculpture served as a constant reminder of the long-gone past. Italian pride in ancient Rome is attested by the fact that many noble families claimed a blood-tie with the Roman patricians.

The intensified secular spirit affected every sphere of mental activity. In art it inspired both painters and sculptors with a new interest in nature and in the human body. No longer was natural beauty regarded as a snare of the devil, but as the gift of a loving God to his children. Furthermore, the changing attitude toward the world and toward man as a citizen of the world quickened that interest in natural phenomena which eventually led such scientists as Copernicus, Galileo, Vesalius, and Harvey to lay the foundations of modern science. It likewise led to a new conception of the universe, to the development of anatomy and physiology, and finally to the age of experimental science which began in the seventeenth century. Another manifestation of the growing secular spirit was the vast expansion of geographical knowledge. Though much of this knowledge was gathered by explorers who were searching for riches and new markets, there was an intense curiosity about the unknown world apart from that aroused by commercial motives. Thus Thomas More, in his *Utopia*, has the mythical Raphael Hythlodaye join the expedition of Amerigo Vespucci "for the desire that he had to see and knowe the farre Countreyes of the worlde." In the realm of political thought Machiavelli presented in *The Prince* a thoroughly secular view of politics, disregarding completely the basic theories of medieval thought. In the field of literature the secular spirit manifested itself, first, in an increasing expression in vernacular literature of purely human interests, of the mundane loves and hates, fancies and desires, of man; secondly, in an intense enthusiasm for the literatures of ancient Greece and Rome.

ITALIAN LITERATURE

Italian was not the first Romance language to attain the dignity of a literary language; toward the end of the thirteenth century both Spanish and Provençal were much more developed than the Tuscan dialect which became the literary language of Italy. One reason for this tardiness was the persistent strength of the Latin tongue in Italy. The glorious traditions of Rome made Latin more satisfactory than any dialect to many Italians, and for centuries the best intellects of Italy were content to express themselves in that language. Another reason for the slow progress of the Italian language was the political condition of the country. After the dismemberment of the empire, Italy was parceled out in numerous pieces that lacked common relations, mutual coöperation, or any reason for cultivating a common language. In the fourteenth century, however, the Tuscan vernacular, already on the way to becoming the literary language of Italy, gained a decided preëminence over the other claimants and at the same time became the vehicle of a literature more mature and more impressive than any theretofore produced in the other national languages of Europe. This was achieved principally by three men, customarily classed together as the triumvirate of early Italian literature: Dante, Petrarch, and Boccaccio. Literary historians have bestowed on them respectively the titles of "creator of Italian literature," "author of the greatest Italian lyrics," and "father of Italian prose."

Dante Alighieri (1265–1321), the greatest name in Italian literature, is also one of the great poets of all time. His masterpiece is the *Divine Comedy*. For it he created a poetic idiom which enabled the Italian language to express the sublimest thoughts;

Italian poetry at once soared to a height it can hardly hope to surpass. To present any adequate idea of this poem in a brief analysis is utterly impossible. Its themes are the mysteries of the invisible world as revealed by a journey through Hell, Purgatory, and Paradise. Dante saw the other world in spirit and related in the poem what he saw. The conception is essentially medieval; it is symbolical, mystical, and scholastic. The poet is the great interpreter of the theology of the Middle Ages, and the poem has been called a synthesis of medieval Catholicism. It clothes in poetic garb the *Summa Theologica* of St. Thomas Aquinas, in which the theology of the Middle Ages attained its highest development; in fact, the technical phrases of Aquinas are reproduced with little modification in the third part of the *Divine Comedy*. Theology was still to Dante the sum of all knowledge and the key to all problems of the universe. His primary concern is the salvation of the soul; hence his vivid picture of the horrors of Hell, the expiatory punishments of Purgatory, and the glories of Paradise. He named the poem *Commedia* because after many adventures it ends happily. His compatriots, regarding the title as too mean for its content, soon prefixed the word *Divina* to the original title, and thus it became known as the *Divine Comedy*.

Though Dante looks backward to the Middle Ages in his "swan-song of scholasticism," his attitude toward the heathen poets is in some respects indicative of the growing interest in the secular literature of the ancients. True, the fact that he quotes Virgil some two hundred times and Ovid about half as often merely illustrates the characteristic medieval tendency to commingle examples from sacred literature and pagan mythology. But his profound admiration of Virgil and his thoroughly human depiction of this Latin poet herald the enthusiasm for humane letters which was soon to be the outstanding characteristic of educated Italy. Of Virgil, who was his guide through the infernal regions, he wrote:

> "Art thou that Virgil, then? the fountain-head
> Whence roll the streams of eloquence along?"
> Thus with a bashful front I humbly said—
> "O light and glory of the sons of song!
> So favor me as I thy page have sought
> With unremitting love and study long!
> Thou art the guide and master of my thought."

In general, his thorough and loving study of the Latin poets points to the revival of the ancients. In *De Vulgari Eloquentia* he wrote: "The closer we imitate the regular [ancient] poets the better we shall write poetry."

Far more sensitive to secular values than Dante was Francesco Petrarca, or Petrarch (1304–1374). In his *Canzoniere*, a collection of more than three hundred sonnets and forty-nine odes (canzoni), he abandoned the scholasticism and allegory of Dante and became more human and secular. Most of the poems were written to celebrate Petrarch's love for Laura, of whom he became enamored upon seeing her at mass. The identity of the lady whose beauty so moved the poet has not been finally established. It appears that she was a married woman and that nothing came of the affair but the tender sonnets themselves. Though Dante's love-poems for Beatrice are perhaps more beautiful than those of Petrarch for Laura, the object of Petrarch's affections is a living, breathing woman while Beatrice is a vision, a dream. Against the background of lovely landscapes Laura is represented in countless attitudes. Her "gentle face," "rosy fingers," "lovely feet," "milk-white bosom," and "golden tresses" inspired Petrarch ever anew. Thus after her death in 1348 he wrote:

> Those eyes my bright and glowing theme erewhile;
> That arm, those hands, that lovely foot, that face,
> Whose view was wont my fancy to beguile,
> And raise me high o'er all of human race;
> Those golden locks that flowed in liquid grace,
> And the sweet lightening of that angel smile,
> Which makes a paradise of every place.

Though Petrarch's sonnets are composed with exquisite art, he himself attached little value to them, stating that they were mere pastimes written to express the overflowings of his heart. Their appeal was universal. Not only were they imitated in Italy for centuries, but throughout the whole of Europe they were regarded as models of lyric poetry.

The first great Italian prose writer was Giovanni Boccaccio (1313–1375). His most famous book is the *Decameron*, a collection of a hundred novellas or tales written during the period when the Black Death raged in Europe. Ranging in plot from farce to tragedy, they are ingeniously united under the supposition of an outing. According to the author seven ladies and three men left

Florence in 1348 to escape the ravages of the plague. Retiring to a country house, they agreed that, to beguile the time, each person should daily tell a story for ten days. Hence the title *Decameron* (Ten Days). Few if any of the plots are original. They were drawn from many sources, including folklore and classical and oriental writers. But into these stories Boccaccio wove the details of the life of his time. They are concerned with the world of human things, everyday events that constitute the common experience of mankind. In them an infinite variety of people from every class of contemporaneous society are portrayed, giving the reader a vivid insight into the life of fourteenth century Italy. With the exception of the mystical, the subject matter is all-inclusive in its human interest and sympathy. Though the gross and the vulgar element is prominent, the *Decameron* also depicts the traits of courtesy, humanity, and generosity.

Boccaccio's *Decameron* is the first enduring work to break completely with the ascetic and mystical spirit of the Middle Ages. In contrast with the *Divine Comedy* of Dante it is frequently called the "Human Comedy" of Boccaccio. Its spirit is one of love for mankind, of wide tolerance for human error and weakness. From the standpoint of influence it has been one of the most important books in literary history. Previously crude and undeveloped, Italian prose as matured in the easy elegance of Boccaccio's style became a model for later storytellers. The book also left its mark on the development of French, German, Spanish, and English literature, and particularly on the development of the short story and the novel. By many Boccaccio is regarded as the founder of the modern novel. Such great personages in the history of literature as Chaucer, Shakespeare, Goethe, and Tennyson found the *Decameron* a source of inspiration.

After Boccaccio the development of Italian literature was interrupted for a long period by the efforts of the so-called humanists to revive the civilization of Rome and Greece, and to make classical Latin the literary language of Italy. As a result, the use of the Italian language as a literary medium was discouraged. Even Dante, Petrarch, and Boccaccio, the trinity that raised the Tuscan dialect to the dignity of the literary language of Italy, had insisted upon the unapproachable superiority of Latin. From the death of Boccaccio to the end of the fifteenth century not a single masterpiece in vernacular literature was produced in Italy.

In the interval the best minds of the age turned to the recovery
and appropriation of ancient culture.

ITALIAN HUMANISM

Although classical civilization had declined with the Roman
Empire, knowledge of the classics had not perished in western
Europe during the Middle Ages. This was particularly true of
Latin literature. Such writers as Virgil, Ovid, Horace, Terence,
Livy, and Cicero were known and read in the monasteries. Cita-
tions from and references to them abound in the ecclesiastical,
scholastic, and historical works of the time. Through such ecclesiastical compilations as were made by Isidor, bishop of Seville,
ideas and extracts from the Latin classics circulated widely. Classical Greek, on the other hand, except for a rare student here and
there, had become practically extinct,[1] and the literature of
ancient Greece survived only in Latin translations of some of the
works of Plato and Aristotle.

Since the content of this classical literature was pagan, it was
regarded by many leading churchmen as inimical to Christianity.
Thus Gregory, bishop of Tours, advised his generation to "forego
the wisdom of sages at enmity with God, lest we incur the doom
of endless death by sentence of our Lord." This attitude is illustrated also in a story of Odo, abbot of Cluny. After reading Virgil
he saw in a vision a vase of extraordinary beauty filled with serpents bent on strangling him. Concluding that the vase represented the book of Virgil and the serpents its false teachings, he
thenceforth ceased reading this Latin master. But not all churchmen repudiated the classics; many continued to cherish them, and
sought to accommodate them to the essential teachings of the
Church by deleting objectionable passages or by allegorical interpretations. Thus Socrates and Plato were made into precursors
of Christianity, and the works of Aristotle were interpreted by
Albertus Magnus and Thomas Aquinas in such a fashion as to
furnish the logical basis for Catholic theology. In all periods of
the Middle Ages, however, there were scholars who, with the imperfect means at their disposal, pursued the study of the classics

[1] Two exceptions may be noted. Some study of Greek was fostered in the Irish
monasteries; also the inhabitants of southwestern Italy, who were the descendants
of Greek colonists, possessed a practical knowledge of the language. They had,
however, little familiarity with the ancient literature of Greece.

for intrinsic meaning and as an end in itself. The mere fact that leaders in the Church found it necessary to combat this disposition gives some indication of the interest displayed.

As the secular spirit grew and the moral authority of the Church declined, study of the classics attained an independent existence. Works were no longer studied primarily for what theological meanings might be read into them or for style alone, but for the conception of life they presented. In the classics the man of the Renaissance found a secular view of life which supported and strengthened his own. Hence the classics became for many a practical school of life, almost a new religion. From the Latin words *litterae humaniores* (humane letters, literature dealing with humanity) such study of the classics is known as humanism, and those who pursued this study are called humanists. Most of the humanists were laymen, but there were many in the Church whose interests were centered in "humane letters" rather than in "divine letters." Among them were such popes as Nicholas V, Pius II, and Leo X; also the papal secretary Lorenzo Valla, Cardinal Bembo, and many bishops. The example of these higher ecclesiastics did not fail to influence the whole ecclesiastical hierarchy under them.

Though signs of the coming revival of antiquity had long preceded him, Francesco Petrarch may be regarded as the first representative humanist. From an early age the classics, particularly the works of Cicero, had been his chief interest. His father, however, resolved to make a lawyer of him, and sternly repressed his predilection for classical literature. For a time, therefore, first at Montpellier and four years later at Bologna, young Petrarch was compelled to study law; but, having no inclination whatever for this pursuit, he spent the time supposed to be devoted to law in perusing his favorite classics. Petrarch himself relates that one day his father, who had come upon him unexpectedly while he was reading the classics, threw the books into the fire; but moved by the tears of his son, he relented sufficiently to snatch from the flames a copy of Virgil and Cicero's *Rhetoric*. In 1326 his father's death set Petrarch free to follow his own bent. Forthwith he turned to writing poetry and to humane studies, having secured a means of livelihood by taking minor orders in the Church. His poetry soon gained him such fame that in 1341 he was crowned poet laureate in Rome, an honor which Dante had coveted in vain.

Although Petrarch is chiefly remembered in the history of literature as the author of the *Canzoniere*, he has a wider claim to glory
through his prodigious labors in awakening an interest in antiquity. Dominating the period of early humanism in Italy, in
many respects he showed the way to later humanists. His discourses and writings kindled an interest in that antiquity which
he so enthusiastically admired. Because of his influence many
powerful and wealthy friends became patrons of humanism.
Moreover, he instilled his own passion for the classics into a
chosen circle of disciples, foremost among them Boccaccio. As a
writer he professed to despise the vernacular, and if it had not
been for the necessity of using a language which Laura could
understand, he probably would have written exclusively in Latin.
As his models he chose Virgil and Cicero. "I have loved Cicero
and Virgil so well," he wrote, "that I could have loved none better. . . . I felt a filial affection toward the one, and a brotherly
love for the other. . . . My friendship could hardly have been as
great for living men I have seen." Petrarch was no mere imitator;
he sought rather to copy the manner than the matter of his models.
His claim to immortality, he believed, rested on his Latin writings,
particularly on his *Africa*, an epic written in hexameters and
glorifying the achievements of Scipio Africanus. It is paradoxical,
indeed, that the Italian poems which he considered mere trifles
should be remembered, while the *Africa* is not.

The best energies of Petrarch's life were spent in discovering
classical manuscripts and purging them of mistakes. He was particularly eager to recover the lost writings of Cicero, and in 1333
had the good fortune to find at Liège two speeches of the great
orator. A few years later he experienced the supreme joy of discovering the letters of Cicero to Atticus. Today they are preserved
through a single copy made from Petrarch's own manuscript.
Altogether Petrarch succeeded in collecting about two hundred
volumes, many of which are still in existence in European libraries.
Among them were some Greek manuscripts. In his *Letter to Homer*
he wrote, "I have not been so fortunate as to learn Greek"; yet
the Greek writers were as much his personal friends as the Latin
authors. The mere possession of a manuscript of Homer transported him with delight, and he prized a Greek manuscript of sixteen of the dialogues of Plato. Thus Petrarch was a pioneer in the
recovery of Greek literature. Great as was his enthusiasm for the

classical writers, however, it had little of the paganism which characterized the later humanists.

Most distinguished among Petrarch's disciples was Boccaccio. Through his admiration for Petrarch he early took up the study of the Latin classics, and was the first humanist to become familiar with some of the works of the Roman historian Tacitus. It was not until 1350 that he met Petrarch, who was at the time on his way to win the indulgence of the Jubilee in Rome. The meeting marked the beginning of an intimate friendship which lasted until Petrarch's death. On the advice of Petrarch, Boccaccio took up the study of Greek in middle life and became the first Italian to succeed, in a measure, in mastering Greek. In 1342 Petrarch had made an attempt to acquire some familiarity with Greek, under the tutelage of Barlaam, a Calabrian by birth, but he did not go beyond mastering the alphabet. Persuading Leontius Pilatus, a pupil of the same Barlaam, to come to Florence, Boccaccio received him in his house and proceeded to learn what Greek Pilatus could impart, which was little beyond the Byzantine Greek of the time. Together, however, teacher and pupil rendered the first complete modern version of Homer's *Iliad* and *Odyssey* in Latin, a notable achievement. This translation, presented by Boccaccio to Petrarch, was hailed by the latter as a precious boon. Tradition has it that Petrarch died while annotating it.

An event of outstanding importance in the history of humanism was the arrival in Italy of Manuel Chrysoloras (c. 1355–1415), a Byzantine of noble family and the most accomplished Hellenist of the age. His coming marked an epoch in European learning, for he was to be responsible for the revival of Greek on a wider scale. Hitherto the literature of ancient Greece had been studied through Latin translations; now, as a result of Chrysoloras' teaching, scholars became acquainted with Attic masterpieces in the original. Among his pupils in Florence, where he taught for four years, were such eminent men of letters as Poggio Bracciolini, Carlo Marsuppini, and Leonardo Bruni. The last-named achieved renown for his translations from Plato, Aristotle, Demosthenes, and Plutarch, as well as for his Latin *History of Florence*. It was through Bruni's translations of Plato's *Republic* and Aristotle's *Politics* that the political thought of Greece became more widely known in Italy. In his *Commentaries*, Bruni wrote:

"Letters at this period grew mightily in Italy, seeing that the knowledge of Greek, intermitted for seven centuries, revived. Chrysoloras of Byzantium, a man of noble birth and well skilled in Greek literature, brought to us Greek learning." Other Italian cities—Milan, Padua, and Venice—were also to enjoy the benefits of Chrysoloras' teaching. But his influence was not limited to teaching. He prepared an elementary Greek grammar which was the earliest modern text of the kind, and which long remained the only written introduction. Erasmus used this text while teaching Greek at Cambridge.

The influences initiated by Petrarch, Boccaccio, Chrysoloras, and others spread rapidly. Groups of men soon toiled unremittingly at the task of collecting manuscripts of the ancient writings. Many of these searchers were in the employ of rich merchants, princes of the blood, and other wealthy patrons of learning who vied with each other in acquiring manuscripts and founding libraries. Bibliophilism—and with some it was bibliomania—became one of the passions of the age. To find Latin manuscripts it was not necessary to go to distant lands, for most of them had remained for centuries in western Europe. All that was needed was to bring them to light from their hiding places, in the libraries, the damp cellars, the dusty attics, or the lumber rooms of monasteries and cathedrals. So intense and successful was this activity that by the last quarter of the fifteenth century new works by such Latin authors as Pliny, Cicero, Tacitus, Ovid, Nepos, Plautus, and others had been added to those already known during the Middle Ages. Substantially all that we possess of the Latin classics today was recovered at that time. As for the Greek manuscripts, of which there were relatively few in Italy, their number was augmented by additions from the East before the downfall of Constantinople. Guarino of Venice, a pupil of Chrysoloras, alone brought some fifty manuscripts in 1408. The greatest single addition to the stock of Greek manuscripts in Italy was made in 1423 when Aurispa, a Sicilian, came to Venice with two hundred thirty-eight volumes of profane authors, including copies of almost every work that was ever to be discovered.

Among those collecting manuscripts may be mentioned Pope Nicholas V (1447–1455), who acquired about five thousand, paying little attention to price when it was a matter of possessing a coveted treasure. By adding these to the original papal collection

he became the founder of the present Vatican Library. Another
famous collector was Cosimo de Medici (1389–1464), the most
celebrated patron of learning of the age. He spent vast sums, employing innumerable commercial agents who were scattered in
many countries, ever on the alert for new manuscripts. He also
erected buildings to house the new treasures, and through his
aid a number of libraries were either founded or enriched. His
personal collection formed the nucleus of the famous Medicean
Library.

The newly discovered manuscripts were copied and recopied,
collated, edited, and criticized, work which gave employment to
an endless number of scribes, editors, and librarians. As early as
1450 Italy had itinerant scholars who were engaged in the Latini-
zation of Greek writings, to assure them a wider circulation. Many
humanists held posts of influence because of their skill in the use
of Latin for correspondence and state documents. Popes, princes,
the aristocracy, and the great merchants employed them as secretaries, teachers, and ambassadors. Since eloquence was highly
prized, humanists also served as orators. But they did not stop
here; they pushed on to creative efforts in their desire to capture
the very spirit of antiquity, and tried to write as the ancients had
written, to think as they had thought. Almost every subject of
human interest is included in the thousands of pages they penned
in an heroic but vain attempt to make classical Latin a living
language.

In the third quarter of the fifteenth century the art of printing
became a factor in the diffusion of the New Learning, making the
classics accessible to cultivated persons of moderate means. In
1464 the first printing press was set up by two Germans at
Subiaco, and soon thereafter similar establishments were opened
at Rome, Florence, Venice, Milan, and other places. By the end
of the century more than four thousand separate editions had been
printed. The most famous printing house was the Aldine Press,
founded in 1490 by Aldus Manutius or, as he is also known, Aldo
Manuzio, a humanist by training. Having early devoted himself
to the study of Greek and Latin, Aldus conceived the idea of printing the masterpieces of Greek literature. Accordingly he set up a
press in Venice. Since Greek type was not to be had, he cast his
own and also made his own ink. Furthermore, he gathered a
group of Greek scholars who carefully compared manuscripts and

weighed different readings before a text was printed. Between 1493 and 1515, the year of his death, he produced twenty-seven first editions of Greek and Latin classics. All were of a quality theretofore unknown. Not only was the text as accurate as it was then possible to make it, but the form of each volume was of a beauty that set a new standard. Withal the price was so moderate as to insure wide circulation. Modern book-publishing methods may be said to begin with the books of small format which Aldus issued.

At the end of the fifteenth century Florence, long foremost in the study of classical antiquity, yielded to Rome its position as capital of humanistic culture, in the brief final period of Italian humanism. Though the humanists had at first been the chief source of the knowledge of antiquity, their importance had been lessened by the appearance of numerous printed editions of the classics. And once the humanists were no longer indispensable, their exaggerated notions and undoubted faults were soon held up to ridicule and censure. The principal accusations against them were self-conceit, profligacy, and irreligion. Italian humanism was accompanied not merely by indifference to religion, but also by positive immorality and license. Study of the classics undermined the Christian morality of numbers of humanists without substituting the ethics of the ancients. While it is true that many professed to be following the Stoic way of life, they were in reality wallowing in unbridled sensuality and licentiousness. The result was that the whole class fell into deep disgrace. Other factors, too, contributed to the decline of humanism. The march of Charles VIII of France on Naples in 1494 initiated a period of turmoil in which foreign armies used Italy as a battleground. Because of more pressing concerns the patrons of learning, upon whose liberality the very existence of the humanists depended, found it impossible to continue their support. Rome itself was spared for some decades; hence classical learning continued briefly to flourish there. But during its capture and sack in 1527 by the army of the Emperor Charles V, many humanists perished by the sword or by disease, while others were scattered far and wide. As a movement, Italian humanism thereby came to an end.

Some of its contributions, however, were enduring. First, in recovering the wisdom of the ancients and the varied interests of Greek and Roman life, Italian humanism widened man's intellectual horizon, stimulated and fertilized the mind, and opened a larger and freer conception of life. Secondly, Italian humanism restored the study of Greek and replaced the uncouth Latin of the schoolmen and monastic writers with classical Latin. Thirdly, it reëstablished in prose and verse good standards of style which were to have a powerful effect on the development of modern literature. Fourthly, Italian humanism stimulated a critical spirit which, if not profound, at least laid the foundations of historical criticism. This spirit was already manifest in Petrarch, in his comparison of alternative readings of classical authors with a view to establishing a sound text. But the outstanding instance of an awakened critical spirit operating on historical problems was Lorenzo Valla's exposure of the so-called Donation of Constantine, a document which had been the basis of the papal claim to temporal power, as a gross forgery. In 1440 Valla (c. 1406–1457) definitively demonstrated on philological grounds that the document, accepted for centuries as unquestionably genuine, was not written in the fourth century as purported, but in the eighth.

Finally, the influence of the humanists also made itself felt in education. Mention has already been made of the well-rounded training which it was believed would develop whatever was best and characteristically human in the individual, a program taken largely from the authors of antiquity, particularly from Quintilian. In general, the humanists sought a free and full development of the natural faculties of the individual, and to this end founded many schools. The older schools and universities, having become strongholds of scholasticism, were at first inhospitable to the New Learning, but gradually opened their doors to it. Before the close of the fifteenth century it had found a secure place in the universities of Florence, Rome, Padua, Pavia, Milan, and Ferrara, and not long after was admitted to most of the other universities of Italy. In time the study of classical literatures and languages replaced the former grammar, rhetoric, and dialectic as the central feature of academic education. Latin and Greek grammar, literature, poetry, history, and philology became known as the humanities because they were regarded as the best means for developing humanity or the highest state of human culture in the individual. Once firmly established in the schools, these studies remained the staple of education until forced to give way before the advance of scientific studies in the nineteenth century.

On the other hand, the limitations inherent in the movement must not be overlooked. Humanism was not popular in character, for its influence was restricted almost entirely to the intellectuals. Furthermore, in its later period Italian humanism was distinctly unprogressive. Dogmatists regarded the classics as the one standard of learning and the one instrument of education, as offering the final solution to all mysteries of thought and life. An indiscriminate avidity for everything classic was the consequence, inferior classics being prized more highly than the best current vernacular works. This gave rise to a reaction against the Middle Ages which spread from Italy to the rest of Europe.

It soon became a common practice to divide history into three periods: ancient, medieval, and modern or contemporary. The medieval or middle period was regarded as the dark, dreary period between a brilliant antiquity and an enlightened present. Rabelais, for instance, wrote: "Out of this thick Gothic night our eyes are opened to the glorious torch of the sun." Scholasticism was styled "inane and arid," and the names of some of the scholastic philosophers were used as terms of reproach. Thus the word *dunce* derives from Duns Scotus. Even in Italy the chairs for the study and elucidation of Dante which had been established in the fourteenth century were abolished during the later Renaissance, and the *Divine Comedy* was labeled "barbarous and unintelligible." Gothic architecture became an object of derision and the adjective *Gothic* was used as a synonym for *benighted, ludicrous,* or *grotesque.*[1]

Moreover, the enthusiasm for classical culture that was present in the writings of early humanists like Petrarch and Boccaccio as a liberalizing force later degenerated into mere formalism. Style became the prime consideration, with theme and content of minor importance. So occupied were the later humanists with outward form that the spirit of antiquity completely eluded them. Even in the matter of form their interest became circumscribed as attention was gradually concentrated on a few models

---

[1] Such views regarding the Middle Ages and things medieval were given new life by the Protestants, who, because of their opposition to the Catholic Church, scorned the Middle Ages. Later the Enlightenment of the eighteenth century was likewise to view the medieval period as one of barbarism and superstition. Not until the second half of the eighteenth century did certain forerunners of the Romantic movement approach the study of the Middle Ages with some degree of sympathy. Among them were Herder, Justus Moeser, and Goethe.

of composition, particularly Cicero. Ciceronianism decreed that the structure, vocabulary, and metaphors of all Latin writing be taken from Cicero. He was the standard of excellence, the voice of authority, for many later humanists in much the same way that Aristotle was for the schoolmen. Hence their writings, now covered with the dust of oblivion, were little more than dilettante collections of model passages from that author. Beyond the Alps the humanistic writers took a saner view of the classics.

THE NORTHERN RENAISSANCE

Humanism developed later in northern Europe than in Italy. Interest in classical literature had been growing since the fourteenth century, but it was not until the fifteenth that the New Learning gained a real foothold in Germany, England, and France. The influence that quickened the intellects of northern scholars came from Italy. Attracted by the fame of eminent humanists, students made their way to Italian lecture rooms and later returned home as missionaries of classical learning. The councils of Constance, Basel, and Florence, at which northern scholars and Italian humanists met on common ground, also helped to spread an enthusiasm for the classics among the former.

Although varying in each of the countries in which it manifested itself, northern humanism everywhere had certain qualities which distinguished it from Italian humanism. Like the Italian, the northern humanists were attracted by the charm of the classics, but their approach was more conservative. Sensuous pleasures, which moved the Italians to abandon themselves to a pagan enjoyment of life, did not greatly influence northern scholars. Besides, except in France, where the court of Francis I and his successors cultivated a brilliant secularism, the humanists north of the Alps were not so indifferent to the teachings of the Church as their fellows in Italy. Furthermore, northern humanism was practical. Scholars, particularly those of Germany and England, were motivated by a desire to purify the social and religious life of the time, and in their studies the Church Fathers and the Bible found a place beside the classical authors. For many, in fact, study of the Bible was of greater importance than study of the classics. They prized a knowledge of Greek as a means of reading the classical authors in the original, but even more as a means of discovering new truth and beauty in the Greek New Testament.

One result of their studies was the publication of the Bible in its original languages and in a new Latin translation; another was a demand for a simpler form of Christianity. By placing the Bible in the hands of the educated classes and by turning a stream of criticism on the abuses of the Church, the humanists prepared the way for the Protestant Reformation. Nevertheless, the religion of these humanists had a distinct secular quality. It centered about the historical Jesus. All problems transcending the human were either avoided or pushed into the background. To Erasmus, for example, morality and social conduct were much more important than the question of the hereafter.

In Germany, where the influence of Italian humanism first made itself felt, the Renaissance was restricted mainly to humanism; in German art the stirrings of the Renaissance spirit are most evident in painting, but even there naturalism and a sense of beauty were often secondary. Moreover, German humanism was short-lived. While the new movement extended over a period of two centuries in Italy, it covered, roughly speaking, only the last quarter of the fifteenth century and the first quarter of the sixteenth in Germany. Thereafter German thought was largely absorbed by the Reformation.

The first group of German humanists endeavored to bring about a revival of classical learning and to introduce a new system of education. They were mostly schoolmasters, so to speak. At no time did they permit their culture to expand beyond the confines of Roman Catholic doctrine. Outstanding among this group was Rudolph Agricola (1443–1485), of whom Erasmus declared, "He was the first to bring us a breath of higher culture out of Italy." The second group have been styled the "rational humanists" because they adopted a rationalistic view of the Church and its dogmas. They did not stop at scourging such practices as indulgences, simony, pluralities, and the misuse of the Church's temporal power, but attacked scholasticism itself in an endeavor to replace its intricate theology and its sacramental rites with a simpler ethical Christianity. The leaders of this circle were Reuchlin and, in a sense, Erasmus.[1]

Johann Reuchlin (1455–1522) studied in Italy in his youth,

---

[1] Erasmus was hailed by the German humanists as their leader. He was also regarded as a compatriot because he had been born in the Netherlands, which were part of the Habsburg empire.

becoming so adept that he was soon regarded as the ablest Greek scholar of Germany. Scarcely slighter was his reputation in Latin. He published at the age of twenty a Latin dictionary which in less than three decades went through twenty-five editions. But his chief service to the advance of humanism was his introduction of the study of Hebrew into Germany. Animated by a desire to read the Hebrew writings, particularly the Old Testament, he took up the subject about 1490 with Jewish rabbis as his tutors. To him the language was important not only as the most ancient (as he thought), but also as the holiest. In order to make a knowledge of it available to other non-Jewish students, he published in 1506 his epoch-making Hebrew grammar and lexicon entitled *De rudimentis hebraicis.*

Through his interest in Hebrew, Reuchlin became involved in a controversy which embittered the closing years of his life. Johann Pfefferkorn (1459–1522), a convert from Judaism whom Erasmus described as "a bad Jew and a worse Christian," had endeavored to show his zeal for his adopted religion by advancing a plan to destroy all Hebrew literature, except the Old Testament, as subversive of faith and morals. When Reuchlin's opinion of the plan was requested he vigorously denounced the indiscriminate destruction of Hebrew literature, particularly of the Talmud, and went so far as to advocate the founding of chairs of Hebrew in German universities. The result was a furious controversy between the Reuchlinists on the one hand and Pfefferkorn and his supporters, styled by their opponents "the obscurantists," on the other. The chief allies of Pfefferkorn were members of the theological faculty of Cologne, mainly Dominicans. Through their leader, the papal inquisitor, Jakob von Hochstraten, Reuchlin was accused of having made heretical statements. This accusation was given support by the fact that he had studied under Jewish rabbis. Summoned to appear before the Inquisition at Mainz, Reuchlin succeeded, by an appeal to the pope, in having his case transferred to Rome. It dragged on for years. Finally in 1520 he was condemned to silence, after which the question was forgotten in the agitation caused by Luther's attack on papal authority.

Meanwhile humanistic studies had taken root in German education. For a time the German universities had responded grudgingly to the classical influence; the study of theology remained their paramount concern. But by the end of the fifteenth century a number of universities, including Heidelberg, Ingolstadt, and Erfurt, had founded chairs for humanistic studies, and by the close of the first quarter of the sixteenth century all the German universities had followed their example. During this period a number of new universities, among them Wittenberg, were founded on a humanistic basis.

Northern humanism produced no more outstanding figure than Desiderius Erasmus. This prince of humanists, as he was hailed, was distinguished for the fertility of his mind, the brilliance of his wit, and the charm of his personality. With these qualities he became the most influential scholar of his age, ruling the republic of letters as Petrarch had done in his time, and as Voltaire was to rule it in the eighteenth century. A Dutchman by birth, Erasmus was cosmopolitan in spirit. Indeed, his life and influence are more closely connected with Germany, France, England, Italy, and Switzerland than with the land of his birth. As his works were written exclusively in Latin, they could be read by all educated persons in Europe. He corresponded with scholars of all countries who consulted him as an oracle. To many he appeared as the perfect embodiment of humanistic ideals. Philip Melanchthon published a poem in 1516 which depicts Zeus entertaining Apollo and the Muses with a reading from Erasmus' poetry; Ulrich von Hutten styled him "the German Socrates"; and Mutianus of Gotha said: "Erasmus surpasses the measure of human gifts. He is divine, and must be worshipped in pious devoutness."

Erasmus was probably born in Rotterdam about 1466, the child of an unwed mother. He was educated in the school of the Brethren of the Common Life at Deventer, famed as the first school in northern Europe to come under humanistic influence. Although the pedagogic methods filled him with distaste, the training grounded him in Latin, taught him the rudiments of Greek, and probably awakened that love of letters which became the dominant motive of his life. The religion fostered by the brotherhood stressed the inner spirit rather than the outer form and emphasized life rather than doctrine, a fact which goes far to explain Erasmus' dislike of formalism and outward observances in later life. Persuaded by his guardian to enter an Augustinian monastery in Steyn about 1487, he had opportunity there to read the classics and the Fathers. He was ordained to the priesthood in

1492, but as neither that nor the monastic mode of life appealed to him, he soon set forth on his travels about Europe. After studying at the University of Paris for some years, he visited England in 1499. This was the turning point of his career. Through his acquaintance with prominent scholars, particularly with Colet, Grocyn, Linacre, and Sir Thomas More, he was encouraged to improve his knowledge of Greek and to turn his efforts to religious studies.

Erasmus was now over thirty and had as yet published little of importance. In 1500 the *Adages* appeared and was enthusiastically received by the literary world. A collection of about eight hundred proverbs from classical authors, with brief explanatory remarks by Erasmus, the *Adages* introduced ideas of antiquity to a wider circle of readers. The final edition contained more than four thousand sayings from Greek and Latin authors with a commentary explaining their meaning and origin, and also illustrating their use. The year 1504 witnessed the appearance of the *Handbook of the Christian Knight*, which sets forth Erasmus' idea of a normal Christian life. According to his own statement, it was written to correct the error of those whose religion depends on "ceremonies and observances of a material sort, and who neglect the things that conduce to piety." A Christian Renaissance—in other words, a return to the simpler Christianity of the early Fathers of the Church—was his great aim, and almost everything he wrote was designed to promote it.

The work which won for him primacy in the contemporaneous republic of letters, and also enduring fame, was his *Praise of Folly*, illustrated by Holbein and published in 1511. In it Erasmus poured satire, as biting in its mockery as that of Voltaire, on the abuses and follies of his age. He skilfully scourged the princes who had no regard for the public welfare; he directed his satirical shafts at scholastic pedantry; and he ridiculed, above all, the formalism, credulity, hypocrisy, and superstitions of his time. The worship of images, the sale of indulgences and pardons, the irreverence of mock mysteries, and the outward conformity in ritual and ceremonial practice to the detriment of true piety, all come under his lashing pen. By his brilliant humor and keen satire he did more than any other man of his age to make people conscious of their follies and superstitions. The book passed through twenty-seven editions in the lifetime of the author. More than a century later Milton could still write: "Everybody in Cambridge is reading it." As early as 1517 it appeared in French and since then has been translated into most European languages. Still translated, edited, and read, it gives its author rank among the great satirists of all time.

Next to the *Praise of Folly*, his *Familiar Colloquies* (1516), in which he continued his attack on the credulity and hypocrisy of his age, is probably best known. When this book was condemned by the Sorbonne in 1525, it became so popular that 24,000 copies were sold in a few months. Under the satire and mockery of both books is the deeper purpose of showing men a better life.

Meanwhile Erasmus had paid his second visit to England, made a journey to Italy, and returned to England, where for a time he taught Greek at Cambridge. In 1514 he had journeyed to Basel to arrange for publication of his Greek New Testament, his chief contribution to scholarship. Issued in 1516, it was the first printed Greek text of the New Testament, and was accompanied by a Latin translation which exposed many errors that had crept into the Vulgate. Because of its low price it had a wide circulation. After the publication of this work, Erasmus spent much of his time in Basel as editor and general adviser of Froben's press, which with his aid became the outstanding printing house of Europe. He died at Basel in July, 1536, and was interred there.

In England the Renaissance was limited largely to humanism, for there was little Renaissance painting or sculpture, and the revival of architecture did not take place until the seventeenth century. The beginnings of a humanistic spirit are already visible in the later writings of Chaucer, who, like Boccaccio, was an exponent of the secular view of life. But the period after Chaucer was not favorable to the New Learning. In the fifteenth century the Wars of the Roses and the persecutions of the Lollards kept the country in a state of turmoil. During the second half of the century a number of English scholars studied in Italy, but their influence on the course of English scholarship is hardly discernible. Not until Henry VII had restored peace and order, and the rapidly expanding commerce and industry had brought wealth and leisure for intellectual pursuits, did conditions favor the spread of the new culture. Then interest in classical learning was quickened by a group of notable men, often known as the Oxford Reformers.

The outstanding members of the group were Grocyn, Linacre, Colet, and Sir Thomas More. All but the last had studied in Italy in the later years of the fifteenth century, and had brought back to England an enthusiasm for the classics. The interests of the Oxford Reformers were primarily religious. They took up the study of Greek mainly for a better understanding of the New Testament. Like Erasmus, they were trying to restore Christianity to its primitive purity. Though they failed in their immediate purpose, these Christian humanists helped stir up a critical spirit which led to a change of the old order. They were more immediately successful in winning a place for the classics in the education of the time. William Grocyn (1446–1519) taught Greek at Oxford, where his classes were attended by prominent scholars. Thomas Linacre (1460–1524) also taught at Oxford, and was physician to Henry VIII and tutor to the Princess Mary. More notable was John Colet (1466–1519), who for six years lectured at Oxford on the Epistles of St. Paul, introducing the novel idea of a critical handling of Biblical subjects. As dean of St. Paul's, to which position he was called in 1504, Colet rendered his greatest service to classical learning by refounding at his own expense St. Paul's Grammar School, the first school in England devoted expressly to the New Learning. His choice of the Company of Mercers as trustees of the school set a precedent by making St. Paul's the first English school under non-clerical management.

The outstanding figure in English humanism is Sir Thomas More (1478–1535), a pupil of Grocyn and Linacre. After preliminary studies at Oxford, More turned to law and reached the highest rank in that profession, becoming lord chancellor. Nevertheless, he retained his ardor for classical studies. Among his accomplishments are to be listed translations of Greek epigrams into Latin elegiac verse; also portions from Lucian into Latin prose. But his greatest achievement is his *Utopia*, published in Latin in 1516, which embodies his conception of an ideal commonwealth or, in other words, of a paradise here on earth. In Utopia, the Land of Nowhere, there is no private property, labor is transformed into recreation, poverty is unknown, money is used only in transactions with other nations, war is outlawed except for self-defense, and all men are brothers. Indirectly, More's book is a trenchant indictment of the society of his time and an attempt to bring about various readjustments. The abuse of power in high places, the dynastic wars, the wretched poverty of the working classes, the evils resulting from enclosures, and the cruelty of the criminal law, are all pilloried by the author. So patent was the satire in the book that it could not be published in England, but was printed in Louvain under the editorship of Erasmus. Curiously enough, no English version was published during the lifetime of More, the earliest appearing in 1551. For the notion of an ideal commonwealth More was probably indebted to the *Republic* of Plato, while the actual framework of the *Utopia* owes much to Amerigo Vespucci's account of a land free of political and social ills which he claimed to have visited on his voyages. More's *Utopia* became one of the world's classics, exerting a deep influence on later writers. Significantly, the name Utopia has come to stand for political and social ideals which are forward-looking but impracticable.

The efforts of the foregoing humanists centered largely in Oxford, but the New Learning soon gained entrance into Cambridge, too. No less a person than Erasmus promoted the study of Greek at Cambridge by his teaching from 1510 to 1513. Thus humanist studies gradually displaced scholastic learning in the English universities. In the lower schools also they made progress. Everywhere in England new schools were founded after the model of St. Paul's. More than sixty were opened during the reign of Henry VIII, and almost as many under Edward VI. Under Elizabeth numerous translations of the ancients and of the Italian writers of the Renaissance appeared, making them accessible to those of fair education outside the universities and schools. Humanism was also one of a number of new influences in the rise of English literature.

In France the University of Paris, a stronghold of scholasticism, so dominated the intellectual life of the country as to hinder for a time the progress of learning. Though humanism had penetrated into France some time after 1460 through the same channels as in the other countries, its progress was slow until near the turn of the century. The real beginning of the French Renaissance may be dated from the Italian expedition of Charles VIII, which established direct intellectual contacts with Italy, thus accelerating the introduction of Italian ideas into France. Charles brought back from Italy a group of artists and workmen, and several humanists. His successors, Louis XII and Francis I, continued his policy of encouraging art and learning and of inviting Italian artists and men of learning to France. Particularly Francis I, with his love of glory and display, became an active supporter of the Renaissance. At no other court of the time were artists and scholars more honored. Erasmus wrote in 1517: "How happy is France under such a prince!" In the upper layer of society there developed a definite secular mode of life; and a new idea of culture, based largely on Castiglione's *Book of the Courtier*, set the standard for the aristocracy generally. In the arts the highest development was reached in architecture, examples of which are the Louvre (1515) and the Renaissance wing of the Château of Blois. Neither in painting nor in sculpture did the French Renaissance produce a name of the first rank. France's greatest contribution to the Renaissance was her men of learning.

The leading figure among these was Guillaume Budé or Budaeus (1467–1540), a man of wide interests and profound erudition. Erasmus called him "the wonder of France." Among his achievements are his translations into Latin of many of Plutarch's *Lives;* his commentary on the Pandects of Justinian (1508), which initiated a new era in the study of Roman law; and his treatise on Roman coins and weights, which was the first serious study of that subject. Through his writings he was instrumental in stimulating an interest in Greek literature, also. Furthermore, he rendered signal service to the cause of scholarship by persuading Francis I to found the Corporation of Royal Readers, which later became the Collège de France. Likewise the establishment of the Bibliothèque de Fontainebleau, the nucleus of the Bibliothèque Nationale, was due to his initiative.

While in Italy humanism had checked the development of vernacular literature, in France it had the opposite effect. The New Learning fertilized and stimulated the minds of many authors, inspiring them to original expression. The most outstanding was François Rabelais (c. 1495–1553), humanist, priest, physician, satirist, and obscene jester. In his life and work he summed up many aspects of the Renaissance. Among other things, he was representative of that encyclopedic humanism of the Renaissance which ranged over the whole field of classical learning; he also shared the Renaissance distaste for the mysticism, scholasticism, and formalism of the Middle Ages; but above all he possessed in an eminent degree the secular spirit of the Renaissance which regarded life as really worth living for itself. Probably no other writer of the era save Boccaccio had such a zest for life in all its phases. As a young man he entered a monastery, took the vows of a monk, and was ordained a priest. Here his primary interest was study. Besides acquiring a knowledge of Arabic, Hebrew, and Greek, he read omnivorously both in the classics and in contemporary works. But his desire to be free of rules and restraints moved him to abandon his cloistered life. The year 1530 saw him studying medicine at Montpellier, and two years later he became physician to the Lyons Hospital. As his salary was modest, he supplemented it by editing medical treatises, and in 1532 also prepared an edition of a popular romance. The popularity of this romance, of which Rabelais himself said that "more copies of it have been sold in two months than there will be of the Bible in nine years," seems to have encouraged him to write the first book of *Pantagruel*, published in 1533. His *Gargantua* appeared in 1535. It was not until eleven years later that the second book of *Pantagruel* was published, followed by the third in 1552. The last book of *Pantagruel* was published posthumously. Because of the inferiority of its style and the acid spirit of its satire, many critics have advanced the opinion that it was written only partly by Rabelais.

The romantic adventures of Gargantua and Pantagruel are a strange medley of popular tales handed down from French tradition, coarse buffoonery, and wide erudition. The humor is often so coarse that it repels many readers. But under the gross jests and indecent mockeries is a high seriousness. Rabelais was a social reformer who used this method to escape the usual penalty of the gallows or the stake for attacking corruption and inefficiency in high places. Under the cloak of his buffoonery he poured mockery on the opinions, errors, crimes, and follies of his age. He hurled barbed shafts at fanatics, schoolmen, pedants, quack doctors, bad kings, and bad priests, making Calvin and Geneva as well as Rome and the Catholic Church a target. In short, like Erasmus he heaped ridicule on the follies of the age. But while Erasmus had written in Latin, which could be read only by the learned, Rabelais wrote in the French vernacular. He was a deliberate vulgarizer who expressed his ideas in a language which the common people, the bourgeoisie, and the upper classes could understand. Men shook with delight over his coarse burlesque, but they also realized the sharp satire inherent in it. Thus both Erasmus and Rabelais helped to kill obscurantism with laughter. By some Rabelais has been denounced as an obtrusive mocker and by others he has been hailed as one of the great emancipators of modern thought, as a worthy forerunner of Voltaire, Montesquieu, and Anatole France.

As a creative artist Rabelais ranks high. Coleridge ranked him with Shakespeare, Dante, and Cervantes as a great creative mind. Many of the characters he created have become types; for example, Panurge, Grandgousier, Father John, Gargantua, and Pantagruel. His knowledge of human nature has seldom been excelled. A great artist in the use of the French language, he wrote in a style often magnificent in its contrasts, its exuberance, and its exaltation. With Calvin he shares the honor of being the founder of modern French prose. To his writings modern French is indebted for more than six hundred words. The historian Michelet says of him: "What Dante accomplished for Italian, Rabelais did for French. He used and blended every dialect, the elements of every period and province developed in the Middle Ages, meanwhile also adding a wealth of technical expression."

The last significant member of the Renaissance school of French writers was Michel Eyquem de Montaigne (1533–1592), famous for his *Essays*. Montaigne was representative of the Renaissance in at least three respects. First, he had not only a deep love of the classics but also a wide knowledge of them, which fertilized his mind and stimulated his imagination. Secondly, he was a thorough individualist, so much so that he made himself the subject of his *Essays*. Thirdly, he was also deeply interested in everything connected with human life in general. Member of an old family of Bordeaux, he received a sound education in the classics, learning Latin as if it were his native tongue. Later he studied law, becoming a magistrate and a member of the Parlement of Bordeaux. Having acquired a large fortune by marriage, he retired from public life in 1570 to spend the next eight years reading, meditating, and writing. The results of his meditations were his *Essays*, which in their final form embody a lifetime of profound study and keen observation. They have moved some critics to style Montaigne a sceptic, and others to call him an epicurean. It is impossible, however, to put a definite label on his ideas, for he did not long hold to any one thesis. In so far as his *Essays* have any unity, it lies in the fact that they are all concerned with the nature of man, which the author illustrated by his own example. He was, however, a sceptic in the sense that he despised most convictions because he thought so little of man's capacity to know the truth. To keep himself from making dogmatic assertions he inscribed on the rafters of his house such mottoes as "To every reason there is a good counter-reason," "I take no definite view," and "It is possible and yet impossible."

Montaigne's *Essays*, which first appeared in 1580 and in a final augmented form eight years later, hold a high rank in European literature. It has been said of them that they "first taught Europe the delights of the essay." In France Pascal, Molière, La Fontaine, Montesquieu, and Rousseau, among others, were influenced by them. Across the Channel, where they soon appeared in a translation, the *Essays* were read by Bacon and Shakespeare, and later by Addison and Sterne. Bacon probably conceived the idea of writing his own *Essays* after reading those of Montaigne, and for Shakespeare they were the inspiration of numerous passages. In America Montaigne's *Essays* became influential in molding the thought of many writers, particularly Emerson and Thoreau. Emerson, speaking of his discovery of the *Essays* in his father's library, said: "It seemed to me as if I had myself written the book in some former life, so sincerely it spoke to my thought and experience." In general, their graceful and charming style, their dry humor, refined satire, delicate raillery and homely common-sense, gave them a popularity which has survived the passing of centuries.

THE INVENTION AND SPREAD OF PRINTING FROM MOVABLE TYPE

An important factor in the diffusion of secularism was the invention of printing from movable type. During the early period of the Renaissance the New Learning was confined to a few thinkers, but the improved art of printing distributed books widely among the laity as well as among the clergy. Until the invention of movable type, books had been produced by two methods: laborious copying of manuscripts, and printing from wooden blocks. Even in ancient times books were prepared for sale by large staffs of trained scribes. In the Middle Ages the monks, serving as copyists, produced books in such numbers that monasteries and universities often possessed hundreds of volumes. But so long as they had to be copied by hand on parchment or vellum, they were costly and their possession was only for the few.

About the fourteenth century block-printing was introduced into Europe from China, where it had been practiced for centuries. This method involved cutting the desired picture or text in relief on a block; next the face of the block was inked, and impressions were then made on some soft material that would receive color. The earliest known Chinese block-book, now in the British Museum, dates back to A.D. 868. The technique employed in its making is so advanced as to indicate a considerable period of evolutionary development. The Asiatics also used block-printing to make paper money and playing cards. The latter may have been the means of transmitting the art to Europe. Soon after its introduction into the Occident, it was used to print pictures for popularizing Bible stories or events from the lives of saints, often with a short text beneath the picture.[1] Later crude books were made by combining a number of these pictures. Useful as this method was for reproducing small picture books, it was inadequate to the demands of the time. Not only was it impracticable for the printing of longer books because of the time necessary to carve the plates, but it also had its drawbacks for the printing of small non-picture books. Once a block had been carved, there was no possibility of changing or correcting the text, except by carving a new block. Thus need existed for a new method of bookmaking, by which books could be multiplied more rapidly and cheaply to supply the demand for knowledge created by the Renaissance.

All the essentials for working out the practical problems of an improved method of printing were at hand. The first of these was an adequate supply of paper. Paper made of fibers and old rags had been invented in China at least as early as A.D. 105. After remaining the exclusive monopoly of the Chinese for centuries, the process was introduced into the Mohammedan world in the eighth century—according to tradition by Chinese who had

[1] The earliest dated woodcut of this kind appeared in 1423 and pictured St. Christopher fording a stream with the child Jesus on his shoulder. Underneath the picture was the couplet:

"Each day that thou the likeness of St. Christopher shalt see
That day no frightful form of death shall make an end of thee."

been taken captive in a battle with the Arabs (A.D. 751). Near the end of the century the famous caliph Harun-al-Raschid established a paper factory in Bagdad. Soon other factories sprang up in all the Islamic countries. In Egypt the use of paper had become so widespread by the end of the ninth century that a letter of the time closes with the words, "Pardon the papyrus." From Egypt the manufacture of paper was introduced into Spain, probably in the tenth century. About the middle of the twelfth century there was a paper-mill at Fabriano in Italy, and before long paper-making spread to the other countries of Europe.

For some time before the advent of printing, paper had been used in the preparation of manuscript books. An improved ink, made of boiled linseed oil and lampblack, had also been invented. This ink, developed through the use of oil in painting, had the quality of adhering to metal surfaces, from which it could be transferred to paper and vellum under pressure. A press adaptable to printing was already in common use as a wine or cheese press. Finally, metalworkers possessed the knowledge necessary to make the proper alloy for metal type, cut the dies, and cast the type. Only the idea of movable type was lacking.

So simple is the idea of printing from movable type that one wonders the method was not developed earlier. Such printing was in fact practiced in Asia centuries before it was discovered by Europeans. The first known type was made in China of earthenware (china) sometime during the years 1051–1059; a little later, type was made of tin; and a detailed record written in 1314 tells about printing with wooden type. There is no evidence that the use of movable type in the Orient had any connection with its invention in the West. Alphabetic type and the printing press are probably independent European inventions. It is, however, still a moot question as to who first cast movable type in the Occident. At some time or other almost every European country has put forward a candidate for the honor of inventing movable type. In recent decades the list has narrowed down to two men. The question today is: Did Lourens Janszoon Coster invent printing with movable type at Haarlem (Holland) about 1430, or was it invented by Johann Gutenberg either at Mainz or Strasbourg sometime during the decade after 1440? The earliest printings from movable type bear neither dates nor signatures, and such other records as exist are far too scant for any final conclusion.

Though the weight of the evidence favors Gutenberg, it is possible that Coster preceded him. If so, he did not carry his invention beyond the experimental stage. It was Gutenberg and his associates who first demonstrated the practicability of movable type for the printing of long books. The first such book printed from movable type by them was the Latin Bible, probably the so-called Forty-two Line Bible, which consists of 641 printed leaves.

Since the improved art of printing met a universal need, it spread rapidly. From Mainz it was carried first into other cities of Germany and then to other countries. Its spread was undoubtedly hastened by the capture and sack of Mainz in 1462, an event which scattered the printers and typesetters of that city. The result was that by the end of the third quarter of the century typographical presses were at work in no less than seventy towns in eight countries. Almost every large German city had its printing establishment, producing chiefly books of a theological character. As early as 1464, two Germans carried the art of printing into Italy, and five years later three German printers set up a press at the Sorbonne. Like the Italian printers, the French printed both Greek and Latin classics and the works of contemporary writers. The greatest early publishing house of France was that of the Estiennes or Stephani. For nearly a century after 1504, the year in which its first book appeared from its press, this house led the publishing business in France. In 1551 it published an edition of the New Testament in which the chapters were divided into verses, a precedent which has been followed by most Bible printers since. In Switzerland the first printing establishment was probably opened in 1472 by a German who had been employed in Gutenberg's shop. The most famous publisher in Switzerland was Johann Froben of Basel (d. 1527), who had no less a personage than Erasmus as his literary adviser. In Spain also, as in most countries of the continent, the first printers were Germans; the first book was probably printed at Valencia in 1474 or 1475. The earliest Dutch books are signed and dated at Utrecht in 1473. During the sixteenth century printers of the Netherlands issued great numbers of Bibles and controversial religious pamphlets, many of which were exported.

In England the first printing press was not set up until 1476. But the earliest English book had previously been printed at Bruges either in 1474 or 1475. It was the *Recuyell* (or summary) *of the Historyes of Troye,* and the printers were Colard Mansion and William Caxton. The latter, an Englishman, after translating the popular medieval romance from the French had migrated to Cologne to learn the art of printing, and had then set up a press at Bruges to print the translation. His first ventures in printing English books having proved successful, he transported his press and type to England in 1476 and opened an establishment at Westminster. During the next fifteen years he issued nearly a hundred books, most of them of a popular character. Although they were inferior to those of his continental brethren in workmanship, Caxton's books enjoyed a wide circulation. That they were read and reread until worn out is indicated by their present scarcity. Among the volumes he published were Chaucer's *Canterbury Tales,* Malory's *Morte d'Arthur,* Boethius' *Consolation of Philosophy,* the *History of Reynard the Fox,* and Aesop's *Fables.* Besides being a keen business man, Caxton also possessed literary ability. He translated into English more than twenty of the books he published, and to most of his other publications he added prologues or epilogues.

Thus, not many decades after the invention of movable type, printing had become a regular industry in the chief countries of Europe. Books were being issued in quantities that would have staggered the imagination a century earlier. It is estimated that by 1500 no fewer than ten thousand separate editions had already been printed. In making possible the dissemination of knowledge on a vast scale, printing became a potent factor in the progress of civilization.

CHAPTER THREE

Renaissance Art

RENAISSANCE art was not the result of a sudden outburst of the imagination; it was the fruit of a slow development covering centuries. In this development the discovery of classical models was indeed an influence considerably hastening its growth, but it was only one of a number of shaping factors. The source of inspiration was not so much the far-distant past as a heightened observation of nature. Just as explorers and traders discovered new worlds, Renaissance artists discovered nature and life; and as men became aware of the beauty of the world of nature a more naturalistic form of art developed. Such impetus as issued from classical models was greatest in architecture. In sculpture and painting the influence of ancient art was more limited, inasmuch as the knowledge of ancient sculpture and painting possessed by the early Renaissance artists was derived principally from some few sculptural remains which were not even the classic models of Greece, but Roman copies; from the descriptions of Vitruvius and Pliny; and, somewhat later, from Roman wall paintings which were unearthed.

Medieval art, the direct antecedent of Renaissance art, was in its earlier phases conventionalized and stereotyped. Its primary purpose was not to please the eye, but to illustrate the dogmas of the Church and teach them to those who could not read. Consequently ideals of beauty were subservient to moral values. The staple subjects were Bible stories and allegories from the Fathers.

In time, endless repetition made for highly formalized treatment; and for such subjects as "The Nativity" and "The Crucifixion" standard patterns evolved, from which artists were not supposed to deviate. The chief figures become fixed in type; the human form was depicted as gaunt and stiff, with haggard face, deep-set eyes, and elongated hands, and was posed in unnatural attitudes. The relation of objects in space was merely suggested, and the place of the landscape was filled in by a solid background of gold. The whole treatment was symbolical, with little trace of verisimilitude. To represent the inner world, not the external; to reveal beauty of soul, not of body, was the aim of the medieval artist.

Nevertheless, despite conventions and formulas, a steady advance toward naturalism is noticeable in the development of this art. Austere human forms gradually become softer; faces, gestures, and drapery are rendered with greater precision; figures depart from fixed types and tend more and more to represent individuals. This trend is visible in France in the sculptures of the great Gothic cathedrals as early as the first decades of the thirteenth century. In the statues of the portals, as well as in the carvings which adorned the capitals and pedestals, may be seen a more naturalistic rendering than artists hitherto had expressed. Whether this influenced the development of Italian art is questionable. A more immediate influence was exerted by St. Francis (d. 1226) and the Franciscan movement. If the dawning naturalistic art of Italy was not originally inspired by St. Francis, it was in any case strengthened in its purposes by his glorification of the visible world. All things in nature, even the lowliest, were the objects of his sympathetic attention. The ascetic ideal had discouraged interest in the beauties of nature, but for Francis they were the creation of a loving God for the happiness of man. It was not long before art felt the vivifying touch of his love of nature.[1] Instead of mystical abstractions, objective realities increasingly found place in the representations of artists. Landscapes were substituted for gold backgrounds. The morose and rigid figures of the saints tended to become more kindly and mild; in particular the representations of Mary, which had been so lacking in animation, gradually began to exhibit the finer

[1] The influence of St. Francis and the Franciscan Order can be seen specifically in the development of Giotto (1276–1336) and his followers.

shades of emotion. In short, artists turned into the pathway which led to the art of the Renaissance.

ITALIAN PAINTING

Italian painting of the fifteenth century was still largely religious in subject matter. It was in the treatment of that subject matter that progress was most evident. First may be mentioned the advance in technique, for now a knowledge of the laws of perspective, the effect of light and shade, and human anatomy is reflected in the pictorial art. Secondly, portraits are included in religious paintings, and even madonnas, angels, and apostles are personalized. Nor is this depiction of actual people confined to the heads; it includes the costumes, down to the minutest detail. Joy in nature is expressed, and beautiful and harmonious backgrounds are supplied. Finally, along with religious subjects, genre subjects, illustrative of common life, are painted, and form a cross-section of contemporary life in its manifold aspects.

Florence, Rome, and Venice were the principal centers of Renaissance painting. As in the rise of humanism, Florence also took the lead in the development of painting. Her artists may be regarded as having reached the very pinnacle of Renaissance art, achieving distinction not only as painters but as sculptors and architects, and even as scientists and poets. The painter was in a sense a craftsman who received his training as an apprentice in the shop (bottega) of a master, as there were no art schools at the time. Paintings were made to order; not only was the subject matter prescribed by the patron, but often even the mode of treatment. Both apprentices and shop-assistants took a large share in the actual painting, the master often only sketching in the design and painting the principal figures.

Giotto (1276–1336), a precursor of the Quattrocento (fifteenth century), may be considered as having inaugurated the naturalism in painting which reached its fullest development in Renaissance art. Though his work is still medieval in its allegorical subjects and in its two-dimensional character, it exhibits a definite trend toward naturalism. As Leonardo da Vinci stated in his *Treatise on Painting*, the real value of Giotto's contribution to Italian painting rests on his observations of nature. His first major work was the decoration of the basilica of St. Francis at Assisi, with frescoes depicting a series of episodes from the life of the saint. Of greater importance are his decorations in the Arena Chapel at Padua, setting forth the life of the Virgin and the life of Christ. Giotto imbued his figures with a vitality heretofore unknown, creating an art capable of expressing the whole range of human emotions. His *Death of St. Francis*, for example, introduced into Italian painting a new element of poignancy. Furthermore, his figures are not represented in a void, but in earthly surroundings, albeit of a symbolical nature. Compared with that of earlier artists, his work shows greater harmony of line and color, and a marked improvement in draughtsmanship.

In the work of Masaccio (1401–1428) the constructive genius of Italian painters was carried another step forward. His contribution consists, for one thing, in the analysis of space. Persons, trees, and houses are shown in geometrically determined places, from a fixed point of view, and give a sense of space. In addition, he achieved greater realistic differentiation than any predecessor, surpassing even the work of Giotto in this respect. Particularly did Masaccio excel in depiction of the nude. His studies of the human body formed the basis for the similar work of most later Renaissance artists.

After Giotto and Masaccio a number of artists continued the development of naturalism.[1] At the summit of this development in Italy stand the great painters of the High Renaissance.

The first of these was Leonardo da Vinci (1452–1519). In considering Leonardo as one of the great painters of all time, we must not overlook the fact that his achievement in painting was but one of the many facets in which his extraordinary genius manifested itself. This genius was of such range that it explored the whole realm of mental activity, surveying with sovereign ease and power the intellectual horizon then open to man. Whether as painter, sculptor, architect, engineer, or musician; whether as anatomist, mathematician, chemist, geologist, botanist, astronomer, or geographer, he pushed forward his explorations with unmatched skill and penetration, adding a new content to art, and anticipating many later discoveries in science. His curiosity gave him no rest, ever driving him on to new fields of investigation.

---

[1] Some of the more outstanding were: Fra Angelico (1387–1455), Paolo Ucello (1397–1475), Antonio Pollaiuolo (1429–1498), Fra Filippo Lippi (1406–1469), Botticelli (1444–1510), Domenico Ghirlandaio (1449–1494), Mantegna (1431–1506), and Perugino (1446–1524).

His purely artistic interests, it appears, became subordinate to scientific objects as he grew older. But to admit this is not to deny that his work as a painter was of the very highest.

Leonardo was born in 1452, in the neighborhood of the little mountain village of Vinci which lies between Florence and Pisa. He was the natural son of Piero d'Antonio, a notary. Sometime between 1466 and 1470 he entered the bottega of Verrocchio, the chief Florentine sculptor of the time, who was also a goldsmith, painter, and musician. From him Leonardo received instruction in the different aspects of the art of his day. At the same time the way was opened to other branches of study. Verrocchio's studio was a sort of gathering place for the intellectual as well as the artistic world of Florence. Consequently Leonardo had contact with some of the finest minds of the age. Here he acquired the habit of scientific investigation, the training requisite to become a master draughtsman, and an accurate knowledge of anatomy.

When he left Verrocchio's studio, Leonardo began working as an independent artist. His activities henceforward center mainly about Florence and Milan. After painting his first masterpiece, *Adoration of the Kings*, in Florence, he went to Milan in 1482 as a sort of general factotum to the reigning duke. During the seventeen years he remained there, besides painting the *Virgin of the Grotto* and the *Last Supper*, he continued his studies in anatomy—particularly the anatomy of animals—wrote his *Treatise on Painting*, worked on a colossal statue of Francesco Sforza, executed designs for public buildings, built a dam across the Po, constructed the Martesana Canal, pursued studies in mathematics, rebuilt the fortifications of the city, constructed mechanical toys for the amusement of the court, and improved the battering ram then in use. During his second period in Florence (1503–1506) he painted the *Mona Lisa*, by many regarded as the most celebrated portrait of all time. The next decade was spent in the studios he maintained in both Florence and Milan. In 1516 he was induced by Francis I to accompany him to France where he died in 1519.

Leonardo's work was firmly rooted in a close observation of nature. Such study he held to be the first duty of the artist, commending it to all who would avoid mere imitation of others. He held in disesteem the slavish imitation of classical models, though his own passion for perfection was doubtless nourished by extant

STATUE OF GATTAMELATA
by Donatello

THE CATHEDRAL OF FLORENCE

THE LOGGIA OF RAPHAEL
IN THE VATICAN

LORENZO, DUKE OF URBINO
by Michelangelo

classical works. Probing and investigating all natural forms, the scientist in him laid the solid foundations for his artistic products. But he did not rest content with merely reproducing. Unlike the naturalists of his time, for whom accurate representations tended to suffice, Leonardo fused the idealistic and actual, expressing thereby a higher reality. Childish innocence reached an ideal type in his representations. The subtle flow of light and shade in the modeling of forms was depicted as never before. For the first time in western art, landscape was painted in a thoroughly modern manner. Above all, Leonardo solved difficult problems of composition. His notebooks indicate to what extent theoretical problems engaged his attention, by what logical steps he arrived at his masterly formulations.

A brief consideration of his two chief works will show those qualities for which Leonardo is justly famed. In the *Last Supper*, considered his greatest painting, the motive power derives from the words of Christ, "One of you shall betray me." The varying effects of these words on the assembled disciples, differing according to their temperaments and ages, are depicted with consummate psychological penetration. Their faces reflect horror, silent melancholy, rising anger, sadness, timidity, indignation, pain, and curiosity. Their eloquent gestures give outward and visible shape to the inward and spiritual state. The disposition of the figures is managed by a device none of his predecessors had hit upon. They are divided into groups of three; Christ stands apart, and upon him are focused all the gestures and movements of his disciples. By the play of light his figure is thrown into greater relief than the others.

Da Vinci's most popular painting, the basis for many legends and romances, is the *Mona Lisa*. In externals only a portrait of some contemporary woman, it symbolizes in essence the mystery of woman's nature. As a psychological interpretation of character, it is unrivaled. Mona Lisa has baffled all efforts to penetrate the secret shrouded in her smile. Her hands, too, with their delicate, nervous lines, enhance the subtle charm of the whole, while the background in its mood and coloring forms a fit setting for this unfathomable portrait.

The second great painter of the High Renaissance was Michelangelo Buonarotti (1475–1564), whose towering genius stamped itself like a colossus on the art of his age, forging mighty forms

which are an enduring witness to the creative spirit of man. Like
Leonardo, he was a man of varied gifts, though not in so many
fields. Painter, architect, and sculptor, he achieved supreme distinction in all three endeavors. In Michelangelo's mind his work
as sculptor was always paramount. He never tired of repeating
that he had imbibed the sculptor's art from the milk of his nurse,
who was a stonecutter's wife. On his own admission he felt himself in his element only when wielding hammer and chisel. Thus
when the pope summoned him to paint the Sistine Ceiling he
vigorously protested against being forced into the trade of painter
when by inclination he was a sculptor. How deep this sculptural
cast of his mind went is shown in the paintings themselves, which
have not inaptly been described as "painted sculpture."

Born at Caprese, near Florence, in 1475, Michelangelo became the assistant of Domenico Ghirlandaio at the age of thirteen,
and under him learned the technique of fresco painting. Later he
became one of the protegés of Lorenzo the Magnificent, and as
such had an opportunity to study the antique models assembled
in the Medicean Gardens. Through the kindness of a friendly prior
he had access to a cell in a monastery, where he dissected human
bodies in an endeavor to penetrate the mysteries of structural
form. He also studied the sculpture of Donatello and the paintings of Masaccio.

With painting as with sculpture, it was from first to last the
nude that engrossed him; he used it to symbolize the highest
spiritual truths. The culmination of his work as painter is seen in
the Sistine Chapel. On its ceiling he painted the story of Genesis
from the Creation to the Flood. For more than four years he
labored unceasingly at this colossal task, harassed by such personal
cares and hostile intrigues as would have daunted a less staunch
spirit. Lying on his back on a mattress, he toiled on at this stupendous work practically unaided, save in minor details. The
representation consists of four larger and five smaller "fields"
which depict: (1) the division of light from darkness; (2) the
creation of sun, moon, and stars; (3) the creation of waters;
(4) the creation of man; (5) the creation of woman; (6) the temp-
tation and expulsion from Eden; (7) the sacrifice of Noah; (8) the
deluge; (9) the drunkenness of Noah. The design covers about
ten thousand square feet of surface and includes three hundred
forty-three figures, some of them twelve feet in height. The per-

fect balancing of its architectural relations, the mighty intellectual force inherent in the conceptions, and its idealized form make this work the greatest single masterpiece in the history of painting.

In 1534, twenty-two years after the completion of the ceiling frescoes, Michelangelo started work on the *Last Judgment*, which covers the great wall over the altar. This vast fresco, fifty-four feet six inches in height and forty-three feet eight inches broad, occupied him more than seven years. The central figure is a Herculean Christ in the act of judgment, surrounded by celestial hosts. Below, the dead are rising from their graves and becoming flesh. On the left are pictured the lost, hurled to eternal damnation, while on the right the blessed rise heavenward. The work lacks the unity which characterizes the Sistine Ceiling. The colossal figures of which it is composed give the impression of being separate masses rather than parts of a whole. It also lacks the freshness of inspiration and the poetic fervor of the earlier paintings. Yet by contemporary artists it was enthusiastically acclaimed. The huge writhing, twisting figures appeared to them to contain the whole grammar of the representations of the human body. Vasari wrote: "It is obvious that the peerless painter did not aim at anything but the portrayal of the human body in perfect proportions and most varied attitudes, together with the passions and affections of the soul. That was enough for him and here he had no equal." Unfortunately the effect of the work was marred soon after it was finished by the placing of draperies on some of the nude figures.

The third of the immortal trio of High Renaissance painters was Raphael Santi (1483–1520), regarded by some as the prince of them all and by others as a lesser figure whose chief excellence resides in his mastery of composition. Unquestionably he did not possess the creative faculty of Leonardo or Michelangelo. In figure-painting he was surpassed by the Florentines, and in the use of color by the Venetians. His strength lay rather in great assimilative power, in ability to select unerringly the good qualities of others and use them for his own purposes. In short, he was a derivative genius of the highest order. His career was concentrated largely on perfecting his technique of painting. In this he differed from Leonardo, so much of whose energies were spent in scientific study and experimentation, and from Michelangelo, who preferred sculpture and who consumed much time in altercations with his employers and in such mere routine undertakings as quarrying marble.

Raphael was born at Urbino, in Umbria, in 1482. His father, Giovanni, himself a painter of some attainments, probably was young Raphael's first teacher. The painter who first influenced him deeply, however, was Perugino, the most celebrated Umbrian master of the time. So great was his impress on Raphael that the latter's early works are scarcely distinguishable from those of the master. Having assimilated all he could learn from Perugino, Raphael turned to Florence and in four years there advanced far toward maturity. The more dramatic style of the Florentines gave force to his own. From Leonardo he acquired greater subtlety in psychological representation; from Fra Bartolommeo greater dignity; from Donatello and Pollaiuolo a greater adeptness in treatment of the nude. Among his works of this period may be mentioned the *Madonna of the Grand Duke, La Belle Jardinière, St. Catherine,* and *St. George and the Dragon.*

His style reached maturity in Rome, whither he was invited in 1508. From his studies of the Sistine Ceiling, part of which was unveiled in 1509, and of ancient relics unearthed there during building operations, he gained assurance and strength. All that he had learned of expression, composition, classical grace, and monumental background was fused in his Vatican frescoes. The *Dispute of the Sacrament,* the first of these paintings, shows his enlarged mental horizon. In *Parnassus* and the *Galatea,* the classical spirit in its joyous mood is represented; while the more serious side of antiquity may be seen in the *School of Athens,* which also shows the massive quality derived from Michelangelo. In his execution of portraits, too, Raphael showed steady improvement. Notable examples of this period are the likenesses of Pope Julius II, Pope Leo X, and Baldassare Castiglione. In the painting of madonnas, for which he is especially famed, he reached his peak in the *Madonna of the Chair* and the *Sistine Madonna.* The latter, painted on canvas for the monks of San Sisto at Piacenza, depicts the Madonna and Child floating down from heaven. A true religious fervor animates the conception of both the Mother and the Child.

The paintings of Raphael earned him so great a popularity that his work suffered from the demands made on him. To fill the huge orders that came pouring in, he was compelled to rely upon the assistance of others. In many instances his own part was limited to sketching in the design and retouching the product when his assistants had finished. In addition to his labors as painter, he allowed himself to be made surveyor of Roman antiquities and architect of St. Peter's. All facts considered, it is surprising that the quality of the paintings of his last years remained as high as it did. His strength overtaxed by his multifarious duties, he died prematurely in 1520, at the age of thirty-seven.

In draughtsmanship Leonardo and Raphael, and particularly Michelangelo, had reached a degree of perfection beyond which it was hardly possible to go, but color was a less explored field. This became the peculiar province of the Venetians, who in their use of color attained an unrivaled splendor. By the early sixteenth century Venetian art had become thoroughly worldly, spiritual or religious aspirations playing little part in it. Devotional piety had given way to a pagan naturalism. Though madonnas and saints were still painted, they were less the expression of a spiritual than of a mundane ideal; they were beautiful young women and handsome young men, filled with the joy of life. In general, Venetian painting reflected the pageantry of Venetian life. To the artists their own environment with its rich and picturesque materials was an endless source of inspiration.

The greatest painter of the Venetian school was Tiziano Vecelli, called Titian (c. 1477–1576), in whom its various phases are summarized. In the use of color he has had few peers in the history of painting. During a life of extraordinary length, spanning almost a century and devoted exclusively to painting, he produced so much that even his important paintings cannot all be mentioned here. One thing that strikes the observer is his well-nigh all-embracing subject matter. Characteristically, ascetic subjects are lacking. With equal ease and freshness of imagination he painted earth, sea, and sky, faces, costumes, and gleaming flesh. And always his grasp of reality was firm, whether in altarpieces, portraits, historical pictures, or mythological and allegorical representations. Real men and women look out of his portraits, vivid in external appearance as in their inner life. It matters not whether the subject was old or young, king or peasant; the same vitality is present.

Of the many subjects he treated, the mythological was peculiarly adapted to give free rein to his imagination. Here the exuberant joy of life which the Venetians shared with the ancients could find ample representation. Here full scope for modeling the human form was granted. Thus in the *Bacchus and Ariadne* the figures are instinct with life, the color dazzles in its splendor. Similarly in his *Venus of Urbino* Titian reveals that power to express sensuous beauty which was so characteristically his. In his sacred pictures he admirably reflects the Venetian conception of religion which centered in ceremonies. To the Venetians church festivals were primarily occasions for a display of pomp and magnificence. This spirit is mirrored in such paintings as the *Assumption of the Virgin* and the *Pesaro Madonna*, the former being regarded by some as the greatest oil painting in the world save perhaps Raphael's *Sistine Madonna*. Occasionally, however, Titian rose above mere pomp and pageantry. In the *Tribute Money*, which represents the conversation between Christ and the Pharisee, he struck a new note in spiritual feeling. Only Leonardo surpassed him in representation of the gentleness, intellectuality, and majesty of Christ. The same high spirituality is seen in the *Ecce Homo* and the *Crowning of Thorns*.

The happiest blending of all of Titian's faculties is to be found in his portraits, which equal if they do not excel those of Raphael and Rembrandt. Here, as elsewhere, it is his masterful interpretation that gives them their supreme quality. Titian had the gift of infusing the spark of life into his characters, of revealing their inwardness of feeling, of painting with consummate skill the texture of skin and hair, and of posing his subjects in exactly right positions. Notable examples of his accomplishments in this realm are his portraits of Emperor Charles V, Philip II of Spain, Pope Paul III, Francis I of France, and Pietro Aretino; to which should be added his *Man with the Glove*, which ranks among the world's masterpieces of psychic interpretation. His gift for genre he displayed in such portrayals as those of St. Christopher and St. John, for which peasants and boatmen served as models. Titian's development continued long after the age when most men have ceased to create. Some of his best pictures were painted after he had passed threescore and ten. Working to the end, he succumbed to the plague which desolated Venice in 1576.

ITALIAN SCULPTURE

Italian sculpture of the Renaissance presents certain traits which set it apart from any preceding work. Thus Greek sculpture of the classical period may be said to have given imperishable form to the outward semblance of man, but individuality, in the modern sense of the word, was a quality it did not seek to attain. The aim of classical sculpture was the expression of universal types, and any representation of individuality was accidental. In Renaissance sculpture the ideal advanced a step to include the play of human emotions within the framework of bodily representation. Expression of character is fused with beauty of form in products of true individuality. This gives Renaissance sculpture a dynamic quality in contrast to the repose which was the ideal of classical antiquity.

Of the many figures in the history of Italian sculpture only the most outstanding can be mentioned. Niccolo Pisano (c.1205–1278?) may be regarded as the pioneer of the movement which flowered so magnificently in the work of Michelangelo. The pulpit which he created for the baptistery of Pisa is a landmark in the history of Italian sculpture. Its six panels, sculptured in high relief, depict scenes from Biblical history. Though the representations are still medieval in that they lack essential vitality, they have a vigor and a classical grace hitherto unknown in the sculpture of Italy.

After Niccolo Pisano a naturalistic style was gradually developed, by observation of nature and by imitation of classical forms, which was more adequate to the expression of personal and individual experience. The first Florentine sculptor of note was Lorenzo Ghiberti (1378–1455), famous chiefly for his bronze doors of the baptistery at Florence, which Michelangelo pronounced fit to be the gates of paradise. Yet even Ghiberti's style was largely medieval.

The outstanding sculptor of the early fifteenth century was Donatello (1386–1466). He occupied the place in sculpture which Masaccio held in painting; together they dominated the art of the period. By some modern critics Donatello is placed among the greatest sculptors of all time. He was supreme in the representation of character, for which he often sacrificed beauty. An excellent technician, whether in bronze or marble, he utilized to the full the possibilities of his material. Furthermore, with him sculpture became an independent art, whereas in earlier times it had been an integral part of architecture, confining itself to ornamental reliefs and statuettes. His statue of David is probably the first example of a free-standing figure. In addition, it is the first bronze figure to be treated in the nude. By his masterly blend of realism and classical ideas of form, Donatello pointed the way to a development which was to be the peculiar earmark of Renaissance sculpture. His originality reached its zenith in the equestrian statue of the condottiere Gattamelata, considered by many his maturest work in point of skill and subtlety. It was the first equestrian statue since Roman times, and one of the two great equestrian statues of the Renaissance, the other being Verrocchio's Colleoni. Donatello exerted a marked influence in both sculpture and painting. His representations of the nude and his studies of anatomy and drapery greatly stimulated the naturalistic trend.

Benvenuto Cellini (1500–1571), sculptor, goldsmith, medalist, braggart, liar, thief, libertine, duelist, poet and writer of prose, is probably better remembered today as a figure in literary history than as a great artist. His *Autobiography* is a curious mixture of frankness, valor, and acuteness, with a liberal admixture of bluster, braggadocio, and falsehood. Written in a racy style, it is a record of Cellini's achievements and weaknesses, a unique work in its candid revelation. Of moral sense he had little. His virtues and vices, his daring exploits, his amours, his intimacies with the well-known and well-born, are all related with the same gusto. More than the autobiography of a picturesque character, the book is a mirror of the age in which its author lived. It presents an unvarnished picture of a characteristic phase of Renaissance life in which unrestrained passion, vitality, and abounding creative energy have free play. If not the most accurate portrayal of the period, it is probably the most vivid. No less a personage than Goethe regarded it so highly that he put aside his creative work to translate it into German.

Apart from his literary work Cellini is distinguished as the most eminent goldsmith of the Renaissance period, as a skilled medalist, and as a worker in bronze. The variety and versatility of his achievements are characteristic of the age. His work includes masterpieces of minute and delicate tracery in gold and silver and statues in bronze and marble. Of his surviving bronzes his Perseus is the most famous. It was generously acclaimed by his contemporaries, but at the same time did not pass without some pertinent criticism. As one acute critic remarked, the Perseus has "the body of an old man and the legs of a girl." Special interest attaches to this statue for the method of casting which Cellini employed and which is fully described in his autobiography.

Towering above all other Renaissance sculptors is Michelangelo. But, like the achievement of lesser men, his art did not spring forth full-fledged. His sculpture shows a well-defined progression from his early style, in which his figures were constructed from direct observation and the study of classical models, to his mature style, which passed beyond the blend of the naturalistic and classical to a more original technique, in which nude figures were made the vehicle of certain abstract thoughts and emotions that were not embodied in classical sculpture. An example of his early style in its classical phase is the Sleeping Cupid. According to a popular story this statue was so skilfully wrought that, after having been buried in the ground for some time, it passed for a genuine antique and was sold as such to Cardinal Raffaelo Riario. The work of this period which raised Michelangelo to the front rank of contemporary sculpture was the Pietà in St. Peter's at Rome. Done in marble, the Pietà has a singular purity of feeling. The Mother holds the dead Christ on her knees, supporting his shoulders with her right arm; with her left, which is uplifted, she admonishes beholders as if to say, "Behold and see!" Its expression of the emotion of pity, with which Christian art had grappled for long centuries, set it above anything theretofore achieved in this realm.

Soon after the completion of the Pietà, Michelangelo returned to Florence (1501), where he produced his colossal David, popularly known as the Giant. From a block of marble which another sculptor had already begun to chisel he carved a perfectly balanced statue of heroic proportions. With a small wax model eighteen inches high as his sole guide, he completed the work with such exactitude that the entire slab of marble was utilized. This he indicated to his employers by leaving a vestige of the old carving on the top of David's head. The statue is the embodiment of youthful daring, second only in majesty to the Olympic Zeus.

In its angularity and suppleness it suggests adolescent youth. An example of his later style is his Moses. The mighty lawgiver, heavily bearded and draped, and represented as double life-size, is shown with the table of laws in his right hand while the left grasps his beard. An impression of irresistible force is conveyed in every detail.

The climax of Michelangelo's style was reached in his monuments to two members of the Medici family, Giuliano, duke of Nemours, and Lorenzo, duke of Urbino. These statues show the influence of painting in their reliance on effects of light and shade. The stone in some places is highly polished to give the impression of high light, and in others is left unfinished to indicate shadow. The statues of the deceased are conceived in an abstract manner and symbolize eternal types. It is commonly thought the statue of Giuliano conveys the spirit of action and that of Lorenzo the brooding spirit of contemplative life. At the feet of Giuliano recline two allegorical figures known as Night and Day, and at those of Lorenzo, Twilight and Dawn. These figures form a series of abstractions into which Michelangelo has crowded his own highest thoughts. As the Greeks established a canon for plastic representation to embody the ideal of material form, so Michelangelo established one which harmonized the spiritual and the physical. Unfortunately, in the work of later sculptors his canon was grossly misunderstood and led to the debasement of sculpture.

RENAISSANCE ARCHITECTURE

Renaissance architecture is not a single, definite style; it is rather an ensemble of styles. For this reason it is impossible to characterize the whole by a few typical details. Unlike Gothic architecture, which was the product of a communal impulse, Renaissance architecture was individualistic in character. The only tie which linked the diversity of forms was the use of Graeco-Roman elements. Nevertheless, though many of the forms of Renaissance architecture are classical in origin, its dependence upon ancient architecture must not be unduly stressed. Far from being mere imitators, architects adapted certain elements to their special needs. The resulting products were original to a high degree.

The new architecture evolved slowly. As in literature, there was inherent in architecture throughout the Middle Ages a classical strain which gradually gained strength in the general ferment of the times. There was no abrupt or complete departure from medieval architecture; rather, existing forms were modified by a fresh creative spirit, and upon them were grafted classical forms and principles until the classical character became predominant.

The beginnings of Renaissance architecture may be dated from the activities of Filippo Brunelleschi (c.1377–1446), a Florentine. Dissatisfied with the confusion of existing architecture, he journeyed to Rome, where for some years he assiduously studied the ancient Roman buildings. The purpose of his studies was to discover the secrets of the construction, grandeur, and beauty of Roman architecture rather than to learn how to reproduce the actual Roman forms. Upon his return to Florence in 1418 he obtained the commission to erect the dome which was still lacking over the crossing of the cathedral of Florence. The height of the dome itself is about one hundred twenty feet, and its diameter is nearly one hundred forty. Octagonal in shape and raised without centering, it is important in the history of architecture because it is raised on a high drum, and also because the exterior is not covered. It became the prototype for the many beautiful domes which were erected later, including that of St. Peter's in Rome.[1]

A work in which the influence of Brunelleschi's Roman studies is more manifest is the Pazzi Chapel in the cloister of Santa Croce. This was probably the first ecclesiastical building to be erected in the Renaissance style. In plan not unlike certain Roman temples, it managed, as a whole, to strike an original note. Two other examples of architecture showing the classical influence are the churches of San Lorenzo and Santo Spirito in Florence, both designed mainly by Brunelleschi, though the former was not completed and the latter was not built until after his death.

After Brunelleschi Florentine architects continued to dominate Italian architecture until the sixteenth century, when Florence lost its cultural and artistic ascendancy to Rome. There Renaissance architecture reached its zenith. The leading spirit in the first part of the century was Bramante (1444–1514), whose great work, the basilica of St. Peter, marks the culmination of the

---

[1] Others are St. Paul's in London, the Panthéon of Paris, and the Capitol in Washington, D.C.

Renaissance in church architecture. The foundations were laid in 1506, according to his plans, in the shape of a huge Greek cross. When Bramante died in 1514, Raphael and a number of others successively took charge of the construction, devising innumerable plans which altered the original conception; but in 1546 Paul III gave the supervision of the work to Michelangelo, who returned to the main outlines of Bramante's plan. Already seventy-two, Michelangelo devoted the remaining years of his life to this undertaking. His design introduced a square east front with a portico for the chief entrance; also more massive central piers to support the imposing dome which he himself designed. He did not live to see the completion of the dome, which was carried out from his designs in a somewhat modified form.

When the conditions which had brought it forth changed, the art of the Renaissance declined in Italy. An important factor in this was the decreasing prosperity of the Italian cities caused by a shift of the trade routes from the Mediterranean to the Atlantic. The influence of the Italian artists had penetrated the countries north of Italy, however, and there continued effective for some decades.

FLEMISH AND GERMAN ART

Fresco painting, so widespread in Italy, was for several reasons comparatively rare in the northern countries. One reason was the peculiar architecture of most churches. Built so as to admit the greatest amount of light, the northern Gothic churches had few wall-spaces sufficiently wide to permit the free treatment of subjects requiring breadth. Thus an angel with spreading wings, a group, or a procession could not be treated. Another reason was the dampness of the climate, which was detrimental to fresco painting. Hence northern painting sought other media.

Of the northern peoples the Flemings were the first to develop the art of painting. After a time during which the treatment was symbolical and the color crude, Flemish art took a great stride forward in the work of the Van Eyck brothers, Hubert (1366–1426) and Jan (1386?–1440). Their joint masterpiece, the *Adoration of the Lamb*, in the chapel of St. Bavon, in Ghent, stands in the same relationship to Flemish art as the frescoes of Masaccio to Italian art. In it, as in the paintings of Masaccio, naturalism and glowing color are interwoven with the medieval conception. The painting is done in the new oil medium. Though oil painting was known as far back as the tenth century, the Van Eycks were the first of the new epoch to perfect oil as a medium for mixing colors.

During the sixteenth century Flemish painting gradually came under the influence of the Italian masters. Flemish artists visited Italy regularly and adopted the Italian manner to such an extent that they were known as "Italianizers." From their contact with Italian artists the Flemish painters showed an advance in certain particulars—for example, in the depiction of the beauties of the human body and in improved composition; but, in the main, imitation gradually supplanted the true creative spirit.

Early in the seventeenth century Flemish art regained its native vigor in the work of Peter Paul Rubens (1577–1640), who opened a new golden age of Flemish painting. In synthesizing the various tendencies of the age, he was to the seventeenth century what Raphael had been to the sixteenth. At the very beginning of the century he spent some years in Italy, where he was influenced by the works of the great masters, and particularly by the Venetian use of color. Returning to Antwerp in 1608, he entered upon a prolific career covering three decades, during which, with the help of his pupils, he completed over 2200 paintings, some of colossal size, including sacred and mythological subjects, portraits, landscapes, and animals. His early works, such as the *Raising of the Cross* in the Antwerp Cathedral, show Italian influence to a marked degree. They are characterized by glowing color, dramatic composition, and muscular tension in the figures. After some years, however, Rubens developed a style characteristically Flemish. Among the canvases which established his reputation are the *Descent from the Cross, Adoration of the Magi, Fall of the Damned, Assumption, Diana Returning from the Chase,* and *Castor and Pollux Carrying Off the Daughters of Leucippus.* Probably the most outstanding are the series of paintings executed for Marie de Medicis, wife of Henry IV, composed of twenty-three depictions of episodes in her life. It is a pageant of history and mythology, for nude genii, gods, and goddesses mingle with historic personages. As an embodiment of the visual imagination it takes its place with Giotto's Arena Chapel at Padua and Michelangelo's Sistine Chapel. In general, the work of Rubens marks a change from the spirituality of the old masters to a frank delight in the sensuality of the flesh. Even in his religious pictures the purely human aspect dominates his treatment. By the mastery of his composition, the splendor of his color, and the excellence of his drawing he became a power not only in Flemish art but in the art of Europe as a whole.

In Germany the painters of the fifteenth century were crafts-men rather than self-conscious artists. As the burghers were the chief patrons of art, the painters sought to meet their demands by narrative and realistic details instead of by formal aspects of line, pattern, and color. In short, it was an illustrative art. As a whole, German painting of the fifteenth century was crude in compari-son with that of Italy and Flanders. The paintings were over-crowded and lacked unity. The figures were comparatively stiff and angular. Traces of medievalism lingered also in the gold background which delayed the development of aerial perspective. Only by contact with Italy was the scope of German art widened. Taste became more refined, and theoretical knowledge was aug-mented, making the pursuit of painting more than mere crafts-manship.

Albrecht Dürer (1471–1528), painter, draughtsman, and en-graver, rose above the limitations which had characterized Ger-man art in the fifteenth century. The outstanding figure of German art, he combines the most diverse qualities, those of the dreamer dwelling in a world of strange fantasy and those of the realist seizing the simplest aspects of life. Like Leonardo he was essentially an inquirer, who took up the study of anatomy, botany, and other scientific subjects with great zeal. For him, too, nature was the great teacher. After his journey to Italy, Italian influence is clearly visible in his work. His idealized *Adam and Eve* shows his improved knowledge of the human form, as does his *Lucretia*, one of his rare mythological representations. In general, his paintings exhibit great force of imagination and emotion, and are rendered with precision and realism. Among his chief works are his *Self-Portrait, Jerome Holzschuher, Trinity,* and *Portrait of a Man.* Unlike his predecessors, Dürer did not work mainly to fulfill a commission, but to express a certain power within him. His advance over contemporaneous painting is also seen in the fact that he approached his problem from both the psychological and the formal aspect. He was lacking, however, in a feeling for color, and for this reason his paintings do not ap-peal to many.

Dürer's highest attainments are found in his engravings, through which he has won a world-wide reputation. Here more than in his paintings are revealed his mastery of design and his rich creative fancy. Here also he shows his astonishing grasp of natural forms, all of his numerous drawings, portraits, and studies of animals and plants being rendered with due regard for the science of form and with great depth of thought. His studies of animals were unsurpassed until Rembrandt's *Carcass of an Ox* more than a century later. Of his many copperplate etchings, the *Knight, Death, and the Devil* is perhaps the best known. Other notable examples are his *Melancholia, St. Jerome in His Study*, and *Vision of St. Hubert*.

Next to Dürer the greatest German artist of sixteenth century Germany was Hans Holbein the Younger (1497–1543). He typifies the worldly and urbane painter, without a trace of mysticism. After receiving some instruction from his father, Holbein went from Augsburg, his birthplace, to Basel, where he became a friend of Erasmus. Soon after this he made the pen-and-ink sketches, eighty-three in number, which illustrate Erasmus' *Praise of Folly*. But it was through his portraits that he earned his high position in art. His *Madonna of Burgomaster Meyer*, painted about 1526, is among the finest altarpieces of all time. He excelled also in woodcuts and etchings, in which he illustrated such subjects as the *Dance of Death*, and, in a satirical vein, such abuses of the time as the sale of indulgences. In England, where he spent some years, he was appointed court painter by Henry VIII. His many portraits include those of Erasmus, Sir Thomas More, Jane Seymour, Anne of Cleves, Prince Edward, Catherine Howard, and Henry VIII. Holbein's art is characterized by certainty of draughtsmanship, by ability to suggest character with a few masterly strokes, and by unusual skill in combining rich and harmonious colors. After Dürer's death and Holbein's migration to England, German art—largely because of the confusion and exhaustion caused by the religious controversy and the civil wars—declined sharply.[1]

[1] For Spanish and Dutch art see pp. 284–287 and 314–316 respectively.

CHAPTER FOUR

The Age of Exploration

AT THE opening of the fifteenth century, European knowledge of geography was limited largely to Europe itself. Men did not question the fact that the earth is a sphere; for throughout the Middle Ages textbooks of astronomy had taught this. But as to the various continents beyond Europe their knowledge was only vague. The existence of the American continent was, generally speaking, unsuspected. Though the Norsemen had already reached the coast of America, their achievement bore little fruit. It is possible, however, that some stories of their exploits may have persisted, and that on these exploits rested conjectures concerning the existence of land in the west.[1] With the exception of a narrow strip along the Mediterranean, Africa was an unknown continent; and Asia, except for the frontier that touched on Europe, was known only vaguely from the accounts, often largely fantastic, of ambassadors, merchants, missionaries, and travelers. The most famous story was *The Book of Ser Marco Polo concerning the Kingdoms and Marvels of the East*, a record of the travels of the Venetian Marco Polo (1254–1324), who toward the end of the thirteenth century had spent many years at the court of the Great Khan. To Europeans it proved fascinating, revealing in vague outline the existence of lands unknown to them. But its influence on the progress of geographical knowledge was slight.

[1] Charles Duff in *The Truth about Columbus* (1936), p. 26, cites instances of maps which, before Columbus, indicated the existence of land across the Atlantic.

NICCOLO MACHIAVELLI

PETRARCH

AN EARLY PRINTING
ESTABLISHMENT

PRINCE HENRY THE NAVIGATOR

VASCO DA GAMA

CHRISTOPHER COLUMBUS

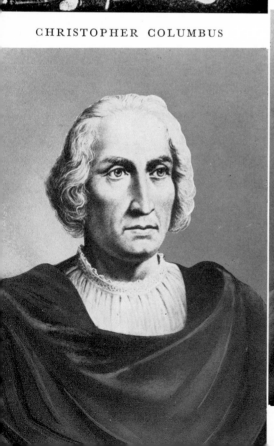

FERDINAND MAGELLAN

How imperfect and distorted this knowledge was, even as late as the fifteenth century, may be seen from the maps of the time. Thus on the map of the globe prepared by Martin Behaim in 1492 only a few localities were given their true situations.

But before Behaim's map appeared, a new age of discovery had opened—an age which was not only to increase geographical knowledge vastly, but also to alter profoundly the life and thought of Europe. One factor predominates among the elements which combined to make the fifteenth and sixteenth centuries an era of geographical discovery: the desire to find all-water routes to the East. By establishing direct contacts with the fabulous Orient, such routes would eliminate the exorbitant profits the middlemen derived from the eastern trade. For nearly two centuries the hope of finding such routes continued to serve the representatives of various nations as an incentive for further exploration and discovery.

Until the late fifteenth century, when the discoveries finally led to the opening of a new route, trade from the East to Europe followed, in the main, one of three well-established paths. The first or southernmost was largely a water route. Starting from the rich trading centers of the western or Malabar coast of India, the way led across the Indian Ocean and through the Red Sea to its northern end, where the goods were unloaded and carried by caravan to Cairo and Alexandria. The second route lay somewhat to the north; it too started from the Malabar coast and passed through the Persian Gulf, whence the wares were transported by caravan either to the Black Sea or to the Mediterranean. The third or northernmost way extended directly westward from China across the Gobi desert, through such cities as Samarkand and Bokhara, to the region of the Caspian Sea. At this point one branch led to the southwest through Asia Minor and Syria to the Black Sea and the Mediterranean, another went northward around the Caspian and terminated on the Black Sea, while a third ran northward into Russia. Goods were necessarily restricted to the more precious and portable kinds because of the great distances to be traversed and the many hardships of travel. Naturally, merchants were willing to carry only goods on which the profits were likely to be commensurate with the risks.

Despite the handicaps involved, considerable quantities of merchandise did finally reach the Mediterranean; from here they were distributed over much of Europe. The cargoes consisted largely of spices which grow only in the East—pepper, cinnamon, ginger, nutmegs, cloves, and allspice. Other Eastern imports were diamonds, pearls, and other precious stones, medicaments, dyes, silks, tapestries, glassware, porcelain, and rugs. These goods were conveyed by Moslems to the Mediterranean, where they were sold to European traders. Owing to the advantages of their natural position, Italian merchants from Venice, Genoa, Pisa, and Florence controlled the bulk of this trade, but French and Spanish merchants also shared in it. The Italian merchants sent a great part of their goods across the Alps to Nuremberg, Augsburg, Ulm, Regensburg, Constance, and to other cities in the valleys of the Danube and the Rhine. They also distributed them in France, the Netherlands, England, and even in Poland and the countries on the Baltic. Italian cities battened and grew powerful on this trade. So rich was the harvest they reaped from it that other nations sought to participate in the returns. But the Italians held a virtual monopoly of the trade passing over the old trade routes. Therefore it became necessary for the competing nations to search for new ways of access to the East. Hence the many voyages of discovery in the fifteenth and sixteenth centuries.

These voyages of discovery were facilitated by certain great advances in navigation, and particularly by the introduction of the mariner's compass. Ancient and medieval sailors had been forced to hug the shores because of the difficulty in adhering to a fixed course. Their only guide was the sun or the north star in clear weather; but when the sky was overcast, even such aid was denied them. The discovery that the magnetic needle indicated polar tendency unshackled navigation. As early as the twelfth century a crude type of compass, a magnetic needle floating in a straw on water, came into use. In the improved form in use by the opening of the fifteenth century, the needle was attached by a pivot to a card on which the various points of the compass were indicated. Now mariners were enabled to steer bolder courses into the open sea. Map-making as well as navigation was revolutionized by the compass. The directions of coast lines and the positions of countries in relation to each other were indicated for the first time. A further aid to sailors was the astrolabe, by means of which latitude could be calculated. As scientific information progressed other aids—astronomical mathematics, tables of the sun's declination, and devices for measuring time—were employed. All these advances greatly enhanced both the safety and the scope of navigation, and made possible the extensive explorations of the fifteenth and sixteenth centuries.

Portugal took the lead in the work of discovery and exploration. While most of the other states were occupied with disturbing domestic problems, Portugal enjoyed comparative quiet. At the beginning of the fifteenth century it was the best unified nation in Europe, containing fewer elements of dissension than the other countries. Castile, the only threat to Portuguese independence in the Peninsula, had been overcome with the help of the English, and by the end of the fourteenth century peace had been concluded. Thereafter Portugal, cut off from communication and trade with Europe by land routes, turned to the sea. Its long Atlantic seaboard with excellent harbors was a particular asset for maritime exploration and trade. The era of exploration and discovery was initiated by Prince Henry (1394–1460), youngest son of King John I. Although Henry never personally embarked on any voyages of discovery, his sustained assistance to men actively engaged in exploration earned for him the title of "the Navigator." He devoted all his energies to the undertaking. When he was a young man he built an observatory at Sagres on Cape St. Vincent, and there he remained for the rest of his life. He gathered about him a group of trained pilots and mathematicians, and at great expense engaged the services of Jayme of Majorca, who was a cartographer, maker of nautical instruments, and skilful navigator. In the neighboring port of Lagos he supervised the construction of stouter and larger vessels, equipped with the compass and the improved astrolabe. These ships, supplied with the best available nautical apparatus, he sent out year after year to explore the western coast of Africa.

In fitting out these expeditions Prince Henry was governed by various motives. As Grand Master of the Order of Christ he desired to keep alive the crusading spirit against the Moors. Not satisfied with ousting the Moors from their domains, the Portuguese had carried the struggle into Africa, and in 1415 captured Ceuta, the African counterpart of Gibraltar. Prince Henry, who had participated in this capture, conceived the idea of continuing the struggle against the infidel. Hence, from one point of view, his expeditionary activity was a phase in the general crusading move-

ment against the Moors. Through explorations along the coast, he
hoped to ascertain the extent of the Moorish dominions in Africa
and determine if it were possible to strike at them from behind.

But the crusading motive was by no means Prince Henry's
sole reason for sending out expeditions; if it were, he might more
fittingly be called Henry the Crusader. He was keenly alive to
the possible advantages of a wider field for his country's trade,
and as a matter of fact was more successful in the expansion of
Portuguese commerce than in the propagation of the faith. The
explorations became more and more the important factor in the
development of trade. Opportunities to establish trading posts
were never overlooked. To that end, the coast beyond Cape
Bojador, hitherto an unknown region, was explored, in order
that markets to which no Europeans had yet penetrated might be
obtained.

The hope of reaching the kingdom of Presbyter or Prester
John was probably also a powerful incentive to Prince Henry,
as it was to many other explorers. During the twelfth century
the belief grew throughout Europe that somewhere in the dim
East reigned a powerful Christian ruler, known as Prester John.
The existence of the Christian kingdom of Abyssinia may have
given rise to the fable; but whatever its origin, it persisted in the
fourteenth and fifteenth centuries. Even at the end of the fifteenth
century King John II of Portugal still regarded as his first object
the opening of communication with this brother sovereign.

The first decade of Prince Henry's activities witnessed the
rediscovery of the Madeira Islands and the Azores and the beginnings of permanent settlements on them. Each captain who sailed
down the coast toward Cape Bojador was urged to outstrip his
predecessor. Prince Henry was unremitting in his encouragement.
When one of his captains, terrified by the surf and winds at the
Cape, and by lurid tales of what dangers lay beyond the seething
waters, turned back, he was rebuked by the Prince in these words:
"Go out again and give no heed to their opinions, for, by the
grace of God, you cannot fail to derive from your voyage both
honor and profit." Finally in 1434 Gil Eannes not only passed
the Cape but sailed nearly two hundred miles beyond it. Once
the myths regarding the supposed perils lurking in those regions
had been exploded, a succession of captains added even more
fruitful results. Before Henry's death in 1460 the coast had been

explored almost as far as the Gulf of Guinea. Thus by his aid and inspiration his captains succeeded in sailing some two thousand miles down the west coast of Africa, enormously stimulating further explorations of a more extended character.

After the death of Prince Henry, interest in exploration lagged for a time. To be sure, trade with Africa and the islands in the Atlantic did not cease, but the Portuguese ships no longer endeavored to push on into the unknown. Not until after the succession of John II in 1481 was the work of exploring the coast of Africa resumed. Portuguese navigators again continued pressing southward, until in 1488 Bartholomew Diaz rounded the southernmost point of the continent. Since there was reason to believe that the long-sought route to the Indies had been found, it was named the Cape of Good Hope.[1]

Soon explorers went out in other directions. One of the boldest was Christopher Columbus. His achievement, measured by standards of that day, was truly staggering. The obscurity that envelops his origins and early life is so dense that he has become almost a mythical figure. Exhaustive modern research has added so little knowledge that only a few facts regarding his early life can be put forward with certainty. Columbus' own writings merely serve the more to confuse scholars, for time and again he contradicts himself in regard to his origin, place of birth, and early activities. Thus he has been claimed by Spain, Portugal, and France, and "evidence" has been put forward in support of these claims. However, it appears beyond reasonable doubt that he was of Italian origin. Born in Genoa, about 1451, of humble parentage, he went to sea at a very early age and during the years which followed gained considerable maritime knowledge. Whether Columbus personally conceived his great project of finding land in the west as a result of scientific considerations or whether the project was suggested to him is a moot question. Whatever the

[1] The story that Diaz named the southernmost point of Africa the Cape of Storms and that King John II rechristened it the Cape of Good Hope after receiving the report of Diaz is, according to E. G. Ravenstein ("The Voyages of Diogo Cão and Bartholomeu Dias," *Geographical Journal*, vol. 16 [1900], pp. 625–655), to be regarded as one of those apocryphal tales often associated with great events. The story rests, he asserts, solely on the statement of João de Barros, who on some points regarding the expedition is undoubtedly in error. Duarte Pacheco, a contemporary, states that Diaz himself gave the Cape its present name. This assertion is corroborated by a marginal note in a copy of Pierre d'Ailly's *Imago Mundi* which was the property of Christopher Columbus.

origin of his vast idea, this much is clear: he was convinced that to the west across the Atlantic there lay land. That he definitely set out to find a western route to India and China, an oft-repeated idea, cannot be proved from the existing documents. The agreement between Columbus and Ferdinand and Isabella merely states that he was setting out "to discover and to gain certain islands and mainland in the ocean."

For years Columbus urged his case, applying first to the king of Portugal and then, when his plan was rejected, turning to the Spanish court. After seven or eight years of pleading and patient waiting, he finally succeeded in winning the support of Ferdinand and Isabella. On August 3, 1492, he sailed from the port of Palos with three small ships, the *Santa Maria* of about a hundred tons, the *Pinta* of fifty or sixty, and the *Niña* of about forty. Ninety sailors made up the crews of all three vessels. Refitting at the Canaries, they continued onward, holding a course which was practically due west. On October 12 the ships came in sight of land. A small island of the Bahamas, probably the one now known as Watling Island, was the place at which they landed. First taking possession of it in the name of the Spanish crown, Columbus continued his voyage, reaching in turn Cuba and then Haiti. These islands, he firmly believed, were in the neighborhood of the Asiatic continent, an erroneous conviction perpetuated by the name West Indies. Although Columbus made three further voyages, on the last of which he actually touched the mainland of America, it is doubtful whether he realized that he had discovered a new continent. It remained for the Florentine, Amerigo Vespucci, to give wide publicity to the idea that this was a new world, though he was not the first to realize the fact. Hence his name was given to the new continent.

Soon after the return of Columbus from his first voyage the Spanish sovereigns petitioned the pope to confirm the exclusive rights they claimed over the lands the intrepid discoverer had found. On May 4, 1493, Pope Alexander VI responded by issuing a bull which drew a line of demarcation from the North to the South Pole "a hundred leagues towards the west and south of any one of the islands commonly called the Azores and Cape Verde Islands." [1] All islands and mainlands to the west and south

---

[1] How a line running straight from pole to pole could pass to "the west and south" of the Azores and Cape Verde Islands was not explained.

of this line, discovered or to be discovered, and not in the possession of a Christian king or prince at Christmas, 1492, were declared the exclusive possessions of the Spanish crown. Subjects of other rulers were not even to cross the line without authorization from the Spanish sovereigns. In 1480, the pope had already assigned to the Portuguese all lands from Cape Bojador on the western coast of Africa to the East Indies. When the Portuguese protested against this new division, three envoys from each nation met at Tordesillas in 1494 and drew up a treaty which placed the line three hundred seventy leagues west of the Cape Verde Islands. The treaty of Tordesillas, confirmed by the pope in 1506, divided the non-Christian world between Portugal and Spain, giving to the former Africa and Asia, except the Philippines, and to the latter the whole of the American continent except Brazil, which was on the Portuguese side of the line. However serious Spain and Portugal may have been in making it, the division was regarded by other nations in the light of their own convenience. As it suited their purposes they respected it, sought loopholes in it, or ignored it entirely.

THE PORTUGUESE EMPIRE

After Diaz demonstrated the possibility of a sea route to the east by sailing around the Cape of Good Hope, internal affairs for a time prevented the Portuguese from continuing their efforts to reach India. Finally, however, the completion of the task was entrusted to Vasco da Gama. Sailing from Portugal in July, 1497, with a fleet of four ships, he rounded the Cape of Good Hope and persisted in his course until in May, 1498, he reached Calicut on the western or Malabar coast of India. At Calicut the Portuguese encountered bitter opposition from the Moslems who controlled the trade with Europe. In order to escape their harassings Vasco da Gama made his way to a neighboring city, where he collected a valuable cargo of pepper, ginger, cinnamon, cloves, and nutmeg, besides rubies and other precious stones; then in August, 1499, he started on his voyage back to Europe. His entry into Lisbon was a triumph. Financially the voyage was eminently successful, for the cargo repaid sixty times the cost of the expedition. In addition, the information which Vasco brought back, regarding the route to India and conditions there, was invaluable. However, the voyage had its debit side as well. Vasco da Gama lost half his ships, his brother, and nearly two-thirds of his men, mainly from the painful and loathsome malady of scurvy. But the quest for a direct route to India had at last been accomplished. The dream of Prince Henry the Navigator had finally come true. The Mohammedan wedge, which for centuries had prevented direct contact with Asia, was at last circumvented, and East and West were united, so "that people might learn to exchange their riches." [1]

Determined to utilize to the full all possible advantages of the new route, in 1500 the king of Portugal sent a fleet of thirteen ships and twelve hundred soldiers, commanded by Pedro Alvares Cabral, to establish commercial stations in India. Cabral, following a more westerly course than that of Vasco da Gama, touched at the coast of Brazil.[2] After taking possession of it in the name of the Portuguese sovereign, he continued on his way to India, where he established trading posts at Calicut and Cochin.

Cabral's voyage was followed by a second one by Vasco da Gama. This time he sailed with a fleet of fifteen ships, determined to secure a permanent foothold on the Malabar coast. After destroying the Moslem fleet in reprisal for the burning of the Portuguese factory (an agency-house for the purchase of spices) which Cabral had established at Calicut, he founded a number of trading posts at other ports, two of which he strongly fortified.

Such fortified trading posts were the bases of the Portuguese Empire, which was not colonial, but commercial. It consisted of a chain of fortresses strategically located both for trade and for military purposes. In some localities, as at Goa and Diu, the Portuguese controlled small districts around their trading posts. They did not, however, press into the interior to acquire territories or to rule the natives. Their primary purpose was merely to establish stations along the seaboard to which the native traders could bring their wares and where the purchased goods could be loaded aboard vessels for shipment to Lisbon.

---

[1] The voyage of Vasco da Gama supplied the foundation for the national epic of Portugal, the *Lusiads*, written by Luiz de Camoëns (1524–1580). The author also worked into the poem, which appeared in 1572, many other incidents from Portuguese history.

[2] The question as to whether the Portuguese knew of the existence of Brazil before Cabral's voyage is ably discussed by Charles E. Nowell, "The Discovery of Brazil—Accidental or Intentional?" *Hispanic American Historical Review*, vol. 16 (1936), pp. 311–338. The conclusion reached is that Cabral's "discovery" was not accidental and that he was not the first Portuguese to visit Brazil.

The real founder of Portuguese dominion in the East was Affonso d'Albuquerque, who became "Governor of India" in 1509. He carried the old crusading spirit into his office, conceiving his task as a battle against the whole of Islam. "The first ground of our policy," he wrote, "is the great service which we shall perform to our Lord." Among the far-flung fantastic designs he cherished were a proposal to capture Mecca, a plan for carrying off the remains of Mohammed from Medina as a ransom for the city of Jerusalem, and a project to cripple Moslem power in Egypt by diverting the Nile into the Red Sea, thereby destroying the fertility of the soil. His accomplishments were more sober, and aimed to drive the Moslem traders from the Indian Ocean. The capture of Goa in 1510 by Albuquerque enabled the Portuguese to control the ports along the Malabar coast which were the centers of exchange between the merchants from the farther East and the Moslem traders who carried the goods to the Mediterranean. Secondly, by the seizure of Malacca in 1511, Albuquerque broke the monopoly of the Moslem trade in the Far East. There he built a fort which controlled the route to the farther East and which also served as a base for Portuguese penetration into the Moluccas or Spice Islands. As a final step in his program Albuquerque sought to close the old trade routes from India to the Mediterranean through the Persian Gulf and the Red Sea, which the Moslem traders controlled. In this he was only partially successful. For though, after a severe struggle, he managed to capture Ormuz, the key to the Persian Gulf, he failed to take Aden, which commanded the entrance to the Red Sea. In 1515, two years after his death, when the Turks wrested Egypt from the Mameluke Sultans, this last highway also was closed. The Portuguese had finally gained a virtual monopoly of the coveted Indo-European trade.

But the Portuguese did not hold their monopoly long. A small nation of not more than a million souls, it was impossible for them to keep a sufficient force to back up their power in the East. The battles waged against the Moslems had decimated their numbers, while scurvy, cholera, malaria, and dysentery had thinned their ranks even more perilously. Even before 1525 they were forced to resort to the expedient of pressing convicts, criminals, and half-grown lads into service. Efforts to augment the number of Portuguese in the East by establishing colonies there met with little success. The one colony of any size was established at Goa. The few Portuguese who settled at other places were soon enervated by the climate and the oriental mode of life. Another expedient, that of encouraging alliances between Portuguese men and native women, resulted only in a population of degenerate half-breeds. As the extent of the empire grew, such meager forces as the Portuguese controlled were scattered too widely to insure the necessary protection. That Portugal was able to uphold its power as long as it did against the aggressions of the other European nations was due solely to its fleet. When this fleet lost its effectiveness, the maritime nations of northern Europe were able to step in and supplant their rival. Already on the wane when Portugal was united with Spain in 1580 in the person of Philip II, Portuguese power in the East collapsed during the period of union, under the determined and persistent attacks of the Dutch and the English. When Portugal again became independent in 1640, it lacked the necessary strength to regain what it had lost.

The Portuguese were ultimately more successful in Brazil, which owes its name to the discovery there of a valuable reddish dyewood similar to the brazilwood of the East. At first preoccupied with the gains that could be derived from the flourishing trade of India, the Portuguese paid little attention to Brazil, with its poor and uncivilized natives. In fact, official abandonment was contemplated for a time because no precious metals were found. In the early decades of the sixteenth century the region, for the most part, served as a penal colony for the mother country. Twice a year a ship would carry convicts and women of ill-repute there, and would return laden with different varieties of wood and parrots. Gradually colonists of a better caliber began to migrate to Brazil, among them many Jews who fled from Portugal to escape the terrors of the Inquisition. Spurred on, no doubt, by the growing interest that France manifested, Portugal slowly grew aware of the possibilities of Brazil. The first effort to establish an organized government was made by John III in 1532 when he divided the territory into fifteen sections or captaincies, each under a captain who held the land as a feudal fief of the Portuguese crown. When this system failed to realize the hopes of the home government, the king in 1549 concentrated the executive power in the hands of a governor-general who resided at Bahia, for the next two centuries the capital of Brazil. In the sixteenth century several other towns were founded, including Rio de Janeiro (1567). About the middle of the century the cultivation of sugar-cane was introduced, and soon large plantations, worked by slave labor, sent their products to the markets of Europe. As this Portuguese colony began to show signs of prosperity settlers came from the mother country. By the end of the century, it has been estimated, there were as many as forty thousand Portuguese in Brazil. During the sixty years (1580–1640) that Portugal was under the rule of the king of Spain, Brazil was largely neglected because of the belief that the Spanish colonies were greatly superior in wealth. But the Portuguese administration continued to function as before. When Portugal regained independence (1640), the Portuguese realized that Brazil was the most valuable colony they still possessed.

SPANISH ENTERPRISE

All this time the Spaniards had been busy exploring and making settlements in the half of the globe the pope had allotted to them. The first Spanish settlement in the New World was on the island of Haiti, called Hispaniola, which Columbus had discovered on his first voyage. Founded on the south coast of Hispaniola in 1504, the city of Santo Domingo became the first capital of Spanish America. For a decade it served as the base for the movement of expansion which resulted in the subjugation and occupation of the neighboring islands. In 1509 Jamaica was conquered, and in the next year Ponce de Leon established a permanent settlement on the island now called Puerto Rico. Cuba, the largest island of the West Indies, was also gradually brought under the dominion of Spain. In 1511 Diego Velasquez founded Havana on the north coast, and by 1514 had succeeded in extending his sway over the entire island. Although Ferdinand and Isabella had issued instructions to the effect that the aborigines were to be treated kindly, their orders had little effect upon the conduct of the Spanish conquerors, customarily called *conquistadores*. The natives, powerless against the firearms of the Europeans, were subdued by the most atrocious cruelties and then were apportioned among the Spaniards by the process of allotment and forced into slavery. Sugar-cane had very early been brought from Spain to Hispaniola, and from there its cultivation spread to the other islands. Much attention was also given to the breeding of cattle and horses, so that the sugar-mill and the stock-farm soon became the true source of wealth for the settlers after they had taken what gold the natives had. Those restless adventurers who were still intent on thrilling adventures, on discovering fabulous stores of gold, or on winning fame were forced to turn to the unknown regions of the mainland.

One of the most picturesque of these soldiers of fortune who sought fame and wealth on the continent of America was Ponce de Leon. Having been told by the Indians of a land to the north called Bimini where there was gold aplenty and, what was even more alluring, a river which had the power of restoring health and youth, Ponce de Leon set out in 1512 with several ships to find this fabled land. For months the ships cruised about, finally approaching a land which Ponce de Leon named Florida, probably because it was discovered on Easter Day (Pascua Florida). Failing to find either gold or the "Fountain of Youth," and finding the Indians inhospitable, the expedition returned to Puerto Rico. A second expedition in 1521, also headed by Ponce de Leon, encountered vigorous opposition from the natives of Florida. After a bloody battle in which many of his men were slain, and in which he received a wound, Ponce de Leon, discouraged and broken in spirit, returned to Puerto Rico to die. Spanish rule in Florida was not definitely established until the founding of St. Augustine in 1565.

Soon after Ponce de Leon left with his first expedition, Vasco Núñez de Balboa sailed from the West Indies to the Isthmus of Panama to seek the ocean of which the Indians had told him. He and his men slowly made their way through the malarial swamps and the dense undergrowth of the almost impenetrable tropical forest of the isthmus until, after incredible hardships, they reached a mountain ridge whence stretched out before them a vast expanse of water. It was the ocean that Magellan later named the Pacific. The expedition continued on to the shore, where Balboa officially laid claim to the ocean and all the islands in it for his master, the king of Spain. This discovery of the Pacific convincingly demonstrated that the lands previously sighted by Columbus were no part of the continent of Asia. In questioning the natives Balboa learned of the great extent of the land southward, and was also told that some of its inhabitants were fabulously wealthy. The truth of this information was later corroborated by a member of Balboa's company, Francisco Pizarro.

It was a time of romantic exploits. Diego Velasquez, governor of Cuba and an enterprising and ambitious man, sent out an expedition westward after reducing that island to Spanish control. In 1517 this expedition reached the great peninsula of Yucatan, where the inhabitants were of a much higher state of civilization than any hitherto encountered. The report to Cuba stated that these natives lived in masonry houses, "went about clothed in cotton garments," "possessed gold," and "cultivated maize fields." This news led to the epic march of Cortez into Mexico, a story which reads more like a fairy tale than actual history. Setting out from Cuba in 1518 with a fleet of ten small ships, an infantry of about six hundred, sixteen horses, and some artillery—assuredly a small force considering all he accomplished with it—Cortez sailed to the mainland, where he founded a Spanish settlement called Vera Cruz. The sight of the Spaniards, who with their strange ships, cannons, horses, and trumpets seemed like veritable gods, filled the natives with awe. Montezuma, their ruler, fearful lest the Spaniards enter his capital, tried to dissuade them from venturing farther inland by giving them presents of gold. But the sight of gold only excited the cupidity of the Spaniards and confirmed Cortez in his resolve to continue on to Mexico City, the capital of the Aztec Empire. To make sure his men would not turn back, Cortez destroyed the ships before his departure. Then he redoubled his forces by enlisting natives hostile to the Aztecs; thus strengthened, he started toward the capital.

At the sight of Mexico City the Spaniards were amazed. "We were astonished," a member of the expedition wrote, "and kept saying it was like the enchanted things which they tell of in the book of Amadis—great towers and temples and buildings of solid masonry rising out of the water; some of our soldiers were asking whether that which they saw was not a dream." To the small force of Spaniards the city appeared impregnable. But fortune was on their side. Montezuma, thoroughly intimidated by now, decided to propitiate the approaching Spaniards by inviting them into the capital. Once within the city, Cortez seized Montezuma and forced him to acknowledge the sovereignty of the king of Spain and also to pay a huge tribute in the form of gold and jewels. The cowardly behavior of the ruler in yielding to the Spaniards so enraged the Aztecs that they deposed him and rose against their conquerors. So doggedly did they fight that the Spaniards were forced to retreat from the city. His force augmented by the arrival of more Spaniards and also by natives who were enemies of the Aztecs, Cortez attacked Mexico City the next year and succeeded in taking the proud capital in August, 1521, after some fierce fighting. In the course of the next three years the surrounding tribes were forced to submit to Spanish rule, and Cortez was master of Mexico with all its wealth. In 1524 he continued his daring march, going through the province of Tabasco to the Gulf of Honduras. At the same time one of his subordinates made his way through Nicaragua. Thus the Spaniards under the valiant if ruthless leadership of Cortez added to the Spanish crown the great realm from Mexico to Panama. Later expeditions went out toward the north from Mexico City to explore the territories which are now, roundly speaking, California and Texas.

While Cortez' force was subjugating the land of the Aztecs, another Spanish force under the leadership of Ferdinand Magellan was occupied with a notable maritime enterprise. Magellan had served under the flag of Portugal in the East Indies and probably participated in the exploration of the Spice Islands, an expedition undertaken after Malacca had been captured by Albuquerque in 1511. Probably it was then he became convinced that the Spice Islands could be reached by sailing west from Europe, either around South America or through a passage he believed existed south of Brazil. In despair of winning support for his project from Portugal, Magellan applied to the king of Spain, offering to demonstrate the shortest route to the Moluccas or Spice Islands, and to acquire these islands for Spain. After wearisome negotiations King Charles I (Emperor Charles V) finally agreed to enter into a compact with him, stipulating, however, that he was not to trespass on the Portuguese sphere.

In September, 1519, Magellan sailed from Seville with five ships. After touching at the Cape Verde Islands, he struck across the Atlantic to the shores of Brazil. Coasting down the American continent, he discovered the waterway still known as the Straits of Magellan. By this time only three ships of the original number remained, for one had foundered on the rocks and the other had covertly turned back to Spain. The remaining ships passed through the straits; then, holding to the northwest, they went far beyond the many islands that dot the Pacific—so named by Magellan in witness of the calm weather he experienced in crossing that vast body of water. In the course of the voyage across this great ocean Magellan and his men suffered intense privations, the record of which has come down to us from one of Magellan's men, the Venetian Antonio Pigafetta. His description of the crossing of the Pacific reads in part:

"We were three months and twenty days without getting any kind of fresh food. We ate biscuit, which was no longer biscuit, but powder of biscuit swarming with worms, for they had eaten the good. . . . We drank yellow water that had been putrid for many days. We also ate some ox hides that covered the top of the mainyard to prevent the yard from chafing the shrouds, and which had become exceedingly hard because of the sun, rain, and wind. We left them in the sea for four or five days, and then placed them for a few moments on top of the embers, and so ate them; and often ate sawdust from boards. Rats were sold for one-half ducado apiece, and even then we could not get enough of them. But above all the other misfortunes the following was the worst. The gums of some of our men swelled, so that they could not eat under any circumstances and therefore died. Nineteen men died from the sickness. . . . Twenty-five or thirty men fell sick during that time, in the arms, legs or in another place, so that but few remained well. . . . Of a verity I believe no such voyage will ever be made again." [1]

At length Magellan reached a group of islands inhabited by natives so rapacious that the Spaniards called their abode the Ladrones (Isles of Robbers), a name which they still retain. Thence they sailed westward, and at a distance of three hundred leagues discovered the Philippines, so named in 1542 in honor of Prince Philip of Spain, later Philip II. There Magellan, becoming involved in a quarrel among the natives, was killed on April 27, 1521. The survivors continued to Borneo and to the Moluccas, and finally reached Seville in 1522, having completed the first circumnavigation of the globe. Of the five ships that had started, only one finished the voyage.

Magellan's voyage is one of the most impressive of all maritime

[1] Antonio Pigafetta, *Magellan's Voyage around the World*, translated by J. A. Robertson, vol. 1 (1906), p. 83.

achievements. It was the first concrete demonstration of the theory that the earth is a sphere, and it definitely established the extent of the earth's circumference. The voyage also irrefutably exposed the fallacy of Columbus' belief that the West Indies were in the neighborhood of Asia. But however valuable from a theoretical standpoint the voyage had been, its practical results were negligible. The vast expanse of the Pacific, extending farther than visioned by Magellan, made the new route unsuitable for commercial purposes. For centuries Da Gama's route to the East remained the only practicable one. It was not superseded until 1869, when the Suez Canal was opened. Moreover, after much wrangling, it was found that the Spice Islands, which Spain claimed, lay in the sphere that had been assigned to Portugal by the treaty of Tordesillas. The only gain which Spain derived from the memorable voyage was the Philippines, which finally became part of her dominions after a struggle which lasted a century and a half.

Ever since the Indians had told Balboa and his men of a land of great wealth to the south, there had been much talk of finding it. When an expedition sent out in 1522 was unsuccessful in its quest, Francisco Pizarro, a man of robust constitution, high courage, and great determination, decided to venture forth in search of the fabled land, which had come to be known as Peru. His first expedition, launched in 1524, met with no success; but with characteristic doggedness Pizarro refused to abandon his plans, and soon started again. For three years he continued the search, periodically sending back a ship for reinforcements and provisions. Finally the expedition landed at Tumbez, about where modern Ecuador and Peru join. The report brought back by the messenger sent to the Indians confirmed the Spaniards in their most extravagant hopes concerning the fabled El Dorado. Pizarro then decided official recognition would be better; so he sailed for Spain to make direct application to the crown before embarking on his conquest of the Inca Empire. The necessary sanction was granted on the condition that he pay the crown one-fifth of whatever treasures he might obtain. Pizarro returned to Tumbez burning to begin his inland march. His force consisted of less than two hundred men and about fifty horses. Like that of Cortez, it was insignificant in comparison with the vast hordes of natives, but it conquered the Incas without much difficulty.

The Incas controlled a vast empire which extended from north to south for a distance of more than two thousand miles and included most of the territory which now forms Ecuador, Peru, Bolivia, and northern Chile. The reigning Inca at the time was Atahualpa, who, when he heard of the presence of white men in his territories, consented to meet them for a friendly interview. Pizarro, however, taking his cue from Cortez, met these friendly overtures with treachery. His plan was to seize Atahualpa; for he hoped that without their leader the Incas would be unable to resist his force. The plan was wholly successful. When the sovereign came forth in all his splendor to meet Pizarro, little suspecting any treachery, he was quickly made prisoner. For his release Atahualpa offered a huge ransom which Pizarro accepted in seeming good faith, but instead of releasing the ruling Inca, he had him put to death after a mock trial. All efforts of the Incas to resist the invaders were thwarted, and once vanquished they never recovered their power. In their search for gold the Spaniards plundered the palaces and temples, finding greater stores of riches than they had ever dreamed of.

When the first ships laden with Peruvian gold arrived in Spain (1534), adventurers began to flock to Peru in large numbers, lured by the prospect of ready gain. These adventurers became the dominant group in the country. For their livelihood they depended on the labor of the natives, who were forced to work in the mines and on the plantations. As in the other Spanish colonies, representatives of the Catholic Church came with the settlers, and soon various religious orders were actively engaged in missionary activities among the natives. At first the missionaries were handicapped in their efforts by civil dissensions among the conquerors themselves, but ultimately they succeeded in converting the natives to Christianity. The capital of Peru was in Lima, founded by Pizarro in 1535, six miles from the shores of the Pacific. When Pizarro was murdered by a group of conspirators in 1541, a viceroy was sent from Spain to take his place.

From Peru and other points expeditions set forth at various intervals to explore the vast interior of South America. In 1535 Almagro, first the partner and later the enemy of Pizarro, led a party through what is now Bolivia to Chile, but he found no treasure. The country was so poor that for a time it was abandoned. A second expedition, sent out by Pizarro in 1540, pushed its way into this area and in 1541 founded Santiago. Previously the district which comprises modern Ecuador had been occupied. Other expeditions explored the territories which are now Colombia, Argentina, and Paraguay. The hardships encountered were often so terrible as to defy description, and the cost in both men and money was large; but the hardy explorers gathered much knowledge concerning the interior of South America and also founded many settlements.

Thus Spain became the first exploring and colonizing nation of America. More than a century before the other European states gained a foothold in the New World, it had laid the foundations for a vast colonial empire. By the year 1574, according to an official report, there were already more than two hundred towns and settlements in Spanish America. For purposes of administration the vast possessions of Spain in America were divided into two kingdoms, each one ruled by a viceroy appointed by the king.[1] Broadly speaking, the first kingdom comprised the mainland and the islands north of the Isthmus of Panama; it was called New Spain. The other, known as Peru, included all the territory of South America from New Spain to Patagonia, except Brazil.

ENGLISH DARING

Meanwhile Englishmen were not inactive. In delimiting the spheres of influence of Spain and Portugal, the papal edict had specifically mentioned the "west and south," but had not referred to possible discoveries of trade routes elsewhere. Hence the English felt free to consider a northwestern or a northeastern passage. Of course the Spaniards and Portuguese did not admit any such right on the part of the English, but the latter were not deterred. Indeed, only three years after Columbus returned from his first voyage the English entered the arena. John Cabot, a Venetian residing in Bristol, was commissioned by Henry VII to make a voyage to the northwest in the hope of reaching Asia by that direction. In the spring of 1497 he sailed from Bristol in a small ship with a crew of only eighteen, and ultimately reached the coast of America near Newfoundland or Nova Scotia. Though finding no rich cities—in fact, no inhabitants at all—Cabot did not doubt that he had actually touched the coast of Asia, and that he could eventually reach its rich marts by sailing southward.

[1] The first viceroy was sent to New Spain in 1535 and to Peru in 1543.

But he was forced to turn homeward by a shortage of provisions. In 1498 he made a second voyage, but no details are known. The practical outcome of Cabot's voyages was the discovery of the rich fishing grounds in the vicinity of Newfoundland.

As it became evident that the new land was not Asia, the possibility of reaching the East by sailing around this land beckoned. The first attempt to find a northwestern passage around America was made by Sebastian Cabot, second son of John, but he found only masses of ice which forced him to turn back. In 1527 Robert Thorne wrote a treatise in which he advocated a northwestern route passing directly over the North Pole. "Now then," he wrote, "if from the said New Found Lands the sea be navigable, there is no doubt but sailing northward and passing the pole, descending to the equinoctial line, we shall hit these islands, and it should be a much shorter way than either the Spaniards or the Portugals have." In subsequent years several expeditions sailed in quest of the northwestern passage, but as they achieved no tangible results interest in the venture gradually lagged.

Search for a northeastern route was now begun. Sebastian Cabot, returning to England after having served the king of Spain for almost thirty years, advised the merchants of London to strike out a path for themselves by sailing to the northeast. As a result of his advice a company was formed to initiate the venture, and in 1553 three ships set sail under the command of Sir Hugh Willoughby, with Richard Chancellor as second in command. A violent storm off the coast of Norway separated Chancellor's ship from the others. Willoughby, with two ships, continued along the coast of Russia, and in the bitter cold of the arctic winter perished with his men, who numbered about seventy. The following summer the two ships with all the bodies were found by some Russian fishermen. Willoughby's diary, in which he kept a record of the voyage, was also found. Chancellor, failing to reëstablish contact with Willoughby, sailed into the White Sea and, with the aid of some Russian fishermen, eventually reached Archangel. From there he journeyed overland to Moscow, where he obtained from the Russian sovereign, Ivan the Terrible, permission to trade in the territories of Russia. When Chancellor returned to England, this concession led to the formation of a new company, established for the purpose of trade with

Russia. Its effect was to discourage further search for a northeast passage. In 1554 Queen Mary gave the new company, known as the Muscovy or Russian Company, a charter which granted it a monopoly of the trade with Russia. Trading stations were soon established at various points in that country, and despite the loss of a number of ships the company prospered for a time. The chief article exported from England was woolen cloth, in return for which the English received furs, tallow, wax, train-oil, timber for masts and spars, cordage, and other commodities. The Muscovy Company was the first of a series organized to develop world markets for England.

Toward the close of the sixteenth century the English, feeling the need of a larger outlet for increasing manufactures and capital, turned once again to the dormant project of a northwestern passage. In 1576 Martin Frobisher set sail with two ships, and reached what is now known as Baffin Land. The bay into which he sailed still bears his name. Convinced that it was a passage between America and Asia, he returned to England and announced that he had found the long-sought route. But interest in the new passage quickly became secondary when some ore which Frobisher had brought back was reported to contain gold. The prospect of inexhaustible sources which would far eclipse the mines of Spanish America completely captivated men's minds, and the company formed to support Frobisher's original venture now turned to furthering the search for gold. However, after two expeditions, headed by Frobisher, had transported many shiploads of the ore to England, it was found to be worthless. The fiasco threw the company into hopeless bankruptcy and prevented it from resuming the search for a northwest passage.

Some years later John Davis made three attempts (1585–1587) to sail around the northern part of the American continent. He was convinced that the channels in the strait (still known as Davis Strait) between Greenland and Baffin Land led to Asia. Modern discovery has shown that Davis was partly right. Two of the four channels he discovered do run around the north of America, but they are not navigable because of the perennial ice. Davis's failure to reach Asia, added to Frobisher's failure, discouraged further attempts at sending out expeditions. English merchants, eager to share in the trade with the East, now turned their attention in another direction.

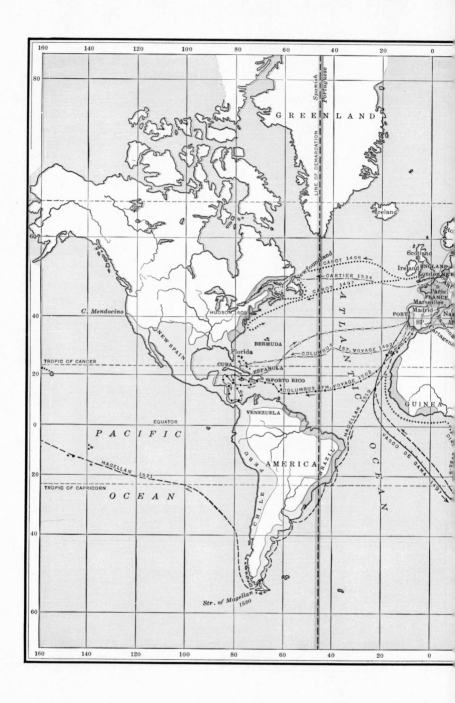

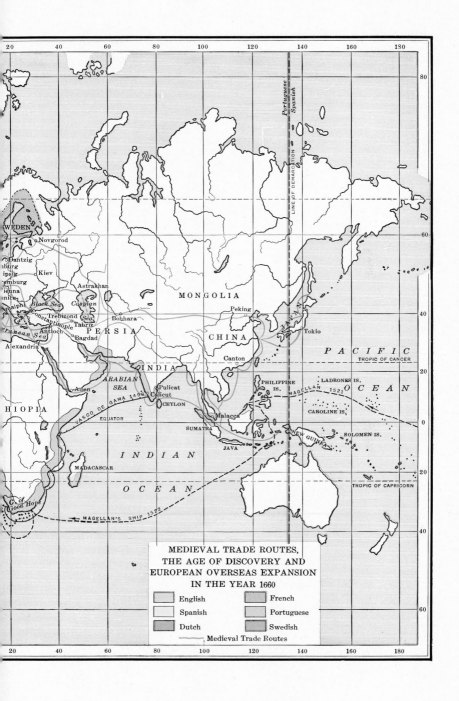

MEDIEVAL TRADE ROUTES,
THE AGE OF DISCOVERY AND
EUROPEAN OVERSEAS EXPANSION
IN THE YEAR 1660

English
Spanish
Dutch
French
Portuguese
Swedish
Medieval Trade Routes

While the explorers were busy with the search for a northern passage, a class of adventurers had arisen who, with the tacit encouragement of the English government, undertook to destroy the commercial monopoly of Spain.[1] Prominent among these adventurers was John Hawkins (1532–1595). As a youth Hawkins made some voyages to the Canary Islands, where he heard that there was a great demand for slaves in Hispaniola (Haiti). Lured by the prospects of gain from the slave trade, he resolved to try his fortunes in it. His first voyage (1562) to Guinea was successful, for he obtained three hundred Negroes, "partly by the sword and partly by other means," and sold them to the Spanish planters at Hispaniola. Despite Spanish objections, Hawkins sailed again in 1564, making a handsome profit from the venture. This time he took the slaves to the Spanish Main [2] and to the Gulf of Mexico. But his third voyage ended disastrously. Disposing of his cargo of slaves, Hawkins proceeded to enter the port of San Juan de Ulua, where he was suddenly attacked by a Spanish fleet. Three of the largest of his five ships were destroyed. Only the two smallest reached England, with Hawkins on board one and Francis Drake, his principal assistant, on the other.

The attack was neither forgiven nor forgotten by the Elizabethan seamen. It gave rise to retaliatory measures in which Francis Drake took a leading rôle. To avenge the murder of his comrades as well as to recoup himself for his personal losses, Drake resorted to piracy or, as it was later called, buccaneering. His first successful venture was the capture of a Spanish treasure train laden with thirty tons of silver as it crossed the Isthmus of Panama. The success of this expedition incited Drake to a still more daring enterprise. Setting sail again in 1577, he at first followed the route Magellan took on his circumnavigation of the globe. After passing through the Straits of Magellan he sailed up the west coast of South America as far as California, seizing as many Spanish vessels as he could. Presumably Drake had the idea of finding a northern passage to England, but after sailing north from California for some time he abandoned the search. Instead of sailing home the way he had come, he turned westward,

---

[1] The contention of the English that they had a right to trade with the Spanish colonies anticipated the Open Door policy claimed by modern European states.

[2] That portion of the Caribbean Sea adjacent to the northeast coast of South America.

touching the Philippines and the Spice Islands. From there he took a route around the Cape of Good Hope, and in 1580, two years and nine months after his departure, landed in England. The cargo of gold, silver, spices, and silks which he brought back was unequaled in the annals of Spanish adventuring. For his services Drake was knighted by Queen Elizabeth.

English commerce took great strides forward thereafter. Among the factors which promoted this growth were the loss of respect for the papal awards to Spain and Portugal and particularly the growing disregard of the English for the naval power of Spain. The last lingering fear was shattered when the "Invincible Armada" was ignominiously defeated in 1588. The effect of Drake's voyage upon the future of English commerce was also far-reaching. It silenced those who were inclined to regard the English galleons as inadequate for the long trip to the East. In fact these swift-sailing ships proved themselves superior to the slow-moving Portuguese carracks. Moreover, the information Drake brought back was encouraging to English hopes, revealing as it did the hostility of the native princes to the Portuguese. Emboldened by these circumstances, the English set resolutely to work to grasp what share they could in the world's richest trade. The first English squadron, financed by a group of London merchants, was commissioned in 1591 and sailed around the Cape of Good Hope into the Indian Ocean. Though this voyage ended disastrously because of an unhappy combination of storms, mutiny, and disease, another fleet was equipped by the London merchants in 1599. The returns from this voyage doubled the amount of capital invested, whereupon the thrifty merchants petitioned the crown for a charter. Thus was founded on December 30, 1600, the English East India Company, destined to be the greatest trading and empire-building corporation in English history.

FRENCH EXPLORATIONS

The French also participated in the explorations of the sixteenth century. In fact, they very early reaped benefit from the discovery of the New World. As early as 1504, hardy fishermen of Brittany and Normandy undertook voyages to Newfoundland fishing grounds; and after 1509, fishing expeditions went out yearly. With a plentiful supply of fish and a wide demand because of the many fast days of the Church, fishing became a lucrative business. All expeditions were financed by private interests, for the government was either too indifferent or too preoccupied with politics and wars to engage in such ventures as participation in explorations. Finally, however, Francis I (1515–1547) entered the contest for the discovery of a westward route to China and the Spice Islands. In 1524 he sent out Giovanni Verrazano, a Florentine, who explored the eastern coast of North America from New Jersey to Cape Cod searching for such a passage. When the explorer returned to France, he found the king too immersed in difficulties to give any further attention to exploration.

A decade later, during a lull in his wars with Charles V, Francis I renewed the French efforts to find a westward passage to China when he sent out Jacques Cartier. With two ships Cartier sailed to Newfoundland; he then continued slowly up the eastern coast of the island, passed through the Strait of Belle Isle, and finally reached a point near the mouth of the St. Lawrence. There the ships encountered heavy tides and adverse winds, and as the season was late Cartier decided to return home lest he be forced to spend the winter on the barren coast of the New World. The hope that he had found a way to China led him to return in the following year to the place where he had turned back. Proceeding up the St. Lawrence, he came to the Indian village of Hochelaga, near a mountain which the French named Mont Réal (now Montreal). To the west he saw rapids which prevented him from sailing on. The belief that these rapids barred the way to China is perpetuated by the name La Chine (China). Though Cartier's efforts to reach China were unsuccessful, he did discover the fertile lowlands of the St. Lawrence. For more than half a century thereafter the French government did nothing further, its energies being absorbed by religious dissension and religious wars. But early in the seventeenth century a new era opened for New France with the founding of settlements at Port Royal in Nova Scotia (1604) and at Quebec (1608).

In summary, after Prince Henry ushered in the age of exploration by sending out his sea captains to explore the coast of Africa, the work of discovery was carried on by other countries, which were primarily concerned with finding new routes to the East. As the explorers went out in search of these new routes, they discovered parts of the globe theretofore unknown to Europeans. In this way they added to the fast-growing knowledge of the habitable world. In quick succession Diaz sailed around the Cape of Good Hope, Columbus discovered the New World, Vasco da Gama sailed to India, and Cabral landed on the coast of Brazil. After the pope confirmed the right of the Portuguese to the East and the right of the Spaniards to the West, the former established a supremacy in India which lasted to the end of the sixteenth century, while the latter became the great exploring and colonizing power in America. Such explorers as Ponce de Leon, Balboa, Cortez, and Pizarro explored vast territories in the New World and laid claim to them for the Spanish crown; on the sea Magellan achieved the astounding feat of circumnavigating the globe. Though the English and French made no permanent settlements in the New World during the sixteenth century, they did send out explorers, particularly in quest of a northern passage to India. From England the Cabots, Martin Frobisher, and John Davis, and from France Verrazano and Cartier, went out to explore the coast of North America in the hope of finding a passage to the East, while the English Willoughby-Chancellor expedition sought to discover a northeast passage to India. The result of these explorations was that by the end of the sixteenth century the Europeans had learned the general outlines of the greater part of the world. Also they had opened a new world of commerce and had found vast wealth in the form of precious metals. Both the new commerce and the new supply of precious metals gave a great impetus to the rise of capitalism, a development which will be discussed in the next chapter.

CHAPTER FIVE

Capitalism, Banking, and Mercantilism

THE BACKGROUND OF MODERN CAPITALISM

CAPITALISM, like most "isms," is susceptible of many interpretations. The various definitions agree only in the one respect that capitalism involves the use of capital. In a broader sense, capital is everything that produces or is used to produce an income, but in a more specific sense it is wealth other than land; it is fluid, negotiable wealth, and implies the existence of a money economy. Thus capitalism may be defined as a system of using wealth other than land on a large scale for the definite purpose of securing an income.

The use of capital on a large scale is not a distinctly modern phenomenon. In some form or other it has existed wherever money economy has been dominant. Hence elements of capitalism are evident from very early times. In essence the older capitalism was the same as the modern variety, the difference between the two being primarily quantitative. Most attributes of modern capitalism, such as the accumulation of wealth, the investment of capital in commerce and industry, the lending of money for interest, production for profit, and the employment of hired labor, have existed since ancient times. In Greece capitalistic finance and commerce were not uncommon, and even capitalistic production was not unknown. Because of the risks involved in commercial enterprises the rate on loans for that purpose ranged from twelve to twenty per cent, and in some instances rose as high as thirty. In the Roman Republic, and also in the Roman Empire, capitalistic enterprise was more highly developed. Though industry was least affected—since the larger markets were supplied by small craftsmen, while slave labor provided for local needs—there were industries carried on by freedmen for which men of wealth furnished the capital and whose profits they shared. Thus the manufacture of glassware and pottery, of silver and bronzeware, was organized on lines of capitalistic production. There were also partnerships and joint-stock companies for the operation of mines and saltworks. Furthermore, the Roman bankers were not merely money-changers; many of them received deposits, paid interest on them, and made loans on notes and real estate. At first the rate of interest for loans was high, but in 50 B.C. one per cent a month was made the legal rate for the whole empire. Some banks even had branches or correspondents in other cities and were therefore able to issue bills of exchange. Yet in comparison with the vast extent of the empire and the size of its population the capitalistic transactions of the time were relatively insignificant.

The fall of the Roman Empire put an end to most of the business development of the preceding age. After the fourth century the towns largely ceased to be centers of a flourishing trade and thenceforth served principally as the homes of a purely agricultural population. Except in Italy and the Netherlands, the economic life of Christian Europe was for more than five centuries restricted primarily to the manor. In the absence of markets each manor aimed to produce, so far as possible, everything necessary for the subsistence of the lord of the manor and of the villeins and serfs who lived on it, including food, clothing, implements, and weapons. The attainment of complete self-sufficiency was, of course, impossible. Certain wares essential to existence and work had to be purchased from traders outside the manor or village. One such item was salt; another was iron, necessary for agricultural implements. A traffic in wine was also sustained. In one part of western Europe foreign trade did not cease after the fall of the empire. It was not until late in the eighth century that Islam closed the Mediterranean so completely that commerce along the Mediterranean coast of Gaul was blighted. Thereafter, until near the eleventh century, foreign trade on a large scale did not exist in western Europe. At no time, however, did it cease entirely. During the whole period from the eighth century to the eleventh, Jewish and Syrian merchants carried on a limited trade in oriental luxuries. Under these conditions the use of money was not nearly so general as it had been in the foregoing period. The peasant made his payments to the lord of the manor in produce or in service. Such trade as existed on the manor was maintained largely on the basis of barter. Even wars could be waged without a large outlay of money, for each knight equipped himself from his own resources. Before modern capitalism could emerge it was necessary that a money economy should arise.

The development of this money economy, which took place by slow degrees after the tenth century, was accelerated by the Crusades. On the one hand, the crusaders needed a ready means of exchange for the purchase of equipment, supplies, and transportation; and on the other, the merchants required a standard and stable coinage for the expanding trade between the East and the West. Gradually the precious metals which had been locked away, particularly by the Church, were made mobile, and more were added from other sources. But the medium of exchange was still largely silver. It was not until the thirteenth century that gold was coined on a large scale. With this minting of gold the monetary system of modern Europe may be said to begin. Much of the gold for this coinage probably came to the West from the Byzantine Empire. After the capture of Constantinople (1204), the Venetians not only took from the conquered city a huge treasure in gold but they also received as their share of the spoils three-eighths of the territory of the Byzantine Empire. In this way they gained control of the Crimea, probably the only district producing gold at the time. The first gold coin, however, was not minted by Venice, but by Florence, then the city of bankers. It was the famous gold florin which appeared in 1252. Venice followed suit in 1280 with a gold coin of the same weight as the florin, called a ducat (later, sequin), and in the fourteenth century most European states issued gold coins.[1] Since the supply of precious metals was still far from sufficient for the needs of the expanding com-

---

[1] The need for a heavier silver coin than the denarius or penny which was the chief current coin in silver during the Middle Ages led to the minting by Louis IX of France (1266) of the *gros tournois*, a coin which was soon imitated in other countries, resulting in the appearance of the German *Groschen*, the Italian *grosso*, the Flemish *groot*, and the English *groat*.

merce, mining was pursued more vigorously, particularly in the fifteenth century. Shafts in Italy, southern France, Spain, England, Austria, Silesia, Hungary, and Bohemia,[1] none of which was unusually rich or worked with any degree of technical skill, produced considerable amounts of bullion. Still the production of precious metals could not keep pace with the expansion of commerce. But the discovery of rich sources of gold and silver in America put an end to the shortage of bullion. Thereafter capitalistic trade flourished and capitalistic industry developed in new directions.

In the new towns which had grown as a result of increased commercial activity after the tenth century, and in the old towns which had again become active, the restrictions placed on both trade and industry were at first unfavorable to capitalistic enterprise. Each town formed a separate economic unit within which both industry and trade were controlled by gilds or associations of persons engaged in the same calling. These gilds, particularly the craft gilds, restricted the use of capital by individuals. They held their members in close regulation, minutely prescribing the rate of wages, the hours of labor, the materials and methods to be used, the quality of the finished product, and even the amount of goods each master could produce, the number of apprentices and journeymen he was permitted to employ, and the price he could charge for the finished product—he could take only the "just price," no more and no less.

After the thirteenth century, however, the gilds declined. The internal causes of their decay included a growing exclusiveness. Whereas formerly most of those desiring to practice a trade were able to become masters in the gilds, now only a select number were admitted as masters, the rest being unable to rise higher than journeymen. Furthermore, the increasingly minute gild regulations left no room for inventive skill and improved methods of production. This was contrary to the trend of an age in which the expanding markets demanded increased production and better methods of manufacture. Since the gild system was inadequate for these markets, privileged establishments, protected by the state, were founded in some cities, or craftsmen who were not gild

---

[1] From silver mined in the valley of St. Joachim in Bohemia there was coined in 1519 the *Joachimsthaler* or *Thaler*, the father of the "almighty dollar" of the United States.

members opened establishments outside the towns, often with funds supplied by capitalist merchants. Thus capitalism developed largely outside the gilds. A distinction must be made, however, between the gilds which produced for local use and those which produced for export. The latter, which will be discussed in the next section of this chapter, early became capitalistic.

Prior to the decline of the gilds opportunities for the use of capital had been increasing gradually for those who succeeded in accumulating a surplus from money-lending, mining, and foreign trade. Export trade was dominated by capital even before the thirteenth century. Thus modern capitalism was born much earlier than is generally assumed. The capitalistic spirit, which a number of writers date from the age of the Reformation, is definitely to be found centuries earlier. True, capitalism did not exercise a preponderant influence on the economic life of these centuries, but the evidences for its existence are unmistakable. The period of early capitalism may be said to have lasted, broadly speaking, from the thirteenth century to the eighteenth. This capitalism was largely commercial, though instances of industrial capitalism are not wanting.

COMMERCIAL CAPITALISM

The story of modern capitalism begins with the merchants of Venice, Florence, Genoa, and Pisa. The trade of these cities with Constantinople and the Mohammedan cities of Africa and the East, which had already begun to flourish before the Crusades, expanded rapidly after they started. While engaged in the transportation of pilgrims, crusaders, and supplies with large merchant fleets built for the purpose, the merchants of the Italian cities missed no opportunity to establish depots or trading quarters in the cities taken by the crusaders. When the Crusades ended they had important trade connections with the cities of Syria and Palestine, and virtually controlled many cities on the Aegean and on the Black Sea. The trade was conducted by professional wholesale merchants who sold only to smaller merchants and to shopkeepers; not directly to the consumer. A wholesale merchant, of course, needed considerable capital and often owned the ship which transported his cargo.

As early as 1200 there appeared the sedentary merchant, who possessed a larger amount of capital than the traveling merchant.

Whereas the latter probably owned only one ship, the former had a fleet of ships. The sedentary capitalist did not go on trading voyages, but remained at home to direct various ventures in which his capital was invested. In comparison with the traveling merchant he was a man of big business. Trusted agents, working either on salary or on commission, did the actual buying and selling and supervised the transportation of the goods. Though many resident merchants acquired only modest fortunes, others attained to the status of merchant princes. The demand in Europe for Levantine and oriental wares was so great that it gave the Italian merchants an almost unlimited opportunity for commercial development. From this commerce there was accumulated the capital which, in turn, made possible an ever increasing volume of trade.

The commercial activities of the Italian cities and merchants were reproduced by other cities and merchants of Europe. In the north a number of German cities had formed a Hanse or society, called the Hanseatic League, for trading purposes. Though the first step toward its formation was taken in the twelfth century, the Hanseatic League did not assume its definitive character until the fourteenth century. Thereafter until the second half of the sixteenth century it played a decisive part in the trade of northern Europe. At the height of its power and prosperity the League included from sixty to eighty cities, of which the more important were Lübeck, Cologne, Hamburg, and Danzig. Trading posts and warehouses were also established at Bruges, London, Bergen, and Novgorod. Some of the products bought and sold by Hanseatic merchants were fish, grain, furs, leather, skins, wool, a great variety of timber, iron and copper ore, wax, tallow, pitch, and tar. But since trade was limited primarily to the North Sea and the Baltic, the activities of the League were more restricted, and its rewards more limited, than those of the Italian cities, which had access to the rich eastern markets.

An example of the rise of capitalism in both commerce and industry is furnished by the buying of wool and the finishing and sale of woolen cloth in Florence as early as the thirteenth century. Two of the seven great gilds (*Arti Maggiori*) of Florence, the *Arte della Lana* (Gild of Wool) and the *Arte di Calimala* (Gild of Merchants in Foreign Cloth), controlled the sale of woolen cloth. Though the territory about Florence was rich in sheep, the former gild imported vast quantities of wool from England, Spain, and Flanders, a commerce which required much capital. Wool was bought in the north because it was impossible to weave fine cloth from the coarse native product. On one occasion the agents of the Arte della Lana bought the prospective yield of England for two years in advance. In the fourteenth century the two hundred wealthy masters of this gild exercised arbitrary power over about thirty thousand Florentine workers. The Arte di Calimala, forbidden by statute to deal in homemade cloths, refinished coarsely worked foreign cloth, which was unsheared, unrefined, and dyed in fading colors. Capitalist merchants invested large sums in these rough Flemish and Dutch cloths, transported them to Florence, and distributed them to a number of masters who hired wage-earners to refine, dye, and enrich them. When the work was finished, the capitalist merchant, after paying the masters, returned the cloth to the domestic and foreign market. Gradually the industry assumed such proportions that the wage-earning proletariat, with fixed wages and hours of labor, formed a large part of the population. But since the work was done in homes and small workshops, there was no massing of workers in large factories. Other examples of the capitalistic export industry of Europe in the later centuries of the Middle Ages may be found in the woolen industry of Flanders and England, the linen industry of the Lake Constance region, and the silk-weaving of certain Italian cities.

After the discovery of the New World and the new route to India, the center of commercial activity gradually shifted from the Mediterranean to the Atlantic. In other words, the Atlantic seaboard became the main street of the world's commerce, while the Mediterranean declined to the status of a side street. The spices, drugs, and luxuries of the East which had formerly passed over the old routes to the Mediterranean were largely diverted by the Portuguese to the route around the Cape of Good Hope, which remained the chief path of trade from India, China, and the Spice Islands until the opening of the Suez Canal in the second half of the nineteenth century. With the change of the center of the world's commerce to the Atlantic the leadership in trade passed from the Italian cities to Portugal, Spain, the Netherlands, France, and England.

It is noteworthy that a well-rounded capitalism emerged neither in Portugal, which for some decades held a monopoly on the new route to India, nor in Spain, which was the recipient of vast quantities of gold and silver from the Americas. Occupied in securing a footing in the East and in transporting vast cargoes of goods to Lisbon, the Portuguese made no attempt to develop their trade in northern Europe. The business of distributing the goods they brought from the Indies was left to others. Neither was anything done to develop the industries of Portugal. The Jews who might have done so were expelled, and the more ambitious Portuguese departed to make their fortunes in the eastern trade. In Spain the situation was much the same. The Spaniards were conquerors, adventurers, seekers of gold, and missionaries rather than successful merchants or manufacturers. As early as 1503, regular shipments of precious metals began to arrive in Spain from Hispaniola, Cuba, and Puerto Rico. Later the booty from Mexico and Peru was sent to Spain, and after 1545 the vast output of the silver mines of Peru and Mexico. Thus more gold and silver entered Spain in the sixteenth century than had been accumulated in all previous history. Yet this wealth did not go far in stimulating industrial production at home. Most of it went to enrich the nations that supplied Spain with the necessaries and luxuries of life. It has been said that the gold and silver from America served only to make the Spaniards indolent.

The country which first replaced the Italian cities as the seat of commercial capitalism was the Netherlands. Capitalist methods which had been developed in Italy were quickly adopted in the Netherlands, whose merchants became the merchants of Europe. Even earlier the commerce of the Low Countries had been capitalistically organized, though not on so large a scale as that of the cities of Italy. In cities like Bruges, Liège, Ghent, Brussels, and Ypres the manufacture of cloth and brass for sale in distant markets was largely controlled by exporting traders who bought the raw materials and sold the finished products. Bruges in the fourteenth century had been the greatest market in northern Europe, but as its restrictions on trade became more onerous and its harbors began to silt up in the fifteenth century, much of its commerce was diverted to Antwerp. This change, added to the shifting of the center of trade from the Mediterranean to the Atlantic seaboard, made Antwerp with its magnificent harbor the greatest port of the world in the sixteenth century. Its liberal commercial policy and easy conditions of citizenship brought a rapid influx of foreigners. Most of the great merchant and banking houses of Europe opened branches there. It was the center to which a great part of the spices which the Portuguese brought to Europe from the East and many of the products collected by the Spaniards in the New World ultimately found their way.

At the height of its prosperity, with hundreds of vessels arriving and departing daily, Antwerp was the scene of a concentration of commerce such as the world had probably never before witnessed. Here was opened the first great bourse or exchange, where merchants dealt in wares without displaying or transferring them. From every part of Europe merchants came to this bourse to carry on their trade. But the prosperity of the city was short-lived. During the wars of the Netherlands against Spain it suffered as did all other Flemish towns. After its sack in 1585 by the troops of Philip II of Spain, it soon declined and its trade was absorbed by Amsterdam, London, Hamburg, Frankfort, and other cities.

Toward the end of the Middle Ages the joint-stock company was revived. Those who possessed capital were given an opportunity to invest it in some undertaking, either temporary or permanent, directed by paid officers. If the undertaking was limited to a certain period, the original capital plus a proportionate share of the accrued profits was returned to the investors; otherwise dividends were paid at stated times. In permanent companies the system of transferable shares enabled a stockholder to regain his capital at any time by selling his stock. One of the earliest examples of a joint-stock company was organized in Genoa in 1347 for the purpose of seizing the island of Chios to exploit its supply of alum. Other companies of this kind were founded for mining and public banking. In time oversea trade became the principal field of activity of the joint-stock companies. Two notable examples are the Dutch East India Company organized in 1602 and the English East India Company founded in 1600.[1] Such companies usually held a monopoly of the trade of a certain part of the globe. Without the permission of the Dutch East India Company, for example, no Dutchman was

---

[1] The English East India Company was founded as a regulated company, but was gradually converted into a joint-stock company during the first half of the seventeenth century. In a regulated company each member paid an assessment for the protection of the company and for the use of its facilities, but carried on trade with his own resources, subject to certain regulations drawn up by the group as a whole.

permitted even to sail beyond the Cape of Good Hope, to say
nothing of engaging in trade. All Dutchmen, however, could
share in the profits of the company by investing capital in it.
This type of association was to dominate the commercial life of
the seventeenth and eighteenth centuries. By the end of the
seventeenth century there were no fewer than one hundred forty
joint-stock companies in England and Scotland. The largest were
the East India, Hudson's Bay, African, and New River companies.

Other important factors in the rise of capitalism were the
widening of markets and the introduction of new commodities
and luxuries as a result of the discovery of America and the route
to the East around the Cape of Good Hope; also the increased
consumption of such known products as spices, silks, and cotton.
Some of the first wares to become important in the transatlantic
trade were the derivatives of sugar-cane. Introduced into Spain
and Portugal from the East some time after the Crusades, sugar-
cane was transplanted early in the sixteenth century to the
western hemisphere, where it found the soil and climate congenial. Soon each year saw the imports of raw sugar, molasses,
and rum increase until they reached vast proportions.[1] The colonies which produced most of the sugar-cane were Hispaniola
(Haiti) and Brazil.

Another article of the first importance for trade was American
tobacco. Some of the earliest Spanish conquerors had learned the
use of the weed from the Indians, and once the custom of smoking
and taking snuff was introduced into Europe, it spread rapidly.
Tobacco was the main produce of the colony of Virginia for a long
time and was even used as money. Still other commodities which
in the seventeenth century became articles of trade were cocoa or
chocolate from tropical America, and tea and coffee from the
East. Such fruits, vegetables, and other foodstuffs as oranges,
lemons, limes, bananas, pineapples, preserved fruits, lima beans,
yams, tapioca, and rice were imported into Europe in increasing
quantities. Imports of other kinds included dyes like brazilwood,
indigo, and cochineal; sandal, ebony, and sapan woods; drugs and
medicines—particularly quinine, which is derived from cinchona
or Peruvian bark; also furniture, rugs, carpets, tapestries, furs,
ostrich feathers, and ivory. From this trade the capitalist mer-

---

[1] In the sixteenth century Antwerp was an important sugar-refining center.

chants realized enormous profits, in some instances in excess of 200 or even 300 per cent. The English East India Company made profits of 195, 221, 311, 318, and 334 per cent on some of the early voyages, and for almost two centuries the Dutch East India Company paid dividends ranging from 12½ to 50 per cent. Not infrequently the products were simply taken from primitive peoples who were unable to defend themselves against the superior weapons of the European traders.

Another source of enormous profits was the African slave trade. In western Europe slavery had practically disappeared during the later centuries of the Middle Ages, only to be revived again in the fifteenth century by the Portuguese in the form of Negro slavery. The founder of the European trade in African slaves was Prince Henry the Navigator. In 1441 Antam Gonsalves, one of the mariners of Prince Henry, brought back the first group of ten or twelve Africans, and thereafter few explorers returned home without a cargo. When it was discovered that the Negroes of Africa could endure exertions impossible to Europeans in a hot climate, large numbers were captured to provide the Portuguese with cheap labor. Two hundred unfortunate Africans were transported to Portugal by a fleet of ships in 1444. Soon Negroes were captured in even larger numbers, so that by the end of the century the number in the population of Portugal was considerable. In southern Portugal, where the population had been depleted by the wars with the Moors, many large estates were speedily brought under cultivation by slave labor. Negroes also worked as domestics and stevedores, for which purposes as well as for agricultural work many were also sold in Spain.

Whatever qualms the Portuguese may have had over the seizure of the African natives were allayed by the thought that it was really a kindness to the primitive Negroes to send them where they could be converted to Christianity, and thus escape everlasting perdition. For a long time the Portuguese held a monopoly of the profitable slave trade, with Lagos in southern Portugal as the great slave mart. Yet the market would have been speedily saturated had America not been discovered.

It was in the New World that the slave trade assumed vast proportions. Soon after their arrival the Spaniards, determined to wrest as much wealth as possible from the mines and fields of America, impressed the natives of the West Indies, Mexico, and

Peru into forced labor. The men were confined to arduous toil in the mines, and the women were used for husbandry and tillage on the plantations. Being weak of constitution and by temperament unfitted for slavery, the aborigines died in frightful numbers under the brutal oppression of the Spaniards. Large numbers were also slaughtered in the ruthless warfare in which the well-armed Spaniards opposed the poorly armed natives. Smallpox and other diseases introduced by the Europeans increased the mortality rate until the Indians were threatened with extinction in some of the Spanish possessions. The Bahamas were virtually depopulated by 1510 and in Hispaniola the natives were reduced by two-thirds within a few years. Though many of the clergy denounced the barbarities inflicted upon the wretched tribesmen, their efforts achieved little. The Spaniards who took the profits of slave labor hardened their hearts against the censure of the clergy, and continued the cruel oppression with a supreme contempt for the lives of the Indians.

One clergyman, however, continued to work untiringly to save the natives from their oppressors. He was Bartolomé de las Casas, called the "Apostle of the Indies." Las Casas saw men and women forced to drag or carry loads beyond their strength, and to perform labor utterly beyond their endurance. He saw hands and feet hacked off and bodies otherwise mutilated because the unfortunate victims had displeased their masters. This ferocious cruelty, which took the lives of innumerable Indians and drove others to suicide, moved him to devote himself to the task of trying to save the aborigines from extinction. After his polemics and missionary enterprises proved futile, he went to Spain in 1517 to intercede with the authorities there. As a final effort to save the Indians he placed before the government the proposal made by a group of masters, that they would willingly release the Indians if each colonist were permitted to import a dozen Negroes from Africa.

Permission was granted, but the scheme failed of its purpose. The importation of Negro slaves did not end the slavery of the Indians. Later, when informed of the cruelties perpetrated by the Portuguese in capturing the Negroes, Las Casas deeply regretted having made the suggestion. Though the traffic in Negro slaves was undoubtedly stimulated by the proposal, it is erroneous to lay the introduction of Negro slavery into America at his door.

The first contingent of Africans for work in the mines of Hispaniola had already arrived in 1502, and their number was augmented in the years immediately following. In 1510 Ferdinand of Spain, in response to the appeal for laborers, had ordered the Casa de Contratación, the board in charge of commerce, to send out two hundred fifty Negroes. Negro porters accompanied Cortez on his expedition into Mexico and even carried the loads of Balboa across the Isthmus of Panama in 1513.

In 1517 Charles V himself authorized the traffic in slaves by granting a number of patents, one of which carried the right to supply four thousand Negroes annually to Hispaniola, Cuba, Jamaica, and Puerto Rico. If the statements of Las Casas can be taken at face value, the African slave trade grew so rapidly that by 1560 some forty thousand Negroes had been sold in Hispaniola and one hundred thousand to the other American colonies. The license or royal assent required to engage in the slave trade, known as an *asiento*, figures prominently in the history of Europe and America during the seventeenth and eighteenth centuries.

Meanwhile slavery was also introduced into other parts of the New World. In the Portuguese colony of Brazil its establishment came about in much the same way as in the Spanish possessions. When thousands of Indians, obtained by raids into the interior of the country, either ran away or died, the Portuguese planters imported Negroes from Africa to replace them. The first cargo of slaves to what is now the United States was landed at Jamestown, Virginia, in 1619 by the Dutch. Thereafter all the Christian colonial powers, eager to share in the spoils, participated in the slave trade. During the eighteenth century the English managed to obtain the asiento privilege, thereby gaining the primacy in the trade. The horrible cruelties of many slave traders, who regarded the African natives as anything but human, defy description. Not infrequently thirty or forty per cent of the Negroes died during the voyage from Africa to America, a mortality rate of twenty per cent being regarded as fair. This nefarious traffic was not abolished until the nineteenth century.

BANKING

Banking developed toward the close of the Middle Ages as a necessary adjunct of the vigorous trade. The term *bank* derives from the Italian word *banco*, meaning "bench." The early money-

changers in Italy had benches in the market place on which they
kept their coins and plied their trade. When a money-changer or
banker failed, the populace would break his bench, a procedure
which gave rise to the term *bankrupt* ("broken bench"). In another
sense *bank* means a heap or accumulation of money or stock
(perhaps from the German *Banck*) and is synonymous with the
Latin word *mons*, a "mound" or "heap."

Whereas the modern banker is primarily a dealer in credit,
the earlier bankers were money-changers, exchanging one coin
for another. Because of the perplexing variety of coinage that
existed in the later Middle Ages and the absence of a standard
currency, money-changing became a necessity. Not only was it impossible for sellers to evaluate the different coins, many of which
were mutilated by clipping and also debased, but in many cities
they were forbidden to accept anything but the current coins of
the place. Hence merchants took only gold and silver bullion with
them on their journeys, and, as they wished to make purchases,
exchanged it for the coin of the realm. At all fairs and points of international commerce the money-changers plied their trade. From
this business other enterprises gradually developed. The money-
changers soon began to receive deposits for safekeeping, to provide
for the safe transfer of money from place to place, and to make
loans at interest. In taking deposits, which they in turn lent to
others, they gathered much capital which would have been useless from a commercial point of view.

The first to develop banking on a wide scale were the Italians.
The bankers of Italy soon followed Italian trade into all countries,
giving their activities an international character. They bought
and sold bullion, coins, bills of exchange, and promissory notes;
and also negotiated loans for merchants. One of their earliest and
most important functions was the collection of the papal revenues
in the various countries of Europe. Throughout western Christendom the pope derived enormous revenues from tithes, annates,
Peter's pence, indulgences, and numerous payments and dues.
These payments could best be collected and transferred to Rome
through those who dealt in money. For such transactions the
bankers charged five to six per cent or more. As early as the twelfth
century, for example, the pope utilized the Italian bankers to
collect the papal dues in England. They further lent money to
the popes, kings, and others. They also provided rulers with the

necessary means for hiring mercenary troops or for organizing disciplined armies. In fact, whenever the treasury was empty and money was urgently needed, a king or ruling prince could turn to the bankers to replenish it. At times some of the larger cities borrowed money for civic improvements. As security for a loan, the bankers often demanded the right to collect the taxes or customs dues.

The Church's prohibition of usury, however, still put obstacles in the way of money-lending at interest. During the Middle Ages all direct payments for loans were styled usury and therefore condemned as sinful. Usury was regarded as so grievous a sin that it was punishable by excommunication. As late as 1179 Pope Alexander III publicly excommunicated all usurers. Theoretically the stand of the Church was based on the prohibitions of usury in the Old Testament (Leviticus 25:36; Deuteronomy 23:20; Psalm 15:5) and upon the statement of Aristotle that money in itself is unproductive (*Pecunia pecuniam non parere potest*). The practical justification rested on the fact that under the conditions of primitive economy which existed in the early Middle Ages a person usually borrowed money only when he found himself in need.

As the Jews did not come under the immediate jurisdiction of the Church and were expressly permitted by their own laws to take interest from non-Jews, the business of lending money was largely conducted by them. The rate of interest they were permitted to charge ranged up to 43⅓ per cent per annum. Considering the lack of security and the risks of the money-lenders, this rate was probably not excessive. Since they were socially ostracized, the Jewish money-lenders not only had to pay large sums for protection, but were also frequently unable to collect their money. Converted Jews were, of course, forbidden to engage in the business. Consequently, when the money-lenders became indispensable to some of the ruling princes, the latter objected to all attempts to convert the Jews to Christianity. The kings of England and France went so far as to demand financial compensation for the conversion of Jewish bankers, and until 1281 the king of England declared forfeit the property of any Jew who permitted himself to be converted.

Since the business of money-lending was profitable and not too strenuous, Christians gradually became money-lenders de-

spite the prohibitions of the Church. The pioneer Christian lenders
were the Lombards, a name given to Italians from Milan, Genoa,
Lucca, Pisa, and Florence, who in time absorbed the higher
kinds of money-lending while the Jews became merely pawnbrokers and small money-brokers. Lombard Street in London
still marks the district where the early bankers congregated. As
the economic life of Europe developed, the Church became more
liberal in its interpretation of the laws against usury. If a loan was
not paid by the specified time, the Church permitted the imposition
of a fine. Furthermore, the lender was given the right to collect
damages which he might have suffered because of the loan. Thus
the bankers who did not openly ignore the laws of the Church
had means of circumventing them. Often loans were made under
the guise of a temporary partnership. But gradually the prohibitions of the Church ceased to be effective and loans became daily
commonplaces.[1] The interest on loans to princes, cities, or officials
of the Church was seldom less than twenty or twenty-five per cent,
and at times as high as fifty or sixty. Before the sixteenth
century the rate of interest was not generally legalized in Europe.
In England Henry VIII set it at ten per cent; in Spain, some
years later, Philip II established it at twelve. In other states of the
continent money could be borrowed at a lower rate.

As the widening opportunities for trade naturally demanded
larger amounts of capital, various means were employed for
supplying it. One of these was the so-called sea loan, which had
endured from the days of classical antiquity. The merchant who
borrowed the funds for the purchase of a cargo of goods to be
used to trade in the East or for the direct purchase of wares in the
East promised to repay the loan plus an additional premium for
the risks involved in trading at sea. The rate charged rose as high
as fifty per cent, varying according to the distance of the venture.
For a trading voyage to Syria, for example, it was fifty per cent,
while to Sardinia or Corsica it was only ten to twenty per cent.
There are some cases on record in which the borrower, instead of
paying a set rate, simply shared the profits with the lender. If the
goods purchased with the funds were lost at sea, the borrower was
not obliged to repay the loan. Thus the sea loan filled a real need
during a period when commerce was rapidly expanding. It not
only supplied merchant or mariner with money to outfit his ship

[1] Both Luther and Ulrich von Hutten decried the usury of their time.

or buy a stock of goods; it also insured him against the perils of the sea. On the other hand, it offered to the possessor of idle funds an opportunity to make immense profits. During the fourteenth and fifteenth centuries the sea loan was used in Venice, Barcelona, Marseilles, and particularly in Genoa. It may be regarded as the earliest form of maritime insurance. When risky ventures were to be undertaken, a group of men would divide the risks, each "underwriting" a share of the undertaking.

The greatest progress in financing trade was made by the use of the bill of exchange. Medieval transport facilities were so poor, and the risks of transporting money from place to place so enormous, that the safeguarding of the money in transfer was decidedly expensive. To obviate the necessity of transporting specie, the bill of exchange was used. A banking house having branches or agents in each of the great trading centers would receive the money in one place and would issue a bill of exchange redeemable in another city or wherever that specific banking house had agents. Such bills of exchange appeared in Italy as early as the twelfth century and by the thirteenth were employed quite generally all over Europe. It was the Italians who most developed their use; in fact, the chief advances in financial technique were made by them. In the thirteenth century their financial powers became so great that their field of enterprise included the whole of western Christendom. They became the bankers of Europe. The early banking houses were for the most part family businesses. Some firms, however, were composed of a number of families, the name being taken from the oldest or most prominent.

Florence, the artistic and intellectual capital of the Italian Renaissance, was also the first banking city of Europe during the thirteenth, fourteenth, and fifteenth centuries. Its wealth was derived primarily from the wool trade and the sale of woolen goods. Besides wealth, an important factor in its banking operations was the standard value of its coinage. At a time when gold was comparatively scarce, the city annually, after 1252, issued from 350,000 to 400,000 gold florins, which were dependable as to weight and purity. They served as a standard of value not only in Florence and in other cities of Italy but also in France, Spain, and Germany. With vast wealth at their command the Florentine bankers became so eminent that in the fourteenth century the money transactions of almost every country of

Europe passed through their hands. It is said that there were eighty banking houses in Florence about 1350. But as there was a tendency to nationalize capitalist banking, the Florentines had no easy time holding their international supremacy. In the fifteenth century the French managed to dispense with them for a time just when they were enjoying their greatest prosperity. Jacques Cœur (c. 1395–1456), a Frenchman who had accumulated a large fortune from the Levant trade, established connections with the French government and made large loans to Charles VII for carrying on his wars. After his death, however, the French were forced to turn again to the Florentines.

In the history of Florence there are two great eras of international banking. The first centers about the Bardi and the Peruzzi, two mercantile and banking families. At the beginning of the fourteenth century the former had branches as far north as England and as far east as Rhodes, while the Peruzzi had more than one hundred fifty branches and agencies in Europe and the East. Both advanced large sums to Edward II and Edward III of England, at times virtually controlling the financial administration of the country. Edward III used a part of the money to start the Hundred Years' War, and when his early military efforts failed, stopped payment to his creditors in 1339. Before the Florentine bankers could recover from this blow they were forced into bankruptcy when the king of Sicily also defaulted in 1341. It was one of the most sensational bankruptcies in history. In the words of Giovanni Villani, "The immense loans to foreign sovereigns drew down ruin upon our city, the like of which it had never known." Not until the Medici reached the height of their power in the fifteenth century did Florence recover its former prosperity.

Though the Medici family had long been engaged in banking, Giovanni di Medici (1360–1429) was the first to gain eminence. Gifted, diligent, and prudent, he further increased the great wealth he had inherited from his father. The sphere of his business activity included France and Flanders besides the states of Italy. All the important monetary affairs of the popes were transacted by him. His equally skilful son, Cosimo (1389–1464), continued where he left off. Cosimo established branches in all the countries of the West, becoming the ruler of the European money market. The head of the richest family of Florence, he added personal ambition to wealth, and in 1434, as already stated, became ruler of the city. It was under Lorenzo the Magnificent (1448–1492) that the ascendancy of the family reached its highest point. Eminent as statesman, financier, diplomatist, poet, scholar, and patron of the arts, Lorenzo was one of the outstanding figures of his age. But changing economic and commercial conditions, and his aversion for the intricacies of finance, combined to decrease the fortune of the family during the last years of his life. His death coincided with the great discovery of 1492 which was inevitably to shift the tide of progress westward and deprive Florence of its financial supremacy. Thereafter the fortunes of the Medici declined until the family ceased to be a power. The memory of the house is perpetuated in the sign displayed by pawnbrokers, the three golden balls adapted from the six red balls on the gold field of the Medici coat of arms.

The great banking and mercantile house of the sixteenth century was the Fugger family of Germany. At first weavers of cloth, the Fuggers of Augsburg became wholesale merchants of silk and spices early in the fifteenth century, gradually building up a business which became famous throughout the world. The most distinguished member was Jacob Fugger (1459–1525), known as Jacob the Rich, who by some is regarded as the great financial genius of the early capitalistic period. Under him the firm combined the activities of banker, mine owner, and wholesale merchant. He particularly furthered its interests by opening relations with the house of Habsburg and with the princes of Germany. In repayment of a loan, Archduke Sigismund of Tyrol gave the Fuggers the yield of the Tyrolean silver mines. Later they also acquired extensive copper mines in Hungary. The income from both sources rapidly increased the fortune of the family, so that "rich as a Fugger" became a common saying. For a time they virtually controlled the copper market of Europe. After the beginning of the sixteenth century they gave most of their attention to the money market, making large loans to various governments.

As the Habsburgs such as Charles V and Philip II were always in need, the Fuggers became deeply involved in financial transactions with them. It was the money they advanced which enabled Charles to bribe the electors and thus gain the imperial throne over his rival, Francis I of France, in 1519. Indirectly they were also connected with the beginnings of the Protestant Reformation, for it was to them that Albert of Brandenburg, archbishop of Mainz, owed the funds which he attempted to repay by selling indulgences, thereby moving Luther to post his ninety-five theses. During the three decades after the death of Jacob the Rich in 1525 the fortunes of the house reached their zenith and then declined. In the seventeenth century the Fuggers lost most of their wealth in the great national bankruptcies of Spain and Holland.

In the sixteenth century numerous banks were opened in various parts of Europe, but the one which served as a model for many of the later European institutions was the Bank of Amsterdam. It was founded in 1609 by the merchants of Amsterdam, which had become the center of the international trade of Europe, to correct the prevalent financial disorders and meet the needs of the Dutch trade. Since money flowed in from many lands, its merchants accumulated light-weight, worn, and clipped coins. These they took to the bank, receiving credits in standard coin. Such credits came to be known as "bank money." For practical purposes it was preferred to coins, and because of its standard value it soon commanded a premium. All foreign bills of exchange were also paid in "bank money," a procedure which raised the value of bills on Holland in foreign countries. For generations it was unquestioningly accepted in Amsterdam and throughout the commercial world. But toward the close of the eighteenth century it was discovered that the bank had been permitting certain customers to overdraw their accounts and had also lent vast sums to the Dutch East India Company. Public confidence was undermined by these disclosures, and in 1819 the bank was finally closed by royal decree. Previously, in 1814, the Bank of the Netherlands had been organized to replace it.

The establishment of the English banking system was a seventeenth century development. Its forerunners were the London goldsmiths, who began to act as bankers about the middle of the century. Besides collecting rents for customers, they received money and valuables for safekeeping in their vaults and strongboxes. On time deposits they usually paid six per cent interest, lending the money, in turn, to merchant companies and to the government. The customers' practice of giving written orders on their goldsmiths even gave rise to a kind of checking system. In 1694 the Bank of England was established by act of Parliament.

A SIXTEENTH CENTURY
BANKER *by Holbein*

A HANSEATIC SHIP

THE EMPEROR CHARLES V AND
THE BANKER FUGGER

FRANCIS I   *by Titian*

CLEMENT VII

SULEIMAN THE MAGNIFICENT

BARTOLOMÉ DE LAS CASAS

It was founded not as an aid to commerce and business, but merely as a convenient device for raising a long-period loan. Being in need of a loan, the government adopted the plan that £1,200,000 should be borrowed at eight per cent interest. As an inducement to capitalists to subscribe, the subscribers were incorporated as the "Governor and Company of the Bank of England," with extensive but not exclusive privileges. The bank was empowered to buy and sell coin and bullion, to deal in bills of exchange, to borrow at four per cent, and to make loans on proper security. But it could not borrow or give security in excess of the amount of its loan to the government. Neither was it to engage in direct trade operations of any kind. Thus as a result of the political exigencies of the time England acquired a central banking organization which gave financial stability to the government, marketed the government's securities, and maintained the circulating medium of the country.

MERCANTILISM

A direct outgrowth of the expansion of trade and the rise of capitalism was mercantilism. In so far as it can be defined, mercantilism is the sum total of the means employed by the statesmen of the period from the end of the fifteenth century to the second half of the eighteenth to create strong commercial and industrial states. It may be regarded as the economic counterpart of political unification. In practice the aim of the mercantilist was twofold. He endeavored, first, to strengthen his state by the concentration of national economic life under the direction of a powerful central government; and second, to increase the strength of his state against that of the other national states. The means employed varied in the different countries according to time and circumstance. Mercantilism was therefore not a system, but rather a tendency. There never was a mercantilist philosophy in the sense of a definite school of thought. Hence such phrases as the "mercantile system," "mercantilist theory," and "mercantilist doctrines" are misleading if they are interpreted to mean a definite body of thought or doctrines espoused by a specific group of theorists. Yet in most states of Europe, including England, France, Portugal, Spain, Russia, and Scotland during the aforementioned period, there was a certain unity of economic policy which gives the word *mercantilism* meaning.

It is not surprising that the state should endeavor to make its authority as decisive in the economic as in the political sphere, for with the expansion of commerce and of economic interests in general, economic unity became the natural corollary of political unity. The supporters of economic particularism were the great feudal lords and the more or less independent towns. Feudal lords still levied tolls wherever they could, along roads and inland waterways, at bridges, and at markets and fairs. The Rhine, for example, averaged one toll station to every ten miles, and the Loire one to every five miles. The toll on a load of salt transported on the Loire from Nantes to Nevers, a distance of about two hundred sixty miles, was four times the original cost of the cargo. Furthermore, many of the feudal lords had their own mints, their own systems of weights and measures, and their own codes to regulate commercial practices. This was true also of the towns. In addition, the towns regulated industry within the territory they controlled, protecting it against competition from other towns by tariffs. Commerce was therefore organized on a municipal rather than a national basis. The establishment of a national economic system necessitated the suppression of feudal and municipal rights and practices, including feudal and municipal tolls, weights, measures, and coinage. But the efforts of the mercantilists in this direction were only half-hearted.

Much more important to the mercantilist was his second aim—promoting the power of his state in relation to other states. The best means for achieving this end, the mercantilist believed, was the accumulation of wealth. By this he meant precious metals rather than commodities. The importance of precious metals derived from the fact that they could most easily be converted into the commodities desired, and, in the words of a seventeenth century mercantilist, "they are not perishable, nor so mutable as other commodities, but are wealth at all times and in all places." They were of special importance in times of war, which the mercantilists were always anticipating. A saying frequently repeated in mercantilist writings was: "Money is the sinews of war." An English writer of the seventeenth century expressed the same thought thus: "In the common opinion, that state that abounds in money hath courage, hath men, and all other instruments to defend itself and offend others, if it have wisdom how to make use of it." [1]

---

[1] Rice Vaughan, *A Discourse of Coin and Coinage* (1675), p. 59.

Hence it was that the precious metals came to be identified with power. This same idea is stated succinctly by Colbert: "It is only the abundance of money in a state that determines its greatness and power." A seeming proof of this contention was the political influence wielded by Spain during the sixteenth century despite its meager natural resources. The precious metals which flowed into the royal coffers from the New World enabled the Spanish rulers to outfit armies, build ships, and pay bribes; in fact, to dominate Europe. Spurred on by the example of Spain, mercantilists everywhere endeavored to obtain as much gold and silver as possible, as all the great colonizing powers joined in the mad chase for precious metals.

But only Spain was successful in discovering rich mines. The other countries had to seek other ways and means of obtaining bullion. Hence it came about that the mercantilists outside of Spain turned to trade as the only possible means of increasing national wealth. The dominating objective was to establish a so-called "balance of trade." In other words, much must be exported and little imported, the difference flowing into the country in the form of coin. To make the balance as large as possible the consumption of foreign goods was restricted to a minimum. Only raw materials were to be imported, and after they had passed through the process of manufacture the finished product was to be exported. The price received abroad for the finished product above the cost of the raw materials was considered clear gain. When the materials were native, the profit to the nation was regarded as one hundred per cent.

Since a favorable balance of trade could be had only if a country had a large capacity for production, manufacturing was encouraged and subsidized. To obviate the necessity of importing foreign goods, native industries were created for the manufacture of products previously imported. Moreover, tariff barriers were raised against the outside world for the protection of the native industries and the home markets,[1] and also to prevent the transportation of precious metals out of the country. There was, however, at least one important exception to the policy of excluding foreign products. The importation of the appropriate necessities for war was encouraged by low tariffs or even by the payment of bounties. Conversely, the exportation of such necessities was for-

[1] The Dutch who remained free traders are an important exception.

bidden. Thus, while placing emphasis on production in order to have things to sell abroad, the mercantilist also aimed to achieve national self-sufficiency for times of peace and times of war— ultimately for the latter.

This desire for self-sufficiency played an important part in the colonial policy of the European states. The colonies received protection from the mother country, but were in turn expected to complement her industries and to supplement her needs. They were required to send their raw materials to the mother country and to buy her finished products. Furthermore, they were forbidden to produce anything the mother country had for sale. England, for example, prohibited the manufacture of woolen goods for export both in Ireland (1699) and in the American colonies (1719). Since the mother country desired to exploit her colonies for her own benefit, foreign traders were excluded from colonial markets, often through the creation of privileged companies which were given monopolies of the trade of certain colonies. As both the colonies and the trade required protection, much attention was given to the question of adequate sea power. Thus shipbuilding was promoted by means of subsidies, the cutting of trees was restricted to insure a plentiful supply of timber for shipbuilding, and the consumption of fish was encouraged to increase the available number of hardy seamen.

All this was not enough, however, for the mercantilist. He further desired to create a demand for the products of his country. This, he believed, could be done by the manufacture of quality goods. All products of his country must be superior to those of other countries. To achieve a uniform high quality, systematic regulations were laid down for production—regulations which were by and large a continuation of the regulations of the old craft gilds. They stated what things could be made, who was to make them, and what materials were to be used; they also minutely prescribed the processes to be followed, from the treatment of the raw materials through the subsequent stages of manufacture until the product was finished. The system of regulation was least extended in England and carried to the greatest lengths in France. It was Colbert who, in an effort to achieve a national unified control, inaugurated the most comprehensive state control of manufacture. This phase of mercantilism is still known as Colbertism.

Mercantilism reached its peak in the seventeenth century and declined in the eighteenth. Toward the end of the latter century the Physiocrats and Adam Smith (in his *Inquiry into the Nature and Causes of the Wealth of Nations*, published in 1776) derided the idea of the balance of trade and the importance which the mercantilists put upon the precious metals. By this time, however, the conditions which had originally inspired the mercantilists were no longer the same. The nations of Europe were increasingly interested in finding markets for the products of their expanding industries rather than in the mere acquisition of bullion, of which there was no longer a dearth.

Since the extent to which the mercantilist principles were applied varied with such circumstances as the wealth of a country, the degree of political centralization, the power of the central authority, and the extent of its foreign trade, mercantilism did not have the same effect in all countries. Yet it may be said that, in general, the majority of mercantilist measures failed to achieve their ultimate purpose. Most successful were the regulations which aimed to unify foreign trade. Others, particularly those for the production of quality goods, tended to hamper rather than to facilitate the development of commerce and industry. Furthermore, the efforts of the mercantilists to put order into the chaos of customs, tolls, weights, and measures were successful only to a limited extent. Even Colbert was able to abolish the interprovincial duties in only about three-eighths of France. The multiplicity of river and highway tolls, of weights and measures, continued much as before. The completion of this unifying process in France and in the other continental states was postponed until the era of laissez faire. It began during the French Revolution and was finally carried out in the nineteenth century. In England a large measure of economic unity had been established before the age of mercantilism.

CHAPTER SIX

The Empire of Charles V

EUROPEAN affairs in the sixteenth century revolved principally about the fortunes of the house of Habsburg. Its
position of eminence had largely been achieved through a
series of fortunate marriages. So successful were the Habsburgs
in their policy of territorial aggrandizement through marriage
that their good fortune became a byword.[1] Purely fortuitous circumstances, which included even the discovery of the New World,
added more territory to already huge possessions held by the
Habsburgs. The result was the creation of the largest domain
ruled by one man in modern times, a conglomerate empire so
vast in extent that it was said the sun never set on it. Its ruler
was Charles, eldest son of Juana, daughter of Ferdinand and
Isabella, and of Philip the Fair, son of Emperor Maximilian I.
Although he was the first ruler of that name in Spain and the
fifth in the Holy Roman Empire, Charles was born in Ghent in
the Netherlands, February 24, 1500. The enumeration alone of all
the territories and titles he inherited would require pages. Through
his mother he became king of Spain, of Naples and Sicily, and
ruler of the Spanish dominions in Africa and America. Through

---

[1] The idea was stated in the distich:

Bella gerant alii! Tu, felix Austria, nube,
Nam quae Mars aliis dat tibi regna Venus.

(Let others make war. Thou, happy Austria, marry, for Venus gives
thee those realms which on others Mars bestows.)

his father he fell heir to the German possessions of the house of Habsburg and to the territories of the house of Burgundy. The Habsburgs had acquired the latter through the marriage of Emperor Maximilian I, Charles's paternal grandfather, to Mary of Burgundy, daughter of Charles the Bold. In 1506 the death of Philip the Fair left Charles, a child of six, ruler of the possessions of the house of Burgundy, which comprised Flanders and Artois, Franche-Comté (county of Burgundy), Luxemburg, and the provinces of the Netherlands.

Though far from handsome, Charles has been described as "graceful and well-built." His appearance was marred by the characteristic projecting underjaw of the Habsburgs. Jutting and unwieldy, it not only disfigured him; it prevented him from enunciating clearly. In spite of these drawbacks, even as a boy he had an undoubted air of distinction. His formal education never went far beyond the elementary stage despite the fact that he had excellent tutors. Particularly in the study of languages, a knowledge of which would have been a decided asset to the future ruler of a polyglot empire, he showed little aptitude. Consequently he knew no Spanish when he became king of Spain, though later he made good this deficiency. He was to rule over Germany for more than three decades without ever mastering German. Head of the Holy Roman Empire, his knowledge of Latin remained rudimentary. He was most at home in French, which he learned as a child, but his use of even that language lacked polish. The zeal he lacked in learning was applied instead to such pursuits as riding, fencing, wrestling, and marksmanship.

SPAIN

At the age of sixteen Charles was called on to rule Spain, Naples and Sicily, and the Spanish colonial possessions in Africa and America. The death of his maternal grandfather Ferdinand in 1516 would ordinarily have left his mother Juana (often called Juana la Loca) next in succession, but as she was mentally unfit to rule, the inheritance passed on to Charles. Upon his arrival in Spain in 1517 he was not received with cordiality. A number of factors were responsible for this. Even before he arrived on the scene, he was regarded with suspicion because he was a foreigner. The animosity toward him was aggravated by the fact that after the death of Ferdinand, Charles had postponed his departure from the Netherlands until September of the following year. In addition, his inability to speak Spanish was taken as a deliberate affront. Spanish resentment was further heightened because Charles had brought with him as advisors a group of Flemings who prevented free access of the Spanish subjects to the king. These Flemings, intent primarily on filling their own pockets, were appointed to many lucrative posts, both civil and ecclesiastical.

The Spaniards were not slow to express their indignation. The Castilian Cortes, meeting at Valladolid in November, 1517, agreed to recognize Charles as ruler only after he had sworn to respect its rights. The Cortes of Aragon proved even more intractable, insisting that in the event of Juana's recovery she should be sole sovereign.[1] Soon the question of the imperial succession arose to complicate matters further. The death of the Emperor Maximilian in 1519 made Charles, as head of the house of Habsburg, the logical successor to the throne of the Holy Roman Empire. Close association with the empire was not regarded as an advantage by the Spanish people, and, above all, they wanted no absentee king. Disregarding their evident displeasure, Charles proceeded to take the necessary steps to insure his election by sending large sums of money to Germany for the purpose of bribing the electors. At the news of his election and of his intended departure the people were filled with dismay and urged him to abandon his plans; but Charles, turning a deaf ear to the entreaties, summoned a meeting of the Cortes of Castile to obtain the necessary sums for his journey to Germany. The Cortes acceded to his demands only after exacting a promise from him that he would not appoint foreigners to Spanish benefices or political offices. Hardly had the Cortes voted the subsidy when Charles flagrantly broke his promise by appointing his Flemish tutor, Adrian of Utrecht, his representative during his absence.

Soon after Charles left Spain the smoldering discontent flared into open revolt. From Toledo, where it started, the revolt quickly spread to other cities or communes, venting itself on government officials and on the deputies who had voted the subsidy. In August, 1520, representatives of the rebel cities convened at Avila and there organized the Santa Junta which forthwith deposed

---

[1] Officially Juana was joint ruler with Charles, though she took no part whatever in the actual government of Spain.

the regent and his council, and declared itself the supreme authority. It next drew up a memorial demanding that Charles return to Spain and make his permanent residence there; also that foreigners be barred from all Spanish offices and benefices. Foreign traders were equally hated by the Spaniards, because they feared that Charles might permit all his subjects to participate in the American trade. For a time many of the nobles sympathized with the uprising, but when the Junta attacked also their privileges, the nobility at once took the field against the rebels. In the beginning the revolt had been directed against the crown. Now it assumed the nature of a class war. In the end the communes were unable to withstand the opposition of the nobles, whose fighting power was superior, and the uprising was quelled. Thanks to this circumstance, Charles's cause triumphed without his presence or assistance.

The king's absence from Spain was not without its good effects, for during this period he made great progress in the art of state-craft. The more conciliatory attitude noticeable on his return in 1522 reflected itself by a decidedly improved relation between him and his subjects. With but few exceptions, Charles now conferred all benefices and other posts of honor on native Spaniards. He even showed a willingness to please his subjects in the question of his marriage. The Cortes of Castile had ventured to suggest Isabella, sister of the king of Portugal, as his bride; this alliance was desirable from the point of view of Pan-Iberian unity, toward which Ferdinand and Isabella had consistently striven, and from the aspect of the large dowry that would come with the bride. Charles accepted the suggestion, and the marriage was celebrated in Seville, March 10, 1526, amid great popular rejoicing. Though it was contracted for reasons of state, the marriage proved happy. Isabella died in 1539, and Charles was left disconsolate. During the remainder of his life he expressed his loyalty to her memory, whenever it was possible, by starting the day with a mass for her soul and by remaining cold to all suggestions for a second marriage. Their son, who succeeded his father as Philip II, later based his claim to the throne of Portugal on his Portuguese ancestry.

Charles's great aim was the unification of the different small kingdoms that comprised Spain. True, he did not propose to amalgamate the states into one, but he did try to lessen the differences between them. The mere fact that the crowns of Castile

and Aragon were joined in his person was already a step in that
direction. In foreign affairs he strove to make Spain dominant in
Europe. This policy involved him in many wars which seriously
drained the financial resources of the country. Even the vast
quantities of wealth which flowed into the royal treasury from
Mexico and Peru were insufficient for his needs. Hence he was
forced to issue many edicts to increase the royal revenue. Not
only did he find it necessary to treble the taxes during his reign
but at his death he left a huge deficit. The draft on the man power
of Spain was no less severe. Thousands left the country to participate in the wars in Italy, the Netherlands, Germany, and Africa,
to say nothing of the numbers who went to the Americas.

GERMANY

On the death of Maximilian in 1519 a lively contest ensued
over the succession. Despite the fact that it carried little direct
power, the imperial title was still the most coveted in Europe. The
two principal aspirants were Francis I, king of France, and Charles
of Spain, grandson of Maximilian. In seeking the imperial dignity,
Francis was motivated by a desire not only to obtain the overlordship of Europe, but also to prevent Charles from gaining too
great a predominance. The candidates vied with each other for
the favor of the electors by offering huge bribes, until it seemed
that the election would finally go to the king with the larger purse.
Though Charles as a Habsburg had the initial advantage, his
chances were weakened by the lack of necessary funds, a respect
in which Francis was more fortunate. The latter's position was
also strengthened by the support of the pope. In the end, however,
the fear that the financial resources of Francis might make him
too powerful, and the consideration that Charles was a Habsburg,
threw the weight of opinion in favor of Charles. His election was
finally assured when the pope withdrew his support from Francis,
and when Charles signed a formal deed in which he acceded to
certain demands of the electors. Among other things, he promised
to respect their rights and privileges, to use German or Latin for
the official business of the empire, to confer all offices on native
Germans, to call no meetings of the diet outside the limits of
the empire, and to bring no foreign troops into the country.
Elected emperor by the unanimous vote of the electors, Charles
did not arrive in Germany until the following year. At Aix-la-

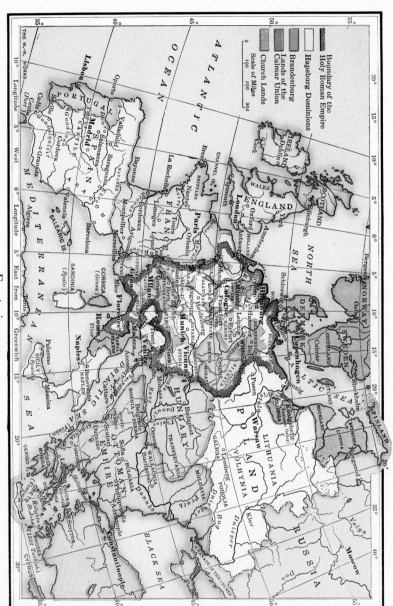

Europe in 1519

Chapelle in October, 1520, he was duly crowned Holy Roman Emperor with the golden diadem of Charlemagne.

Before Charles returned to Spain he summoned the diet to meet at Worms in 1521. Though the presence of Luther at this diet was in the public eye the outstanding event, other questions of importance were also considered. On the one hand, the princes wished to strengthen the reforms inaugurated under Maximilian; and on the other, Charles sought to obtain money and troops for the imminent war against France. Earlier Charles, in order to gain the support of the electors, had promised to form a representative central government which was to have charge of imperial affairs during the absences which were necessitated by his being king of Spain. The princes now wanted a permanent council which should decide all imperial questions whether or not Charles was absent. But they realized only part of their program. After much debate it was decided that a council of regency be appointed to exercise authority when the king was away. In spite of the council's power, Charles even so reserved for himself decisions on more important cases. The diet also reconstituted the imperial court of justice (*Reichskammergericht*), but no new provisions for financing it were made. Since the common penny voted under Maximilian had failed to provide sufficient revenue, the idea of levying a duty on all imports into the empire was entertained for a time. If it had been adopted, this proposal would have led to the founding of a kind of customs union which might have opened the way for a closer political union between the different parts of the empire. However, the opposition of the towns, which believed import duties would ruin their trade, was so determined that the diet abandoned the scheme and revived the system originally voted in 1507 of collecting funds known as *matricula*, from the separate states. Charles, for his part, also did not obtain the resources he desired. He did not receive a permanent revenue and he got considerably fewer troops than he had anticipated. The diet granted him only a levy of 24,000 men for the war against France. The affairs of the diet of Worms concluded, Charles turned to one of the great tasks of his reign, the war with France.

HABSBURG AND VALOIS RIVALRY

The outcome of the imperial election made war between Charles and Francis inevitable. It was not merely that Francis was

chagrined by his failure to obtain the imperial crown; he felt
that his country's position was vulnerable, hemmed in as it was
by Habsburg states. In addition, each ruler laid claim to territories in the possession of the other. Francis claimed the kingdom
of Navarre, a part of which Ferdinand had seized for Spain, and
also the kingdoms of Naples and Sicily. Charles, on the other
hand, demanded the restitution of the duchy of Burgundy which
Louis XI had appropriated. There was also the question of
Milan. At the beginning of his reign Francis had led an army into
Italy, and by a brilliant victory at Marignano gained control of
Milan, territory which Charles regarded as a fief of the empire and
was determined to regain. A more deep-seated cause for war lay
in the dynastic rivalry between the crowns of Spain and France,
with ill-feeling that dated from the conflict between Ferdinand
and a succession of French kings. Finally, the rivalry between the
Austrian Habsburgs and the French house was an element that
could not be overlooked.

Charles would have avoided war if possible, but to Francis it
seemed an auspicious time to launch an attack. Internal affairs
had brought Spain and Germany, Charles's two principal possessions, into a state of upheaval. In Spain the Santa Junta was in
rebellion, and in Germany the spread of Lutheranism was disrupting the social order. Encouraged by these disruptions the
French took the offensive and in the spring of 1521 invaded
Spanish Navarre. On the strength of this aggression Charles was
able to form a league with the pope and Henry VIII for the purpose of curbing the ambitions of the French king. A long, aimless
struggle ensued, which, though it was interrupted by occasional
periods when hostilities were suspended, was not concluded until
the treaty of Cateau-Cambrésis (1559) nearly forty years later.
At first the French army was successful in the conquest of Navarre,
but it was later driven out by the imperial forces. The French
position was greatly weakened when the commander of the military forces, Charles, duke of Bourbon, a great general who had
been suzerain over the whole of central France, became estranged
from his sovereign and decided to throw in his fortunes with the
emperor.

The principal seat of the war was Italy. After a combined force
of imperial and papal troops succeeded in ousting the French
from Milan, the tide turned definitely against the latter in the

battle of Pavia (1525). Francis had crossed the Alps at the head of a strong army and had laid siege to this city. The imperial forces, though numerically weak, were able to hold the city until the arrival of fresh troops from Germany under the duke of Bourbon. Thus reinforced the imperial troops were able to strike a shattering blow at the French army. In telling his mother of the overwhelming disaster Francis wrote, "Of all I possessed only my honor and my life are saved." To add to the ignominy of the defeat, Francis was made prisoner and taken to Spain. After many months of imprisonment he gained his release by signing the treaty of Madrid in 1526. According to its terms Francis renounced all claims to the Italian provinces as well as the suzerainty of Flanders, Artois, and Tournay. He also promised to restore the territories he had confiscated from the duke of Bourbon and to use his influence with the French Parliament to procure the cession of the duchy of Burgundy to Charles. To make the treaty binding, Francis swore an oath on the Gospels and gave his word as a knight that he would return to captivity if the treaty was not fulfilled in every respect within a specified time. The agreement was further to be sealed by the marriage of Francis with Charles's sister Eleanor. But Francis had not the slightest intention of abiding by the terms of the treaty. As soon as he reached French soil he took occasion publicly to repudiate it, claiming that a treaty made under duress is not binding. This breach of faith so embittered the emperor that he challenged Francis to a duel in the conviction that "God would show his justice without exposing so many Christians to death."

The other states now feared that Charles was growing too powerful. Hoping to protect themselves they formed a league composed of the pope, the duke of Milan, and the cities of Florence and Venice. England, without being an active participant, gave it moral support. Formidable on paper, the league actually amounted to little. It was too much lacking in zeal for the common cause to be an effective weapon. Its force was otherwise weakened; for Francis, to make up for his dreary months of imprisonment, quite lost sight of his military purpose in an endless round of pleasures. Meanwhile a large imperial army of Spanish and German troops under the command of the duke of Bourbon actively prosecuted the war by marching victoriously through northern Italy. When Bourbon was unable to pay his troops they took matters into their own hands and decided to recompense themselves by plunder. As Florence was too well defended to be taken easily, the plundering hosts turned toward the less impregnable city of Rome. During the siege, Bourbon, the one man who might in a measure have restrained the troops, was killed. Once the city was taken, the army, augmented by hordes of Italians equally thirsty for booty, pillaged and looted Rome without hindrance. For eight days, during which thousands lost their lives, the sack continued unabated. It was the culminating blow of a long series of disasters which had been inflicted on Italy by invading armies since the invasion of the French king, Charles VIII, in 1494. Though the emperor pretended to be horrified by the excesses perpetrated by his soldiers in Rome, and expressed deep regret at the plight of the supreme pontiff, he made no move to release the pope, who was held captive in the castle of St. Angelo.

The news of the sack of Rome bestirred Francis from his pleasure-seeking, and he sent another French force into Italy. In a short time this army made itself master of the whole of Lombardy except Milan. The success of the French and the indignation aroused in Spain and in England by his treatment of Pope Clement VII (1523–1534) finally moved Charles to agree to release the sovereign pontiff on the payment of an indemnity. Further conditions were that the pope promise to remain neutral henceforth, and also refuse his consent to the "divorce" of Henry VIII. After this the fortunes of Charles took a turn for the better. His superior troops soon vanquished the French army, which had been decimated by plague and gravely hampered by a lack of supplies. But Charles, though victorious, was unable to take full advantage of his victory. As he wished to have a free hand to deal with the spread of Lutheranism in Germany and the threat of the Turkish invasion, he was eager to terminate the struggle with the French. Hence the treaty concluded at Cambrai in 1529 was less severe than the treaty of Madrid which Francis I had repudiated. The terms were the same as those of the former treaty except that Francis was permitted to retain the duchy of Burgundy.

Peace was not long maintained. Almost immediately Francis began preparations for another war by strengthening his military resources and by negotiating important alliances. He enlisted the aid of Denmark, Sweden, the German princes who were hostile to the emperor, and also the sultan of Turkey. The alliance of a Christian state with the Turks was a startling innovation in the history of modern Europe and was regarded as "an ignominious blot" on the honor of France by the other European nations. Ultimately it lost Francis the support of the Protestant princes of Germany. But undeterred by the indignation this alliance provoked, the king of France continued his preparations, and was not long in finding a pretext for another outbreak of war. An opportunity presented itself in the death of Francesco Sforza, duke of Milan, in 1535. Francis proceeded to claim the duchy for his second son and forthwith sent an army to occupy it. The war, prosecuted spasmodically, was terminated by the treaty of Crespy (1544), and the death of Francis in 1547 prevented recurrence of hostilities. The treaty did not end the warfare between the two rival houses, however. At a later date Henry II, the successor of Francis I, resumed the contest for the so-called balance of power.

THE TURKISH MENACE

Meanwhile Charles's empire was menaced by the Turks. The Ottoman Turks, so called after Osman, their first outstanding leader, were originally a small Asiatic tribe that had embraced Mohammedanism. Under a succession of able leaders this tribe expanded its power until it dominated Asia Minor. Not content with this supremacy, the Ottomans crossed the Bosphorus and about the middle of the fourteenth century gained a foothold in Europe. As the Eastern or Byzantine Empire was at this time in an advanced state of decay, it could offer little resistance to the invaders, and within two decades the Ottomans succeeded in so reducing it that only the city of Constantinople remained. Finally this, too, fell in 1453 before their persistent attacks. The last vestige of the Byzantine Empire having been destroyed, the Ottomans proceeded to consolidate the various provinces of the Balkan Peninsula.[1]

[1] A regular feature of Turkish policy in the conquered districts was the gathering of recruits from the Christian population to supplement their military force. These troops were known as Janissaries (a corruption of the Turkish *Yeni Cheri*, new troops). Each year a certain number of young Christian boys were taken from their parents, converted to the Mohammedan faith, subjected to a rigorous training for a military life, and finally enrolled as Janissaries. In time the organization formed the special guard attached to the sultan and obtained supreme control of the affairs of the Turkish Empire. Their power remained unbroken until their organization was finally dissolved by Sultan Mahmud II in 1826.

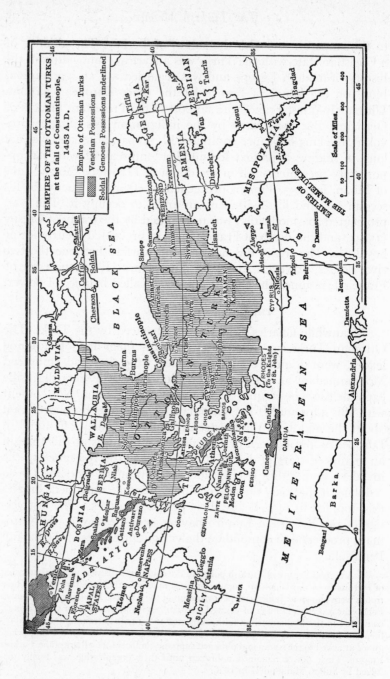

EMPIRE OF THE OTTOMAN TURKS
at the fall of Constantinople,
1453 A. D.

Empire of Ottoman Turks
Venetian Possessions
Genoese Possessions underlined
Soldai

The empire thus established reached its zenith under Suleiman the Magnificent (1520–1566). Ascending the throne in 1520, at the age of twenty-six, Suleiman ruled for almost half a century. His predecessor, Selim the Grim (1512–1520), had already added Egypt to the Turkish Empire by conquest. Soon after his accession, Suleiman made two important additions. In 1521 he captured Belgrade, the key fortress in Hungary which had hitherto successfully resisted the attacks of his predecessors, and thereby made the Turks a definite menace to the Habsburg territories. In the following year he took the island of Rhodes, which, as the stronghold of the Knights of St. John, had for more than two centuries been the base of attacks on Moslem commerce. Its capture assured Moslem control of the eastern Mediterranean. Suleiman followed up these successes by the conquest of a large part of Hungary, which had served as a buffer state against Turkish aggression. In the decisive battle, fought at Mohacs in 1526, the Christian forces were completely routed. The king of Hungary, Louis II, lost his life by drowning while fleeing from the scene of battle, and Hungary, except the western part, now became subject to Suleiman.

But the sultan was not permitted to hold it uncontested. The Archduke Ferdinand of Austria, as the brother-in-law of the late king, laid claim to the throne of Hungary, invaded the country, took Budapest, and dispossessed Suleiman's regent. Retaking Budapest with a large army, Suleiman decided to crush Ferdinand by striking at the heart of his power. In 1529 he invaded Austria and laid siege to Vienna. The Austrian garrison fought so valiantly that Suleiman was forced to raise the siege, but three years later he returned to the neighborhood of Vienna with a larger army. This time Charles V himself collected a formidable force. Suleiman, loathe to risk an open battle, signed a truce in 1533 by the terms of which Hungary was divided between the sultan and Ferdinand. The latter, however, was dissatisfied with the division and in 1540 made an attempt to gain the whole of Hungary. Once again Suleiman returned, in 1541, to inflict a crushing defeat on Ferdinand at Budapest, and then went on to conquer most of Hungary. Finally, in 1547, a truce of five years was concluded on Ferdinand's promise to pay an annual tribute for the portion of Hungary he still held.

In the meantime Europe was harried from another side by Kheireddin Barbarossa, a vassal of the mighty Suleiman and a pirate of extraordinary power. Few men have inspired such terror as did Barbarossa among the inhabitants of the northern coast of the Mediterranean. His bases of operation were Algiers and Tunis. Surrounded by a band of Moors, many of whom had been expelled from Spain, Barbarossa plundered and ravaged the Mediterranean coasts of Europe, killing many of the inhabitants and enslaving thousands of Christian subjects. With the aid of a fleet entrusted to him by Suleiman he was able to continue these raids unchecked. Charles, who regarded himself as the protector of Christendom, was determined to rid the Mediterranean of the Moorish pirates. With a fleet of more than three hundred ships and an army of 30,000, collected from various parts of his empire, he captured Goletta, the fort which protected the channel of Tunis, in the summer of 1535, taking a fleet of eighty-two Moorish galleys. From there he continued on to Tunis, where he routed the army of Barbarossa, took the city, and in reprisal for the depredations inflicted by the Moorish pirates gave it up to plunder after setting free the Christians who had been enslaved by the Moors. This freeing of his coreligionists, the number of whom has been estimated as high as twenty-two thousand, was one of the happiest events in his life. Hailed as the savior of Christendom, Charles resolved to attack Algiers in the following year, but a fresh war with France prevented him from carrying out his resolve until 1541. When he finally launched an expedition, it proved unsuccessful. A storm which arose as the army was disembarking before Algiers wrought such havoc among the troops that the plan of attack was abandoned. With as much of his expedition as he could salvage, Charles set sail for home.

THE LAST YEARS OF CHARLES

During 1545 and the years immediately following, Charles reached the pinnacle of his power. After 1544 he was at peace with his chief antagonist, Francis I, who was too ill to engage in any further contests with him. The death of the French king in 1547, and also of Henry VIII in the same year, gave a reasonable expectation of peace among the Christian states of Europe. Furthermore, in the same year, the signing of a five-year truce with the sultan freed him from the nightmare of Turkish invasion. In Spain his power was firmly established, and in Italy his viceroys were dominant. In Germany, too, the situation seemed well within his grasp, for the battle of Mühlberg (1547) had broken the opposition of the Smalkald League, formed by the Protestant princes for the protection of their common interests; it had also resulted in the capture of his two chief opponents, John Frederick of Saxony and Philip of Hesse. The dogmatic differences, Charles was confident, would be composed by the General Council summoned to meet at Trent.

Actually, however, his security was illusory. By 1550 the tide had turned and disaster was descending upon him from every side. The religious question in Germany was no nearer a solution than before. The Interim, a code of doctrines issued by Charles in 1548 as a temporary expedient until the Council of Trent should make a final decision, was unsatisfactory to Catholics and Protestants alike. Nor was his proposal for unifying Germany by a league of all the German states acceptable to the diet. Catholics would not join with Lutherans, and both feared the increased power it would give the emperor. Moreover, his political strength in Germany collapsed with the defection of Maurice of Saxony, one of his main supporters. When he could no longer count on acquiring more territory by continuing in the emperor's service, Maurice rose against Charles, forcing him to flee the country. How deeply despondent the emperor was is revealed in a letter to his brother. "I find myself," he wrote, "actually without power or authority. I find myself obliged to abandon Germany, not having anyone to support me there; and so many opponents, and already the power is in their hands. What a fine end I shall have for my old age!" The death of Maurice in 1553 did not relieve the situation. Henry II of France, who had fomented much of the opposition in Germany by entering into a league with Maurice and by supplying him with soldiers and funds, continued to harass Charles. He signed an agreement with the Protestant princes of Germany whereby he was to receive the three bishoprics of Metz, Toul, and Verdun in return for his assistance to the Protestant cause. When he proceeded to occupy them, Charles was forced to take the field against him with such forces as he could muster. Elsewhere, too, Henry had brewed trouble by encouraging Ottavia Farnese, the son-in-law of Charles, to raise the standard of revolt in Italy, and in the Mediterranean the pirate captains of the sultan were again despoiling the coasts and enslaving many captives.

To Charles, broken in spirit and health, the difficulties of the situation appeared insuperable. For thirty years he had striven for supremacy in Europe, for peace, and for religious unity. His efforts had all been in vain. He was now seized with a longing to withdraw from the strife, to spend his declining years in peace and solitude. His son Philip and his brother Ferdinand stood ready to assume the burden of ruling his vast domains. He had begun his career as ruler in the Netherlands and it was there that he took the first steps toward closing it. In the autumn of 1555 he summoned his son Philip to Brussels and turned over to him the rule of the Netherlands, beseeching his subjects to render to his son the love and obedience they had shown him. According to one witness "the hearts of all were touched by the words of the emperor. Many wept and others sobbed aloud." A last minute regret that he had deprived his son of his rightful heritage by having turned over the Holy Roman Empire to his brother Ferdinand came too late to permit him to alter the situation he had himself created. As early as the diet of Augsburg in 1530 Charles had urged the electors to choose Ferdinand, and now neither Ferdinand nor the electors were minded to change the succession. Hence Charles went through with the original plan and in 1556 completely transferred the Holy Roman Empire to his brother, who had been ruling in his name. In this same year he abdicated the crowns of Spain and of the Italian possessions in favor of his son Philip, and was ready to retire.

Some notion of the varied scenes his life had witnessed may be gleaned from his own words: "My life has been one long voyage. Nine times have I been to Germany, six times to my Spanish realm, seven times to Italy, and the Netherlands I have visited ten times; four times have I entered France, twice have I crossed over to England, and again twice to Africa; and in order to accomplish all this my navies have taken me eight times across the Mediterranean and three times across the Ocean. . . . This time will be the fourth voyage, to end my days in Spain." In September, 1556, Charles embarked for Spain, where he retired to the seclusion of a small building near the monastery of San Yuste. There, surrounded by the masterpieces of his favorite painter, Titian, he spent the rest of his days tinkering with clocks, studying the many maps he had collected, walking in his garden, and zealously attending to his religious devotions. On September 21, 1558, he quietly died.

Charles was not great, nor was his mind of an original cast. Though he was an absolute monarch who ruled over a surprisingly large number of states, he was unable, in the last resort, to impose his will on any of them. Most of the wars in which he participated were not of his own making. Had he followed his natural inclination, he would have pursued a policy of peace. But he did not fail to utilize such opportunities as the wars he engaged in offered for promoting his own ends. In other words, he was alive to his advantages, firm in his purpose; and if he was slow in reaching a decision, he was tenacious in adhering to it when finally he arrived at it. Charles himself said, "I am by nature obstinate in sticking to my opinions." The vacillation characteristic of his later years may be ascribed to his failing health. Of his honesty of purpose there is hardly a doubt, but Charles had the faculty of persuading himself that what he wanted was right. In trying to do what he regarded as his duty he went against the current of his times in many respects. In an age of rapid changes he tried to preserve the old order both in politics and in religion. He clung to the imperial idea when the rising nationalism in Germany made its failure a foregone conclusion. He persisted in striving for religious unity, having recourse even to force, when Lutheranism was already firmly entrenched. In the opinion of Napoleon Charles missed the rare opportunity of becoming the leader of a united Germany by failing to embrace Lutheranism. Such a move would not only have been contrary to Charles's deepest convictions, both religious and political; it would also have lost him the allegiance of his Spanish subjects. In the matter of religion his faith sprang from his heart. The subtleties of contemporary theological controversies were foreign to his mind; hence in all questions of doctrine he was ready to defer to the authority of the pope. But he would brook no interference in what he considered his rights and privileges in the management of church affairs within his dominions.

Charles was a brave man, but in little things absurdly timorous. He could not, for example, overcome his fear of mice and spiders. His true mettle was shown at critical times when he rose to great heights of calmness and courage. Of his morals it may be said that, although they were not altogether beyond reproach, they were decidedly above those of contemporary monarchs. At all times he showed a proper regard for the proprieties, never permitting his irregularities, like those of Henry VIII and Francis I, to become public scandals.[1] In most of his habits Charles showed exemplary temperance, but he was unable to curb his appetite for food. He particularly relished the highly spiced Flemish dishes which he washed down with large quantities of fine wine. Even the severe attacks of the gout from which he suffered put little restraint on the enormous quantities of food he continued to consume. Hence there is much truth in the statement that Charles ate himself to death.

THE TIMES OF CHARLES V

The period from 1494 through the sixteenth century was, as has been shown in part, a time of war and of preparation for war in most countries of Europe. As a result of the lively interest in things military, numerous changes were wrought both in the mode of warfare and in the constitution of armies. The two outstanding changes of the period are the increasing importance of firearms and the general use of standing armies. Cannon were known early in the fourteenth century, but the first ones, made of wrought iron, were crude. The process of charging, and then of cleaning off the incrustation left by the powder, was so slow that each gun could fire only six or seven shots per hour. Although cannon were considerably improved by the sixteenth century, they were still stationary or, at best, semi-portable. It remained for the great artillerists of the sixteenth century to mount them on traveling carriages which could be drawn by horses. As a result they became part of the regular equipment of every army. The same period also saw great improvements in handguns. Compared with the weapons of today, the handguns of the beginning of the sixteenth century were still primitive, being scarcely more than mere tubes which were discharged by applying a match to the touch-hole. But during the sixteenth century a number of striking developments took place. The match-lock,[2] which had been invented in the fifteenth century, came into wider use, the wheel-lock was invented and improved, the process of rifling barrels was adopted generally, and a standard caliber was fixed for guns. The invention

---

[1] Of his two illegitimate children one, Don John of Austria, rose to fame.

[2] A gun-lock which pressed a lighted match against the powder in the pan, thus discharging the gun. The wheel-lock was a form of gun-lock which ignited the powder by striking sparks from a flint or a piece of iron pyrites with a revolving wheel.

of the wheel-lock was an important factor in the evolution of the pistol because it permitted the carrying of a loaded pistol in a holster.

With the development of firearms the armored knight, whose prestige had already been undermined by the crossbow, became obsolete. His place was taken by standing armies of professional soldiers or mercenaries. Many rulers had previously maintained personal guards of a considerable size, but the first standing army was the twenty Compagnies d'Ordonnance which Charles VII kept permanently after the close of the Hundred Years' War in the fifteenth century. During the period that followed, other rulers formed standing armies. In general, they were not national armies in the modern sense, but armies of mercenaries who fought for the highest bidder. The most famous and most desired were the Swiss, who were noted for their valor and their endurance. Toward the end of the fifteenth century Emperor Maximilian I collected an army of mercenary soldiers known as *Landsknechte* or lansquenets, who seem to have been largely of German origin. Landsknechte also formed part of the army of Francis I which fought against the army of Charles V in Italy. Thus Swiss fought against Swiss, and Landsknechte against Landsknechte. The latter appear to have been the bane of both the rulers and the people. When their wages were not paid promptly, they plundered friend or foe, an example being the previously described sack of Rome in 1527. Contemporary accounts are filled with complaints of their arrogance and moral depravity. Thus Sebastian Franck, a contemporary German writer, denounces them as "the curse of Germany," as "unchristian, Godforsaken folk, whose hand is ever ready in striking, stabbing, robbing, burning, slaying, gaming, who delight in wine-bibbing, whoring, blaspheming and in the making of widows and orphans." During the early part of the sixteenth century the infantry was the most important branch of the army, but when the cavalry adopted such improved weapons as the arquebus, the carabin, and the pistol, it again became prominent in the armies of Europe.

While the development of new weapons of warfare was depriving the nobles of their military importance, the dissolution of the economic order of feudalism was impoverishing many of them, particularly the members of the lesser nobility. In some countries the scions of the nobility either married the daughters of wealthy burghers or turned to commercial pursuits to replenish their dwindling fortunes. But in Germany the nobles scorned trade and industry as unknightly, and regarded the bourgeoisie with contempt. Rather than devote themselves to the arts of peace, many erstwhile knights became robber-knights—in other words, highwaymen and brigands. Since the wealthy merchants and the merchants' caravans were their chief prey, the robber-knights infested the trade routes between the larger cities. Any merchant they captured was held for ransom. If the ransom was not paid, the robber-knights would frequently murder the unfortunate captive or mistreat him in such a way that he would die soon after being released.

A famous robber-knight was Goetz von Berlichingen, who preyed on the merchants in the vicinity of Augsburg and Ulm and whom Goethe later immortalized in his drama of the same name. Robber-knights who were in financial straits even robbed traveling craftsmen, one Thomas von Absberg going so far as to cut off the right hands of his victims if they did not yield enough booty. The natural consequence of the activities of the robber-knights was a perpetual feud between them and the inhabitants of the towns and cities. Summary punishment was meted out to those whom the burghers caught. On occasion larger campaigns were organized against them in reprisal for their attacks. Thus the Swabian League, a commercial league of the towns of Swabia, sent out in 1523 a force which destroyed twenty-four strongholds and hanged such robber-knights as it captured. In general, the lack of a strong central authority in Germany made it difficult to bring them to justice; hence they remained the scourge of commerce until the power of the local princes developed to a point where they could establish law and order.

If the dislocation of the medieval order by the development of commerce was ruining the lesser nobility, it was heaping comfort and luxury upon the merchant class. The wealthy burghers of the early sixteenth century lived in greater comfort than had Charles the Great. Houses were no longer built primarily for defense. The revived use, in the later centuries of the Middle Ages, of chimneys and window glass, both of which were in use during ancient times,[1] greatly improved living conditions. The

---

[1] An oven with a chimney not unlike those of the present day was unearthed in the ruins of Pompeii. The origin of glass is lost in antiquity. Glass articles dating

same end was served by the use of lead instead of tin for underground pipes and for soldering, a practice which permitted more permanent underground plumbing.[1] A drawing by Leonardo da Vinci indicates that glass lamp chimneys were at least known if not widely used by 1500. The first reliable mention of glass mirrors silvered with tin or lead occurs in a document of the thirteenth century, though they may have been used much earlier. Before 1500, they had largely been hand mirrors, but during the sixteenth century large wall mirrors, made by the Venetians and set in gilt wood frames, found their way all over Europe. In some homes all the walls of one room were lined with these large mirrors. Catherine de Médicis helped to set the style by covering the walls of one room of her Paris mansion with one hundred nineteen of them. Besides chimneys, glass windows, and mirrors, the wealthy burghers had rich tableware of silver, fine Venetian glassware, metal-wrought dishes, fine damask tablecloths, and in some instances porcelain from China. Their furniture, and often the wainscoting of their houses, were richly ornamented with carvings, the walls of their houses were covered with costly tapestries, and their beds were furnished with linen sheets and enclosed with silk or satin curtains.

The homes of the poorer classes had also improved, but still remained primitive, the huts of the agricultural laborers being little better than hovels. Even the houses of the peasant owners were still rude structures built of timber frames, laths, and plaster. Window glass was widely used by the prosperous, but was still far from common among the poorer classes. When Montaigne traveled in Switzerland in 1580 he was struck by the fact that all the houses, even the little cottages, had glass windows. But upon arriving in Italy he wrote: "The houses in Italy are very inferior; there are no good rooms; and the large windows have no glass or other protection against the weather but an unwieldy shutter which excludes the light at the same time that you use it to keep off the wind and rain."[2]

back to about 2500 B.C. have been found in the tombs at Ur. Definite mention of window glass and magnifying glasses is to be found in the *Natural History* of Pliny the Younger (A.D. 77). See F. M. Feldhaus, *Die Technik der Antike und des Mittelalters* (1931), p. 173 seq.

[1] The use of lead pipes and of lead for soldering had been fairly common in Roman times.

[2] The diary of the journey was written alternately by Montaigne and his secretary.

In England, it appears, chimneys did not become common until the reign of Elizabeth. William Harrison in his *Description of Britaine*, written during the decade after 1577, tells with pride of the many chimneys put up in his day, stating that there are old men who still remember the day when there were not more than two or three chimneys in most uplandish towns. Yet he by no means accepted chimneys as an unmitigated blessing. "Now we have manie chimnies and yet our tenderlings complaine of rheumes, catarhs and poses. Then we had none but reredosses, and our heads did never ake. For as the smoke in those daies was supposed to be a sufficient hardning for the timber of the house; so it was reputed a far better medicine to keepe the goodman and his familie from the quack or pose, wherewith as then verie few were oft acquainted." In Germany stoves seem to have been commonly used for heating and cooking, but in the other countries fireplaces were the rule. Montaigne remarked in 1580 that he much preferred the German stoves because the smoke of the French fireplaces caused him so much discomfort. Later in the century, according to Harrison, stoves were introduced into the homes of the gentry and wealthy citizens of England.

Also in the furnishings of the homes considerable improvement was made in the sixteenth century, with more tasteful furniture displacing the rude household arrangements. In England Harrison noted especially the wider use of mattresses and beds. "Our fathers, yea and we ourselves also," he wrote, "have lain full oft upon straw pallets, on rough mats covered only with a sheet, under coverlets made of dagswain or hopharlots, and a good round log under their heads instead of a bolster or pillow." Pillows, he states, during the early part of the century were thought meet only for women in childbed. Montaigne still found mattresses scarce in some parts of Germany in 1580, but remarks that feather beds were in common use as coverings. The dishes and utensils in most homes were made entirely of wood, but before the end of the century pewter dishes became more common in Europe. Wooden spoons also gave way to spoons made of tin or, for those in better circumstances, of silver. In Switzerland, according to Montaigne, "they always place as many wooden spoons with silver handles as there are guests, and no Swiss is ever without a knife which he uses to take up everything." Forks were used for cooking purposes but not at the table.

Though the wealthy enjoyed many delicacies and imported luxuries, the food of the average European was coarse. During the winter months the diet consisted in large part of preserved meat—smoked, dried, or salted—for in the fall the absence of root crops for winter fodder made it necessary to slaughter all the cattle except a small number that were kept for breeding purposes. Fish, both fresh and cured, was an important food since meat was forbidden on Fridays and throughout Lent. For those who could afford them, herrings were a staple during Lent. The choice of vegetables was limited, in the main, to peas, beans, beets, onions, lentils, and cabbage. The last, in the form of sauerkraut, was a staple food in Germany. Most foreigners who traveled in that country commented on the frequency with which it was served. Potatoes were not introduced into Europe until near the end of the sixteenth century, and then did not become popular for some time. Turnips, parsnips, and carrots were cultivated in Holland during the late sixteenth century, and from there were gradually introduced into other European countries. Among the fruits, cherries and strawberries were popular, but there is also frequent mention of apples, pears, plums, and grapes. The last two, in the form of prunes and raisins, appear in many of the cooking recipes of the time. Though the bread of the more prosperous was made of fine flour, the poorer classes ate oat-bread, made of a mixture of rye, lentils, and oatmeal. Most foods were highly spiced, and among the peasants garlic was much used.

Of amusements, sports, and pastimes there were many kinds. While the nobles still had their tournaments, the lower ranks had various competitive sports. On Sundays, holidays, or summer evenings crowds of citizens would gather on a meadow outside the town to watch the apprentices and journeymen compete in running, wrestling, archery, spear-throwing, or fencing. There were also other sports. Sir Thomas Hoby, who spent some time at the French court near the middle of the sixteenth century, wrote: "The French king shewed my Lord Marquess great plesure and disport, sometime in playing at tenice, sometime in shooting, sometime in hunting the bore, sometime at the palla malla, and sometime with his great boisterlie Britons wrastling with my lorde's yemen." [1] It was not only the nobility who delighted in

---

[1] *The Life and Travels of Sir Thomas Hoby, 1547–1564,* ed. by E. Powell, p. 72. Pall-mall was a game played in France and England, in which a boxwood ball was driven

hunting and hawking; many merchants and traders who had the opportunity took advantage of it. Another favorite pastime was dancing. Dances were held in the gild halls or out on the green if the weather permitted. About the middle of the fifteenth century, after the introduction of block-printing from the East, card-playing became popular with men and women of all classes. Also dice and gambling found favor with many. Mystery and miracle plays were often presented, especially on religious holidays, but as the sixteenth century progressed they were gradually displaced by plays of a more secular type, presented by professional actors. Important occasions for family festivities were baptisms, weddings, and funerals. Wedding festivities among the wealthy often lasted for weeks and brought together a large number of guests who vied with each other in the display of fine clothes.

Extravagance in dress among all classes, particularly among the bourgeoisie, was a distinguishing mark—nay, the curse—of the fifteenth and sixteenth centuries. The growth of civic prosperity had created a love of display which became so inordinate that laws were passed in many towns of France, England, and Germany to set a standard beyond which it was unlawful to go. But such laws seem to have been largely ignored. Among the wealthy burghers both men and women outdid one another in displaying costly clothes. Materials of the richest quality, embroidered with gold and silver, ornamented with furs and feathers, and adorned with jewels, were worn by both sexes. In the second half of the sixteenth century silk stockings added a further touch of luxury. Queen Elizabeth is often given the distinction of having been the first to wear them, but others before her—among them King Edward VI—seem to have possessed them. Both for men and for women bright colors, especially red, were the favorites. Even more striking was the wearing of parti-colored clothing, with sleeves of different colors and hose that were red and blue on one leg and yellow and green on the other. Fynes Moryson wrote in his *Itinerary*, "The Gentlemen delight in light colours and when I persuaded a familiar friend that blacke and darke colours were more comely, he answered me that the variety of colours showed

through an iron ring suspended at some height above the ground in a long alley. The player who, starting from one end of the alley, could drive the ball through the ring with the fewest strokes won the game.

the variety of God's workes." [1] For some an orgy of colors was not sufficient; they attached little bells to various parts of their clothing as a further means of attracting attention. The shoes worn by both men and women were often bizarre, with points so long that in extreme cases they had to be tied to the knees to permit the wearer to walk. As a result of the more natural treatment of the human body by Renaissance artists, clothing, with the exception of women's skirts, became more tight-fitting, displaying or even emphasizing the natural lines. When the garments of the men became so tight that they impeded natural movements, slits which revealed the silk linings were made in them. First the slits were placed at the elbows and knees, then in other parts of the clothing, until he who had the most slits in his clothing was the most fashionable.

Velvets, silks, satins, and gold brocades notwithstanding, the sixteenth century was not an age of personal cleanliness. In this respect it probably shows a decline over the preceding centuries. During the fifteenth century there were many bathing establishments in the cities of Germany and France. Nürnberg, for example, had thirteen, Augsburg seventeen, Vienna and Frankfort-on-the-Main twenty-nine, and Paris an even larger number. But since the members of both sexes were often permitted to bathe together, the public baths were denounced by the clergy as centers of moral corruption. Moreover, physicians declared them to be the breeding-places of disease and epidemics. In consequence many of the bathing establishments were closed by the municipal authorities early in the sixteenth century, and others disappeared because the fear of contracting disease kept patrons away. Thereafter bathing became a "lost art" except for those who were ill or had private baths. The lack of personal hygiene was common also in other countries. Jerome Cardano, celebrated Italian physician of the sixteenth century, wrote in his memoirs, "Men and women, even those of superior attractions, swarm with fleas and lice; some stink at the armpits, others have stinking feet, the majority a stinking breath." [2] In England Cardinal Wolsey, the minister of Henry VIII, made it a practice to carry with him when he went to Westminster Hall an orange in which was concealed a sponge saturated with essences, "the which he most commonly smelt

[1] Vol. 4, p. 208.
[2] Cited by M. von Boehn in *Modes and Manners*, vol. 2 (1932), p. 205.

into" to avoid the pestilent odors from the suitors.[1] In 1526 Henry VIII ordered that the tattered and filthy garments of the scullions in the royal kitchens be replaced with whole garments "without such uncleannesse as may be the annoyance of those by whom they shall passe." Erasmus, who otherwise liked England, describes the floors of English homes as strewn with rushes under which lie unmolested for many years remainders of fish, discarded beer, excrement of dogs and humans, spittle, and other nasty things.

An interesting commentary on the manners as well as the habits of the sixteenth century are the "books of etiquette" and poems written for the purpose of teaching good manners to the children of the nobility. Among the "don'ts" prescribed by those dealing with table manners are the following: Don't pick your teeth with your knife; don't throw bones on the floor; don't claw your back as if after a flea, or your head as if after a louse; don't pick your nose or your ears; don't belch near a person's face; don't blow your nose on the napkin; don't spit over the table; don't open your mouth too wide while eating; don't sup your soup too loudly; don't pick up a morsel from the dish with your tongue; don't smack your lips or gnaw your bones; don't butter your bread with your thumb; don't laugh with your mouth too full; don't wipe your teeth or your eyes with the tablecloth; don't poke your fingers into eggs. Regarding demeanor, one may read in Richard Weste's *Booke of Demeanor* such lines as:

> Let thy apparell not exceede to passe for sumptuous cost,
> Nor altogether be too base, for so thy credit's lost.
> Be modest in thy wearing it, and keep it neat and cleane,
> For spotted, dirty, or the like, is lothsome to be seene.
> Nor imitate with Socrates to wipe thy snivelled nose
> Upon thy cap as he would do, nor yet upon thy clothes.
> But keepe it cleane with handkerchiffe, provided for the same,
> Not with thy fingers or thy sleeve, therein thou art to blame.

Despite the bad state of the roads and the lack of security for travelers, there were many who traveled for pleasure. The most common modes of travel were on foot and on horseback. In the sixteenth century carriages became increasingly popular. Covered and open carriages had been used for centuries, but they were hardly made for comfort because the body of the carriage rested

[1] *Manners and Meals in Olden Times*, ed. by F. J. Furnivall (1868), p. lxvi.

directly on the axles. Early in the sixteenth century the carriage was improved by swinging the body in straps, thus eliminating much of the jolting. Carriages first became popular, it appears, in Germany and from there were introduced into England, France, and Spain. In all countries they were at first regarded as too effeminate a conveyance for men. In Brandenburg and Brunswick the lesser nobility were forbidden to use them because it was feared that skill in riding would die out. In Spain a member of the Cortes advocated in 1623 that their use be prohibited. "With respect to coaches," he wrote, "great evil is caused and offence given to God, seeing the disquiet they bring to women who own them; for they never stay at home, but leave their children and servants to run riot, with the evil example of the mistress being always gadding abroad. The art of horsemanship is dying out, and those who ought to be mounted crowd, six or eight of them together, in a coach talking to wenches rather than learning how to ride. Very different gentlemen, indeed, will they grow up who have all their youth been lolling about in coaches instead of riding." [1]

On the road travelers could find lodging at the inns or avail themselves of the hospitality offered by the monasteries. The cheaper hostels were often dirty, disreputable places; and the better inns, according to the statements of many travelers, were expensive. Montaigne, who seems to have taken lodging only at the better ones, said of the inns of Switzerland: "The bed-chambers are very indifferent. There are curtains to the beds, and you always have three or four beds in a room, standing side by side. . . . They are very ill-provided everywhere with what we consider bed-chamber necessaries. He is a very lucky man who can get hold of a white sheet; and what sheets there are never cover the bolster; indeed, the most ordinary covering is a sort of thin feather-bed and that is very dirty." On the other hand, he does state repeatedly that the cooking was good. Of the inns in Italy the diary records that they "are far less convenient than those in France and Germany. . . . The bedrooms are mere cabins and the beds wretched pallets. Heaven help him who cannot lie hard! There is a great deficiency of linen, too."

In the sixteenth century, superstitions permeated most phases of human life. Not only were disease and all misfortune still widely

---

[1] Cited by Martin Hume in *The Court of Philip IV* (1908), pp. 130–131.

regarded as the work of the devil, but for the learned as well as for
the illiterate the air, the woods, and attics were peopled with ghosts.
No ghost story was too fantastic to find acceptance. The German
knight Hans von Schweinichen, for example, writes in all seriousness in his memoirs of a ghost that had appeared at an inn two
days before he arrived there; it had washed all the rooms clean,
made the beds, and put the whole house in order. Three days
later this same ghost appeared before Schweinichen's bed with
a club-like thing in its hand with which it drove away the flies
that were molesting him. When Schweinichen became frightened
and commended himself to God Almighty, the ghost retreated
into a corner, where it stood grinning at him.[1] He also tells how
as a boy he was prevented from fighting with another lad by the
grunting of a phantom sow. The grunting of phantom swine seems
to have been common, for it was heard also by other men, including the Italian physician Cardano.[2] Various means were
prescribed for driving away ghosts and evil spirits. Thus "if a
soul wander in the likenesse of a man or woman by night, molesting men, with bewailing their torments in purgatory, by reason
of tithes forgotten, etc. and neither masses nor conjurations can
helpe; the exorcist in his ceremonial apparel must go to the tomb
of that body, and spurn thereat with his foot, saying: *'Vade ad
gehennam'* (Get thee packing to hell!): and by and by the soul
goeth thither, and there remaineth forever."[3]

   An outgrowth of the belief in the devil and in evil spirits was
the belief in witchcraft. It was believed that certain persons,
mostly women, were endowed by the devil with powers which
enabled them to perform supernatural acts. There were witches,
who could raise hail, tempests, lightning, and thunder or procure
barrenness in man, woman, or beast; others could draw down the
moon, foretell the future or instill inordinate love or hate in men's
minds; again others could pass invisibly through the air from
place to place or cause objects or beings to do so. Johannes
Butzbach, a wandering scholar of the early sixteenth century,
states that when he desired to return quickly from Bohemia to
his ancestral home on the Main a witch offered to provide him
with a black cow on which he could ride home through the air,

---

[1] *Leben und Abenteuer des Ritters Hans von Schweinichen* (1907), p. 89.
[2] Cardano, *The Book of My Life*, trans. by Jean Stoner (1930), p. 205.
[3] Reginald Scot, *The Discoverie of Witchcraft* (1584), p. 219.

but fear of the devil prevented him from accepting the offer.[1] The
belief in witches was not new, but near the end of the fifteenth century new life was given to it through the publication of the *Malleus
Maleficarum* or *Witches' Hammer* by Heinrich Institoris and Jacob
Sprenger. In it minute descriptions of every type of witch were
given, as well as directions for counteracting their influence.
Above all, it urged upon everyone the duty of exterminating
witches as heretics. The result was a perfect frenzy of witch-
finding and witch-burning. This frenzy did not diminish with the
coming of Protestantism, for Protestants were as zealous in hunting
down witches as were their Catholic neighbors. Witches were
either burned or hanged. Since those accused of witchcraft were
often tortured until they stated that they were guilty, the accusation was almost tantamount to a death sentence. It was in Germany that the witch mania wrought the greatest destruction of
human life. In Lorraine, for example, nine hundred persons were
executed for witchcraft during a period of fifteen years. In 1591
seventy-two persons were hanged or burned for witchcraft in the
little town of Ellingen near Nürnberg. The passing of the sixteenth century did not abate the zeal of the witch-hunters; in
fact, in some districts it became more intense in the next century.

The sixteenth century made little progress toward a more
humane administration of justice. "Common" criminals were still
treated with a cruelty that beggars description. For such crimes
as perjury, libel, smuggling, and persistent vagrancy men had
their cheeks branded, their right hand or their ears cut off, or their
hands mutilated. The punishment for heresy, various kinds of
theft, highway robbery, murder, treason, and counterfeiting was
death, and it was carried out by hanging, drowning, decapitation,
quartering, impaling on the stake, burning at the stake, boiling
in oil or water, or by burying alive. In England, for example, an
act was passed in 1530 which decreed that all poisoners were to
be boiled alive.[2] In some parts of Germany a person convicted
of blasphemy might have part of his tongue cut off. Criminals
were still broken on the wheel or their limbs were crushed one
by one with an iron bar. Harrison says regarding England: "We

---

[1] *The Autobiography of Johannes Butzbach*, trans. by R. F. Seybolt and P. Monroe
(1933), p. 75.
[2] The statute was later repealed, but only after several culprits had suffered
death under its provisions.

have use neither of the wheel nor of the bar as in other countries;
but when wilful manslaughter is perpetrated, besides hanging,
the offender hath his right hand commonly stricken off before or
near the place where the act was done, after which he is led forth
to the place of execution, and there put to death according to the
law." Executions were generally public because it was believed
that they had a deterrent effect. But the death penalty was inflicted so frequently in the larger towns and cities that it ceased
to arouse a sense of horror. In Nürnberg, and this was probably
not exceptional, 1159 executions took place in twenty-four years.
In many places executions were gala occasions when crowds
gathered about the scaffold or the stake in a sort of festive mood
and the town wits endeavored to make humorous remarks at the
expense of the condemned.

During the sixteenth century, imprisonment as a punishment
for crime became a more widespread custom than previously, but
it was still largely dominated by the idea of inflicting physical
pain on the criminal. Hence imprisonment was often hardly more
humane than being broken on the wheel or burned at the stake.
In many places the gate towers or the cellars of old buildings were
used as gaols, and prisoners were chained in dark damp cells
which swarmed with vermin and rats and were so foul that the
expression *squalor carceris* (prison squalor) became proverbial. As
a punishment and to prevent escape prisoners were often weighted
down with such heavy irons that they were unable to stand. While
those who had means could get better food and bedding, others
who had none were allowed only mouldy straw to lie on and
were furnished with just enough food to enable them to live. The
more populous cities of continental Europe and England had
larger prisons, but even in these the conditions were often horrible
beyond belief. Clement Marot, the French poet of the sixteenth
century who was imprisoned in the Conciergerie, the prison
which was later to be the last dwelling-place of Marie Antoinette,
stated that it is impossible to conceive of a place on earth that
was more nearly like hell. In the second half of the century houses
of correction and workhouses began to appear in England and
Holland, but drastic reforms of prisons and criminal laws came
only after a group of eighteenth century writers denounced the
inhuman treatment of criminals.

An important contribution of the sixteenth century to later

ages was the Gregorian calendar, so called because it was sponsored by Pope Gregory XIII. Up to that time the Julian calendar, originally drawn up by order of Julius Caesar, was universally accepted throughout Christendom. Although the Julian calendar was a great improvement upon the preceding calendars, it was not accurate. Its year of $365\frac{1}{4}$ days was eleven and a fraction minutes longer than the true length of the solar year. Over a short period the discrepancy caused no difficulties, but by the sixteenth century it amounted to ten days, so that the vernal equinox fell on the 11th instead of the 21st of March. This confusion led to difficulties regarding the proper date for the observance of Easter. After the question of calendar reform was discussed by several General Councils, it was finally taken up by Gregory XIII. A committee of astronomers and mathematicians was appointed to consider the question, and on the basis of its report the pope promulgated the Gregorian calendar. The official decree, issued in February, 1582, directed that the ten days between October 4 and October 15, 1582, be omitted from the calendar. To prevent similar irregularities in the future, the Gregorian calendar provided for the elimination of leap year at the close of each century (centurial year) except those that are divisible by 400 without remainder. The calendar was adopted in Italy, Spain, Portugal, and France in 1582, and in Switzerland, the Catholic states of Germany, and the Catholic Netherlands the following year. But the Protestant states adhered to the Julian calendar a long time. Finally, in 1700, Denmark and the Protestant states of Germany adopted the new style, and Sweden gradually introduced it by omitting the leap years from 1700 to 1740 inclusive. In Great Britain and its dominions (including the North American colonies) the Calendar New Style Act (1750) provided for its adoption in 1752. At the same time January 1 was also fixed as the official date for the commencement of the new year, the official date having previously been March 25. In the countries professing allegiance to the Greek Orthodox Church the new style was not adopted until the twentieth century (Bulgaria, 1915; Soviet Russia, 1918; Rumania and Yugoslavia, 1919; Greece, 1923).

CHAPTER SEVEN

The Protestant Reformation

ORGANIZATION OF THE ROMAN CATHOLIC CHURCH

AT THE opening of the sixteenth century the Roman Catholic Church was the most important institution in Europe. Its authority was recognized everywhere except in Russia, Greece, and the Balkans, where the Orthodox Church held sway. Practically every inhabitant of western Europe was born into the Church and remained a member for life. Worship was everywhere conducted according to the same rites and in the same language (Latin). The pope, as bishop of Rome, was at once the supreme lawgiver, the supreme judge, and the supreme administrator of the Church. As supreme lawgiver he issued, whenever the occasion demanded, edicts called bulls (from *bulla*, the Latin word for the seal which was attached to the edicts) or decretals. In this capacity he could also grant dispensations from ecclesiastical laws. As supreme judge he passed final judgment in all ecclesiastical lawsuits; while as supreme administrator he supervised the management of the affairs of the entire Church. According to the teachings of the Church, the authority which the pope exercised was conferred by Christ on Peter, who was recognized as the first bishop of Rome; and Peter transmitted his authority to those who succeeded him in his office.

Under the supreme authority of the pope was an elaborate organization for administration of the affairs of the Church. The immediate assistants of the sovereign pontiff were the members of the papal curia, which included the household officers, the various administrative assistants, and the cardinals, all of whom were appointed by the pope. As individuals the cardinals performed various functions in the papal government; as a body they constituted the Sacred College or the College of Cardinals. Before 1586, the year in which the pope decreed that the number of cardinals should never exceed seventy, the size of the Sacred College varied from a mere handful of cardinals to a total of fifty-three. The chief function of the Sacred College was to elect a new pope upon the death of the reigning pontiff.

Next in the hierarchical scale was the archbishop, also called the metropolitan because his cathedral was usually in a large city. He was the head of a province, the largest unit of territory in the Church. His chief duties were to enforce the observance of ecclesiastical law, to summon and preside over provincial synods, and to act as court of appeal from the diocesan courts. His special mark of distinction was the pallium, a band of white wool embroidered with small black crosses and worn loosely around the neck. The pallium could be obtained only from the pope, and until an archbishop received it he could not exercise any jurisdiction.

Subordinate to the archbishop was the bishop. He was the executive and responsible head of a diocese, a subdivision of a province. Whatever the manner of his nomination, the bishop possessed no power until his nomination had been confirmed by the Holy See. It was his function to watch over purity of doctrine, to maintain discipline among his clergy, and to administer the sacraments of confirmation and ordination. He also administered the great landed possessions of the Church in his diocese. The pope and the metropolitans were bishops, each having his own diocese. Below the bishop was the priest, who was at the head of a parish, the smallest unit of division. To him was entrusted the "cure of souls." His chief duties were to rule and instruct his flock, to offer the sacrifice of the mass, to hear confessions, to baptize, to solemnize marriages, and to administer extreme unction to the dying.

Because they lived in the world (*saeculum*) and busied themselves with the spiritual cares of men, these churchmen were known as the secular clergy, as distinguished from the regular clergy (monks and friars), who lived under a monastic rule (*regula*). The secular clergy in their ministrations concentrated upon the performance of certain acts known as sacraments. A sacrament was defined by the Church as a "visible sign of invisible grace, instituted for our justification." The sacraments, except baptism, could be administered only by a properly ordained priest. In number they were seven: baptism, confirmation, penance, marriage, ordination (orders, holy orders), the eucharist, and extreme unction. By baptism man was cleansed from the stain of original sin on his soul when he came into the world; by confirmation he was admitted into the full membership of the Church; and by penance he was freed from the penalties of sin which he had committed since baptism. In the eucharist, around which, as the central mystery of Catholic worship, the other sacraments revolved, the priest, according to the teachings of the Church, miraculously transformed bread and wine into the body and blood of Christ, a change called transubstantiation. Extreme unction was the anointing of a person in immediate danger of death in order to remove the last stain of sin and to prepare the soul for eternal life. These five sacraments were obligatory for all members of the Church; the remaining two—marriage and ordination—were optional. By the sacrament of marriage the priest rendered the family tie a religious one. Through the sacrament of ordination or holy orders a candidate was inducted into the priesthood, receiving thereby a divine commission which had been carried down to him by an uninterrupted succession from the apostles.

If a person disobeyed the laws of the Church, he could be excommunicated—that is, excluded from the fellowship of the Church and from the benefits of the sacraments which it taught were necessary for the salvation of man. If the offender remained impenitent, a more powerful weapon, the interdict, through which the administration of the sacraments might be suspended in a certain territory, could be employed. This weapon was used largely to compel obedience from a prince or ruler who refused to recognize the authority of the Church. By these means the Roman Church succeeded for centuries in maintaining at least an outward religious unity throughout most of Europe. In the sixteenth century, however, this unity was disrupted by the movement known as the Protestant Revolt or, more familiarly, Reformation.

BACKGROUND OF THE PROTESTANT REFORMATION

The Protestant Reformation was a complex and far-reaching movement. Like the Renaissance, it was a phase of the general reaction against medieval civilization, but it entered more profoundly into the life of the nation because most people were more interested in religion than in art and letters. Looking back to the teachings of Christ and Paul and Augustine, it exalted primitive Christianity over medieval Catholicism, but it also opened the way for many modern developments. Primarily a religious movement, the Protestant Reformation contained social, intellectual, political, and economic aspects as well, which were far removed from the history of religion. Though it appears to have started suddenly, it was in reality the product of a long previous development. Among the factors which prepared the way for it and insured its success were:

First, the existence of abuses in the Church. One of these was simony or the sale of spiritual offices, an abuse augmented by the fact that offices were often sold to the highest bidders regardless of their fitness. Connected with simony was pluralism, or the holding of more than one office by one person, a practice which made the proper fulfillment of duties impossible even though the incumbent had the ability and the desire. There were also abuses in connection with the laws and doctrines of the Church. People of influence or means could obtain dispensations which exempted them from fulfilling certain laws, such as the law of celibacy and the law forbidding marriage within a certain degree. Another notable abuse was the sale of indulgences, or the remission of the temporal punishment of sin for money. For this purpose pardon-sellers traveled about Europe, often resorting to exaggerations and lies in order to induce people to buy. Other abuses which excited the moral indignation of pious Christians were the rampant worldliness and immorality among the clergy. Many secular clerics led lives of uselessness and ease, with a complete disregard of the laws of celibacy. This moral decline was also manifest among the monks. Monasteries which had once been famed as centers of learning were now sunk in ignorance and vice. The extent of the abuses can be exaggerated. The lives of the worldly and immoral priests and monks were more than offset by the lives of the good priests and monks. But the abuses were nevertheless real.

These abuses, a source of grievance to many, were not new. Many had existed for centuries. Devout leaders in the Church, among them John Wyclif (1324?–1384) in England and John Huss (1369–1415) in Bohemia, had repeatedly denounced them to little avail. During the first half of the fifteenth century councils had met at Pisa (1409), Constance (1414–1418), and Basel (1431–1449) for the purpose of reforming the Church "in head and members," but these endeavors had proved for the most part abortive. Gradually the demand for reform became more widespread; by the end of the fifteenth and the beginning of the sixteenth century, awareness of the need for it appeared both in the learned and in much of the popular literature. The papacy, which should have taken the lead in effecting reforms, was so intent upon the expansion of its political power in Italy that it had little time or inclination for these more pressing matters. In fact, many popes stood in the way of reform; for, instead of setting a good example, they strayed further and further from the moral ideals set up by their predecessors in earlier ages. Indeed, the men who occupied the papal throne toward the end of the fifteenth century were regarded by their contemporaries as capable of almost any vice or crime. In consequence the prestige of the papacy waned, and discipline in the Church suffered accordingly.

A second factor which prepared the way for the Protestant Reformation was the influence of humanism. As has been noted in an earlier chapter, there was a difference between the humanism of Italy and that of the northern countries. In Italy most of the humanists tended either toward indifference to religion or toward complete paganism. The pagan temper of mind as it manifested itself at the papal court was of no small aid to the Reformation in its early stages, because it furnished the reformers with a target for their attacks. Many of the northern humanists keenly satirized, subtly ridiculed, or openly denounced the corruption in the Church. They scored the ignorance of priests and monks, derided the stultifying scholasticism of the Middle Ages, and mocked the elaborate rituals of the Church, advocating a return to a simpler form of Christianity. More than this, they directed the resources of the new learning to the study of the Bible. By their scholarly work they not only put the Bible in its original languages into the hands of the educated classes (the New Testament through Erasmus, the Old through Reuchlin), but they also helped to undermine the authority of the Church by raising that of the Bible, which was to become the basis of the new Protestant faith. In 1516 Erasmus went so far as to advocate that the Bible be made accessible to all. "I fight absolutely," he stated, "the opinion of those who refuse to the common people the right to read the divine letters in the popular language, as if Christ had taught unintelligible mysteries, understood only by some theologians." In short, the humanists, by fostering intellectual freedom, by encouraging a spirit of inquiry, and by emphasizing the personal factor in religion, aroused opposition to the spiritual power claimed by the Church and, in particular, by the pope, and thereby gave strength to the movement for reform.

A third factor was the opposition of the European states to the universal claims of the Church. The Roman Church, modeled after the Roman Empire, was in organization an international or, rather, supra-national state. As such it claimed both a spiritual and a temporal supremacy over the states of Europe. This assumption involved repeated interference by the papacy in affairs over which the temporal sovereigns claimed sole jurisdiction; in fact, on the basis of the twofold supremacy no sphere of human interest or activity was exempt from the authority of the Church. Its claims included even the right to depose a ruler, to absolve subjects from their allegiance to him, and to bestow his territories on another. Such assertions, however, went counter to the political tendencies of an age which witnessed a remarkable growth of national consciousness and an increasing concentration of political power in the hands of the temporal sovereigns. Consequently, relations between church and state were strained in most countries of western Europe. Secular rulers, seeing in the universal claims of the Church the chief obstacle to the concentration of all political power within the state and, more specifically, in themselves, sought to limit the sphere of the Church's power purely to matters of religion and morals. In this attempt they were also motivated by the desire to control the right of appointment to the lucrative ecclesiastical offices and to obtain the landed possessions of the Church.

Finally, there was the economic conflict between church and state. At the end of the fifteenth century the wealth of the Church was enormous. Throughout western Europe it owned numerous manorial estates from which it derived a large income. Since the alienation of church property was forbidden and more property was constantly being added by gifts from pious individuals, the wealth of the Church continued to increase. In addition to the income from its property, the Church collected from the laity the tithe, a ten per cent income tax. Another source of revenue was the fees charged by the priests for the administration of the sacraments. Complaints against the tithes and the imposition of charges for the sacraments became more loud-spoken and insistent during the period immediately before the revolt against the Church, engendering considerable anticlerical sentiment which was favorable to the success of the Protestant movement.

The complaints were directed not so much at the prodigious sums garnered by the Church as at the fact that a considerable part of this income regularly flowed out of the country in which it was collected and into the papal treasury. Beyond his regular income the pope also reaped a rich harvest from the bestowal of the pallium on archbishops, and from the incomes of all vacant benefices. Furthermore, the papacy received large sums from the tax called Peter's pence, from the sale of indulgences and dispensations, from contributions raised in support of crusades, from fines levied in the ecclesiastical courts, and from the payment of annates, or the first year's income, demanded of each new incumbent of a benefice. The Emperor Maximilian, perturbed over his own pecuniary straits, declared that the Roman curia derived from Germany a revenue a hundred times larger than his own. To many others the papacy appeared as a foreign power bent on fattening its coffers at the expense of the various European states. In general, the continuous demand for money on the part of the popes aroused for the whole papal system a distaste which was an important factor in hastening the ultimate breach with Rome.

It is possible that the breach might have been avoided or, at least, postponed by a reform of the most glaring abuses and by agreements delimiting the spheres of both church and state. While such agreements would have given the state a large measure of control over the clergy and their wealth, they would have permitted the Church to retain some part of its influence and possessions. The rulers of the larger states who were engaged in consolidating their dominions did not desire to support religious changes which might cause disorder and division in their states. Hence they were not averse to negotiations with the Roman curia. A concordat was, in fact, concluded between the pope and Francis I of France in 1516. It gave the state a large degree of control over the clergy by transferring to the king the power to appoint the bishops, abbots, and priors, though the pope reserved the right to veto the appointment of such as did not fulfill the canonical conditions. But in Germany, where the ecclesiastical abuses were more common than in the other countries, there was no strong central power to conclude such an agreement. Some princes undoubtedly would have been willing to arrange a concordat with the Church, but others were eager to free themselves entirely from the overlordship of the pope and seize the church lands, in order to consolidate their power against the emperor or still the cries of their subjects for reform. It was the latter who gave to the Protestant movement the support and protection it needed in order to be successful.

LUTHERANISM

The leading figure in the opening phase of the Protestant Reformation was Martin Luther. Luther was not a deliberate revolutionist who intended from the start to organize a new church. He was by nature and temperament a conservative. His original purpose was nothing more than to reform certain evils in the Church. It was the unwillingness of his opponents to see the need of the reforms he advocated that drew him into the struggle and made him the focal point of the new movement. Meanwhile those whose ideas he unwittingly expressed urged him on, and a number of princes who opposed the universal claims of the papacy zealously supported him. Gradually Luther came to regard the situation as a God-given opportunity and seized the leadership of the movement with zeal and determination. Thereafter until his death he was its dominant figure. Yet it was not Luther himself, but the support of the German princes and the German people, that made the movement a success. Without the backing of his countrymen his attacks against the pope would have been tantamount to throwing a pebble against a granite cliff; with popular support, his attack amounted to an avalanche that swept the papal authority out of a large part of Germany.

Luther was born in Eisleben, a little village in Saxony, on the 10th of November, 1483, the son of a peasant miner. Because of the severity of his upbringing, his youth was far from happy. Both at home and in school he was punished summarily for even the slightest offenses, a discipline which was rooted in the legalistic religion of the day. In consequence young Luther was harassed by religious anxieties. He was tortured by an ever-present fear of God, whom he conceived as the implacable judge who inexorably punishes every infraction of His laws. The question of how he could please God soon became uppermost with him and ultimately determined the course of his life. His father wished young Martin to become a lawyer, in order that he might rise in the social scale. Accordingly Luther, at the age of eighteen, was sent to Erfurt, at that time the most famous university in Germany. An intelligent and hard-working student, he took the degree of master of arts in 1505 and made ready to pursue the study of law. But the question of how he could please God caused him so much mental anguish that he suddenly decided to become a member of the Augustinian friars, a mendicant order of monks. In the monastery at Erfurt he devoted himself unremittingly to winning favor in the eyes of God by the customary discipline of fastings, prayers, and scourgings. Nevertheless, he found no peace of soul. The idea of a righteous God still continued to haunt him. Peace finally came when, as a result of his studies of the Bible and of the writings of St. Augustine, he formed the conviction that man is saved from the wrath of God not by faith and good works, but solely by faith in God's grace and mercy. This momentous doctrine of justification by faith, discovered anew by Luther, was to form the cornerstone not only of Luther's beliefs but also of Protestant theology.

At that time, however, this doctrine made little outward difference in Luther's life, for he continued in the usual path. In 1508 he was called to the University of Wittenberg, newly founded by Frederick the Wise of Saxony, where he first taught philosophy and later lectured on the Bible. His teaching was interrupted in 1511 by a journey to Rome on business of his order, a visit destined to influence his subsequent career. He was profoundly shocked by the many abuses he saw in the Holy City. Although at the time his faith in the Church remained unshaken, the remembrance of this visit later roused him to launch a vigorous attack on the evils he had witnessed. In Rome he pursued the usual course of visiting the most celebrated shrines in order to take advantage of the indulgences granted to pious pilgrims. The opportunities for this procedure were so many that he half regretted, as he later confessed, that his parents were not dead; for to pray them out of purgatory would have been easy. His return to Wittenberg found him as devoted to the Church as ever, and his promotion in its ranks followed. In 1515 he was appointed to the office of district vicar and placed in charge of eleven monasteries of his order. He might have gone on to the end of his days as a pious Catholic, had not a series of events roused him to action and literally forced upon him the leadership of the reform movement.

The initial step was provoked by the activity of John Tetzel, a Dominican friar engaged in the sale of indulgences near Wittenberg. According to Catholic doctrine, an indulgence is the extra-sacramental remission of the temporal punishment of sin. Temporal punishment remains after the eternal punishment has been removed, and this the sinner must undergo either in the present life or in purgatory. Release from it is secured when the Church draws upon the inexhaustible treasury of merits created by the sufferings of Christ and the good works of the saints, and applies them to the souls of repentant sinners. It does this by granting indulgences. In earlier times indulgences had been granted for participation in a crusade or for such acts of personal piety as prayers and good works. Later in the Middle Ages the practice arose of granting them for money. On the present occasion Tetzel sold, under the auspices of Albert of Brandenburg, archbishop of Mainz, indulgences proclaimed by Leo X. Stamped with the papal seal, they insured to those who bought them complete forgiveness of sin and freedom from purgatory. The purpose of the sale was to raise money to defray the debt owed by the archbishop to the Fugger banking house, and also to complete St. Peter's Cathedral in Rome. Tetzel, in his eagerness to obtain as much money as possible, was selling the indulgences carelessly, without first insisting on the penitence of the buyer. To Luther this sale of the promise of forgiveness, grace, and heaven, without insistence upon penitence, was an unmitigated evil against which he felt compelled to inveigh. He voiced his protest in ninety-five theses which, according to academic custom, he posted, on October 31, 1517, on the door of the Castle Church in Wittenberg. His immediate concern was with correcting the flagrant abuses attendant upon the sale of indulgences, not with doctrinal points.

The effect which the ninety-five theses produced was electric. With unprecedented speed they were printed and spread broadcast through Germany. Soon people of all ranks were discussing them. On the one hand, they aroused the sympathy of many; on the other, they moved faithful churchmen to attack Luther for his stand. A heated controversy arose. The pope, who was at first inclined to consider the whole matter a monkish quarrel, finally summoned Luther to Rome to answer for his arrogance. However, through the mediation of Frederick the Wise, elector of Saxony, it was arranged that Luther's trial be held on German soil. Hence in 1518 Luther journeyed to Augsburg, where he met the papal legate, Cardinal Cajetan. The interview settled nothing, for when Cajetan insisted that Luther retract his opinions, the latter promptly refused. A second messenger of the pope, Charles von Miltitz, by exercising great tact, managed to persuade Luther to refrain from further attacks, on condition that his opponents also remain silent.

But the truce was short-lived. The second step in Luther's break with the Church was precipitated by the renowned Dr. Eck in the famous Leipzig Disputation of 1519. When Eck challenged Luther to a debate, the latter willingly accepted the opportunity to express his views in public. The debate began on June 27, 1519, and lasted a week. In the course of it, Eck skillfully drew from Luther the admission that the Church had erred in condemning Huss, who was burned by the Council of Constance in 1415 for his views. This admission exposed Luther, too, to the accusation of heresy, and implied a definite break with the Church. There remained only to declare Luther a heretic publicly, and to excommunicate him. Eck's application for a bull of excommunication did not long remain unanswered. Although it was not published in Germany until some months later, it was issued as early as June 16, 1520. It condemned forty-two propositions taken from Luther's writings, ordered all of Luther's books burned, forbade him to preach, and demanded recantation of his errors within sixty days under pain of excommunication. When the bull reached Wittenberg, Luther took the spectacular step of burning it in the public square in the presence of a large gathering of professors, students, and citizens. Thus he publicly severed his connections with the Church. That Luther was able to take this step with impunity indicates how strong, at least in some parts of Germany, the will to resist the pope was.

Meanwhile Luther, upon receiving information of the proceedings against him, had started to put his case before the people, without waiting for publication of the bull in Germany. His means was the printing press. Among the writings which he published in the year 1520 three treatises stand out. The first, entitled *Address to the Nobility of the German Nation*, was a call to the Germans to unite and demolish the power of the pope over the German states. It may be styled the political and social manifesto of the Lutheran Reformation. In it Luther offered a number of suggestions for reform, among others the creation of a German National Church, the abolition of the mendicant orders, the improvement of moral conditions among the priests, and a reduction of the excessive number of holy days. The second, *On the Babylonian Captivity of the Church*, subjected the entire sacramental system to a searching criticism. In consequence he rejected all the sacraments but two, baptism and the Lord's Supper (eucharist), though he did ascribe to penance a certain sacramental value. The other so-called sacraments, he concluded, were but ceremonies of human institution. Moreover, he attacked what he regarded as three abuses of the Lord's Supper: the withdrawal of the cup from the laity, the doctrine of transubstantiation, and the teaching that the mass is a sacrifice. In the third treatise, *The Freedom of a Christian Man*, he briefly expounded the idea of the priesthood of all believers. Though many details were to be added later, the broad outlines of Luther's theological system were drawn in these three treatises. Thousands of copies of these writings circulated throughout Germany and won large numbers of supporters for Luther's cause.

Conditions generally were favorable to the success of the movement. Charles V, who might have offered a solid check to it, was too deeply preoccupied with the affairs of his vast domains, particularly with the wars against France, to devote any time to its suppression until too late. When he took a hand in it in 1521, the movement had reached such proportions that Luther could no longer be condemned without a hearing. He was therefore summoned to give an account of his position before the Diet of Worms, which was to meet in the same year. Together with the summons, Luther received letters of safe-conduct from the emperor and from the various princes through whose territories he must pass.

The journey to Worms was in the nature of a triumph, for all along the route throngs turned out to acclaim and encourage him.

On April 16, having arrived at Worms, Luther was ushered into the hall where the diet was assembled. As he stood before it, he was not "a poor, humble monk opposed by the whole world"; rather, he was the champion of an influential party which was represented by a small but powerful minority. Nor was he a simple-minded monk with only his faith to guide him. He was by this time already a warrior of considerable experience. Previous to his appearance before the diet, he had certainly discussed with his advisers, who were no less sagacious than those of the emperor, the best way to meet the situation. The first question he was asked was whether he had written the books that were arranged on a table before the emperor. After the title of the books had been read, Luther answered in the affirmative. When asked if he was willing to retract what he had written, he requested that he be given time to frame a suitable answer, and was granted a delay of twenty-four hours. The next day he replied to the question at some length. Tradition has added to the drama of the scene by having Luther conclude his refusal to recant with the words: "Here I stand; I cannot do otherwise. God help me. Amen." His actual words were dramatic enough: "Unless I am convicted of error by the testimony of Scripture or by clear reason (for I can trust neither the popes nor the councils, since it has been established that they have often erred and contradicted themselves) . . . I cannot and will not recant anything, since it is neither safe nor honest to act against one's conscience. God help me. Amen."

Having given his answer, Luther was dismissed. During the days immediately following his appearance before the diet, a commission held a series of conferences with him in the hope of effecting some kind of settlement. But as the monk of Wittenberg would not budge from the stand he had taken, the negotiations proved vain. Charles V, who was both amazed and shocked by Luther's resolute stand, finally issued the Edict of Worms, which put Luther under the ban of the empire. The edict declared that "the said Martin Luther shall hereafter be held and esteemed by each and all of us as a limb cut off from the Church of God, an obstinate schismatic and manifest heretic." It ordered that Luther be delivered to the imperial authorities at the expiration of the safe-conduct, and forbade everyone, under severe penalties, "to give the aforesaid Luther house or home, food, drink or shelter" or to read, print, or sell his books.

On the return journey to Wittenberg Luther suddenly disappeared. As he was passing through a wood an armed troop of horsemen, secretly sent by Frederick the Wise, carried him off to the Wartburg Castle near Eisenach, to protect him from the impending danger. In the Wartburg, where he remained in seclusion for almost a year, Luther worked incessantly, writing letters of advice and encouragement, a commentary on the Psalms, and an elaborate treatise entitled *On Monastic Vows*, in which he condemned their validity. He also began his translation of the Bible. A Bible in the German vernacular was not a novelty. A considerable number of translations had appeared before this time; but since they were all based on the Vulgate, they were unacceptable to the reformers. Luther's translation was based on Greek and Hebrew texts. Though the complete work did not appear until 1534, the New Testament was published as early as 1522. It circulated widely and was no small factor in winning support for Luther's cause. Because of its literary beauty it has become as much a classic as the English Authorized version.

Luther's sojourn in the Wartburg was terminated suddenly in March, 1522. During his absence from Wittenberg an iconoclastic group under the leadership of another professor, John Bodenstein of Carlstadt, and the Augustinian friar, Gabriel Zwilling, both of whom believed that Luther's reforms had not gone far enough, had introduced further changes. In themselves the changes were not important, but they were attended by riots and outbreaks. Luther, who discountenanced the use of force to achieve reforms, was alarmed at the progress of this more radical movement. Returning to Wittenberg, he preached a series of sermons against this group and succeeded in quieting the disturbances. Meanwhile the imperial authorities took no action regarding the ban, nor was it enforced later. On the other hand, since it was never rescinded, Luther remained theoretically under the ban for the rest of his life.

A noteworthy event of the next period of his life was his marriage in 1525 to Katharine von Bora, an ex-nun who had run away from a convent after reading Luther's treatise, *On Monastic Vows*. In taking this step Luther was motivated in part by the desire to oppose the practice of clerical celibacy by his personal example. From his opponents this marriage between an "apostate monk" and a "renegade nun" evoked much denunciation. That the physically infirm Luther found married life a source of comfort and happiness is evidenced by the many sermons he preached on the blessings and joys of the married state.

After his return to Wittenberg Luther's services in behalf of reform were not so dramatic. He again took up his abode in the Augustinian monastery, now deserted by the rest of the monks, to continue his indefatigable labors as author, teacher, preacher, and organizer. Since he had renounced the ecclesiastical system of the Roman Church it became necessary to organize a new church system. As Luther viewed it, this new church was essentially the old one, with certain unessentials and outer trappings discarded. Nevertheless, among the doctrines rejected by Luther and the church that took its name from him were a number of fundamental beliefs, including those regarding the headship of the pope, transubstantiation, purgatory, good works, indulgences, relics, and the adoration of saints. Of the seven sacraments only two, baptism and the Lord's Supper, were retained. The basic doctrine of the new church was, of course, justification by faith; and the sole source of all doctrines was the Bible. The clergymen of the new church were permitted to marry and to live more like laymen. In general, the lines which sharply separated the clergy from the laity in the Catholic Church were less distinct in the Lutheran Church. The question of church government was settled by giving the supreme power, except in questions of doctrine, to the governments of the German states and cities.

Important changes were also introduced in the forms of worship, which were organized more on popular lines. The Latin service of the Roman Church was replaced by one conducted entirely in German. It consisted, in the main, of preaching, Bible-reading, and hymn-singing. So that there would be a greater variety for the congregational singing, Luther prevailed upon his friends to write hymns. He himself wrote a large number, many of which are prosaic. Among them, however, there is one that is really great—the hymn *A Mighty Fortress Is Our God*, which the German poet Heinrich Heine called the *Marseillaise* of the Reformation. For the religious education of the common people Luther wrote two summaries of the Lutheran doctrines, the Longer and Shorter Catechisms, both of which were published in 1529. These books, particularly the Shorter Catechism, were used so successfully to indoctrinate the common people that the Catholics followed Luther's example by publishing catechisms of their own.

Up to the year 1524 the Lutheran movement steadily gained strength in Germany, thus indicating the ultimate conquest of the whole country. But a series of events was soon to rob the movement of much of its force, so that in the end the influence of the Lutheran Church in Germany was confined largely to the northern part of the country. The first of these events was the Peasants' War. The fundamental causes of this rebellion were similar to those which had precipitated numerous local revolts in Germany during the generation preceding the uprising of 1524. Though the majority of German peasants were free, the number of serfs was still considerable. Of the free peasants only comparatively few were independent owners of the land they cultivated. The rest owed to the lord of the manor dues ranging from a simple ground rent to a multiplicity of payments and services. Some were so overloaded with dues and services that their condition was little better than that of serfs; in fact, in some districts of Germany free peasants were being reduced systematically to a state of serfdom. Among the most vexatious dues and services were the forced labor on the personal estate of the lord, the unrewarded service of beating the bushes for the lord during the chase, and the heriot or death tax.[1] There were also many complaints against the three tithes—the "great tithe" on corn, the "small tithe" on fruit, and the "flesh tithe" on domestic animals. Furthermore, the peasants were forbidden, under severe penalties, to hunt, fish, or cut wood in the forests. A more serious grievance was the seizure of the common lands by the nobility. Since the middle of the fifteenth century the lords had been adding the common lands to their personal estates. For the peasants, who were thereby deprived of the pasture lands on which they had formerly raised their cattle, the task of earning a living and paying the manorial dues became increasingly difficult. In years of poor harvests many were forced to borrow money from the money-lenders at exorbitant rates in order to pay the landlord. As a result foreclosures became so common that many contemporary writers, including Luther, were moved to inveigh against the avarice of the money-

---

[1] According to custom the lord had the right, upon the death of the head of the family, to claim the best article the deceased had left; for example, a horse or an ox. By the sixteenth century the heriot had largely been commuted to money payments.

lenders, and also against the exploitation of the peasants by the nobility.

Thus there was no lack of causes for the dissatisfaction and unrest among the peasants. An additional cause for the revolt of 1524 was the general ferment produced by Luther's writings, particularly by the doctrine of Christian liberty, from which the discontented peasants drew inferences applicable to their own conditions. More than this, they looked to Luther, "the son of a peasant," to champion their cause. The insurrection, which started in extreme southwestern Germany in May, 1524, spread quickly and by the following year had reached formidable proportions. In March, 1525, the peasants presented their demands in Twelve Articles. The demands included abolition of serfdom, the heriot, and all tithes but the "great tithe" on corn; restoration of the common lands; reduction of oppressive feudal services and exorbitant rents; and extension to the peasants of the right to hunt, fish, and cut wood in the forests. Luther, who was not unsympathetic to the peasants, attempted at first to mediate between the two parties by advising mutual concessions. But when the revolt got out of hand and the peasants began to sack and burn castles and monasteries, Luther withdrew. Theoretically opposed to all forms of violence, he vehemently denounced the peasants in the pamphlet, *Against the Murderous and Thieving Rabble of the Peasants*, calling upon the nobility to crush the revolt, root and main. "Rebellion," he stated, "is not merely wicked murder but a sort of conflagration, which devastates the land, brings bloodshed and creates widows and orphans. Therefore, whoever can, should smite, strangle or stab, secretly or publicly." The princes and nobles, who needed no urging, put down the revolt so ferociously that many thousands of peasants [1] perished, either in battle or at the hands of the executioner. In consequence Luther's cause lost the support of the peasants who survived the insurrection. Furthermore, many of the nobles of southern Germany turned against the Protestant leader because they regarded the revolt as the natural result of his teachings.

In the years after the Peasants' War the Lutheran movement suffered further losses as a consequence of the break between Luther and the humanists. At first it had seemed as if the spirit of the Northern Renaissance and that of the Reformation might

---

[1] Estimates run as high as one hundred thousand.

unite in ushering in a new age. But the interests of the reformers soon clashed with those of the humanists. Many of the humanists who had hoped Luther would usher in an era of intellectual freedom were sorely disappointed as he continually grew more dogmatic; they were also repelled by his violence. Among them was Erasmus. Because of his trenchant attacks on the prevailing abuses in the Church, Erasmus was, in a sense, the intellectual father of the Protestant movement. As the saying has it, "Erasmus laid the egg which Luther hatched." But when Luther launched his attacks against the Church, Erasmus did not join hands with him. The aim of Erasmus was primarily educational, not religious. In a letter to Luther he wrote, "I keep myself, so far as I can, neutral in order that I may better serve the reviving cause of letters." Nor were Luther's methods his. Temperamentally averse from violent methods, he was repelled by Luther's impetuosity and vehemence. Moreover, he was alarmed at the possible consequence of organized religious animosities. Gradual enlightenment through humanistic studies, Erasmus believed, would be much more effective in abolishing the evils which were afflicting society. "I would," he wrote, "that Luther had followed my advice and abstained from those violent and opprobrious writings. More would have been gained and with less odium." Wishing to remain on good terms with both parties, Erasmus at first avoided committing himself finally to either side. In time, however, he yielded to the persuasions of the Catholic party and firmly stepped out as the opponent of Luther by writing his *Diatribe on Free Will*. Luther's determined answer was not calculated to be conciliatory, and the rift became irreparable. In consequence most of the humanists who still supported Luther's cause deserted it, while others were confirmed in their antipathy to it.

In 1530 Charles V, having made peace with France, turned again to the task of effecting a settlement of the religious question. This time he was resolved to reconcile the contending parties once for all, little realizing that the cleavage was too deep to be mended except by concessions which neither side was willing to make. In the previous year the Catholic party, emboldened by the emperor's victory over Francis I, had passed a decree at the Diet of Spires demanding that the Edict of Worms be executed. The Lutheran members of the diet had responded by publishing a protest, and by virtue of this action had become known as the

"Protestants." When Charles arrived in Germany he asked the Protestants to draw up a statement of their beliefs, to be read before the imperial diet summoned to meet at Augsburg in the same year. This statement, known as the Augsburg Confession, was largely the work of Philip Melanchthon, next to Luther the leading figure of the Lutheran movement; but it was submitted to and approved by Luther. Melanchthon had drawn up the statement in a conciliatory spirit, putting the emphasis on the doctrines the two parties held in common and stressing the conservative nature of the changes that had been made. After reading the statement, Luther himself wrote, "I cannot walk so softly or lightly." Yet it was unacceptable to the Catholic leaders. They insisted that the Protestants yield completely. Charles V charged a group of Catholic theologians to prepare a confutation of the Augsburg Confession and when it was ready ordered the Protestants to accept it by a given time.

Fearing that the emperor would use force to achieve his end, a number of Lutheran states and cities formed the Schmalkaldic League, a defensive union. The advance of the Turks, however, prevented the emperor from executing his threats, and a truce was agreed upon between the two parties. This armistice lasted until 1546 when Charles V was able to return to the problem of suppressing Protestantism. Despite Luther's efforts to preserve peace, the so-called Schmalkaldic War broke out in February, 1546, four months after his death. For a time it seemed as if the Protestant cause were doomed, but in the end Charles' attempt to crush Protestantism failed once and for all. The peace of Augsburg which terminated the war in 1555 was in effect a compromise. Each prince was given the right to decide which of the two faiths was to be permitted in his territory, on the principle *cuius regio, eius religio* (whose territory, his religion). All dissentients were to be given an opportunity to emigrate. Thus Lutheranism received legal recognition in Germany.

Meanwhile Lutheranism had taken root also in the Scandinavian countries, where in time it spread more widely than in Germany because of its intimate connection with politics. The Swedish king, Gustavus Vasa (1496–1560), actuated in large degree by a desire to secure the vast wealth of the Church for his impoverished treasury, early espoused the Lutheran cause. Lutheranism was formally sanctioned at the Diet of Westeras, 1527, and at the same time the property of the Church was surrendered to the king. Religious changes, however, were introduced only gradually, and the reforms effected were more conservative than those of the Lutheran Church in Germany. The archbishop of Upsala, shorn of much of his judicial power, remained the head of the Swedish Church, and the episcopal titles were retained for Lutheran incumbents. It was not until 1544 that the organization of the Swedish Lutheran Church as the national church was finally effected. Thereafter the Catholics in Sweden gradually declined to an insignificant number. In Finland, at the time a dependency of Sweden, the Reformation took practically the same course.

Contemporarily, similar changes were introduced in Denmark. After Frederick I (1523–1533) granted toleration to Lutherans, in 1527, and permitted the marriage of priests, Lutheranism spread rapidly. The next king, Christian III (1536–1559), abolished the authority but not the title of the bishops, and also confiscated the church lands in 1536. In the following year Johann Bugenhagen, one of Luther's associates, arrived from Wittenberg to assist the king in the work of reorganizing the Danish Church according to Lutheran principles. The new constitution which Bugenhagen prepared was officially adopted in 1539. Soon after, Norway, which was under Danish rule from 1380 until 1814, and Iceland, a Danish possession, were also Lutheranized by royal decree.

CALVINISM

A reform movement that was independent of Luther had meantime started in Switzerland. Nominally a part of the Holy Roman Empire, Switzerland was a confederation of thirteen small, virtually autonomous cantons. Thus the political organization of the country rendered it comparatively easy for local leaders such as Ulrich Zwingli, the originator of the reform movement in Switzerland, to influence the inhabitants.

Only a few weeks younger than Luther, Zwingli was born on New Year's Day, 1484, at Wildhaus, a village in the upper valley of the Toggenburg. His early life was free from the grinding poverty and the spiritual struggles which marked the boyhood of the German reformer. At no time in his life does Zwingli seem to have been troubled by the agonizing sense of sin which tortured Luther. He had little of the mystic in him, being more representative of humanistic culture. At the University of Basel, where he took his master's degree in 1506, he became deeply interested in the classics and decided to enter the priesthood. In making this decision he was probably impelled more by humanistic than by religious motives, for as a priest he could continue his humanistic studies. His first charge was Glarus, where he remained for ten years before he was called to Einsiedeln. Here he began his work as reformer by preaching against indulgences and pilgrimages. He did not attack them with the impetuosity of Luther, however, but rather sought to ridicule them out of existence.

A wider opportunity for his efforts presented itself when in December, 1518, he accepted the post of vicar at the cathedral church of Zurich. Wealthy and powerful, with a population of about seven thousand, Zurich was the most eminent city in Switzerland. Soon Zwingli became a person of influence there, assuming the leadership in all important spiritual matters. In 1519 he was able to force Bernard Samson, a seller of indulgences, to leave Zurich. During the years which followed, he searched more deeply into the current abuses in the Church, deriving much support for his own convictions from his reading of Luther, although he himself probably would have denied that he was ever a disciple of the Wittenberg professor. At any rate, his work of reform bears the impress of Luther's ideas.

The great turning point in Zwingli's career was a series of debates which were held in 1523 before the city council in Zurich. As the basis of discussion Zwingli drew up sixty-seven theses containing the essence of his reformatory ideas. In them he asserted the sole authority of the Bible and affirmed the doctrine of salvation by faith. He rejected all the characteristic peculiarities of the Catholic creed, such as the papacy, mass, invocation of saints, fasts, festivals, pilgrimages, monastic orders, the priesthood, auricular confession, absolution, indulgences, penances, and purgatory. Before six hundred people, both laymen and clergymen, he so ably defended his position that he won the sympathy of the council, which henceforth gave him its full support. Changes more radical than those of Luther, and anticipating Calvin, were rapidly introduced in Zurich. Mass was abolished; statues, pictures, crucifixes, altars, and candles were removed from the churches; relics were buried; holy water was done away with; and even the frescoes were covered with whitewash.

Though in practice the reforms of Zwingli were much more thoroughgoing than those of Luther, both reformers were in substantial agreement on most of the cardinal doctrines of Protestantism. On the doctrine of the eucharist (Lord's Supper) there was, however, a radical difference of opinion. Luther, nearer to the Catholic view, held that the words of institution, "This is my body," must be interpreted literally. His is the theory of consubstantiation as against the Catholic belief in transubstantiation.[1] Zwingli, on the other hand, regarded the eucharist as merely a devout commemoration of Christ's death and work. The bread and wine were to him only signs or symbols of the body and blood of Christ. The controversy in which Luther and Zwingli engaged on these doctrinal points, at the instigation of the Strasbourg divines who were eager to have the points cleared up, was bitter. Neither could convince the other. Finally, at the suggestion of Philip of Hesse, the reformers met at Marburg in 1529 to adjust the doctrinal difference. But the difference proved irreconcilable. Luther refused to budge one iota from the literal interpretation which to Zwingli was only a relic of Catholicism. Even when it became evident that no common ground could be reached, Zwingli extended the hand of fellowship to Luther, but the latter refused it, stating that the Swiss were of another spirit. This disagreement marked the beginning of the division of Protestantism into the two branches, Lutheran and Reformed.

Meanwhile Reformed Protestantism had spread in Switzerland until it embraced all but the five forest cantons.[2] The two groups of cantons, Protestant and Catholic, regarded each other with such uncompromising hostility that leagues were formed and preparations made for war. Though actual fighting was prevented in 1529 by a truce, neither side was satisfied with its terms. Two years later war actually broke out. The forces of Zurich, greatly inferior to those of the forest cantons, were defeated on October 11, 1531, and Zwingli, who had accompanied the men of Zurich

---

[1] *The New Catholic Dictionary* (1929) defines *transubstantiation* as "the marvellous and singular changing of the entire substance of the bread into the entire substance of the Body of Christ and of the entire substance of the wine into His Blood." *Consubstantiation* (according to *The New Schaff-Herzog Religious Encyclopedia*, vol. 3 [1909], p. 260) denotes the view that "the bread and wine remain bread and wine; though, after the consecration, the real flesh and blood of Christ coexist in and with the natural elements, just as a heated iron bar still remains an iron bar."

[2] Uri, Schwyz, Unterwalden, Lucerne, and Zug.

into battle as their chaplain, lost his life. The peace which followed gave to each canton the right to adhere to its religion. Thereafter Protestantism made no further advances in the Catholic cantons.

The reform which Zwingli started at Zurich was carried on later at Geneva by John Calvin, who can thus be said to belong to the second generation of reformers. He was born at Noyon, in France, on July 10, 1509. His father, Gerard Calvin, who held the posts of secretary of the Noyon bishopric and attorney for the cathedral chapter, destined him for the priesthood. When only twelve years old young Calvin was granted the income from a small benefice to defray the cost of his clerical education, and a few years later the income from a second one was added. In his studies for the priesthood Calvin progressed as far as taking the tonsure and preaching occasionally, though he was not ordained. Suddenly, his father decided that the law offered better prospects, and ordered him to forsake theology for jurisprudence. Young Calvin did as he was bidden, and took up the law. It has been said the legal studies were uncongenial to him; however this may be, they left a mark on his mind which later became evident both in the form and in the content of his theology. After the death of his father in 1531, he turned to the study of the humanities. The fruit of this study was a commentary on Seneca's *De Clementia*, published in 1532. Shortly after the appearance of this work his "sudden conversion" (to use his own expression) took place. As to the circumstances in which it occurred Calvin has left posterity entirely in the dark. Also the events of the next few years of his life are obscure. However, he was now openly in sympathy with the Reformation, and in 1534 he severed his connections with the Roman Church completely by resigning his benefices. Shortly thereafter he went to Switzerland since France was by this time no longer safe for professing Protestants.

The early months of the year 1536 saw him in Basel, where he published *The Institutes of the Christian Religion*, the book which gave him rank among the reformers. The first edition, consisting of only six chapters, contained but the germ of what was ultimately to be known as Calvinism; in the edition of 1559, expanded to eighty chapters, its doctrines were fully developed. But even in its earliest form the book gave unity to the ideas of the Protestant Reformation, and in this resides its importance. For its material Calvin was, in the main, indebted to others, particularly to Luther.

Originally written in Latin, the book was translated into French by the author in 1541 and dedicated to Francis I in an effort to bring the French king into sympathy with the new doctrines. The effort failed. In 1542 the book was condemned as heretical by the Parlement of Paris and publicly burned.

The doctrines of Calvin's *Institutes* are in substantial agreement with those of Luther. Like the Wittenberg reformer, Calvin insisted upon the sole authority of the Bible in matters of faith and conduct, upon the sinfulness of man and his impotence to save himself, and upon the doctrine of justification by faith. There were, however, important points of difference. Whereas Calvin sought to suppress everything not directly sanctioned in the Bible, Luther permitted everything not specifically forbidden in it. Then, too, Calvin's idea of God rested upon the Old Testament concept of the majesty of God, while Luther's revolved upon the New Testament concept of the love of God. In his interpretation of the Lord's Supper Calvin took a position midway between those of Luther and Zwingli, teaching a spiritual presence. But the central and peculiar dogma of Calvinism, distinguishing it from all other Protestant creeds, was the doctrine of predestination. This doctrine teaches that, though salvation is by faith, not everyone can be saved, but only those whom God has predestined from all eternity. The number of those predestined to eternal bliss is unalterable. They were chosen not because God foresaw good in them, but because it was His will to bestow on them the gift of salvation for the manifestation of His glory. The rest of mankind He has left to suffer the penalty which they justly deserve because of their sins. In its main outlines this doctrine was not new. It had been stated by both Augustine and Luther, but neither had carried it to its ultimate conclusions of admitting divine determination for those who were lost. It was Calvin's unique distinction, driven as he was by his pitiless logic, to accept in full all the dire consequences of man's inability to save himself. But how can a person know if he is predestined to be saved? Calvin's answer was that those "who are chosen unto life are chosen unto good works." In other words, the elect strive toward perfection, toward complete freedom from the slavery of sin. They zealously endeavor to fulfill to the last iota the moral laws as found in the Bible, particularly in the decalogue. The obligation of the elect does not, however, stop with themselves. It is also their duty to make other men moral, to refashion their community and the world in accordance with God's will. Thus the Calvinist has a "divine mission," one which "implies the call of the best, of the sanctified, of the minority, to dominion over the sinners, the majority." Hence the militantly aggressive character of Calvinism.

Soon after he published the first edition of the *Institutes*, Calvin was to find an opportunity to "refashion a community after God's will." While traveling through Switzerland in 1536, he stopped at Geneva, intending to remain there only a short time. As it turned out, he remained there the rest of his life, with the exception of one short period. The city of Geneva, which lies between the Jura Mountains and the Alps, on the south border of Lake Leman, comprised at that time a population of about thirteen thousand, mainly of French, German, and Italian elements. Earlier in the century the city had revolted against its bishop, and when Calvin arrived there he found the reformer William Farel occupied with the task of establishing a Protestant church. More zealous than tactful, Farel had been unable to cope with the elements of disorder. He was, however, shrewd enough to see that the author of the *Institutes* would be a valuable ally, and he therefore induced him to remain. Together the two men set about making Geneva into a model Christian community. Their discipline was so severe that in 1538 the people rose in rebellion and both Calvin and Farel were banished from the city. But the three years of Calvin's exile in Strasbourg were not a period of peace and order in Geneva. The incessant strife of the various factions created such disorder that in 1541 the council urgently requested Calvin's return. For some time Calvin hesitated, because, as he said, "I feel unequal to the difficulties which await me there." Finally, however, he decided to go back.

In September, 1541, Calvin reëntered Geneva to resume at once the task of completely reforming all departments of society. At his suggestion and under his supervision, the famous Ecclesiastical Ordinances were prepared, which provided for a consistory of six (later twelve) clergymen and twelve elders (appointed by the council) to "supervise" the morals of the citizens of Geneva. Though in theory the jurisdiction of the consistory in civil affairs was only advisory, in fact Geneva became a theocracy under its rule. The guiding spirit of the consistory was Calvin himself. He it was who formulated the laws, founded entirely on the Bible, to regulate the life of every citizen in its minutest details. Thus the Bible was the final authority not only in religion but also in politics. The laws included, besides matters ordinarily regulated by law, provisions for such things as church attendance, behavior, dress, amusements, and luxuries. Punishments for transgression were severe. In extenuation of this severity it might be stated that punishments were generally heavier in the sixteenth century than they are now; nevertheless, blue laws were never so blue as they were in Geneva. Women were imprisoned for wearing an exaggerated headdress or clothes of forbidden stuff. Dancing was prohibited, and musicians were permitted to remain in the city only if they promised not to play dance music. Stage plays were tolerated solely if they dealt with Scriptural subjects. Parents were forbidden to give certain names, including those of saints and legendary heroes, to their children. To such lengths did this regulatory passion go that a father who was imprisoned for naming his new-born son Claudius was released only when he consented to change the name to Abraham. Everyone was compelled to attend church services and to listen to Calvin's sermons, but to laugh during these sermons was considered a crime. Wearing jewelry if one was a spinster, playing cards, singing frivolous songs, saying *Requiescat in pace* over the grave of one's husband, betrothing one's daughter to a Catholic, and being ill for three days without sending for a minister were also labeled penal offenses.

Thus Geneva, under the theocratic rule of Calvin, became outwardly "a city of God"—"the most perfect school of life that was ever on earth since the days of the apostles," said John Knox. Others are of the opinion that the Draconian discipline did not make the people good, but merely served to drive sin beneath the surface. At that, there was no dearth of transgressors. The records show an enormous list of fines, imprisonments, and banishments between the years 1541 and 1559. Even sterner punishments were being meted out. In Geneva, as in the rest of Europe, the belief in witchcraft still prevailed. It has been calculated that for this reason more than fifty persons were condemned to death during a period of five years. Then there was the question of heresy. Though heresy was regarded as treason, those guilty of it were in most cases not put to death. A notorious case in which the death penalty was imposed is that of the Spaniard, Michael Servetus. It is the darkest shadow on Calvin's career. Early in

1553 Servetus, who was practicing medicine at Vienne in southern France, anonymously published a book entitled *The Restitution of Christianity*, in which he assailed certain doctrines held by both Catholics and Protestants, particularly the doctrine of the trinity. When the authorship of the book became known Servetus was seized by the Catholic authorities, brought to trial, and condemned to death by a slow fire. But he managed to escape and one Sunday suddenly appeared in the congregation of the cathedral at Geneva where Calvin was preaching. Just why Servetus went to Geneva is unknown. In view of the fact that he had previously carried on acrimonious discussions by letter with the Genevan reformer and had been warned not to come to Geneva, it was a foolhardy venture. Calvin, upon being informed of Servetus' presence, ordered his arrest and filed charges of heresy and blasphemy against him through one of his servants. Then he prosecuted the case against Servetus with remorseless severity. For two months and a half the trial dragged on. In the course of it the two men debated doctrinal points with great zest and vigor, and with mutual denunciations and recriminations. Finally, the Genevan council condemned Servetus to death by fire. He met his fate manfully, adhering steadfastly to his opinions. The general intolerance of the age was such that most theologians applauded the sentence.

In prosecuting Servetus, as in everything he undertook, Calvin was fortified by the conviction that he was doing the work of God. "It would be hypocrisy," he said, "not to own that the Lord has been pleased to employ me." Hence when he felt himself summoned to avenge what he called "the honor of God" he gave no quarter. Had he done so, he would have been the first to accuse himself of betraying the sacred trust imposed on him as one of the elect of God. Because of his unbending zeal, Calvin is to many a synonym for all that is stern and gloomy. Yet Calvin's nature had a kind side. In his relations with the people of his parish he often displayed a gentleness that was almost feminine. He grieved with them in their sorrows and rejoiced with them in their joys. A wedding or the arrival of a baby aroused in him a warm personal interest. Among the men and women who lived in intimate daily association with him he was a much loved man.

From the time he came to Geneva until his death, Calvin's life was one of incessant activity. Besides carefully supervising the lives of the inhabitants of Geneva as "a vigilance committee of one," he pursued intense and protracted mental labors, frequently at the expense of his health, which was never robust. His writings, which include five editions of the *Institutes* and expository commentaries on practically every book of the Bible, fill most of the fifty-nine quarto volumes of the *Calvini Opera*. At all times his correspondence was staggering in volume. In addition to all this, he preached about three hundred times a year and in his later years also taught in the Academy of Geneva. Finally, however, his feeble health gave way under the burden of his arduous labors. Prematurely worn out, he died on May 27, 1564, a few weeks before his fifty-fifth birthday. On the next day he was buried without pomp or ceremony in a plain wooden coffin. For a time after Calvin's death, the theocracy he had organized was carried on by his successor, Theodore Beza, but as Beza lacked the iron qualities of Calvin the town council managed gradually to free itself from the spiritual rule.

The historical importance of Calvin lies not so much in the work he undertook in Geneva as in the influence which he and the Genevan reform exerted upon Protestantism in general. Though very different estimates may be formed of his character, it cannot be denied that he rendered a powerful service to the cause of Protestantism. He was in a sense the supreme arbiter of the Reformed churches. Appeals for help and advice poured in from Protestant communities in all parts of Europe. His writings were translated into various European languages and were widely read by both clergy and laity. His fame attracted large numbers of Protestants to Geneva from all parts of Europe and many later returned to their native countries to spread his teachings. A further means of spreading his influence was the Academy which he reorganized in 1559 and which later became the University of Geneva. During Calvin's time the higher departments of this Academy were primarily a training school for Calvinistic ministers. Among the thousands of students who attended the Academy there were many foreigners who, after they had been imbued with Calvin's doctrines, went forth to preach them in other countries of Europe. Through such means Calvin inspired John Knox, William the Silent, Admiral Coligny, and Oliver Cromwell, and molded the thought and ideals of Protestantism in many countries.

Next to his interests in Geneva, Calvin was most concerned

with the establishment of his ideas in France, an aim which he
pursued with tireless energy. The French Protestants or Huguenots, in turn, looked to him as their leader. As such Calvin sent
encouragement, rules of discipline, and models for confessions to
the struggling Huguenot congregations. He also translated his
important works into French [1] for the benefit of his French followers, and in his Academy gave special care to the training of
ministers for the work of founding new Huguenot congregations.
By 1559 there were already so many congregations in France that
representatives from them gathered in Paris to organize a national
synod and to adopt a confession which had been drawn up by
Calvin. Thus Calvin was the real founder of the French Reformed
Church.

More widespread and lasting was the influence of Calvinism
in Scotland. Though Protestantism had taken root in Scotland
earlier, the organization of the Scottish Kirk was effected largely
under the leadership of John Knox (1515–1572), a disciple of
Calvin. Knox, an ordained priest, first publicly professed the
Protestant faith about 1545. After preaching in the town of St.
Andrews for some years, he reached England in 1549, where he
served as minister of the Church of England for the next five
years. Through his association with Cranmer and other reformers
he appears to have exerted some influence on the course of the
English Reformation. Upon the accession of Mary Tudor, an
ardent Catholic, Knox crossed the Channel, finally reaching Geneva, where he became pastor of the English refugee congregation in 1555. There he often had occasion to converse with Calvin,
whose doctrines he accepted with some modifications. All this
time Knox's principal interest was the progress of Protestantism
in Scotland. He was in constant touch with the Protestant movement in the land of his birth, and it was under his direction that
the Protestants of Scotland drew up the First Scotch Covenant in
1557. Two years later Knox returned to Scotland to assume the
leadership of the Protestant party and to lead an active campaign
against the Catholic Church and the government. When the regent Mary of Guise died in 1560, the Protestant leaders summoned
a free parliament which renounced the doctrine, worship, and
government of the Catholic Church and established the Reformed

---

[1] The precision and simplicity of Calvin's French prose contributed materially
to the development of the French language, which was then in its formative period.

Kirk of Scotland. With the assistance of others Knox drafted for
the new church a confession of faith based, in the main, on the
doctrines of Calvin, and also a constitution known as the First
Book of Discipline. The Calvinistic system of church government
as it was developed in Scotland vested complete control of the
Kirk in representative councils, known as presbyteries, composed

Extent of the Reformation, 1524–1572

of ministers and elders (presbyters). This was called the Presbyterian system. By the time Mary Queen of Scots returned from
France in 1561 to take over the personal rule of Scotland, the
Scottish Kirk was so firmly established that she was powerless
against it.

Calvinism took root also in other countries of Europe. After
the death of Mary Tudor in 1558 Protestant exiles returning to
England brought back a Calvinistic Protestantism which spread

rapidly among the middle classes, taking form in the movement known as Puritanism. In Germany, too, Calvinism won a following, particularly in the Rhenish Palatinate, whence it spread to other states; but it was not to gain legal recognition until the end of the Thirty Years' War in 1648. About the middle of the sixteenth century Calvinism also penetrated into the Netherlands. Introduced by Reformed preachers from France, it soon absorbed the converts which Lutheranism had made and even spread among the Catholic population. Ultimately the southern provinces, now included in the kingdom of Belgium, remained Catholic, but in the northern provinces Calvinism became the national religion of the Dutch. Like that of Germany, the Calvinism of the Dutch Reformed Church was milder than that of Geneva.

From Europe Calvinism made its way to America in the seventeenth century. The Pilgrim Fathers, the Dutch Burghers, the Scotch Presbyterians, the French Huguenots, and the Germans from the Palatinate carried their Calvinistic creeds to the New World where they stamped their influence deeply upon Protestant morality. In general, Calvinism trained men who, confident of their own election, set out aggressively to accomplish what they regarded as the will of God, emphasizing chastity and temperance.

CHAPTER EIGHT

The Catholic Reformation

B Y THE year 1560 Protestantism had spread until it seemed certain to triumph in most countries north of the Alps. It was firmly rooted in northern and central Germany, and had won many adherents in the southern portions. Scandinavia as a whole had fallen away from the Catholic Church. In Scotland Calvinism was gaining the ascendancy, in England the Elizabethan settlement was soon to establish a national church, and in Switzerland most of the cantons had welcomed the doctrines of Zwingli and Calvin. Furthermore, most of the nobility of Poland had accepted Protestant opinions. Protestantism was also spreading in Hungary, the Netherlands, and France; even in Spain and Italy it had won numerous converts. But the tide was about to be stemmed. Toward the middle of the century there arose in the Roman Catholic Church the movement known as the Catholic Reformation or Counter-Reformation, which aimed to eliminate from the Church the abuses that had been the objects of complaint, to infuse new spiritual life into Catholicism, and to recover the territory lost to the Protestants. In all respects the Catholic Reformation achieved a large measure of success. Besides purging the Church of its worst abuses, the movement was instrumental in regenerating Catholicism in some parts of Europe, and in regaining much of the ground temporarily abandoned. At the end of the first quarter of the seventeenth century Catholicism was again supreme in southern Germany, Poland, the southern Netherlands, Hungary, Moravia, and Bohemia; in Spain and Italy, Protestantism had disappeared entirely.

In Spain a Catholic reform movement, born of the religious zeal engendered during the centuries of conflict with the Moors, had already preceded the Protestant Reformation. Its leader was Ximenes de Cineros, confessor of Queen Isabella and grand inquisitor of the Spanish Inquisition; its aim was the extirpation of heresy and improvement of the morals and education of the clergy. With the support of the Spanish rulers, who desired to make Spain a model Catholic state, Ximenes brought the religious orders under the control of the secular authorities and introduced such rigor into monastic life that many monks left the country. He also forced a stricter discipline upon the clergy generally. Seeing the need of a better-educated clergy, he urged them to study the Scriptures. A monument to his promotion of biblical learning is the Complutensian Polyglot Bible, prepared under his supervision. It presented the Old Testament in Hebrew, Greek, and Latin, and the New Testament in Greek and Latin. To offer better opportunities for education he also founded the University of Alcala in 1498.

At the time, this reform movement had little influence outside of Spain. It was not until near the middle of the sixteenth century that the pope created or sanctioned the agencies which were to introduce it into other parts of Europe. The agencies were: (1) the Council of Trent; (2) the Index and the revived Inquisition; (3) the Society of Jesus.

THE COUNCIL OF TRENT

The idea of a general council as a means of reforming the evils from which the Church was suffering, and of settling the disputed questions, was not new. Since the inception of the Protestant movement there had been a widespread demand for such a council. Not only had Luther and the German Diet advocated one, but Charles V also was particularly eager to see it summoned, regarding it as the best agency of both reform and reconciliation. The popes, however, were hesitant about convoking a reformatory council. They feared that it might again endeavor to declare itself supreme over the papacy. Finally, Paul III summoned a council to meet at Mantua in 1537. Hardly had the summons been issued when war broke out between Charles V and Francis I

MARTIN LUTHER   JOHN CALVIN

ULRICH ZWINGLI   JOHN KNOX

IGNATIUS LOYOLA   LEO X   *by Raph...*

THE COUNCIL OF TRENT   *by Ti...*

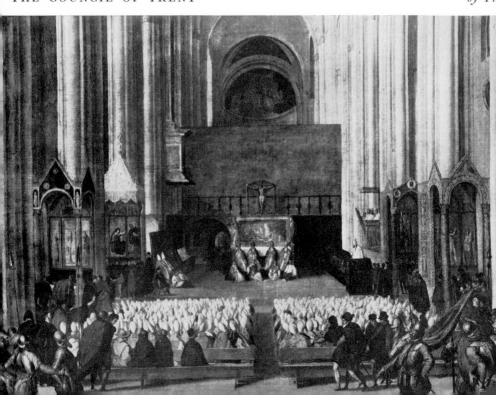

for the third time, preventing the holding of the council. Later the pope called a council to meet in 1542 at Trent, a city in Austria, just across the border from Italy. After various delays the sessions finally opened in December, 1545. When an epidemic broke out in 1547 the meeting place was transferred to Bologna, where a few unimportant sessions were held. In 1551 the council reassembled at Trent, suspended its sittings for ten years in 1552, and finally adjourned in 1563. The number of prelates attending the sessions varied, only thirty-four who had the right to vote being present at the first. At no time was the number very large and in all the sittings the Italian and Spanish prelates preponderated.

From the beginning two opinions were held as to the purpose of the council. The pope was opposed to any compromise in favor of the Protestants. He wished the council simply to define the doctrines of the Catholic Church in answer to the innovations of Protestantism, so that the Church could take a firm stand against all heresy. As the Roman Inquisition had been established in 1542 to uproot heresy, it was a matter of primary importance for the inquisitors to know just what the Church could tolerate and what was heretical. To Charles V, on the other hand, the matter of fundamental importance was the peaceful restoration of unity between the Lutherans and the Catholics. The internal strife caused by the Protestant revolt was weakening the empire and preventing it from offering effective resistance to external foes. Hence Charles desired the council to make such reforms and such modest concessions in doctrine as might be necessary to induce the Lutherans to re-enter the Church. During the second series of meetings in Trent the Protestants, upon the urgent insistence of the emperor, were twice invited to attend. They were offered the right of discussion, but were refused the right to vote. Nothing definite, however, came of the invitations.

In the end the wishes of the pope prevailed, for the council definitely rejected all compromise. After emphatically condemning the dissenting Protestant views, it formulated the doctrines of the Roman Church in a manner which rendered reconciliation with the Protestants impossible. It was unanimously agreed that the traditions of the Church are no less binding, as the source of faith, than the Bible. Justification was declared to be by faith and good works as against the Protestant doctrine of justification by faith alone. The council further decreed the Vulgate to be the only authoritative version of the Bible. No copies of the Scriptures were to be printed or circulated without authorization from the proper ecclesiastical officials. The right of interpreting the Scriptures was also reserved for the Church, and all private judgment in matters of faith and morals was expressly rejected. The seven sacraments were reaffirmed in opposition to the Protestants, with special emphasis on the doctrine of transubstantiation. The council also condemned the celebration of mass in the vulgar tongue, perpetuated the practice of withholding the cup from the laity, and confirmed the excellence of the celibate state. Finally, it maintained the doctrines of purgatory, indulgences, invocation of saints, and veneration of relics and images. The council closed with "anathema to all heretics, anathema, anathema."

Besides definitely formulating the vital doctrines of the Church, the Council of Trent effected a number of important reforms. Though they were not so drastic as many ardent Catholics had wished, they did eliminate the abuses which had been the principal targets of censure. The council decreed a thorough reformation of monastic life, and strict supervision of the subordinate clergy by the bishops. It denounced the appointment of disreputable and incompetent men to ecclesiastical positions and ordered that those elevated to the higher positions in the Church be men of good morals. The need for a better-educated clergy was recognized, and plans were made to establish seminaries for the education of priests. The abuse of pluralities was checked, and the clergy were commanded to preach frequently to the people.

In its achievements the Council of Trent was one of the most important gatherings in the history of the Roman Catholic Church. It accomplished three objects. First, it formulated the faith and practices of the Church in a clear, compact, and authoritative statement. Since a great diversity of opinion had existed in the writings of the medieval Church, such a statement of doctrine as a criterion of orthodoxy was widely desired. It obviated controversial questions by definite doctrines and replaced doubtful traditions with dogmatic certainties. Second, the council strengthened the organization and centralized the government of the Church, so that Catholicism could henceforth present a united front to its enemies. Finally, it drew up a program of reform which freed the Church from most of the abuses which had given strength to the Protestant movement. With its scattered forces collected, the Roman Church could now move to reconquer some of the territory it had lost.

THE INDEX AND THE INQUISITION

Among the tasks which the council left to the pope, one of the most important was the preparation of an Index of Prohibited Books (*Index librorum prohibitorum*), a list of works which Roman Catholics were forbidden to read. This was not a radical departure. The Church since early times had used various means of preventing the reading and spread of heterodox literature. Popes, councils, and even emperors had issued prohibitions regarding books dangerous to the faith. Thus the reading of pagan books, of the writings of Arius, and of the Talmud was interdicted at various times during the Middle Ages. The easiest way to prevent the circulation of heretical volumes was to confiscate and burn them. The Council of Constance (1415), for example, ordered that all the books of John Huss be burned publicly, and directed the bishops to make a diligent search for hidden copies. So long as copies of books were multiplied slowly by scribes and the number in circulation was small, their suppression was comparatively easy. But after the invention of printing, thousands of copies could be turned out in a short time. To meet the changed conditions Pope Alexander VI inaugurated a new censorship of books by his bull in 1501, forbidding the printers of Treves, Mayence, Cologne, and Magdeburg to publish books without permission of the respective archbishops. In 1515 a decree of the Fifth Lateran Council forbade the printing of any book in any diocese in Christendom without permission of the proper ecclesiastical officials.

These prohibitions, however, were of no avail in restraining Protestant printers. When they released a veritable deluge of books regarded as dangerous by the Church, new methods had to be devised to keep Catholics from reading them. Hence the lists of forbidden books. The first Indexes appeared at Louvain, at Cologne, and at Paris in the decade before 1550 and were only of local importance. The first papal Index or list of prohibited books for the whole Church was issued by Pope Paul IV in 1559. As it was unsatisfactory for a number of reasons, the Council of Trent took the matter in hand. It appointed a commission which drafted a set of ten rules by which writings were to be judged, but left the actual preparation of the list to the pope. The new Index, published by the pope in 1564, proscribed without distinction all books condemned during the Middle Ages, all writings of here-siarchs, all books tending to corrupt morals, and all literature dealing with astrology, necromancy, and occultism. In 1571 Pope Pius V created at Rome the Congregation of the Index, whose business it became to examine all suspected publications and to place on the forbidden list those adjudged dangerous to faith or morals. The Index issued in 1596 remained, with some additions, the standard until the middle of the eighteenth century. Since its first issue the Index has passed through about a hundred editions.

In 1897 Leo XIII stated that the penalty for reading pro-hibited books was *ipso facto* excommunication. Permission might, however, be obtained to read or possess forbidden books. Among the more famous authors whose names have appeared on the Index and whose works are forbidden either entirely or in part are: Joseph Addison, Francis Bacon, Balzac, Bergson, Giordano Bruno, Comte, Descartes, Alexander Dumas, Anatole France, Edward Gibbon, Oliver Goldsmith, Heinrich Heine, Thomas Hobbes, Victor Hugo, David Hume, James I of England, Kant, Locke, Maeterlinck, John Stuart Mill, Milton, Montesquieu, Leo-pold von Ranke, Ernest Renan, Rousseau, George Sand, Spinoza, Stendhal, David F. Strauss, Tolstoy, Voltaire, and Émile Zola.[1] In 1917 Benedict XV suppressed the Congregation of the Index, leaving its duties entirely to the Holy Office.

Another instrument for combatting heresy had been set up by Pope Paul III in 1542 when he authorized the establishment of a "Supreme Tribunal of the Inquisition." It was not a new organ-ization, but simply an adaptation of the older Papal Inquisition to new conditions. The Papal Inquisition, a special tribunal for the detection and punishment of heresy, was founded in the thir-teenth century because the ordinary episcopal courts were unable to cope with the alarming spread of heretical beliefs. Entrusted to the Dominican and Franciscan monks, it at first moved from place to place. Later inquisitorial districts were formed in central Europe. In England and Spain it did not gain a foothold. On the whole, it exercised jurisdiction only over those who had fallen away from the Catholic faith. Because of the extreme rigor of its

[1] For a more complete list see *The Roman Index of Forbidden Books Briefly Explained* by Francis S. Betten, S. J. (2nd rev. ed., 1932).

proceedings, its use of torture, and the unfairness of its trials according to modern standards, it has been severely denounced. The guilt of the accused was assumed before the trial began. If the accused confessed his real or imputed guilt a comparatively mild punishment was imposed. If not, various means, including moral subterfuges and weakening of physical strength, were employed to gain a confession. Torture was the last expedient. Those who confessed under torture were condemned to imprisonment for life. If the accused still remained obdurate, he was handed over to the secular power to be burned alive. Heresy, it must be remembered, was regarded as more terrible than murder or treason. Innocent III stated that "it is infinitely more serious to offend against the Divine Majesty than to injure human majesty." By the fifteenth century the heresies which had called the Inquisition into being had been so largely repressed in central Europe that there was a tendency to suspend its functions.

But late in the fifteenth century the Spanish Inquisition took its rise. Whereas the rulers of the Spanish states had previously refused to permit the introduction of the Papal Inquisition, Ferdinand and Isabella in 1480 consented to the establishment of the so-called Spanish Inquisition at Seville. The Spanish Inquisition, being strictly under the control of the government, was as much a political as a religious agency. Probably its most notorious head was Thomas de Torquemada, an austere Dominican monk who was made grand inquisitor in 1483. His chief aim was to make the Inquisition more effective by establishing other tribunals in addition to that at Seville; and the courts were increased until by 1538 there were no fewer than nineteen. How many persons were punished by the Spanish Inquisition can only be conjectured. It is estimated that at least two thousand were condemned to the flames during the eighteen years of Torquemada's tenure of office, while tens of thousands suffered milder penalties. Like Ferdinand and Isabella, their successors, Charles V (Charles I of Spain) and Philip II, also believed that religious unity was the best guarantee of political unity; therefore, they continued to protect and to foster the Inquisition. So harshly did this tribunal do its work that Protestantism was completely crushed in Spain.

It was the success of the Inquisition in Spain which suggested to Pope Paul III the idea of setting up an Inquisition to supervise the whole Church in 1542. Six cardinals were appointed inquisitors-general, with authority on both sides of the Alps "to try all causes of heresy, with the power of apprehending and incarcerating suspected persons and their abettors, of whatever estate, rank or order, of nominating officers under them, and appointing inferior tribunals in all places, with the same or with limited powers." Thus the Roman Inquisition could proceed against anyone denounced to it. It could punish heresy with imprisonment, confiscation of property, and death. From its judgments there was no appeal except to the pope. But since the Inquisition could not function without the support of the secular powers, its sphere of activity was on the whole limited to Italy. In France the efforts of Henry II to introduce the Roman Inquisition were frustrated by the resistance of the Parlement of Paris. In Italy the Inquisition was successful in suppressing Protestantism or at least in driving it underground. Some renounced their heretical beliefs, others left the country, and a few were put to death. Although set up on the Spanish model, the Roman Inquisition was comparatively mild, the death penalty being imposed only in a small number of cases.

THE SOCIETY OF JESUS

Besides combatting heresy, reforming the abuses in the Church, and converting heretics, it was also one of the purposes of the Catholic Reformation to revive the spiritual life in the Catholic Church. All these objects were in some degree combined in the activities of a number of religious orders founded in the sixteenth century. One of the most influential was the Oratory of Divine Love, founded in Rome during the last years of the pontificate of Leo X (1513–1521) by a group of about sixty clerics and laymen, including some of the most learned priests of the Roman Curia. The fame of the order spread rapidly in Italy, and led to the formation of branch movements in other cities. Thus the Oratory of Divine Love may be said to have begun the regeneration of Catholicism in Italy. In succeeding decades other religious societies were formed for similar purposes, but not one of them can compare in effectiveness with the Society of Jesus, more popularly called the Jesuits, which combined war with religion, fighting heresy with all known weapons and striving by every possible means to awaken religious sentiment in the Roman Church.

The Society of Jesus owes its existence to a young Spanish nobleman, Don Iñigo López de Recalde, better known as Ignatius Loyola, who was born in the castle of Loyola, in the Basque province of Guipuzcoa. Little is known of his life up to the age of thirty. Even the year of his birth is doubtful, 1491 being the most generally accepted date. His education was limited to the ability to read and write. At an early age the ambition to perform great deeds impelled him to adopt the profession of a soldier. While fighting in defense of the fortress of Pampeluna (1521) against the French in the war between Charles V and Francis I, his right leg was smashed by a cannon ball, an injury which left him permanently lame. The leg was set so badly that it was twice broken and reset, all of which Loyola bore with heroic fortitude. During his prolonged convalescence he asked for romances of chivalry, which were then in vogue, to while away the time. As there were none at hand, he was given a Life of Christ and some Lives of the Saints. The books fired his imagination until, under the excitement of reading, he saw visions, the Virgin appearing to him with the infant Jesus. He resolved thenceforth to devote his life to God and the Church, and to emulate the deeds of the saints. As soon as he was able to travel he made a pilgrimage to the shrine of the Virgin at Montserrat, where he hung his sword and poniard on the altar as a votive offering. He also gave away his rich clothing, donned sackcloth, and spent a year in prayer and penance. It was probably during this period that he worked out the broader outlines of his *Spiritual Exercises*.

In 1523 Loyola made a pilgrimage to Palestine, where he would have remained to convert the infidels if the local authorities had permitted it. The experiences of this pilgrimage convinced him that he lacked the necessary knowledge to carry out the plans he had conceived. So at the age of thirty-three he returned to Spain to prepare himself for his life-work. After three years of study at Barcelona, during which he mastered the elements of Latin, he attended the University of Alcala, and later that of Salamanca. At both places difficulties with the Inquisition, because he was preaching on the streets and giving religious instructions without proper authorization, led to his temporary imprisonment. This so embittered him against the land of his birth that he went to Paris to continue his studies. Here his plan for organizing a society matured. In August, 1534, he and six similar-minded comrades, among them Pierre Lefèvre and Francis Xavier, repaired to the Abbey of Montmartre, where they all solemnly took the vows of poverty and chastity, and pledged themselves to labor for the conversion of infidels in the Holy Land. As the war between the Venetian Republic and the Turks prevented their going to Palestine, the little band journeyed to Rome in 1537 to offer their services to the pope. They were kindly received by Pope Paul III, but found it difficult to overcome the opposition of the higher clergy to the formation of another religious order. Undaunted, Loyola continued his representations until Paul in 1540 issued a bull confirming the society.

Loyola was by unanimous vote elected general of the new order, which adopted the name Society of Jesus, "organized to fight against spiritual foes" and composed of "men devoted body and soul to our Lord Jesus Christ, as well as to his true and legitimate vicegerent on earth." Its growth was extraordinarily rapid. At the time of Loyola's death in 1556 the society already counted a thousand members scattered over twelve provinces. During the last years of his life Loyola drew up a constitution which, however, was not finally approved until after his death. Despite his years of study he was not a man of profound learning, but he did possess clear judgment and was alert to the circumstances of the time. Moreover, he was a man of extraordinary will-power, able to sacrifice all other interests to the attainment of his goal, the aggrandizement of the Roman Catholic Church. His vivid imagination exalted the Church to such a degree that opposition to it was in his mind tantamount to opposing God himself. He was beatified in 1609 and canonized in 1622.

The Society of Jesus differed from most other monastic orders in that its members were not shut up in monasteries. Whereas withdrawal from the world had been the ideal of most medieval orders,[1] the object of the Jesuits was intervention in the affairs of the world for spiritual purposes. Members of the society were not forced to undergo fasts, scourgings, or other ascetic exercises which might interfere with their work. They wore no distinctive habits, but dressed like the clergymen of the country in which they were working. In common with other monastic orders the Jesuits took the vows of poverty, chastity, and obedience. To these the select members of the society added a fourth vow of

[1] The Dominican and Franciscan orders were outstanding exceptions.

special obedience to the pope, promising to go without questioning or hesitation wherever he might send them. Great care was exercised in choosing members. Sound health, pleasing appearance, good intelligence, worldly wisdom, and stability of character were as important as goodness and piety. Candidates of low intelligence, however virtuous, were not accepted. Once accepted into the order, the members were counseled to sever every tie which bound them to their fellow men in order that they might devote all their efforts to the purposes of the society.

The supreme virtue of the order was absolute obedience. In his letter on "The Virtue of Obedience," which in 1604 every Jesuit was ordered to read every two days, Loyola wrote: "We may the more easily suffer ourselves to be surpassed by other religious orders in fastings, vigils and the rest; in the roughness of food and clothing which each according to its own rites and discipline holily receives; but I am particularly anxious, dearest brethren, that you who serve in this society be conspicuous for true and perfect obedience and abdication of will and of judgment." As soon as a person became a member of the order he laid aside all right of individual judgment. Thereafter positive unquestioning obedience to the established authority of the Church and to the superiors of the order became the first principle of life. In his *Spiritual Exercises* Loyola states that if the Church decides that "the white which I see is black, we must forthwith hold that it is black." Orders of the superiors were to be obeyed blindly, without inquiry into their reason or object.

The basis of the spiritual training of the members of the order was the *Spiritual Exercises* of Loyola. This little book, the fruit of Loyola's spiritual struggles, consists of meditations grouped in four divisions or weeks. In the first week the novice is bidden to think of the hideousness and the terrible consequences of sin. During the second week he is asked to meditate upon the life of Christ up to Palm Sunday; during the third week upon Christ's suffering and death; and during the last week upon his resurrection and ascension. All ideas are to be pictured by the novice as vividly as possible. For example, in the first week he is directed to see with the imagination the great blazing fires of hell; to hear the shouts, blasphemies, and laments of the damned; to smell the smoke, the brimstone, and the putridity of hell; to taste the bitterness of tears and melancholy, and the worm of conscience; to feel the burnings of the eternal fires. The object of all this was to impress deeply upon the mind a hatred of sin. Soon after the *Spiritual Exercises* were first published in 1548 they were recommended to the faithful by the pope. Since then they have been not only the principal instrument of the Jesuits in securing a thorough discipline, but a great influence in the Church at large.

The internal organization of the Society of Jesus was rigid. Its supreme dignitary, in whom all authority was centralized, was a general elected for life and resident in Rome. He appointed all officials of the order and could also depose them. For a cabinet he had a Council of Assistants, numbering from four to six members. In the different countries in which the order had a footing the provincials served as his viceroys. The members, as a whole, were divided into four classes. In the lowest class were the novices, who during a period of two years were tested for fitness to take the monastic vows. Before a novice could advance to the next class he was trained in obedience and thoroughly examined to make sure that he was mentally, physically, and spiritually fitted to the purposes of the society. If he passed the tests, he was permitted to take the three vows and become a scholastic or scholar. He now underwent a protracted course of training in the various branches of secular and theological learning. If he showed promise, he was promoted to the third class, that of the coadjutors. As such he could still be either a cleric or a secular. Those designated as seculars served as cooks, gardeners, hospital attendants, or in some other capacity. The clerics devoted themselves to the instruction of youth in the schools and colleges of the society, or served as priests and missionaries. After many years of trial the ablest of these were received into the highest class, the professed (*professi sunt*), so called because they took the fourth vow, that of unconditional obedience to the pope. The number of the professed was always comparatively small, about two per cent of the membership. From this inner circle were chosen the higher dignitaries of the order.

Although the society was not founded with the conscious design of counteracting the teachings of Luther and Calvin, it became the backbone of the Catholic Reformation. Its aim as expressed in the motto of the order was *Omnia ad majorem Dei gloriam* (All for the greater glory of God). The greater glory of God was identified in the most absolute way with the universal dominion of the Roman Church. In other words, the united energy of the order was unwaveringly directed to the strengthening and spread of Catholicism. This included bringing the heathen under the sway of the Church, fortifying those who were in the faith, and leading back into the Church those who had strayed from it.

While the Jesuits took part in all the efforts to strengthen the Church and to stop the spread of Protestantism, their success was founded principally upon preaching, the use of the confessional, and the promotion of education. From the beginning the society gave special attention to preaching as a means of winning Protestants back to the faith. Jesuit preachers were taught to make their sermons short, simple, forceful, and applicable to contemporary conditions. Services in Jesuit churches were made as attractive as possible, with the best music obtainable. Furthermore, confession was changed by them from a simple sacrament into a means of soul-guidance. Sparing neither flattery nor assurances of devotion to win the favor of princes, they managed in a short time to become confessors in the imperial court and in many courts of Europe. Once their influence was established they were not slow to direct the policies of the state to their own ends. Thus at Vienna, Warsaw, Lisbon, Madrid, and at many of the smaller Italian and German courts they established a predominant influence. In France they were the power behind the throne from the time of Henry IV to the reign of Louis XVI.

But it was through their educational activities that the Jesuits exercised the greatest influence. Very early the society recognized the great opportunity which education offered for gaining a lasting hold on the minds of the young. Their saying regarding the influence of early education is well known: "Give me the child and I care not who has the man." At the time of Loyola's death the order already had thirty-five schools. As it increased in numbers, schools were opened all over Europe. The education offered by the Jesuits was free. Though their pedagogical methods did not differ radically from those of the other schools of the time, they taught with enthusiasm, giving care to the individual needs, the physical training, and the morals and companionship of their pupils. This quickly earned the Jesuit schools a high reputation. Large numbers of young men flocked to them, particularly from the aristocratic families, and most of them remained throughout life warm supporters of the schemes of the order. Even Protestants sometimes sent their sons to Jesuit schools, where they were naturally won over to the Catholic faith. By the middle of the seventeenth century, Jesuits controlled all the higher schools in Italy, Portugal, and Poland, and a majority in Spain, France, Hungary, the southern Netherlands, and Catholic Germany. At the opening of the eighteenth century the colleges and universities of the order numbered 769; they were found in almost every region of the globe, and had an enrollment of 200,000 students.

Through their zeal and ability the Jesuits succeeded in saving the Catholic faith in some localities by hemming in the further advances of the Protestant movement; in others they blighted, and even suppressed entirely, the Protestantism which had flourished there. In Italy, Portugal, and Spain, where Protestantism was not deeply rooted, they aided in stamping it out. They reconquered Poland, where Protestantism had gained the ascendancy among the nobility, expelled Protestantism from the Spanish Netherlands, and won Hungary back to the Catholic fold. In France, where the two faiths were struggling for predominance, their influence helped to decide the issue in favor of Catholicism. Even in England they won converts despite the stringent laws against them. In the seventeenth century Charles I was influenced by them, and James II fell entirely under their sway. One of the notable triumphs of the order was to turn the tide in favor of the Catholic religion in southern Germany, where Protestantism had dominated the universities and claimed the adherence of a large part of the nobility and many towns. Shortly after the middle of the sixteenth century the order managed to gain control of the universities of Vienna and Ingolstadt, which thereafter served as centers of Jesuit influence. A decade later most of the institutions in Bavaria and the Tyrol, Franconia and Swabia, and a large part of the Rhenish provinces and Austria were in their hands. During the first half of the seventeenth century the lands of the Habsburgs, which had formerly seemed ready to abandon the old faith, were reclaimed so completely that Protestantism virtually disappeared from them.

Nor did the Jesuits confine their activities to Europe. Enthusiastic missionaries went to all parts of the world, including America, India, China, Japan, and Africa. The most famous was Francis Xavier (1506–1552), who baptized great multitudes in India and in Japan. Though his work of conversion has been decried as superficial, his example served as an inspiration to many who came after him.

In the eighteenth century the society degenerated. It turned away from its former ideals to banking and commercial enterprises. Its schools declined badly, and its high-handed and ruthless measures, even to successfully plotting the assassination of kings, aroused widespread condemnation. To civil rulers the Jesuits became such a menace that the society was expelled from Portugal in 1759, from France in 1764, and from Spain in 1767, nearly six thousand priests being deported from Spain alone. Finally, in 1773, the pope dissolved the society, stating that the peace of the Church made such a step necessary. Catherine II of Russia and Frederick the Great of Prussia refused to permit publication of the bull of dissolution because they could not replace the Jesuits as educators, and the remnants of this once powerful order sought refuge in these two countries. The dissolution proved to be only temporary, however. In 1814 the Society of Jesus was again restored by Pope Pius VII.

CHAPTER NINE

The Tudor Monarchy

HENRY VIII AND THE BREAK WITH ROME

THE period of the Tudor rulers in England is known as the era of strong monarchy. Henry VII, the first Tudor, had been able to obtain for the crown an authority such as no monarch had exercised since Henry II (1154–1189). This power he bequeathed to his son and successor, Henry VIII, who strengthened it and handed it on to his children. Though their rule is frequently referred to as despotic, the Tudors were not despots after the manner of the princes of the Italian Renaissance. In exercising their authority they never ignored popular sentiment; hence their government can perhaps be more accurately described as a popular dictatorship or as an absolutism founded on popular approval. The basis of this approval was the fact that the Tudors represented in a general sense the spirit and policy of the entire English people. But to a special degree they represented the spirit and policy of the middle class, whose support was an important source of their strength. The Tudor monarchs could do what they liked, but they were careful that their desires were in harmony with the aims and needs of this class. Furthermore, they depended largely on the bourgeoisie for their advisers. The great ministers of the period, including Thomas Cromwell, the Cecils, and Walsingham, were upstart gentry. Elizabeth herself, in fact, was the great-granddaughter of a London merchant.

Though they exercised their power with almost unlimited absolutism, the Tudors did so in parliamentary form. They did not, it is true, call Parliament as frequently as it had been summoned in the later Plantagenet era. Henry VII summoned it but seven times in twenty-four years, and Elizabeth convoked it only ten times in a reign of forty-five years. But no attempt was made to supersede Parliament or to abrogate the constitution. The old limitations upon the royal authority still remained: (1) the king could make no laws, nor could he repeal any statutes; (2) the king could impose no new taxes without the consent of Parliament; (3) the king could not commit a man to prison or punish him except by due process of law. Beyond these limitations, however, Parliament had no power over royal policy except in so far as it could control taxation and thus limit the income of the ruler. Hence the Tudors, to evade the curb of Parliament, found other means of replenishing the royal purse when the regular taxation proved insufficient for their needs; and at all times they were careful to avoid friction with Parliament, particularly in regard to finances. Henry VII set the precedent in this respect, and his example was followed by his son, Henry VIII.

Seldom has the accession of a king been greeted with such open expressions of delight as was that of Henry VIII (1509–1547). Happy that the rule of Henry VII had come to an end, the people looked to the new monarch with the highest expectations. Since Henry united in his person the blood of the rival houses of York and Lancaster, and the rebellious noblemen of former times were now submissive courtiers, the danger of a revival of the civil conflicts was remote. The expanding trade gave indications of an even more prosperous reign than that of Henry VII had been. Above all, the people had unbounded faith in the person and ability of the new king.

Just eighteen at the time of his accession, Henry was tall, fair-haired, dignified in bearing, and unusually handsome. A Venetian ambassador was later to pronounce him "handsomer than any other sovereign in Christendom." Those who came in contact with him were charmed by his frankness, gaiety, and geniality. In addition to his good looks and personal charm he possessed accomplishments of both body and mind. Stalwart of frame and well-proportioned, he was skilful in the manly exercises of the time, excelling in horsemanship, tilting, and jousting. He was likewise well versed in theology, for until the death of his older brother, Arthur, he had been educated with a view to ecclesiastical preferment. He spoke French, Spanish, and Latin, and was generally fond of learning. He also performed well on the organ, lute, and harpsichord. Because of these many-sided interests the various classes saw in him the champion of their respective causes. Scholars, for example, were enthusiastic over his love of learning, churchmen extolled the purity of his life and his devotion to religion, and statesmen discerned in him an extraordinary capacity for dealing with matters of state. Though Henry was to disappoint many expectations and shatter many dreams, he never lost entirely the popularity with which his reign began.

During the first part of his rule Henry gave but little attention to the details of government. For nearly twenty years the affairs of England were in the hands of his minister, Thomas Wolsey, who was some years Henry's senior. Of middle-class parentage, Wolsey had received a good education and was eventually appointed chaplain at the court of Henry VII. When Henry VIII became king he recognized valuable qualities in Wolsey, and in 1511 admitted him to his council. Thereafter Wolsey's rise was rapid. In 1515 Henry appointed him chancellor, the highest position in the kingdom next to the king. In the same year he was raised to the rank of cardinal by the pope and in the following year was made papal legate (i.e., the pope's official representative) in England. Thus Wolsey held the highest offices in both church and state which a subject could hold in England. Henry was pleased that he had an able man to perform the irksome duties of government while he devoted himself to sports and recreations or wrote treatises on theology. Gradually the king gave more and more power to Wolsey, until the latter was more king than Henry himself, and a Venetian ambassador could state without much exaggeration that Wolsey "rules both the king and the entire kingdom." The cardinal, who was essentially a politician and not a churchman, emphasized his position by surrounding himself with princely pomp and regal magnificence, and by generally assuming a royal state. This did not, however, prevent him from applying himself diligently to the conduct of governmental affairs. Thoroughly devoted to the interests of his master, he labored incessantly to advance the prestige of the crown, on which his own greatness rested. But his haughty and arrogant manner made him unpopular with the people, despite the fact that he possessed many excellent qualities and was a true friend of the poor.

Wolsey's chief title to statesmanship rests upon his conduct of foreign affairs. His primary object was to win for England a position of equality with Spain and France, at this time the principal nations of Europe. Since England was smaller, poorer, and weaker than either, it was to its interest to maintain a balance of power between the two, so that neither should grow so powerful as to dominate Europe and threaten the independence of England. Both powers desired the help of England for the impending struggle[1] and were ready to promise much to obtain it. Instead of definitely committing himself to either side, Wolsey schemed and intrigued, craftily playing one power off against the other in order to preserve a certain equilibrium between the two without involving England in war. This policy was so successful that as long as Wolsey remained in office England was the chief arbiter of Europe. But Wolsey was not permitted to exercise a free hand in matters of state indefinitely. As time went on the king interfered in the government more frequently, making demands which Wolsey was often sore pressed to fulfill. Finally the so-called "divorce" case of Henry caused his chancellor's downfall. It also marked the beginning of the Reformation in England.

It is paradoxical, indeed, that the man who severed the bonds which joined the English Church to Rome, thereby paving the way for doctrinal reform, took infinite pride in his theological orthodoxy. The Venetian ambassador wrote that the king "was very religious, heard three masses daily when he hunted, sometimes five on other days, besides hearing the Office daily in the Queen's chamber, that is to say, Vespers and Compline." From the beginning of his reign Henry had zealously suppressed heresy in his domains, going so far as to encourage the burning of Lollards. His government took drastic steps to curb the spread of Luther's doctrines, and Henry personally undertook the task of refuting Luther's *On the Babylonian Captivity of the Church*, written in 1520. In his *Defence of the Seven Sacraments against Martin Luther* the English king attempted to disprove Luther's heretical statements point by point, applying to him by way of emphasis such appellations as "pernicious pest," "poisonous serpent," "wolf of

[1] See pp. 151–155.

hell," and "limb of Satan." So pleased was Pope Leo X with the treatise that he bestowed on Henry the title of "Defender of the Faith" and granted to all readers of Henry's defense an indulgence of ten years.

It was therefore not religious but personal and political motives which impelled Henry to sunder the connection with the papacy. The king desired to procure an annulment of his marriage with Catherine of Aragon. Yet this desire to be rid of Catherine was not the cause of the rupture with Rome; it merely supplied the occasion for it. The essential causes of the English Reformation go deeper than the whim of the monarch. They were much the same as those which lay at the root of the Reformation on the continent. The abolition of papal authority in England was a change which a majority of Englishmen desired. It was the logical conclusion of a gradual growth of anti-papal feeling since the time of William the Conqueror. Had it lacked the moral support of the nation, the separation from Rome could never have become a permanent fact. The English people would have resisted it as stoutly as they later did the absolutism of the Stuarts.

After living happily with his wife, Catherine of Aragon, for many years, Henry began to have misgivings about the legitimacy of their marriage. The misgivings were probably aroused by the lack of a male heir to insure the future of the Tudor dynasty and the peace of England. Of the six children that had been born of the marriage, all had died in early infancy save one, Mary. And the rule of a woman was without precedent in England. Since the Conquest only one woman, Matilda, the daughter of Henry I, had laid claim to the crown, thereby starting a civil war which lasted fourteen years. Besides, the marriage of a woman ruler would surely raise serious problems. If she married an English subject the jealousy of the other nobles might give rise to civil war; if she married a foreign prince England might become the appanage of another nation; if she did not marry at all, the civil conflicts over the succession might break out afresh. Hence Henry's ardent desire for a son, a desire which became virtually an obsession. As long as there was any possibility of a male heir, Henry made no move to put Catherine away. But now that the queen was past childbearing he felt that it was imperative for him to take a new wife in the hope of having a son. Having decided to dissolve his marriage, Henry found religious reasons for such a step. Did not the Bible state in *Leviticus* XX, 21: "And if a man shall take his brother's wife, it is an unclean thing . . . they shall be childless"? Had not all his sons died in infancy? What further proof was necessary to show that the curse of God rested on the marriage? Henry's scruples regarding his marriage to Catherine were undoubtedly intensified by the fact that he had fallen in love with gay and vivacious Anne Boleyn, one of the queen's ladies-in-waiting. He determined to make Anne, who was twenty years younger than Catherine, his wife, and ordered Wolsey to obtain from the pope an annulment of his marriage.

When Henry applied to the pope he did not anticipate any obstacle in obtaining the requisite pronouncements. Only a few years earlier a pope had permitted Louis XII of France to put away his wife on account of sterility. Special difficulties, however, were inherent in Henry's case. Though the proceedings are often referred to as "divorce" proceedings, there was, in fact, no question of a divorce. The canon law of the Church did not permit divorces. What Henry wanted from the pope was a declaration that his marriage with Catherine had been null and void from the beginning or, in other words, that the dispensation of an earlier pope which had permitted him to marry his brother's wife was invalid. Henry's request put the pope in a serious predicament. To accede to it, the pope would have to invalidate the act of a recent predecessor. Such a reversal would undermine the power and prestige of his office. Nevertheless, if that had been all, some technical ground might have been discovered for revoking the decision of the earlier pope. A greater difficulty remained. Clement VII was at that time in the power of Emperor Charles V, the loyal nephew of Catherine of Aragon, and did not dare offend him by granting Henry's request. Neither did he want to lose the favor of the king of England. While Henry, impatient by nature, was chafing under the delay, the pope temporized, hoping that some turn of events would enable him to extricate himself from his difficult position. Finally, however, it became obvious that an adverse decision was merely a matter of time.

For Wolsey the failure to carry the negotiations with Rome to a successful conclusion spelled disgrace. After being deprived of his offices, he was ordered to retire to his archbishopric of York. Only his death in 1530 saved him from being brought to trial for treason.

Wolsey's failure to obtain an annulment did not move Henry to give up the idea of freeing himself from Catherine. On the contrary, he now decided to take the question of annulling the marriage into his own hands. Upon the death of the archbishop of Canterbury in 1532 he had made sure that the new archbishop would be on his side by choosing Thomas Cranmer. Authorized by the king to take up the question of an annulment, Cranmer convoked an archiepiscopal court at the end of March, 1533; and after long discussions this court declared in May that Henry had never really been married to Catherine. The king had anticipated this decree four months previously by secretly marrying Anne Boleyn, and the new queen was already pregnant. As astrologers had assured him the child was a son, Henry eagerly awaited its birth. The child was born in September, but to the infinite disappointment of the parents it was not a son; it was the future Queen Elizabeth.

Henry next turned to Parliament to legalize what had taken place. Parliament obliged by passing the Act of Succession, which vested the succession in the offspring of Anne Boleyn and declared any slander of the marriage to be high treason. In the years since it had first met in 1529 the so-called "Reformation Parliament" had been busily engaged in curtailing the authority of the pope over the English Church. Among other enactments, it had forbidden any appeals from English courts to be carried to Rome, prohibited the payment of annates or the first year's income of a bishopric to the pope, and given the appointment of bishops to the crown. Now the king proceeded through act of Parliament to repudiate the papal authority entirely. In November, 1534, the Act of Supremacy was passed, declaring "that the King, our sovereign lord, his heirs and successors, kings of this realm, shall be taken, accepted and reputed the only supreme head in earth of the Church of England, called the Anglicana Ecclesia." In this way the English Church became an independent national body under the absolute rule of the king, with the archbishop of Canterbury as its highest ecclesiastical official. The Act of Supremacy was accompanied by a new Treason Act which forbade anyone on penalty of death to call the king a "heretic, schismatic, tyrant, infidel, or usurper."

The separation from Rome was accepted with comparative equanimity by most of the people of England. Some, however, resolutely adhered to the principle of papal supremacy to the extent of giving their lives for their convictions. Among these were Sir Thomas More and Bishop Fisher of Rochester. When both repeatedly refused to take the oath to the Act of Supremacy, they were tried, condemned, and beheaded.

After making himself "Supreme Head of the Church" Henry proceeded to suppress the monasteries and to confiscate their property. In the Middle Ages monasteries and nunneries rendered invaluable services to the communities in which they were situated. Besides copying books and promoting agriculture and cattle-raising, the monks had discharged the humanitarian duties of society. For example, they cared for the sick and dying when hospitals were few, and in the absence of schools taught the children of the poor. Gradually, however, other agencies took over these duties. Having outlasted their usefulness to society, many monasteries degenerated from the principles on which they were founded. Many monks became lax in their adherence to the monastic vows, education was neglected, and some were even guilty of gross misbehavior. In short, English monasticism was evincing unmistakable signs of decay. But Henry had other and, from his point of view, excellent reasons for destroying it. The monasteries were strongholds of papal influence in England. Furthermore, the monastic property would not only provide money for the royal coffers but also lands which could be used to win supporters for his policy. The idea of suppression in itself was not new. During the two preceding centuries religious orders had frequently been the targets of attacks. In the fifteenth century a number of men of high station had even projected the idea of dissolving them, and earlier in Henry's reign Cardinal Wolsey had already taken the first step in that direction when he had obtained permission from the pope to suppress monasteries with less than seven inmates and to use their revenues for educational purposes.

The execution of the king's decree was entrusted to Thomas Cromwell who, as chief adviser to Henry since Wolsey's death, was the author of the various measures which had destroyed the papal power in England. In 1535 Cromwell sent out agents to inquire into the conditions of the monasteries—more specifically, to ferret out damaging evidence against them. On the basis of their findings Parliament in 1536 passed an act for the suppression of all monasteries with an income of less than £200 a year or with

less than twelve inmates. But the days of all monastic establishments in England were numbered; and during the years immediately following, the larger monasteries shared the fate of the
smaller. As a whole, the monks and nuns suffered but little. The
older monks, for example, were pensioned, while many of the
younger ones became secular clergymen or accepted other posts
which were sometimes more profitable than those they had abandoned. All the monastic property—lands, buildings, money and
plate—and also the proceeds from the sale of cattle, furniture,
and bells, passed into the possession of the king.[1] This enormous
wealth was used for various purposes. Some of it was put into the
royal treasury for general expenses; some of it was used to endow
schools and also six new bishoprics; a portion was appropriated
for the navy and for coastal defense; and the remainder was given
to noblemen and to members of the middle class to bind them to
the king and his new policy.

Although the papal jurisdiction had been abolished and the
monasteries suppressed, neither the king nor his subjects regarded
themselves as less Catholic. In the Church of England the hierarchy still existed as before, except that the king had taken the
place of the pope as its head. Beyond this substitution there had
been no renunciation of Catholic doctrines. There was now, it is
true, a group with definite Protestant leanings, but most of the
people remained attached to the old teachings which the king
was determined to uphold. The one material advance in the direction of reform during Henry's reign was his order that a translation of the Bible be placed in every church, so that anyone who
desired might read it. Further than this he refused to go. To prevent all deviations from Catholic doctrines, Parliament in 1539
passed, at Henry's behest, the Act of the Six Articles which reaffirmed transubstantiation, the sufficiency of communion in one
kind, the celibacy of the priesthood, the necessity of the vows of
chastity, and the value of private masses and auricular confession.[2] Obedience to the conditions laid down by the Six Articles
was insisted upon throughout the country. All heretics who denied

---

[1] With the dissolution of the monasteries the abbots disappeared from the House
of Lords.

[2] It stated, in other words, that the bread and wine are changed into the body and
blood of Christ, that communion in both kinds is not essential to salvation, that the
marriage of priests is unlawful, that the monastic vow of chastity must be observed, that
prayers for the dead are beneficial, and that auricular confession should be retained.

transubstantiation were to be burned at the stake without opportunity for recantation, and those who publicly attacked the other
articles were to be executed as felons. The king was now absolute
master with ready weapons to strike down all opposition. On the
one hand, he could burn as heretics those who deviated from Catholic doctrines and, on the other, he could behead for treason those
who clung to the old Catholic belief in the spiritual supremacy of
the pope.

Not only questions of creed vexed Henry. Among others there
was also the bugbear of the succession. Henry's second marriage
did not allay his fears regarding it, for, after the birth of Elizabeth, Anne failed to bear other living children. Consequently his
affections toward the woman for whom he had braved so much
began to cool. He was determined to have another spouse so that
he might do his duty to the nation. Hence in 1536 Anne was accused of adultery and incest, found guilty by a court ever ready
to oblige the king, and beheaded on May 19. A short time later
Henry married his third wife, Jane Seymour, who gave him what
he had so ardently desired, a son and heir, the future Edward VI.
But the newborn prince was a delicate, sickly little boy who was
not likely to live long. A few weeks after Edward was born, Jane
Seymour died, leaving Henry free to seek another wife.

This time Cromwell acted as matchmaker. To counterbalance
an alliance which had been concluded between Spain and France,
he advised Henry to enter into a league with the Protestant princes
of Germany. As the first step toward this political league Cromwell arranged a marriage between Henry and Anna, daughter of
the duke of Cleves. The bride-to-be had already lost the first
bloom of youth, was stout of figure, simple in mind, sadly lacking
in social graces, in all respects grossly unattractive. Cromwell,
however, to achieve his purpose, told Henry that she was good-
looking; he also had Holbein paint a flattering portrait of her.
When Henry saw Anna his disillusionment was instantaneous.
Her physical qualities were so repellent to him that he dubbed
her "the great Flanders mare." It was only with difficulty that he
was prevailed upon to go through the ceremony of marriage.
Thereafter he would have nothing to do with her, and a few
months later the marriage was dissolved. To make matters worse
the projected alliance between England and the Protestant princes
of Germany did not materialize. Henry, who had reached the

stage when he could brook no opposition to his will, felt that he had been duped. His fury vented itself on Cromwell. The minister who had served him so faithfully for twelve years was suddenly arrested on a charge of treason and executed on July 28, 1540. On the same day Henry married his fifth wife, beautiful Catherine Howard, who was so young that she had been named for Henry's first wife. Fifteen months after her marriage Catherine was charged with immoral conduct and was beheaded February 14, 1542, on the same spot where Anne Boleyn had been executed five years before. The next year Henry concluded his matrimonial ventures by taking as his sixth wife comely Catherine Parr, a gentle, discreet, and pious widow who had already survived two husbands and whose private life was beyond reproach. Possessed of an infinite store of patience and the ability to humor the weak points of the king, she faithfully nursed and tenderly mothered the ageing Henry in his last painful years, surviving him long enough to marry a fourth husband.

Accustomed to having his own way, Henry became more and more wilful and cruel in his last years. Whoever had the courage to oppose him was sooner or later sent to the block. In money matters he was as lavish in his expenditures as before. Despite the vast sum his father had left him, and the immense spoils which flowed into the treasury when the monasteries were suppressed, Henry found himself so heavily in debt, so desperately in need of money, that he was compelled to debase the coinage by ordering that less gold and silver than their face value be put in the coins. As a result prices fluctuated and commerce suffered greatly. Physically, Henry was prematurely old. Always a great eater, he grew corpulent in his last years, and his body became bloated and swollen with increasing disease. Yet he continued to work until almost the last day of his life. Before his death he signed his elaborate will and testament which passed the succession to the throne successively to Edward, Mary, and Elizabeth, if neither Edward nor Mary should have direct heirs. On January 28, 1547, at the age of fifty-five and after a reign of nearly thirty-eight years, the king passed away.

To this day Henry's character and achievements are subjects of heated controversy. For his moral character little can be said. He was brutal, crafty, hypocritical, self-willed, and, above all, self-centered. His better qualities were in time submerged by the selfishness that was the motive force of his thoughts, actions, and vices. When he labored to make England great, it was not because of any love of his people, but for self-advancement. His own glory was always his first aim. So self-absorbed was he that he was incapable of deep devotion to others. If he ever had any affection for anyone but himself, it was of a transitory nature. Few kings had been served by more faithful ministers than he; yet he was only too ready to demand their heads when they displeased him. But whatever one might think of the man, it must be conceded that as king he was one of the most successful rulers in English history.

REFORMS UNDER EDWARD VI

The English Reformation, which under Henry VIII was limited primarily to a rupture with Rome, entered its second phase, that of doctrinal and liturgical change, in the reign of Edward VI. In fact, the predominant question of the reign was the controversy between the Catholic and Protestant groups over the reformed doctrines. When Henry felt his end approaching he had appointed by his will a Council of Regency consisting of sixteen members which was to conduct the affairs of England during the minority of his son Edward, who was not yet ten years old. Edward, though intellectually precocious and serious beyond his years, was an invalid physically, and too young to be allowed independent judgment. Henry tried to choose the members of the council from the various shades of religious opinion so that all religious parties would be fairly balanced, but the majority were of Protestant leanings, and Edward himself had been brought up in the reformed opinions. Within a short time one member, Edward Seymour, earl of Hertford, an uncle of the young king, succeeded in having himself appointed Protector of the Realm. He also managed to have himself made duke of Somerset, the name by which he is generally known.

Somerset, as virtual dictator of England and head of the Protestant party, proceeded to advance the cause of Protestantism, a work in which he was aided by Archbishop Cranmer. After Parliament had cleared the way by repealing the Act of the Six Articles, the Latin mass was replaced by a communion service in which the laity was given the cup as well as the bread. Various ceremonies, such as the use of candles, ashes, palms, and holy water, were also done away with by royal proclamation. Images were everywhere destroyed, and pictures which had been painted on the walls of churches were covered with whitewash. Parliament also renewed and enforced the Chantries Bill of 1545, decreeing the confiscation of all property belonging to gilds and chantries which had been established for such purposes as saying masses for the souls of the dead. Though part of this property was used to endow grammar schools or to refound hospitals, much of it went into the pockets of the courtiers, the Protector himself appropriating a liberal share. Meanwhile Cranmer had been busy preparing his Book of Common Prayer—now known as the First Book—based on the old Latin service books which had been in use for many centuries. Written in dignified and solemn English, it permitted such latitude of opinion that Lutherans, Calvinists, and Catholics could use it without unduly straining their consciences. By the first Act of Uniformity, passed in 1549, this book was made the only legal service book in England under penalty of fine and, eventually, imprisonment.

Though Somerset succeeded in his religious reforms, he was unequal to the task of governing England. He was a man of considerable ability, well-meaning and idealistic, opposed alike to religious persecution and the oppression of the lower classes. But he was greedy, self-seeking, and haughty, offensive to those about him and unpopular with the people at large. Both his foreign and his internal policy failed. Fruitless efforts to effect a union with Scotland merely involved him in a war with France. At home there was widespread discontent caused by the rise of prices and the debasement of the currency, and particularly by the "enclosures." When Somerset issued a proclamation against enclosures, the masses of peasants took matters into their own hands and began their demolition. Uprisings occurred in various parts of England, the most formidable being Kett's rebellion. Instead of adopting drastic measures to suppress this revolt, the Protector chose to parley with the insurgents. This displeased the council, which thereupon sent a force under the earl of Warwick against the insurgents. Not only was Somerset censured for his lack of action against the rebels, but the revolts themselves were imputed to the feebleness of his policy. Gradually the earl of Warwick, better known as Northumberland,[1] gained an ascendancy over

---

[1] After his rise to power he had himself created duke of Northumberland.

the council. Somerset was forced to resign his position. When he later schemed to recover the protectorship, he was tried, convicted of felony, and beheaded in 1551.

For the remainder of Edward's reign Northumberland, a man of boundless ambition, played the leading rôle in the government. In internal affairs the unrest and disturbances continued and Northumberland was soon even more disliked by the people than Somerset had been. In questions of religion he sided with the reform party, largely from motives of self-interest; and with the support of the king, who by this time had very decided Protestant opinions, he undertook to give the Church a definite Protestant character. The Second Prayer Book, which was issued in 1552, definitely rejected the doctrine of transubstantiation by stating that the elements of Holy Communion were not to be accepted as real flesh and blood, but merely as commemorative of Christ's suffering and death. Public worship was simplified by the abolition of the pomp and show of medieval ritual.

In 1553 the sickly young king became mortally ill. Northumberland, who saw that the accession of Mary would mean his downfall, formed the ambitious design of obtaining the crown for his own family. He played upon Edward's fears of a Catholic restoration under Mary until the dying king named as his successor Lady Jane Grey, a descendant of Henry VIII's sister Mary and as such a distant heir to the throne. Lady Jane Grey was then married to Northumberland's fourth son, Guilford Dudley. When Edward died in 1553 at the age of sixteen, Northumberland had Lady Jane proclaimed queen. But she remained queen only nine days. As Mary and her troops approached London, Northumberland's supporters melted away. He himself was arrested, convicted of treason, and beheaded, while Lady Jane Grey and her husband were confined to the Tower. Later in Mary's reign they, too, were sent to the block.

THE REACTION UNDER MARY

Mary was in her thirty-seventh year when she became ruler of England. Ill-health and adversity had left their mark on her plain features, and her bearing was prematurely grave. A Venetian ambassador described her in the following words: "She is rather of little than of middle stature, thin, and delicately formed, with lively eyes, short-sighted, and has a strong deep voice like that of a man. . . . Her passions, public and domestic, often throw her into deep melancholy." She inherited the obstinate will of her father and her mother's deep devotion to the Roman Catholic faith. The events of her life had intensified this devotion, for during an unhappy childhood, followed by years of neglect, her religion had been her only consolation. To the rise of Protestantism she could ascribe many of her early misfortunes. The work of the reformers had brought disgrace on her mother, Catherine of Aragon, and had put the stamp of illegitimacy on Mary herself; in fact, it had nearly deprived her of the succession to the throne. Hence she nursed a deep resentment against all reformers and against all the ecclesiastical changes that had been inaugurated. The restoration of the Catholic faith as it had existed early in the reign of Henry became an overmastering passion which made all else in home or foreign politics appear insignificant to her.

When Parliament met, it showed itself tractable to the wishes of Mary by repealing all laws of the reign of Edward VI which related to religion or the Church. The Book of Common Prayer was discarded, together with communion in both kinds and the marriage of the clergy, and the Catholic service as it had existed in the last years of Henry VIII was restored. Yet for Mary this was not enough. In her mind the restoration of Catholicism involved acceptance of papal supremacy. But the English people were of a different opinion. Though their Protestantism was scarcely more than a veneer, and easily penetrable, they were decidedly averse to a return to papal rule. Such considerations, however, did not restrain Mary. In 1554 she succeeded in having a packed parliament repeal the anti-papal legislation of Henry VIII. Soon thereafter, Cardinal Pole arrived from Rome as the pope's representative to absolve the English from their heresy and to receive them back into communion with the Church of Rome. But on one point Parliament remained adamant. It refused to restore the lands which had been taken from the Church when the monasteries were suppressed. Moreover, it insisted that a guarantee of these lands to their new possessors be incorporated in the act which reëstablished the papal supremacy. Though the pope demurred, he was finally compelled to waive the restoration of the church lands lest he frustrate the reunion with England.

Mary was still not satisfied. Feeling that her work would not be finished until all heresy was eradicated and every Englishman had accepted the Catholic faith, in 1555, after Parliament had re-enacted the old laws against heresy, she inaugurated the persecutions by faggot and stake which were calculated to restore religious unity in England. Nearly three hundred Protestants who refused to abjure, suffered death by burning during the four years which have attached the epithet "bloody" to the name of Mary. The most prominent of the martyrs were Bishops Latimer and Ridley and Archbishop Cranmer.

But the effect of the persecutions was exactly opposite to Mary's intention. Instead of promoting the spread of the Catholic faith, they aroused a strong antagonism against it, for most Englishmen, including those who were not Protestant in sentiment, were opposed to burning people for their opinions. Had Mary proceeded with discretion and moderation; had she been satisfied to stop with the reëstablishment of Catholicism as the official religion, it might have been possible for her to win England for the Church of Rome. As it was, her fiery determination to dictate religious thought permanently alienated the English people from the Church of Rome and assured the future of Protestantism in England. Aside from this aspect, the Marian persecutions differed from later ones in England in that they were purely religious. Most of the victims were not men of political importance; they were burned solely because of their religious convictions, which were no threat to Mary's rule. Later persecutions were avowedly political in their motivation, however much the religious factor entered into them.

Mary's second mistake was her marriage with Philip of Spain, in spite of the objections of her people. To Mary, whose mother was Spanish, the prospect of marrying the son of the Emperor Charles V was particularly attractive. Besides fulfilling her desire to be allied to her mother's house, the marriage promised the support of the strongest power of Europe for her efforts to reëstablish and perpetuate the Catholic faith in England. To the emperor, on the other hand, the marriage meant the aid of England for his struggle against France, and an alliance that could be depended on under all circumstances. But the majority of the English people were opposed to the union. There was a general fear that any such connection would endanger the independence of England; that in consequence of the alliance England might become a part of the monstrous empire of Charles V, and English soldiers be called upon to sacrifice their lives for the glory of a foreign power. The Commons went so far as to entreat Mary to select a husband from the nobility of the realm. Even among Catholics it was deemed desirable that Mary should marry an Englishman. All protest and entreaties, however, proved unavailing. When the English statesmen saw that Mary was not to be dissuaded, they endeavored to hedge the marriage about with as many restrictions as possible in order to prevent Philip from gaining any direct power in England. It was finally agreed that he was to have no part in the rule, nor were any of his countrymen to hold office of any sort. The negotiations completed, Philip set out for England; and in July, 1554, soon after his arrival, the marriage was celebrated.

The marriage was not a happy one. Mary, whose life had been without love, longed for affection from her husband. Having already fallen in love with her ideal of him before she saw him, she grew to love him for his own sake. Philip, for his part, felt little affection for his doting queen. To him the marriage to Mary, who was eleven years his senior and no beauty at best, had been primarily one of policy. He was more intent upon winning the favor of the English people, with whom he was personally unpopular, than the love of his middle-aged wife. When he saw that Mary's persecutions were outraging public opinion he disavowed all responsibility for them, urging Mary to moderate her religious zeal. But the knowledge that she could not hold her husband's love only moved her to persecute more fiercely than before. The marriage failed also in another respect: it produced no heir. Pathetically eager for a son who would carry on the tradition of a Catholic England, Mary at one time, in a mistaken belief that her desire was about to be gratified, made open and ostentatious preparations for the event. It was even announced on one occasion, with ringing of bells, processions, and rejoicings, that a male child had been born to the queen. Finally even Mary, who obstinately refused to give up hope, realized that she was mistaken, thus making it possible for Philip to leave her side. Impatient to be off, Philip departed in the autumn of 1555, to return only once for a brief stay.

Philip's return in 1557 was not in response to the pleadings of Mary, but solely from political motives. He came to seek the aid of England in his war against France. In the previous year he had become Philip II of Spain. Now he was determined to administer a crushing blow to Spain's great rival. Mary was still desirous of pleasing her husband; consequently he was able to persuade her to declare war against France, in spite of English opposition to a war in the interests of Spain. Disaster resulted. In 1558 the French took Calais, which had been in the possession of the English since its capture by Edward III more than two centuries before. The English felt the loss of this last remnant of what had once been an extensive English domain on the continent as a deep disgrace, and Mary's unpopularity increased. Already ill when she received the news, the loss of Calais broke the queen's spirit completely. With the realization that her most cherished endeavors were doomed to failure she sank into a deep gloom. She knew, however much she might try to dissemble, that her efforts to reëstablish the Catholic faith had failed, and that her successor, Elizabeth, the daughter of her mother's supplanter, would reverse her religious policy. Childless, detested by her people, deserted by the husband whom she loved so fondly, she died of dropsy on November 17, 1558.

THE REIGN OF QUEEN ELIZABETH

Unlike her half-Spanish predecessor, Elizabeth was thoroughly English and took pleasure in speaking of herself as being "mere English." Twenty-five years old at the time of her accession, she was moderately tall and well proportioned in figure, with a face that was pleasing rather than beautiful. She had a fine though somewhat olive complexion, golden hair, striking light blue eyes, and a nose that was high and slightly aquiline. Her attraction lay not so much in her feminine charm as in the power of her compelling personality. Elizabeth was incredibly vain. So insatiable was her thirst for adulation and flattery that she demanded fulsome praise from her courtiers and reveled in it even though she well knew that the words addressed to her were but hollow compliments. Having been forced to dress plainly before her accession, she now indulged her penchant for personal adornment and display. Jewelry of all kinds, fans, combs, ruffs, veils, embroidery, and laces in profusion formed part of her daily attire. When she died she left more than a thousand dresses. To impress her people and to strengthen her popularity she employed splendid pageants and masques, for which she had a decided taste. This love of display she retained even in later life. As the years advanced she surrounded herself with greater state, and bedecked herself with more finery, perhaps in an effort to hide the ravages of time. But despite her love of feminine adornment, Elizabeth was not a womanly woman. There was in her make-up a definite masculine strain, a certain unfeminine hardness. Coarse-minded and coarse-tongued, she delighted in free jokes, and swore and spat like a trooper. As Sir Robert Cecil said, she was "more than a man, and sometimes less than a woman."

The new queen was eminently fitted, nevertheless, to rule England. She was a natural leader with gifts few rulers have possessed. Endowed with a keen intellect, she had been carefully and fully educated, despite the fact that her birth had been such a disappointment to her father. Her naturally keen mind was further sharpened by thorough instruction in the school of adversity. Through the years of her youth she had lived in an atmosphere of jealousy, suspicion, and danger. When Mary became queen she was distrustful of the daughter of Anne Boleyn, regarding her as the center of all plots against the throne. Once Elizabeth was even confined in the Tower with the prospect of being sent to the block. Only her craft and consummate caution saved her. The difficulties of her early days taught her prudence, self-control, and self-reliance; they also gave her a deep knowledge of human nature and convinced her that she could trust only in herself and must depend solely on her own judgment. Forced to hide her thoughts and sentiments, she emerged a master in all the arts of dissimulation, utterly deceitful and unscrupulous. Yet with all her vanity and deceitfulness Elizabeth had the love of her people and kept it to the end. She realized the value of popularity and overlooked no opportunity to strengthen her own. Having witnessed Mary's mistakes in opposing the wishes of the people and her consequent failure to hold their esteem, she identified herself so completely with her people that their interests became hers.

Elizabeth had need of all her gifts and abilities to wrestle successfully with the tremendous problems which faced her. The most urgent were the settlement of the religious question, the termination of the war with France, and the restoration of the finances and of national credit. In addition such other problems as the defense of England against invasion, the protection of her throne against a pretender, and also the question of her marriage required attention. Her first step toward the solution of these problems consisted in selecting able advisers, an important factor in her subsequent success. As her principal minister she chose William Cecil, Lord Burghley (1520–1598), who served her faithfully for forty years. Burghley, a man of Protestant sympathies, combined a detailed knowledge of the workings of the government with an amazing capacity for hard work. Impervious to bribes, calm, cautious, and methodical, he had more influence than any other person during the first years of Elizabeth's rule, in which the course of the reign was charted. But Elizabeth was certainly no figurehead who moved only when Burghley gave the command. If he was the helmsman who steered the ship of state through the troubled waters of economic disorganization, religious dissension, and diplomatic intrigue, she herself remained at all times the captain of the ship. Burghley was undoubtedly the author of many policies of the reign, but the final decision as to their adoption rested with the queen. Though Elizabeth relied on the reports of her ministers for a knowledge of affairs both at home and abroad, her decisions were largely independent. From the moment of her accession to the end of her life, she firmly held the reins of government in her own hands.

Having chosen her ministers, the new queen proceeded with their aid to work out a religious settlement. In this, as in other matters, Elizabeth moved with extreme caution. Lacking religious feelings herself, she thought religious arguments and religious zeal tiresome and ridiculous. Like her brother Edward she had been instructed in the tenets of the reformed faith, but she was fond of the ritual of the Catholic Church. Even after she had definitely cast her lot with Protestantism, she retained the crucifix and candles in her private chapel, much to the sorrow of the reformers. Political considerations dictated her ecclesiastical policy. Both her public action in religious matters and her private practice varied with the exigencies of the moment. Naturally, she cherished a sincere opposition to the idea of papal supremacy. Her imperious will was not inclined to brook papal interference in the affairs of England, and as the daughter of Anne Boleyn she could scarcely be expected to entertain affection for a system which had pronounced her illegitimate and therefore unfit to occupy the English throne. On the other hand, she regarded with little patience the ideas of ecclesiastical self-government sponsored by the Calvinists. Her wish was to allay the religious animosities which had been excited during Mary's reign. To this end she judiciously chose the middle way between the two extremes of Catholicism and Calvinism. Her goal was a national church which was at once Catholic and Protestant and as such would claim the allegiance of the majority of the English people. While she believed outward conformity essential to national unity, she wished to permit at the same time a certain freedom of private opinion.

When Parliament met in 1559 it repealed the reactionary laws which had been enacted during the reign of Mary and passed a new Act of Supremacy which declared the crown to be "supreme in all causes ecclesiastical as well as civil," putting the constitutional form of the Church back to the condition in which Henry VIII had left it. There was, however, one notable change. Lest the title of "Supreme Head of the Church" offend the consciences of some of her subjects, Elizabeth declined to accept it, piously declaring that it belonged to Christ alone. As a compromise she assumed the title of "Supreme Governor." Parliament next passed the Act of Uniformity by which the Prayer Book, slightly modified from the Second Prayer Book of Edward VI, became the only legal form of common worship. For the second time it abolished mass and established the Church of England as it still exists, with the ruler of England as its head, with English as the language of its worship, and with a clergy which is permitted to marry.

The Elizabethan settlement was acceptable to the bulk of the English people. After the extremes of the two preceding reigns with their attendant excesses Englishmen were content to adopt the queen's compromise. Of the ten thousand English clergymen, only some two hundred refused to accept the Prayer Book. Two groups, the Calvinists and the Catholics, regarded the settlement as merely temporary. The former looked forward to the time when the Church would be purged of such un-Calvinistic practices as making the sign of the cross and the use of all vestments except the surplice; the latter worked for an early return to the fold of the Roman Church. At first both parties were hopeful that their respective demands would be met. But when they discovered that the government would make no further concessions in either direction the conflict with the Church of England became more definite and open. After 1570 the situation became more difficult for the Roman Catholics. In that year the pope excommunicated Elizabeth and absolved all Catholics from their allegiance to her;

but instead of promoting the cause of Catholicism in England, the bull of excommunication served to make England more emphatically Protestant than before. Many Englishmen who had wavered in their loyalty between the pope and the government now sided with the state. Thenceforth adherence to papalism was regarded not only as dissent from the Church, but also as disloyalty to the English nation. Elizabeth and Parliament answered the papal bull by making the laws against Catholics more severe and enforcing them more rigorously.

Another problem which urgently demanded a solution was the financial confusion and the consequent loss of national credit. One of the causes of this disorder was the state of the coinage, which had been debased during the reigns of Henry VIII and Edward VI. During the early years of Elizabeth's rule the impure coin was gradually called in by the government and a pure coin was minted to replace it. Although this restoration of the coinage to its standard value failed to bring about a drop in prices, it did restore the national credit in the continental money market, thereby greatly benefiting English trade. On the whole, Elizabeth's reign was a period of commercial and industrial expansion and prosperity. English merchants and adventurers went to all parts of the world to sell their goods and to bring back new products. John Hawkins, for example, set out to supply the Spanish plantations with slaves. Richard Chancellor reached Moscow by way of the White Sea, and established trade relations with Russia which resulted in the founding of the Muscovy Company.[1] Likewise the Levant Company for trade in the eastern Mediterranean, the Eastland Company for trade in the Baltic, and the Guinea Company for trade in western Africa were founded at this time. The last years of the reign saw the establishment of the East India Company, which was destined to become by far the most important of the English companies.

English industry profited greatly from the arrival of immigrants who had been driven from the Low Countries and from France by religious troubles. These foreign artisans infused new life into the old industries and also founded new crafts. Even the manufacture of cloth, the staple industry of England, was benefited. In consequence of the immigration of Flemish cloth-makers the number of cloth works, fulling mills, and dye works increased.

---

[1] For an account of the exploits of the Elizabethan seamen see pp. 114–118.

What is more, the quality of English cloth improved. Whereas English woolen cloth had formerly been exported in a coarse or half-finished condition, it now became sufficiently fine to compete with the French make. New crafts established by foreign artisans included the manufacture of lace, felt, thread, glass, and needles, and the weaving of silk. This expansion of industry led to a change in the nature of trade, for as the sixteenth century progressed less raw material and more manufactured articles were exported. Besides encouraging the immigration of foreign artisans, the government sought to promote industrial development in other ways. The home consumption of fish, for example, was increased by a decree which forbade the eating of meat on certain days of each week and throughout Lent. Such encouragement of both industry and commerce was an outstanding feature of Elizabeth's reign.

To understand the economic policy of Elizabeth's government it is necessary to keep in mind the fact that this was an age of mercantilism. Like other governments of the time, Elizabeth's advisers aimed to build a powerful, economically self-sufficient state on the basis of mercantilist principles. Since the fourteenth century the rulers of England had shown a mercantilistic tendency. In Elizabeth's reign this policy became increasingly definite and comprehensive. The outstanding example of the government's attempts to regulate English economic life was the Statute of Apprentices of 1563, by which the economic regulations of the period since the fourteenth century were consolidated and codified. This statute dealt primarily with what is now known as the labor problem. To check the unsettled state of labor it decreed that a workman must be hired for a period of a year and that no workman might leave his employer except at the end of this time. To secure good workmanship and protect a qualified workman from unskilled labor, it fixed the period of apprenticeship at seven years for all crafts. Finally, it ordered the justices to fix fair wages for laborers in their respective districts.[1] This statute, which with some modifications remained in force until the second decade of the nineteenth century, was supplemented in 1601 by the Great

---

[1] The wages set by justices were maximum and minimum rates. The purpose was rather to protect employers against excessive demands for wages than to protect the interests of the laborer. An employer who paid more than the maximum was to be punished by ten days' imprisonment and a fine of five pounds.

Poor Law, a summary of the Poor Law statutes of the preceding period. Its main provisions affirmed the legal claim of the destitute to relief and bestowed on the justices the power to impose a compulsory poor-rate on the inhabitants of any parish under their control. Those who could work were to be given employment, while vagrants were to be sent "to the house of correction or common gaol." This statute remained the basis of Poor Law administration until 1834.

The agrarian problems of Elizabeth's government were like those of the previous reigns. Since enclosures still continued, poverty and want remained widespread in the country districts. From the different parts of England the government was besieged with complaints against the practice, but an effective remedy was not forthcoming. Actually the enclosures do not seem to have inflicted so much hardship on the country as did the rise of prices resulting from the influx of silver from the Mexican and Peruvian mines, but public opinion seems to have blamed the enclosers for the difficult times. Toward the end of Elizabeth's reign the progress of enclosures slackened somewhat. Still enclosing did not cease entirely, but continued as a source of many complaints and much unrest.

In foreign affairs the first move of Elizabeth's government was to end the war with France in which England had become embroiled for the sake of Spanish interests. On the verge of exhaustion, with its army disorganized and its navy in a state of decay, England needed a period of tranquillity to restore its finances and to put the country in a state of defense. Since France and Spain also wanted peace, a treaty was concluded between the three countries at Cateau-Cambrésis (1559). By its terms Calais remained in the hands of the French. The loss of this last possession on the continent, regarded by many Englishmen at the time as humiliating to the English pride, was probably a blessing, for it relieved England of a great expense and made withdrawal from foreign complications easier. In the same year Elizabeth sent an English force to Scotland to assist the Protestants in freeing that country from French domination. By the treaty of Edinburgh (July, 1560) negotiated between the English and the French, the latter promised to withdraw from Scotland, thus assuring the ascendancy of the Reformation party. Thenceforward to the end of her life Elizabeth endeavored to keep Scotland in firm alliance with England in order to prevent France or Spain from obtaining the upper hand in Scottish affairs, and thus to secure the English borders against an invasion from Scotland.

With the treaty of 1560 England entered upon the longest period of official peace it had enjoyed since the thirteenth century. However, there was no lack of tension between it and other governments. Its principal opponents were the two great continental powers, Spain and France. Both were dissatisfied with the state of affairs in England. Spain wished to regain the influence it had wielded there during Mary's reign and to reëstablish Catholicism. France, also eager to see England restored to the fold of the Roman Church, regarded Mary of Scotland as the rightful queen of England.

The great danger lay in a combination of France and Spain against England. To forestall such an alliance Elizabeth launched a succession of consummate intrigues, playing off one power against the other. Her methods were wholly devoid of scruples. Although her age was characterized by a statecraft unhampered by moral considerations, she was without a peer in the matter of unprincipled diplomacy. No politician of the time, not even Catherine de Médicis, was her equal in the art of double dealing, of employing craft and subterfuges, and of telling plain lies. Averse to adopting a bold course, she gave her orders in such a way that she could disavow them, couched her messages in language so ambiguous that they were subject to various interpretations, and planned her course in such a way that retreat was always open. Of her methods the Spanish ambassador wrote: "Your lordship will see what a pretty business it is to treat with this woman who I think must have a hundred thousand devils in her body, notwithstanding that she is forever telling me that she yearns to be a nun and to pass her life in prayer."

Despite Elizabeth's efforts, a Franco-Spanish alliance against England might have materialized if internal troubles had not crippled both countries. Seeing the safety of England in the continuation of these disturbances, the English queen helped to aggravate them. When the first of a series of religious wars broke out in France in 1562 she sided with the French Protestants or Huguenots against the French ruler, giving them encouragement and furnishing aid. Again, when the Netherlands rose in revolt against Spain she sent money to William of Orange, permitted

English volunteers to enlist under the banner of revolt, and later sent an army under Leicester to aid them. Notwithstanding the help she lent to dissidents, Elizabeth did not regard herself as the champion of Protestantism, a rôle which Protestants have assigned to her. Political considerations were always predominant in her foreign policy. She supported the Huguenots and Dutch Protestants not because they were Protestants, but because in so doing she distracted and weakened her adversaries. Her principal aim was to keep herself on the throne and to guard against an invasion of England. Even then she could not suppress her natural hatred of rebellion enough to aid or encourage consistently subjects who were in revolt against their lawful sovereign. She gave them just so much help as would prevent them from being crushed. In 1564 she concluded a pact with France and thereafter assiduously cultivated friendly relations with the French rulers. For the rest of her reign her efforts were centered upon abating the power of Spain. A bitter hostility soon grew up between the two governments and between the two peoples. Though religious factors entered into the situation, the most potent cause of the Englishman's hatred of the Spaniard was the bar which Spain tried to place in the road of England's commercial expansion. While England was outwardly maintaining the fiction of peace, English seamen preyed on Spanish commerce and the queen herself was not beyond sharing in the spoil when a Spanish galleon was seized. Nevertheless, open war between the two governments did not break out until Philip sent his "Invincible Armada" against England.

In her conduct of foreign affairs the question of her marriage was an invaluable diplomatic asset to Elizabeth. It was naturally assumed that the queen would marry, for in that age every woman did so if the opportunity presented itself. As Elizabeth was the great prize of Europe, and in her younger days not personally unattractive, virtually every eligible prince in western and central Europe—among them the kings or future kings of Spain, France, Denmark, and Sweden—proposed to her. Realizing the value of her position in the marriage market, the English queen was ever seemingly contemplating matrimony and always ready to entertain proposals; yet in every case she found specific objections to the particular offer. Her suitors were merely pawns in the game of politics, and according to the political exigencies she either prolonged her courtships or terminated them quickly. Almost to the end of her days, even when she was a withered old woman, she continued to act coquettishly and to invite young gallants to deluge her with flattery and bid for her hand. More than once she was almost forced by circumstances of her own making into taking a consort. But her gambler's luck did not desert her. She was always able to retreat, though it was at times difficult. The reason why Elizabeth finally did not marry remains a subject of conjecture. It may have been that she was averse to sharing her power with a husband or it may have been some other reason. The "Virgin Queen" guarded her secret successfully.

In its relations with the Irish, Elizabeth's government made no more progress than the governments of previous English rulers. Although Ireland had been granted to England by the pope as far back as the twelfth century, English sovereigns before the accession of the Tudors exercised authority over only a small part of it. This was the so-called English Pale, a district immediately surrounding Dublin and largely owned by nobility of English descent. The rest of Ireland remained in the hands of half-civilized tribes who waged incessant warfare with one another and with the English. Finally Henry VII decided to extend the royal power in Ireland; for this purpose he sent Sir Edward Poynings, together with a body of English officials, to Ireland in 1494. The new deputy prevailed upon the Irish parliament to pass the statute known as Poynings' Law, which declared that laws passed in England were effective also in Ireland. Another provision of the same law stated that no parliament was henceforth to meet in Ireland except by permission of the English king and his council. Needless to say, this unpalatable law caused widespread resentment. Henry VIII, who in 1541 assumed the title "King of Ireland," aroused further antagonism by attempting to introduce into Ireland the ecclesiastical changes he effected in England. But because the Irish associated it with the rule of foreign tyranny the Reformation made little headway in Ireland. The Irish became more devoted than ever to Catholicism. Elizabeth, determined to reduce Ireland to obedience, employed repression instead of conciliation. Uprisings were savagely put down; the land of the rebels was confiscated and granted to Englishmen who often remained absentee landlords. Despite the brutal manner in which they were quelled, the uprisings continued. Thus, instead of subduing Ireland, the high-handed methods of the Tudor sovereigns fomented the bitter racial enmity, religious antagonism, and incessant strife which became the heritage of later rulers.

In addition to the many other difficulties with which she had to cope, Elizabeth had to ward off a threat to her throne. Should Elizabeth die without children the nearest heir to the throne was Mary Stuart, perhaps better known as Mary Queen of Scots. But Mary was not content to wait until Elizabeth died. A devout Roman Catholic, she shared the belief of her Church that, as an illegitimate child of Henry VIII, Elizabeth was a usurper. Accordingly, upon Elizabeth's accession to the throne Mary at once assumed the arms of England and Ireland as though she were the lawful sovereign of both, but without attempting to enforce her claim. This action marked the beginning of a rivalry between the two which ended only with Mary's execution a quarter of a century later. A great-granddaughter of Henry VII, Mary was the daughter of James V of Scotland. Very early in life she was taken to France, where she was brought up at the French court and in 1558 was married to Francis II, the sickly son of Henry II and Catherine de Médicis. When Francis died in 1560 after a brief reign of seventeen months, Mary decided to return to Scotland to rule that country.

Not yet nineteen when she arrived in Scotland, Mary with her dark brown eyes, chestnut hair, and comely figure was attractive in person, charming in manner, and naturally gay and vivacious. On the other hand, her long sojourn at the French court in an atmosphere of luxury, deceit, and corruption had made her self-indulgent, adept in the arts of dissimulation, and as unscrupulous as Elizabeth. The equal of Elizabeth also in coolness and courage, she lacked the discretion of her English cousin. Having become thoroughly French, she had little in common with her Scottish subjects and did not understand them. In a country where a strict form of Calvinism was established by law, her Catholic religion became a source of friction. True, she was not a fanatical Catholic; for the time being she contented herself with having mass celebrated in her own chapel. Yet her subjects, led by the fiery John Knox, suspected her, and not unjustly, of designs to restore the old religion to its former supremacy. Despite all these differences, her influence gradually increased and the prospects for a peaceful reign appeared fair. In 1565 the Scottish queen married her cousin, Lord Darnley, an English nobleman who after herself was the next lineal heir to the English throne. Of this marriage was born the child who became James VI of Scotland and James I of England. Mary's claim on the English crown was now stronger than ever, for she had a son to succeed her, whereas Elizabeth was still unmarried.

But the marriage which had promised so much was to be one of the main causes of her downfall. It was the first act of a drama of love, hate, passion, and intrigue in which Mary lost her crown, her liberty, her reputation, and finally life itself. Darnley, a handsome youth of twenty when he became Mary's husband, was a person of considerable accomplishments, but without brains or morals. His superior airs, his inability to refrain from interference in the government, and his taste for low vices soon alienated the affections of his wife, who began to give her confidence and trust to her secretary, David Riccio. Jealous of Riccio's influence, Darnley caused him to be brutally assassinated. Concealing her loathing for her husband, Mary called to her side the earl of Bothwell, a man of reckless audacity, but without a scruple and without the ability to consider the consequences of his actions. One night in February, 1567, while Mary was attending the wedding of a servant at Holyrood, Darnley's house was blown up with gunpowder and Darnley was found dead in the garden near by. In the minds of the people there was no doubt as to the identity of the murderer. Placards proclaiming Bothwell the perpetrator of the deed were even hung on the walls of Edinburgh to inform the government that the people knew who was the guilty man.

Whether or not Mary was a party to the plot for Darnley's assassination is still a matter of dispute.[1] Her conduct at the time was imprudent enough to confirm the worst suspicions. Almost immediately after the murder she showered lands and power on Bothwell, permitted him to abduct her with a show of force, and

[1] Mary's complicity in the plot to murder Darnley is apparently proved in the so-called Casket Letters, purportedly exchanged between her and Bothwell. The authenticity of the letters, however, is doubtful. Since the originals have disappeared the question will probably remain open. The present tendency of scholarship is to regard them as letters written by Mary, in which liberal alterations and interpolations have been made by others. In any event, the importance of the letters is chiefly biographical. If they are forgeries, they leave unanswered the question of Mary's guilt or innocence in the murder of her husband; if genuine, they prove beyond doubt her participation in the plot to assassinate him. They did not affect the politics of the time, for the revolution in Scotland was an achieved fact and foreign opinion had already been formed when they were discovered.

finally married him. By this act Mary outraged the feelings both of her subjects and of the peoples of Europe and wrought her own ruin. The Scottish lords at once rose in revolt, took their queen captive, and confined her in Lochleven Castle. There she was compelled to sign a deed of abdication in favor of her son, who became king as James VI. After an imprisonment of ten months Mary contrived to escape and rally a few supporters about her. But her small army was hopelessly defeated. Broken, discredited, and friendless, she then sought refuge in England, protesting to Elizabeth that "next to God I have no hope but in your goodness." Elizabeth was hardly pleased over the presence of her ambitious rival in England. Seeking to restore Mary to the Scottish throne, the English queen soon discovered that the Scottish lords were determined not to take her back. So she remained a prisoner in England until her death almost two decades later.

Mary in England was a more perplexing problem than Mary in Scotland. From the moment of her imprisonment she became the rallying point of malcontents, the focus of all the conspiracies against Elizabeth's life and throne. Outside of England there was much sympathy for Mary's cause, a state of affairs which made Elizabeth fear the formation of a league against her. Fortunately for Elizabeth, both France and Spain were occupied with troubles at home. In England plot followed plot to dethrone Elizabeth, some of them financed with French or Spanish funds. Finally Mary, whose imprisonment was made more and more rigorous, became extraordinarily rash in her intrigues, snatching eagerly at every opportunity which promised liberation. The consequences were tragic. In the spring of 1586 a plan known as the Babington plot was devised to assassinate Elizabeth and to enthrone Mary with the help of Spain. Elizabeth's secretary, Walsingham, who seems to have known of the plot from its very inception, permitted it to develop until he had obtained definite proof of Mary's complicity. Then Mary was brought to trial before a special commission, found guilty, and condemned to death. With great reluctance Elizabeth finally affixed her signature to the death warrant, and on February 8, 1587, Mary was beheaded.

With Mary dead, Philip II of Spain realized that there was only one way to reclaim England for Catholicism and to stop the English attacks on Spanish commerce; that was by force. Hence he prepared to invade England. No longer, however, would he attack England in behalf of Mary's line of succession. Prior to her execution Mary had bequeathed to him her claims to the English throne, and Philip was now determined to conquer England for himself. After extensive preparations Philip's fleet, which the Spaniards had named the "Invincible Armada," sailed from the Tagus in May, 1588, with disastrous results for Spain.[1] The danger of invasion had drawn all Englishmen together. English patriotism was excited to a high pitch, and Roman Catholics and Protestants stood together to beat back the attack of the enemy. The crushing defeat administered to the Spaniards shattered once and for all the tradition of Spanish invincibility. No longer need England fear invasion. Conscious of their supremacy at sea, the English turned on the Spaniards with greater fury, preying on Spanish commerce, plundering Spanish possessions, and even burning Spanish towns. English trade increased rapidly, and English discoverers were sailing on every sea.

The defeat of the Armada was the climax of Elizabeth's reign. During the last fifteen years of her life she increasingly lost touch with the new generation. In Parliament an opposition was forming against the absolute government of the Tudors, presaging the struggle between the crown and Parliament which was to break out after the accession of the Stuarts. Only the tact and popularity of the aged queen held the conflict in abeyance. When Elizabeth in 1601 asked Parliament for a large grant of supplies for the Irish war, Parliament voted them, but in turn vehemently protested against the granting of monopolies—that is, the exclusive right of making or selling a specified article. These monopolies, which included such articles as wine, oil, tin, steel, and even such necessities as salt, starch, and vinegar, were an intolerable burden on the nation. So determined was the House of Commons in the matter that Elizabeth was forced to give way. In her most gracious manner she informed the House that she would immediately revoke all illegal grants of monopolies. Her message so pleased the Commons that one hundred forty members went to Whitehall in a body to convey their gratitude to her. Addressing them at some length, the queen thanked the members for making the grievance known to her and expressed her affection for her people. It was her last public speech.

During the last years of Elizabeth's life the loneliness of old

---

[1] For a brief account of the "Invincible Armada" see pp. 269–273.

POSVI DEVM ADIVTOREM MEVM

SEMPER EADEM

QUEEN ELIZABETH

HENRY VIII   *by Holbein*   EDWARD VI   *by Holb*

SHAKESPEARE AND HIS CONTEMPORARIES

age oppressed her. Without husband, children, or near relatives, she was almost alone in the world. Her faithful old ministers had passed from the scene, and their successors were seeking to make their future secure by planning how to win the favor of the new ruler when he should ascend the throne. It was in these years that the queen said: "To be a king and wear a crown is more glorious to them that see it than it is pleasure to them that bear it." Her one favorite, Robert Devereux, earl of Essex, caused her only heartaches. A man of good appearance but of mediocre gifts and an exaggerated notion of his own ability, Essex had enjoyed the favor of the queen from the time he came to court. When a serious rising in Ireland threatened the English ascendancy, he was sent to put it down. But instead of taking vigorous action, Essex dallied until his forces were decimated by disease and desertion, and then returned to England in disregard of the queen's express prohibition. For his gross insubordination he was dismissed from all his offices and banished from court. In an effort to force his reinstatement at court, Essex foolishly attempted a revolt in London. Elizabeth, much as she may have wished to do so, did not save him from the block. The tragedy seems, however, to have robbed her of much of her spirit. Melancholy and fretful, she lived but two years after the execution of Essex. On March 24, 1603, the last and greatest representative of the house of Tudor passed quietly away. How amazed her contemporaries were that she, a woman, could achieve such greatness is indicated in a popular ballad written at the time of her death:

> She rul'd this Nation by her selfe,
> And was beholden to no man:
> O she bore the sway of all affairs,
> And yet she was but a woman.

ELIZABETHAN LITERATURE

The chief glories of Elizabethan England are the exploits of the Elizabethan seamen and the literary works of the Elizabethan writers. Of the two, the latter ultimately contributed more to the national reputation. The period preceding the reign of Elizabeth was, comparatively speaking, an age of literary barrenness. Because of the distractions caused by religious questions, little was produced that might be styled creative literature except Thomas More's *Utopia*, and that was not translated from Latin into English until 1551. The period of Henry VIII and the earlier years of Elizabeth were, however, a time of exploration, experiment, and adventure in literature as in life. A new era began in English verse with the publication in 1557 of Tottel's *Miscellany*, a collection of songs and sonnets by Sir Thomas Wyatt, the earl of Surrey, and others. This was soon followed by that part of *The Mirror for Magistrates* which contained the poems by Thomas Sackville. In prose the middle years of Elizabeth's reign brought John Lyly's *Euphues*, which established a new, though artificial, style. More important, perhaps, was the advent of Philip Sidney, whose name, next to that of Shakespeare, is significant of the spirit and meaning of English taste and ideas in the expanding age of Elizabeth. Elizabeth had been on the throne two decades before the first of the great literary works of her reign appeared. The ensuing period, however, was one of rare fertility, boasting such names as Spenser, Marlowe, Bacon, and, above all, Shakespeare. Partly from indifference and partly from parsimony, Elizabeth herself did little for that wonderful group of writers that made her reign famous. Spenser, who wrote his *Faerie Queene* in her honor, was forced to content himself with a meager reward. There is a story that Shakespeare wrote *The Merry Wives of Windsor* at Elizabeth's behest, but her reaction to it is unknown. Beyond that she seems to have done little to encourage the development of a national literature. Nevertheless, critics have given the name "Elizabethan" to the literary productions of a period extending far beyond her reign. In point of time the work of some of the great Elizabethan authors belongs to the reign of James I, but the spirit which pervades their writings is that of the reign of Elizabeth.

Elizabethan literature was, on the whole, secular in spirit. Though theology found a place in it, notably in the writings of Richard Hooker, its dominant interest was man as a citizen of this world. In other words, the spirit of Elizabethan literature was akin to that of the Italian Renaissance. The Renaissance desire to make the most of life upon earth, its enthusiasm for the Greek and Latin classics, its accentuation of reason rather than of faith, the new ideals of beauty, the desire to extend the limits of human knowledge, the adventure of geographical discovery, are all reflected in the new writing. It is the literature of the age of Drake, Hawkins, and Frobisher. The same heroic, romantic, adventurous spirit that impelled the Elizabethan seamen also animated the Elizabethan writers. The exploits of the seamen gave a decided stimulus to the imagination of the age, and the sea figures prominently in the literature of the period. Elizabethan literature is furthermore a patriotic literature. It is the expression of an age in which Englishmen were intensely proud of being English; in which they gloried in their defects as well as good qualities. Elizabethan literature is, above all, as exuberant as the life of the period. Masterpieces were produced in such numbers that no other contemporary nation offers nearly so many. It was, however, a literature which belonged almost exclusively to the upper classes, despite the fact that literary productions could be spread throughout the land by means of the printing press; for but few Englishmen of the lower classes were able to read. Nevertheless, Elizabethan literature was brought to the people in at least one form. In the theaters, of which there were no less than eleven in or near London during the latter part of Elizabeth's reign, the man in the street could enjoy the finest productions of the Elizabethan playwrights.

The number of the important literary figures of the Elizabethan age is so large that only a few of the most outstanding can be considered here. One of the foremost was Edmund Spenser (c.1552–1599), whose best known works are *The Shepheards Calendar* and *The Faerie Queene*. The latter is the great epic of Elizabethan England. It was dedicated to Elizabeth herself, "the most high, mightie, and magnificent Empress, renowned for Pietie, Vertue, and all Gratious Government." The central motive of the book, according to its author, was "to fashion a gentleman or noble person in vertuous and gentle discipline"; in other words, to portray the twelve virtues of the perfect knight. It is the goal of Castiglione's *Book of the Courtier*. For his subject Spenser chose the history of King Arthur, a theme familiar to most readers of the time. As originally planned the work was to comprise twelve books, each consisting of twelve cantos. Only half of it was completed; the first three books were published in 1590 and the next three in 1596. The six present the legends of Holiness, Temperance, Chastity, Friendship, Justice, and Courtesy. When the poem appeared it was accorded immediate and enthusiastic admiration, and Spenser was acclaimed the first poet of his generation. The beauty of some of its stanzas moved his contemporaries to bestow on him the title of "the heavenly poet." Written in a stanzaic form that has become one of the great forms in English poetry, *The Faerie Queene* is as rich and fine and elevating in language and thought as anything in English.

While Spenser was writing his *Faerie Queene*, Christopher Marlowe (1564–1593), the greatest of the considerable group of English dramatists before and contemporary with Shakespeare, was enriching English literature with his dramatic works. A writer of vivid imagination and vehement passions, he produced during his brief and tragic life a number of plays which bear the stamp of genius. His first work was the tragedy, *Tamburlaine the Great* (1587). Though marked by a crude violence, it immediately made Marlowe the reigning dramatist of the day. During the five years that followed he produced, among other plays, *Doctor Faustus*, *The Jew of Malta*, and *Edward the Second*. The last is probably the best historical play in English literature before Shakespeare, while *The Jew of Malta* is notable for its vivid representations of malignant human passions. But it is his *Doctor Faustus*, a succession of scenes rather than an organized drama, which probably best reflects the genius and experience of Marlowe. Its theme—which Goethe was later to use in his *Faust*—is man's overpowering desire for knowledge and power. Dr. Faustus sells his soul to the devil for the privilege of enjoying certain powers during a period of twenty-four years. As a master of the forces of nature he travels about the globe, performing miracles of every sort and playing tricks upon scholars, friars, princes, the emperor, and the pope; at last he returns to Wittenberg, where the devil claims his soul. The final scenes are among the most pathetic and the most grandiose in the history of drama—scenes which were not eclipsed even in the works of Shakespeare or Goethe. In 1593, at the age of twenty-nine, Marlowe was killed in a tavern brawl. The early death of this stormy genius would have been an irreparable loss had he not been succeeded by the greater Shakespeare.

William Shakespeare is not only the outstanding figure in English literature but also the greatest writer of drama in any language. No man before or since his time has possessed his sublime mastery in this field. But despite his preëminence, we have less positive knowledge of his life than of the lives of many small poets and playwrights. Not one of his acquaintances took the trouble to record the facts of his life; neither did he himself jot down for posterity any information about his personal affairs. So great is the dearth of facts regarding his life that it has given rise to various theories concerning the authorship of his plays, which have even been ascribed to various of his contemporaries. Almost nothing is known about his life before he reached the age of thirty. It is certain that he was baptized at Stratford-on-Avon on April 26, 1564; that he was the son of John Shakespeare, a general storekeeper of that little town; and that he married Anne Hathaway in 1582 and that three children were born of the marriage. All other information regarding his life before 1592 is tradition or conjecture. Reliable data concerning his education, the exact time he went to London, and the year in which he joined the stage are lacking. Whatever the facts of his previous experience may have been, by 1592 he was established as an actor and a playwright of some reputation. Upon his arrival in London he joined a company of actors and began his career both as actor and dramatist. During the next two decades he wrote so much that limitations of space permit no more than a listing of his more important works, which include almost every type of dramatic writing known at that time.

The years 1590 to 1594 were the period of his apprenticeship. At first he seems to have devoted his talents to reworking old plays, but soon he turned to writing his own. By 1594 he had written several, including *Love's Labour's Lost, Comedy of Errors*, and *Two Gentlemen of Verona*, and also two narrative poems, *Venus and Adonis* and the *Rape of Lucrece*. During the second period (1594–1600) he concentrated on the writing of historical plays and romantic comedies. The year 1595 saw the appearance of *Richard II*, one of his greatest historical dramas. Next came the tragi-comedy, *The Merchant of Venice*. Other plays of this period are: *Midsummer Night's Dream, Romeo and Juliet, The Taming of the Shrew, King John, Henry IV, Henry V, Much Ado about Nothing, The Merry Wives of Windsor, Twelfth Night*, and *As You Like It*. The last, a pastoral comedy, is by many regarded as the loveliest of Shakespeare's plays. The third period (1600–1608) is characterized by the great tragedies. It saw the appearance of *Julius Caesar, Hamlet, Othello, King Lear, Macbeth*, and *Antony and Cleopatra*. The three plays of his final period (1609–1611), *Cymbeline, The Winter's Tale*, and *The Tempest*, are all idyllic romances with happy endings. About 1611 he seems to have retired to Stratford where he lived the life of a gentleman until his death in 1616. His remains, in obedience to his well-known epitaph, have remained undisturbed in the old church by the Avon.

Shakespeare is not only the greatest but, in a sense, also the most popular of English writers. As it was his purpose to please the entire audience, he wrote for the common people as well as for the cultured nobility. He possessed the supreme ability of giving a distinctive individuality to each of his characters. They may differ in age, sex, and passions, vices and virtues, but they are all vitally alive. No dramatist has written with a deeper understanding of human nature. Love, joy, ecstasy, friendship, pity, avarice, malice, envy, jealousy, hatred, revenge, remorse, and their interactions are all presented in his dramas. Shakespeare wrote for his time and not for posterity; yet, in the words of Ben Jonson, he is "not of an age, but for all time." Had the survival of his plays depended on him, they probably would have perished. During his lifetime they appeared only in cheap quartos, the texts of which had been purloined from the prompter's copy or taken from the lips of the players. Only sixteen of the thirty-seven plays commonly ascribed to him were published before he died. It was not until seven years after his death that the first collection, known as the First Folio, appeared, through the endeavors of two of Shakespeare's actor-friends.

A third great figure in the Elizabethan age is Francis Bacon (1561–1626), statesman, lawyer, philosopher, and man of letters. Bacon's career as an official carried him to the position of lord high chancellor (head of the legal system of England) with its manifold duties; nevertheless he managed to find time for his literary work. His *History of the Reign of Henry VII* has served as a basis for the writings of most historians who have subsequently treated that period. A more imaginative work is his *New Atlantis*, an incomplete sketch in the manner of More's *Utopia*. But the most widely read of Bacon's writings are his *Essays*, which immediately acquired a popularity they have maintained to the present. Bacon himself said: "Of all my other works they have been most current; for that, as it seems, they come home to men's business and bosoms." The earliest collection, containing only ten essays, was published in 1597. Their general title was borrowed from Montaigne; and imitating Montaigne, Bacon continued working at them for the rest of his life, ever adding and correcting until the edition of

1625 contained fifty-eight essays. Bacon's essays differ in spirit, however, from Montaigne's. While Montaigne wrote copiously in a personal vein and tended to philosophize on anything related to man, Bacon is crisp and curt, wholly impersonal, and averse from pure speculation. The *Essays* are distinguished for their brilliance, polish, and conciseness; for the gems of pregnant thought they contain; and for their wealth of practical suggestions. Many statements found in them have become proverbs; for example: "Some books are to be tasted, others to be swallowed, and some few to be chewed and digested"; "Reading maketh a full man, conference a ready man, and writing an exact man"; "The folly of one man is the fortune of another"; "A wise man will make more opportunities than he finds"; "Many a man's strength is in opposition"; and "Money is like muck, not good unless it be spread."

Early in life Bacon had planned a vast work to be called *Instauratio Magna* or *The Great Renewal*. It was meant to be a comprehensive review and encyclopedia of all knowledge, in harmony with Bacon's statement: "I have taken all knowledge to be my province." Inevitably, only portions of the work were completed. These included *The Advancement of Learning*, published in English in 1605, and the *Novum Organum*, published in Latin in 1620. Both are merely fragments. The former contains the basic principles of Bacon's thought, while the latter, though it contains suggestive observations on science, deals mainly with the fallacies or errors which stand as obstacles in the path of a true understanding of nature. To these errors he gave the Platonic name of "idols," and divided them into idols of the tribe, idols of the cave, idols of the market-place, and idols of the theater. Though the influence of the *Novum Organum* has been exaggerated,[1] it did contribute toward inculcating in science a spirit of unbiased, accurate, and careful observation and experimentation. King James likened it to the "peace of God" because "it passeth all understanding."

By the end of the second decade of the seventeenth century the impetus which had given birth to Elizabethan literature was largely spent. George Chapman produced one of the few poems of that period that are still read, his translation of Homer. Ben Jonson, the dominant figure among men of letters immediately

---

[1] See Morris R. Cohen, "The Myth about Bacon and the Inductive Method," *Scientific Monthly*, vol. 23 (1926), pp. 504–508.

after Shakespeare, gave to drama a turn from the romantic to the realistic, enriching English literature with *Every Man in His Humor, Volpone, The Alchemist,* and other plays. He also gave it some of its finest lyrics, such for instance as "Drink to Me Only with Thine Eyes." But the interests and energies which for a time had been concentrated on literature were being absorbed by political questions. The Elizabethan spirit had made its contributions to the progress of culture. It had produced one of the greatest literary epochs in the world's history.

CHAPTER TEN

Spain under Philip II and Its Decline in the Seventeenth Century

PHILIP II AND HIS AIMS

IN THE eyes of the contemporaries of Charles V, Spain with its vast empire appeared the greatest of world powers. It was said that "when Spain moves, the whole world trembles." The power of Spain was the dread of European nations, and the destruction of its might became one of the principal aims of European statesmen. Under Philip II, Spain still retained the ascendancy in Europe by virtue of the almost fabulous riches which flowed into the country from the New World, and Europe continued to fear Spanish power; but as his reign drew to a close, signs of internal decay were becoming increasingly manifest.

Philip II was born in Valladolid, May 27, 1527, the son of Charles V and Isabella of Portugal. He early gave evidence of the qualities which were to characterize him as a man. The great hero of his youth, and also of his later life, was his father, whom he imitated in every possible way, even copying his gravity and dignity. But, whereas his father could be jovial when the occasion demanded, Philip was cold and reserved, giving way to geniality only in private, in the company of those he knew intimately and liked. As a child he was already obstinately self-willed, presaging the man who was to be impervious to the influence of others, once his mind was made up. Philip the man was below middle size in stature and slight of figure. His features bore a strong resemblance to those of his father, but in Philip the Habsburg protrusion of the lower jaw was more marked than in Charles. Philip lacked the vigor which had characterized his father even past middle life. Such pastimes as jousting and hunting—in fact any form of physical exercise—held little attraction for him. Whereas Charles had been a warrior who delighted in danger and the clash of arms, Philip's armies were led by others; and so deficient was he in martial spirit that his courage was suspect. Yet he was a favorite with the Spanish people; for in contrast to his father, who had been more cosmopolitan, Philip was a Spaniard to the core.

In 1543, at the age of sixteen, Philip married the Portuguese princess Maria, his first cousin. The marriage, which was popular in Spain, was calculated to multiply the chances of uniting the whole Iberian Peninsula under one rule. Of this union was born in 1545 a son, the tragic Don Carlos,[1] but Maria died in giving him birth. Though the succession of the Habsburgs now seemed assured, Philip's father, Charles V, began to look about for a second advantageous marriage for his son, one which would strengthen the position of his house. His final choice was Mary Tudor. It had been reported to Philip that Mary was very unattractive, "skinny, pimply, and sickly," but he raised no objections. "I very well see the advantage that might accrue from the successful conclusion of this marriage," wrote this dutiful son to his father.

As stated in Chapter Nine, the marriage which was successfully concluded in 1554 was not successful in itself. His hopes for an heir blasted, Philip left his wife in 1555 to go to Brussels, whither he had been summoned by his father. There, on October 25, 1555, Charles invested his son with the rule of the Netherlands. Previously he had conferred upon Philip the rule over the kingdoms of Naples and Sicily, and the duchy of Milan, so that he would not have to go to England a landless prince. Early in

---

[1] Don Carlos, weak physically and mentally as a child, showed definite signs of insanity as a young man. He cherished such a hatred for Philip that he even contemplated murdering him. He died suddenly in 1568 under mysterious circumstances, after making preparations to flee from Spain. Some writers, without proof, have gone so far as to accuse Philip II of murdering his son. Among others, Schiller and Alfieri have written dramas based on the life of Don Carlos.

1556 Charles also abdicated the Spanish crown. Actually there was no crown of Spain, nor was there a unified Spanish kingdom. Castile and Aragon, which comprised Spain, were two independent kingdoms united only in the person of the king, each having its peculiar laws and organization. With the crowns of these states Philip also assumed the rule of their vast dependencies. Thus he found himself the monarch of an immense empire which, besides the territories already mentioned, included Franche-Comté (the county of Burgundy), five ports and fortified places in Africa, and the vice-royalties of Peru and Mexico in America. That Philip did not inherit the German Empire was indeed a blessing, for it would have added considerably to his difficulties.

During the first two years of his reign Philip was occupied with the war against France which had broken out afresh in 1557. Assisted by the troops of Mary Tudor, he invaded France and administered two crushing defeats to the French forces at St. Quentin and Gravelines. However, instead of marching on Paris after the victories, Philip sued for peace. His treasury was empty and his soldiers were unpaid. Furthermore, both Philip and Henry II of France desired peace in order to proceed against the Protestant heresy which was spreading in their dominions. By the treaty of Cateau-Cambrésis, concluded in 1559, the year after Mary Tudor's death, Spain and France restored everything they had taken from each other since 1551, while England lost Calais to France. Philip, now nearly thirty-two, also agreed to marry Elizabeth of Valois, the fourteen-year-old daughter of Henry II of France, hoping through this marriage alliance to isolate Elizabeth of England, who had refused his offer of marriage. At peace now with France, Philip spent some time organizing the administration of the Netherlands before he returned to Spain, never to leave the Iberian Peninsula again. With his return to Spain in 1559, his personal rule may be said to begin.

When Philip took personal control of the government of Spain he was not lacking in definite opinions regarding his kingship. He firmly believed that his right to rule had been bestowed on him by God and that he was accountable for his actions to God alone. Earlier he had made clear that he regarded his power as absolute, when he told the Cortes of Castile that he would rule without their aid if he desired to do so. Nor was he at this time without practical experience as a ruler. At the early age of sixteen, during his father's absence from Spain, he had served as co-regent with Cardinal Tavera. At all times Charles V had taken great pains to instruct his son in the art of government, even to drawing up minute instructions for his guidance. In these instructions two principles were stressed: Philip was counseled to listen to the opinions of everyone but to trust no one; and, secondly, to avoid hasty decisions because they were usually bad. As king he put both principles into practice literally. Distrustful and suspicious by nature, he feared to rely on his subordinates, aspiring to do everything himself. He was his own chief minister; and every matter, however trifling, had to be brought to his attention. With colossal industry Philip plodded laboriously on. Painstakingly he read the voluminous reports and petitions, drafting replies to the petitions with his own hand and copiously annotating the reports. Since he was unable to distinguish between weighty and inconsequential affairs, he frittered away hours on minutiae while neglecting serious matters. To him all of his work was important because it was God's work. Moreover, as Philip was irresolute and vacillating, his slowness in arriving at even minor decisions caused interminable delays which almost paralyzed the government. Even though the case was pressing, he could not be hurried. In one instance, under critical circumstances he left the dispatches of his ambassadors unanswered for eight months.

Basically, Philip's policies were the same as his father's. Like Charles he strove to uphold the supremacy of Spain in Europe and to maintain the various scattered territories he had inherited. Since the other European powers viewed Spain's predominance with envy, they made use of every opportunity to lessen it. In consequence Philip was almost constantly at war. Charles, recognizing the folly of perpetual warfare, had counseled his son to avoid armed conflict whenever possible. Moreover, Philip himself detested war; but the policy he adopted, and to which he adhered to the end, made it inevitable. Hence Spain, already burdened with debt at Philip's accession, was overburdened at his death. Always in need of money to finance his wars, Philip employed whatever means he could, good or bad, to secure it. Old taxes were collected to the last penny, and new ones were imposed over the protests of the cortes until the country was groaning under the ever increasing burden. He even resorted to such expedients as the sale of offices and patents of nobility, the levying of contributions on the clergy, the raising of voluntary and forced loans, and the sale of a monopoly on playing cards—all this despite the enormous sums which flowed into the royal treasury from the mines of Mexico and Peru.

Determined as Philip was to pursue the political objectives of his father, he was even more determined to uphold the Catholic faith. His mother had inculcated on him an intense devotion to the Catholic religion, and Charles had repeatedly exhorted his son to stand firm in the Catholic faith, to "love God above all else and serve Him devotedly." Philip early became convinced that God had chosen him to combat the forces of evil in the world, which to him were synonymous with opposition to the Roman Catholic Church. To maintain the supremacy of Catholicism became one of the great aims of his life, and mercilessly to trample down every shoot of heresy his most sacred duty. "I would rather," he declared, "reign in a desert than in a country peopled with heretics." Ideas of the reformers, in his opinion, were not only pernicious heresy; they were a form of resistance to his authority. Hence he issued vigorous orders for the persecution of heretics in Spain and in his other possessions. The Inquisition, with its *auto-da-fé*, was given a free hand. With the majority of Spaniards this policy was popular. After many centuries of warfare against the infidel, they shared Philip's desire for religious unity and rejoiced in his efforts to eradicate heresy.

Philip's religious zeal and uncompromising orthodoxy did not, however, keep him from quarreling with the Holy See. As long as the pope was in full agreement with his designs Philip was obedient and submissive. But when the vicar of Christ opposed him in any way or refused to aid him, the Spanish king retaliated against the supreme pontiff with great harshness. Philip did not fear papal excommunication, though he wished others to stand in dread of it. Jealous of his royal prerogatives, he was moved to demand that the pope exercise power in Spain only through him. At no time did he permit the head of the Church to interfere in the affairs of his states beyond the degree he thought proper. He was inflexible, for example, in his insistence that no papal bull be published in his domains until he had examined it and given his approval. When the decrees of the Council of Trent were promulgated, Philip accepted them only in so far as they did not infringe on his royal prerogative.

THE PROBLEMS OF PHILIP'S REIGN

One of the serious internal problems of Philip's reign was the revolt of the Moriscos or converted Moors who lived in the southern and eastern provinces of Spain. These were chiefly engaged in silk-weaving and agriculture, most of the other occupations being closed to them. Their social status was probably somewhat like that of the colored population in the lower South of the United States at the present time. As the Moriscos had been forced to accept Christianity, their conversion was naturally superficial. Outwardly they conformed to the practices of the Catholic Church, but at heart they remained strongly attached to their former religion and to Moorish customs. The Spaniards accused them not only of being insincere in their acceptance of Christianity but also of surreptitiously celebrating Moslem rites. It was further alleged that the Moriscos were in treasonable contact with the Turks and the Barbary pirates. There seems also to have been much resentment against the Moriscos because they were willing to work for low wages and were satisfied with small profits in trade. After repeated representations of their obstinate and incurable infidelity had been made to Philip, he finally yielded to the demands of the clergy against them by issuing an edict in 1566 which proscribed the use of Arabic and ordered all Moriscos to learn Castilian within three years. Furthermore, the wearing of Moorish clothes was prohibited, women were commanded to appear in public unveiled, and the use of Moorish names and surnames was forbidden; also the taking of hot baths according to the custom of the Moors was interdicted.

In 1526 a similar edict had been issued, but the Moriscos had succeeded in freeing themselves from its restrictions by bribery. This time the Spanish officials were more determined to enforce the decree. With professions of loyalty to the king, the Moriscos remonstrated that none of the usages which were forbidden had the remotest religious significance, that women wore veils from modesty, and that baths were for cleanliness only. Philip, however, turned a deaf ear to all their protests and entreaties. He would hear of nothing less than complete submission. In 1569 the accumulated hatred of the Moriscos burst into open rebellion. Though their attack on the city of Granada failed, the insurgents were able to hold out in the mountainous regions against the Spanish forces for two years. In 1570 Don John, the king's half-brother, took command of the punitive forces and by the next year succeeded in suppressing the insurrection. By an edict issued in 1570 Philip decreed that everyone who was not a Spaniard and a Christian must leave Andalusia. As a result the Moriscos were scattered in other parts of Spain. But their opponents were by no means satisfied. After the death of Philip II his successor, Philip III, was prevailed upon in 1609 to sign an edict for the total expulsion of the Moriscos from Valencia. In subsequent years similar edicts drove them from the rest of Spain. The number of those expelled has been variously estimated from 500,000 to as high as 3,000,000. Over against these estimates stands the figure of 101,694, exclusive of nursing infants, which was compiled by the commissioners who supervised the deportation. The findings of more recent scholarship indicate that this figure is "apparently much more complete than economic historians have believed." [1]

Outside of Spain Philip had to deal with the Turkish menace in the Mediterranean. Suleiman the Magnificent died in 1566. His successor, Selim II, though lacking the vigor of his father, continued the policy of conquest. In 1570 the Turks took the Venetian island of Cyprus and were thus in a position to threaten all the Christian states on the Mediterranean. Although Europe had for some time been alarmed over the progress of the Turks, mutual jealousies prevented the states from agreeing to any common action. At length in 1570 representatives of the pope, Venice, and Spain met in Rome to form a league against the Turks. The object of the league was the reconquest of Cyprus. Don John of Austria, Philip's half-brother, was made commander-in-chief of its forces. By the summer of 1571 a considerable fleet, composed of 264 vessels of all kinds, 29,000 men at arms, and 50,000 sailors and rowers, had been collected at Messina. Special prayers were offered throughout Catholic Europe for the success of the expedition, which moved against the Turks under a sacred banner sent to Don John by the pope. Every man fasted, confessed, and was absolved in preparation for the combat. On October 7, 1571, the fleet met the formidable Turkish navy of some 300 vessels and more than 100,000 men at Lepanto in the Gulf of Corinth. After some four hours of fighting Don John and his forces won a

---

[1] E. J. Hamilton, "The Decline of Spain," *Economic History Review*, vol. 8 (1938), pp. 168–179.

splendid victory. It was the first time the Turks had been defeated at sea.

The victory at Lepanto was greeted with universal jubilation throughout Europe. It made Don John the idol of Christendom. At the news of the victory the pope gave expression to his joy in the words of the Bible: "There was a man sent from God, whose name was John." But the fruits of the victory were not commensurate with the exultation it excited. The Turks, it is true, made no further advances, nor did they again threaten the northwestern shores of the Mediterranean. This, however, was due in greater measure to the internal decay of the Ottoman Empire than to the defeat at Lepanto. The advantage which the league gained by the victory was not improved. Don John was eager to sail immediately for the Dardanelles to intercept the Turkish ships which had managed to escape, and then to attack Constantinople. He dreamed of procuring for himself an independent kingdom at the expense of the Turks, and desired also to aid the Christians of the Ottoman Empire in throwing off the Turkish yoke. After Venice refused to participate in the venture, Don John appealed to Philip for support. The king of Spain vetoed the project from motives either of jealousy or of prudence. In 1573 Venice blasted all hopes of concerted action against the Turks by making a separate treaty with them. At length Philip put an end to all proposals by recalling Don John from the scene of his triumph and sending him to the Netherlands to put down the revolt which had broken out there.

The most vexing of Philip's problems was the revolt of the Netherlands. In 1566 they rebelled against his rule, and during the remainder of his reign the question of how to quell the uprising overshadowed all his other difficulties. Besides severely draining the royal treasury, the Dutch rebellion also affected Philip's relations with other rulers, particularly Elizabeth of England, who aided the Dutch. In the end his efforts met with only partial success; he managed to win back the allegiance of the Belgian Netherlands, but failed to subdue the Dutch. Assisted by the natural defenses of their country and by outside aid, the small Dutch nation fought savagely against Spain's strongest armies and ablest commanders until complete independence was achieved in the middle of the seventeenth century.[1]

[1] See the next chapter for an account of the Dutch War of Independence.

Though unable to reduce the northern provinces of the Low Countries to obedience, Philip did succeed in another undertaking. In 1580 the throne of Portugal became vacant and the Spanish monarch, taking advantage of a temporary lull in the affairs of the Netherlands, turned his attention to the problem of obtaining the Portuguese crown. He laid claim to it through his mother, the eldest daughter of King Manuel of Portugal. Others could present better claims, but Philip had an army with which to assert his. He needed his army. So great was the traditional hatred of the Portuguese people for the Spaniards that they declared another candidate king, in an attempt to forestall Philip, and armed to prevent the ruler of Spain from seizing the throne. It was all to no avail. The duke of Alva invaded the country at the head of a Spanish army, defeated the opposing forces without much difficulty, and proclaimed Philip king. At last the whole of the Iberian Peninsula was united under one sovereign. Besides Portugal itself, Philip annexed also the vast Portuguese dominions in America and India. But the union of the Iberian states was only temporary. Sixty years later the Portuguese freed themselves from Spanish rule.

Despite his newest success, Philip was surrounded by troubles which threatened to overwhelm him. The Netherlands were in revolt, Naples had risen against the financial oppression of its Spanish rulers, and disaffection was widespread in Portugal. Philip was also engaged in a struggle with the pope over the supremacy of the Church in Spain. In addition there was trouble from another side. Although the governments of Spain and England were professedly at peace, English seamen were inflicting indignities on the Spanish colonies in America and on Spanish shipping. Drake and Hawkins, and their comrades and imitators, did not stop at carrying on a contraband trade with the colonies of Spain in violation of Philip's regulations; they also plundered and destroyed Spanish settlements and preyed on Spanish commerce and treasure ships. This intolerable state of affairs drove Philip to action. He evolved a plan the execution of which, he believed, would recoup his fortunes at one stroke and compensate him for the failure of his previous projects. He would build a gigantic armada with which he would deal England a crushing blow. Once master of England, he could insure the ultimate triumph of Catholicism in that country. Soon the various ports of Spain were busy with the preparations for the great fleet, which the Spaniards, confident of its success, styled the "Invincible Armada."

Although Philip tried to conceal his intentions, they quickly became known in England. Elizabeth immediately entered into negotiations with representatives of Spain to avert the attack. But Philip did not trust Elizabeth's diplomacy, interpreting her negotiations as a ruse to delay the sailing of his fleet so that she might gain time for defense measures. The intrepid Drake, deciding that he could best defend his country by carrying the war to the enemy, collected a small squadron of ships and set out for the Spanish coast. In April, 1587, he suddenly sailed into the harbor of Cadiz and, as he later boasted, "singed the king of Spain's beard." He burned the galleons which lay in the harbor, seized some of the valuable stores that had been collected for the Armada, and destroyed the rest. He also demonstrated the impotence of the Spanish galleons against the English ships with their long-range guns.

But the lesson was lost on Philip. Undaunted by the English demonstration of might, he continued his preparations. Finally on May 30, 1588, the great flotilla sailed under the command of the duke of Medina Sidonia, whose qualifications for the post consisted of little besides courage. Hardly had the Armada put to sea when its troubles began. A storm damaged some of the ships so badly that a return to a Spanish port for repairs became necessary. It was July 12 before all the vessels were ready to resume the voyage. At the last moment Sidonia advised Philip to abandon the enterprise, but the king, having once determined upon the plan, turned a deaf ear to the advice. From every church and altar in the land fervent prayers arose for the success of the expedition. Philip himself spent hours each day upon his knees, and even arose during the night to implore divine aid.

The Spanish fleet numbered about 130 vessels carrying some 19,000 soldiers and 8000 seamen.[1] Most of these ships were armed merchant vessels. Less than half were efficient men of war. It was not Philip's object to crush England at sea. The Armada was essentially a monster convoy which was to transport an army to the shores of England for the purpose of conquering that country by a land campaign. According to the general scheme the Spanish

[1] The total tonnage of the 130 ships was 57,868, which is less than that of the Cunard liner *Queen Mary.* See R. T. Davies, *The Golden Century of Spain* (1937), p. 214.

fleet was to sail into the English Channel and effect a contact with the duke of Parma, who was in the Netherlands with a force of 17,000 troops. After Parma's army had been taken on board, the fleet was to proceed to a point on the English coast near London where the troops were to disembark for the invasion of England. But the plan left too much to chance. It did not allow for a naval battle with the English or seriously take into account the inevitable presence of the English navy in the Channel. It seems to have been based on the strange supposition that the English would not attack or that they would flee precipitately at the sight of the Spanish ships. It also omitted the definite selection of a suitable point at which the junction with Parma's army was to be made. Above all, the plan ignored Parma's suggestion that the Armada seize a harbor—Flushing, for example—where it would be protected from the onslaughts of the enemy during the embarkation of the Spanish troops.

England was not unprepared for the coming attack. The delay in the sailing of the Armada occasioned by Drake's feat at Cadiz gave the English an opportunity "to set doune such meanes as are fittest to putt the forces of the Realme in order to withstand any invasion." The patriotic spirit of the English was aroused, and all creeds and classes vied with each other in making preparations to resist the Spaniards. Militia was trained, fortified camps were established, and beacons and bonfires were made ready to inform the people of the advent of the foe. Since the English royal navy consisted only of thirty-four ships, every effort was made to find other ships and arm them. Various seaports contributed, and privateers increased the number until the aggregate reached almost two hundred. In total tonnage there was little difference between the rival fleets; but in nautical skill and in gunnery the English had a decisive advantage. The smaller and lighter English ships moved much faster and were more easily handled than the clumsy galleons. Furthermore, the English ships were built with a low forecastle, whereas the high upper works of the Spanish galleons made them easy targets for the English guns, which could fire three times to the Spaniards' one. Lord Howard of Effingham, an experienced and courageous officer, commanded the English fleet. His judgment, coolness, and caution were in no small degree responsible for the defeat of the Spaniards. As assistants he had three of the bravest and most expert seamen of the age: Sir Francis Drake and Captains John Hawkins and Martin Frobisher.

After their attempts to meet the Spanish fleet off the coast of Spain were frustrated by storms, the English commanders decided to await the Armada in the Channel. Late in July it finally hove in sight off the English coast and on July 30 entered the English Channel. From one end of England to the other, beacon fires announced the arrival of the enemy. The English troops marched to their allotted stations along the coast; even the country people, according to an eyewitness, "forthwith ranne doune to the seaside, some with clubs, some with picked stones and pitchforks." The English fleet did not immediately attack the Armada. Lord Howard believed that because of their size the Spanish ships would have the advantage in a close fight, and therefore contented himself with following the Armada with the intention of harassing it at every opportunity. Utilizing their speed and long-range guns the English ships bombarded the Spaniards, at the same time keeping out of range of the enemy. By these tactics they succeeded in disabling several ships and in inflicting considerable damage on others. At the end of a week the Armada anchored off Calais. Here they found that Parma was not ready to join them, a Dutch fleet having prevented him from making the attempt. Meanwhile the English commanders had called a council of war and agreed that they must force a decisive engagement before Parma could join the Spanish fleet. On the night of August 7 they took eight ships, filled them with pitch, sulphur, and other combustible materials, set them on fire, and sent them with the wind against the Spanish fleet. When the Spaniards saw the fire ships approaching, panic seized them. Anchors were lifted or cables hastily cut, and the ships drifted away to the north. Two were set on fire in the confusion, others ran afoul of one another, and several were badly damaged.

The next morning the English attacked the Spaniards in force off Gravelines. During the greater part of the day the battle raged fiercely. The Spaniards, whose one advantage lay in hand-to-hand fighting, were not swift enough to grapple with the speedy craft of their opponents. The English raked the Spanish ships with broadside after broadside, riddling their hulls and turning their decks into charnel houses. By nightfall they had sunk four Spanish ships and taken or disabled others. The Spanish fleet was not destroyed, but Medina Sidonia realized that he was hopelessly beaten. The morale of his men was shattered, his ammunition was exhausted, and many of his ships were unfit for further combat. Fearing the destruction of his entire force, he abandoned further attempts to carry out the enterprise and headed his battered fleet northward to return to Spain around the west of Ireland. On the homeward journey wind and waves wrought the final ruin of the "Invincible Armada." A violent gale arose, scattering the ships far and wide. Nineteen were wrecked on the coasts of Scotland and Ireland, and their crews were butchered by the Irish or by English officials. Thirty-five other ships disappeared without a trace.

When the remnants of the once mighty Armada straggled into the ports of Spain, it was found that sixty-three ships had been captured or destroyed. The loss of life was proportionately great. Besides those who were killed in battle, drowned, or butchered, many died of disease, cold, and famine. No accurate statistics of the total loss of life have ever been published. A moderate estimate sets the number at about 10,000. So ended Philip's projected invasion of England. The sole achievement of the Armada had been the capture of a few English pinnaces laden with fish, homeward-bound from their fishing grounds. In the whole series of actions the English ships had incurred only slight damages and lost only about a hundred men. But the English suffered heavy losses from the spread of a pestilence in the fleet on the way back to Plymouth from the North Sea.

The defeat of the Armada did not end the war between Spain and England. English buccaneers continued to harry the Spanish trade routes, while Drake sacked Vigo and Corunna, and Lord Howard later attacked Cadiz, destroying its docks and arsenals. Philip, far from crushed by the defeat of his plan, stubbornly set himself to make another attempt to conquer England. The opportunity, however, did not present itself. His attention, which had been centered on England, was again divided between England, France, and the Netherlands. Particularly in the situation in France he saw the possibility of regaining some of the prestige he had lost. If he could dominate France or at least keep it divided, he would have no great rival on the continent. So he sent an army to aid the Catholic League in its fight against Henry of Navarre. But Philip's hopes were blasted when Henry, seeing that the people of France as a whole would not accept him as king unless he became a Catholic, abjured Protestantism and entered the Catholic Church, a move which won for him the hearts of the French people. In the summer of 1598 Henry IV and Philip II signed the treaty of Vervins, by which each restored all conquered territory and relinquished all claims to the possessions of the other.

The last days of Philip were indeed trying. While his body was being consumed by a lingering disease, his mind was tortured with anxieties about the future of his country. On almost every side he saw his ambitions wrecked, his prayers unanswered, his dreams dispelled, and his hopes frustrated. When he felt his end approaching, he had himself carried in a litter to the Escorial.[1] There for nearly two months his body was racked by the most excruciating pains. In various parts of his body there appeared great gangrenous ulcers teeming with maggots and discharging putrid matter which filled the room with a stench that only the most robust of his attendants could bear. But Philip endured it all with unflinching fortitude. Not a word of complaint escaped his lips. To the end he remained as serene and impassive as ever. After making arrangements for his own funeral down to such details as the order of the procession, Philip died on September 13, 1598, at the age of seventy-one.

Although regarded by his contemporaries as the most powerful monarch in Christendom, Philip was, on the whole, a glorious failure. He was always on the verge of great accomplishments, but was able to carry few plans to a successful conclusion. Staking all upon the predominance of Spain in Europe and upon the victory of Catholicism, he labored strenuously and conscientiously, only to fail in the end. Yet Philip was immovable in the conviction that his policy was right because, as he believed, he was on the side of God. His far-reaching plans were not national, but religious and dynastic. They aimed solely at extending the influence of the Catholic religion and the power of his house. To his Spanish contemporaries he was Philip the Prudent, an estimate in which neither the non-Spaniards of his time nor later generations have concurred.

[1] A gigantic structure, which was at once a monastery, a palace, and a mausoleum, built by Philip in the bare, wind-swept hills near Madrid.

THE DECLINE OF SPAIN

The century after the death of Philip II was for Spain in many respects a period of rapid decline. During Philip's reign Spain, at least until the disaster of the "Invincible Armada," still appeared the greatest of world powers. The Spanish army was regarded as the most formidable in Europe, and on sea only the Turk had dared to contest the Spanish supremacy, with disastrous results. But the forces of disintegration were at work, though unobserved. Even after the failure of the Armada had demonstrated that Spain's mode of naval warfare was obsolete, the glamour of the Spanish name veiled the decay of Spain from the eyes of Europe for a long time.

During the last quarter of the sixteenth century symptoms of Spain's economic decline had already manifested themselves, but the condition did not become general until the beginning of the seventeenth. One of its causes was the long and costly wars in which Spain was involved. The fruitless attempts of Charles V and Philip II to dominate Europe not only drained the country of its precious metals but also necessitated constant borrowing on usurious terms from the great banking houses of Europe, with a consequent increase in the national indebtedness and the burden of taxation. Nevertheless, the successors of Philip II were to continue the wars throughout the seventeenth century, with only brief intervals of peace. In the sixteenth century the cost of the expeditions had been offset to a large extent by the vast sums that flowed into the royal treasury from the mines of America; but by the beginning of the following century the income from this source was failing, and by the middle of the century it was to decline to only a small fraction of its former volume. Moreover, in the seventeenth century the Spanish nation no longer had the recuperative power to repair the economic losses of the wars through its industrial production.

Spanish industry, it appears, was able to hold its own during most of the sixteenth century.[1] If the growth of population in such important industrial cities as Burgos, Segovia, and Toledo during

[1] The present state of historical knowledge does not permit final statements regarding the economic conditions in Spain during the sixteenth century because, as E. J. Hamilton states (*American Treasure and the Price Revolution in Spain, 1501–1600*, p. 295), "only scanty data concerning the activity of agriculture, industry, and commerce in the sixteenth century are accessible."

the period from 1530 to 1594 is a criterion, industry even expanded considerably. The manufacture of silks, linens, and woolens flourished at least during the first half of the century. But the rise of prices resulting from the influx of Mexican and Peruvian silver reacted unfavorably upon production. The consequent rise in wages caused an increase in the cost of manufacture which placed a handicap on Spanish goods in competition with the goods of Holland, England, and France. Foreign merchants in time even gained control of the home markets of Spain because they could furnish goods of the same quality much cheaper despite the high tariffs on imports. What remained of the native industries was further crippled by the *alcabala* (a tax on every article sold within the realm) and by internal customs duties. Of the sixteen thousand looms which had been turning out silk and wool at Seville in the reign of Charles V, only four hundred remained at the death of Philip III in 1621. Toledo, which in the sixteenth century had boasted fifty woolen manufactories, had only thirteen in 1665. Ultimately, the manufacture of woolen cloth declined until only a few factories remained, and these produced but a poor, coarse type of cloth. Woolen cloths of a better grade were imported from other countries despite the superb quality of Spanish wool.

Like Spanish industry, Spanish commerce also declined sharply in the seventeenth century. In the previous century Spain had boasted the second largest merchant marine in Europe, being outranked only by the Dutch. But the seventeenth century tells a different story. To commerce as well as to industry the rise of prices was detrimental, decreasing exports and even the building of ships. By the end of the century shipbuilding had virtually ceased; and with the exception of the trade with the Spanish colonies, what remained of Spain's commerce was largely in the hands of foreigners.

In the seventeenth century agriculture also went the way of industry and commerce. Previously cotton, sugar-cane, rice, and the mulberry tree (on the leaves of which the silkworm feeds) had been widely cultivated in southern Spain. Enough olives had been produced to supply the needs of Spain, Spanish America, and a large part of Europe for olive oil. From Cadiz and Seville large quantities of wine had annually been exported, particularly to Spanish America, where the cultivation of the grapevine was prohibited. But after 1575 Spanish agriculture began to show signs of a decline which became more rapid in the seventeenth century. Undoubtedly the expulsion of the Moors was one cause of the agrarian decay, but it was not the primary factor, as is so often stated. More potent were the excessive taxation, the deleterious effects of the law of primogeniture, which made for large-scale landholding, and the preservation of certain lands by ordinance as ox pastures, swine fields, and meadows for non-migratory sheep. Still another cause was the herding privileges granted to the association of sheep-owners, called the Mesta, whose "flocks of merinos migrated every spring from the grassy plains of Andalusia and Estremadura to the mountains of the Asturias and the kingdom of Leon and whose object was to preserve the whole intermediate country as grazing ground, without which such migrations would not be possible." By the end of the century, however, the Mesta itself was decadent. Whatever the exact combination of causes, the fact remains that Spanish agriculture declined rapidly in the seventeenth century. The production of olive oil dropped to a fraction of the former output, and the number of mulberry trees decreased until they threatened to disappear entirely. According to a report of the year 1619 the number of livestock in the bishopric of Salamanca had decreased by sixty per cent since 1600. It appears, however, that the agricultural decline was less severe than the industrial, notwithstanding the contemporary complaints that Spain was fast becoming an uncultivated desert.

Besides the industrial, commercial, and agricultural deterioration there was also a decline in the population. In spite of the emigration to the New World and the heavy losses of life in the continuous wars, the population of Spain, exclusive of Portugal, appears to have increased by approximately fifteen per cent in the sixteenth century, but the first decade of the next century saw the population diminishing rapidly. A junta or council appointed by Philip III in 1618 to suggest a remedy reported that "the depopulation and want of the people in Spain is at present much greater than was ever seen or heard of before . . . it being in truth so great that if God does not provide a remedy for us . . . the crown of Spain is hastening to its total ruin and destruction." The Cortes of Castile, alarmed over the decrease in the population, stated in 1621 that "there will soon be no peasants to work on the land, no pilots on the sea, none to marry." To supply the lack of farm hands, foreign laborers were imported, particularly from France. Such workers were but "birds of passage," remaining only from seedtime until harvest, when they would depart with whatever gains they had been able to accumulate.

Various explanations have been put forward to account for the decline of the population. The expulsion of the Moors was responsible in part. Furthermore, the wars in which many thousands of young men lost their lives constantly drained the population. But the basic cause is probably to be sought in the economic conditions of the time. As these conditions grew worse, large numbers of Spaniards went to America in the hope of improving their lot. The marquis of Villars wrote to Louis XIV that in 1681 no less than six thousand emigrants left in one fleet because they were unable to subsist in Spain. As a result of the economic decline the number of marriages also decreased. Many young Spaniards who were oppressed by economic worries and government taxes sought the protection of the monasteries or joined the secular clergy. As early as 1603 Philip III met with leading theologians of the Spanish Church to devise means of checking the increase in the number of clerics. Though entrance into religious orders was made more difficult, it did not effectively limit their growth. According to one computation there were nine thousand monasteries in Spain at the end of the seventeenth century, and about 150,000 monks and priests who were devoted to a life of celibacy. All of the foregoing factors combined to reduce the population of Spain at least a quarter, and perhaps as much as a third, during the century after the census of 1594.

The economic conditions in Spain were rendered more critical by a widespread aversion to honest labor. This was true particularly of the nobles, for they generally regarded all work as beneath their dignity. A similar attitude prevented even the hidalgos or inferior nobles from practicing a craft or entering one of the professions. Since, according to the law of primogeniture, the eldest son inherited the family estate, the younger sons entered the service of the Church or the state, or spent their lives in poverty and idleness. In no other country were there as many nobles in proportion to the total population. For example, it has been calculated that at the end of the seventeenth century there were four times as many nobles in Spain as in France, which had a much larger population. Their contempt for labor did not fail to affect the lower classes. A French lady, during her travels in Spain about the middle of the seventeenth century, wrote: "The peasants will more willingly endure hunger and all severities of life than work." On the other hand, many persons who were willing to work could hardly earn the bare necessities and were forced into the ranks of the shiftless by oppressive taxation. Little wonder, then, that the vagabonds and vagrants increased until they became the curse of the land, while fields lay untilled for the lack of laborers.

Finally, the century after the death of Philip II was also a time of political decadence. Charles V and Philip II had closely supervised the government of their realms, but under their less diligent successors the rule passed into the hands of ministers and favorites who were more concerned with their own good than with the welfare of the state. Thus Philip III (1598–1621), son of Philip II, was a well-meaning but weak ruler who was little more than the tool of his favorites. His father had undoubtedly foreseen this when he said shortly before his death: "God who has given me so many kingdoms has denied me a son capable of ruling them." Indifferent to the widespread distress among the people, Philip III and his unscrupulous minister, the duke of Lerma, continued to squander the revenues which the tax collectors squeezed out of the impoverished country. The next king, Philip IV (1621–1665), was, if anything, even weaker and more frivolous than his predecessor. As the financial distress grew more and more acute both Philip III and Philip IV did not hesitate to resort to currency inflation, with the result that the other nations drained the gold and silver from Spain until the coinage of the country consisted largely of copper, the value of which the government sought to sustain by law. To prevent the outflow of specie, Philip IV in 1624 decreed the penalty of death and confiscation of property for all who were guilty of exporting it or of aiding others to do so, but even this decree proved ineffectual. Meanwhile the government continued its efforts to carry on the foreign policy of Philip II, thereby becoming involved in wars which drained Spain of blood and treasure without winning for it any lasting benefits.[1] In

[1] The wars in which Spain was involved in the seventeenth century, after the truce with the Dutch in 1609, were the Thirty Years' War, which was continued as a war between France and Spain until 1659, and the wars with Louis XIV. See pp. 342–350, 473–480.

the Iberian Peninsula the power of the Habsburgs was diminished by a successful revolt of the Portuguese in 1640, who chose the duke of Braganza as their king. In general, the story of the reigns of Philip III and Philip IV is one of inefficiency and exhausting wars.

The last of the Habsburg line was Charles II (1665–1700), also known as Charles the Bewitched. Sickly in mind and body, he was wholly incapable of directing the government. How steady the progressive degeneration of the Habsburg rulers had been is indicated by the statement "that Charles V was a warrior and a king, Philip II only a king, Philip III and Philip IV not even kings, and Charles II not even a man." Appropriately the reign of Charles II has been characterized as one of "royal anarchy" at home and of disaster abroad. As it appeared that Charles II would be the last of the line and that he might die at any moment, he was constantly surrounded by intrigues for the purpose of securing the succession. His death in 1700 was the signal for the outbreak of a general European war.[1] By this time the Spanish nation had declined to the status of a second-rate power.

SPANISH CULTURE

The period from the defeat of the Armada to the opening of the eighteenth century, though one of political and economic decadence for Spain, was nevertheless an era of great intellectual and artistic achievement. It may rightly be termed the golden age of Spanish culture. To this period belong most of the great writers and artists Spain has produced, and during it Spain made its greatest contributions to the intellectual and artistic wealth of the world.

The first of the great writers of the golden age was Miguel de Cervantes Saavedra (1547–1616). Little is known of his early life and education. Though his formal education appears to have been limited, he must at some time have read widely to have gained his thorough acquaintance with the literature of his country. The deep knowledge of contemporary life which he capitalized in his writings he acquired from experience. After 1570, the year in which he became a soldier, his life was for some years one of adventure. He participated in the battle of Lepanto with conspicuous bravery, receiving three gunshot wounds, one of which

[1] See pp. 477–479.

THE SPANISH ARMADA

PHILIP II

MARY TUDOR

TOLEDO *by El Greco* ST. JEROME *by El G*

THE SURRENDER OF BREDA *by Velasq*

crippled his left hand. This crippled hand was responsible for his nickname, "El Manco" (The One-handed), an appellation in which he gloried. Don John of Austria, the commander of the fleet, personally commended him for his valor. Some years later he was captured by the Algerian pirates and did not succeed in obtaining his release for five years. Upon his return to Spain, he could find no permanent employment. Therefore he decided to devote himself to literature. Previously he had written a number of sonnets, but now he turned to prose, publishing the novel *La Galatea* in 1585. When the "Invincible Armada" was being fitted out he interrupted his literary labors to act as agent for the collection of supplies. Sometime during the years that followed he began to work on his masterpiece, *Don Quixote*. Harassed by poverty and other troubles, he labored on until the first part was published in 1605. The untimely appearance of a spurious "Second Part" in 1614 moved Cervantes to write one himself and to publish it in 1615. In the following year, on April 23, he died. It is a curious fact of history that Cervantes and Shakespeare died not only in the same year, but within a period of ten days. Though Shakespeare may have read *Don Quixote* it is tolerably certain that Cervantes died without hearing Shakespeare's name.[1]

The plot of *Don Quixote* is well known. A Spanish nobleman becomes so absorbed in reading the chivalric novels which were in vogue at that time that his mind grows unbalanced. Believing himself to be a knight-errant, he sets forth to right all wrongs and to establish justice. As the word *quixotic*, which derives from Don Quixote, indicates, he is ridiculously chivalrous and extravagantly romantic. His antithesis is the unromantic and plebeian Sancho Panza, a simple peasant whom Don Quixote induces to accompany him as a squire. The narrative relates the adventures of these two heroes. Its primary purpose was simply to ridicule the chivalric romances of the day. As the author himself wrote at the end of the book: "My desire has been no other than to deliver over to the detestation of mankind the false and foolish tales of the books of chivalry." But the work developed into a graphic panorama of contemporary Spanish life, including all classes of society.

[1] Writers have often stated that both died on the same day. Although the date given for Shakespeare's death is the same as that of the death of Cervantes (April 23, 1616) they did not actually die on the same day. The date of Cervantes' death is according to the Gregorian calendar, whereas that of Shakespeare is in the old style. By the new reckoning, Shakespeare died on May 3.

Cervantes' *Don Quixote* is the most important single contribution of Spain to world literature. The book immediately became a favorite. During the first few months after its publication five editions of the first part appeared; the second part was no less a success. Few books have enjoyed such uninterrupted popularity —a popularity which continues unabated today. In the words of a leading Cervantes scholar: "The consensus of opinion of three hundred years has found in the world of Cervantes a note of universality, a wide humanity, a generous sympathy with the frailties and aspirations of all men. Every new and changing generation has recorded the living appeal of his great book." [1] Few books have been translated into more foreign languages. By many literary critics it is considered the greatest novel ever written. It made its author one of the great personages in the literary history of the world. In Spanish literature he occupies the place which Shakespeare holds in English, Goethe in German, and Dante in Italian. Even if he had not written *Don Quixote* he would hold a high place among Spanish novelists because of his *Exemplary Tales*, which appeared in 1613. His poetry and dramas, however, are only mediocre.

The second great literary figure of Spain's golden age of culture was Lope Felix de Vega Carpio (1562–1635). Among Spanish dramatists he was the most universal in his genius, uniting in his plays all the tendencies of his predecessors. As a young man he enlisted in the "Invincible Armada" and was assigned to the galley *San Juan*, one of the few that survived the disaster. Having begun to write plays while attending the University of Alcala, Lope de Vega devoted himself entirely to literature after his return from the fateful expedition. His powers of production were prodigious. One of the most voluminous writers of all time, his works comprise a whole literature—novels, epistles, epics, innumerable sonnets, odes, elegies, ballads, and, above all, dramas. The number of plays he wrote is almost incredible. According to his own statement, he finished many of them within twenty-four hours. An early biographer has estimated that he wrote 1800 comedies (*comedias*) and 400 religious plays (*autos sacramentales*), an estimate which is based on the statements of Lope himself. This number appears to be greatly exaggerated. The most trustworthy list of Lope's writings includes the titles of 723 comedias, some of

[1] R. Schevill, "Cervantes and Lope de Vega," *Spanish Review*, vol. 3 (1936), p. 14.

which are of doubtful authenticity. It cannot be denied, however, that many of his dramas may have disappeared. Only 426 of his comedias and about 50 autos sacramentales of unquestioned authenticity have survived. To Lope the writing of dramas was a kind of amusement which he refused to take seriously. Like Shakespeare, he did not think them of much artistic value. Yet it was his dramas that have established his fame. Among his nondramatic works there is not a single one that is outstanding.

As Lope's dramas were written hastily in response to popular demand they lack the philosophical depth and the smoothness of finish which only deliberate and careful execution can produce. The principal characteristic of these pieces is their national inspiration. Whereas Shakespeare's work is unbounded by the limits of race and age, that of Lope remains essentially Spanish. Two of the most characteristic of his comedies are *The Widow of Valencia* and *The Peasant Girl of Xetalfi*. Many of his plots were taken from the Bible, the lives of saints, novels, ballads, and chronicles, but he could create new plots about as fast as he could rework old ones. His power of invention was inexhaustible; his imagination so fertile that he anticipated most of the dramatic situations which have been used since his time. He also possessed an extraordinary mastery of dialogue and a rare facility in versification. Lope dazzled Spain with his creative powers. Few men of letters have experienced such popularity, such a succession of triumphs as he enjoyed. Though his private life was a series of scandals, he was idolized by the people and honored by the king of Spain and the pope. His domination of the contemporary world of Spanish letters is comparable to that exercised by Voltaire in France at a later time. When he died in 1635 he was interred with pomp befitting a king. Lope de Vega gave to the Spanish theater the stamp which long continued to characterize it. Almost all the Spanish dramatists for centuries after his death were deeply indebted to him.

Another great figure of the golden age is Pedro Calderon de la Barca (1600–1681). Like his predecessor Lope de Vega, Calderon in his turn dominated the Spanish literary world for many decades. His talents, however, were less varied than those of Lope. He wrote nothing of importance outside of his dramas, which number about 120 comedias and 70 autos sacramentales. His dramas are more finished, more mechanically perfect than those of Lope, and he also excels in the greatness of his conceptions.

His style is brilliant, but at times somewhat labored and pompous. Calderon lacked the creative genius which characterizes Lope's work. Rather than invent a new plot, he preferred to recast an old one. Often he took the most extreme liberties with historical facts. His dramas are also more serious and abstract than those of his great predecessor. Furthermore, they are without humor. He was like Lope, however, in being preëminently Spanish. The ideals of his land and people afforded the chief inspiration of his plays, and it is upon the fact that he portrayed the essential traits of the Spanish mind that his greatest claim to fame rests. He added no new forms of dramatic composition to the Spanish theater; nor did he effect any important changes in those established by his predecessors. With Calderon's death the golden age of Spanish literature came to an end. The phenomenal fertility of its writers gave way to a spiritual exhaustion which lasted until the second half of the eighteenth century.

While Spain was declining economically and politically, its art as well as its literature attained its finest growth. Spanish painting, because of the country's close political connection with Italy, had been considerably influenced by the Italian masters in the sixteenth century. So great was the admiration for Michelangelo, Leonardo, Raphael, and other artists of the High Renaissance that their works became the great ideal of Spanish painters. The Italian influence was beneficial in many ways. For example, it led the Spaniards to a more careful study of drawing and composition. But blind admiration caused many to lose their individuality and become mere imitators who conformed to the Italian manner so thoroughly that they were known as Mannerists. Little by little, however, a native Spanish art developed which was the peculiar expression of the character of the Spanish people, particularly of their religiosity, their asceticism, and their ecstatic sensuality. These qualities, rendered with the frankest realism, gave a distinctive note to Spanish paintings of the golden age. Since the Church and royalty were the chief patrons of art, portraits and religious subjects predominated.

The greatest Spanish painter of the late sixteenth and early seventeenth centuries was Domenico Theotocopuli (c. 1547–1614), commonly called El Greco (the Greek) because of his Cretan birth. His work expresses more the spiritual than the naturalistic spirit of Spanish art. Having studied for some time in

Italy, where he was impressed by the coloring of the Venetian paintings and the forms of Michelangelo, he journeyed to Spain and settled in Toledo. His first paintings show the Italian influence strongly; but as his art developed, he slowly acquired a manner of his own. His paintings became more and more subdued in color and showed a heightened emotional intensity. El Greco had entered on the phase of his career in which he was concerned chiefly with the expression of mysticism, of which he is the foremost exponent in Spanish painting. The masterpiece of this period is the *Burial of Count Orgaz*, probably his most famous picture. It depicts the body, supported by St. Augustine and St. Stephen, being lowered into a vault surrounded by a group of high dignitaries. Above, the firmament is open and Christ and the Virgin are awaiting the spirit of the departed, while a host of angels hover about. The painting is a strange combination of realism and of visionary power. In his later work this trend becomes more accentuated. The chief effect aimed at is the imaginative, and to achieve this he sacrifices verisimilitude. His color becomes harsh, his lines exaggerated, and his figures elongated and twisted, in utter disdain of outward reality. His *Toledo in the Storm* may be regarded as the forerunner of imaginative landscape painting. Though modern painters have found him a source of inspiration, many of his contemporaries viewed his work as that of a madman. At El Greco's death the trend toward realism in Spanish painting had become so strong that he left few disciples.

The great representative of Spanish painting of the seventeenth century, one of the masters of all time, is Diego Velasquez (1599–1660). His fame is of recent origin, for until the first quarter of the nineteenth century his works were unappreciated. Today he is recognized as the painter who anticipated to some extent nearly every movement in modern painting. His early training was acquired in the studios of several painters of Seville, the city of his birth. To his practical work in the studios he added scientific study to enable him to portray facial and bodily movement better. He was a realist from the start, aiming in his work to give a true, living representation of what he saw. He possessed the rare gift of being able to omit unnecessary details and to include only the essentials of a scene. His early works were genre and religious subjects. They include the *Old Woman Cooking Eggs* and *Christ in the House of Martha*.

In 1623 he settled in Madrid. A portrait of Philip IV which he painted in the following year so delighted the Spanish king that he not only engaged Velasquez as court painter but also granted him the exclusive right of painting the royal features. As court painter, a position he held for thirty-seven years, Velasquez was occupied largely with portraits of the royal family, fine examples of which are those of Don Carlos and the Infanta. He painted his royal patron no less than thirty times. Two brief trips to Italy, which broadened and deepened his taste, interrupted his long residence at Madrid. In the two decades following his first visit he painted besides portraits a number of hunting scenes, one of which is the *Great Boar Hunt*. On his second visit to Italy in 1648 he painted the portrait of Pope Innocent X, considered one of the greatest portraits ever painted. In the last period of his life he developed a style remarkable for its rendering of instantaneous impressions. His chief aim, in his own words, was to achieve "unity of vision"; that is, to represent only what the eye can take in at a single glance. It is in this respect that he is close to the modern impressionists who have turned to him for guidance and inspiration. One of his most famous pictures is the *Maids of Honor* (*Las Meninas*), which shows the Infanta Margarita Teresa surrounded by her court, with the figures of the king and queen, who are spectators of the scene, reflected in a small mirror in the background. The whole painting suggests an instantaneous photograph.

Peculiarly representative of the religious spirit of seventeenth century Spain was Murillo (1617–1682). Whereas Velasquez in his paintings was dominated by the natural, Murillo moved in the sphere of the supernatural. The relatively few religious pictures which Velasquez painted were treated in a realistic manner. In contrast, the spirit which pervades Murillo's work is mystical, combined with a realistic execution. Murillo was probably at his best in his representations of the Immaculate Conception, which he painted no less than fifteen times, earning for himself the title of "the painter of Conceptions." His models were the girls of Seville, but he surrounded them with the idealism of the teachings of the Church. Thus his representations truly express the Spanish comprehension of the Virgin Mother. Since the dogma of the Immaculate Conception was peculiarly the province of Spanish theologians, and was honored no less by the nation as a whole, his paintings took a deep hold on the hearts of the Spanish people. As pictorial translations of the dogmas of the Roman Catholic Church, Murillo's paintings have always had a wide popular appeal. Regarding them solely as works of art, critics have pointed in disparagement to the painter's want of technique, force, and originality. In the field of genre Murillo achieved considerable success with his portrayals of beggar boys, frowzy flower girls, and ragamuffin gipsies as he saw them in Seville.

As the death of Calderon marked the end of the great age of Spanish literature, so the passing of Velasquez and Murillo brought to a close the great age of Spanish art. The painters who followed them ushered in an epoch of imitation and affectation. Much art was produced, but it was largely devoid of both originality and vitality. There was to be no notable figure in the history of Spanish art until the appearance of Goya toward the end of the eighteenth century.

CHAPTER ELEVEN

The Rise and Decline of the Dutch Republic

THE NETHERLANDS BEFORE THE REVOLT AGAINST SPAIN

THE Netherlands or Low Countries, so called from their depressed position, included at the opening of the sixteenth century those territories between France and Germany which now comprise the kingdom of Belgium and the kingdom of the Netherlands (often loosely termed Holland). Ruled by many lords during the Middle Ages, the provinces of the Netherlands were gradually united under the rule of the dukes of Burgundy, and passed into the possession of the Habsburgs in 1477 through the marriage of Mary of Burgundy, the only child of Charles the Bold, to Maximilian of Austria, who later became emperor of the Holy Roman Empire. For administrative purposes the Netherlands were not one state, but seventeen provinces, each of which had its own laws, its own administration, and its own assembly of Estates. Some of the provinces also had their own stadtholder or local governor. There was, it is true, a States-General which met from time to time to consider problems affecting the country as a whole, but its power was strictly limited. The individual states were proud of their autonomy and zealously guarded it. When Charles V assumed the rule of the Netherlands, he sought to establish a more centralized system of government; but realizing how jealous the provinces were of their rights he proceeded with caution. He organized a number of councils to supervise justice, the police, and finances, and also formed a Council of State, composed chiefly of the greater nobles of the Netherlands, to exercise a general supervision over the other councils and also over foreign affairs. Nevertheless, the Netherlands still remained a loose confederation of provinces. In language the northern provinces were Dutch and the southern Flemish and Walloon.

The importance of the Netherlands lay in the fact that they were the seat of flourishing industries and a thriving commerce. Centrally situated between the northern and southern parts of Europe, at the mouths of the Rhine, the Meuse, and the Scheldt, the Netherland provinces were a natural center of trade. There the merchants from the north and the south brought their goods, either to sell them or to exchange them for other wares. In consequence the Netherlands became the general market of Europe, boasting such important cities as Antwerp,[1] Amsterdam, Ypres, Ghent, and Bruges. The southern provinces produced linens, woolen goods, laces, carpets, and tapestries. Many of these industries were to decline later in the sixteenth century, but during the first half of the century Brussels and Mechlin laces and Brussels carpets were famous throughout Europe, and Flanders still produced the finest kinds of cloth. Other important manufactures were Liège weapons, Namur leather work, Mons cloths, and the copper utensils of Dinant and Namur.

The most important industry of the northern or Dutch provinces was fishing. About 1380 an improved method of curing and barreling herrings, which permitted them to be preserved indefinitely, had been discovered by an obscure fisherman of Zeeland named William Beukels (d.1397). Such was its significance that Charles V later ordered the erection of a large monument over Beukels' grave at Biervliet. It was a most timely discovery, for the large shoals of herrings which had formerly frequented the coasts of Norway, Sweden, and Denmark had suddenly moved to the Dutch and British coasts. With their huge dragnets the Dutch gathered unlimited quantities of the fish, and preserved them for distribution throughout Europe. Because meat was forbidden on Fridays, on the many church holidays, and during the forty days before Easter, they found a ready market. The industry expanded

[1] See pp. 128–129.

until it employed thousands of fishermen, and also thousands of other persons who built and rigged the ships and fitted them with nets, casks, and salt. The rise of Amsterdam (by 1550 next to Antwerp the leading port in the Netherlands) was due largely to the fishing industry—a fact that is picturesquely expressed in the Dutch saying, "The foundation of Amsterdam was laid on herring bones." Another important consequence of the expansion of the fishing industry was the construction of the Dutch mercantile marine, which later threatened to monopolize the carrying trade of Europe.

On the whole, the inhabitants of the Netherlands were hardworking and prosperous, successful in agriculture as well as in commerce and industry. For the Habsburgs they were an important source of income, the richest jewel in the imperial crown. From them Charles V annually drew about two-fifths of the enormous revenue he squandered on his dynastic wars. But in the second half of the sixteenth century they rose in revolt against the rule of Philip II. After a bloody and devastating struggle the southern provinces were to remain subject to the king of Spain, while the northern or Dutch provinces were to fight on until their independence was unreservedly recognized in 1648.

The revolt was the result of a combination of causes, some religious and others political in nature. The outstanding religious cause was Philip's determination to extirpate all heresy in the Netherlands. Soon after Luther revolted against the Church, his ideas—and after them Anabaptist teachings—had penetrated into the Netherlands. Later, zealous Calvinist preachers who migrated to the Netherlands from France were gradually successful in supplanting Lutheranism and in making many converts among the Catholics. Charles V had viewed this spread of Protestantism with anxiety, and as early as 1522 he had taken steps to curb the diffusion of Protestant ideas by prohibiting the printing and sale of Luther's writings in the Netherlands and by organizing an Inquisition to search out heretics. Subsequent years saw the publication of nearly a dozen edicts against heresy, each increasingly severe. The harshest was the "Edict of Blood," issued in 1550, which decreed death for all who were guilty of possessing, selling, or copying heretical books; of destroying or in any way injuring the images of the saints; or of disputing on the Scriptures either privately or in public. Had the edicts been strictly enforced, they would have claimed a large part of the population as victims. As it was, hundreds were executed, the majority being Anabaptists who were social and political radicals as well as religious heretics. When Philip II succeeded his father, he organized a more determined campaign against heresy. Besides ordering the strict enforcement of the edicts against heresy which had already been promulgated, in 1560 he introduced a more effective Inquisition. This of course aroused a fierce resentment in those who had accepted Protestant doctrines.

In 1559 Philip excited further opposition to his rule by increasing the number of bishoprics in the Netherlands from three to fifteen. A change of this kind had been planned earlier in the century by his father, but had never been carried out. It was a much-needed reform, for the three old dioceses had been so unwieldy as to prevent efficient administration; but this was not the reason for Philip's action. There is no doubt that he was largely motivated by a desire to combat heresy more effectively, and also to strengthen his rule in the Netherlands. It was the latter aim which aroused apprehension. Since the bishops were to be nominated by the crown, it was feared that they would serve as its agents. Both the Catholics and the Protestants, therefore, protested loudly when the increase was announced.

Important as the purely religious issues were, they were thus not the primary causes of the rebellion. The number of those who opposed Philip II for purely religious reasons was comparatively small, for in the northern provinces as well as the southern the Catholics were in the majority. At bottom the revolt was an uprising against the absolute rule of a foreign dynasty. The Netherlanders regarded Philip II as narrow and cruel, but, above all, as an alien. This was particularly true of the Dutch, among whom a national feeling, based on a common tradition in language, literature, and art, in seamanship and in economic pursuits, was stirring. Philip's efforts to maintain the Catholic religion, many of the Dutch were convinced, were only a blind to conceal his real objective, the establishment of absolute rule in his dependencies and the consolidation of his empire. A number of facts, besides the increase in the number of bishops, gave strength to this belief; especially Philip's attempt to rule without consulting the native nobles. Whereas the nobles were trying to gain a larger part in the government for the Council of State, Philip's aim was to make this body a mere appanage of the crown. He chose other advisers for the regent, his half-sister Margaret of Parma, thereby virtually excluding the great nobles from a share in the government. In general, in the conduct of the government, Philip preferred to rely on his ministers or even upon foreign upstarts rather than upon the native nobility; and this in spite of the fact that he knew how intense were the hatred and distrust of foreign officials in the Netherlands. When it was reported to him that the Netherlanders objected to the foreign officials he remarked, "I, too, am a foreigner. Will they refuse to obey me as their sovereign?"

Had someone responded "Yes!" the answer would have been largely correct. As events turned out, the Netherlanders did refuse to obey Philip, and the reason was, in part, that he was a foreigner. Under Charles V there had been grumblings and complaints about the measures adopted for the repression of heresy, the vast sums levied on the people, and his efforts to centralize the government of the provinces. But Charles was a Fleming by birth, was raised in the Netherlands, cherished them as his homeland, and was regarded as a native prince. Philip, on the other hand, was to the Netherlanders a foreigner who knew neither Flemish nor Dutch. Moreover, he was cold, haughty, and inaccessible in comparison with his father. Hence, everything that Philip did was viewed with mistrust and suspicion. Finally the growing discontent vented itself in open rebellion.

THE REVOLT AGAINST SPAIN

In April, 1566, some four hundred nobles from the various provinces of the Netherlands congregated in Brussels to present to the regent Margaret of Parma a petition which they had drawn up. The petition requested that the Inquisition and the edicts against heresy be moderated and that the States-General be convened at regular times; it added that there was great danger of revolt if this were not done. According to report, when Margaret of Parma promised to give serious consideration to the petition one of her counselors exclaimed: "Is it possible that Your Highness can fear these beggars!" When this derisive remark reached the petitioners they adopted the name "Gueux" (Beggars), which gradually became the designation of all those who opposed Philip's government. Soon the cry of "Vivent les Gueux!" was heard not only in noble circles but also among the burghers generally.

While the petitioners were awaiting the answer of Philip, who according to his wont was temporizing, religious riots broke out. In Antwerp mobs roused to a high pitch of excitement by Calvinistic preachers entered the Catholic churches of the city, smashed the images and statues which adorned the buildings, broke the stained glass windows, defaced the paintings on the walls, and wrecked many altars. The wave of iconoclasm spread to other cities, and for a time many districts were in a state of turmoil. More sober leaders of the opposition, like the prince of Orange, exerted themselves to the utmost to repress the furious iconoclastic outbursts, and with their help Margaret of Parma was finally able to restore order. Besides inflicting incalculable injury on treasures of medieval art, the outbreaks compromised the cause of the patriots by prompting many Catholic nobles to withdraw their support from it.

When Philip was informed of the outrages, he firmly resolved to avenge them. He sent the duke of Alva to the Netherlands at the head of a force of some 10,000 veteran troops, with orders to punish summarily all those who had taken part in the disturbances. The powers conferred on Alva were those of a military dictator. The very announcement of his arrival spread consternation in the provinces, causing many to seek safety in flight to other countries. Some still hoped that he would be lenient. All such hopes were dissipated, however, when Alva organized a special tribunal, officially known as the Council of Troubles but popularly called the Council of Blood, to root out heresy and to try those who had participated in the riots or been in any way responsible for them. Margaret of Parma, finding herself superseded, resigned, warning Alva before she left for Italy that his policy would antagonize the people of the Netherlands. But he continued his bloody work. Often the accused were hailed before the council in batches, given trials that were farces, and then condemned to death. The property of the condemned was confiscated for the royal treasury. No one was safe from the accusations of enemies or paid informers. So severe were Alva's methods that the pope, and also most of Philip's advisers, protested against them. Alva himself boasted of having put to death more than eighteen thousand during the period he held sway in the Netherlands. It appears, however, that he exaggerated the number of his victims.

Among the members of the higher nobility who died on the scaffold were Counts Egmont and Horn. The execution of these leaders excited such wide indignation that many joined the ranks of the opposition to Spanish rule. Both had been found guilty of stirring up a plot against the king. The fact that their trial and condemnation violated a law confirmed by Philip himself, which stated that Knights of the Golden Fleece were to be tried only by their own order, seemed to raise no scruples in Alva's mind. William, prince of Orange, would have shared the fate of Egmont and Horn had he not fled to Germany. When he did not heed the summons requesting his return, his property was confiscated and he was publicly declared an outlaw.

The climax of Alva's tyranny was reached in 1569 when, to pay the expenses of his system, he imposed a tax of one per cent on all real or personal property, five per cent on the sale of landed property, and ten per cent on the sale of all movable goods. The last tax, which was not actually collected until 1571, proved so harmful to commerce and caused such widespread suffering among the working classes that protests poured in upon Philip from all sides. Gradually the opposition to the tax became so violent that Alva was forced to declare all raw materials and many textiles exempt, and finally to abolish it altogether. After six terrible years of oppression, he was relieved of his post in 1573, having failed to please his master, to placate the people of the Netherlands, or to suppress heresy in the Low Countries.

Meanwhile William of Orange, also called William the Silent, had been energetically raising money and troops in Germany. In 1568 he had definitely opened the war against Alva by taking the field at the head of a small force composed of French Huguenots, German mercenaries, and exiles from the Netherlands. But the early efforts of William and his small force met only with defeat. The first successes were to be won on the sea. In his capacity as sovereign prince of Orange, William had in 1569 issued letters of marque to a number of vessels which preyed on Spanish commerce under the name of "Sea Beggars" (Gueux de Mer). Soon the coasts were swarming with rovers who swept all Spanish shipping out of the North Sea and the English Channel. They also sought to avenge Alva's acts of cruelty by attacking Spanish settlements and by dealing sharply with the crews of the vessels they captured. Lacking harbors in which to take refuge, they had at

E SYNDICS OF THE CLOTH HALL *by Rembrandt*

WILLIAM THE SILENT

THE DUKE OF ALVA *by Titian*

A DUTCH SURGEON'S SHOP IN THE SEVENTEENTH CENTURY

A QUACK SELLING HIS CURE-ALL IN SEVENTEENTH
CENTURY HOLLAND

first used English ports with the connivance of Queen Elizabeth. But when the protests of the Spanish ambassador to England forced the queen to forbid them her harbors, the Sea Beggars seized the town of Brielle at the mouth of the Meuse in 1572. Emboldened by this success, the Estates of the province of Holland met at Dordrecht and openly declared William their governor (stadtholder), invested him with wide powers, and voted him supplies to conduct the war.

After Alva was recalled in 1573 the Spanish nobleman Don Luis de Requesens was sent to the Netherlands as governor-general. Requesens, a good soldier, firm administrator, and, above all, a proponent of moderation, suppressed the Council of Blood and attempted to effect a settlement of the differences between Philip and the people of the Netherlands. But his efforts were futile. The struggle continued with the Spanish forces under the leadership of Requesens administering a number of reverses to the "Beggars." Fortunately for the cause of the Netherlands, Requesens died in 1576 before he could gain a decisive victory. During the time that elapsed before the arrival of the next governor-general, representatives of both the Catholic and the Protestant provinces entered into an agreement known as the Pacification of Ghent. By this agreement, based on a religious compromise, the provinces pledged their mutual support to expel the Spaniards from the country at any cost. Hence when Don John of Austria, the half-brother of Philip and hero of Lepanto, arrived in the same year to take the place of Requesens, he found himself opposed by a united Netherlands. Nevertheless, his conciliatory attitude augured well for an early settlement. Don John had brilliant dreams of quickly pacifying the Netherlands, after which he intended to use the country as a military base for an invasion of England. His dreams were soon dispelled. On the one hand, William of Orange and his supporters refused to trust his promises; and on the other, Don John fell out of favor with Philip, who feared his ambition. Thwarted on all sides, he died in 1578, at the age of thirty-nine.

Circumstances were more favorable to Spain when the new governor-general, Alexander Farnese, prince of Parma, arrived in the Netherlands. Religious dissension had arisen in the States-General between the Catholics and the Calvinists, the former claiming that the latter were violating the religious pact by proselyting among the Catholics. Farnese made the most of the situation by playing on the fears of the southern Catholics and also by using his troops to force William of Orange to loosen his hold on the southern provinces. As he moved northward with his army, he drove the Calvinists of the southern provinces to seek refuge in the north, thereby greatly strengthening the Calvinist element there and giving to the Catholics undisputed sway in the south. In the end he succeeded in detaching the southern provinces completely by forming the League of Arras (1579) for the defense of the Catholic religion. The answer of the seven northern provinces[1] was the Union of Utrecht, which united them in defense of their rights against the rule of Philip. Although this union was regarded as only temporary, the articles of union became the constitution of the United Provinces. Henceforth the southern and northern provinces went their separate ways, the former again professing allegiance to Spain and the latter continuing their struggle to be free of it. From the Union of Utrecht to the proclamation of independence was only a short step. This was taken when in 1581 the representatives of the seven provinces completely renounced their allegiance to the king of Spain. The act of abjuration, often called the Dutch Declaration of the Rights of Man, was a pioneer utterance and set the model for declarations issued during the Puritan Revolution, the French Revolution, and the War of American Independence. The opening statement reads: "The people were not created by God for the sake of the Prince . . . but, on the contrary, the Prince was made for the good of the people." The relationship between ruler and subject, the declaration contends, is defined by the law of the country, and since Philip has not observed this law, the Dutch are justified in deposing him.

In 1584 the cause of the United Provinces received a severe blow in the death of William of Orange at the hands of an assassin. Philip, believing that William was the great obstacle to the reconquest of the Dutch provinces, had offered a large sum of money, and also a part of William's property and a title of nobility, to anyone who would either capture or kill the leader of the Dutch provinces. With these inducements as an incentive several unsuccessful attempts were made on the life of William. But in July, 1584, a young Burgundian, Balthasar Gerard, spurred no

[1] Holland, Utrecht, Friesland, Zeeland, Gelderland, Groningen, and Overyssell.

less by religious fanaticism than by the hope of the reward, managed to gain entrance to William's house in Delft and killed him with a pistol shot. Few persons in history have been as much over-eulogized or over-slandered as William the Silent, who for almost two decades resisted the power of Philip II. He was not, like Washington or Cromwell, a great military leader. As a soldier he had only fair success, but as a statesman and diplomatist he occupies a foremost place among his contemporaries. Moreover, in an age of religious fanaticism he stood on the side of moderation, strongly disapproving of the iconoclasm of his coreligionists. Philip II himself gave testimony to the importance of his doughty opponent as a leader when he placed such a high price on William's head. By the Dutch, William of Orange is gratefully remembered as "Vader des Vaderlands."

When Philip heard the news of William's death, he rejoiced, believing that the last obstacle to reconciliation between Spain and the Dutch Netherlands was removed. But Philip was miscalculating. Although the affairs of the United Provinces were at a critical stage, the guidance of William the Silent was not indispensable to the Dutch cause. William's place as military leader was taken by his second son, Prince Maurice, since his eldest son was a prisoner in Spain. While Prince Maurice gradually drove the Spaniards out of Dutch territory by his determined attacks, the Dutch fleets continued their raids on the commerce of Spain and Portugal, which since 1580 had been under the rule of Philip II. Yet, despite their successes and the many rich prizes they captured, the Dutch desired peace to settle their internal difficulties, and to make the most of their opportunities for commercial expansion.

So long as Philip II was ruler of Spain, peace was out of the question, except on the basis of complete submission by the Dutch. But after Philip II's death in 1598 negotiations were opened with his successor. Because the Dutch would accept nothing short of unconditional independence, the negotiations dragged on. Finally in 1609 a truce was concluded which provided for a general cessation of hostilities for twelve years. When the truce expired the Thirty Years' War was raging in Germany, and Spain was involved in it. Hence the Dutch had allies in the final phase of their struggle. Peace between Spain and the Dutch Republic was signed at Münster in January, 1648. Its terms declared the United Provinces free and independent, permitted the Dutch to retain

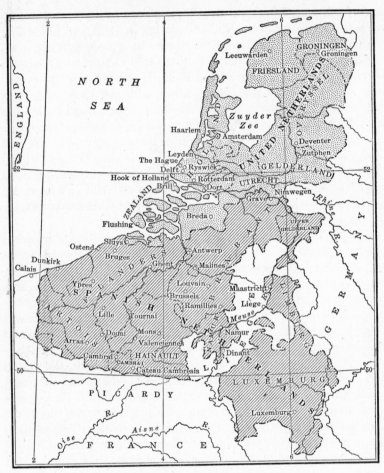

The Netherlands at the Truce of 1609

their conquests, and specified that the Scheldt was to remain closed. Thus terminated the long but successful struggle for independence by a small country of about three million inhabitants against one of the most powerful nations of Europe.

No sooner had the war endēd than internal disputes arose, for there were in the union of the northern provinces elements of dissension which were to cause almost constant strife. The so-called Dutch Republic was not a compact, homogeneous state, but a loose confederation of provinces, each of which remained a sovereign state with its own form of government. The confederation, in which Holland outweighed all the other states both in wealth and in importance, was based on the Union of Utrecht, which was drawn up under conditions of war and was ill-suited for a permanent government. So complicated was the organization of the government that it was difficult to tell just where the sovereignty resided. The States-General, which met at The Hague and was composed of representatives of the seven provinces, had supreme control of military and naval affairs. Actually, however, the members of the States-General could do nothing on their own authority. They received their instructions from the provinces they represented and could only act accordingly. A majority in the States-General could make a decision, but the decision was not binding for those who did not vote in favor of it. Besides the States-General there was also a Council of State, consisting of the stadtholders or governors of the provinces and a total of twelve deputies from the seven provinces.[1] This council exercised some power in military affairs and supervised the collecting of funds from the provinces for the common defense. Within the separate provinces the government was conducted by the stadtholders and by the provincial Estates composed of representatives of the nobility and the bourgeoisie.

With such a medley of overlapping and conflicting authorities unity of action would have been impossible without the steadying influence of the princes of the house of Orange, who gradually assumed the direction of foreign affairs and the general supervision of the administration of the republic. During the War of Liberation William the Silent and his successors had won so much prestige as leaders of the Dutch against Spain that they exercised an authority exceeding that of the offices they held. William the Silent had been the stadtholder only of Holland and Zeeland. Maurice (1584–1625) had become stadtholder of five provinces, and his successors, Frederick Henry (1625–1647), William II (1647–1650), and William III (1672–1702), were stadtholders in six. All were men of exceptional ability—probably the most able line of rulers of the seventeenth century. Gradually they attained to such dignity and influence that they were regarded both by foreigners and by the Dutch people themselves as the heads of the Dutch Repub-

---

[1] Three from Holland, two each from Gelderland, Zeeland, and Friesland, and one each from the other three provinces.

lic. During their tenure they were fairly successful in curbing the local feeling which constantly tended to hamper the unity of the United Provinces.

ECONOMIC EXPANSION

In the long and bitter struggle against Spain the Dutch had prospered, but the commerce and the industries of the southern provinces had suffered irreparable harm. The prosperity which was visible in Flanders and Brabant about the middle of the sixteenth century was only a memory when the seventeenth century opened. The iconoclastic outbursts, the raids of the Dutch, and, above all, the destruction wrought by the Spanish troops had blighted the prosperity of the cities of the south. Antwerp, the great center of European trade, started on the path of decline when it was besieged and captured by the Spanish army in 1585. As the Spaniards not only set out to eradicate Protestantism by closing all schools and churches, but also levied insufferably high taxes on the people, practically all the Protestants and many Catholics migrated to other places—particularly to the Dutch Netherlands. Almost twenty thousand merchants and artisans left Antwerp at one time, most of them settling in Amsterdam. Thereafter the Dutch completed the ruin of Antwerp by building forts on the Scheldt to intercept all ships bound for that port. Finally they blocked the approach to Antwerp entirely by sinking vessels loaded with stone in the channel of the river. Much of the commerce which had been the source of Antwerp's prosperity and greatness was thereby diverted to Amsterdam, which became the new commercial, industrial, and financial center of the Netherlands. In short, by the beginning of the seventeenth century the Dutch provinces had succeeded in wresting the economic supremacy of the Netherlands from the Spanish provinces.

Dutch industries, comparatively insignificant before the war, developed so tremendously during the struggle against Spain that the Dutch became the greatest industrial nation of Europe. This industrial preëminence was due in large part to the immigration of skilled artisans from the Spanish Netherlands. Textile workers from Flanders, Artois, and Brabant soon enabled the Dutch to produce some of the finest textiles in the world, including the serges of Leyden, the linens of Haarlem, and the velvets of Utrecht. Other important Dutch products were the beer of Haarlem, the tiles, chinaware, and pottery of Delft and Gouda, and the books and paper of Leyden. The great center of industry was Amsterdam, noted for goldsmiths and silversmiths who supplied Europe with fine jewelry, and for its marble works, tanneries, soap factories, sugar refineries, sawmills, and oil mills. A Dutch industry that merits special mention was shipbuilding. Already important in the middle of the sixteenth century, this industry expanded until it annually built more ships than all the other yards of Europe combined. Toward the end of the sixteenth century the output was reputedly two thousand ships a year; and this despite the fact, as Sir William Temple observed, that "they have no native commodities toward the building or rigging of the smallest vessel; their flax, hemp, pitch, wood and iron, coming all from abroad, as wool does for clothing their men." [1] The Dutch industry was standardized through specialization and division of labor, until the parts used in one ship would fit any other as well. Consequently ships could be built faster and more cheaply than in other countries. Shipbuilding naturally gave rise to many subsidiary industries which turned out such necessary products as rope, sails, anchors, cables, and nets. The fact that much of their machinery was driven by windmills, well suited to the country because of the prevalence of winds, gave the Dutch a great advantage in industry. Another important aid to industry was the excellent system of canals which permitted cheap transportation to and from the very doors of the factories.

During the war with Spain the Dutch continued to develop their fisheries, so that the annual income from this source had increased enormously by the beginning of the seventeenth century. Sir Walter Raleigh estimated the number of Dutch ships engaged in fishing along the coasts of England, Scotland, and Ireland at three thousand. "These three thousand fishing ships and vessels of the Hollands," he wrote, "do employ near nine thousand other ships and vessels and one hundred and fifty thousand persons more by sea and land to make provision to dress and transport the fish they take." [2] About the middle of the sixteenth century the Dutch had also turned to whale fishing, having learned from the

---

[1] *Observations upon the United Provinces of the Netherlands* (1668), p. 60.

[2] "Observations touching Trade and Commerce with the Hollander," published in his *Remains* (1681), p. 195. Raleigh's estimates are high. The actual number of ships engaged in fishing was probably nearer two thousand than three.

Basques how to boil down blubber. At first whales were abundant
in the vicinity of Spitzbergen, where both the Dutch and the English founded whaling stations. In the seventeenth century the
Dutch, because of a scarcity of whales there, were forced to move
northward to Davis Strait and the coasts of Greenland. Though
this made whaling more hazardous, they continued to realize
large profits despite the high losses in ships each year because of
the ice. The writer Pieter de la Court, whose book *Interest van Holland* was published in 1662, estimated that about twelve thousand
fishermen annually went north in pursuit of whales.

The greatest advance made by the Dutch during their struggle
against Spain was in commercial development. Commerce, in
fact, was the principal source of their prosperity. Having been international carriers on a moderate scale since the Middle Ages,
the Dutch during the century after 1550 developed the carrying
trade until their mercantile marine was unsurpassed. The wide-
bellied Dutch ships could carry more goods than those of other
countries and were also more easily manned, making transportation possible at much lower prices than their competitors charged.
In addition, the cleanliness and businesslike methods of the Dutch
won many friends. The French engaged Dutch vessels for both
their outward and homeward trade, and the English permitted a
large part of their exports and imports to be carried in Dutch
bottoms; much of the carrying trade of Scotland, Germany, Denmark, and Norway was also in Dutch hands. After the War of
Liberation ended, the Dutch gained a substantial share of the
carrying trade of Portugal and Spain. The transportation of grain
from the Baltic ports (Danzig, Lübeck, Riga) to other parts of
Europe, a profitable business which had formerly been controlled
by the Hansa towns, was gradually absorbed by the Dutch after
the middle of the sixteenth century. About the middle of the seventeenth century this trade in grain alone kept as many as seven or
eight hundred ships busy. By this time Dutch commerce had expanded until it seemed as if it would monopolize the carrying
trade of Europe.

Dutch trade, indeed, grew until it included most of the countries of the globe. The eagerness of the Dutch merchants to gain
new customers was proverbial. It was said that they would send
their ships into hell itself if they did not fear the burning of their
sails. In 1645 twenty times as many Dutch ships as those of other

nations sailed into the Baltic to sell or take on cargoes. To the northern countries the Dutch took spices, salt, wines, sugar, silks, and other textiles, returning with cargoes of cattle, wood for shipbuilding and casks, hides for fine leathers, furs, wool, caviar, arms, iron, copper, lead, tar, pitch, saltpeter, potash, honey, fat, and wax. Of great importance was the trade in wood from the Baltic regions, for the Dutch supplied not only their own ship-yards but also those of France and Italy. Shipments of tallow and wax were valuable because of the wide demand for candles, es-pecially for ecclesiastical purposes. Dutch traders were active also in other parts of Europe. Early in the seventeenth century their trade in the Mediterranean, which already included France and the cities of Italy, was extended by commercial treaties with Morocco and Turkey. Furthermore, hundreds of vessels were en-gaged in the river trade along the Scheldt, the Meuse, and the Rhine. The trade with Hamburg, also, was particularly heavy. It has been estimated that three thousand ships were plying be-tween Hamburg and Netherland ports in 1642.[1]

At the end of the sixteenth century the Dutch had also entered the eastern trade. Until Philip II closed Lisbon they had been the European distributors of the spices and other goods brought from the East by the Portuguese. But after Philip extended his rule over Portugal he tried to ruin the lucrative trade of his rebellious Dutch subjects by excluding them from Lisbon (1581). Confronted with the alternative of losing their trade or going straight to the source of supply, the Dutch, with their usual energy and enterprise, chose the latter. In 1594 a fleet of four ships appeared in the Indian Ocean under the direction of Cornelius Houtmann, who had formerly been in the Portuguese service in India. Though the ex-pedition was not a great success from the mercantile point of view, since Houtmann lost two ships and two-thirds of his men, others soon followed. Admiral van Neck, sent out by the merchants of Amsterdam with a fleet of eight ships in 1598, made treaties with the native rulers of Java and other islands, expelled the Portu-guese from some of their settlements, established Dutch factories, and finally returned to Holland with a valuable cargo of spices and silks. The success of this venture led other groups of Dutch merchants to dispatch fleets, so that no less than sixty-five ships were sent out before 1601.

---

[1] P. J. Blok, *A History of the People of the Netherlands*, vol. 4 (1907), p. 82.

Competition between the various Dutch companies became so keen and their interests so confused that it was decided to amalgamate them into one large corporation, the Dutch East India Company. From the States-General the company received a charter granting it a monopoly of the trade with the East. It was empowered to make war or peace, maintain fleets and armed forces, establish colonies, erect forts, and make treaties in the name of the Dutch government, but the States-General reserved the right of assuming control of the company at any time. As a governing board sixty directors were chosen from the various chambers of commerce which had joined the enterprise. Since this was too large for practical purposes, the actual direction of affairs was given into the hands of the Council of Seventeen or, as they were called, the Messrs. XVII. This council determined the size and equipment of the fleets which were sent out annually, the time of their departure, what goods were to be brought back, and where they were to be marketed. In the East the seat of the company's government was established at Batavia on the island of Java. There the Dutch governor-general, appointed by the Council of Seventeen, resided, and from there he directed the eight governments which sprang up in the various parts of the Dutch Empire of the East (Celebes, Amboyna, Banda, Ternate, Macassar, Malacca, Coromandel, and the Cape of Good Hope).

Under the direction of a series of energetic governors-general, the Dutch Empire was rapidly extended and consolidated. The chief scene of the early activities was the Moluccas or Spice Islands. As the native rulers hated the Portuguese, many of them joined forces with the Dutch to put an end to Portuguese rule. A fierce and bloody struggle ensued, which finally resulted in the expulsion of the Portuguese and Spaniards from the Moluccas. The Dutch East India Company vigorously pursued the expansion of its "empire." In 1641 its forces wrested Malacca from the Portuguese and with it the control of the trade with eastern Asia; in 1658 they expelled the Portuguese from Ceylon and in 1661 from the Celebes. Thus the Dutch gradually deprived the Portuguese of nearly all their eastern possessions. Other activities of the Dutch East India Company included the planting in 1640 of a colony in Formosa which became an important center for trade in such products as silk, lacquer work, and carpets. In 1652 the Dutch also founded a colony at the Cape of Good Hope, which had strangely been neglected by the Portuguese. This was to serve as a sort of halfway station to the East, a place where the ships could replenish their supply of fresh water, vegetables, and fresh meat. As early as 1634 the company had established trade relations with Japan, but in 1641 the Japanese government confined its trading operations to the island of Deshima and subjected the Dutch traders to humiliating restrictions. Nevertheless, the trade with Japan, of which the Dutch held a monopoly, for a time proved profitable.

At first the Dutch had consented to share the trade of the Moluccas with the English, but scarcely were they firmly intrenched there when they sought to expel the English as well as the Portuguese and Spaniards. Their determination, backed by a superior naval force, finally compelled the English to give way. This contest for the Spice Islands, particularly the massacre of Amboyna (1623) in which the forces of the Dutch East India Company put to death an English garrison of twelve men, aroused the bitter hostility of the English toward the Dutch and later helped to bring about a series of wars between the two nations. By 1632 the Dutch were supreme in the Moluccas, and for the time being the activities of the English were limited to India and the adjoining countries.

Since it was the primary aim of the directors of the Dutch East India Company to furnish the largest possible revenue, they sought to keep up prices by limiting the supply of spices. Not only did they burn the surplus in years of good harvest, but they also destroyed the clove and nutmeg trees in the areas they could not easily control. In this way, and by the forced labor of natives, the directors were able to garner enormous sums from the spice trade. The profits from this trade, and from the trade in silks, cottons, precious stones, and fine woods, were so large that the company was able to pay annual dividends ranging from $12\frac{1}{2}$ to 50 per cent for almost two centuries. As a result the value of the shares of the company had risen 500 per cent by the middle of the seventeenth century.

In 1621 the Dutch had also formed a West India Company. Earlier in the century Henry Hudson, an English seaman in the employ of the Dutch East India Company, had explored the coast of North America in search of a northwest passage to India and in 1609 had sailed up the river that still bears his name, claiming the region in the name of the Dutch Republic. Five years later the Dutch founded a settlement on Manhattan Island, calling it New Amsterdam, while the larger territory about it was named New Netherland. To combine the various interests of trade and settlement the West India Company was organized after the model of the East India Company and given the exclusive right to trade on the west coast of Africa, the east coast of the Americas, and on all islands between these coasts. Though the West India Company declared high dividends for a time, payments were not steady. The income of this company was necessarily precarious, for its larger profits were made from smuggling among the islands of the West Indies and from piratical raids upon Spanish and Portuguese shipping, particularly the Spanish treasure fleets. Within a period of fifteen years its ships captured no less than 545 Spanish and Portuguese vessels. During the War of Independence armed forces of the company also took a large part of Brazil from the Portuguese. But when the Portuguese became independent of Spain in 1640, they attacked the Dutch so vigorously that the latter, who were not being properly supported by the home government, were forced to abandon Brazil in 1654. Though the treaty of 1661 gave the Dutch freedom of trade with Brazil and Portuguese Africa, this was not enough to save the tottering corporation.

The only prosperous venture of the company was New Netherland. Under the vigorous rule of Peter Stuyvesant, who became governor in 1647, this colony flourished and its population increased until by 1660 it numbered about ten thousand. New Amsterdam, the capital, had about sixteen hundred inhabitants, the rest being distributed on Manhattan Island and along the banks of the Hudson. But the English, who had never conceded the rights of the Dutch to New Netherland, took the colony in 1664 and renamed it New York. Thereafter the Dutch West India Company survived for only a decade.[1] In part its failure was due to lack of support from the home government and also to a lack of colonists. So long as the Dutch could make an easy living at home, they showed little inclination to settle in an uncivilized country where life was hard and precarious. As for the Dutch government, its primary interest was in the East Indies, which yielded immediate and large returns.

---

[1] A new company was established on the ruins of the old one, but it did not receive a trade monopoly.

The failure of the Dutch West India Company may be said to mark the beginning of a general decline of the Dutch Republic. Having reached its peak about 1650, Dutch prosperity declined slowly toward the end of the seventeenth century, and more rapidly after 1700. While the Dutch were building up their commercial and industrial supremacy, England and France had been distracted by civil and religious dissensions. About the middle of the seventeenth century quiet was restored in both countries and the energies of both nations were more and more devoted to pursuits in which the Dutch were predominant. Both England and France, envious of the prosperity of the Dutch, began to contest for what they regarded as their rightful share of the world's business, and to do for themselves what the Dutch had previously done for them. Thus they proceeded to build merchant marines to carry the goods which had been transported in Dutch bottoms. In consequence the carrying trade which had been the backbone of Dutch commerce dwindled. This decline was hastened by the English Navigation Act of 1651, which decreed that no products of any other country in Europe should be imported into Great Britain or Ireland or any English possession except in British ships, owned and manned by British subjects, "or in such ships as were the real property of the people of the country or place in which the goods were produced, or from which they could only be, or most usually were, exported." Feeling between the Dutch and the English ran so high that war broke out in 1652. After a struggle of two years in which the Dutch were the heavier sufferers, peace was concluded in 1654. A second fierce maritime war broke out in 1664, lasting until 1666. Again in 1672 naval warfare was resumed for a period of almost two years. Though in the actual fighting the Dutch were a match for the English, Dutch commerce was more vulnerable because of its greater extent. In the end the greater resources of the English prevailed, and by the middle of the eighteenth century England's commercial supremacy was an established fact.[1]

In the eighteenth century Dutch trade suffered a general decline. The English absorbed much of the commerce with Russia, Sweden, Denmark, Portugal, and Brazil. The trade of the last

[1] For a brief account of the Anglo-Dutch wars see pp. 401–402, 414–416.

two countries, gained by the Dutch through the commercial treaty of 1661 with Portugal, was transferred to the English by the famous Methuen treaty in 1703, which opened the Portuguese markets to British goods in return for the admittance of Portuguese wines at a duty one-third less than that levied on French and German wines. Some idea of the diminution of Dutch trade may be gained from the toll records of the Dutch ships passing through the Danish Sound into the Baltic Sea. Between 1697, when more than four thousand Dutch ships passed through the Sound, and 1780, the number decreased about half, and fell still lower in the years immediately following. In like manner the eastern trade of the Dutch declined as that of England and other nations was extended. After 1700 the Dutch East India Company was able to maintain itself only with difficulty. Since its bookkeeping was a mystery to all except the highest officials, and its credit was therefore still good, it was able to borrow money to keep up the appearance of large profits and pay dividends until 1782. In 1798 it was finally dissolved. The enormous debts of the company were assumed by the Dutch government.

The Dutch sphere of economic activity was narrowed also in other respects. Aggressive rivalry on the part of the other nations crippled the Dutch industries. Not only did these competitors begin to manufacture many of the articles formerly made for them by the Dutch, but they also sought to exclude all Dutch products by high protective tariffs. The tariffs promulgated by Colbert in 1664, for example, practically barred many Dutch products from France. As his policy was adopted by other countries, the market for Dutch manufactures became more and more restricted. Not satisfied with handicapping the Dutch products by import duties, other nations also placed export duties upon raw materials which were indispensable to the manufactures of the Netherlands. All this ruined some industries and heavily injured others. The Dutch government itself hastened the decline by oppressive imposts and various restrictions. While clinging to the idea of free trade, it sought to liquidate the national debt incurred in the wars with England and France by the imposition of taxes on native products. On some of these, taxes were paid several times. Thus grain was taxed when it was sold; later the flour was taxed, and also the bread that was made from it. According to Sir William Temple no fewer than thirty taxes were paid on a certain fish sauce before it reached the table. The saying became proverbial in Holland that a dish of fish was paid for seven times —once to the fisherman and six times to the government. This handicap opened even the home markets to foreign competition, since the state levied no import duties. Dutch industry threatened to disappear altogether. Thus, of the three thousand looms which were turning out cloth in Leyden at the end of the seventeenth century, only about two hundred were in use in 1753. By the end of the eighteenth century only such manufactures remained as were not exposed to foreign competition.

Dutch fisheries suffered as well. After the first two decades of the eighteenth century they declined steadily. In the whaling industry the English and the Danes became competitors, while other nations soon began to supply herrings to markets formerly held by the Dutch. The great rivals of the Dutch in the herring trade were the Swedes, but other countries also realized the value of the fisheries. The English herring fisheries soon assumed great commercial importance, for English bloated or half-salted herrings seemed to please customers more than the pickled herrings of the Dutch. In some countries tariff barriers were raised against Dutch herrings, or their importation was entirely prohibited. By 1746 the number of Dutch ships engaged in the herring fishery was less than two hundred. Naturally, shipbuilding and its affiliated industries suffered severely. Gradually quiet settled upon districts in which the shipyards had formerly bustled with activity.

Although the eighteenth century saw their prosperity diminish on all sides, the Dutch did manage during much of it to retain their supremacy in banking. The enormous surplus which had been accumulated from commerce and industry in the seventeenth century enabled them to remain the great money-lenders of the world, with Amsterdam as the chief banking center. Since there was little opportunity for the Netherlanders to use the money in their own country, vast sums were invested in foreign securities and holdings throughout the world. Almost all the countries of Europe borrowed money from the Dutch. As the rate of interest was higher than at the present time, profits were considerable. But the latter half of the century witnessed grave financial crises, each of which caused the failure of a number of banks. Finally the Bank of Amsterdam itself, as previously stated, was forced into bankruptcy.

The economic decadence was accompanied by a decline of political and military power. The Dutch Republic, which in the seventeenth century had been one of the arbiters of Europe, sank in the eighteenth to the rank of a third-rate power. In the seventeenth century a succession of able stadtholders had controlled the forces of political disruption, but after the direct line of the house of Orange died out with the passing of William III in 1702, decentralization became the order of the day. Not only did each province act as an independent republic but the larger cities also asserted sovereign rights. The Dutch army, which under William III had been a potent instrument of war, was reduced in numbers and efficiency until it became an object of derision to other nations. When the French Revolution developed into a European war, the Dutch remained neutral until the French opened the passage of the Scheldt in 1792. Late in 1794 Pichegru led a large French army into the United Provinces. In an effort to save their country the Dutch again cut their dikes as they did when Louis XIV tried to conquer it. But this time the severe frosts of winter converted the water into solid ice over which the French army marched to take town after town. Amsterdam fell and the French cavalry even captured the Dutch fleet, which was frozen in the ice. Then the French drew up a new constitution, modeled on that of France, and transformed the old Dutch Republic into the new Batavian Republic. Various changes of government followed until, on the downfall of Napoleon, the great powers created the kingdom of the Netherlands.

DUTCH CULTURE

The material development of the Dutch during the century after 1550 was paralleled by an equally remarkable intellectual development. As early as 1575 William the Silent had founded the University of Leyden, and before the middle of the seventeenth century universities had been established in other cities (Franeker, 1584; Groningen, 1614; Utrecht, 1636; Harderwijk, 1646). Famed for the study of philology, these seats—particularly the University of Leyden—drew students from all parts of Europe. Furthermore, the migration to the United Provinces of some of the choice intellects of Europe, attracted by the freedom of thought offered them there, acted as a spur to intellectual life. The degree of toleration enjoyed by those outside the Dutch Reformed Church varied, it is true, according to local circumstances, but, in general, dissenters were not aggressively persecuted if they did not attack the state or proselytize openly. Sir William Temple wrote: "No man can here complain of pressure in his conscience, of being forced to any public profession of his private faith, of being restrained from his own manner of worship in his house or obliged to any other abroad." [1] The theories professed by Baruch Spinoza (1632–1677) would in any other country probably have meant imprisonment or even the stake. It was this freedom of thought, accorded particularly to foreigners, which made the United Provinces a haven for those who were being persecuted for their beliefs in other countries. Both Descartes and Locke took refuge there to develop their "systems" of philosophy. The large measure of liberty granted by the Dutch also permitted the publication in the United Provinces of many books which were forbidden elsewhere. Among the famous foreigners who published writings there during the seventeenth and eighteenth centuries were Galileo, Descartes, Pascal, Comenius, Hobbes, Locke, Montesquieu, Voltaire, and Rousseau.

The age of Dutch prosperity was also a golden age of Dutch literature. In the midst of the struggle for independence a succession of writers appeared who were instrumental in raising the Dutch language from a German dialect to the literary language of the Netherlands and in laying the foundations for a national literature. Many of the greatest figures in Dutch literature lived during this period. Among them were Roemer Visscher (1545–1620),[2] Pieter Cornelis Hooft (1581–1647), and Jacob Cats (1577–1660), who was affectionately known to his readers as Vader Cats and whose collected poems were often styled the "Household Bible." The greatest literary figure of the period, and also the greatest of Dutch poets, was Joost van den Vondel (1587–1679). His dramas, which combine dramatic power with lyric beauty,

---

[1] *Op. cit.*, p. 205.
[2] Visscher was an epigrammatist called the Dutch Martial by his contemporaries. Perhaps in no other period of history were so many epigrams produced as in the Dutch literature of this time. The purpose of most of them was moral. But Visscher wrote many that were characterized by humor or exaggeration. One of his compositions reads:

"Jan sorrows—sorrows far too much—'tis true;
A sad affliction hath distressed his life;
Mourns he that death hath taken his children two?
Oh no! he mourns that death hath left his wife."

are examples of Dutch imagination and intelligence at their highest development. His *Lucifer*, a tragedy written in verse, is the greatest poem in the Dutch language. In this respect Vondel is to Dutch literature what Camoëns is to the literature of Portugal. A resemblance between certain parts of Vondel's *Lucifer* and the greater *Paradise Lost* of Milton has led many students of literature to believe that the English poet had read the Dutch work before writing his own. *Lucifer* was published in 1654, four years before Milton is supposed to have started on *Paradise Lost*, which appeared in 1667. Of the Dutch writers Vondel alone, through his influence on Milton, entered the broader stream of European literature. The influence of the rest was limited to the small class in the United Provinces which had both culture and leisure.

Though he can hardly be said to belong to Dutch literature, since he wrote most of his great works in Latin, Huig van Groot, better known by the Latinized form of his name, Hugo Grotius, is the most famous Dutch writer of the period. Born at Delft on April 10(N.S.), 1583, young Grotius became one of the greatest prodigies in the annals of precocious genius. At the age of nine he wrote good Latin verse, at twelve he entered the University of Leyden, and at fifteen he received the degree of doctor of laws and was hailed by Henry IV of France as "the marvel of Holland." When the States-General decided in 1603 to appoint an official historiographer to preserve for posterity an account of the Dutch struggle against Spain, it chose Grotius, then only twenty years old. Although a jurist by profession, Grotius was also deeply involved in the theological controversies of the time. His support of Johan van Olden-Barneveldt, the leader of the Remonstrants against the Calvinists, led to his arrest with Barneveldt in 1618. Later Barneveldt was condemned to death while Grotius was sentenced to imprisonment for life in the castle of Loevestein. After he had spent about two years in the castle, his wife succeeded in liberating him by a stratagem. He was successfully smuggled out in a chest supposed to contain borrowed books and soiled linen, and in the disguise of a mason made his way to Paris. The remainder of his life was spent in exile. When his attempt to return to Holland in 1631 failed he accepted the invitation of the Swedish chancellor, Oxenstierna, to act as the ambassador of Sweden at the French court, a post which he held until 1644. Grotius died at Rostock, in Germany, August 29, 1645. His remains were sent to his native country, where they were interred in the Nieuwe Kerk at Delft, beside those of William the Silent; and upon the man whom it had refused citizenship in life the Dutch Republic bestowed the highest honors in death.

Hugo Grotius was a thinker of stupendous erudition. He distinguished himself as a scholar of great versatility, a writer of Latin verse, a liberal theologian who sought to reconcile Protestantism and Catholicism, a writer of commentaries on the Old and New Testaments, and, above all, as a jurist. It was his juridical writings that won world-wide renown. As advocate for the Dutch East India Company he wrote a short treatise entitled *Mare Librum* in which he repelled Portuguese claims to the eastern waters and argued that the ocean was free to all nations. His greatest work was *On the Law of War and Peace*, first published in 1625. It was the period of the Thirty Years' War, and as Grotius himself states, he was induced to write this book by the license, barbarity, and ruthlessness he saw throughout the Christian world in the conduct of war. His purpose was to found the conduct of war and the intercourse of nations upon principles of humanity. He was not the first to write about modern international law, but he did treat the subject more fully and fundamentally than the writers who preceded him. Even in Grotius' lifetime *On the Law of War and Peace* became a classic, and chairs were established in various universities to expound its principles. Throughout the seventeenth and eighteenth centuries it continued profoundly to influence ethical and legal thought, being studied less only after its principles had won general acceptance. Though it is an overstatement to call him the father of modern international law, the scientific study of the subject may be dated from the appearance of this epochal work.

During this period science also blossomed in the Netherlands as never before. A great influence was exerted upon the thought of the United Provinces by the sojourn of René Descartes, who had left France to escape the persecutions of his enemies. During the two decades (1629–1649) he remained in Holland, Descartes gave new life to the study of natural science. It was there that he wrote his notable *Discourse on Method*, published in 1637. In the seventeenth and eighteenth centuries Dutch instrument-makers were noted for the excellence of their scientific instruments. From their workshops mathematical, astronomical, microscopical, and nautical appliances were exported to all parts of Europe. They were particularly famous for their skill in grinding lenses for telescopes and microscopes. Many of the lens-grinders became amateur scientists, studying microscopic life, a pursuit in which the names of two men stand out. They were Anton van Leeuwenhoek (1632–1723) and Jan Swammerdam (1637–1680), both of whom contributed much to the advance of science through their studies.[1] The most celebrated Dutch scientist of the time was Christian Huygens (1629–1695), physicist, astronomer, mathematician, and expert maker of instruments, who may be regarded as the connecting link between Galileo and Newton. Among his contributions to science may be listed: the application of the pendulum to the regulation of clocks, the invention of a kind of micrometer for use in fine measures at the telescope, the discovery of the ring of Saturn, and mathematical studies of the higher curves. His greatest contribution was the wave theory of light, which was further developed in the nineteenth century.

In painting, as in science, this was for the Dutch the age of highest development. No period in Dutch history has produced so many names of outstanding artists as the decades from the Declaration of Independence to Rembrandt's death in 1669. Before the northern provinces had separated themselves from the southern and severed their allegiance from Spain, Dutch painting was hardly distinguishable from Flemish. The same subjects appear in both, and the technical methods employed were similar. But with the growth of a national spirit in the United Provinces there arose an independent art which was essentially national in its inspiration. It grew from the character of the people and from the conditions of their life. Since Calvinism banned all imagery from its churches, there was little demand for religious paintings. Similarly, the sturdy republicanism of the Dutch discouraged the representation of ceremonials reminiscent of court life. Hence Dutch art was thoroughly secular, dominated by the republican tastes of the bourgeoisie or wealthy burghers who were its patrons —a fact of no little consequence for the particular forms it assumed. These burghers created a demand for small paintings which might be suitable for their dwellings, and the subjects treated reflect their taste. As the puritanical strain of Dutch Calvinism frowned on pagan myths and even upon historical subjects, the life of the people in all its minutiae became the subject matter

[1] See pp. 374–375.

of Dutch painting. It was essentially an art of portraiture. Interiors, tavern scenes, village festivals, pastures, farms, seascapes with shipping, were depicted with loving and often matchless artistry, with the utmost precision and at the same time with the greatest simplicity. For the first time on a large scale the facts and scenes of everyday life were made objects of artistic representation, creating an art which might be called the glorification of the ordinary. Every wealthy burgher family had its portrait gallery and its collection of paintings which immortalized every notable event in the life of the family. Civic life was represented in portraits of corporations and groups. There were few boards or military gilds that did not possess paintings of their members. However, the wonderful perfection of this art must not blind us to the fact that much of it lacked inner intensity and meaning, a certain imaginative quality which alone can lift art to the level of a vital creation.

Frans Hals (c. 1580–1666), the first great painter of the Dutch national school, has been called the father of genre painting. Delighting in portraying life in its lighter aspects, he represents humor in the widest possible range, from the boisterous to the quietly mirthful. His themes include market women, wandering musicians, fisher boys and girls, and particularly his own children. Examples of this art are his *Jolly Trio* (in the Metropolitan Museum, New York), *Toper*, *Laughing Cavalier*, *Gipsy*, and *Portrait of Hille Bobbe*. He is famous also for his portrait groups of military gilds. Living when Holland was fighting for independence, and himself a veteran of the struggle against Spain, Hals represents in this phase of his art the militant spirit of the Dutch. After Rembrandt, Hals is the finest portrait painter of Holland.

The greatest Dutch painter, and one of the commanding figures in the history of all art, is Rembrandt van Rijn (1606–1669). The difference between the joyous, spirited work of Frans Hals and the weighty, soul-searching art of Rembrandt is one of subtle psychological penetration. Whereas the former is concerned with outward appearances, the latter probes into man's spiritual nature. All that visual art can reveal of man's inner life has been encompassed by Rembrandt. He is representative of the modern spirit in its concern with the soul. The technical means by which Rembrandt achieved his artistic purpose was his use of chiaroscuro. To this he owes his unique position in the history of painting. By the interplay of light and shade he sheds a peculiar radiance on objects, and transfigures them. An enveloping luminosity lifts all into the realm of the spiritual.

Born in Leyden, Rembrandt removed as a young man to Amsterdam, where he spent the rest of his life. Among the best-known of his early portraits are those of himself and his family. Other portraits of his early years are his *Money-changer*, *Naval Architect and His Wife*, and the group portrait known as the *Anatomy Lecture*, which depicts a post-mortem examination by the anatomist Nicholas Tulp before a group of associates. As his personal misfortunes multiplied, beginning with the death of his children, followed by that of his wife, and including bankruptcy, Rembrandt withdrew more into himself. But adversity only strengthened his artistic purpose, and art became the language through which he expressed his emotions, particularly pain, pity, and kindness. Examples of this expression are the various representations of the Holy Family, the *Supper at Emmaus, Jacob Blessing His Grandsons*, and the *Return of the Prodigal Son*. At this time, too, he turned to the painting of landscapes, in which his poetic feeling found inspiration. His landscapes, of which the *Mill* is probably best known, show him as the great master of atmospheric effects. Among Rembrandt's achievements must be mentioned etching, in which he has seldom, if ever, been surpassed, either in technical skill or in beauty of conception. Notable examples of his work are *Christ Healing the Sick* and the *Presentation to the People*. As the art of Rembrandt's later years was beyond the range of the sympathies of the Dutch, he lived in the greatest isolation, and died poor and forgotten. A remarkable group portrait of his old age is the *Syndics of the Cloth Hall* (1661). Earlier he had painted another well-known picture of contemporary life, the *Sortie of the Banning Cock Company*, formerly known as the *Night Watch*.

Toward the end of the seventeenth century arts, letters, and science, as well as political and economic affairs, entered upon a period of decadence. In the realm of the intellect the subsequent century was an age of imitation rather than of originality. As in the other countries of Europe, the French court became the great exemplar after which the Dutch upper classes modeled their culture, tastes, and fashions. Ornamentation and ostentation superseded simplicity in art, and literature was composed largely of translations, imitations, and adaptations of the masterpieces of French drama.

CHAPTER TWELVE

The Rise of Absolute Monarchy in France

THE WARS OF RELIGION

THE history of sixteenth century France consists largely of religious strife and civil wars. During the early part of his reign Francis I (1515–1547) remained on friendly terms with the party of reform, hoping to receive aid against Charles V from the Lutheran princes of Germany and the Zwinglian cantons of Switzerland. But this was only a temporary policy necessitated by the political situation. As the concordat of 1516 with the pope had given the king the right to nominate most of the higher ecclesiastical officials in France, any religious change was a menace to the authority of the crown over the clergy. Moreover Francis, whose motto was *Un roi, une foi, une loi* (One king, one faith, one law) had no desire to foster a movement that would rend the religious unity of his kingdom. Hence, toward the end of his reign he energetically repressed all efforts in the direction of religious change. After 1535, royal edicts followed each other in rapid succession, ordering state officials to root out Protestantism as a crime against the state. Soon the fires of persecution were burning brightly all over France. In 1547 the Chambre Ardente or "Burning-Court," a kind of Inquisition tribunal, was added to the Parlement of Paris to try those accused of heresy. It lived up to its name by pronouncing the same sentence upon all found guilty—death by fire. The policy of persecution inaugurated dur-

ing the reign of Francis I was continued by his successor, Henry II
(1547–1559), who even endeavored to establish the Inquisition in
France; but his plans shattered on the strenuous opposition of the
Parlement of Paris.

Despite the efforts of the government to suppress it, Protestantism spread widely in France. In form it was Calvinist, and
its adherents were called Huguenots. Ardent Calvinists held clan-
destine meetings and secretly sold or circulated Calvinistic books,
with the result that the number of Huguenots increased rapidly,
particularly during the reign of Henry II. They are said to have
numbered about 400,000 by the year 1560. Converts were drawn
from the upper and more particularly the middle classes, the
lower classes remaining firmly attached to the old religion. The
Huguenots, meeting at first in separate groups, were early organized by Calvin himself into an ecclesiastical and political party
which demanded freedom of conscience and freedom of worship,
and was ready, if necessary, to fight for these ends. As both sides
were equally determined, the religious differences caused a long
period of civil wars. In the end, however, Catholicism proved itself the more firmly intrenched.

When Henry II died in 1559 of a wound accidentally received
in a tournament honoring the approaching marriage of his daughter Elizabeth to Philip II of Spain, he was succeeded, in turn, by
his three sons, Francis II (1559–1560), Charles IX (1560–1574),
and Henry III (1574–1589). What France needed above all at
the death of Henry II was a wise and strong ruler who could preserve peace by repressing the immoderate zeal of both Huguenots
and Catholics. Instead there came a series of three weak monarchs,
wholly unfitted to cope with the situation. France was submerged
in a sea of bigotry, anarchy, and civil war.

During the brief reign of Francis II, a dull boy of fifteen and
the husband of Mary Stuart, the conduct of state affairs was in
the hands of Mary's two uncles, the duke of Guise and the cardinal
of Lorraine—who was also of the house of Guise. As feeble in
health as in character, Francis II died after only seventeen months
on the throne and was succeeded by Charles IX, a lad of ten. The
regent during Charles's minority was the queen-mother, Catherine
de Médicis, offspring of the powerful and ambitious Italian family
of Medici. Catherine, who was cast in an eminently masculine
mold, was fond of hunting and manly exercises; above all, she was

eager for power. To wield the dominating influence in France became the primary object of her life. From Machiavelli's *Prince*, which was dedicated to her father, she had learned that in matters concerning the state the laws of morality were not binding. Hence, in her strivings for power, she did not hesitate to use any means, however questionable or evil. Craft, intrigue, and assassination were her favorite weapons because she believed them to be most effective. Once she had established her influence in France, she retained it until her death in 1589. To keep it she even went so far as to foment quarrels between her children and to encourage them in debauchery. Her object in holding the reins of power was not the welfare of the French people, but solely the gratification of her inordinate ambition. Regarding religion as a mere instrument of government, she at first tried to retain the support of both the Catholic and the Huguenot party by making concessions alternately. But when this policy resulted in both sides distrusting her, she finally went over to the Catholic party. As the Huguenots grew stronger, she opposed them not so much for religious as for political reasons, regarding them as a threat to her power. Her feelings toward them grew ever more bitter, until finally her hatred culminated in the wanton massacre of St. Bartholomew.

In 1562 the first of the Wars of Religion broke out between the Huguenots and the Catholic party. Its immediate cause was the massacre at Vassy perpetrated by Francis, duke of Guise, the leader of the reactionary Catholics in France. While passing through Champagne the duke's attention was attracted by the singing of a Protestant congregation of about six or seven hundred gathered for worship at Vassy in defiance of an edict forbidding such public meetings. He immediately sent his retainers to order them to disband. But the Huguenots refused, reviling the men sent by the duke with such names as "papists and idolators." When the duke and his men tried to force their way into the building, the unarmed worshippers began to hurl stones, one of which struck the duke himself. In retaliation his infuriated retainers fell upon the Protestants, killing more than fifty and wounding over a hundred. At the news of the massacre Huguenots everywhere took up arms under the leadership of the prince of Condé and Admiral Coligny. All efforts to quell the discord failed, and war began. After almost a year of fighting, Francis, duke of Guise, died from a wound inflicted by a Protestant who had entered his camp, and Catherine became generally recognized as the head of the Catholic party.

Though the Huguenots, on the whole, met reverses during the wars, which were separated by intervals of peace, their party seemed to increase in strength. Seeing that it was useless to prolong the struggle, Catherine adopted a policy of conciliation. By the Edict of Saint-Germain (1570) the Huguenots were granted limited rights of public worship and admission to all employments, and were also permitted to retain possession of four cities as "places of safety." Furthermore, the Huguenot leader, Admiral Coligny, a man of high character and political wisdom, was made a member of the royal council. Coligny, eager to see a united France offer a bold front to enemy nations, made the most of his opportunity by converting the king to his views of healing the breach between the two religious groups. Charles IX entered into the project with zeal. The marriage of the king's sister Marguerite, a Catholic, to Henry of Navarre—an able prince who, after Coligny, was the outstanding leader of the Huguenots, and also the next in succession to the French throne if Catherine's sons had no male issue—was one of the proposals for reconciling the two religious factions.

In the midst of the preparations for the wedding, however, Catherine became alarmed at Admiral Coligny's growing influence over Charles, fearing that her own would come to an end. Coligny, she decided, must be put out of the way at all hazards. One day as he was entering his house he was wounded, though not seriously, by a would-be assassin attached to the house of Guise, with which Catherine had secretly joined hands against the admiral. When the king solemnly swore before Coligny that the attempted murder would be investigated, Catherine was thoroughly agitated lest her part in the plot be discovered. She now projected a plan to destroy all the leading Huguenots at one blow. Feeble Charles IX at first shrank from the horrible proposal, but under the stinging taunts of his mother finally consented to the plan on condition, as he told her, "that you do not leave a Huguenot alive in France to reproach me." Thus the origin of the massacre of St. Bartholomew must be sought primarily in Catherine's jealousy of Coligny's influence over the king.

Circumstances favored Catherine's plan, for most of the Hu-

guenot leaders were just then in Paris for the wedding of Marguerite and Henry of Navarre. It was arranged that at a given signal
armed bands would go from house to house to slay every Huguenot
they could find. About two o'clock on Sunday morning, August 24,
1572 (the festival of St. Bartholomew), the church bells of the
city tolled the signal and the assassins began the slaughter. To
make sure that Coligny did not escape death a second time,
Henry, duke of Guise, personally supervised his murder. Of the
Huguenot leaders only two were spared, the young prince of
Condé and the king's brother-in-law, Henry of Navarre; all others
were systematically slain. The spirit of murder soon spread, and
private enmities and greed were given full vent as the mobs went
about killing every Huguenot man, woman, and child they could
find and looting the houses of the dead. From Paris the massacre
spread to other towns and districts until a large part of France was
in a state of turmoil and horror. The number slain will never be
known, for there are no records of the massacre. A moderate estimate sets it at ten thousand. To at least one person the slaughter
was an occasion for joy. When Philip II of Spain received news of
the ghastly affair he is said to have laughed in public—something
he did only on rare occasions.[1] Charles IX survived the massacre
less than two years. He died in May, 1574, at the early age of
twenty-four, haunted on his deathbed, it is said, by visions of the
dying and their pleadings for mercy.

The results of the massacre, however, were not so decisive as
its instigators may have hoped. Coligny and many leaders of the
Huguenots had been slain, but new leaders soon rose up to take
their places. Instead of breaking the back of the Huguenot movement, the slaughter only roused the Protestants to fight harder.
During the reign of Henry III, who was as weak as his brother
Charles and much more debauched, the War of the Three Henrys
broke out. It was so called from the names of the three leaders:
Henry III, leader of the moderate Catholic party or Politiques;
Henry of Guise, head of the reactionary Catholic party which had
organized the Holy League for the extermination of Protestantism;
and Henry of Navarre, energetic and able leader of the Hugue-

---

[1] St. Goar, the French ambassador wrote, ". . . he (who otherwise never laughed)
began to laugh, and showed the greatest satisfaction and content." Moreover, Philip
ordered a Te Deum and commanded all bishops to have processions and thanksgiv-
ings in their dioceses.

nots. With the support of Philip II of Spain the duke of Guise gradually became so powerful that he was more king than Henry III himself. To free himself from this domination, Henry III caused the duke to be assassinated in 1588. Then, to protect himself from the vengeance of the League, he joined hands with Henry of Navarre, and together they laid siege to Paris, the stronghold of the League. But in August, 1589, Henry III fell under the dagger of an assassin, a Dominican friar who believed it his sacred duty to free the country from so detestable a monarch. With the death of Henry III the Valois line came to an end and the house of Bourbon obtained the crown. Before his death the king acknowledged Henry of Navarre as his legitimate successor and urged the French people to accept him as such. He also exhorted Henry of Navarre to adopt the religion of the majority. "You will have many troubles unless you make up your mind to change your religion," the dying king is reported to have said.

HENRY IV

Though Henry of Navarre at once took the title "Henry IV," he had the support of only a small part of the French people, for the majority refused to submit to a heretic king. Moreover, Philip II, who had no desire to see the French throne occupied by a Protestant, had sent an army under Parma to hold Paris against Henry. But the French people, weary of civil war, anarchy, and foreign intervention, were ready to accept Henry as king if he would consent to become a Catholic. Since religious opinions had always been more a matter of family tradition than of deep conviction, Henry willingly made preparations to change his faith in order to strengthen his position as king. On July 25, 1593, in the abbey church of St. Denis, he solemnly abjured Protestantism, read his new profession, and vowed to live and die in the Catholic Church. No sooner had he accepted the Catholic faith than one city after another came over to his side. Even in Paris the tide of public opinion turned to him; the gates were opened, and Henry made his entry with but little resistance. The mobs there, who had long admired his valor, acclaimed him joyfully. With the support of Paris, Henry was recognized as king by most of France. The Spanish garrison now had no other course but to retreat from Paris; this it was permitted to do without hindrance. Henry himself, viewing the departure of the Spanish soldiers, called out to them: "Gentlemen, commend me to your master, but do not come back." The final treaty of peace between France and Spain was not signed, however, until May, 1598 (treaty of Vervins).

The new king was a man of charming personality, with a genius for handling men. His simplicity of manner and human qualities made him one of the most beloved of French kings. He was quick at repartee and always ready for a joke; many of his pointed remarks became proverbs. On the other hand, he was lacking in refinement, his manners often resembling those of a coarse peasant. Yet his wit, intelligence, vivacity, and good fellowship were such that his weaknesses were overlooked. Of medium height, he had a vigorous manner and a robust constitution. He delighted in strenuous sports, particularly hunting. His favorite diversion throughout life, however, was the pursuit of women, the story of his private life being a chronicle of scandals; yet he never allowed women to interfere in the affairs of state.

When Henry was firmly established on the throne, he set to work to heal the many wounds France had received during the civil war. For more than three decades armies had ravaged the country, often plundering friend and foe alike. Many districts had been frightfully devastated, and both commerce and industry had suffered severely. Villages and cities had been destroyed, roads torn up, and bridges burned. In many parts of France human life was extremely insecure. Robber barons terrorized certain districts and robber bands roamed the countryside, making public highways unsafe. Social life was disturbed by hatreds and jealousies, intrigues and cabals. The all-sufficient explanation of the general disorganization is to be found in the fact that there had been no government strong enough to compel obedience and guarantee order and security. Thus Henry was confronted by a twofold task: first, to reëstablish the royal authority; and second, to rehabilitate agriculture, commerce, and industry.

The absolute power which Louis XI and Francis I had won for the monarchy had been thoroughly undermined by the Wars of Religion. Powerful nobles had developed the habit of ignoring the absolute claims of the crown. In the words of a contemporary: "A large portion of the nobility no longer desires a king." Henry could only begin the work of reëstablishing the royal authority in France, which Richelieu later completed. The smaller nobles were forced to submit, and more formidable men were induced with gold or titles to surrender the powers they had seized. Autocratic in temper, Henry did not give the Estates-General an opportunity to dispute his will, for he did not summon it during his reign. Upon the parlements he kept a tight rein. To the Parlement of Toulouse he said: "I must insist on being obeyed." The most representative gathering of his reign was the meeting of notables at Rouen in 1596, and that did little more than inform the king of the grievances of the country.

For the work of reconstruction Henry IV was fortunate in having a number of able assistants, the most important of whom was Maximilien de Béthune, baron of Rosny, better known as the duke of Sully. A faithful supporter of the Bourbon cause through the vicissitudes of the civil wars, Sully had long been closely attached to the person of Henry of Navarre. When Henry adopted the Catholic religion Sully had been strongly in favor of the change, but he himself had remained a staunch Calvinist. The two men were unlike in many respects. While Henry IV was gay, affable, good-humored, and warm-hearted, Sully was morose, arrogant in bearing, ungracious in manner, and harsh in speech. An austere Calvinist, he abhorred the laxity of the court and did not hesitate to say so. Both men, however, had at least one trait in common: a deep devotion to the welfare of the French people. Both were also determined to raise France from its state of anemia to one of prosperity and well-being. The king recognized the exemplary fidelity, the untiring industry, and the practical ability of Sully by making him his chief minister, and by retaining him as such against all efforts of the court to dislodge him. Only Sully could repeatedly contradict the king, chide him for his extravagances, or berate him for some foolish love affair. He was in important respects Henry's other self. So closely did king and minister work together that it is impossible to separate their work.

Though no financial genius, Sully as "the watch-dog of the treasury" was extraordinarily successful in restoring the finances of France. When Henry IV began his reign the coffers were empty and the government was heavily in debt. The long civil wars had necessitated vast expenditures, and large foreign loans had been contracted to meet them. Moreover, the king needed large sums to pacify the great nobles, and until after the treaty of Vervins the army was a heavy expense. For all this Henry had only a meager income from an impoverished country. Taxes were gathered by *fermiers* who paid the government a lump sum and kept for themselves whatever they could collect beyond it. The whole system was so honeycombed with abuse, graft, and corruption that the treasury received only about one-fourth of the sum which the people annually paid in taxes. In his efforts to improve the finances, Sully introduced no innovations; he simply reformed the existing methods. Though he did not abolish the system of farming out the taxes, he did uproot many of the attendant evils. He introduced a strict method of accounting whereby frauds could be easily detected, and he also inaugurated a more equitable distribution of the taxes by compelling those who had received improper exemptions to pay the taille. So successfully did Sully husband the finances of France that by 1610 he had not only greatly reduced the national debt, but after spending large sums on roads, bridges, canals, and public buildings, he had amassed a considerable reserve.

Both Henry IV and Sully were deeply interested in restoring and improving agriculture. Indeed, of all the kings of France Henry was probably the most solicitous for the welfare of the common people. He wanted them to be prosperous because he believed that this would make the state strong, particularly in time of war. His aim, as he expressed it, was "to put a chicken in the pot" of every peasant family for the Sunday dinner. As early as 1595 he revived an ancient ordinance which forbade the seizure of livestock and farm implements in payment of debt. But the most beneficial of his acts for the improvement of agriculture was a decree which permitted the free exportation of grain from France, except in times of scarcity, thereby giving the peasant a surer market in plentiful years. Under the supervision of Sully, who believed that French prosperity depended "on the cow and the plough" rather than on industry, new methods of tillage were introduced, the breeding of horses and cattle was encouraged, and much land was put under cultivation through draining the extensive marshes in various parts of France.

While Sully was supervising the improvement of agriculture, Henry IV devoted great care to the promotion of industry. In harmony with the spirit of the age, his ideas were mercantilistic. In this respect he was the most important forerunner of Colbert. The king's object was to keep in France the large sums which were annually sent to other countries for imported products, particularly for articles of luxury. To this end he encouraged the manufacture of tapestries, carpets, fine glassware, wrought leather, velvets, satins, silks, and cloth of gold and silver by government bounties and by prohibiting the importation of goods which might compete with them. So long as these new industries were subsidized by the government, they were fairly prosperous; but when the subsidies ceased after Henry's death, many of them failed.

Though Sully was opposed to the manufacture of luxuries in France, on the ground that they tended to encourage idleness and excessive expenditure, he coöperated heartily with the king in the restoration of commerce. New roads and bridges were built, and old ones were repaired. Since transportation on land was still costly, plans were drafted for joining the rivers of France by a system of canals which would have made it possible to transport goods on water from the Atlantic to the Mediterranean. However, only a small part of the project was completed during Henry's reign. A reform that would have been of the greatest benefit to commerce, had it been carried through, was the suppression of the multiplicity of internal tolls; but in this respect the efforts of Henry and Sully did not go very far. Since the king needed the income from the royal tolls, they were left untouched; only a number of private tolls were abolished. Henry also endeavored to foster oversea commerce and colonization. In 1608 Champlain was sent to Canada, where he established Quebec and laid the foundations for a New France in America. Slowly France was beginning to assume a place of importance in the economic as well as in the political affairs of Europe.

Meanwhile Henry had not forgotten his former coreligionists. In April, 1598, he signed the Edict of Nantes, which gave the Huguenots, a small minority of the French people, a generous measure of civil and religious liberty. It granted them liberty of conscience in all parts of France, and freedom of worship in all places where they had enjoyed it during the two preceding years, with the exception of Paris and five leagues about that city. It further declared Huguenots eligible for all public offices, guaranteed their admission to all schools, colleges, and hospitals, and permitted them to open schools of their own and to set up printing presses in the towns in which they might legally hold their worship. To secure them against unfair treatment in the courts of law, all cases in which Protestants were involved were to be tried by special tribunals composed of judges of both faiths. In addition, the Huguenots were permitted to retain political control of La Rochelle and about a hundred other fortified towns. This privilege made them a sort of state within the state, disrupting the centralization of the royal power.

On the whole, the edict granted such a generous measure of freedom and toleration that it stands as a landmark in an age of intolerance. Yet upon its promulgation it was denounced in almost equal measure by Catholics and Huguenots. The former regarded the concessions as too liberal, and the latter as too meager. The edict was to many Catholics a proof of the insincerity of Henry's conversion, while to many Huguenots it seemed a betrayal of his former brethren. To Henry it was a means of bringing internal peace to France, and as such was well enforced during his reign. By it the French king declared that Catholics and Protestants alike had religious rights which must be mutually respected.

By 1610 the fruits of Henry's efforts were everywhere visible. Order and tranquillity had been restored and the French people were prospering. He now thought the time ripe to check the power of the Spanish and Austrian Habsburgs, whose domains encircled France;[1] and though his plans were regarded with little favor by his advisers, he pushed preparations for war. But only a few days before he was to leave at the head of his army, he fell under the dagger of an assassin. François Ravaillac, a religious fanatic, apparently acting on his own initiative, had become obsessed with the idea that Henry was an enemy of the Catholic Church and had vowed to kill him. Approaching the royal carriage as the king was riding through a narrow street of Paris, he stabbed him twice in the region of the heart. Henry, who is reported to have said, "*Ce n'est rien, ce n'est rien* (It is nothing)," died on the way back to his palace. By his death the French people lost a great friend and an able king.

As Henry's marriage with Marguerite of Valois had been childless, and in every way a failure, the pope had annulled it in 1599. In the following year the king had married Marie de Médicis, the second member of that house to occupy the French throne.

---

[1] The idea that Henry IV was the author of or ever seriously entertained the so-called "Grand Design," a scheme for uniting the states of Europe in one great confederation, which Sully describes at length in his memoirs, has been pretty thoroughly discredited. See David Ogg's introduction to Sully's *Grand Design of Henry IV* (Grotius Society Publications, no. 2., London, 1921).

Though this union was far from happy, it achieved its political purpose, for in September, 1601, Marie gave birth to the dauphin, who was later to become Louis XIII. At the time of his father's death Louis was not yet nine years old; hence the Parlement of Paris proclaimed Marie de Médicis regent of France during her son's minority.

Marie de Médicis was a large, phlegmatic, narrow-minded woman, with little ability for the task of ruling France. Thus the strong rule of a strong man gave way to the weak rule of a weak woman, and much of the work which Henry had accomplished was to be undone during her regency. Instead of choosing able advisers to aid her in her difficult task, she permitted herself to be controlled by two vulgar favorites—the handsome, scheming Concino Concini and his wife, Leonora Galigai, both like herself Italians. Upon Concini, whose ascendancy over her was almost complete, she showered offices, titles, and wealth. The fact that the queen, herself a foreigner, chose two arrogant upstart foreigners as advisers gave great offense. Sully, the one statesman who might have helped her carry on an orderly government, found his influence at an end, and retired to his estates soon after the death of Henry IV. In the foreign affairs of France Marie de Médicis reversed the policy of her husband by signing a marriage treaty with Spain in 1612, by which Louis XIII was betrothed to Anne of Austria, the daughter of Philip III of Spain. At home the government declined rapidly. When the nobles revolted under her lax rule, she bought them off with offices, appointments, and ready money—the easiest way to secure peace. Through lavishing the royal income on her favorites and using it to pacify her nobles, she soon exhausted the reserve which Sully had so industriously accumulated. Things rapidly grew worse, and finally a meeting of the Estates-General was summoned to suggest remedies.

In 1614 almost five hundred deputies met as representatives of the clergy, the nobility, and the Third Estate, but they accomplished nothing. The Third Estate demanded such reforms as a reduction of the taxes; the establishment of a uniform system of weights and measures; the abolition of tithes, feudal aids, and the petty feudal rights and servitudes; and termination of the exemption of the clergy and nobility from certain taxes. The clergy and nobility, however, were too intent upon securing their own privileges to coöperate with the Third Estate. The principal result of the meeting was that the Estates-General completely discredited itself by its indifference to the general welfare. Though the Revolution was still a long way off, its causes were already at work, and its coming was foreshadowed in the refusal of the two higher estates to permit any reform. Prophetic were the words of a spokesman of the Third Estate who declared that "the people were weary of being the anvil; let others have a care lest they become the hammer." Finally the queen, to whom the deputies of the Third Estate had looked for assistance in their efforts to inaugurate reforms, grew tired of the harangues and sent all the deputies home. The Estates-General was not to convene again for one hundred seventy-five years, until that fateful meeting of 1789 which was to usher in the French Revolution.

RICHELIEU

Though the Estates-General did nothing to better conditions in France, its convocation gave Richelieu, a representative of the clergy, the opportunity to draw the attention of Marie de Médicis to himself. The son of lesser nobility, Armand Jean du Plessis de Richelieu had at the early age of twenty-one been consecrated bishop of Luçon after receiving a special dispensation from the pope because he had not reached the canonical age of twenty-five. Luçon was a small diocese and one of the poorest in France. For six years Richelieu had ministered to the needs of his flock, using his spare time to write theological tracts. Chosen representative of the clergy of Poitou in 1614, the bishop of Luçon impressed the queen so favorably that he was asked to remain in Paris after the dismissal of the Estates-General. He soon won her confidence and became one of her chief advisers. It was due to the efforts of Marie that her favorite minister was finally elevated to the cardinalate in 1622. In the meantime both he and the queen encountered the king's displeasure. In 1617, when Louis XIII was sixteen, he revolted against the tutelage of his mother. He had Concini murdered, Leonora Galigai tried for sorcery and beheaded, and both his mother and Richelieu banished from the court. But in 1622 a reconciliation was effected between the king and his mother on condition that Richelieu be named a member of the royal council. As a member of the royal council Richelieu, through the liberal use of craft, managed to become the supreme power in France by 1624.

Having achieved the position of supreme power, Richelieu was able to hold it until his death in 1642, directing the policies of France both at home and abroad. His influence was so preponderant that it suspended the exercise of the royal power. Hence Richelieu may be regarded as the real successor of Henry IV in the development of the French monarchy. Yet to retain his ascendancy it was necessary for him to exercise a perpetual vigilance and to watch constantly the whims and changing fancies of his royal master. Louis XIII disliked Richelieu and would have rid himself of his chief minister if the latter had not made himself indispensable. Though the king was a man of small ability, he did not wish to appear to be a do-nothing king. Hence Richelieu humored Louis by constantly consulting him and by giving the impression that his plans were really those of the king. So precarious did Richelieu regard his own tenure of power, however, that he seldom remained out of the king's sight for any considerable period, lest someone else gain control over Louis's mind. In 1630, on the so-called Day of the Dupes, the king actually dismissed Richelieu, but after a few hours countered the order, saying to his minister, "Continue to serve me as you have done, and I will maintain you against all who have sworn your ruin." The French people, both high and low, hated the cardinal. Conspiracies against his power were frequent, but all schemes devised for his downfall failed of accomplishment. Richelieu's agents were everywhere, and the conspiracies they ferreted out were ruthlessly suppressed without regard for rank or person. Richelieu sent no less than twenty-six members of the aristocracy to the scaffold, including five dukes and a favorite courtier of the king. As a statesman, he was courageous, resolute, sagacious, and tireless in his activity. His weaknesses included love of pomp and splendor, personal vanity, fondness for applause. In his policies he was no innovator; he simply followed established traditions. His aim was twofold: (1) to make the royal power supreme in France; (2) to make France supreme in Europe.

The task of making the king supreme in France involved the abolition of the political and military rights of the Huguenots and the repression of the rebellious nobility. Richelieu struck first at the Huguenots. Though the Edict of Nantes had terminated the Wars of Religion in France, it had not established national unity, for the privileges of the Huguenots set them apart from the rest of the nation. Their possession of fortified towns garrisoned by their own troops not only was an obstacle to the unity of the monarchy; it also tempted them to oppose the absolutism of the king or to coöperate with other rebellious factions and even with the foreign enemies of France. Richelieu was not intolerant of the faith of the Huguenots, but he regarded their political privileges as a constant danger to internal peace. "So long as the Huguenots have a foothold in France," he wrote, "the King will never be master at home, nor able to undertake any glorious action abroad." When the Huguenots rose against the government in 1627, the cardinal minister personally directed a siege of the Huguenot stronghold, La Rochelle. The English fleet which came to relieve the beleaguered city was unable to break the great mole with which Richelieu had closed the harbor; and after one of the most heroic resistances of history, starvation finally forced the Huguenots to surrender in October, 1628. Soon after this the Huguenot opposition collapsed completely with the surrender of the remaining places they held. The peace of Alais (1629) concluded this last religious war in France. It abolished the political and military privileges of the Huguenots, but confirmed their religious and civil rights.

The only threat to the absolute power of the king now came from the great nobles who resented the authority of the crown and intrigued for personal advantage and power. Though the absolute power of the crown had long been established by law, the nobility had been submissive only under strong kings. Richelieu and his successor Mazarin crushed their power so completely that they remained submissive thereafter. In 1626 the former issued an edict for the destruction of all castles and fortifications not necessary for the defense of the kingdom. Thus a great number of castles which had been centers of local tyranny were razed. Yet their possibilities as strongholds of rebellion against the central government may easily be exaggerated, for an army with cannon could have demolished the walls of the formerly impregnable castles in a short time. Richelieu also forbade private wars and the practice of dueling, which he regarded as a remnant of private warfare. How prevalent dueling was in France is seen from the fact that in 1607 four thousand gentlemen were killed in duels. Edicts against duels had existed but had not been enforced. Richelieu now forbade duels on pain of death; and to show that he meant the edict to be obeyed, he had the count of Bouteville, a member of the powerful family of Montmorency, beheaded for fighting a duel in the Place Royale.

Richelieu's destruction of the castles and his prohibition of private warfare were only preliminaries to a reorganization of the system of the local administration. By an edict of 1637 he appointed royal functionaries known as *intendants* to take charge of the financial, judicial, and police administration of the provinces, thus transferring the powers which had formerly been exercised by the territorial nobility to a kind of middle-class civil service. Since the intendants were the nominees and direct agents of the crown, Richelieu held in his own hands all the threads of the administration. Richelieu was not the originator of the system of intendants; he only established it firmly. It was his greatest achievement in the work of centralization.

Richelieu's foreign policy was but a continuation of that of Henry IV. He wished to crush the power of the Habsburgs, who, through a close alliance of the Spanish and Austrian branches of the house, dominated the affairs of Europe. Once this was accomplished France would hold the predominance. When the Thirty Years' War broke out in Germany (1618) Richelieu watched it anxiously, fearing that the complete success of the Austrian Habsburgs might mean the creation of a strong, unified German state which would be a menace to France. When Christian IV of Denmark failed in his invasion of Germany, Richelieu encouraged Gustavus Adolphus to enter the lists against the Habsburg emperor and paid him a subsidy to do so. But when the Swedish king was killed at Lützen in 1632, the cardinal decided it was time for France to engage in the contest as an active participant; this it did in 1635. The stern minister did not live to see the final triumph of his policy, but at his death the task of weakening the Habsburgs was accomplished in all essentials and France was wielding a greater influence in the affairs of Europe.

Richelieu died on December 4, 1642, at the age of fifty-seven. Despite his physical weakness and his chronic ill-health he accomplished much. What he achieved for France was done by Richelieu the statesman, not Richelieu the cardinal. He did not permit his religion to control his statesmanship. He was ever ready to support a Protestant minority against their Catholic sovereign when it would be to the advantage of France to do so.

Thus he supported the Protestant states of Germany against the emperor, thereby probably saving Protestantism in Germany. In ecclesiastical matters his policy was one of opportunism; when necessary, he did not hesitate to attack the powers of the pope. At the papal court he was called "Pope of the Huguenots" and "Patriarch of Atheists."

One patent weakness in the statesmanship of Richelieu was his failure to reorganize the vicious financial system of France. Having been a member of the Estates-General of 1614 he knew full well the desires of the French people for financial relief, stated by the deputies of the Third Estate in plain and emphatic terms. Yet he permitted most of the abuses to remain. Whatever reforms he may have planned in the first year of his ministry were soon put aside under the stress of martial cares and the work of centralization. The antiquated and corrupt methods of farming the taxes and also the unjust distribution of the taxes remained. Indeed, tax abuses were increased under Richelieu by the sale of offices carrying with them certain tax exemptions. Had Richelieu vigorously attacked the financial disorders, he might have saved France from the Revolution. As it was, an immoderate portion of the taxes was diverted by the tax farmers, and what was left proved insufficient to pay the costs of the war against the Habsburgs. Consequently the deficit grew larger year by year. From ten million livres in 1624 it increased to fifty-six million in 1639. This deficit Richelieu passed on to his successors, who in turn passed it on until it grew to proportions which spelled national bankruptcy.

Richelieu was not sufficiently enlightened to realize that the interests of the state and those of the people were identical. He preferred the glory of the dynasty to the public weal. Little, therefore, that he did contributed directly to the welfare and happiness of the French people. Schemes for universal education, for example, found no place in his policy. On the contrary, because he thought that education was keeping many from devoting themselves to commerce, he drafted a plan to limit the number of institutions of higher learning in France, but the plan was not carried out. In 1635, however, he founded the famous Académie Française, an institution to regulate and purify the French language; membership in this Académie is still the highest honor that can be offered a French man of letters. In his economic policy Richelieu was a mercantilist. He concluded commercial treaties with Russia, Sweden, and Denmark, and attempted to build a merchant marine and develop the French colonies. But the result of his efforts was meager. As ruler of France he was not loved by the people; nor did he love them. The masses saw in his policy only heavier taxes and perpetual wars. He, in turn, was cold and severe toward their sufferings, fearing that they would be disobedient if things went well with them. "If the people were too much at ease," he said, "it would not be possible to hold them within the rules of their duty." While the masses were being impoverished, he lived in royal splendor. Besides rebuilding his ancestral château in Poitou, he built for himself not only the magnificent Palais Cardinal in Paris (later the Palais Royal), but also a palace at Rueil. Since obedience to him was based on fear, the news of his death evoked no sorrow from the masses. Instead, many bonfires were lighted as if in celebration of a joyful event. During the French Revolution a mob violated his tomb and carried his head through the streets of Paris on a pike.

MAZARIN

The power Richelieu had gained was passed on to his successor and disciple, Jules Mazarin, an Italian by birth. Mazarin first came to France as a papal legate. Entering the service of Richelieu in 1639, he became a naturalized Frenchman and two years later was made a cardinal through Richelieu's influence. So thoroughly was Mazarin initiated into Richelieu's system of government that the latter, shortly before his death, recommended his protégé to the king as the only person capable of carrying on his political system. Five months after the death of Richelieu, Louis XIII himself died, leaving the crown to his son, Louis XIV, a child of less than five years. By the will of the dead king his wife, Anne of Austria, a rather dull woman of lethargic temperament, became regent, but she allowed Mazarin to govern in her place. In policy he carried on and completed the work of Richelieu. He did not, however, rule with the same iron hand as Richelieu, depending more on craft and intrigue to overcome obstacles.

In internal affairs the rule of Mazarin was marked by a revolt known as the Fronde. A fronde was a sling used by the boys in the streets of Paris, and the term, it seems, was first applied in mockery to the movement against the government; but soon it became the permanent designation. Those who participated in the movement became known as Frondeurs, the name applied to street urchins who delighted in slinging clods of mud at the occupants of passing coaches. Three distinct elements participated in the revolts: (1) the Parlement of Paris, which had long desired a share in the government; (2) the higher nobles, who had not yet reconciled themselves to being social ornaments; (3) the dissatisfied taxpayers who were staggering under an ever increasing burden of taxes. All three parties were united in their hatred of Mazarin because he was a foreigner and the favorite of a foreign queen, but especially because he was continuing a policy that was fatal to the ambitions of the nobility and the Parlement of Paris, and oppressive to the people. A court lady of the time states that "it was the fashion to hate Mazarin." To drive him out of office became the primary aim of the movement against the government.

The revolt may be divided into the First and Second Fronde. The First Fronde centered about the Parlement of Paris, the highest judicial tribunal of France, which had charge of the official register of the laws. Having long claimed the privilege of imposing a practical veto on the decrees of the king by refusing to enter them into the official register, the Parlement of Paris was encouraged by the success of the English Parliament to seek recognition of its claims. The Parlement of Paris was not, however, like the English Parliament, a representative assembly; it was a closed corporation of magistrates who had bought or inherited their judicial positions. Its motives in opposing the absolutism of the king were not so much concern for the public welfare as the desire to secure privileges for itself. In 1648 a charter was presented to the regent in which the Parlement demanded that no new taxes be levied or new offices be created without its permission; that the extortions of the tax farmers be investigated; that the intendants be abolished; and that no one be kept in prison for more than twenty-four hours without being tried. When Mazarin ordered the arrest of the leaders of the Parlement, the people of Paris raised barricades in the streets. Later civil war broke out. At first the Parisian mob gained a few successes, but gradually the royal forces under the command of Condé put down the resistance and a treaty ended the war on the first of April, 1649.

But the peace proved to be only a truce. Since the principal

object of the movement, the expulsion of Mazarin from office, remained unachieved, the treaty was not satisfactory to the Frondeurs. No sooner had the first war ended when the party of the new
Fronde was organized among the higher nobility. Its outstanding
leader was Condé, who had gone over to the opposition because
he was dissatisfied with his position at court. The Second Fronde
did not, like the first, aim at constitutional reform; neither did
the nobles desire to dismember the kingdom. What the dukes,
counts, marquises, and princes of the blood wanted was to overthrow Mazarin and to secure for themselves provincial governor-
ships, pensions, and gifts of money. The beginning of the revolt
may be dated from the arrest of Condé and two other leaders of
the movement by order of Mazarin in January, 1650. Soon the
Parlement of Paris and a faction of the people of Paris joined the
nobility against Mazarin, thus uniting all the disaffected parties.
For a time the Frondeurs under Condé were supreme in Paris,
but gradually, when the people realized that the nobles were bent
only on the advancement of their own interests, a reaction set in.
Encouraged by this change, Mazarin, with the invaluable assistance of the great general Turenne, who had deserted the cause of
the Frondeurs, gradually overcame the forces of the nobility and
the Second Fronde was over. The triumph of the royal cause was
decisive. The system of intendants was restored, the Parlement of
Paris was forbidden henceforth to take any part in state affairs,
and Paris was deprived of the right to elect its municipal officials.
It was the last attempt until the Revolution to limit the absolutism of the crown.

Mazarin died on March 9, 1661. He had succeeded in suppressing the rebellion against the authority of the monarchy and
in raising the prestige of France in Europe. But the condition of
the masses in France was pitiable indeed. Mazarin had been so
busy suppressing revolts and completing the program of Richelieu
that he had found no time to give thought to the problem of financial reform or to the welfare of the people. If the financial administration had been bad under the rule of Richelieu, it was even
worse under Mazarin. In this respect the rule of Mazarin was but
another step in the decline and its inevitable consequence, the
Revolution.

CHAPTER THIRTEEN

Germany and the Thirty Years' War

GERMANY BEFORE THE THIRTY YEARS' WAR

IN GERMANY the period after the peace of Augsburg (1555) was, on the whole, one of decadence. The religious movement which had seemed to promise a new era of national life effected the direct opposite: it dismembered and disrupted Germany, dividing it into a number of hostile religious camps. After a period of vitriolic attacks and endless petty disputations, pent-up feelings which had gradually become more heated burst into physical combat in the Smalkald War (1546–1555). The peace of Augsburg, which ended the war, further divided Germany by giving to the ruler of each petty state the right to decide the religious beliefs of his subjects. Thus, while the larger states of western Europe were trying to establish a national policy by remaining attached to the Roman Church or by accepting Protestantism as the state religion, Germany took a course toward decentralization and particularism in matters religious and political. Religious dissension existed not only between the Catholics and the Protestants, but also within these two divisions. The disagreement among the Catholics regarding religious and political aims was not so fundamental, however, as the breach within the ranks of the Protestants. While the Jesuits were uniting the Catholics, the differences between the Lutherans and the Calvinists were becoming increasingly rigid and uncompromising. Luther, who had appeared as a liberator, ended as the founder of a new orthodoxy based on scripturalism instead of papalism; and Calvinism soon settled into a dogmatism no less inflexible. In consequence the adherents of the two sects often quarreled violently, overwhelming one another with malediction, though in the main their differences were merely secondary.

In such an atmosphere of religious intolerance and party strife the development of a vigorous German culture was hardly possible. Polemics, theological bickerings, and sectarian hatreds consumed the energy that had previously been devoted to art and literature. The result was an age largely barren of intellectual and artistic achievements. In the Netherlands Rubens, Van Dyke, Hals, Rembrandt, and their fellow artists were producing masterpieces, but Germany had no painters worthy of consideration. In literature, this was the age of Cervantes and Lope de Vega in Spain; of Ariosto and Tasso in Italy; of Rabelais, Ronsard, Montaigne, Bodin, and Charron in France; of Marlowe, Sidney, Spenser, Jonson, Bacon, and Shakespeare in England; but with the exception of Hans Sachs, hardly a noteworthy name appears in German literature between Luther's death and the Thirty Years' War. In the latter part of this period, German literature was little more than a poor imitation of foreign literatures. In short, while England produced the great literature of the Elizabethan age and France became the cultural dictator of Europe, German culture grew less and less attractive to the upper classes, and also to many members of the middle class. They turned to the cultures of other countries, particularly France. Even the German language was regarded as crude, and by the opening of the seventeenth century French was supplanting it as the language of polite conversation in Germany.

In the universities the study of theology overshadowed all other subjects. The humanistic impulse of the late fifteenth and early sixteenth centuries, with its promise of academic freedom, had spent itself, and methods of study reminiscent of scholasticism were enthroned in both Catholic and Protestant universities. Many German universities became centers of religious polemics and propaganda rather than schools for the study of science and the liberal arts. Earlier in the century Melanchthon had said: "Learning and letters have come to be loathed in Germany in consequence of religious squabbles." As the century progressed this condition became increasingly true. Both the Protestants and the Catholics sought more and more to propagate their type of Christianity, with little regard for liberal culture. But the decline was not restricted to the quality of the education; it affected also the number of students attending the universities. Before the middle of the century the enrollment of the smaller universities had already decreased considerably, and toward the end of the century even the University of Wittenberg saw the number of its students diminish. Like the universities, the secondary schools (Gymnasia and Latin schools) were dominated by theological learning and the sectarian spirit. This was as true of the new schools founded by the Lutherans as of the old schools controlled by the Catholic Church. Even in Austria and Bavaria, which had remained faithful to the Roman Church, most of the schools sank to a low level. Furthermore, the number of pupils attending the secondary schools decreased. As early as 1562 Emperor Ferdinand I wrote to the Council of Trent: "In the German Gymnasia one can now hardly find as many pupils, counting all together, as formerly attended one of these institutions. In place of five hundred or four hundred students who formerly attended one of them we can find hardly more than twenty or thirty." Such conditions moved a contemporary to write that of the many schools which had formerly been devoted to the liberal arts there remained "nothing but miserable corpses."

Besides the decay of culture and education, the period after the peace of Augsburg also witnessed the decline of German commerce and industry. At the beginning of the sixteenth century Germany was a prosperous country. The great banking houses of the Fuggers and the Welsers lent money to the princes and merchants of Europe, the Hansa controlled the Baltic trade, and the merchants of southern Germany and the Rhine provinces carried on a flourishing trade in goods purchased from Italian merchants. But this changed during the second half of the century. In the north the very success of the Hanseatic League was, in a sense, responsible for its downfall. Its prosperity awakened a commercial spirit in other countries, and stimulated the merchants of the lands served by the league to enter into competition with the Hansa traders. The decline of the league's trade may be dated from 1535, the year in which Denmark and Sweden opened the Baltic to the ships of all peoples. Thereafter the Dutch and English gradually gained much of the northern commerce; the Dutch displaced the Hanseatic League in Sweden and Denmark, while the English concluded commercial treaties which brought them much of the Russian trade. In 1598 Queen Elizabeth dealt a fatal blow to the trade between the Hansa and England by closing the London Steelyard which had served as trading headquarters for the German merchants for five centuries. Though the league was not formally dissolved until 1669, only three of its towns, Hamburg, Bremen, and Lübeck, continued to be centers of a thriving commerce after the sixteenth century.

While the trade of the Hanseatic League was declining in the north, the trade of southern Germany was decreasing because the Atlantic Ocean had replaced the Mediterranean as the highway of the world's commerce. As long as the Italian cities controlled the routes to the East, the cities of southern Germany and of the Rhine Valley thrived from the trade which passed over the Alps. When the eastern trade was diverted to Lisbon, commercial decay set in. Such important centers as Nuremberg, Augsburg, Cologne, and Ulm lost much of their trade, retaining a measure of their prosperity only through their banking activities and the output of certain industries. But the numerous bankruptcies of the last decades of the sixteenth century undermined the prosperity of the banking houses. The Welsers suspended business in 1614, and the fate of the Fuggers, though they struggled on, was sealed about the same time.

The basic explanation of the decline of its commerce is to be sought in Germany's political division as well as in its geographical position. The German merchants lacked the national assistance which permitted the merchants of Portugal, Spain, Holland, and England to make the most of commercial opportunities. Had the Hanseatic League enjoyed the support of a strong government it might have been able to resist the encroachments of the rising national states upon its trade. Without such backing the Hanseatic League was easily dispossessed. In brief, if some unity of action had been possible Germany might have participated in the scramble for riches, colonies, trade routes, and markets in the seventeenth century. Success in this competition, however, could be achieved only with the aid of national armies and fleets and through a unified financial and economic system. In Germany economic unity was as little possible as political. Each petty sovereignty pursued its own advantage without thought for the welfare of the German state as a whole. The various principalities began to impose duties on goods wherever and whenever they could. Consequently Germany soon became a checkerboard of clashing economic interests. This state of affairs was of course an invitation to the rising commercial nations to establish and carry out policies harmful to German commerce. Thus the Dutch arrested German trade on the Rhine by virtually closing the mouth of that river through ever increasing tolls. The outlets of other rivers that were the natural thoroughfares of German commerce likewise passed under foreign control, with the result that the inland cities were shut off from the sea and the great commercial highways.[1]

The decline of German trade was accompanied by a decay of German industries. Continual civil and religious strife and foreign competition proved ruinous factors. Thus cloth-weaving, one of the principal industries of Germany, was crippled when the cloths of other countries gradually claimed not only the foreign but also the home markets of the German trade. In the Netherlands and particularly in England woolen cloths of the finest and medium grades were manufactured at a price the cloth-makers of Germany could not meet. When the English flooded the German markets with their woolens, the ruin of the industry in both the north and south of Germany was inevitable. Similarly, even the finer varieties of German cotton cloths were superseded in the sixteenth century by the products of Flanders and France. Some of the German industries, however, were able to retain their importance and prosperity, despite the industrial decline. The craftsmen of Augsburg, Nuremberg, and other cities famous for the excellence of their arms and equipment continued to supply a large part of Europe with their products; also the manufacture of gunpowder and the hardware and linen industries continued to prosper.

With the rise of prices in the sixteenth century, agriculture became more profitable for landowners, but the condition of the German peasants remained deplorable. After the disastrous failure

---

[1] While the trade of the inland cities was declining, that of Hamburg and Bremen increased. These two ports, commanding the mouths of the Elbe and the Weser, became more and more the great outlets for the exports and the ports of entry for the imports of Germany.

of the insurrection of 1525 the peasants were thrust back into subjection to their ecclesiastical or noble masters. A few of the lords
were farsighted enough to remove the worst of the grievances
which had been responsible for the revolt, but most of them re-
imposed on their unfortunate subjects all the old burdens, including forced labor and inordinate taxation. Indemnities for
damages incurred by the nobles in the insurrection were relentlessly wrung out of the more prosperous peasants, with the result
that few remained independent owners of the land they cultivated.
Hosts of free peasants were forced into serfdom, and much of the
common land was confiscated by the lords. Whenever possible
the feudal lords increased the burdens of the peasantry. The way
to fresh exactions was open in many cases because the deeds and
charters on which the dues were recorded had been destroyed
during the insurrection. Thus the revolt of 1525, which had promised a measure of freedom, only made the miserable estate of the
peasants more hopeless. The lord was virtually the absolute master of the life and property of the peasant who was bound to the
soil. A serf could not even marry without his lord's consent. In
some parts of Germany the fact that a man was a peasant was
sufficient in jurisprudence to prove his serfdom. And the lot of
the peasant was not improved during the second half of the century; if anything, it grew worse. The lords missed no opportunity
to increase the amount of forced labor the peasants owed them.
In 1580 the elector of Saxony found it necessary to issue the following decree: "The poor peasants must not be forced to do soc-
age work or perform other services on Sunday, a day on which
even the cattle and oxen are permitted to rest." This degradation
of the peasants was bound to react on the life of the German
people as a whole. In the words of a German historian: "The
peasants form so large—moreover so fundamental—a part of the
nation as a whole that their impoverization and demoralization
must needs poison the life of the entire nation." [1]

THE THIRTY YEARS' WAR

After many decades of general decline, war, with its destructive fury, descended on Germany in 1618. The Thirty Years' War
was in reality a series of four wars which only their close con-
secutiveness permits us to regard as one. Each of the four periods

[1] W. Roscher, *Geschichte der National-Oekonomik in Deutschland* (1874), p. 123.

of the war—the Bohemian, the Danish, the Swedish, and the French—was almost a complete unit in itself, arising from peculiar causes and bringing new actors on the scene. That the struggle was renewed at the end of each period was due entirely to the interference of some foreign power. Strictly speaking, it was not a religious war. Other causes and motives played an important part. Indeed, as the war progressed the initial religious issues were overshadowed by those of political moment. Wallenstein, for example, pushed religious questions into the background, and Richelieu and Mazarin were actuated primarily by a desire to weaken the power of the Habsburgs and to increase the territory of France at Germany's expense. Restricted at first to Bohemia, the war soon expanded into a general European conflict in which all the powers of western Europe became involved at some time or other. Its basic cause was the bitter rivalry between the Catholics and the Protestants, which was aggravated by a number of questions the peace of Augsburg had left unsettled. Once it had started two other causes made for the continuation of the war: (1) the determination of the emperor to make his rule a reality in Germany; (2) the ambitions of certain European rulers, including Richelieu, Christian IV of Denmark, and Gustavus Adolphus of Sweden.

While effecting a compromise between the Catholics and the Lutherans, the peace of Augsburg had failed to satisfy either party. In the first place, when the treaty was made there were no princes of the Calvinistic confession; therefore it recognized only the Lutherans. Since that time Calvinism had spread widely while the energies of Lutheranism had faltered; as a result the Calvinists demanded legal recognition in Germany. Furthermore, the peace of Augsburg had decreed that all church lands seized before 1552 (Convention of Passau) were to remain secularized. Disputes had arisen, however, as to the interpretation of this provision for the future. While the Protestant princes claimed the right of further secularization of church lands within their states, the Catholics insisted that all lands secularized after 1552 be restored. Finally, the terms of the so-called Ecclesiastical Reservation, which ordained that benefices should be vacated by incumbents who embraced Protestantism, were repeatedly violated, since the Protestants refused to recognize the Reservation. Many of the clergy who became Protestant had secularized the lands which they had controlled as bishops and abbots. Feeling grew so bitter that both sides began to prepare for an appeal to force. In 1608 a Protestant League was organized, but because of the existing hostility between the Lutherans and the Calvinists only the Calvinistic states of the Rhineland and a number of free cities joined it. The next year the Catholics also organized a league under the leadership of Maximilian of Bavaria. In contrast with the Protestant League, this union was characterized by unity and vigor from the start. After numerous threats of war the conflict broke out in 1618.

The war began over the denial of rights bestowed on the Protestants of Bohemia. In 1609 the Emperor Rudolph II, who was also king of Bohemia, granted to the Bohemians a royal charter (*Majestaetsbrief*) which gave to the adherents of certain recognized Protestant creeds rights almost equal to those enjoyed by the Catholics. When his successor Matthias, who became ruler of Bohemia in 1611, endeavored to restrict these rights the Bohemian nobles, who were largely Protestant, bore with him, vowing that after the death of this old and sickly ruler they would choose one more favorably inclined toward Protestantism. But in 1617 the Bohemian Diet was informed by the emperor that the monarchy was not elective. Ferdinand of Styria, ardent Catholic and partisan of the Catholic League, was designated the legitimate successor of Matthias. No sooner had Ferdinand been crowned hereditary monarch of Bohemia than the controversy over the religious question came to a head. When several Protestant churches were destroyed, the Protestants appealed to the emperor and their charter. Receiving no satisfaction, they rose in revolt. In Prague a band of noblemen entered the room where the king's regents were seated, seized them, dragged them to the window, and "according to the good old Bohemian custom" (as a contemporary account has it) threw them out. Though they dropped more than fifty feet, the two regents and their secretary escaped without serious hurt, their voluminous cloaks and a convenient dunghill breaking their fall.

The so-called "defenestration" seems of slight importance when compared with the violence of the times; yet it was the signal for the beginning of the Thirty Years' War. On the one hand, Ferdinand was furious and resolved to punish his refractory subjects; on the other, the Bohemians declared they would no longer tolerate him as their king. In August, 1619, the Bohemian Diet met and formally deposed Ferdinand, who in May of that year, on the death of Matthias, had also become emperor as Ferdinand II. Frederick, elector of the Palatinate, leader of the German Calvinists and son-in-law of James I of England, was chosen as the new king of Bohemia. Eager to obtain the royal dignity, he accepted the throne despite the warnings of his close friends; but he was to retain it only a short time. Maximilian of Bavaria, the Catholic League, and Spain at once came to the aid of Ferdinand, while Frederick's cause evoked little response. The assistance he had hoped for from the Protestant states was not forthcoming; even his royal English father-in-law sent him no help. Lacking both an army and military skill, Frederick mustered such forces as he could to oppose the imperial army which had invaded Bohemia under the able leadership of General Tilly. At Weissenberg, on November 8, 1620, Frederick's army was decisively routed. Frederick himself was forced to flee to The Hague for safety. The emperor, not content with driving Frederick out of Bohemia, proceeded to conquer the Palatinate, conferring it, together with the electoral dignity attached to it, upon Maximilian of Bavaria as a reward for his assistance. In Bohemia Ferdinand followed his victory by a policy of confiscation and religious oppression calculated to crush the Protestant resistance once and for all. Most of the leaders of the Protestant party were executed and their property was confiscated; the Protestant clergy were expelled from the country, Protestant worship was forbidden, and thousands of Protestants were forced into exile.

The emperor had prevailed with the help of the Catholic League. But the supremacy of the emperor and the league was viewed with anxiety by the German Protestant princes. Many who had kept aloof from the troubles in Bohemia realized that steps must be taken if the independence and privileges of Protestants were to remain secure. Aid soon came from the outside. Christian IV, king of Denmark, championed the cause of Protestantism and opposed the growing power of the emperor. Besides being a Lutheran, Christian IV, as duke of Holstein, was a prince of the empire; he also had a family interest in several Protestant bishoprics which were bound to be claimed by the Catholics as having been taken in violation of the Ecclesiastical Reservation. When the English offered to pay him £30,000 a month, if he would invade Germany, the Danish king accepted the offer. No sooner had the Danish army entered Germany than the Emperor

Ferdinand realized that if his forces were to offer effective resistance another army must be put into the field. His finances, however, were in such straitened condition that it would have been
difficult for him to equip a single additional regiment. At this
point Albrecht von Waldstein, better known to history as Wallenstein, offered to collect an army of 20,000 men without any cost
to the emperor. Ferdinand eagerly accepted the offer.

Wallenstein was a Bohemian nobleman who had become one
of the largest landowners of Germany through a fortunate marriage and the acquisition, at very little cost, of vast stretches of
land confiscated from the Bohemians. In the Bohemian war he
had rendered such valuable services to the emperor that he was
made duke of Friedland in 1623. His motives for offering the
services of an army to the emperor were not religious. By origin
a Protestant, he was nominally a Catholic; actually he believed
in little but his own rising star. His mind was filled with daring
schemes, mostly for his own aggrandizement, though the expulsion of the foreign armies from Germany and a united empire in
which all creeds were to be tolerated had a place in them. As a
military leader he was a consummate organizer and a strategist
of high ability. The army which he collected with the utmost ease
was a cosmopolitan aggregation. Soldiers from all parts of Europe
and from every faith quickly filled his ranks, attracted by the high
pay and the opportunity for adventure. By the autumn of 1625
Wallenstein found himself at the head of 50,000 men, united only
in their allegiance to him. This army, which was to be supported
by compulsory levies upon the districts through which it passed,
actually supported itself in large part by pillage. Despite its motley composition, under Wallenstein's leadership it was an effective
instrument of war. It not only defeated the Danish forces but
drove them out of Germany. Christian IV was happy to sign a
treaty of peace at Lübeck on May 22, 1629. By this treaty he retained his hereditary possessions but relinquished all claims to
the bishoprics held in the empire by his family. Thus the so-called
Danish period of the war came to an end.

Instead of attempting to heal the breach between the two factions in the empire by conciliatory measures, Ferdinand, flushed
with his victory over Christian IV, peremptorily issued the Edict
of Restitution (1629), which decreed the restoration to the Church
of all ecclesiastical property secularized since the treaty of Passau

(1552). The territories involved were two archbishoprics, twelve bishoprics, and about one hundred twenty smaller ecclesiastical foundations, some of which had been secularized more than half a century before. It was an ill-advised measure of which even Wallenstein openly disapproved. Besides alienating the loyalty of many Germans, it roused the Swedish king, Gustavus Adolphus, to intervene in the war.

Gustavus Adolphus (1594–1632) was a devout, simple, courageous king. His motives for engaging in the war combined a desire to save Protestantism with a desire to advance the fortunes of his house. As a fervent Lutheran he was moved by the plight of his coreligionists in Germany. He saw the cause of Protestantism in jeopardy if the Habsburgs were to triumph. As king of Sweden, Gustavus aspired to control the Baltic; he had already fought for eighteen years with Denmark, Poland, and Russia for that end. Now he saw his aim imperiled by an imperial victory. Encouraged by Richelieu, Gustavus in 1630 landed his army on German shores. His army was not large, but it was an efficient force. The mere fact that it was a national army inspired by patriotic motives gave it a great advantage over the mercenary troops of the opposition. It was also of one mind in religion, an army which prayed and fought with equal zeal. Moreover, it was probably the best-drilled army of Europe, with a discipline that was unique for the times. Because they were well drilled and well versed in military tactics, Gustavus could move his forces with a swiftness unattainable by his opponents. Even the musket used by the Swedish troops was a great improvement upon that of the imperial forces. Finally, the Swedish king also had pecuniary support. Early in 1631 Richelieu, who had no desire to see Germany united even under the leadership of a good Catholic, concluded a treaty with Gustavus; he promised to pay the Swedish king a large subsidy on condition that the latter maintain an army of 26,000 men in Germany and that he refrain from interfering with the exercise of the Catholic religion.

When Gustavus entered Germany the Protestants for a time refused to join him, because they feared that their aid might help to establish a Swedish ascendancy in Germany. Not until the imperial army captured the thriving city of Magdeburg and reduced it to blackened ruins did Brandenburg and Saxony join hands with the invader. The "Lion of the North," as Gustavus came to be called, could now take the offensive. In September, 1631, he met Tilly's army, hitherto unbeaten, at Breitenfeld near Leipzig, and inflicted upon it an overwhelming defeat; Tilly died soon afterward from wounds received in battle. As Wallenstein had previously been dismissed by the emperor, who feared his growing power and ambition, Germany now seemed at the mercy of Gustavus. Ferdinand realized that he was lost unless he could induce his deposed general to reassume the command of which he had been relieved. Wallenstein was willing to return, but on his own terms. He demanded among other conditions the withdrawal of the Edict of Restitution, absolute freedom of action in military matters, including the right to appoint his own officers, and a guarantee that there should be no other commander of his rank. In his distress, the emperor was compelled to accede to these unwelcome demands.

In a short time Wallenstein again collected a heterogeneous army and proceeded to attack the Swedish forces. The two armies met at Lützen (1632). After a day of fierce fighting Wallenstein withdrew his troops from the field, recognizing the Swedes as victorious. But to the Swedes the victory was costly indeed. In the heat of the battle Gustavus, failing to temper courage with discretion, fought his way almost single-handed into the midst of the enemy and was killed. The loss of the Swedish leader whom Napoleon was to list among the eight great generals of all time was irreparable.[1] Soon the Swedish army, which had hitherto been held in strict discipline, was to sink to the level of the other armies of Germany. With Gustavus out of his way, the emperor no longer stood in such great need of Wallenstein. He was more than ever alarmed over the personal power of this general who was making grandiose plans which have remained largely enigmatic to this day. This much is certain: that Wallenstein was tired of war and was plotting with the Swedes to arrange a general peace. There is also some indication that he wished to retain for himself the crown of Bohemia. But before he could carry out his plans, he was dismissed, in 1634. Shortly afterwards he was assassinated by one of his own officers.

When it seemed that the war was about to end, Richelieu stepped in, determined to crush the Habsburgs so completely that

[1] Liddell Hart, in *Great Captains Unveiled* (1928), p. 151, styles Gustavus Adolphus "The Founder of Modern War."

they would be unable to contest the power of France for a long time. Since the Swedes were too weak to continue the struggle without the brilliant leadership of Gustavus Adolphus, Richelieu sent a French army into the field in 1635. With the French and Swedes on one side, and the Austrians and Spaniards on the other, the war dragged out its devastating course another thirteen years. At first the French army met with a series of reverses; later, however, the two eminent French generals, Condé and Turenne, dealt the imperial army such severe blows that Emperor Ferdinand III consented to the measures necessary to end the conflict. For the task of making a settlement the first modern peace congress was convened at Münster and Osnabrück. After a protracted session the powers finally signed in 1648 what has become known as the Treaty of Westphalia.

This treaty of peace settled the religious difficulties of Germany by extending to the Calvinists the religious freedom and civil equality previously given to the Lutherans. It further adjusted the question of the ecclesiastical lands by specifying that the Protestants were to retain all lands they had taken before the first day of 1624. More difficult of solution were the problems connected with territorial compensation. Eventually the following settlement was adopted: (1) Maximilian of Bavaria was given permission to add the upper Palatinate to his duchy and to retain the electorate. (2) Charles Louis, son of the hapless Frederick who for a brief time had been "king of Bohemia," received the title of elector together with the lower Palatinate, an eighth electorate being specifically created for him. (3) Sweden obtained western Pomerania, which Brandenburg had claimed, as well as the districts at the mouth of the Oder and the bishoprics of Bremen and Verden. (4) Brandenburg, besides gaining eastern Pomerania, was compensated for western Pomerania with the bishoprics of Halberstadt, Minden, and Camin, and the greater part of the archbishopric of Magdeburg. (5) France gained the right to annex the bishoprics of Metz, Toul, and Verdun and acquired Alsace, excepting Strasburg and certain other parts. (6) Switzerland and the United Netherlands were formally recognized as independent states.

The peace of Westphalia, in a sense, gave the deathblow to the Holy Roman Empire. By its terms the various states were permitted to make alliances not only with one another but also with foreign countries. Although a clause declared that such alliances must not be made against the empire, the emperor, or the peace of the land, it was so vague that it could easily be circumvented. Actually each state was now independent, having its own army, its own toll and customs system, and its own mint. Thenceforth the empire continued more as a name than as a state.

The peace of Westphalia did not, however, terminate the war between France and Spain. Between these two countries it was continued for another eleven years with little vigor on either side. While Spain was weak from misgovernment and economic decay, France was in the throes of the civil war known as the Fronde. Finally, in 1659 the two countries signed the treaty of the Pyrenees, a kind of supplement to that of Westphalia. By its terms France retained its conquests, which included Rousillon, Artois, and Cerdagne. The treaty also provided for the marriage of Louis XIV to Marie Thérèse, the daughter of Philip IV. It was stipulated that in return for a large dowry Marie Thérèse was to resign all claims to the Spanish throne. The fact that the dowry was never paid later gave Louis XIV an excuse for trying to annex the Spanish Netherlands.

THE EFFECTS OF THE THIRTY YEARS' WAR IN GERMANY

After three decades the war finally came to an end. In Germany it produced every misery, woe, and tragedy which accompanies war, and gave scope for all manner of savage and brutal indulgence. Hundreds of villages and towns were destroyed and whole districts laid desolate by marauding armies with their bands of camp followers. Pouncing upon homes and villages like vultures on a carcass, the scourging hosts would often wantonly destroy what they could not carry away. Indescribable cruelties were inflicted on the peasants in order to force them to divulge the places where they had hidden what valuables they still possessed. The toll of lives was large. Besides the hundreds of thousands slain in battle, many times that number were carried off by the famines, pestilences, and plagues which stalked the land. Commerce and industry suffered severely, and the general moral tone of the German people was lowered.

Terrible as were the effects of the Thirty Years' War, they may nevertheless be exaggerated. German historians of the nineteenth century, in endeavoring to account for the economic backward-

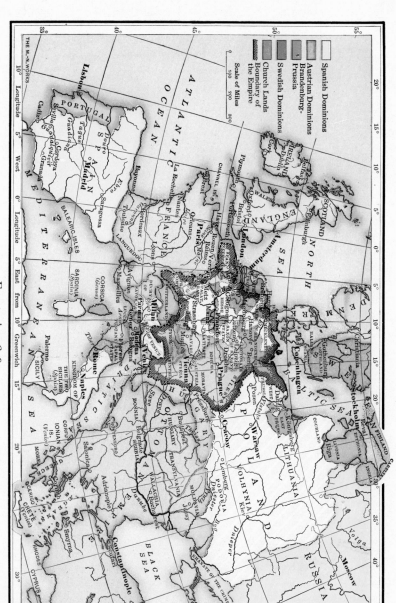

Europe in 1648

ness of Germany in the two centuries after the Thirty Years' War, ascribed it to the destructive effects of the war. The belief that the Thirty Years' War "made a gap in the national development of Germany such as we find nowhere else in history" became a historical dogma. Every tale of horror was readily accepted and often "improved" by the addition of more superlatives. Thus one may read such statements as: "Men climbed up the scaffolds and tore down bodies of those hanged and devoured them. The supply was large. Newly buried corpses were dug up for food. Children were enticed away, that they might be slain and eaten." [1] The opinion still prevails in wide circles that the Thirty Years' War descended suddenly on a prosperous and flourishing country, destroying the material and intellectual civilization so completely that Germany was thrown back at least a century (or even two) in its development. "What did the endless war make out of the flourishing and highly cultured Germany! A desert, a heap of ruins, a depopulated wilderness. Many rich and happy towns had disappeared entirely; it was often even impossible to find the place where they had formerly stood. Some of the districts which had been among the richest and most populous were inhabited only by wolves. Whoever had the courage to go there could travel for days without finding even a trace of a human being." [2]

Any attempt to estimate the destructive effects of the war must consider the fact that a general decline of German civilization was already far advanced when the war began. In some phases of German life the nadir of decline was reached before the war broke out. Hence the entire blame for the condition of Germany in 1648 cannot justly be laid at the door of the Thirty Years' War. The war undoubtedly accelerated the decline, but it was not its primary cause. Furthermore, it must be remembered that not all parts of Germany were equally affected by the war. Some districts suffered severely, while others were affected only slightly. No part of Germany remained the scene of war continuously for

---

[1] A. MacDonald, "Suggestions of the Peace Treaty of Westphalia for the League of Nations," *Reformed Church Review*, ser. 4, vol. 23 (1919), p. 482. F. Julian, in "Angebliche Menschenfresserei im dreissigjährigen Krieg," *Mitteilungen des historischen Vereins der Pfalz*, vol. 45 (1927), pp. 37–93, concludes, after a careful investigation of their sources, that the tales regarding cannibalism during the Thirty Years' War are, with one exception (the siege of Breisach, 1638), fictitious. Such stories, he states, were used for purposes of propaganda or were based on superstition or phantasy.

[2] R. Quanter, *Kulturgeschichte des deutschen Volkes* (1924), p. 529.

three decades. Even in the districts hardest hit, there were periods
of comparative quiet, often covering many years. In the south of
Germany the Austrian crown lands, excepting Bohemia, Moravia,
and Silesia, remained largely untouched by actual warfare; also
the whole of northwestern Germany experienced little of the destruction of the war. Hamburg, in fact, made considerable progress in the development of its trade.

In turning from the towns which escaped the ravages of the
war to those which suffered heavily, caution must be exercised
lest one accept literally the statements of the damages wrought
by the war. As a number of nineteenth century historians pointed
out, the local reports often contained willful exaggerations—exaggerations which were motivated by the blind confessional hatred
of the time. Protestants accused the leaders of the "Catholic" or
imperial armies of the most horrible deeds; Catholics in turn portrayed the Protestants as the scum of humanity. A contemporary
statement has it that the Protestant Swedes destroyed five thousand villages in Brandenburg at a time when that duchy contained
only half that number. Other overstatements can be traced to the
desire to excite sympathy, to obtain a reduction of the war burdens, or to escape further payments of subsidies or levies of troops.
A tendency to exaggerate is characteristic of the age. In the words
of Karl Lamprecht: "There is no doubt that many of the individual accounts are highly exaggerated, if for no other reason because the age of baroque spoke in hyperboles." [1]

It may be true that in certain districts the population declined
to a small fraction of its former size, but this condition was not
universal in Germany. In Saxony, for example, the population
was considerably larger a few years after peace was concluded
than it had been before the war broke out. Frequently at the approach of the armies all the people of a district would migrate to
other sections, thereby causing merely a displacement and not a
general decrease of the population. For this reason the oft-repeated
statements that the war devoured three-fourths, two-thirds, or even
half of the population stand in need of revision. A contemporary
statistician, estimating in round numbers the casualties of each
battle, arrived at a grand total of 325,000 slain during the war.[2]

[1] *Deutsche Geschichte*, vol. 6 (1904), p. 341.
[2] Cited by K. T. von Inama-Sternegg in "Die volkswirtschaftlichen Folgen des
dreissigjährigen Kriegs," *Historisches Taschenbuch*, vol. 5 (1864), p. 15.

Even when it is granted that the number who fell victims to the plague and famine was many times greater, the total is still far from such estimates as half or two-thirds of a population of about eighteen or twenty millions. Of course the empire lost a considerable part of its population in 1648 through the cession of large territories to France [1] and through the recognition of Switzerland as an independent state.

In like manner the material destruction of the war has been exaggerated. Much as they may have consumed or destroyed, the foreign armies did not live in Germany solely by plunder. France, Holland, Spain, England, and the pope sent prodigious sums into Germany for the support of both native and foreign armies. The soldiers of Gustavus Adolphus were forbidden to plunder, and later Oxenstierna, the Swedish chancellor, increased the pay of his soldiers to meet the rise of prices in Germany. Other generals, also, forbade their soldiers to ravage the country. A contemporary chronicle says of Tilly's soldiers during the period they remained in the vicinity of Hanover: "For the most part they bought their provisions and all kinds of supplies in Hanover with money." [2] Furthermore, in rebuttal of such statements as "thousands of villages disappeared completely," it had been shown that many communities which, according to tradition, were supposed to have disappeared during the Thirty Years' War had really ceased to exist as early as the thirteenth and fourteenth centuries.[3] Of the numerous villages burned by the various armies, only a few were not rebuilt before the end of the war or soon thereafter. In the whole of Brandenburg not one village was permanently destroyed. Neither did the war turn large sections of Germany into wilderness. No class of the population suffered as much as the peasants; yet their losses were not irreparable. The fertility of the soil, which was the source of their wealth, was not destroyed by the armies. When the armies did ravage an area, the devastation was in most cases only temporary. Wherever the soil was fertile there was a speedy resuscitation of agriculture as soon as the armies had

[1] While the territories that were ceded to Sweden nominally remained part of the Holy Roman Empire, those given to France were severed from the Germanic body.
[2] Cited by H. Schmidt in "Die Stadt Hannover im dreissigjährigen Kriege," *Niedersächsisches Jahrbuch*, vol. 3 (1926), p. 100.
[3] See H. Beschorner, "Wiederaufbau der meisten im dreissigjährigen Kriege zerstörten Dörfer," *Studium Lipsiense* (1909), pp. 73–88.

passed. To counterbalance accounts painted in the blackest colors we meet such statements as the following, made in 1646: "The people of this part of the country (duchy of Berg) have become so accustomed to war that they pay little attention to it. Their fields are cultivated and they have thrashed their grain and hidden it away." [1] Englishmen traveling in Germany shortly after the war reported in most parts of Germany not scenes of devastation but thriving villages, well-cultivated fields, and plentiful crops.[2]

Neither were German letters, learning, and science blighted as completely as is frequently stated. The German literature of the war years is not inferior to that of the preceding period. In fact, a gradual improvement in quality is perceptible in the literature of the seventeenth century, beginning with the appearance in 1617 of Martin Opitz' *Aristarchus, or On the Neglect of the German Language*, which, though it was written in Latin so that it could be read by the learned men of Germany, was an earnest protest against the neglect of the mother tongue. "You must love it," Opitz wrote, "if you do not wish to foster enmity against your fatherland or, in other words, against yourself." The writings of Opitz and his followers ushered in a movement to raise the standard of German literature, to improve the German language, and to encourage the use of German by the so-called cultured classes. In the same year in which Opitz' book appeared, the *Fruchtbringende Gesellschaft* (Fruit-Bearing Society) was organized for the purpose of restoring and preserving the purity of the German language. It combatted the use of French by the upper classes and also the practice of padding the German language with foreign words (*Sprachmengerei*), both of which are often set down as results of the war. This society not only was active during the war but continued to grow in membership and influence. In science Germany produced in this period Johann Kepler, one of the great astronomers of history, and Otto von Guericke, inventor of the air pump. On the other hand, the universities suffered a great loss of students, particularly toward the end of the war; consequently many—among them Heidelberg—were forced to close their doors. Some decades were to elapse before the damages of the conflict to education were repaired.

---

[1] Cited in B. Erdmannsdörffer's *Deutsche Geschichte, 1648–1740*, vol. 1 (1892), p. 103.

[2] See I. Hoffmann, *Deutschland in Zeitalter des dreissigjährigen Krieges: Nach Urteilen und Berichten englischer Augenzeugen* (1927), p. 117.

HENRY IV AND MARIE DE MÉDICIS
by Rubens

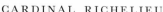

CARDINAL RICHELIEU

WALLENSTEIN   *by Van Dyke*

GUSTAVUS ADOLPHUS   *by Van Dyke*

GALILEO

ISAAC NEWTON

LAVOISIER AT WORK

In summary, the war was not the basic cause of the cultural and economic decline of Germany. It was but an incident in that decline. Long before the war broke out the springs of the intellectual life of the country had begun to dry up and German commerce and industry had started their downward trend. What the war destroyed was only a fraction of the economic prosperity Germany had enjoyed at the beginning of the sixteenth century. The rest had disappeared before the war began. Furthermore, the low estate of German commerce and industry during the two centuries after the war was due not so much to the destruction of the war as to the inability of Germany to recuperate from the long decline that had started about the middle of the sixteenth century. When the treaty of Westphalia confirmed the territorial independence of the German states it effectively barred the way to economic recovery. In France a recovery was made within a short time after the civil wars of the sixteenth century, but in Germany the political and economic decentralization prevented any vigorous commercial or industrial policy. While the commerce within Germany was hampered by innumerable tariff barriers, much of the foreign commerce was at the mercy of such national states as Holland, Denmark, Poland, and Sweden, which occupied the mouths of most of the German rivers in the north, shutting German merchants off from the sea and the markets of the world. So long as each of the rulers of the three hundred odd German states pursued his selfish and independent policy, German commerce and industry were unable to compete with those of the unified national states of Europe. Not until some measure of economic and political unity was established in the nineteenth century did German commerce and industry, as a whole, become prosperous again.[1]

[1] C. V. Wedgwood's excellent study, *The Thirty Years' War* (1939), which was published after this book had been set, substantiates the views on the effects of the war expressed here. According to the estimate cited by Miss Wedgwood (p. 516), the population of the Holy Roman Empire decreased by one-third during the period 1618–1648. Recently published studies and sources indicate that even this estimate is high. An important recent study is Elmer-A. Beller's *Propaganda in Germany during the Thirty Years' War*, which analyzes the different types of propaganda produced for the various social classes.

CHAPTER FOURTEEN

The Beginnings of Modern Science

THE beginnings of modern science go back to the late Middle Ages. In the early Middle Ages there was a definite lack of scientific interest in natural phenomena. Theology dominated learning, and formulation of the dogmas of the Church absorbed men's intellectual energies. Since preparation for the hereafter was regarded as the primary purpose of life, whatever "earthly" knowledge a man might gain was considered valueless in comparison with "divine" learning. From the tenth century on, however, there is discernible a slowly increasing scientific interest in nature; and from the twelfth and thirteenth centuries down to the present, one can follow a historical continuity in the study of natural science. For centuries, it is true, learned men relied on the authority of Aristotle in philosophy and science, of Galen in medicine, of Ptolemy in astronomy, and of Pliny the Elder in natural science; nevertheless intellectual curiosity bestirred itself, and the study of nature was often accompanied by independent scientific observations. By the thirteenth century there were indications of the forthcoming divorce of science from theology; men were beginning to ponder the problems which later centuries were to solve.

The most advanced stages of science in the late fifteenth century and in the early sixteenth are perhaps best summarized in the scientific notebooks of Leonardo da Vinci, who is most frequently thought of only as a great artist. Spurred on by an insatiable curiosity about man, animals, plants, and the physical universe, Leonardo did not confine himself to reading the authors of his own and the preceding age; in addition he made some astounding independent observations. Thus, in an age which generally believed that the sun revolved about the earth, Leonardo wrote: "The sun does not move." Another statement reads: "The earth is a star." Of the moon he said, "I say that the moon has no light in itself and yet is luminous; it is inevitable that its light is caused by some other body." In addition to his observations of the heavens, Leonardo made a close study of human anatomy, dissecting more than thirty bodies of men and women. His detailed knowledge is revealed in the series of magnificent anatomical drawings he left to posterity. From his representations of the valves of the heart, it is assumed that he may have known the circulation of the blood a century before Harvey, but he did not know the laws involved. Versed also in all branches of military science, he left sketches of a mortar for throwing bombs and shrapnel and evolved plans for a submarine which, however, he refused to describe "on account of the evil nature of men, who would practice assassination on the bottom of the seas by breaking the hulls of ships." He even turned over in his mind the possibility of employing poisonous gases in warfare. In an effort to discover the secret of flight Leonardo studied birds and every creature that flies; on the basis of his observations he made sketches of "flying machines." Leonardo also left a drawing of a parachute with the comment: "Any person who possesses a stiff canvas tent of twelve ells height and breadth may let himself fall from any height, no matter how great, without fear of injury." Among his aphorisms were the following: "Practice should always be founded on sound theory"; "Motion is the cause of all life"; and "Every act of nature is accomplished by her in the quickest possible time and most direct manner." Leonardo jotted down in his notebooks his observations, opinions, and conclusions, dealing with an encyclopedic range of topics. More than 5300 sheets have been found, closely covered with notes and sketches on one or both sides. But, since he did not publish his observations, Leonardo gave no noticeable impetus to the advance of science.[1]

---

[1] Leonardo did, it appears, have some influence on the development of the science of anatomy through the naturalism of his art. Writes Charles Singer, in *The Evolution of Anatomy* (1925), p. 92: "The atmosphere created by Leonardo and the

THE CONFLICT OF SYSTEMS

The first great advance in the history of modern science was made with the publication of the heliocentric theory of Copernicus in 1543. The medieval conception of the universe was predominantly geocentric. This theory had been firmly established by Claudius Ptolemaeus, more commonly called Ptolemy, an astronomer who lived in Egypt during the second century after Christ. So closely was his name associated with the geocentric theory that it became known as the Ptolemaic system. Ptolemy declared that the earth was an immovable sphere, fixed in the center of the universe, with the sun and the stars revolving about it. For many centuries the Ptolemaic system was almost undisputedly accepted. Not only did it seem to agree with the perception of the senses but it was also in harmony with the homocentric doctrine of theology, which recognized man as the principal object of divine concern. The entire universe was conceived as having been created to serve man's needs. Hence it was but natural to regard the earth, the abode of man, as the center of the universe. The view is perhaps best expressed by Peter Lombardus (1100–1160), who wrote: "Just as Man is made for the sake of God, in order that he may serve Him; so the Universe is made for the sake of Man, that it may serve him; therefore is Man placed at the center of the Universe, that he may both serve and be served."

Although the belief that the earth was an immovable sphere in the center of the universe was universal in the Middle Ages, such was not the case in classical antiquity. Among the ancients a number of philosophers believed in the earth's motion. Thus the Pythagoreans taught that the earth revolved upon its own axis; a few went so far as to state that it revolved around the motionless sun. Aristarchus, for example, taught that the earth moves in a circular course, revolving around the sun as a center. But these ideas had never become popular because they seemed contrary to the observation of the senses. Ptolemy endeavored to refute them by stating that if the earth moved it would gradually gain speed and soon the objects on its surface would be hurled

great artist anatomists did certainly bear fruit. In that sense the work of Leonardo was not wholly lost, and there are even instances in which the actual mode of representation adopted by Vesalius bears some resemblance to that of Leonardo."

into space; that if the earth did move with great speed an object thrown into the air would fall to the ground east of its starting point. So apparently final were the arguments of Ptolemy that when Nicholas of Cusa in the fifteenth century propounded the doctrine of the earth's motion his ideas were not seriously considered. It remained for Copernicus to develop the heliocentric system and for his successors to secure its acceptance.

Nicholas Copernicus was born February 19, 1473, in Thorn, a little town on the Vistula. Founded by the Teutonic Order, at the time of Copernicus' birth it was under the rule of the king of Poland. It is still a matter of controversy whether his father, a merchant, was German or Polish. Little is known regarding the childhood and youth of Copernicus. After receiving his elementary training in Thorn, he entered the university at Cracow, but in 1496 he crossed the Alps to matriculate at Bologna. In the following year he was appointed canon in the cathedral chapter of Frauenburg in his native land. This position assured an annual income sufficient for his needs, and a leave of absence from his duties permitted him to stay in Italy. The professor of astronomy in Bologna while Copernicus was there was Domenico di Novara (1454–1504), who had the courage freely to criticize the theory of Ptolemy. It is reasonable to suppose that young Copernicus may have acquired his doubts concerning the correctness of the Ptolemaic system from this teacher. Copernicus' stay in Italy, broken by at least one visit to his homeland, lasted nine or ten years. During this time he pursued studies in theology, philosophy, logic, medicine, mathematics, and astronomy. In the spring of 1506, at the age of thirty-three, he settled in Frauenburg, which remained his home until his death in 1543. Of his personal life during these years there is but scant information. For posterity he exists largely in his work.

Since his duties as canon were not arduous, there was sufficient time to practice medicine, to continue his studies in astronomy, and, above all, to ponder his objections to the Ptolemaic system. His chief objection was its complexity. Convinced that the laws of nature were simple and harmonious, he began casting about for other explanations of the universe. In the writings of the classical philosophers to which he turned for enlightenment, Copernicus discovered that a number of early thinkers actually had attributed some form of motion to the earth. With this idea as a starting point he developed his daring hypothesis. The sun, he concluded, was the center of the solar system; the earth was but one of a number of planets that revolved around the sun at varying distances, rotating on their axes. Yet he retained certain current false notions. Thus, since he did not discard Aristotle's theory of the uniform circular motion of the heavenly bodies, he thought the planets moved in regular orbits around the sun. In developing his heliocentric theory Copernicus made occasional observations outdoors, but for the most part his results were obtained indoors in his study. He was primarily a philosopher and mathematician, not an observational astronomer. His instruments were poor and his eyesight was weak; hence his observations were somewhat inaccurate. That he desired accuracy is demonstrated by the fact that he compared his results with the recorded observations of the past.

Copernicus embodied the results of his thinking and observations in a book entitled *De Revolutionibus Orbium Coelestium* (*Concerning the Revolutions of the Heavenly Bodies*). For almost three decades he worked on the manuscript, revising it and reconsidering its conclusions. Naturally averse to controversy, he feared the reaction which so radical an idea as a heliocentric theory of the universe might cause. Therefore he was reluctant to publish it. "When I considered how absurd my doctrine would appear," he wrote, "I long hesitated whether I should publish my book, or whether it were not better to follow the example of the Pythagoreans and others who delivered their doctrine only by tradition, and to friends." Finally a disciple induced him to permit its publication. The book, dedicated to Pope Paul III, appeared in 1543, and a copy reached Copernicus on May 24, the very day of his death. But the work of Copernicus was issued not as revolutionary truth but as merely another hypothesis. To forestall criticism a fraudulent preface, ostensibly by Copernicus himself, had been prefixed to the work by Andreas Osiander, a Lutheran clergyman interested in astronomy, to whom the task of supervising the printing had been entrusted. The preface stated that the doctrine was entirely hypothetical, and should not be construed as a statement of fact.

It is only natural that such a radical innovation as the Copernican theory, a theory which demanded that man give up the flattering belief that he was living in a homocentric universe, should be opposed, even though it was put forward only as a hypothesis. For more than a thousand years the Ptolemaic theory had been universally accepted. The authority of centuries lay behind it; it also seemed to have the support of Scripture. Hence the theologians particularly opposed the acceptance of the new heterodox system. Luther, as reported in his *Tischreden*, said: "The fool is trying to turn the whole science of astronomy upside down. But, as the Holy Scriptures state, Joshua commanded the sun to stand still and not the earth." Calvin condemned the Copernican theory as a foolish superstition, and to substantiate his declaration he quoted the words of the 93rd Psalm (verse 1): "The world is so established that it cannot be moved." In the Roman Catholic Church no formal move was made against the theory so long as it was not put forward as a serious explanation of the universe; but when Giordano Bruno (1549–1600) made it the basis of his philosophy, the Church declared against it. In 1615 the Roman Inquisition formally condemned the teachings of Copernicus in the following terms:

The first proposition, that the sun is the center and does not revolve about the earth, is foolish, absurd, false in theology and heretical, because expressly contrary to Holy Scripture.

The second proposition, that the earth revolves about the sun and is not the center, is absurd, false in philosophy and, from a theological point of view at least, opposed to the true faith.

The next year Copernicus' book was placed on the Index of Prohibited Books, from which it was not removed for about one hundred fifty years.

But the theologians were not the only group that refused to accept the Copernican system. Important as the new theory was, its essential features still remained to be proved. Not until almost a century and a half after its publication was it generally accepted by astronomers, scholars, and mathematicians. Its final acceptance was due to the contributions of Tycho Brahe, Kepler, Galileo, and Newton. The work of Tycho Brahe (1546–1601), a Danish astronomer, consisted principally of observation. He erected a small observatory at Uraniborg on the island of Hven, given him by King Frederick II of Denmark; there he spent the years from 1576 to 1597 observing the stars and studying the moon and comets. Brahe rejected the Copernican theory, developing instead a theory which placed the earth in the center of the universe. Yet by a strange paradox he indirectly contributed, through his collection of accurate data on the position of the planets, toward the establishment of the system he so staunchly opposed. After Brahe's death his assistant and successor, Johann Kepler (1571–1630), who was deprived of the joy of observation by poor eyesight, deduced the laws of planetary movements from the observations of his predecessor. Kepler completely shattered the Aristotelian thesis of circular motion by showing that the planets moved in ellipses, a discovery which attested the fundamental truth of the Copernican hypothesis. An ardent supporter of the system of Copernicus, Kepler in 1616 published his *Epitome of Copernican Astronomy*, in which he endeavored to demolish all objections to it.

Further proof was added by Galileo Galilei, born in 1564 at Pisa in Italy. Like his two famous compatriots, Michelangelo and Dante, he has become known by his first name, Galileo. His father, an impoverished nobleman, chose a career in medicine for his son. To this end young Galileo entered the University of Pisa. Soon, however, his medical studies were neglected for his interest in philosophy, mathematics, and mechanics. Before he was twenty young Galileo discovered the law of the pendulum: that the successive swings of a pendulum occupy the same time. When he was twenty-five his unusual abilities were recognized by an appointment to the professorship of mathematics at Pisa.[1] Three years later he accepted a better appointment at Padua, where he remained for eighteen years, probably the happiest and most fruitful period of his life. Continuing his investigations of the laws of motion, he solved the problem of the law of falling bodies in terms of a uniform acceleration (1, 3, 5, 7, 9, etc.) as distinguished from uniform velocity. Today the law of falling bodies is still formulated as Galileo established it.

Galileo is perhaps most widely known and remembered for his astronomical studies. Early in life he became a convert to the Copernican ideas, but remained silent. In 1579 he wrote to Kepler: "I have been for many years an adherent of the Copernican

[1] Lane Cooper has written a scholarly little book (*Aristotle, Galileo and the Tower of Pisa*, 1935) to show that the oft-repeated story which has Galileo dropping weights from the Leaning Tower of Pisa to disprove an alleged statement of Aristotle is a myth. The book attempts to show: first, that Aristotle did not say that two bodies of unequal weight would fall to earth with unequal velocities; second, that there is no direct contemporary evidence that Galileo performed the experiment of dropping the weights.

system, and it explains to me the causes of many of the phenomena of nature which are quite unintelligible on the commonly accepted hypothesis." It was not until he made a number of discoveries by means of the telescope that he boldly championed Copernicanism. Apprised that a contrivance had been invented in the Dutch Netherlands by which distant objects could be made to appear much nearer and larger, he set to work and soon constructed a telescope, becoming the first scientist to apply it to astronomical observation. With the new instrument Galileo made a number of important discoveries. He found that the moon, instead of being self-luminous, owed its light to reflection; also he proved its surface was deeply furrowed by valleys and mountains. The latter discovery shattered the Aristotelian idea that the moon was a perfect sphere, absolutely smooth. Especially noteworthy was Galileo's discovery of the four satellites of Jupiter, whose revolutions confirmed by analogy the Copernican explanation of the solar system. Galileo also perceived movable spots on the disc of the sun, inferring from them the sun's axial rotation and by analogy the rotation of the earth on its axis.[1]

After making his discoveries with the telescope Galileo could not restrain his enthusiasm for the Copernican system. So persistent were his activities in behalf of it and so unsparing was his ridicule of its opponents that the Church, which still adhered to the Ptolemaic theory, became alarmed. In 1615 he was ordered by the Inquisition to desist from further advocacy of the doctrine "that the earth moves around the sun and that the sun stands in the center of the world without moving from east to west." Galileo submitted, and for the next sixteen years remained silent. Meanwhile, however, he was writing the great work of his life, which he published in 1632 under the title *Dialogue Concerning the Two Chief Systems of the World*. The main reason for his choice of a dialogue between three persons as the medium for his thought was probably a desire to avoid committing himself openly. The work presented overwhelming proof of the Copernican theory. When it was examined by the ecclesiastical authorities, Galileo was immediately summoned to appear before the Inquisition at Rome. Near seventy and broken in spirit, he was forced in the

[1] The honor of discovering the sun spots is shared by several astronomers. Dark spots previously had been seen with the naked eye, but it was believed that they were caused by the passage of Mercury in front of the sun.

presence of the full Congregation to abjure on his knees the doctrines defined as contrary to the Holy Scriptures. The oath of recantation read in part, "I, Galileo Galilei . . . swear that with honest heart and in good faith I curse and execrate the said heresies and errors as to the movement of the earth around the sun and all other heresies and ideas opposed to the Holy Church; and I swear that I will never assert or say anything either orally or in writing, that could put me under such suspicion." A story has it that after he recited the abjuration Galileo muttered under his breath, "*Eppur si muove* (But it [the earth] does move)." Though the legend is unsupported by historical evidence, it indicates the value of the renunciation which was obtained under duress and expresses the general belief as to what went on in Galileo's mind.

The last years of his life Galileo devoted to the study of dynamics, publishing in 1636 his famous *Dialogues on Motion*, a consolidation of his earlier work on the subject. This book not only laid the foundation for the study of mechanics but specifically served as the preliminary work for Newton's laws of motion. Soon after publishing it Galileo became blind and also partially deaf. Yet he continued to work until his death on January 8, 1642, at the age of seventy-eight. Many historians of science regard Galileo as the founder of experimental science. His investigations of nature discredited dependence upon accepted authority, particularly upon Aristotle. Galileo's fight for the Copernican system did much to promote its acceptance and win supporters for it.

December 25, 1642, almost exactly one year after Galileo's death, Isaac Newton was born at Woolsthorpe in Lincolnshire, the posthumous son of a small farmer. Newton's work was to give acknowledged certainty to the heliocentric theory. As a child he was so frail and sickly that his life was despaired of on numerous occasions. However, he lived to the ripe old age of eighty-four, devoting most of his life to strenuous intellectual and practical activities. During his earlier schooling he evinced little aptitude for study. At this time his interest was centered in the construction of mechanical toys and models such as windmills, sundials, and lanterns. In 1661 he entered Trinity College. Though he attracted little attention as an undergraduate, he did gain a thorough mastery of mathematics. Not until after he received his B.A. degree early in 1665 did he start the career of discovery which was to make him one of the dominant figures in the history of science.

Two years, 1665 and 1666, are unique both in the life of Newton and in the history of science, for in this short period he made the three capital discoveries upon which his title to fame rests. He invented the calculus of fluxions (his own version of the calculus), which is the basis of all modern mathematics; [1] he discovered the law of the composition of light upon which he later built a science of optics; and he formulated his first ideas concerning gravitation. Newton explained these achievements with the remark that "in those years I was in the prime of my age for invention, and minded mathematics and philosophy more than at any time since." In 1669, when he disclosed his discoveries to the scholars of Cambridge University, he was only twenty-seven years old, but he was made professor of mathematics, a position he held until 1695. His professorial duties made such slight demands on him that he had ample time to develop his discoveries, but the University could give him only a modest income. Hence in 1695 he accepted the post of Warden of the Mint, a position for which his knowledge of metallurgy made him peculiarly fitted. After supervising the entire recoinage of the then debased silver currency, he was appointed Master of the Mint. He retained this position until his death. The work of the mint proved so burdensome in his later years that Newton discontinued his scientific activities. Previously he twice represented Cambridge in Parliament; later in 1705 he was knighted by Queen Anne. In 1703 he was chosen President of the Royal Society and thereafter was reëlected annually until 1727, the year of his death. His last years were somewhat troubled by the controversy with Leibnitz regarding the invention of the differential calculus. He died famous. Among those who witnessed his interment in Westminster Abbey was Voltaire.

Newton's best known achievement is probably his discovery of the law of gravitation. Yet Newton's study of the problem was by no means the first. Almost every philosopher since Plato had speculated on the subject. The reason for the return of an object to earth had even been rightly ascribed to the earth's force of attraction. But though the power called gravity was a generally familiar concept it remained for Newton to discover the law regulating it. According to tradition his attention was first turned to

[1] The differential calculus was discovered independently by the German philosopher and mathematician Gottfried Wilhelm Leibnitz ten years later. The methods of notation which Leibnitz adopted are still in use today.

the question of gravity in 1666, when he was living quietly at Woolsthorpe in order to escape the plague. One day when he was in the orchard, an apple fell to the ground.[1] Musing over the possible law involved he began to wonder if the force of gravity extended as far as the moon. The final solution was not reached at once, but was gradually developed by a study of the mathematics of motion. Voltaire states that when Newton was asked how he had discovered the law of gravitation he replied: "By thinking about it ceaselessly." Such was the modesty of one of the greatest intellects of all time that he deferred publication of his discovery for many years. Finally surrendering to the ceaseless urging of his friend Halley, he gave his findings to the world in the *Principia* (*The Mathematical Principles of Natural Knowledge*), one of the greatest works in the history of science. Written in Latin, it was published in 1687.

In the *Principia* Newton stated the law that "the attraction between any two bodies is proportional to the square of the distance which separates them." He shows that the law of gravitation holds for any two masses of the planetary system; the same force which pulls the apple also pulls the moon. In other words, he proved that gravity was a universal property of matter. This law of universal gravitation gave men a new insight into the universe. Instead of a series of disconnected planets, it now appeared as a single whole, united by the all-pervading force of gravity. Among other questions, this law of Newton's explained the ebb and flow of the tides. But what the force called gravity really is neither Newton nor anyone after him has been able to explain.

ANATOMY AND PHYSIOLOGY

The period which began with Galileo and ended with Newton was, as already has been indicated, in many respects a notable era of scientific development. New roads were opened in many directions. During this time the modern classification of the natural sciences as anatomy, physiology, botany, zoölogy, geology, and chemistry began to take shape. The study of these sciences, rooted as it was in man's natural curiosity, received a considerable im-

[1] Once discarded by many writers as legendary the story that Newton's reflections on gravitation were aroused by seeing an apple fall from a tree has recently been shown to rest on fairly good authority. On this point see L. T. Moore's *Isaac Newton* (1934), p. 44 ff.; also A. Wolf's *History of Science, Technology and Philosophy in the Sixteenth and Seventeenth Centuries* (1935), p. 149, and J. W. N. Sullivan's *Isaac Newton* (1938), p. 14.

petus from the art of medicine. As the use of herbs in medicines led the "herbalists" or early botanists to describe the structure of plants so that they might be easily recognized, so the desire to know more about the structure and action of the human body hastened the development of the sciences of anatomy and physiology. Previously the works of Galen, a physician who had lived in Asia Minor during the second century, had been regarded as the final authority on all questions of health and disease. Gradually, however, a number of men began to attack his teachings. Chief among them was Andreas Vesalius (1515–1564), a Fleming by birth, who taught in several Italian universities. Instead of relying on Galen, Vesalius taught anatomy by direct observation of the human body through dissection. His book on anatomy, published in 1543, aroused such opposition that he discontinued his research and became the personal physician of Charles V.

After Vesalius the study of the human body stagnated until William Harvey (1578–1650), an English physician, discovered the circulation of the blood. Since ancient times much had been written about the blood, but there was little definite knowledge of its movement through the body. Previously the arteries had been studied only after death, when they were empty; it was thought they served as air tubes. Michael Servetus, the Spanish physician and theologian who was burned at the stake in Geneva in 1555, had known that the blood circulated through the lungs, but it remained for Harvey to discover the function of the heart in maintaining the circulation. He gained this revolutionary knowledge by observing man and by experimenting on the hearts of birds, frogs, and fishes. For twelve years Harvey lectured to his students on the circulation of the blood without causing a stir, but when he published his findings in 1628, in a brochure entitled *An Anatomical Exercise on the Motion of the Heart and Blood in Animals*, they aroused widespread opposition. However, before his death in 1650 the medical faculties of the universities generally accepted his teachings.

SCIENTIFIC ACADEMIES

As discoveries of scientific facts increased, interest in science grew rapidly. One indication of the developing interest was the organization of societies to further the progress of science. The universities, with the exception of the medical faculties, were slow in manifesting enthusiasm for the new discoveries. Controlled by the Catholic Church or by one of the Protestant denominations, most of them displayed a spirit of conservatism that was unfavorable to scientific progress. Some of the early great scientists, it is true, did occupy chairs in institutions of higher learning. On the other hand, there were as many or even more who were not affiliated with the universities. During the seventeenth century and far into the eighteenth, science largely developed outside the universities. It was the scientific societies or academies that took the lead in fostering the experimental method. The work of these organizations has been summed up as follows:

> The societies concentrated groups of scientists at one place, performed experiments and investigations impossible to individual effort, encouraged individual scientists and gave them both opportunity and leisure, often through financial support, for scientific work. They became centers of scientific information, published and translated scientific books, promulgated periodically scientific discoveries, and thus coördinated the scientific efforts of the various progressive European countries. They concerned themselves about matters of homely interest such as trade, commerce, tools and machinery and tried to improve everyday life by the light of sciences. They contributed to the general enlightenment by dispelling popular errors, and at times endeavored to reach the public by means of lectures. But first and foremost they developed the scientific laboratory, devised, perfected, and standardized instruments, originated and insisted on exact methods of experimentation, and thus established permanently the laboratory methods as the only true means of scientific study.[1]

A number of small scientific societies were formed in Italy about the time of Galileo, but the two most important societies founded in the seventeenth century were the Royal Society of London and the French Académie des Sciences. In England a small group of scientists had begun to meet as early as 1645 for the purpose of discussing scientific questions. Owing to the disturbed conditions of the period they did not constitute a formal organization until 1660, the year of the Restoration. Charles II, who, as Pepys tells us, had a laboratory where, among other things, he dissected human bodies in the company of distinguished surgeons, looked favorably upon such an organization and in 1662 gave it a charter of incorporation as the Royal Society of London

[1] M. Ornstein, *The Rôle of Scientific Societies in the Seventeenth Century* (1928), p. 260.

for Promoting Natural Knowledge. Four years later, in 1666, Louis XIV sanctioned the founding of a similar society in France, the Académie des Sciences. Thereafter, particularly in the eighteenth century, societies were founded in other countries. The first scientific journal to be published was the *Journal des Savants* of the Académie des Sciences, followed a few months later by the *Philosophical Transactions* of the Royal Society. Other journals soon made their appearance in Italy, Germany, Switzerland, and Holland. They served as invaluable aids in disseminating scientific knowledge and in stimulating interest in scientific subjects.

EXACTNESS IN CALCULATION AND OBSERVATION

During the seventeenth century the foundations were also laid for what was to become the outstanding characteristic of modern science: exactness in calculation and observation. A series of remarkable advances in mathematics made exact calculation possible. The invention of the differential calculus by Newton and Leibnitz was probably the most important. Another advance was the invention of logarithms by the Scotsman, John Napier, who published the results of his studies in 1614. This new method greatly facilitated computation by reducing multiplication and division to addition and subtraction, and the extraction of square and cube roots to simple division. A decade later slide-rules were invented; with this device, logarithmic calculations could be read off immediately. In the history of algebra the use of symbols opened up a new age. At the end of the sixteenth century Francis Vieta, a Frenchman, had suggested vowels as symbols for unknown quantities and consonants for given quantities. But it was Descartes' *Geometry*, published in 1637, which set the precedent for using the first letters of the alphabet for given quantities and the last for unknown quantities, a system of notation which has survived to the present. Other notable advances in mathematics were the use of decimal notations for fractions, a practice which became general during the seventeenth century, and the invention of analytic geometry. The latter, which may be defined, in a general way, as the application of algebraic methods to geometrical problems, is generally regarded as having been invented by Descartes, though he was by no means the first to work in that field.

These new methods were of the greatest importance to scientists, aiding them in complicated numerical calculations and permitting precise formulation of many scientific ideas. Mathematics supplied a language in which science could express itself both accurately and compactly. As Francis Bacon stated it: "For many parts of nature can neither be invented with sufficient subtility, nor demonstrated with sufficient perspicuity, nor accommodated unto use with sufficient dexterity without the aid and intervening of mathematics." With the help of higher mathematics scientists have been able to solve some of the most complex problems in astronomy and physics. Without higher analysis Newton's theory of gravity, Laplace's celestial mechanics and Einstein's theory of relativity would have been impossible.

As the advances in mathematics opened the way to greater accuracy in calculation, so the improvement of a number of older scientific instruments and the invention of new ones made for greater accuracy in observation and experimentation. The many inaccuracies in scientific data due to the crude instruments of the observers could now be eliminated. More than this, the new instruments made possible the solution of problems demanding a high degree of precision. Of the instruments which inaugurated the era of exactness the most important were the pendulum clock, the air pump, the barometer, the thermometer, and particularly the telescope and the microscope. Though Galileo discovered the principle of the pendulum, he did not connect the pendulum with a clock. Many clockmakers, it seems, worked on the problem, but the man who first succeeded in constructing a clock regulated by the swing of a pendulum was Christian Huygens, the Dutch astronomer (1656). The pendulum clock was invaluable to observers because it afforded a means of accurately measuring small intervals of time which previously could not be measured at all or only inaccurately. The air pump, which enabled physicists to study the properties of air, was invented by Otto von Guericke (1602–1686), a German physicist. In 1654 he appeared before the Diet of Ratisbon and demonstrated the enormous pressure of the atmosphere by showing that horses could not pull apart two hollow metal hemispheres in which a vacuum had been created, but that the hemispheres would fall apart when air was let in through a tap. In his experiments with the air pump he discovered among other things that animals cannot live in a vacuum, that a flame cannot burn in it, and that sound will not penetrate it whereas light will.

Another important instrument was the barometer, which made possible the observation and measurement of air pressure. It was invented or, better, discovered in 1645 by Torricelli, the disciple and successor of Galileo. In investigating the action of suction pumps to discover why water would not rise higher than 32 or 33 feet, Torricelli decided to experiment with liquids of a greater density than water. After filling a glass tube, four feet in length and open at one end, with mercury (the density of which is $13\frac{1}{2}$ times as great as water at the same temperature), he raised the tube perpendicularly to the horizon and submerged the open end in a vessel filled with mercury. The result was that the mercury fell until the distance between the level in the tube and that in the vessel was about thirty inches. He had constructed the first mercury barometer. Not until afterwards did Torricelli realize that the height of the mercury in the tube indicated the atmospheric pressure on the outside. The standard mercury barometers of today represent improvements only in details of the first crude instrument of Torricelli, the principle of which has never been superseded by a better one for measuring the pressure of the atmosphere. Some years later the connection between the rise and fall of the barometer and the changes in the weather was noted. By the end of the seventeenth century, scales of words indicating what kind of weather was to be expected from the height of the mercury were already attached to the barometer.

Some time before this discovery the thermometer had made its appearance. Though its inventor is unknown, it was probably first made in Italy near the end of the sixteenth century. Its development from a mere toy to a precise instrument covers more than a century. Galileo, it appears, had a crude thermometer described as "a glass containing air and water, to indicate changes and differences in temperature." It worked on the principle that air expands on heating. Some decades later wine or alcohol was used instead of water and the glass tube was sealed, making the thermometer depend not on the expansion of the air but on the expansion of the colored liquid in the tube. From this time on the use of the thermometer gradually spread through Europe. Daniel Gabriel Fahrenheit (1686–1736), a young German scientist who used mercury in his thermometers instead of alcohol, made the first accurate thermometer. In 1721 he adopted a scale in which the freezing point of water was 32 degrees, while 212 degrees was the boiling point. In 1742 another scale was prepared by Celsius, a Swedish astronomer. In its final form this scale indicated the freezing point as zero and the boiling point as 100 degrees. As the intervening space is divided into a hundred grades it is known as the centigrade scale.

More important in its immediate results for the development of science was the telescope. Galileo's use of it has already been noted. That the telescope was invented in Holland at some time between 1590 and 1621 seems certain, but as to the details of its invention no certainty exists. Hans Lippershey, a Dutch spectacle-maker, is the first person who is known to have constructed a telescope. The story, widely repeated with many variations, is that Lippershey discovered the principle accidentally by holding before one eye a concave and a convex lens. Observing that the combination made distant objects appear near, he mounted the lenses in tubes and petitioned the States-General in 1608 for the exclusive right to make such instruments. A little later he improved the invention "so as to enable one to see through it with both eyes" and called it a binoculus. But he did not receive the exclusive right to manufacture the new instruments, for others soon put forward claims that they were the first to make telescopes. Whoever may have been the inventor, Lippershey must be credited with giving the instrument to the world. News of the miraculous properties of the Dutch instruments spread over Europe, reaching Galileo, who constructed his own "optic tube" and became the first to use it for the study of heavenly bodies. By the end of the seventeenth century the telescope had completely revolutionized the science of astronomy.

Just as the telescope disclosed the marvels of the heavens, so the microscope revealed an infinite world of little things. Like the telescope, its origin is veiled in obscurity. That glass balls magnify was known to the ancients. During the Middle Ages Roger Bacon had some idea of the nature and properties of lenses, but before the sixteenth century, when a number of naturalists made use of magnifying glasses to study insects and plants, there are no recorded instances of the use of such glasses for the investigation of nature. It was not until the invention of lenses of a very short focus, at some time between 1590 and 1610, that the simple microscope became a valuable means of research. Zacharias Jansen, a Dutch spectacle-maker, is generally considered the first person to have constructed a microscope. The microscope used by early scientists was either simple or compound. The simple microscope consisted of one lens through which the object was viewed directly; in the compound microscope, the lenses were so arranged that the image formed by one lens was magnified by others. Though the same observer often used both kinds, most of the important discoveries until the early part of the nineteenth century were made by means of the simple microscope.

The use of the microscope opened a new era in the study of biology, zoölogy, botany, anatomy, and physiology. Naturalists could now study in detail the organs of ants, flies, fleas, lice, mites, and other minute forms of animal life;[1] also the structure of plants and the tissues of the human body. Of the many pioneers in the use of the microscope only a few can be mentioned. Galileo, who in 1609 published microscopical observations on minute objects, is by many credited with having made this instrument the common property of science. The first man to solve some of the problems of science with it was Marcello Malpighi (1628–1694), an Italian physician and professor at Bologna. In 1661 he described for the first time the capillary circulation of the blood after he had discovered the capillaries (tubes connecting the arteries with the veins) in the lungs of a frog. This discovery added the final proofs to Harvey's teachings. With the assistance of the microscope he further observed the different stages in the development of a chick and made a detailed study of the life of the silkworm. The latter study, published by the Royal Society of London in 1669, ranks as one of the most famous monographs on the anatomy of a single animal. Besides studying smaller animals under the microscope, Malpighi gave considerable attention to the human body, examining microscopically the structure of the brain and the nerve tissues. He further showed that the human skin consists of different layers, one of which is still known as the "Malpighian layer." In botany Malpighi's microscopic researches of plants founded a new branch of study, that of plant anatomy.

The work of the early microscopists was without a definite ob-

---

[1] It was this study that inspired the oft-repeated lines of Jonathan Swift (1667–1745):

> "So naturalists observe, a flea
> Has smaller fleas that on him prey;
> And these have smaller still to bite 'em;
> And so proceed ad infinitum."

jective. Nevertheless, it was not without influence, for their writings were widely studied. Later microscopists put some order into the bewildering multiplicity of phenomena. In other words, they began to classify plants and animals. Thus Jan Swammerdam (1637–1680), a Dutchman, used the microscope for the systematic classification of insects. His *Bible of Nature*, the title under which all his work was published more than fifty years after his death, is one of the best collections of microscopical observations ever produced by one man. The English naturalist Nehemiah Grew in 1676 pointed out the sex differences in plants, thereby opening the way for the revolutionary work of the Swedish botanist Carolus Linnaeus (1707–1778). Linnaeus based the first systematic classification of plants on their organs of reproduction (stamens and pistils). This classification was superseded only by the "natural" system of grouping plants according to their probable relation in the evolutionary scheme. Not content with classifying plants, he also classified animals, minerals, and even diseases. His writings mark a great advance in the use of scientific terminology, for he attached both a generic and a specific name to each plant and animal.

Perhaps the most indefatigable of the early fathers of microscopy was Antony van Leeuwenhoek (1632–1723) of Delft. Leeuwenhoek made his own microscopes—the number is estimated as 274—but he never sold one or taught anyone else how to make one. It is believed that he made a new instrument for the observation of every new subject. Without concentrating on one topic for any great length of time, he moved through nature to discover an endless series of wonders. Many of the observations he made after 1673—all written in Dutch, for he knew no other language—were published by the Royal Society of London in English or in Latin. In 1679 he was made a member of the society and a medal was presented to him. On the obverse side an inscription from Virgil read: "His work was in little things, but not little in glory." Using only the simple microscope for his studies, he added to the knowledge of the capillary circulation by tracing the capillaries in the tail of a tadpole, in the web of a frog's foot, and in the membrane of a bat's wing. He also described the blood corpuscles (the discovery of which he shares with Malpighi and Swammerdam) of fishes, birds, man, and mammals and devoted much time to the study of the structure of tissues. Most important are his discoveries of protozoa and bacteria or microbes, which he called animal-cules. The former he found in stagnant water and the latter in dental tartar scraped from his own teeth and from those of other persons. His descriptions and the figures he drew leave no doubt that what he saw were really bacteria. It was not until the improvement of the microscope in the nineteenth century that bacteria were seen again.

In the seventeenth century men still believed in spontaneous generation; that is, that maggots, for example, arose spontaneously out of putrid meat, vermin out of filth, and frogs out of mud. This belief, supported by the authority of Aristotle, had been shared by all naturalists up to that time. The study of minute life with the microscope soon showed that reported cases of spontaneous generation had been misinterpreted, and gave ever greater authority to the statement that "every living thing comes out of an egg (*omne vivum ex ovo*)." A long step toward disproving the theory of spontaneous generation (abiogenesis) was taken by the Italian physician Francesco Redi (1621–1697). In 1668 he demonstrated conclusively that maggots arose from eggs that had been laid in meat by flies. The final proof of biogenesis was presented by Spallanzani (1729–1799), also an Italian, when he proved that not even minute forms of life would develop in decoctions previously boiled and sealed against the air. Yet the theory of spontaneous generation was tenacious and received its death-blow only at the hands of Pasteur.

CHEMISTRY AND PHYSICS

Whereas the development of most of the sciences had been extraordinarily rapid during the seventeenth century, chemistry lagged behind. In fact, it did not become a science until near the end of the eighteenth century. The origins of scientific chemistry must be sought in the laboratories of the alchemists. The basis of the beliefs of the alchemists was the Aristotelian doctrine of the four elements—fire, air, earth, and water. These elements were believed to be combinations of four primary qualities: dry, wet, cold, and hot. Fire was regarded as hot and dry, air as hot and wet, earth as cold and dry, and water as cold and wet. Though the alchemists made no attempts to isolate the constituents, all matter was supposed to be made up of the four elements in varying proportions. Thus if a substance had the property of cold and wetness it was regarded as containing water, while cold and dryness signified that it contained earth. The doctrine that all substances were composed of the four elements gave rise to the belief that the proper reagents would change the relative proportions of those elements in a compound and in that way one substance could be changed into another. Specifically, this doctrine accounts for the belief of the alchemists in the possibility of changing base metal into gold. Hence the search over many centuries for the "philosopher's stone" which was to effect the transmutation. In the sixteenth century Paracelsus (1493–1541) gave alchemy a new bent by applying it to the preparation of medicines. Yet the search for the philosopher's stone was by no means abandoned; neither was the Aristotelian heritage renounced. In the course of their search the alchemists discovered by chance a number of useful substances but, as they were limited by the doctrine of the four elements, made no contributions to the philosophy of chemistry.

The final demolition of the Aristotelian doctrine as an active element in scientific thought was started by the Englishman Robert Boyle (1627–1691). In 1661 he published *The Sceptical Chymist*, in which he launched a general attack on the fanciful theories of the alchemists and chemists, showing how foolish it was to base beliefs on supposition instead of on careful observation of phenomena. "Methinks the Chymists," he wrote, "in their searches after truth, are not unlike the navigators of Solomon's Tarshish fleet, who brought home from their long and tedious voyages, not only gold and silver, and ivory, but apes and peacocks too: for so the writings of several (for I say not, all) of your hometick philosophers present us together with divers substantial and noble experiments, theories, which like peacock's feathers make a great show, but are neither solid nor useful; or else like apes, if they do have some appearance of being rational, are blemished with some absurdity or other, that when they are attentively considered, make them appear ridiculous." The particular object of Boyle's attack was the doctrine of the four elements. In denouncing it he posited the axiom that an element is a pure substance which cannot be broken up into anything simpler. None of the Aristotelian elements, he contended, could meet this condition. Earth, for example, could with the proper treatment be resolved into a number of different substances. Looking into the future, he predicted the discovery of many more elements than were recognized at his time. He did not, however, postulate any definite number. Boyle was the first scientist to state clearly that a chemical compound is the result of a combination of two constituents and that a compound possesses peculiar qualities not found in either of its constituents alone.

After Boyle many men took part in making chemistry a science. In 1766 Sir Henry Cavendish announced the discovery of hydrogen, which he called "inflammable air." Eight years later oxygen was discovered independently by Joseph Priestley in England and Carl Scheele in Sweden. But the most outstanding figure in the early history of chemistry is Antoine Laurent Lavoisier (1743–1794), a Frenchman who is acclaimed by some as the father of modern chemistry. As a young man Lavoisier showed such great promise that he was chosen a member of the Académie Française at the age of twenty-five. After serving as director of the government powder works, Lavoisier became a member of the *Ferme-Générale*, the great corporation which collected the taxes in France, paying the government a certain sum for the privilege. This position cost him his life in 1794, for when the arrest of the *fermiers-généraux* was ordered, he was included, though there was no evidence to show that as a tax-collector he had been other than honest and kindly. The specific charge against him was that of "adding to tobacco water and other ingredients detrimental to the health of the citizens." Despite his services to France, which included the improvement of French gunpowder and the standardization of weights and measures, he was sentenced to the guillotine. When a petition was presented in behalf of the scientist, it is reported that Coffinhal, the presiding judge, curtly dismissed it with the remark, "The Republic has no need of savants." It was only when Lavoisier's head had been struck off that the French nation realized that it had lost one of its most brilliant citizens. The feeling of many contemporary scientists was perhaps best expressed in the words of Lagrange: "They needed but a moment to cut off a head the like of which a hundred years will not suffice to reproduce."

Lavoisier's contributions almost amounted to a revolution in chemistry. Making use of the discoveries of other chemists, he conducted experiments which enabled him to announce to the scientific world the oxygen theory of combustion, which is still employed today. Lavoisier discovered that the increase in weight which occurs when metals and other substances are burned is due to the simple chemical addition of oxygen. Continuing his experiments, he found that the total weight of all chemical compounds acting in these processes is the same at the end as at the beginning of every operation; in other words, he discovered the law of the conservation of matter. These discoveries overthrew the phlogiston theory (that all combustible substances possess one component in common which escapes in the act of burning), which had dominated chemical research for more than a century, and cleared the way for the progress of modern chemistry. Following Boyle, Lavoisier defined an element as a substance that cannot be further decomposed. In his *Elementary Treatise on Chemistry*, published in 1789, he listed thirty-three elements, twenty-three of which are still so recognized. In the decades after Lavoisier's death many more elements were added to the list; by 1830 the number had passed fifty.

In the science of physics the eighteenth century built upon the foundations laid by Galileo, Newton, Torricelli, von Guericke, Huygens, and others the century before. Though limitations of space rule out a discussion of the progress in physics at this time, a survey of the beginnings of modern science would be woefully incomplete without some mention of the science of electricity, which today is such a potent factor in human affairs. The man who in early modern times reawakened interest in electricity and magnetism was William Gilbert (1540–1603), first physician to Queen Elizabeth. In addition to practicing medicine, he experimented with the force developed by rubbing a piece of amber on soft cloth. These experiments led him to name it *electricity*, from the Greek word for amber (*elektron*). After conducting a prodigious number of experiments he published his observations in a book called *De Magnete*, thus creating the science of electricity and magnetism. The experiments which Gilbert started were continued by others, but no important advances were made until the second quarter of the eighteenth century, when Stephen Gray, also an Englishman, worked on a multitude of experiments and added much to the knowledge of electricity. He made his most important discovery in 1729 when he discovered that certain bodies conduct the "electrical virtue," as he called it, while others do not. The difference between conductors and non-conductors is one of the basic principles of the science.

After Gray made his discoveries the progress of the science of electricity became more rapid. A very important advance was made about 1745 through the discovery of the Leyden jar,[1] which demonstrated for the first time that electricity could be stored and that it could be generated by means other than friction. With it electricians were able to produce new effects such as firing gunpowder and other inflammables. "Then, and not till then," an eighteenth century writer states, "the study of electricity became general, surprised every beholder and invited to the houses of electricians a greater number of spectators than were ever assembled together to observe any philosophical experiments whatsoever." In England a group of members of the Royal Society was successful in sending electricity through a wire twelve thousand feet long, and in determining that the transmission of electricity was instantaneous. Near the middle of the century Benjamin Franklin, the American statesman and scientist, upon seeing a spark produced by a Leyden jar, concluded that lightning and electricity were identical. Later he demonstrated their identity by experiments with a kite during a thunderstorm. The immediate practical result of Franklin's experiments was his invention of the lightning rod. However, electricity did not become an agent of practical value until the discovery of the voltaic pile or battery in 1799 by Alessandro Volta, the Italian physician after whom the volt (unit of electromotive force) is named. The voltaic pile is the forerunner of the modern electric cell and battery. Before its discovery electricity had been known to the experimenter in fitful flashes, but with the voltaic pile a steady flow could be obtained. By combining no less than two thousand cells of voltaic battery Sir Humphry Davy was able a few years later to demonstrate the electric arc which produced a light of dazzling splendor. Other developments soon followed, leading to such inventions in the nineteenth century as the electric telegraph, the telephone, the electric motor, the dynamo generator, electric railways, the incandescent light, the wireless transmitter and receiver, and the X-ray apparatus.

[1] Named after the city in which it was first exhibited. A number of persons seem to have hit upon the idea about the same time. It was discovered independently in 1745 by Ewald von Kleist, a cathedral dean in Germany, and in the next year by Musschenbroeck of Leyden and his friend Cuneus.

CHAPTER FIFTEEN

The Struggle for Constitutional Monarchy in England

FRICTION BETWEEN KING AND PARLIAMENT

THE accession of James VI of Scotland to the English throne in 1603, as James I of England, marks the beginning of a long struggle between king and parliament. The accord between the two which had been a characteristic of Tudor rule had already, as previously stated, begun to break down in the last years of Elizabeth's reign. The danger from foreign invasion having passed with the defeat of the Armada, and the execution of Mary Stuart having removed the principal center of domestic and foreign intrigue, Parliament became more self-assertive, foreshadowing a conflict over authority. Protests were made to Elizabeth against the abuse of monopolies. When the queen yielded graciously, the Commons, prompted by a certain loyalty to the woman who had grown old in the service of the English people, did not force the issue. But with the passing of "Good Queen Bess" the factor of personal sympathy disappeared. No sooner had the first Stuart king ascended the throne than the Commons became aggressive in their claims to a larger share in the direction of policy. A struggle ensued which gradually turned into a conflict to decide whether the ultimate authority in the state should repose in the crown or in Parliament. Through the triumph of the latter, monarchical absolutism was replaced by the rule of an oligarchy, for Parliament was far from being a representative body in the full sense of the word. The country squires and the merchants and bankers who formed the backbone of the House of Commons were interested primarily in obtaining the direction of affairs for themselves and in forcing their ideas on the country. Nevertheless, the victory of Parliament ultimately proved to be a step in the direction of popular government.

When James, then in his thirty-seventh year, came to England a few weeks after the death of Elizabeth to be crowned, he was warmly welcomed by his new subjects. His progress from Edinburgh to London was a triumphal procession. So happy were the English people over the peaceful succession that they made much of the good qualities of the new ruler. However, the popularity of James gradually evaporated. The very fact that he was a foreigner who spoke with an accent was against him. Furthermore, with his shambling gait, spindleshanks, slavering mouth, ungracious manners, and blundering tongue, he had little of the dignity that is generally associated with royalty. He was also vain, irresolute, and lazy. Yet he had his good qualities, for he was well-meaning and on the whole good-natured. His education was somewhat above the average. He had a fair command of languages and was well versed in theology. But with all his learning he was wanting in the practical wisdom to deal successfully with the problems confronting him—problems which would have taxed the ingenuity of a wise man. It was this lack of practical wisdom, coupled with pedantic interests, that caused the duke of Sully, minister of Henry IV of France, to bestow on James the title of "the wisest fool in Christendom." Having ruled with fair success in Scotland, James felt he could do as well in England on the same principles. But he had reckoned without the English people. How little he knew of English ways was demonstrated by the fact that on his way to London he ordered a cut-purse to be hanged summarily without trial, an arbitrary procedure which had not been known in England for more than a century. James was so certain that whatever the king did was right that he did not even consider the possibility of his being wrong.

This extravagant conception of the kingship was to become the greatest source of discord between the new monarch and his subjects. The absolute rule which the Tudors had exercised by consent, he claimed by divine right. In his *Trew Law of Free Mon-*

archies, published in 1598, he had already expounded this view. "Kings," he wrote, "are the breathing images of God on earth." Hence they are accountable to God alone and are bound by no laws. "Although a good king," he stated, "will frame all his actions to be according to the law, yet he is not bound thereto but of his own good will, and for example-giving to his subjects." Under no circumstances, he said in effect, can a rebellion against a king be justified, for if a king is evil he was sent of God to punish his people. To these views James stubbornly adhered throughout his reign. In 1616 he said in a speech to the judges: "It is atheism and blasphemy to dispute what God can do; . . . so it is presumption and high contempt in a subject to dispute what a king can do or say that a king cannot do this or that." Such ideas were, of course, utterly inconsistent with the temper of the times in England. Had James contented himself with an unostentatious use of the power bequeathed to him by the Tudors, he and his successors might have continued to direct the policy of the English government for some time and then perhaps have solved peacefully the question of the final source of authority. But when he chose to theorize about the royal power, the king opened a rift between himself and Parliament which was to widen until during the reign of his son it became civil war.

The first problem of James's reign was religious dissension. Though a majority of the English people were members of the Anglican Church, two major groups were dissatisfied with the settlement Elizabeth had made. The Roman Catholics felt that the religious changes had gone too far, while the Puritans protested that they had not gone far enough in the direction of Calvinism. Both expected that the accession of James would be followed by measures which would advance their respective interests. In the end the hopes of both were thoroughly dashed; for once the new king was seated on the English throne, he decided to support the existing system. He did relax the enforcement of the penal code against the Catholics in order to prepare the way for a Spanish alliance; but because of plots and rumors of plots, and the increase in the number of recusants, the toleration was withdrawn as early as 1604. A royal proclamation banishing all priests from the country was issued in February of that year, and a few months later Parliament passed an act which confirmed and even extended the penal laws of Elizabeth.

The hopeless situation of the Catholics in England led a group of fanatics to plot to blow up Parliament in the old palace of Westminster on a day when the Lords and Commons would be in session and the king himself would be present. To this end they rented a cellar extending under the old palace, and placed in it thirty-six barrels of gunpowder. But the hesitancy of the conspirators to blow up the Catholic peers along with the rest led to the discovery of the "Gunpowder Plot." On the fourth of November, the day before the king and Parliament were to meet, Lord Monteagle received a note advising him not to attend the session. The note was immediately taken to the king, who instituted a search which ended in the discovery of the gunpowder and the arrest of Guy Fawkes, one of the conspirators, who was keeping watch over it. Though Fawkes refused under torture to name his accomplices, all the leading conspirators were hunted down in the suppression of the plot, which probably aroused more opposition to the Catholics than any other incident since the reign of Mary.

The Puritans had rejoiced at the accession of James I because they thought that his upbringing among Scottish Calvinists must have given him Puritan leanings. While the new king was on his way to London they presented to him a petition embodying the demands of the Puritan clergy. This petition, known as the Millenary Petition because it was supposed to bear the signatures of a thousand clergymen, though in reality not more than eight hundred had signed it, asked for the abolition of certain ecclesiastical practices, such as making the sign of the cross, bowing at the name of Jesus, and using the ring in the marriage ceremony. It also requested that the wearing of the surplice be made optional. James, who found great pleasure in theological argument, arranged a conference at Hampton Court between representatives of the Puritans and officials of the Anglican Church. He himself presided, unhesitatingly taking a stand against the Puritans, for he regarded their democratic ideas of church government as a definite threat to his divine right monarchy. When the Puritan leader used the word *presbyter*, the king, mindful of the trouble the Scottish presbyters had caused him, flew into a rage. "Presbytery," he exclaimed, "agreeth as well with a monarch as God and the devil. Then Jack and Tom, and Will and Dick shall meet at their pleasure, censure me and my council and all our proceedings." After a long harangue he concluded with the threat, "I shall make them conform themselves, or I will harry them out of the land."

The king's threat was followed before the close of 1604 by a proclamation which deprived of their livings all those clergymen who refused to conform to the Prayer Book. One group of irreconcilable Puritans went to Holland, whence they later migrated to America to found Plymouth colony in 1620. The others conformed outwardly, carrying on their worship in secret and awaiting the time when they could introduce the desired changes into the Anglican Church. Instead of dying out after the Hampton Court conference, Puritanism gained ground, particularly among the middle classes. As time went on the opposition of the Puritans to the king became ever more determined. Of all the requests made in the Millenary Petition, the only one of importance which James granted was the petition for a new translation of the Bible. By his order the work was divided among forty-odd competent men who finished it in 1611. The new translation was based not only on the original Greek and Hebrew texts and the Latin Vulgate, but also on the various English translations which had previously appeared. From these early English sources springs that musical and forceful flow of its language which is one of the most impressive attributes of the "Authorized Version." This translation is probably the greatest prose work in the English tongue, one which has influenced subsequent writers of English in every part of the globe.

James I was no happier in his dealings with Parliament than in trying to settle the religious question. From the first the Commons manifested a spirit of opposition to the king and his projects, provoked by his absolutist claims and his attitude toward the Puritans, who were strongly represented in the Commons. Thus his project of uniting England and Scotland under one government met with obstinate refusal. In vain did the king personally point out the advantages of union, indulging in such flights of eloquence as: "What God hath joined, let no man separate." The representatives of the commercial classes were determined that the impoverished Scots should not share the English trade. Soon king and parliament clashed on almost every point. The idea that Parliament should share in the sovereignty was most irritating to James. He knew that it had deferred to the will of the Tudors, and he was determined that it should also give way to him. What he forgot was that the Tudors had studiously avoided coming into conflict with it over the question of rights and sovereignty.

The king's greatest weakness in his struggle with Parliament was his need of money. While the discovery of the American mines had caused the purchasing power of gold and silver to decline almost two-thirds during the sixteenth century, the royal income had not grown commensurately. Even under the careful management of Elizabeth the revenues of the crown had not been sufficient to meet its expenses, which, besides those of the royal court, included the costs of the whole machinery of law and government, and the maintenance of the army and navy in times of peace. Under James the demands upon the exchequer were increased by the fact that, since the king was married, the expenses of the royal household were greater than under Elizabeth. Hence James could not have avoided an annual deficit even if he had been as careful of expenditures as his predecessor. But James was as prodigal as Elizabeth had been thrifty. He not only lived extravagantly himself but he also distributed pensions and gifts to his favorites with a lavish hand. Consequently it was not long before he found it necessary to ask Parliament for additional revenues.

When Parliament, to revenge itself, voted insufficient grants, the king had to look for other means of increasing his income. The revenue of the crown came from two main sources: (1) rents from crown lands and feudal dues payable by tenants-in-chief; (2) duties known as tunnage and poundage—a tax on merchandise imported into England, which was granted to the rulers of England for life. In his need James, without the permission of Parliament, raised the old rates and imposed duties on articles which had hitherto been exempt. He also resorted to "benevolences," or forced loans, and the sale of monopolies and titles—for example, he created the title of baronet, which was sold for about a thousand pounds. All this further embittered the relations between king and parliament.

A foreign policy which had the approval of Parliament might have done much to ease the friction, but even in this respect king and parliament were at odds. Temperamentally averse to violence —so much so that he has been accused of cowardice—James wished to establish a permanent peace in Europe. His first move in that direction was the conclusion of a treaty of peace with

Spain in 1604. Laudable as his ambition may have been in itself, James did not take into consideration the wishes of his subjects. Not only did many Englishmen cherish a dislike for Spaniards, but the commercial class which dominated the Commons had found the piratical raids on Spanish commerce a source of profit and glory. Hence they opposed the king's desire for peace.

Not satisfied with having concluded peace with Spain, James made plans to bind England and Spain together by a marriage between his son Charles and the Spanish Infanta. The idea appalled the Commons, particularly since they feared that a Catholic queen would bring up the heir to the English throne in an atmosphere of Spanish Catholicism. When the Commons petitioned him to choose a Protestant bride for his son, James became irritated over what he regarded as meddling with his affairs. Later he adjourned Parliament and with his own hands tore from the journal of the House of Commons the pages on which the protestation against the Spanish marriage was inscribed. After another year of futile negotiations Prince Charles decided, at the suggestion of the duke of Buckingham, his bosom friend, to travel to Madrid incognito for the purpose of wooing the Infanta in person. The venture, on which Buckingham accompanied Charles, proved a ludicrous failure. The Spanish court had no intention of concluding the alliance except on its own terms, which were impossible because they included the immediate suspension of the penal laws against Catholics in England and their repeal by Parliament within three years. Furthermore, the Spanish Infanta was so resolutely set against marrying a heretic that she threatened to enter a nunnery rather than submit. As these facts were unknown to Charles, he continued his efforts to win the affections of the princess. Finally, after two months, the heir to the English throne became convinced that Spain had been diplomatically playing at courtship after the manner of Queen Elizabeth, and returned to England.

The return of Charles without the Infanta and with a demand for war against Spain was greeted with demonstrations of joy by the English. The parliament summoned in 1624 was eager for war with Spain; yet when negotiations were opened for the marriage of Charles to Henrietta Maria of France, a Catholic princess, it voted only limited subsidies for a conflict. Early in 1625 the king died at the age of fifty-six. His passing evoked little sorrow.

THE APPROACH OF CIVIL WAR

During the reign of Charles, who in his twenty-fifth year succeeded his father as Charles I, the storm which had been gathering was to break. The new king had much in his favor. He was stately and dignified in appearance, blameless in his private life, punctilious in his religious observances, frugal in his expenditures, and industrious and conscientious in his work. He had physical courage and a certain amount of culture and artistic taste. On the other hand, he was lacking in political intelligence, humor, and the ability to cope with the conduct of affairs. Though he sincerely wished his people well, he knew them no better than his father had known them. This deficiency cannot be attributed to foreign birth, for he had been in England since he was four. He did not understand the English people partly because he lacked the ability to understand them and partly because he did not want to understand them. Besides being narrow in his views, he was obstinate in adhering to any course once he had embarked upon it. His ideas of the kingship were even more exalted than his father's had been, and he was consequently more impatient of opposition. Unfortunately, the new king took as his adviser the duke of Buckingham, who encouraged him along the path of absolutism. Buckingham was in fact much more than an adviser; during the first three years of the reign he was the real ruler of England.

When Parliament met in June, 1625, the quarrel which was finally to lead Charles to the scaffold began at once. Since his accession Charles had been married to Henrietta Maria of France, and to please her the penal laws against the Catholics had been relaxed, much to the alarm of the Puritans. Parliament now no longer trusted the king to preserve Protestantism in England, fearing that he himself would turn Catholic. The House of Commons immediately gave evidence of its distrust by granting tunnage and poundage to Charles for one year only, despite the fact that it had been voted to every king for life since the reign of Henry IV. Moreover, it refused to vote adequate supplies for the conduct of the war against Spain because it had no assurance that Charles and Buckingham would use them for that purpose. When the king pressed Parliament for supplies, it countered by attacking Buckingham and was at once dismissed after a session of less than two months. In an effort to recoup their fortunes Charles and Buckingham now invested what money they could borrow in a fleet to be sent against Cadiz in the manner of the Elizabethan seamen. The undertaking failed ignominiously. Far from taking Cadiz, the fleet did not even capture the ships lying in the harbor. The failure of this expedition forced Charles to summon a new parliament in 1626. This one, even more conscious of its strength than the first, proceeded formally to impeach Buckingham. To save his favorite the king dissolved it summarily after a session of three months.

For two years Charles and Buckingham managed to struggle on by raising money in any way they could. In 1628, having exhausted all his means, Charles called his third parliament. The Commons were determined to deal with various grievances before voting supplies. A statement known as the Petition of Right was presented to the king for his signature. It forbade him: (1) to levy "any gift, loan, benevolence, tax, or such like charge without common consent by act of Parliament"; (2) to imprison anyone without bringing a specific charge against him; (3) to billet soldiers in private houses; (4) to declare martial law in time of peace. For a time the king struggled against accepting the Petition of Right, but in the end the need of money forced him to affix his signature. In English history the Petition of Right is important as the first act attempting seriously to circumscribe the powers bequeathed to the Stuarts by the Tudors, and as a great landmark in the progress of popular government. To the Commons it was only the first step in redressing grievances. Immediately after Charles had accepted the Petition of Right they again demanded the dismissal of Buckingham. This time he prorogued the session—that is, he adjourned the meetings temporarily.

In the interval between the sessions of the third parliament Buckingham died at the hands of John Felton, an officer who had served on the Cadiz expedition and had some private grievance against him. To the people his funeral was an occasion of rejoicing; yet the House of Commons did not rest content. Upon reassembling it took up other grievances, particularly the continued collection of tunnage and poundage by the king without the consent of Parliament. The final session was a scene of great excitement. While the king's officers were demanding entrance to the hall in order to dissolve the House of Commons, the speaker was held in the chair by force and the Commons carried by acclamation a resolution against "innovations in religion" aimed primarily at the reintroduction of Catholic practices, and one against the unauthorized collection of tunnage and poundage. Then the doors were opened and Parliament was dissolved.

Determined to show that he could do without it, Charles did not summon the next parliament for eleven years. During this period he found it necessary to practice the strictest economy and to exploit every possible source of income. One of his first moves was to settle his quarrels with Spain and France, because he realized that his meager revenue did not permit military intervention in the affairs of Europe. Thereafter he bent all his efforts to the problem of raising enough money to carry on the government. The collection of tunnage and poundage was continued despite the resolutions of the House of Commons. Old, half-forgotten statutes were resurrected and fines were imposed on all who had not obeyed them. Thus in 1630 the king put in force a law requiring all persons who possessed an estate which yielded an income of more than forty pounds a year to take up knighthood. By imposition of heavy fines on all who had neglected to do so the royal treasury collected £170,000. The king also revived the ancient forest laws which stated that all forests were royal property. Lands which had been under cultivation for three centuries were declared part of the royal domains, and landowners were fined for their "encroachments." Another expedient was the sale of monopolies. As their sale to private individuals had been specifically forbidden, Charles sold them instead to corporations. The monopolies included such widely used commodities as salt, soap, iron, wine, leather, glass, and gunpowder. The large sums which corporations paid for the sole right of selling them were ultimately paid by the consumer in the form of higher prices.

Charles also found it necessary to resort to direct taxation in the form of ship-money, an expedient which caused great discontent. It had been the custom of English rulers in the past to call upon the seaports to provide ships for the defense of the realm in times of danger. In this way, for example, most of the fleet which defeated the Armada had been gathered. The levying of money instead of ships was also not unknown. But under Charles the payment of ship-money, which had formerly been more or less a liability of the maritime towns, was requested from all subjects as

a means of national defense. The first writ of October, 1634, was
addressed to maritime towns only. When it did not yield enough
a writ was addressed in 1635 to inland towns and counties as well.
At first the people paid, but in 1637 a number of persons refused
to do so, among them John Hampden, a country gentleman. His
case was brought into court, and of the twelve judges seven decided against him and five in his favor. It was a victory for the
king; yet he could not eradicate from the minds of his subjects
the belief that Hampden was right in questioning the legality of
the collection of ship-money. In justice to Charles it must be
stated that almost every penny of the ship-money was actually
spent on ships. There was no question of an improper use of the
funds. The strengthening of the royal navy, which had been neglected since the death of Elizabeth, was necessary, for English
shipping was menaced by the ships of France, Spain, and the
United Provinces, and also by pirates. Moreover, the collection
of ship-money had been sanctioned by the regular English courts.
All this, however, did not convince the people, who still regarded
ship-money as a device to enable the king to rule without Parliament.

There were also grievances, real and fancied, in other directions. To carry on his arbitrary government Charles had the assistance of Thomas Wentworth, later created earl of Strafford,
and William Laud, archbishop of Canterbury after 1633. The
former had been one of the leaders of the opposition to the king
during the early part of the reign, but had become a trusted
adviser after the death of Buckingham. In this capacity, and particularly as lord-lieutenant of Ireland, he worked zealously to establish the absolute rule of the king, earning for himself thereby
the bitter hostility of the Puritan opposition. As for Laud, he
sought to compel doctrinal unity and to enforce a ceremonial
uniformity of the narrowest kind, which involved the rooting out
of Puritan practices and the violation of Puritan prejudices. Those
who would not conform to the Prayer Book were dealt with severely. Times became so hard for the Puritans that about twenty
thousand migrated to America. Meanwhile the Catholics were
enjoying considerable freedom because of the influence of Henrietta Maria. This, added to the fact that the king preferred Catholics to Puritans, gave support to the suspicion that Charles and
Laud were aiming to restore Catholicism in England. Conse-

quently Laud's innovations became all the more hateful to the Puritans, even to the extent of evoking popular demonstrations against the government.

In 1637 Charles I and Laud made the fatal mistake of trying to impose on the Scottish Kirk a prayer book like that of the English Church. The resistance of the Scotch was immediate. Everywhere in Scotland the use of the book provoked riots, and people of all ranks united in signing a national covenant for the defense of the Presbyterian faith. Determined to force obedience, Charles sent an army into Scotland. It was ill-armed, ill-equipped, ill-disciplined, devoid of enthusiasm for the king's cause, and generally inferior to the well-disciplined and well-equipped Scotch army. A victory for the Scots was so certain that the king met their demands before any fighting took place. He had no intention, however, of keeping his promises. Wentworth was summoned from Ireland, created earl of Strafford, and given the task of subduing Scotland. Perceiving that this could not be done without a strong army, Strafford advised the king to summon Parliament as a means of securing adequate supplies for a war. And so after a period of eleven years the personal rule of the king came to an end.

The parliament which met in April, 1640, sat only three weeks, and is therefore known as the Short Parliament. It lost no time in demanding redress of such grievances as Laud's religious innovations and the king's unparliamentary taxation. The king, rather than yield to their demands, dissolved Parliament without getting any supplies. Though he now tried desperately to raise funds by all the means at his command, including loans from other nations, little came of his efforts. Consequently the force he was able to gather was small and ill-equipped. When the Scots invaded England they were easily able to defeat the king's army and take possession of the counties of Durham and Northumberland. To stop the advance of the Scots the king was forced to promise them a large indemnity, and this promise necessitated the calling of another parliament.

The parliament which met on November 3, 1640, was the longest in English history and also one of the most memorable. Since it was not formally dissolved until March 16, 1660, it has become known as the Long Parliament. The members assembled in a resolute temper, determined to remove the existing grievances. Their first step was the arrest and impeachment of Strafford. Recognizing in him a leader who was opposed to them on almost every point, the Commons decided that he must be put away before they could obtain redress of their grievances. Accordingly Strafford was accused of having "traitorously endeavored to subvert the fundamental laws and government of the realms of England and Ireland" and was brought to trial before the House of Lords. But as the trial progressed it became increasingly apparent that the charges could not be sustained. Suddenly the Commons in their determination to destroy him voted to drop the impeachment proceedings in favor of a bill of attainder, by means of which, if it was passed, Strafford could be put to death without trial. Though the bill quickly passed both houses, Strafford was still confident that the move would fail, for the bill could not become law without the king's signature. Even this was finally procured. After a howling mob had milled about Whitehall Palace a day and a night clamoring for the blood of Strafford, the king, who shortly before had said that not a hair on his minister's head should be harmed, gave way and sealed the doom of his faithful friend. The sentence was carried out in May, 1641. Laud also had been arrested, but was kept in prison four years before he was executed.

With both Strafford and Laud out of the way, the Commons could now proceed against the king. Soon after it assembled, Parliament had passed the Triennial Act, which required the king to summon Parliament at least once every three years. If he did not do so the sheriffs of the counties were to hold elections on their own initiative. To prevent the king from again nipping their reform efforts in the bud, the houses next passed a bill which ordained that the Long Parliament could not be dissolved except with its own consent. Steps were also taken to prevent the king from raising money or administering justice without Parliament. A bill was passed which declared illegal such means of unparliamentary taxation as exaction of knighthood fines, enlargement of forest rights, and ship-money. Moreover, the king was forbidden to collect tunnage and poundage except by permission of Parliament. All the arbitrary courts, including the Court of Star Chamber and the Court of High Commission, were abolished. In a word, Parliament demolished the machinery of absolutism.

After the worst grievances had been removed, a rift appeared in the Long Parliament. One party felt that the limitation of the king's power had gone far enough, while another wished to continue to restrict it. Charles, who had been waiting for an opportunity to regain some of the ground he had lost, now decided to capitalize upon the dissension. He requested the arrest of the five leaders of the opposition to him in the Commons, charging them with subverting the constitution and with carrying on treasonable negotiations with the Scots. When the Commons refused to permit this as contrary to its privileges, the king, egged on by his wife, decided to go in person to make the arrests, accompanied by several hundred armed partisans. As the five members had been forewarned, they were not present in the Commons that day, and the king, remarking that "the birds have flown," was compelled to return to the palace without achieving his purpose. This attempted interference with the privileges of Parliament spelled the ruin of Charles. It convinced the Commons that he did not mean to be bound by law, that all his promises were but empty words. Soon both sides were collecting their forces for the inevitable conflict. In August, 1642, the king set up his standard at Nottingham, summoning all loyal citizens to come to his support. Parliament likewise prepared for war by voting to raise ten thousand men.

THE CIVIL WARS

The conflict that followed was not only political and ecclesiastical but also economic and social. Men of every class might be found on either side. Generally speaking, the nobles sided with the king, though a considerable minority supported the cause of Parliament. The bulk of the parliamentary army was composed of merchants, tradesmen, and small farmers. Thus the fashionable and pleasure-loving classes sided with the king, while Parliament looked to the wealthy trading classes and the yeomen for its support. From the custom of letting their locks fall over their shoulders, and from their fine dress, the followers of the king were known as Cavaliers. Supporters of Parliament, on the other hand, were scornfully called Roundheads because of their close-cropped hair. There was no sharp geographical division between the two parties. In general it may be said that the northern and western parts of England were for the king, and the southern and the eastern regions, with their populous cities, were for Parliament. From the first, Parliament enjoyed the great advantage of having the support of London, of the navy, and of most of the seaport towns.

Not all Englishmen, however, held either with the king or with Parliament. Whole districts and counties declared themselves neutral. Only a small proportion of the nation engaged actively in the struggle. The total number of men under arms was about two and one-half per cent of the population; the rest contented themselves with the rôle of spectators.

The war began when Charles took the offensive and marched toward London in the hope that he might capture that city with one stroke and thus end the war. At the news of his march the parliamentary forces, commanded by the earl of Essex, moved northward to meet the king. The two armies met at Edgehill and the result was inconclusive. It might well have been decisive if Prince Rupert, the king's nephew and commander of the royal cavalry, had not gone in pursuit of the opposing horsemen, thereby giving the parliamentary footmen an opportunity to escape. The second mistake was that Charles did not make the most of his opportunity by immediately marching on London before his opponents had time to rally their forces. Though the distance from Edgehill to London is only about eighty miles, it was three weeks before the king and his army approached the latter city. A few miles from London trained bands of burghers had entrenched themselves, and rather than risk a battle Charles withdrew to Oxford, which remained his headquarters for the rest of the war. The fighting was at first in favor of the king. This was chiefly because his cavalry, led by the spirited Prince Rupert, was superior to that of the parliamentary army. However, two factors soon robbed the king of whatever advantage he held. The first was an agreement between the parliamentarians and the Scots (1643), whereby a Scottish army was to fight for the parliamentary cause on condition that the Presbyterian form of religion be established in England. The second was Cromwell's "New Model Army," which ultimately was to prove the decisive element.

Oliver Cromwell was born at Huntingdon on April 25, 1599, the son of untitled English gentry. As he himself later said: "I was by birth a gentleman, living neither in any considerable height, nor yet in obscurity." At the age of twenty-one he married and settled down to the quiet life of a gentleman farmer. He was a Puritan, but far removed from the grim, stern type. Throughout life he was fond of music, and enjoyed hunting and hawking as did other country gentlemen. He was not averse to jesting, and on

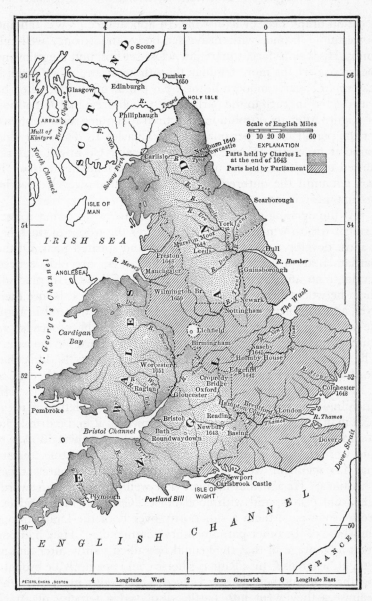

England and Wales in the Civil Wars of the Seventeenth Century

occasion drank beer or light wine. In appearance he was tall and powerful of frame, with heavy-set body and strong, well-knit limbs. His serious face, square jaw, close-set lips, and long flowing locks are perhaps more familiar than those of any other English statesman of early modern history. His public life began when he was elected in 1628 to the parliament which drew up the Petition of Right. After its dissolution he retired to a quiet rural existence for the period of the personal rule of Charles I. When the king found it necessary to call Parliament again, Cromwell was returned to both the Short and the Long Parliament in 1640. It was not until the outbreak of the Civil War, however, that he became prominent.

At the opening of the war Cromwell saw at once that if Parliament was to win a decisive victory over the troops of the king, it must develop a force of well-trained and spirited men. Of the parliamentary troops he said: "Most of them are old decayed serving-men and tapsters and such kind of fellows." In place of them he would "levy men who have the fear of God before their eyes, and will bring some conscience to what they do, and I promise you they shall not be beaten." Accordingly he proceeded to raise a regiment of sternly religious men, full of zeal for the cause. The principle which guided him in his choice was: "I think that he that prays and preaches best will fight best." Paradoxical as it may sound, this proved to be true of Cromwell's troops. His discipline was rigid. As it was reported in a news-letter of 1643: "No man swears but he pays his twelvepence; if he be drunk, he is set in the stocks or worse." Offenses against property and persons were severely punished. Shortly Cromwell was able to state that his regiment was "a lovely company" of "honest, sober Christians." He saw that his men were well equipped with sword, pike, and pistols, and with good horses. Constant drills and exercises soon gave them a superiority over both the king's troops and those of the other parliamentary commanders. They had one great advantage in that they could be rallied swiftly after an onslaught, whereas Prince Rupert's horse could not easily be brought together for another charge. Indeed, Cromwell's men, chanting psalms as they went into battle, displayed a ferocity of attack which has seldom been excelled in warfare.

The combined forces of the parliamentary footmen, the army of the Scots, and Cromwell's cavalry met the royalists on Marston

Moor (July 2, 1644) and won a sweeping victory. In Cromwell's cavalry Prince Rupert found more than his match. He and his men were put to flight by the impetuous charges of the psalm-singing horsemen. In writing about the conflict to his brother-in-law Cromwell states: "We never charged but we routed the enemy. . . . God made them as stubble to our swords." The victory was a severe blow to the king's fortunes, but it was far from decisive. It was in this battle that Prince Rupert gave Cromwell the nick-name Old Ironsides, later transferred to his troops.

His regiment having demonstrated its efficiency, Cromwell was not slow to speak his mind in Parliament regarding the poor quality of the rest of the troops. The result was that an ordinance was passed in 1645 to raise a New Model Army of 20,000 men, patterned after the Ironsides regiment of Cromwell. Sir Thomas Fairfax, a young but capable officer, was given command and Cromwell was made second in authority. In the battle of Naseby (June, 1645) this new force demonstrated its power by utterly destroying the army of the king. When the New Model inflicted a defeat upon the royalists of the southwest at Langport a few months later, the king's cause was doomed. For some time Charles wandered about the countryside almost like a hunted fugitive, still hoping for aid from the Highlands of Scotland and from Ire-land; but in the spring of 1646 he surrendered to the Scots, who the following year delivered him over to Parliament and returned to their own country.

With the king a prisoner, a rift appeared in the opposition to him. There was a general desire to return the crown to him, but there was no agreement regarding the terms. The Presbyterian majority of Parliament was ready to restore Charles on condition that he inaugurate the Presbyterian form of worship. This, how-ever, did not satisfy the Independents,[1] who controlled the army and who desired a religious settlement which would include tol-eration for the various types of Puritanism. To remove the oppo-sition of the Independents, Parliament attempted to reduce the army by half, believing that with the king in their hands the need for a large force had passed. But this move was stoutly resisted by the army. For a long time Cromwell tried to bring about an agree-ment between Parliament and the army. Finally, when his efforts

---

[1] A name given to those Puritans, earlier known as Brownists or Separatists, who rejected episcopacy and presbyterianism alike.

failed, he took the bold step of sending soldiers to gain possession of Charles, so that the army might prevent the restoration of the king except on its own terms. While the army and Parliament continued their controversy, the king contrived to escape and as a last resort entered into an agreement with the Scots. He promised in return for their help to establish the Presbyterian worship in England for a period of three years, after which the question of religion was to be regulated by the crown and Parliament.

The war which resulted, often called the Second Civil War, was soon over. Cromwell and his army met the Scots at Preston in Lancashire, and in an engagement lasting three days completely routed them (August, 1648). Of the large army which had crossed the border but few Scots reached home. The battle was not only a victory over the Scots but it also decided the issue in favor of the army in the contest with Parliament. When Cromwell, upon returning to London, discovered that Parliament had again been negotiating with the king, he proceeded to restore the harmony between that body and the army by expelling its Presbyterian members. His method was anything but constitutional. Colonel Pride was sent to the House with a regiment of soldiers under instructions to turn back all Presbyterian members as they were about to enter (December 6, 1648). The result of Pride's Purge was the exclusion of about one hundred fifty members. The small remnant of fifty-three Independents, later called "the Rump" because it was that part of Parliament which remained sitting, was no longer a representative body in any sense. Its power was derived wholly from the support of the army.

The Rump immediately passed a resolution to bring the king, "that man of blood," to trial. Since the House of Lords refused to participate, the Commons proceeded to appoint a High Court of Justice to try Charles. One hundred thirty-five persons were named, but only some sixty appeared when the trial started. Charles offered no defense, contending that neither that court nor any other had legal jurisdiction to proceed against the king. The verdict of the court was a foregone conclusion. On the fifth day of the trial Charles Stuart was condemned to death as "a tyrant, a traitor, murderer, and public enemy to the good people of this nation." A scaffold was erected against the front wall of Whitehall Palace and there the sentence was executed on January 30, 1649. Walking upon the scaffold with a firm step, the king in a speech to the assembled multitudes disclaimed all guilt for the civil wars and also declared his sentence unlawful. Thereafter he calmly laid his head on the block, prayed silently for a short time, and extended his arms as a signal to the executioner. His head was severed with one blow. It is reported by an eyewitness that when the headsman held up the royal head and according to custom spoke the words, "This is the head of a traitor," there was "such a groan by the thousands then present as I never heard before, and desire I may never hear again."

Charles owed his execution in a large measure to the intensity of his convictions and to his duplicity. Having been taught the doctrine of the divine right of kings since infancy, he adhered to it with a conviction which neither defeat nor prison nor even the approach of death could modify. But it was his duplicity which spelled his doom. Though there were demands as early as 1647 that the king be brought to trial, Cromwell opposed such a move until he became convinced that the king's word was not to be trusted; then the Puritan leader went over to the side of those demanding the king's death. Charles was "a tragic figure because he was born into times he could not understand and to a task that was too hard for him. The tragedy is there rather than in his death, for his execution was largely his own blame."[1] "Charles the Martyr" was more popular than Charles the king had been. His quiet dignity and religious resignation in the face of death excited a widespread admiration. It was a political opponent of the king, Andrew Marvell, who wrote:

> He nothing common did, nor mean,
> Upon that memorable scene.

The sympathy evoked by the king's courage as he faced the executioner soon blotted out the memory of his bad qualities, and many began to wish for the restoration of the Stuart line.

THE COMMONWEALTH AND THE PROTECTORATE

A short time after the execution of Charles, the Rump abolished both the monarchy and the House of Lords, proclaiming England a free Commonwealth. The executive functions were vested in a council of state consisting of forty-one members, of whom all but ten were members of the Rump. Though this gov-

---

[1] John Buchan, *Oliver Cromwell* (1934), p. 317.

ernment was a republic in form, the real power in the state was the army; and Cromwell, as master of the army, was the ruler of England. Few people had any liking for the government. At home, the English people wanted a king; abroad, where the execution was regarded as the height of atrocity, the Commonwealth commanded little respect. The English ambassadors in the United Netherlands and in Spain were murdered by royalist sympathizers, and those in Russia were driven from the court. The Commonwealth had not a friend among the nations of Europe. Yet no nation dared openly to support the Stuart cause. France and Spain were still at war, and the Dutch Republic was troubled by internal difficulties.

One great menace to the stability of the Commonwealth government was the condition of Ireland and Scotland. As the situation in Ireland was most urgent, Cromwell first turned his attention to the "pacification" of that country. The Irish Catholics, the Irish Episcopalians, and the Irish Presbyterians had all united against the government of the Independents. It was feared that if the united forces were successful in taking Dublin from the small parliamentary army stationed there, they would next invade England. To prevent this, Cromwell embarked with an army of 15,000. After storming Drogheda, a stronghold some thirty miles north of Dublin, the army put the whole garrison to the sword, while hundreds of Catholic priests were "knocked on the head," as Cromwell put it. About three thousand perished in the slaughter. The massacre was repeated at Wexford, after which Cromwell's army swept the country like an all-destroying scourge. This expedition to Ireland is the darkest episode in Cromwell's career. He himself seems to have regarded the slaughter of the natives as a just punishment for the uprising of eight years before, when a force of Irish Catholics had attacked the Protestants in Ulster and massacred a large number. "I am persuaded," he wrote, "that this is a righteous judgment of God upon these barbarous wretches, who have imbrued their hands in so much innocent blood; and that it will tend to prevent the effusion of blood in the future." Severity at the outset, he believed, would prevent a long war and further bloodshed. Besides those who were put to death, many were shipped to the Barbadoes, and there consigned to forced labor under the tropical sun. Much of the Irish land was confiscated and given to the supporters of Cromwell. The

Irish did not forget the slaughter, and "The curse of Cromwell on you!" became one of the most terrible imprecations that could be hurled at a foe.

When Cromwell returned from Ireland in May, 1650, another task awaited him. Several months previously Prince Charles, son of the late Charles I, had landed in Scotland and been proclaimed ruler of the three kingdoms (England, Ireland, and Scotland). It was evident that once Charles was the master of Scotland he would try, at the head of a Scottish army, to regain his father's throne. Rather than lead an army to forestall such a move, Fairfax resigned his command and Cromwell was made commander-in-chief. Several days later the new commander-in-chief moved northward at the head of some 16,000 men, filled with zeal both for their religion and for the Commonwealth. At Dunbar Cromwell's army was hemmed in between two Scotch forces in such a way that he himself felt that only a miracle could save him. But when the Scots made the mistake of moving down from a hill which they were holding to attack his army, Cromwell used his cavalry with such devastating effect that he won a complete victory with the loss of but a few men. He took Edinburgh, but even this did not end the resistance of the Scots. The following summer a Scottish army invaded England under the leadership of Prince Charles, who hoped that the English royalists would rally to his cause. In this he was mistaken. The royalists feared Cromwell too much to rise against the government. At Worcester Charles and his army were surrounded by Cromwell's forces and completely routed. Afterwards Cromwell referred to this victory as a "crowning mercy" because it put an end to armed resistance against the Commonwealth. Prince Charles, who barely escaped capture, made his way to a village on the coast of Sussex whence he fled to France. The romantic tale of his escape won many hearts for his cause.

Hardly had the resistance in Ireland and Scotland been put down when a foreign war broke out. Since the beginning of the century there had been an intense trade rivalry between the English and the Dutch. Though the English envied the Dutch their fisheries, they were more concerned about the carrying trade. They found it particularly humiliating that the commerce with their colonies was largely in Dutch hands. To limit the trading sphere of the Dutch, the Rump passed a Navigation Act in 1651 which stipulated that no goods should be imported into England from Asia, Africa, or America except in ships owned and manned by Englishmen; also that no goods should be imported into England or the dominions thereof except in English ships or in the ships of the country that produced the goods. This law and other causes made war between the two nations inevitable. Actual warfare began when Blake, the English admiral, encountering a Dutch fleet under Admiral Tromp off Dover, demanded in vain that the Dutch admiral lower his flag. A fierce combat followed, with Tromp, who had the smaller fleet, withdrawing when darkness fell. In the war which followed, the two fleets fought battle after battle on fairly even terms. But both the Dutch carrying trade and the Dutch fisheries suffered severely. Finally the strain became so great that the Dutch concluded peace in 1654 on terms favorable to the English.

Meanwhile important changes in the government had taken place at home. Not only had the Rump become increasingly unpopular, but it was also at odds with the army. Many of the members were men of ability and character, but the body as a whole seemed more intent upon prolonging its tenure of authority than upon giving England a good government. When the Rump discussed a bill which provided that vacancies in Parliament should be filled only by consent of the existing members, Cromwell lost his patience. Entering the House with a company of troopers, he berated the members and drove them out by force. Fearing the consequences of an appeal to the country at large, he and the other leaders of the army then selected a new body from lists drawn up by the Independent ministers of the three kingdoms. This parliament was composed of 140 members (129 from England, 5 from Scotland, and 6 from Ireland). It was really not a parliament at all, but simply a convention of Puritan notables. In derision the people of England called it Barebone's Parliament, for the first name on the alphabetical list of its members was Praise-God Barebone. Godly and well-meaning men they probably were, but they were also impractical. Soon Barebone's Parliament was more unpopular than the Rump had been. After a session of a few months a group of the more moderate members dissolved the body in December, 1653. With its dissolution the Commonwealth came to an end.

Four days after the dissolution, the leading officers of the army promulgated a constitution known as the Instrument of Government. It is notable as the only written constitution in English history which was ever put in operation. The executive power was vested in a single person, the lord protector, who was to be assisted by a council of state. The legislative powers were entrusted to a parliament of a single chamber in which sat representatives of Scotland and Ireland as well as of England (400 from England and 30 each from Scotland and Ireland). This body also had the right of extraordinary taxation; that is, the voting of subsidies to the protector beyond the fixed revenue for the ordinary expenses of the army and navy and the civil administration. It was to meet not less than once in three years and was not to be dissolved until it had sat five months. Enactments of Parliament, except those which ran counter to the Instrument of Government, became law after twenty days even though they were vetoed by the protector. The right to vote for members of Parliament was restricted by property qualifications, while all who had borne arms against Parliament and all Roman Catholics were excluded. Religious freedom was granted to all professing Christians except believers in "popery or prelacy."

There was of course only one possible lord protector, Oliver Cromwell. On December 16, 1653, he was duly installed in office and for a period of nearly five years remained the chief ruler of England. It is ironical that he who had crushed Charles because he was a despot now found it necessary to do the very things for which the king was put to death. Step by step the man who had so staunchly fought for law and order, who disliked the use of force in government, and who sincerely believed in the government of the people, was compelled to fall back on military dictatorship. He who had put an end forever to "divine right" in England now put "divine might" in its place, for Cromwell believed no less than Charles had that he was called by God to rule England. Rule by force was necessary because Cromwell was ruling without the consent of the nation. On the very day his first parliament met, the Instrument of Government was attacked because it did not insure that parliamentary control of the government for which the Civil War had been fought. Angered by this meddling with "fundamentals," Cromwell managed to exclude about a hundred of the most uncompromising members from the parliament. The move failed, however, to stifle the criticism of his power. For five months the wrangling between protector and parliament continued, and on the first day he was permitted to do so by the constitution, Cromwell dissolved the parliament, styling it a menace to the public good.

Since the Protectorate did not have the support of the majority of the English people, insurrections began to spring up in various parts of England. To prevent such uprisings Cromwell divided England into twelve districts, each of which was put under a major-general. Hence for a period of twenty months, from the autumn of 1655 until the spring of 1657, England was under martial law, a condition forbidden by the Petition of Right. The costs of this system of military police were defrayed by an unauthorized tax of ten per cent on the income of all former Cavaliers. Thus Cromwell in levying arbitrary taxes became guilty of the very injustice he had so vigorously attacked as a member of the Long Parliament.

In the second parliament, called in 1656, the element of opposition was just as strong as it had been in the first until the more defiant members, to the number of one hundred fifty, were excluded. Those who remained hoped to make the government more stable by a restoration of the kingship. Hence they drew up the Humble Petition and Advice, requesting Cromwell to exchange his title of protector for that of king and also to create a new House of Lords. After weeks of indecision Oliver finally declined the royal title, choosing instead to become hereditary lord-protector with the right to name his successor. He did, however, nominate a new House of Lords, largely from among his supporters in the House of Commons. When, after a recess, the excluded members of Parliament returned, and the Commons again proposed amendments to the constitution, Cromwell dissolved both houses in February, 1658.

Though Cromwell's government was unpopular at home, he did strengthen England's position abroad. His New Model Army, the most efficiently trained force in Europe, and a great navy, hardly second in efficiency to the army, gave England enormous prestige. The protector's first act in foreign affairs was to terminate the war with the Dutch (1654) and to enter into commercial treaties with Sweden and Denmark which secured considerable advantages for English trade. He also offered Madrid an alliance against France on condition that the English be accorded religious freedom in Spain, and that English merchants be permitted to trade with the Spanish colonies. When this was refused, in 1657 he entered into an alliance to aid France in its conflict against Spain, a continuation of the Thirty Years' War.[1] The contingent of six thousand Ironsides sent to the Spanish Netherlands helped the French win a number of successes, including the capture of Dunkirk, the best port in Flanders, which was handed over to the English.[2] In the New World an English fleet failed to take Hispaniola (Haiti) but succeeded in capturing Jamaica, which has remained an English possession ever since. Nearer home Admiral Blake achieved a great triumph when he chased the Spanish treasure fleet into the bay of Santa Cruz in the Canaries, silenced the guns of the fortress under which it had taken refuge, and then sank or burned every ship in the bay. As in the age of "Good Queen Bess," Spain again had reason to fear the English. During the reign of Charles II, Pepys was to write: "It is strange how everybody do nowdays reflect upon Oliver and commend him, what brave things he did, and made all the neighbour Princes fear him."

Meanwhile Cromwell's task of governing England grew heavier and heavier. The people were tired of the military despotism and the Puritan severity. Discontent was further increased by the crushing burden of taxes made necessary by the war. Well could Cromwell remark as the difficulties of governing increased: "I can say in the presence of God, in comparison with whom we are but like creeping ants upon the earth, I would have been glad to have lived under my woodside, to have kept a flock of sheep rather than undertake such a government as this." The constant worries and responsibilities of government had incessantly taxed his physical energy, until they undermined his robust constitution. Stricken by a fever in August, 1658, he finally resigned himself to death. "I would be willing," he said, "to live to be further serviceable to God and to His people, but my work is done." As he lay dying a terrible storm raged over England, tearing trees up by their roots and unroofing houses. By his friends the storm was interpreted as God's announcement of the death of His servant Cromwell, but the Cavaliers said it was the devil come to fetch home the soul of the regicide and usurper. On the third of September, the anniversary of his victories at Dunbar and Worcester,

---

[1] See p. 350.   [2] It was later sold to the French (1662).

his "Fortunate Day" as he was wont to call it, he died at the age of fifty-nine.

For almost three centuries Cromwell has been a center about which tempests of blame and praise have raged. His biographers have carefully scrutinized every utterance and disinterred even the smallest details of his life. Yet to posterity he is just as much of an enigma as he was to his contemporaries. Even among those who regard him as one of the greatest statesmen in English history there is little agreement as to the specific nature of his greatness. What has been definitely established by recent scholarship is that he was not a hypocrite. Neither was personal ambition the driving force of his character. A champion of constitutional liberties, he resorted to dictatorship only as a means of obviating what he regarded as greater evils. His central motive was always the welfare of the nation he ruled, not his own glory. To the English people, however, the dictatorship was worse than the evils it was instituted to prevent. Consequently the Protectorate collapsed shortly after Cromwell's death. Nevertheless, while it lasted it saved England from chaos and disruption and raised her high in Europe. In this latter fact lies Cromwell's greatest claim to glory, for he made England's name and power respected as never before since the days of Elizabeth. On the other hand, he displayed little wisdom in dealing with his parliaments, failing with every experiment he tried. But even after all the weaknesses of Cromwell the statesman have been admitted, there still remains much truth in the remark of Lord Clarendon, who said that Cromwell was one of those men "whom his enemies could not condemn without commending him at the same time."

Regarding Cromwell's merits as a soldier there is little room for disagreement. He is the greatest cavalry leader in British history and one of the most inspiring military commanders of all time. The effectiveness of his troops has seldom if ever been surpassed. During his entire military career he was not defeated in battle—indeed, not a single operation failed; yet many of his battles were fought against great odds.

In religious matters Cromwell was, on the whole, far more tolerant than his age—an age in which most religious people regarded any form of tolerance as anathema. He consumed much energy in tempering the persecuting zeal of his fellow Puritans. "I desire from my heart," he stated, "union and right understanding between the godly people—Scots, English, Jews, Gentiles, Presbyterians, Anabaptists, and all." Cromwell permitted the Jews, who had been excluded from England since their expulsion by Edward I in 1290, to return, and also extended protection to the new sect of Quakers. On the other hand, he distributed the endowments of the Anglican Church among the principal Puritan sects, and in 1655 prohibited the use of the Prayer Book, though in general Episcopalians were not molested unless they plotted against the government. The Roman Catholics alone were excepted from the general toleration; yet even the penalties against them were not rigidly enforced.

During his last illness Cromwell had orally named his eldest son, Richard, to succeed him, and immediately after Oliver's death his son was proclaimed protector. Richard was an honest, sensible man, but not strong enough to carry on the work of his father. Whereas Oliver Cromwell had been a military leader who commanded the respect of the army, Richard was a civilian, and a rather unmilitary civilian at that. As such he failed to hold the support of the army, upon which his tenure of office depended. Had he desired to do so, he could have called to his aid the English army of occupation in Scotland under the command of General Monk, and the army in Ireland under his brother, Henry Cromwell. But he would allow no bloodshed on his account. He is reported to have said: "I will not have a drop of blood spilt for the preservation of my greatness, which is a burden to me." Hence, after a rule of nine months, Richard in 1659 resigned his office to retire to private life.

With the resignation of Richard the Protectorate collapsed. In a last effort to maintain its power the army now recalled the Rump, which immediately began quarreling with the officers. Confusion reigned until General Monk marched to London at the head of the troops that had been in Scotland. He recalled all the survivors of the Long Parliament, gave orders that it dissolve itself, and made provision for the election of a new parliament. "I am engaged in conscience and honor," he said, "to see my country freed from that intolerable slavery of a sword government." In the meantime Charles himself smoothed the way for a Stuart restoration by issuing the conciliatory Declaration of Breda which promised: (1) a general amnesty for all persons not specially excepted by Parliament; (2) liberty of conscience according to such laws as Parliament might propose; (3) settlement in Parliament of all claims to landed property; (4) payment of full arrears to the army. On receiving the declaration the new parliament voted that "according to the ancient and fundamental laws of this kingdom the government is and ought to be by King, Lords and Commons." Charles II was then proclaimed king and invited to return to England. On May 29, 1660, he entered London in state amid great rejoicing.

CAVALIER AND PURITAN LITERATURE

In the literature of the period of Charles I and the Civil Wars the spirit of both the Cavaliers and the Puritans found expression. The so-called Cavalier literature was chiefly of a lighter sort—gay, polite, and polished. Probably the most characteristic expressions of the Cavalier spirit are the lyrics of Herrick, Carew, Suckling, and Lovelace, all of whom, except the first, were connected with the court of Charles I. Though Herrick was the greatest poet of the group, Lovelace was the more typical Cavalier. When the war broke out he fought on the side of the king, spending his fortune in the royal cause, but after Charles was beheaded he sank into poverty and finally died in a very mean lodging in London. Most of his poetry is second-rate and tedious, but in two songs, *To Lucasta* and *To Althea*, he touched the universal human heart. The former closes with the chivalrous sentiment:

> I could not love thee, dear, so much
> Loved I not honor more

and the latter contains the familiar lines:

> Stone walls do not a prison make
> Nor iron bars a cage.

Of a totally different nature are the writings in the Puritan spirit. They are solemn and elevated in tone, reflecting the habitual seriousness of the Puritans, their simple tastes, and their reverent behavior. In a word, they are a literature permeated by religious earnestness. The drama found small place in this literature. Not that Puritanism regarded drama as evil in itself, but the Puritans' serious view of life did not admit comedy and pageantry. Hence in 1642 a law was passed to close the theaters. Puritanism found its highest expression in the poetry of John Milton (1608–1674) and the prose of John Bunyan (1628–1688), though neither wrote his great work until the Puritan dream of political domination had been dispelled. These two figures are examples of the wide meaning of the word *Puritan*. Milton, the artist and man of varied learning, represents Puritanism (from which he ultimately broke) in its broadest sense, while Bunyan, a man of the people, exemplifies the fervent belief of many Puritans in a direct personal relationship between God and the individual.

Next to Shakespeare, Milton is the greatest of English poets. As an epic poet he ranks with Homer, Virgil, and Dante. His early poetry includes the *Ode on the Nativity, L'Allegro, Il Penseroso, Comus*, and *Lycidas*. His masterpiece is *Paradise Lost*, composed and dictated to his wife and daughters in the seven years 1658–1665, after he had become blind. As early as 1638 Milton had already determined that the composition of a great poem was to be the chief work of his life. He considered many themes, but finally chose Paradise Lost. The purpose of the epic, as set forth in the prelude, is to "justify the ways of God to man"; its basic theme is the fall of Adam or, in a wider sense, the fall of man:

> Of Man's first disobedience, and the fruit
> Of that forbidden tree whose mortal taste
> Brought death into the world, and all our woe,
> With loss of Eden, till one greater Man
> Restore us, and regain the blissful seat.

No one but the author of the *Divine Comedy* has written a poem that compares with *Paradise Lost* in sublimity of thought. To secure perpetuity of interest for his epic Milton chose a subject which he believed would retain its hold on the imagination of men, but today *Paradise Lost* is more admired than read. Many of its passages, however, are frequently quoted, as for example:

> The mind is its own place, and in itself
> Can make a Heaven of Hell, a Hell of Heaven.

Four years after the appearance of *Paradise Lost* Milton published his *Paradise Regained*, a shorter epic dealing with man's redemption through Christ. The author seems to have preferred it to its predecessor, but posterity has regarded it as inferior in both style and interest despite a number of lofty passages. The greatness of Milton's poetic works has overshadowed his prose, which includes *Areopagitica, A Tractate on Education, Eikonoklastes or the*

Image-Breaker, and *History of England to the Norman Conquest*. Of these his *Areopagitica*, an eloquent plea for uncensored printing, is probably the best known and the most admired. His prose has a marked affinity with his poetry. Unwieldy at times, at its best it is supremely great. Indeed, had he not written one line of verse, Milton's prose would give him rank among the great masters of the English tongue. His last important work was *Samson Agonistes*, a dramatic poem, written in the manner of the Greek tragedies, which tells the story of Samson's captivity and of his revenge upon his oppressors. Since Milton, like Samson, was stricken with blindness, this theme possessed an irresistible attraction for him. The poem accordingly has a distinct autobiographical interest. In 1674 Milton died, having carried on heroically despite physical affliction, the opposition of his contemporaries, and a hopeless sense of a despairing struggle against fate. To him might well be applied the words spoken of the dead Samson by Manoa:

> Samson hath quit himself
> Like Samson, and heroically hath finished
> A life heroic.

Four years after Milton's death the first part of *Pilgrim's Progress* appeared. Its author, John Bunyan, was a man of little education. Having left the Church of England in early manhood to become a Baptist preacher, Bunyan in 1660 was imprisoned in Bedford jail on a charge of preaching in unlicensed conventicles. For the next twelve years, with one short interval, he remained in prison. Since he refused to stop preaching, a second incarceration followed, during which he probably wrote the first part of *Pilgrim's Progress*. Later he wrote a second part which appeared in 1684. *Pilgrim's Progress* is one of the great allegories of literature. Its story is the journey of a Christian from the City of Destruction to the Heavenly Jerusalem. During the first seven years after it was published, the first part ran through ten editions. Since then countless copies of the book have been printed and it has been translated into all the principal languages of the earth. For two centuries after its appearance it was one of the most widely read books in England, though its genuine popularity has perhaps been exaggerated. Macaulay said of its author: "Bunyan is as decidedly the first of allegorists as Demosthenes is the first of orators or Shakespeare the first of dramatists."

CHAPTER SIXTEEN

England from the Restoration to the Death of Queen Anne

THE RESTORATION

THE entrance of Charles II into London was greeted with frenzied enthusiasm. He returned, as Evelyn described it, "with a triumph of above 20,000 horse and foot, brandishing their swords and shouting with inexpressible joy; the ways strewed with flowers, the bells ringing, the streets hung with tapestry, fountains running with wine." The nation was joyful over its release from the strain of military rule and elated by the thought that after the rigors of Puritan government Merrie England had returned in the person of the king. Charles, stunned by the acclaim of the people, said with a smile to one of his company: "It must have been my own fault that I did not come before, for I find no one but declares he is glad to see me." The coronation was celebrated in April, 1661, with great pomp, and in May of the following year Charles married the Portuguese Infanta, Catherine of Braganza. The marriage was purely a political contract, concluded when Portugal offered to provide the Infanta with a dowry of half a million pounds; to cede to England Tangier on the northern coast of Africa and Bombay in India; and to grant certain commercial privileges. The alliance which this marriage initiated between the two countries was to continue for the better part of two centuries. The marriage itself was not successful in that it failed to produce an heir. Neither was the queen able to turn Charles from his infidelities.

Charles reëntered London on his thirtieth birthday. Six feet two inches tall, he was a man of good figure and vigorous health. His face with its swarthy complexion, large mouth, and dark eyes was homely. Charles himself, upon viewing his portrait, said: "Oddsfish! I am an ugly fellow." But he was also likable. Those who came in contact with him were impressed by his engaging personality, his easy disposition, his affability, tolerance, and generosity, and by his keen sense of humor. Indeed, the king's unfailing friendliness moved a contemporary to state that Charles II "could send away a person better pleased at receiving nothing than those in the good king his father's time that had requests granted them." Furthermore, in his rovings and adventures he had gained a knowledge of men which was to serve him in good stead. On the other hand, he lacked the sincerity, piety, and reserve which had characterized his father, and during his exile had acquired a capacity for intrigue and duplicity which later lost him the confidence of his parliaments, though his people did not cease to love him. In religion he had Catholic leanings, but he did not permit religion to interfere with pleasure. His father had been a model of domestic virtue; Charles II was openly immoral.

Charles's ideal in government was the absolutism of his Bourbon cousins in France. Yet he realized that he must tread warily. His saving trait was that he knew when to yield. The years of exile during which he had at times suffered from want had been so unpleasant that he was ready to concede almost anything rather than undergo the experience again. "I am weary of traveling and am resolved to go abroad no more," Charles said. Hence he was careful to hide his Roman Catholic bias and his desire for absolute power. He established the reputation of being an indolent, easygoing king—a pose which was not displeasing to those who remembered his father's determination to control all affairs. Nevertheless, behind the screen of his idleness, frivolity, and insouciance, he worked quietly and persistently to gain freedom for the Catholic religion in England and to maintain and strengthen the ancient prerogatives of the crown. He chose his ministers with consummate skill, and then quietly guided and directed them along the paths of his policy, often without arousing their suspicions as to his designs. For this and for other reasons many historians regard him as one of the most astute rulers in the history of English monarchy.

The Convention Parliament, as the body which recalled Charles is usually known, proceeded at once to settle some of the problems of the restoration. Since Cromwell's rule had convinced the English that a standing army is incompatible with liberty, Parliament immediately paid the arrears due both the soldiers and the fleet and disbanded all the troops except three regiments. This was the end of Cromwell's splendid army. As Charles had promised in the Declaration of Breda, an Act of Indemnity was passed which pardoned all who had opposed the king during the Civil Wars except those who were directly involved in the king's execution and a few others. After a dozen of the regicides had been executed, Charles, who was not vindictive, wrote Edward Hyde (Lord Clarendon), his chancellor: "I must confess I am weary of hanging—let it sleep." By act of Parliament Cromwell's remains were removed from Westminster, suspended from the gallows at Tyburn, and then buried with the bones of common criminals. Parliament next turned to the land question. It was decided that confiscated lands should be restored to their original owners without compensation to those who had bought them, but private sales of land were confirmed. The latter decision caused great disappointment to Cavaliers who had sold their land to aid the royal cause or had been forced to sell it in order to meet the fines imposed on them by the Protectorate government. Another important settlement was that of the royal revenue, so long a subject of quarrels between king and parliament. He was granted a fixed annual revenue, part of which was derived from an excise tax[1] on beer, salt, starch, silks, and other articles of common consumption. The settlement of the religious question was left for the new parliament which was to meet in May, 1661.

The new parliament was nicknamed the Cavalier Parliament because it was composed largely of ardent royalists, men whose fathers had fought under the banner of Charles I. Yet their royalism had its limits. They passed a law which forbade subjects to take up arms against the king on any pretense; yet they did not fail to take the precaution of refusing him permission to retain a

[1] The revenue of this tax, first levied during the Civil Wars, was assigned to the crown in compensation for the feudal dues, which were abolished.

standing army, so that he would be unable to establish an auto-cratic government. They also fixed the king's income at a figure which was barely enough to pay current expenses during peace time. In dealing with the religious question the Cavalier Parliament showed itself opposed both to Puritans and Roman Catholics. The Church of England was restored as it had existed in the reign of Charles I, and a series of acts known as the Clarendon Code was passed to force all into conformity with it. The first was the Corporation Act (1661), which decreed that all holders of municipal offices must receive Holy Communion according to the rites of the Church of England. As the strength of Puritanism lay in the cities, this excluded all zealous Puritans from participation in municipal government. In the next session (1662) the Act of Uniformity was passed, requiring all clergymen to accept the Prayer Book in its entirety. About two thousand refused to do so and were expelled from their parishes. Since many of the dispos-sessed clergymen continued to minister to their flocks by holding services privately, the Cavalier Parliament passed the Conventicle Act in 1664. This forbade the holding of religious services by five or more persons, exclusive of the members of a household, except according to the established forms of the Anglican Church. Pun-ishments for the non-observance of this law were severe—impris-onment for the first two offenses and transportation for the third. When many of the dissenting ministers won the acclaim of the people because they remained in London while many of the reg-ular clergy fled during the outbreak of the Great Plague (1665), Parliament immediately passed the Five Mile Act. It forbade any dissenting minister who refused to take the Oath of Non-resistance to come within five miles of any town or parish in which he had formerly preached.

Meanwhile the second war with the Dutch had begun. The commercial rivalry which had provoked the first war still con-tinued. Moreover, Charles himself had private grudges against the Dutch. Not only had they treated him discourteously, as he believed, during his exile, but they were withholding from his nephew, William of Orange, the hereditary title and office of stadtholder. Hostilities broke out in 1664, when the English took possession of New Amsterdam, and renamed it New York. Though the early advantages were on the side of the English, the Dutch soon gained the upper hand owing to the fact that a large part of the English fleet was laid up because Parliament had voted no funds for its maintenance. In 1667 the Dutch entered the Thames, sailed up the Medway as far as Chatham, burned six men of war, and captured two others. The English felt the shame of the Dutch exploits severely. It was said by many that such a thing would not have taken place had Oliver Cromwell been alive. Soon after this the treaty of Breda was signed, by which England lost her hold on the Spice Islands in the East but retained New York.

While this war was still in its second year (1665), England, and particularly London, suffered from a terrible plague. Within a few months about seventy thousand lives were claimed in the metropolis. To prevent its spread, orders were issued that the door of every house visited by the plague be marked with a red cross and the inscription, "Lord have mercy on us." At night carts made the rounds of the city to collect corpses, the ringing of a bell being the signal for the inhabitants to bring out their dead. After four months the fury of the plague abated somewhat in the capital, but in the following spring it spread to various parts of England. Hardly had it ceased devastating London when a great fire destroyed a large part of the city. For five days, from the 2nd to the 7th of September, 1666, it raged, consuming more than thirteen thousand buildings. Finally the king ordered that a number of houses be blown up to make a gap over which the fire could not pass.

Throughout Charles's reign the problem of finances was a pressing one. As he was chronically impecunious, and did not wish to become involved in strife with Parliament, he turned to France. Charles felt a deep friendship for this monarchy. Not only was he bound to it by ties of blood, but he also sympathized with France for religious reasons. Earlier he had sold Dunkirk to Louis XIV for a goodly sum, and had also received subsidies to supplement his insufficient revenue. Now, in 1670, despite the fact that his advisers had recently concluded the so-called Triple Alliance with Holland and Sweden, Charles entered into a secret agreement, called the treaty of Dover, with the Grand Monarch, binding himself to join France in a war against the Dutch and also publicly to declare himself a Roman Catholic at a proper time. In return Louis was to pay Charles a sum of money and, if the English people resisted the treaty, send a French force to help quell their opposition.

Charles began to carry out his part of the agreement by pro-
voking a conflict with the Dutch. He sent English ships to attack
a fleet of Dutch merchantmen, and the war began in 1672. In
the same year he published a Declaration of Indulgence which
suspended all the laws against Catholics and Dissenters. Although
the act granted only the right of private worship to Catholics
while it allowed Protestant Dissenters to worship in public, men
were convinced that it had been issued solely to further Catholic
interests. When Parliament met, it immediately petitioned the
king to restore the laws he had suspended. For a brief time Charles
stood firm in the hope that he might win. But, finding the leaders
determined, he soon gave way and revoked the declaration. It
was a signal victory for Parliament. Had the king been permitted
to suspend laws at will, he would soon have been able to make
himself an absolute ruler. To fortify its victory Parliament passed
the Test Act, which decreed that all holders of civil and military
office must receive the sacrament according to the rites of the
Anglican Church, and repudiate the doctrine of transubstantiation. The manifest object of the law was to prevent Catholics
from holding office, and for over a century and a half it served to
exclude both Roman Catholics and conscientious Dissenters from
civil and military affairs. On all sides the opposition to Charles's
policy spread. The war against the Dutch grew increasingly unpopular. Englishmen began to regard France rather than the
United Provinces as their real enemy. Many voiced the opinion
that the war was merely a pretense to permit the king to build up
a standing army. Finally in February, 1674, Charles yielded to
the demands for peace, leaving Louis XIV to continue the struggle
alone.

The passing of the Test Act was but one indication of the national dread of Roman Catholicism in England. Men's hearts
were filled with fears of a Catholic plot against their faith, and
nothing was too fantastic to be believed. It was at this anxious
time that Titus Oates, a most singular character and an adroit
liar, returned from the continent with "information" about a
supposed Catholic plot to kill the king, enthrone the duke of York,
who was the king's brother and a professed Catholic, land a French
army, and impose Catholicism upon England by force. The story
was well attuned to popular fears. Charles was unimpressed by
the reports, for in questioning Oates he had detected more than

one untruth in his statements. But two events of the time facilitated the acceptance of this amazing story by the people. The first was the discovery of a secret correspondence between the secretary of the duchess of York and the confessor of Louis XIV upon a scheme to restore Catholicism in England. The other event was the disappearance of the magistrate to whom Oates had first told his story and the finding of his body on Primrose Hill several days later. It was immediately assumed that he had been murdered by papists, and panic swept over England. In London barricades were raised in the streets, guns were placed at important points, and trained bands marched through the city ready to suppress any uprising or to repel invasion. Those accused by Oates of being leaders of the plot were tried, and many innocent victims were put to death. Oates himself was hailed as the savior of the country and rewarded with a pension. The members of Parliament, giving no less credence than the people to the tale, immediately passed a bill excluding Catholics from sitting in Parliament.

After sitting for eighteen years, the Cavalier Parliament was dissolved early in 1679. The new Parliament which met in March of that year soon began the discussion of the Exclusion Bill to debar from the throne James, duke of York, who was the heir since Charles had no rightful son. This time the king stood his ground; and when Parliament continued with the bill, Charles dissolved it in July, 1679. During the discussion of the Exclusion Bill those who supported the Catholic duke of York received the name Tories, which had hitherto applied to a certain class of Catholic outlaws in Ireland. The royalist supporters, in turn, called the exclusionists Whigs, a name hitherto used to designate rabid Scotch Covenanters.

From that time until his death Charles ruled with a firm hand. When the parliament which met in 1680 turned again to the Exclusion Bill, Charles retaliated by dissolving it. As his financial needs made another parliament necessary, the king summoned it to meet at Oxford (1681), where it would be free from intimidation by London mobs. Nevertheless, another Exclusion Bill was introduced. Its supporters were confident of victory because, as they believed, the king would be forced by his need of money to give way. They did not know, however, that Louis XIV had promised Charles a large subsidy. Hence the amazement when the king, to prevent further discussion of the Exclusion Bill, dissolved parliament after a session of only six days. In his address to the members he said: "I will never use arbitrary government myself and I am resolved not to suffer it in others." For the rest of his life he ruled without Parliament. His ascendancy was complete. Yet he was not to enjoy it long. In February, 1685, he was stricken with apoplexy and died a few days later. His sense of humor remained keen to the end, as is shown by his oft-quoted apology to those about him: "I am afraid, gentlemen, that I am an unconscionable time a-dying."

JAMES II AND THE "GLORIOUS REVOLUTION"

The new king, James II, was already in his fifty-third year when he ascended the throne. In appearance he had an advantage over his brother, for he was not only tall but handsome, with regular features and considerable grace and dignity. He also had certain virtues which his brother lacked, such as sincerity and candor. But he did not possess the cleverness and versatility of his predecessor. He was a person of narrow intellect, obstinate, arbitrary, harsh, and relentless. Like his father, Charles I, he was unable to gauge public opinion. As Buckingham had said earlier: "The king (Charles II) could see things if he would, and the duke (James II) would see things if he could." Though he had been in close touch with the politics of his brother's reign, James had failed to learn the lessons it had sketched in bold letters. As king he had two distinct aims: to rule as an absolute monarch and to reëstablish the Roman Catholic Church in England. Both were contrary to the temper of the nation and the times. Charles II had realized that there was a point beyond which he could not go. Thus he had abandoned the treaty of Dover when he saw that it would turn the people against him. He had also waited until he was on his deathbed before professing himself a Roman Catholic. James, on the other hand, went ahead blindly with his plans, disregarding entirely the opinions and prejudices of his people. Charles II had said shortly before his death: "When I am dead and gone, I know not what my brother will do. I am much afraid that when he comes to wear the crown he will be obliged to travel again." Not many years were to pass before this prophecy was fulfilled.

At his accession James was received with general complacency, and for a time it seemed as if he would rest satisfied with very moderate demands. But distrust was aroused when James had mass celebrated publicly for the first time in more than a century and a quarter. The alarm increased when he opened in parliament the question of relaxing the penal laws against Catholics. But an uprising against the king in the southwest of England turned all attention in that direction for the time being. The duke of Monmouth, eldest natural son of Charles II, had landed in Dorset with a small army and proclaimed himself king. As he proceeded his force increased until it numbered about 5000 men. At Sedgemoor, Monmouth encountered the royal troops on July 6, 1685; there his supporters were scattered and he himself was taken prisoner to be executed for high treason.

James II was now at the peak of his power. Since most of the people had remained loyal to him during Monmouth's rebellion, he seemed to feel that nothing could shake their loyalty. The army of some 30,000 men which had been recruited to put down the rebellion was not dismissed, but quartered near London as if to overawe the people of that city. When Parliament declared the army a menace to the nation, and also refused to repeal the Habeas Corpus Act[1] and the Test Act, James angrily prorogued it in December, 1685. Thereafter he went on from blunder to blunder. He appointed an "Ecclesiastical Commission Court" which was practically a revival of the Court of High Commission that had been abolished by the Long Parliament, he gave certain Catholics high commands in the army in defiance of the Test Act, appointed Catholics to important positions in the Anglican Church, and named Catholics as the heads of two Oxford colleges. Finally, without the permission of Parliament, he issued a Declaration of Indulgence (1687) suspending all penal laws against Catholics and Dissenters. The Declaration of Indulgence in itself was a commendable move toward general toleration, but

[1] The writ of Habeas Corpus ("You must produce the body"), by which an imprisoned person could appeal to a judge to determine whether he was being legally confined, dates from early times, but was at first narrow in scope and subject to irregularities. Attempts to establish the legal rights of the individual on a more secure basis culminated in the Habeas Corpus Act of 1679, which, among other things, declared that any prisoner charged with offenses other than treason or felony must, on the issuance of the writ, be brought before the judge within an interval of twenty days to determine whether he should be held for trial or released on bail; that a prisoner accused of treason or felony must be tried at the next gaol delivery or released on bail. The operation of the act was not extended to non-criminal cases until 1816.

the power to suspend laws had previously been denounced in Parliament. Moreover, most Englishmen were convinced that it was only a disguised step to procure toleration for Roman Catholics. In 1688 the king issued a second declaration, this time ordering it to be read in every parish church. Seven bishops who drew up a petition in which they questioned the legality of the dispensing power were committed to the Tower by the king and brought to trial for libel. When the jury after long deliberation finally acquitted them the people cheered the verdict lustily; even James's soldiers added their shouts of approval.

The English people had hitherto tolerated the acts of the king because James was already over fifty and the heir to the throne was his daughter Mary, wife of William III of Orange and a staunch Protestant. The next in the line of succession after Mary was her sister Anne. Both were daughters of James by his first marriage. But after the death of his first wife James had married Mary of Modena, an ardent Catholic. For many years the marriage had been childless, but in the summer of 1688, while the seven bishops were being tried, it was announced that the queen had given birth to a son. Despite the fact that about sixty persons had been present at the birth, the people at first refused to believe the child was the queen's son. It was rumored that he had been smuggled into the queen's bedroom in a warming pan, so that a Catholic succession might be insured. But the fact was really incontrovertible that an heir had been born who took Mary's place as the next in succession to the throne. It was also certain that he would be brought up in the Catholic faith. The prospect of a long line of Catholic rulers moved seven of the leaders of the two parties, Whigs and Tories, to send a letter to William III of Orange inviting him to come to England.

William III of Orange, besides being the husband of Mary, was also the only son of James's elder sister. He was the outstanding Protestant leader of the continent and a distinguished general. His great aim in life was to save the United Provinces from being conquered and annexed to France. When Louis XIV invaded the Dutch Netherlands in 1672 the government of the De Witt brothers had been overthrown and young William III had taken over the task of defending the country. The ambitions of Louis XIV had been curbed temporarily by the League of Augsburg,[1]

[1] See p. 476.

an alliance formed by the Dutch Stadtholder, but William feared an Anglo-French alliance, which he believed would prove fatal to the freedom of Holland. It was the possibility of preventing such an alliance and of enlisting England to fight against France that induced him to go to England. Sailing with a fleet of 600 transports carrying about 16,000 troops, convoyed by 60 warships, he eluded the English fleet, and on November 5 landed at Torbay on the coast of Devonshire.

Meanwhile James was making an eleventh-hour bid for support. He canceled all his Catholic appointments, restored the Protestant bishops, and changed his ministers. But it was too late. The people were awaiting the arrival of the new king. As William with his army advanced toward London, the English leaders joined him in ever increasing numbers. James, on the other hand, was losing his followers by desertion. Finally even his daughter Anne and her husband left him. Convinced that he could not depend on the royal army, he embarked on a ship for France, but was captured and brought back to London. William III, however, did not desire his presence in England, and he was given every opportunity to flee again. Obligingly, James departed for France, where Louis XIV gave him the palace of St. Germain and an annual pension of £40,000. Thus, without bloodshed, was accomplished a change of rulers.

THE REVOLUTION SETTLEMENT

After the arrival of William of Orange and the departure of James II, it became necessary to summon a convention parliament similar to that which had recalled Charles II, for there was no king to issue writs for a regular parliament. At first the Tory members were in favor of merely declaring William and Mary regents in the absence of the king. But when William of Orange stated emphatically that he would return to Holland if no power beyond that of regent was given him, the convention passed a resolution declaring the throne vacant because James II had broken "the original contract between king and people," had "violated the fundamental laws," and had "withdrawn himself out of the kingdom." Then the crown was offered to William and Mary as joint sovereigns with equal rights, on condition that they ratify a "declaration of right," a statement enumerating and declaring illegal the misdeeds of James II. Though William and

Mary were named as joint sovereigns, the administration was vested in William alone. Both accepted the crown on the terms offered, and on February 13, 1689, they were formally proclaimed as William III and Mary II.

By deposing James II and elevating William and Mary to the throne, Parliament established its right both to dethrone and to set up a monarch. It was the final blow at the theory of the divine right of kings. Thereafter all authority centered in Parliament. As stated in the previous chapter, the members of the House of Commons were elected by a very limited suffrage, not by the nation as a whole. Hence the government of the period from 1689 to the passing of the Reform Bill of 1832 may be described as the rule of the aristocracy. The House of Lords, composed of "lords temporal," or peers, and "lords spiritual," or bishops of the Anglican Church, was completely aristocratic. But even the House of Commons was dominated by the aristocracy.

As no changes had been made in the electoral laws since the middle of the fifteenth century, the shift of the population left populous cities unrepresented while towns with few inhabitants retained the right to elect representatives. This accounts for the existence of many pocket boroughs where the few remaining electors were under the sway of some great landowner or rich merchant; and the rotten boroughs, where votes could be bought. In the counties, each of which returned two members, it was not so easy to control an election; but the right to vote was restricted to freeholders who held an estate worth an annual rent of forty shillings. This excluded the copyholders and all agricultural laborers. As the eighteenth century progressed, the House of Commons became less and less representative. The transformation of England from an agricultural to an industrial country shifted the weight of population from the south and east to the north and west, creating more pocket boroughs, while such industrial cities as Manchester, Leeds, Sheffield, and Birmingham were unrepresented. So long as this condition of affairs continued, the aristocratic influence remained paramount in Parliament.

In the houses of Parliament the members were divided into Whigs and Tories, the two parties which had taken form during the reign of Charles II. The Whigs, in a general sense, continued the tradition of the Roundheads while the Tories maintained the principles of the Cavaliers. The main object of the Whig party was the establishment of the supremacy of Parliament through the limitation of the power of the monarch. Because the Whigs drew much of their support from the trading and moneyed classes, they favored the development of trade and a vigorous colonial policy. In religion they championed the claims of the Protestant nonconformists for toleration. The Tories, on the other hand, represented the agricultural interests of the country. Their chief tenets were a wide royal prerogative and the preservation of a strict High Church Anglicanism.

After William and Mary had accepted the throne, the convention, transformed by the new sovereigns into a regular parliament, proceeded to supplement the revolution settlement by a series of parliamentary acts. The declaration of right which it had drawn up earlier was, with some additions, embodied in a formal statute (1689) known as the Bill of Rights. This statute is the most important document of the revolution settlement and one of the most important in English constitutional history. First, it finally deprived the crown of all power to impose taxes without the consent of Parliament, and to suspend laws. Secondly, it declared that the election of members to Parliament ought to be free and that the freedom of speech and debate in Parliament ought not to be impeached or questioned in any court outside the houses of Parliament. Thirdly, it decreed that no sovereign who professed the Catholic religion or who married a Catholic should be permitted to reign. Fourthly, it demanded frequent parliaments and asserted the right of subjects to petition the king. Finally, it declared illegal the raising or keeping of a standing army within the kingdom in time of peace without parliamentary consent. But despite the great popular prejudice against standing armies, the foreign situation made such an army a necessity. The right to enforce discipline was granted to the crown by the Mutiny Act (1689), which authorized the punishment of desertion by martial law. It was to be in force for six months only, but was extended at the end of that time and later made annual. This act has been passed each year since 1701.[1]

In another bill Parliament took up the question of religious freedom for Dissenters. By this time it had become evident to even the most bigoted High Church partisans that it was impossible to

---

[1] It is now known as the Army Act. The act was not passed during the years 1698–1701, but the military machine continued to function, nevertheless.

force the Protestant Dissenters back into the Anglican Church. Now that the government was headed by a Calvinistic king, the question of religious freedom for Protestant nonconformists could hardly be ignored any longer. Yet the High Church party was not ready to broaden the basis of the Church so as to include the moderate Dissenters. After much debate the Toleration Act was passed, giving freedom of worship to Protestant Dissenters who accepted the doctrine of the Trinity. It conferred no privileges on Roman Catholics, Jews, or Unitarians. Neither did it permit nonconformists to hold office, for the Test and Corporation Acts still remained. Nevertheless this act, restricted though its benefits were, marks the beginning of religious toleration in England.

In Scotland and Ireland the revolution settlement was not so peaceful as in England. Most of the Scottish people accepted William III as their ruler, but the Highlanders of the north and west of Scotland rose under the leadership of Claverhouse (Viscount Dundee). A battle took place in the Pass of Killiekrankie in which the Jacobites, as the supporters of James were now called, defeated William's troops. The victory, however, cost the Jacobites their leader, and without leadership the revolt soon collapsed. In Ireland the resistance to the rule of William was much greater. As most of the Irish were Roman Catholics, they sided with James II, and raised an army in his behalf. Informed of the strength of this support, James decided to go to Ireland himself to begin the recovery of his throne. Supporters of William were so few that, unable to meet the Jacobite force in the open, they took refuge in the fortified city of Londonderry. When James laid siege to this city, the defenders held out for over a hundred days before a small English fleet forced its way up the river to relieve the city and break the blockade. In 1690 King William III himself went to Ireland. At the battle of the Boyne his troops scattered the Irish army in the utmost confusion, forcing James to flee in undignified haste and take a ship for France. For some months the struggle continued, but in the following year the Irish submitted on the promise that Roman Catholics should be as free in their worship as in the reign of Charles II. The English government, however, failed to abide by the promise. Only a year later Irish Roman Catholics were excluded from government offices. Other restrictions and harassments were to follow.

Besides the resistance in Scotland and Ireland, England also faced the problem of keeping the balance of power in Europe by blocking the efforts of Louis XIV to gain for France what he considered its natural boundaries. William, as previously stated, had accepted the throne mainly because he wished to enlist the support of England for the coalition he had formed against Louis XIV, called the League of Augsburg. Despite the fact that the English people had been bitterly hostile to the French, his predecessors, James II and Charles II, had been on friendly terms with the French monarchy. The connection between the two dynasties had resulted for a time in the domination of British foreign policy by France. But under the new king England became again the outstanding rival of France. Thus the accession of William not only put an end to absolute monarchy in England but also effected a change in British foreign policy. It marked the beginning of a series of wars between England and France which was to continue for more than a century. Fifty-six of the years between 1689 and 1815 were spent in conflict. At first the English struggle was waged for the balance of power in Europe and, on the part of William, to save his beloved Dutch Netherlands, of which he was still the ruler; later it turned into a contest for commercial and colonial supremacy.

The first war, that of the League of Augsburg, began almost immediately after William's accession (May, 1689).[1] It dragged on until 1697 when a general European peace was arranged in the little Dutch town of Ryswick. The peace, however, proved to be only an armistice. Immediately the former contestants began preparations for the conflict that seemed inevitable over the question of the Spanish succession.

During the war of the League of Augsburg the question of the English succession had come to the fore again. In 1694 Mary had died of smallpox without leaving any heirs. As William's health was in a precarious state it did not seem likely that he would marry again. Mary's sister Anne and her son, the duke of Gloucester, were still living, but this last surviving child of Anne died in 1701. Parliament then passed the Act of Settlement, which provided that in the event of Anne's death without heirs the crown was to go to the Electress Sophia of Hanover [2] and her Protestant heirs. The other surviving branches of the house of Stuart were passed

---

[1] See p. 476.
[2] Her mother was Elizabeth Stuart, daughter of James I of England.

over because they were Roman Catholics. The Act of Settlement included also various provisions regarding the English sovereign. It reënacted the sections of the Bill of Rights which excluded from the throne anyone who was a Roman Catholic or who should marry a Roman Catholic. Moreover, it stated that in the future the English sovereigns were not to retain their particular brand of Protestantism but were to be members of the Church of England. Other clauses stated that English sovereigns might not involve England in war for the defense of territories not belonging to the English crown, that they might not leave the realm without the consent of Parliament, that judges shall hold office during good behavior, and that they can be removed only upon the address of both houses of Parliament.

William III survived the Act of Settlement only a short time. Early in 1702 his horse stumbled in Hampton Court Park, throwing him to the ground and breaking his collar bone. The shock proved too much for his strength, already undermined by years of labor and anxiety, and on March 8, 1702, he died at the age of fifty-one. There was little regret over his passing. Though he was an able statesman and a clever diplomatist, he had been unpopular from the first. Few English sovereigns have had a smaller place in the affections of their subjects. William was a foreigner and remained a foreigner. For Englishmen and English ways he had little sympathy, evincing throughout his reign an undisguised preference for Dutchmen and Dutch customs. Moreover, he lacked personal charm; he was taciturn, unsociable, and morose. Nevertheless, William rendered an immense service to England by piloting the English people through an important constitutional crisis. His acceptance of the throne opened the way for liberal constitutional development, and his foreign policy ultimately gave Great Britain the commercial and colonial supremacy of the world.

THE REIGN OF QUEEN ANNE

Anne, the last of the Stuart sovereigns, was thirty-seven when she became queen in 1702. She was meek, smiling, and cheerful, dark in complexion and stout of figure. Indispositions caused by twenty years of childbearing and her habit of eating without restraint had undermined her health. At the time of her coronation she was suffering from convulsions and gout, and had grown very fat. Because of her weak eyesight as a child, her education had been neglected. "In her youth," the duchess of Marlborough wrote, "she never read, and cards entirely occupied her thoughts." Consequently her interests and understanding were so limited in later life that she was incapable of coping independently with the larger problems of her reign. She was on the whole a rather dull person, ill-qualified to occupy the throne. Usually she was ruled by some stronger or abler mind. The real head of the government during the first part of her reign was the duke of Marlborough, whose wife held for some years an almost complete ascendancy over the queen. Yet Anne was popular with her subjects because she was English. Moreover, in her public acts, with few exceptions, she conducted herself with a dignity which commanded respect. Devout in matters of religion, she was passionately attached to the Anglican Church, a fact which contributed much to her popularity with the supporters of the Church.

The two outstanding events of Anne's reign were the union of England and Scotland in 1707, and the War of the Spanish Succession. During the century since James VI of Scotland had become king of England various schemes for the union of the two governments had been broached, but all had failed of acceptance. Public opinion in Scotland was against a closer association with England. In fact, the members of the Patriotic party of Scotland desired complete independence for their country. This feeling was expressed by the Scottish Parliament in 1703 in a resolution "that, after the decease of her majesty, we will separate our Crown from that of England." On the other hand, many Scots saw great economic advantages in a closer connection with England if the English colonies and markets would thereby be opened to Scottish enterprise. For the English a union of the two crowns and parliaments was indispensable. The existence of an independent Scotland would have been a great danger in time of war, particularly if the Stuarts occupied its throne.

Commissioners appointed by both nations finally agreed on terms of union, and on May 1, 1707, after the Act of Union was passed by both the English and the Scottish parliament, the United Kingdom of Great Britain came into existence. The "Union Jack," combining the crosses of St. George and St. Andrew, became the national flag. Thenceforth Scotland was to be represented in the House of Commons by forty-five members and in the House of Lords by sixteen peers. The Scots were permitted to retain their legal system, and the Presbyterian Church was declared the state church of Scotland, every British monarch being required at his accession to take an oath to protect it. Finally, the Act of Union established complete freedom of trade, at home and abroad, thus permitting the Scots to trade with the English colonies.

In foreign affairs Marlborough carried forward William's plans for checking France in Europe. As a result England became involved in the long War of the Spanish Succession.[1] It was feared that if a French prince should obtain the Spanish crown, and with it the whole Spanish empire, England would be at the mercy of the Bourbons. To prevent this, William had already arranged an alliance consisting of Holland, England, the Holy Roman Empire, and Brandenburg, which Portugal and Savoy joined at a later time. The strife broke out soon after Anne's accession in 1702. Marlborough, a statesman of ability and a distinguished general, was commander-in-chief of the Anglo-Dutch forces. Under his brilliant leadership the British arms gained a series of victories at Blenheim (1704), Ramillies (1706), Oudenarde (1708), and Malplaquet (1709), dealing a severe blow to the military prestige of France. But in England the Tories fostered a growing opposition to the war. When they gained control of Parliament in the election of 1710, they relieved Marlborough of his command on the charge of accepting a bribe from the dealer who sold bread to the army, and the next year opened negotiations for peace. It was not until 1713, however, that the peace of Utrecht was signed. By it the English gained everything for which they had fought except the barring of the Bourbon king, Philip V, from the Spanish throne.[2]

In the year after the peace of Utrecht Anne died at the age of forty-nine, and was entombed in Westminster Abbey. Besides being the last English sovereign to preside regularly over the meetings of the cabinet,[3] she also bears the distinction of having been the last to veto a bill in Parliament.

LITERATURE AND PHILOSOPHY

In social life and in literature, as in political affairs, an inevitable reaction set in after the collapse of Puritan rule. So long as the Puritans held the ascendancy they had forbidden many

[1] See p. 477.　　[2] See p. 479.　　[3] See p. 547.

amusements, but with the Restoration the nation, as if to satisfy its hunger for proscribed pleasures, plunged to the opposite extreme. There was an undisguised pursuit of gaiety, with the king and court setting the pace. In some circles the licentiousness was so shameless that few attempts were made to throw even the thinnest veil over it. This spirit is reflected in the literature of the period; for of course the later works of Milton and Bunyan's *Pilgrim's Progress* were the expressions of an age that was past. Authors now wrote primarily to amuse the courtiers and the pleasure-loving public, and held up Puritanism and its stern morality to mockery and ridicule.

Samuel Butler (1612–1680) probably provoked more mirth than any other poet of the time. In his *Hudibras*, the best burlesque poem in the English language, he exposed to ridicule the worst side of Puritanism. The work was undoubtedly suggested by Cervantes' *Don Quixote*, for, like the chivalrous Don Quixote and his trusty Sancho Panza, Sir Hudibras, a Presbyterian knight, and his clerk, Squire Ralpho, go forth to redress grievances and seek adventure. When the first part of the poem appeared in 1663 it was greeted with salvos of laughter, especially by the Cavaliers, who saw in it the expression of their very thoughts and feelings. Charles II himself was so delighted with the witty poem that he frequently garnished his conversations with couplets from it. If we may believe the statement of Pepys, to be unacquainted with *Hudibras* was as good as being out of England. The following lines from Butler's description of Sir Hudibras may give some idea of the manner in which he caricatured the Puritans:

> For he was of that stubborn crew
> Of errant saints, whom all men grant
> To be the true Church Militant:
> Such as do build their faith upon
> The holy text of pike and gun;
> Decide all controversy by
> Infallible artillery;
> And prove their doctrine orthodox
> By apostolic blows and knocks.

The reopened theaters offered flagrant indecency, glittering wit, biting satire, and bombastic tragedy. The most popular dramas were the comedies, coarse in language and often profane, reflecting a social life in which morality was disregarded. The outstanding literary figure and greatest dramatist of the age was John Dryden (1631–1700). Between 1662 and 1694 he produced no fewer than twenty-seven plays, of which *All for Love*, a tragedy inspired by Shakespeare's *Antony and Cleopatra*, is generally regarded as the best. High-minded in his other writings, Dryden bowed to the taste of the age by including a liberal measure of obscenity in his dramas, especially in his comedies. Besides plays, he found time to write verse dealing with the affairs of his time. Thus in 1659 he wrote a poem lamenting Cromwell's death and in the next year published an ode to celebrate the accession of Charles II. He also wrote a long poem entitled *Annus Mirabilis: the Year of Wonder, 1666*, in which he chronicled the Great Fire, the Plague, and the war with the Dutch. As a satirist he was the most incisive writer of his day, his *Absalom and Achitophel* being one of the finest examples of political satire in English literature. Few writers have equaled his mastery of the English language.[1]

Besides poets, dramatists, and scientists, the period produced two noted diarists, Samuel Pepys (1633–1703) and John Evelyn (1620–1706). Few times are pictured more vividly than is the Age of the Restoration in the diaries of these two men. Actuated by an insatiable curiosity Pepys, a secretary of the Admiralty Board, saw as much as he could, and inquired about everything. He was interested equally in large and small matters. In the words of Jeffrey: "He finds time to go to every play, to every execution, to every procession, fire, concert, riot, trial, review, city feast, or picture gallery that he can hear of. Nay, there seems scarcely to have been a school examination, a wedding, a christening, charity sermon, bull-baiting, philosophical meeting, or private merrymaking in his neighborhood at which he is not sure to make his appearance. He is the first to hear all the court scandal, and all the public news; to observe the changes of fashion and the downfall of parties; to pick up family gossip and to detail philosophical intelligence; to criticize every new house or carriage that is built, every new book or new beauty that appears, every measure the king adopts, and every mistress he discards."[2] Having gathered

---

[1] In the history of science this was the age of Isaac Newton (1641–1724), one of the greatest scientific minds of all time, and of Robert Boyle (1627–1691), one of the founders of modern chemistry. The incorporation of the Royal Society of London by Charles II in 1662 opened a new era in the development of science in England. For further details see pp. 364–377.

[2] *Contributions to the Edinburgh Review* (1875), p. 185.

his budget of information, Pepys would return home to confide it to his diary, which covers a period of more than nine years beginning January 1, 1660. The diary, written in shorthand and bequeathed to Magdalen College, Cambridge, was not deciphered in full until the nineteenth century. It stands unsurpassed both as a vivid picture of an age and as a work of self-revelation, for Pepys hides not even his most private thoughts. Evelyn's diary, like its author, is more dignified and less gossipy and garrulous. It covers the events of his long life. One of the earliest recorded incidents is the execution of the earl of Strafford in 1641. Thereafter Evelyn witnessed the Civil Wars, the rise and fall of the Commonwealth and Protectorate, the Restoration, the Revolution of 1688, and the first part of the War of the Spanish Succession, recording his impressions of them all. Both diaries are invaluable as historical records.

Among English philosophical writers of the seventeenth century John Locke (1632–1704) is the most important figure. His great work is the *Essay Concerning Human Understanding*, published in 1690. Its purpose, as he states, is "to inquire into the origin, certainty, and extent of human knowledge, together with the grounds and degrees of belief, opinion and assent." The idea of analyzing the ultimate powers and limitations of the mind came to him during a student discussion while he was still at Oxford. For more than twenty years it occupied his thought. In his *Essay* Locke finds the origin of all ideas in experience or sense perception, rejecting both the doctrine of innate ideas held by Descartes and the scholastic doctrine which bases the first principles of knowledge on authority. He likened the human mind to a sheet of blank paper (*tabula rasa*) on which the senses inscribe the first impressions. "I see no reason to believe," he declared, "that the soul thinks before the senses have furnished it with ideas to think on." Sensation is necessary to give the mind material; yet it is not the only source of knowledge. Knowledge may also be gained by reasoning or reflecting on the ideas with which the senses furnish the mind. Thus Locke traces all knowledge to sensation and reflection. His *Essay*, the first attempt in modern times to arrive at a comprehensive theory of knowledge, has been of great significance in the development of modern thought. In England it was for a long period probably the most widely read of philosophical works.

Other works of Locke are his *Thoughts on Education, Letters concerning Toleration,* and *Two Treatises on Civil Government.* The first holds an important place in the history of education, for in it are the germs of the ideas later developed by Rousseau in his *Émile.* The political treatises were written to defend King William's title to the English throne. Because of them he has been styled "the apologist of the Glorious Revolution." Holding that government was instituted by a "social contract," he deduced therefrom the right of the subjects to transfer the sovereignty from one person to another. In all his writings he was a strenuous upholder of civil and religious liberty. But his doctrine of religious freedom had exceptions. Toleration was to be extended to all save Roman Catholics and atheists. The former he regarded as dangerous to the public peace because of their allegiance to a foreign power, whereas the latter were to be excluded because they had no satisfactory basis of conduct, all moral law resting on the divine will. Nevertheless, it was Locke's intellectual mission to awaken modern criticism of human conduct. His aim was to supplant blind reliance on authority with a universal reasonableness. The questions he raised regarding toleration, education, the nature of government, and the reasonableness of the Christian religion were taken up in the eighteenth century by the writers and thinkers of America, France, and Germany, as well as of England. Some of the terms in which the American Declaration of Independence is couched were taken from his writings. In Europe, Kant and Hume built up their systems with Locke's ideas as a starting point, Voltaire based his ideas on Lockian conclusions, Montesquieu expounded Locke's ideas in his writings, and Rousseau was in many respects a disciple of Locke. In short, Locke was the apostle of the dawning Age of Reason.

OLIVER CROMWELL   CHARLES I   *by Van Dyke*

MILTON DICTATING "PARADISE LOST" TO HIS DAUGHTERS

RED SQUARE,
MOSCOW, IN THE
EIGHTEENTH
CENTURY

CHARLES XII

MICHAEL ROMANOV

PETER THE GREAT

A CHURCH PRO-
CESSION IN MOS-
COW IN THE
SEVENTEENTH
CENTURY

CHAPTER SEVENTEEN

Russia to the Death of Peter the Great

RUSSIA BEFORE PETER THE GREAT

RUSSIA, extending from the western world to the eastern, was the largest European state at the opening of the eighteenth century. But prior to the reign of Peter the Great its political influence in Europe was negligible. It was virtually a state apart. Poor means of communication with the other countries of Europe accounted in large measure for its isolation. The sea, which was the chief connecting link between other European nations, was a barrier rather than a highway between them and Russia, which lacked an accessible seaport. Travel by the overland routes, also, was difficult, because of the condition of the roads and the necessity of passing through countries hostile to Russia. Consequently the Russians had few contacts with western Europe. Many elements of Russian civilization were drawn rather from Byzantium and Asia. The women of the upper classes were secluded in the terem or Russian harem, and were permitted to appear in public only when heavily veiled. The long hair and beards of the men, and their long-skirted garments, also bore witness to eastern influence. In short, the outstanding aspect of Russian culture and thought before the eighteenth century was its association with the eastern world.

The Russian people, comprising the Great Russians, the Little Russians or Ukrainians, and the White Russians, are basically part of the Slavic family, which also includes the Poles, the Serbs, the Czechs, and the Bulgars; but they have assimilated many members from such alien families as the Finns, Tartars, Letts, Lithuanians, and Germans, and are therefore, like all other nations, a mixture.

Prior to the sixteenth century the Russians were not united in one closely knit state. A number of political centers existed in the territory now called Russia. Each tribe was independent of the others; each had its own peculiar organization. Russian history may be said to begin with the founding of the first of these centers at Novgorod by the Northmen or Varangians about the middle of the ninth century (862 is the date generally given). According to legend the Slavs called in the Northmen to put an end to the discord and strife between the Slavic tribes. Whatever the truth may be, the Scandinavian princes organized the Slavic tribes of that region into a sort of state. After the death of Rurik, the half-legendary leader of the Northmen, in 879, his successor left Novgorod and established himself at Kiev. Here a powerful state developed, becoming the central point for the unification of the Slavs of that region. The name *Russia* derives from the word *Rous* or *Russ*,[1] which was used by the Slavs to designate the Northmen of Kiev. When the Northmen ceased to be aliens and became Slavs in speech and habits, the term *Russ* was applied to the Slavs of that vicinity. As early as the tenth century, chroniclers called the district about Kiev Russia, and thereafter the name gradually spread to the rest of the country that now bears that name.

In the tenth century the Russians, who had hitherto been pagans, were converted to Christianity—not to the Roman Catholicism of the West, but to the religion of the Greek Orthodox Church, which had its seat at Constantinople. Russia became an ecclesiastical province of the patriarchate of Constantinople, with the patriarch appointing the metropolitan or immediate head of the Russian Church. The close connection thus established between Russia and Constantinople led to the incorporation of many elements of Byzantine culture in Russian civilization. Historically the conversion of Russia to the Greek instead of the Roman Church was of the greatest importance; for Christianity,

---

[1] The derivation of the word *Rous* or *Russ* is uncertain. It is possible that the word is a Slavonic form of the Finnish *ruotsi* or the Swedish *rothsmenn*, both meaning "rowers" or "seafarers."

which might have been a bond between Russia and western Europe, acted as a bar to union. When in 1054 the eastern and western churches finally separated, the Russians naturally followed the eastern. Indeed, they were so staunchly partisan that in 1439, when the Greeks agreed to a union with the Roman Church in the hope of getting western aid against the Turks, the Russian Church severed its connections with the Greek patriarch.[1] After the capture of Constantinople in 1453 the conviction grew in Russia that the Russian Church was the legitimate heir of the Greek Church, and therefore the principal guardian of the Orthodox faith.

In the thirteenth century the Mongol-Tartars,[2] the last of the conquering hordes which had periodically swept in from Asia, invaded Russia. This final inroad was not an invasion by primitive nomads; on the contrary, it was a planned campaign carried out by a highly organized army, subject to a rigorous discipline and in military science far superior to the troops of western Europe. It was set in motion by Jenghiz Khan (1162–1227), a leader of surpassing military talent who had united various Tartar tribes and after a series of victories in the East had directed their way to the West. When the Tartar armies appeared from the East under the leadership of Batu, grandson of Jenghiz, the Russian princes, too much divided to offer any effectual resistance, were quickly subjugated. After dividing their forces into two armies, the Tartars continued westward from Russia. The first army met and defeated a combined force of Poles and Germans at Liegnitz in Silesia (1241), while the second routed the Hungarians and ravaged their country. Central Europe seemed doomed. Suddenly, however, upon receiving the news that the Great Khan had died in eastern Asia, Batu ordered a general retirement from Europe. Apparently one of his reasons for turning back was his desire to be present in person at the election of a new Great Khan. Withdrawing to the lower Volga, Batu and his armies, the "Golden Horde," established their capital at Sarai.

Though their control over western Russia lasted only a little more than a century, the Tartars dominated eastern Russia for

---

[1] The definite establishment of a national church in Russia did not take place until 1589 when the metropolitan of Moscow was consecrated patriarch of Moscow.

[2] The original form of this name is Tatar, but from the time they appeared in Europe the invaders were variously known as Tartari, Tartares, or Tartars, probably because the name was associated with *Tartarus*, meaning "hell."

more than two centuries. Yet neither in subjugating Russia nor thereafter did the Tartars violently disrupt the life of the Russian people. In some localities, particularly in the middle Dnieper region, the old administration was supplanted by a new system administered by Tartar officials, but in the main the old political organization was not changed. For the most part, the religion, language, customs, and institutions of Russia also remained undisturbed. There was not even a general military occupation. In most sections the Tartars contented themselves with imposing a heavy tribute on each principality, in proportion to its population, and with levying recruits for their armies. Just how great was the effect of the Tartar domination upon the customs and manners of Russia is impossible to state. Recent scholarship has traced to Byzantine origins many customs—for example, the seclusion of women—which were formerly believed to have been introduced by the Tartars. However, that the Tartars did influence Russian civilization, despite the fact that they made no deliberate attempts to Tartarize it, cannot be denied. After the first resentment over the invasion was allayed, there was a great deal of friendly intercourse between the two peoples, and therefore interaction of customs and manners. The direct Tartar influence, however, was restricted to the princes and the nobles with whom they constantly came in contact. Some Russian historians believe that intercourse with the Tartars brutalized the manners of the upper strata of Russian society, leading to the introduction of torture and floggings with the knout. One thing is certain: the Muscovite state did borrow certain improvements for its financial system and its military organization from the Golden Horde.

In the second half of the fifteenth century the rulers of Moscow finally freed Russia from the Tartar yoke. Kiev, which in earlier centuries had given promise of being the center that would weld all Russian lands, principalities, and settlements into a single organized and centralized state, had declined before the coming of the Tartars, and Moscow had gradually taken its place as the most important political unit. In addition to the natural advantages of its geographical position in the heart of Russia, in the fourteenth, fifteenth, and sixteenth centuries Moscow had a series of energetic rulers. Unscrupulous, grossly superstitious, cruel, and ruthless, they persisted in their purpose of breaking the power of the Tartars and uniting all Russia under their rule. From a small

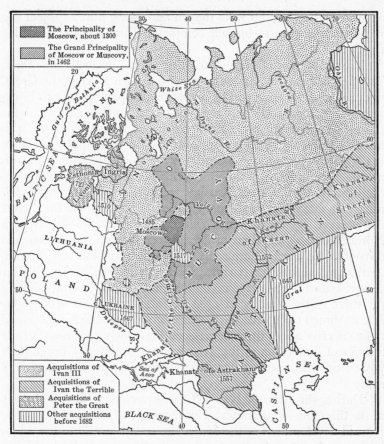

Growth of Russia, 1300–1725

principality dominated by the Tartars they transformed Moscow
into a great and independent empire. At the same time they laid
the foundations of that autocratic power which was wielded by
the Tsars down into the twentieth century. Although the name
Tsar had for some time been applied to the ruler of Moscow in
literary works and even in diplomatic documents, it had not become his formal and official title until the coronation of Ivan IV
in 1547. By this time the government was an established autocracy;
the Tsar controlled absolutely the lives and property of his subjects. To silence all opposition he had recourse to such effectual
arguments as the knout, the torture chamber, the gibbet, and the

axe. So exalted was his rank that in addressing him a subject was required to prostrate himself completely, his forehead touching the floor.

Two of the line of Muscovite rulers stand out above the others. The first is Ivan III (1462–1505), also known as Ivan the Great, under whom the state of Moscow grew conspicuously both in extent and in power. His first important undertaking was to subdue the proud merchant republic of Novgorod and incorporate it in his domains (1478). Later he annexed the principality of Tver (1485). Supplementing conquest with purchase and judicious marriage contracts, by the end of his life Ivan had managed to unite most of the north Russian territories into one state. His reign also marks the final emancipation of Russia from the Tartar domination. By the fifteenth century the power of the Golden Horde was showing signs of decadence. Internal dissension had disrupted the Tartar Empire into three distinct khanates: Kazan, Astrakhan, and Krim (Crimea). Further to weaken the Tartar power, Ivan III neglected no opportunity to foster enmity among the three states. Finally in 1480 he frustrated a last attempt by Khan Ahmed to enforce the Tartar domination which had ceased to be effective about three decades earlier. During the next decade a series of attacks upon the Tartar states completely broke their power, opening the way for their assimilation by the Muscovite state.

During the reign of Ivan III the government turned sharply in the direction of autocracy. This change was due not only to the natural development of the Muscovite state but also to the adoption, principally from Byzantium, of exotic principles and ceremonies. The tendency to regard Russia as the heir of Byzantium was strengthened by Ivan's marriage in 1472 to Sophia Paleologus, niece of the last emperor of Constantinople and heiress to the Byzantine Empire. A clever, ambitious, and cultivated princess, she exercised great influence over her husband. Besides being instrumental in persuading him to introduce many changes in Russia, she seems to have stirred imperial ambitions in his mind. After his marriage Ivan adopted much of the ceremonious etiquette of the former Byzantine court and proclaimed himself the heir of the Byzantine emperors by assuming their emblem, the double-headed eagle, a device which remained the arms of imperial Russia until the fall of the empire in 1917. Thereafter the

Grand Prince of Moscow gradually became more imperious and less accessible. He even referred to himself occasionally as Caesar or Tsar, the name by which the Byzantine rulers had been known to the Russians. The arrival of Sophia in Russia, while it established Byzantine tradition more firmly, also served to bring Russia in touch with western civilization. From Italy, where she had taken refuge after the fall of Constantinople, the Greek princess brought with her a number of highly trained Italians, including artists and architects. In their limited way, they introduced into Moscow various phases of Italian civilization and culture.

The second outstanding ruler of the Muscovite line was Ivan IV (1547–1584) or, as he is better known, Ivan the Terrible. A curious mixture of cowardice, unrestrained passion, and remorseful asceticism, Ivan the Terrible completely disregarded human life. As Tsar of Russia he committed deeds of such extravagant cruelty that his name stands today as a byword for ferocity and fiendishness. His insane destruction of Novgorod, the second wealthiest city of his tsardom, because of a false rumor which he did not stop to investigate, and the coldblooded massacre of many of its inhabitants is one of the most wanton acts of history. Moreover, in a sudden fit of ungovernable fury toward the end of his life he struck his eldest son, a gifted young man of great promise, so hard that the blow proved fatal. After committing such savage deeds he would prostrate himself before his ikons with such fervor that his forehead would be severely bruised. Yet in many respects Ivan was an able and farseeing ruler. He introduced reforms in the morals and habits of the monks and clergy, issued a new code of laws, and improved the administration of justice. He gradually placed almost half of Russia more directly under his rule by appropriating the ancestral estates of the landed aristocracy of central Russia and distributing them among the *oprichniki* or new gentry of non-aristocratic origin with whom he surrounded himself. This change greatly weakened the power of the old aristocracy (*boyars*) and gave greater importance to the small and middle gentry (*dvoryane*). He also continued the work of expansion by conquering the khanates of Kazan and Astrakhan and adding both to his territories. The third of the khanates, the Crimea, passed under Turkish sovereignty before it was annexed to Russia by Catherine II.

In the conquest of both Kazan and Astrakhan, Ivan was aided

by the Don Cossacks who, in general, played a prominent part in
the southward and westward expansion. The origin of the Cossacks is shrouded in obscurity, but the name itself is of Asiatic
origin and signified "freebooter." It was adopted, probably
from the Tartars, by the inhabitants of the southern steppes of
Russia, who organized along military lines for plunder and for
protection against the raids of Tartar horsemen. Ethnologically
the Cossacks were not a tribe or a number of tribes, but were a
mixture of Turks, Tartars, and Russians, including many peasants from northern Russia who joined the Cossacks to escape the
political and economic oppressions to which they had been subjected. The earliest settlements of the Russian Cossacks were along
the river Don, but later Cossack settlements were founded in various parts of Russia.[1] Though the Don Cossacks recognized the
sovereignty of the Tsar after 1570, Ivan did not attempt to enforce his rule absolutely. Consequently the Cossack communities
were practically independent democracies. For a long time the
Cossacks could repeat the saying: "The Tsar rules in Moscow and
the Cossacks on the Don." Even under the later Tsars they were
permitted a certain degree of autonomy in return for military
service. In the early days of Cossackdom the chief means of subsistence were hunting, fishing, cattle-raising, and plunder. Tillage
was despised and forbidden. Gradually, however, the Cossacks
turned to agriculture and a more settled life. The Russian government early recognized their importance for border defense,
and in time their light cavalry formed an important element of
the Russian army.

An event of greater importance ultimately than the conquest
of Kazan and Astrakhan was the annexation and exploration of
Siberia and the opening of its vast expanses to settlement. Two
centuries earlier the traders of Novgorod had established trading
posts in Siberia and had even made some attempts at colonization. But as the better land routes were controlled by the hostile
Tartar Khan of Sibir, access to the interior of Siberia was difficult.
Consequently, as late as the middle of the sixteenth century little
was known in Russia about Siberia. However, in 1582 a band of
freebooters under the leadership of Yermak, a Don Cossack, took
the capital of the Siberian Khan and presented it to Ivan the

---

[1] Other notable Cossack groups are the Dnieper Cossacks, Ukrainian Cossacks,
Ural Cossacks, and Terek Cossacks.

Terrible. Thereafter the conquest of Siberia was undertaken in earnest. Though Ivan died in 1584, his successors continued the work he had started. The leading figures in the extension of the Tsar's power over Siberia were volunteer Cossacks who not only assisted in the conquest but also formed a kind of police force that kept Siberia under the sway of the Tsar. Since the few natives were powerless to stop the invaders, the conquest proceeded so rapidly that the year 1647 saw the foundation of Okhotsk on the shores of the Pacific. Soon after Russia began the extension of its sovereignty over Siberia large numbers of fur traders and trappers, attracted especially by the sable and ermine, entered the country from Russia. Also Russian peasants, provided with horses, cows, and farm implements furnished by the government, began to arrive, though larger agricultural communities were not established until the second half of the seventeenth century. Besides sending colonists to Siberia the Russian government transported convicts and political offenders to prison camps established in the remoter regions. Thus was opened a country which was in itself an empire of vast size, rich in furs, timber, salt, and mineral deposits.

During the reign of Ivan the Terrible closer trade relations were established between Russia and western Europe. In 1553, while searching for a northern route to the East, an English ship under the command of Richard Chancellor found its way through the White Sea to the mouth of the Dvina. Natives took Chancellor to Moscow, where he was cordially received by Ivan. Later Chancellor returned as the representative of the English Muscovy Company, organized for trade with Russia, and negotiated with the Tsar a treaty which gave extensive trading privileges to the English. Shortly after, the Dutch and Swedes also came in. Soon the trade with these nations was of such volume that, though the White Sea was navigable only three months of the year, Archangel at the mouth of the Dvina became a flourishing settlement. But the Russian port was difficult of access and the route perilous. Seeing this, Ivan the Terrible decided to conquer Livonia, so that he would have an outlet on the Baltic. At first his efforts met with success. The Russian army which invaded Livonia in 1558 soon took a number of cities, of which Narva on the coast became an important point of contact with western Europe. Moreover, having obtained new ports, Ivan began the construction of a Russian navy. But his success aroused the fears of other nations. Poland and Sweden intervened, and after a long war Russia was forced to relinquish its hold on Livonia (1582). Poland annexed Livonia, and Sweden took Estonia and Ingria, thus completely isolating Russia from western Europe on that side. Not until the time of Peter the Great was Russia to have a permanent outlet on the Baltic.

In another respect, also, Ivan the Terrible was the precursor of Peter the Great. Like Peter, he felt the necessity of raising the Russian people to the technical level of western Europe. With this end in mind, as early as 1547 he sent an agent to Germany to collect as many skilled workmen as he could. But the project came to nothing. Neighboring countries, fearing that a Russia with flourishing industries would be a menace to their safety, prevented artisans from migrating to Moscow in large numbers. Queen Elizabeth, however, sent the Tsar a physician, apothecaries, engineers, and a number of artisans. These last, together with skilled workmen from Italy and Germany, taught the Russians, among other things, improved methods of making soap, tanning leather, and distilling spirits; also, how to cast cannon. The English further assisted in developing the mining of ore and in building ironworks at Vologda in 1569.

The death of Ivan the Terrible in 1584 ushered in a period of strife and anarchy known in Russian history as the "Time of Trouble." Feodor, the sickly and weak-minded son of Ivan, became Tsar in name, but the power was in the hands of his brother-in-law, Boris Godunov. At the death of Feodor, the last of the line of Ivan, in 1598, Godunov got himself elected Tsar and a struggle for power ensued among several factions. After 1605 it was really a period of civil war, marked by the intervention of Poland and Sweden. Finally in 1613 the representatives of fifty cities gathered in Moscow and, after long and stormy debates, chose Michael Romanov, a young boyar of sixteen, as Tsar. The election of Michael terminated the Time of Trouble and established on the throne the house which was to rule Russia almost uninterruptedly until 1917. During the three-quarters of a century following the accession of Michael, and preceding that of Peter the Great, the influx of personages and ideas from western Europe was accelerated. Attracted by the prospects for trade, industry, and military service, craftsmen, foreign merchants, doctors, and army officers came in larger numbers, spreading foreign customs, ideas, and practices. Many citizens of Moscow adopted these foreign customs, donned foreign garb, and purchased foreign imports, though they were regarded as traitors and apostates by their more conservative countrymen. In general, a greater interest in the civilization of western Europe manifested itself, presaging the wider Europeanization under Peter the Great and the emergence of Russia from its isolation to take an active part in the affairs of Europe.

Despite all the efforts to promote industrial development, Russia was still almost entirely a land of peasants and landowners. Moreover, since the thirteenth century the trend had been not toward greater freedom for the peasant but toward serfdom. While in most European countries the personal bond between landowner and peasant was dissolving, or at least loosening, the Russian peasants were gradually losing their right to leave the land on which they were living. Various tendencies were at work limiting their freedom. Because of the continuous wars and the increase in the number of government officials, the tax burden of the peasants was increased enormously in the sixteenth century. This burden, added to the dues and services they owed for the use of their land, spelled the economic ruin of many. Unless he was able to meet his financial obligations, a peasant householder could not leave his holding, and the number of those who could not do so continually increased. Some peasants even sold themselves into personal bondage in order to escape from the crushing weight of debt. Toward the end of the sixteenth century the government began to restrict the right of the peasant to migrate from one estate to another. Thus 1581 was a "prohibited year," a year in which even solvent peasants were not permitted to leave their holdings. Thereafter other such years were proclaimed. By the time of Peter the Great more than half of the peasants had sunk to a state of serfdom as a consequence of the various limitations on their freedom.

PETER THE GREAT

Peter I, commonly known as Peter the Great, was the only son of Tsar Alexis and his second wife, Natalia. He was born in the Kremlin in Moscow on May 30, 1672. A restless, undisciplined, and neglected lad, he acquired but little formal education. Or-

thography and grammar remained mysteries to him to the end of
his life, and his knowledge of mathematics did not go beyond the
most elementary stage. He cared most for technical subjects, particularly of a military and nautical nature. These interests were
probably awakened by a Dutchman named Timmermann, who
instructed him in the rudiments of mechanics, ballistics, and for-
tification. Timmermann also excited in young Peter that interest
in ships and shipbuilding which later impelled him to create a
Russian navy. Beyond his liking for mechanics, soldiering, and
boating, the future Tsar gave little promise of differing from his
licentious predecessors. When Peter was ten, he and his sickly,
feeble-minded half-brother Ivan were made joint Tsars, with
their sister Sophia as regent. At seventeen, the age of maturity
for a Russian Tsar, Peter, aided by a group of conspirators, seized
the government and sent Sophia to a convent. Though Ivan was
to live a few years longer, he was almost totally incapacitated.
The task of ruling Russia was left to Peter, whose reign is generally dated from the overthrow of Sophia's regency in 1689.

Besides being one of the outstanding rulers in Russian history,
Peter the Great is one of the strangest characters of all time. Endowed by nature with a colossal vigor of body and mind, he was
capable of all extremes of good and evil. Physically he was powerful in frame and of giant stature, being six feet eight and one-half
inches tall. His features were rather handsome, but his appearance was marred by a twitching of the facial muscles due to a
nervous disease. In dress he was slovenly. His garments, often
grotesque, were usually untidy, patched, and mended. His manners were boorish, his tastes vulgar. Throughout life he delighted
in coarse humor, low practical jokes, and rough horseplay. He
was very irascible and subject to fits of rage during which he lost
all self-control, usually becoming brutally violent. At such times
the lives of those about him were not safe, and it was necessary to
post a sentry at his door to prevent anyone from approaching him.
The Saxon minister, writing in 1721, probably expressed the sentiments of many of Peter's subjects when he said: "Happy is the man
who is not obliged to approach him." As a youth he began to
drink excessive quantities of vodka (brandy) and this habit he
continued until the end, priding himself on his ability to drink
most of his companions under the table. As he was himself grossly
licentious and essentially vulgar, he preferred associates who

shared his tastes. Peter also was capable of cruelty which stamped him as the true successor of Ivan the Terrible. To watch writhing victims in the torture chamber, to witness wholesale executions, and even to take part in them, gave him great pleasure. But his love of cruelty and his quenchless thirst for dissipation were not matched by physical courage. Often at the very thought of danger he became so terror-stricken that his body shook violently. Of cockroaches, which abounded in Russian dwellings at that time, he had a horror, the sight of one almost making him faint.

For all his vices, vulgar tastes, and boorish manners, Peter possessed several good traits. He was truthful, simple, and straightforward. Although he had been raised in an atmosphere of eastern pomp and ceremonial, he was the sworn foe of all display. So plain were the arrangements of his court that in this respect only the court of the penurious Frederick William I of Prussia could compare with it. His attendants were few in number and on his travels he often stopped in the humble cottages of his peasants. Furthermore, Peter set an example for his subjects by his diligent application to affairs of state. It is erroneous to infer that his debaucheries prevented him from applying himself assiduously to state business. His remarkable vitality enabled him to labor long and hard at his tasks. Often he rose at four to begin his work, which he continued throughout the day. The peasants said of him: "He works harder than any muzhik." It was impossible for him to be idle. If his restless energy was not occupied with affairs of state, he would engage in some form of manual labor such as carpentry or boatbuilding. In this respect he differed greatly from many of his predecessors, whose round of laziness was broken only by prayer and fasting. But Peter was just as violent and hasty in his work as in everything else he did. He had no time to plan or to evaluate its worth to the Russian people. He simply worked impetuously and precipitately.

Hardly had the death of Ivan in 1696 left Peter sole Tsar when, at the risk of losing his throne, he left for an extended journey in Europe. In the summer of 1696 he had captured Azov, at the mouth of the Don. Now he sought help to hold this conquest and also to wrest more land from the Turks. Hence he sent the Grand Embassy, composed of more than two hundred Russians, to negotiate anti-Turkish alliances with the Christian states of Europe. To this embassy Peter attached himself as plain Peter Mikhailov, for the purpose of satisfying the curiosity regarding the customs and practices of western Europe which his mother had roused in him in boyhood, and which association with various western men had intensified. Peter wanted to see everything, to investigate everything. He visited workshops, factories, shipyards, schools, and hospitals. With a Prussian colonel as his tutor he studied gunnery in Koenigsberg; in Holland he worked in the shipyards as a plain carpenter; in England, also, he spent considerable time in the royal dockyards at Deptford before continuing on to Vienna to present his case against the Turks to the emperor. As he was about to leave Vienna for Italy he received the news that the Streltsi, the Tsar's standing army, had revolted in his absence. Abandoning his plans for further travel and study, he immediately hurried homeward.

Whatever knowledge Peter gained during his visit to Europe was primarily technical. Confirmed in his admiration of foreign handicrafts and foreign technical skill, he returned home with the ardent desire to transplant to Russia many of the improvements he had seen. The culture of Europe left no deep impression on him, for he was unable to appreciate it. Diplomatically, the journey was a failure. The states of western Europe were at that time busily engaged in preparing for the impending struggle between the Habsburgs and Bourbons over the question of the Spanish succession. This fact precluded all interest in the proposed war against the Turks. Recognizing the situation, Peter relinquished the idea of further expeditions against the Turks and turned to the project of driving the Swedes out of the Baltic provinces.

By the time Peter reached Russia the mutiny of the Streltsi had been quelled. But the Tsar was not satisfied. He decided that the Streltsi, whose power at the court of Russia may be likened to that of the Janissaries of Turkey, had outworn their usefulness and must be suppressed. The manner in which this was done shows the most hideous side of the semibarbarian Peter. Only to Sophia and to his wife Eudoxia, both of whom had sympathized with the insurgents, did he show any mildness, and them he permanently immured in a convent. To the Streltsi who had taken part in the rebellion he showed not the slightest mercy, displaying on the contrary a frenzied energy in exterminating them. Torture chambers were opened and the most cruel means employed to extort confessions. Wholesale executions followed, in which Peter participated. As a terrible warning to all, hundreds of corpses were gibbeted along the walls of the city or left unburied on the place of execution. Those whose lives were spared were banished to Siberia. Thus was the corps of the Streltsi annihilated; even its very name was abolished.

Having sat in judgment, Peter energetically began introducing into Russia certain customs and technical achievements which he regarded as not only useful but necessary. As his first "reform" he continued on a wider scale the work of reorganizing the Russian army, an undertaking which his predecessors had started. Thousands of miles of Russian borders were menaced by Turkey, Poland, Sweden, and other powers. If it was not to be at the mercy of its enemies, Russia must be their equal in military strength. Besides, if Peter would gain new ports for Russian trade by driving back the Swedes, he must have an army capable of the task. During his expeditions against Azov he had realized the utter inadequacy of his military forces. Now, after a closer acquaintance with European military methods, he was resolved to raise his army to a level with those of the other states, both in efficiency and manpower. His new regiments were disciplined, clothed, and equipped in the European manner. To secure the desired number of recruits, Peter introduced a system of conscription which marked the beginning of a truly national army for Russia. Each province was required to furnish its quota and to pay for their maintenance. In this manner Peter succeeded in raising by the close of his reign a regular army of over 200,000 men, besides recruiting many regiments among the Cossacks. True, the recruits gathered by conscription were often of such low mentality that hay had to be tied to one leg and straw to the other to teach them the difference between right and left. Yet the Russian army soon commanded the respect of the other nations of Europe.

Peter also built a small navy which fought successfully against both the Turks and the Swedes. At its height the navy consisted of forty-eight large warships, eight hundred smaller vessels, and almost thirty thousand sailors. Throughout his reign the Tsar attempted to make his people realize the importance of the sea to the life of the nation.

The cost of creating the army and navy, added to the cost of the wars which Peter waged during twenty-one years of his reign, resulted in such pressing financial needs that development of the economic resources of the country was a necessity. During his visit to Europe Peter learned something about mercantilism and upon his return home it was explained to him in detail by certain foreigners. He was told that if Russia was to escape impoverishment it must produce all it needed; export as many manufactured articles—but no raw materials—as possible; and import only what was necessary. Peter adopted the theory, seeing in it a means of augmenting the revenues of the state, and proceeded to apply it to Russian industry and commerce. Craftsmen and skilled workers of foreign countries, particularly French craftsmen, who had been famous since the days of Colbert, were offered inducements to migrate to Russia. New industries were created and old industries expanded, principally for the manufacture of arms and ammunition, military supplies, and clothing. Steps were also taken to exploit the untouched mineral resources which were so vital in the conduct of war. Peter's efforts temporarily stimulated Russian industry, but the permanent results were negligible. Many of the industries he founded collapsed before his death; by the second half of the eighteenth century hardly one-tenth still survived. Peter was not, as some historians have claimed, the first to establish factories. Decades before his time glass works, paper mills, iron works, and cloth factories had been built in Russia.

The multitude of new and intricate institutions which Peter created for fiscal, industrial, commercial, and other purposes necessitated a reorganization of the entire administration of government. For this reform he again borrowed principles from western Europe, largely from Sweden and Germany. Collegia or departments of state, corresponding roughly with the ministries of western Europe, were constituted to preside over the various functions of the central government. These departments, ten in number, were supervised by councils in which foreigners were the leading spirits. Peter also endeavored to organize the provincial administration, which before his reign had been in a state of hopeless confusion. The entire empire was divided into provinces or governments (*gubérnii*), administered by governors with the assistance of a council (*Landrath*) elected by the nobles. The towns were given autonomous government.

Peter's educational schemes, so ambitious on paper, were carried out only in a very limited way. For his plans to open elementary schools throughout Russia the funds, the teachers, and the inclination to learn were sadly lacking. Such schools as he did establish in Moscow and St. Petersburg were chiefly military and vocational. One important educational reform accomplished during Peter's reign was the simplification of the Russian alphabet; eight letters were discarded and the form of some of the others was modified.

Some of Peter's reforms attacked Russian customs and manners. After his return from Europe he issued a series of edicts against the long beards and the long-skirted costumes of Russia, both of which symbolized to him that conservatism of Old Russia which he was resolved to uproot. Arming himself with a pair of shears, he personally cut off the beards of those who frequented his court, and also cut their long coats at the knee. Outside the court circles the edicts—from which both the clergy and the peasants were exempted—were carried out by barbers and tailors stationed at the gates of the towns with orders to clip the beards and shorten the cloaks of those who entered or departed. Anyone who refused to comply with the edict was to be "beaten without mercy." It was comparatively easy to introduce the tonsorial and sartorial changes at his court, but the Russian noblemen as a whole were less tractable. Malicious wits among them ascribed Peter's desire to abolish beards to the fact that he could not grow one himself. Orthodox Russians in general regarded shaving the beard as a defacement of the image of God. Nevertheless, Peter was firm. He did, however, under the pressure of economic need, permit the wearing of beards upon the payment of a high annual tax.

Having seen women commingling freely with men in the salons of the West, Peter decided on his return to Russia to shatter the seclusion of the Russian women of the upper classes. He not only ordered them released from the terem but also forbade them to cover their faces with veils. Moreover, Peter gave women the right to marry of their own free will whomsoever they wished, whereas formerly they had been forced to accept as husbands men chosen for them by their parents or guardians. Convivial meetings were held at which the sexes met for conversation and dancing. The Tsar himself, having learned to dance during his stay in the West, taught some of his nobles, who were expected to pass the art on to others. Another custom which Peter introduced was that of smoking. His father had detested smoking so greatly that anyone guilty of it was, according to the code of laws of 1649, to have his nose cut off. Peter himself, however, had contracted the habit on his journey and did all he could to make the use of tobacco widespread in Russia. A further effort to Europeanize Russia was the adoption of the Julian calendar. Whereas the old Russian calendar dated from the creation of the world, the new chronology reckoned from the birth of Christ, and the new year which had hitherto commenced in September henceforth started on the first of January. Finally Peter also abolished the ceremony of striking the ground with the forehead when one approached the sovereign.

Important as they were for the introduction of western customs and practices, it is easy to overstate the originality of the Petrine reforms. They did not, as many historians have declared, suddenly interrupt the natural development of Russian civilization. The tendency toward westernization in Russia was manifest long before Peter took over the reins of government. Since Ivan III most Russian rulers had endeavored to transplant to Russia the technical progress of the countries of western Europe and to effect a more direct intercourse and a closer coöperation with them. During the half-century preceding Peter's rule, Russia had been moving definitely westward. Peter, far from being the instigator of the movement, merely carried out some of the schemes conceived or prepared by his predecessors. Even then his achievements fell short of the extensive programs planned before his time. The first regiments organized on foreign models had already appeared in Russia under Tsar Michael Romanov; Peter's father had launched the project of building a Russian fleet; and the reorganization of the administration and the adaptation of European methods to industry were already under way when Peter ascended the throne. But, whereas the Tsars before him had merely planned these reforms or at most made weak attempts to put them into effect, Peter with his iron determination succeeded in a measure in carrying them out.

Hitherto the process of Europeanization had been one of slow penetration; now, owing to the methods employed by the great Tsar, it became one of revolution. Carried away by his own eagerness, he attempted to change his backward country in one generation, to catch up with Europe at one jump. To accelerate the acceptance of his reforms he used force, frequently resorting to such revolting and unnecessary cruelty as torture, the knout, tearing of the nostrils, and sentences of painful death. These violent methods aroused in most Russians a stubborn resistance which was fortified by ingrained indolence, natural conservatism, and religious scruples. The clergy, steadfastly opposing the innovations from the start, taught the Russians that it was sacrilegious for Holy Russia to abandon its native customs and to imitate the heretics of the West. They assailed the Tsar as Antichrist and interpreted his nervous twitchings as signs of diabolical possession. In answer the Tsar applied still sterner measures, ruthlessly smashing his way through all opposition.

In promulgating his reforms Peter did not proceed according to a systematic plan. He was unable to map his course deliberately and then follow it in detail. His reforms, composed principally of siftings, fragments, and remnants gathered from all parts of Europe, were proclaimed when necessity demanded or at the caprice of the sovereign. But though they followed no regular sequence, they had a general object: they were calculated, in the main, to make Russia a great military power. Political, social, and economic questions were important to Peter primarily because of their relation to the acquisition, equipment, training, and maintenance of new recruits. And it was in the sphere of military and naval organization that his reforms proved most lasting. The numerous commissions and administrative boards he established ceased to function after his death; his efforts to stimulate the industrial and commercial development of Russia were successful only to a limited degree; and his social reforms affected only the higher strata of Russian society. But his military and naval reforms were basic and permanent. In other respects western civilization did not penetrate to larger sections of the Russian people until the nineteenth century. Not one of Peter's reforms was of any benefit to the peasants, who constituted all but a small percentage of the population. On the contrary, their lot was made more deplorable by recruiting agents, and the tax burden, which already weighed heavily, was increased still more by the Tsar's military ambitions.

Since the clergy constituted the chief opposition to his reforms, Peter was determined to restrict the power of the Orthodox Church and to lessen the prestige of the hierarchy. The existence of an independent and hostile institution in the state was contrary to his ideas of absolute monarchy. Hence he did not overlook opportunities to weaken the Church. When the Patriarch Adrian, an avowed opponent of Peter's reforms, died in 1700, the Tsar did not appoint a successor. After leaving the office open for two decades, in 1721 he abolished it altogether and vested the powers of the patriarch in a commission known as the Holy Synod, composed of a number of bishops under the presidency of the procurator-general, a layman who represented the Tsar. This move degraded the Russian Orthodox Church to the position of a mere instrument of the state and made the clergy a class of state officials. Despite his need of money for military purposes, Peter did not lay hands on the wealth of the Church, but he did facilitate the task of recruiting by decreeing that no Russian could become a monk before he had reached the age of thirty. As Peter had no deep-seated religious beliefs he was tolerant toward other forms of Christianity, permitting foreigners to have their own churches. The Jesuits, however, were summarily expelled from Russia in 1710 because of their propagandist activities.

THE NORTHERN WAR

In his foreign policy Peter aimed to "open a window to the west" — that is, to obtain an ice-free port that was easily accessible to Europe; for with Archangel as its only port Russia was landlocked on the European side during most months of the year. Early in his reign Peter had sought this "window" in the Black Sea, which was controlled by Turkey, but after his first journey to Europe he decided to wrest a Baltic port from Sweden. At this time Sweden still wielded the predominant influence in northern Europe which Gustavus Adolphus had won for it by his conquests and victories. In addition to Sweden itself, the Swedish king ruled also Finland, Esthonia, Livonia, Ingria, Carelia, western Pomerania, and a number of smaller territories, most of which were coveted by other nations. Both Russia and Poland desired some of the Swedish territory along the Baltic; Prussia sought to obtain western Pomerania; and Denmark wanted the duchy of Holstein, which was under the protection of Sweden. A propitious time to proceed against Sweden as the common foe was all that was needed to start a general war. The desired opportunity seemed to present itself when Charles XI of Sweden died in 1697, leaving as his successor a son, Charles XII, who was only fifteen. Believing that this young, inexperienced ruler would be unable to defend the Swedish possessions, Denmark, Poland, and Russia formed a coalition against Sweden, with Prussia remaining neutral for the time being. All the members of the coalition hoped to make considerable acquisitions without much difficulty.

But the task of subduing Sweden was not so easy as it seemed. Though he was without military experience, Charles XII proved to be a more capable military leader than the allies had calculated. He had a born love of fighting and was never happier than when he was on the battlefield. When he was apprised of the coalition against him the Swedish king decided not to wait for the enemy to attack. Quickly organizing his military resources, he embarked on that sensational military career which started with a series of brilliant successes but ended in the annihilation of the power of Sweden. His plan was to crush each member of the coalition separately, and the target of his first attack was Denmark. In May, 1700, he invaded that country with an army of 15,000, marching right to the gates of Copenhagen and forcing the Danish king, Frederick IV, to accept a humiliating treaty by which his country withdrew from the coalition. Next the young king proceeded against the forces of Peter the Great which had invaded Ingria and laid siege to Narva, the key fortress of that province. Though Charles XII could pit but 8000 men against the Russian army of nearly 40,000, his was much the superior force. Peter's reorganization of the Russian army had not proceeded very far; hence the Russian troops were mostly raw recruits. Even their equipment was poor, the few cannon they possessed having been purchased from the very Swedes against whom they were fighting. The battle which took place in November, 1700, resulted in a complete rout of Peter's army. It was the most celebrated victory of Charles's career. But the Swedish king did not follow up his victory, though the Tsar's army was completely in his power. Instead, he turned against the third of his enemies. Marching into Poland, he defeated the Polish army, declared Augustus the Strong deposed, and forced the Poles to elect his candidate, Stanislaus Leszczynski, as their king.

Charles XII was now at the pinnacle of his success, hailed by many as "the wonder of the world," but he was soon to ride to a speedy fall. During the seven years the Swedish king spent fighting the armies of Augustus the Strong, arranging the affairs of Poland, and pursuing Augustus into Saxony,[1] the Tsar had not

[1] Augustus was also the ruler of Saxony.

been idle. Eager to wipe out the disgrace of Narva at any cost, Peter had recruited and disciplined fresh regiments without delay. With this new army he had invaded the Baltic provinces of Sweden, overrunning Ingria and Carelia. He even went so far as to lay the foundations for his new capital, St. Petersburg, in the conquered territory near the mouth of the river Neva. When Charles XII had settled his affairs in Saxony, he decided to deal Russia a mortal blow, and for this purpose he collected an army of 30,000 men. Peter tried to induce the Swedish king to give up the plan of invading Russia, but all his efforts came to nothing. So certain was Charles of success that he answered the Tsar's offers by declaring that he would make peace upon his arrival at Moscow. Everything else having proved unavailing, Peter turned to the problem of defense. The plan he adopted was in essence the same as that which was employed a little more than a century later against the vastly larger army of Napoleon. The Russians, instead of giving battle to the Swedes, were to retire before the invaders, stripping the country bare of all food supplies as they went. Moreover, Russian troops were to cling to the flanks of the Swedish army to cut off any foraging groups that might be sent out, and also to harass the enemy as much as possible.

Early in 1708 Charles marched into Russia with Moscow as his objective. From the very first, ill-luck attended the venture. Not only did the bad roads and the severe weather slow the progress of the invaders, but the difficulty of obtaining supplies caused them much suffering. The most severe Russian winter in many decades found the Swedish forces still hundreds of miles from Moscow with food and supplies becoming scarcer and disease decimating their ranks. When spring came the once splendid army of Charles had dwindled to about 20,000 exhausted and demoralized men. Meanwhile the Tsar had collected a large, well-equipped force to oppose the invaders. The lack of provisions and constant harrying by the Russians forced the Swedes farther and farther southward; finally the two armies met in June, 1709, at Poltava, a fortress near the southern border of Russia. The battle resulted in a decisive victory for Peter. Practically the entire Swedish army was destroyed or captured. Only a few hundreds, together with the king, succeeded in escaping to Turkish soil. The king of Sweden who had been the terror of Europe was irretrievably ruined, his empire collapsing like a house of cards.

Nevertheless, the war dragged on for another twelve years. From his place of refuge in Turkey, Charles managed to stir up the Turks to war against Russia (1710). Peter, emboldened by the victory of Poltava, recklessly marched into Turkish territory with the intention of enlarging his boundaries in that direction. On the Pruth, however, the Russian army was hemmed in by the Turks and would have been forced to surrender if Peter had not bought peace by restoring Azov to Turkey. Soon after this Charles emerged from Turkey and returned to Sweden. Marshaling what forces he could, he continued the struggle until he was killed in an obscure conflict in Norway in 1718.

The series of treaties which followed upon the death of Charles, culminating in the treaty of Nystad between Sweden and Russia (1721), relegated Sweden to the position of a second-rate power and gave Russia definite rank among the European states. By the treaties of Stockholm (1719 and 1720) most of the Swedish possessions in Germany were divided between Prussia and Hanover, both of which, together with Great Britain, had joined the coalition against Sweden later in the war. Prussia received most of western Pomerania and the coveted town of Stettin, while Hanover gained possession of Bremen and Verden. Denmark received a money indemnity and the promise that Sweden would acquiesce in a Danish occupation of Holstein. Though Poland made no territorial gains, Augustus was restored to the Polish throne. The largest share of the spoils went to Russia, which by the treaty of Nystad acquired Esthonia, Livonia, Ingria, part of Carelia, and the province of Viborg in eastern Finland.[1] Amid transports of joy the Senate acclaimed the Tsar as "Peter the Great, Father of the Fatherland, and Emperor of all Russias."

PETER'S LAST YEARS AND HIS SUCCESSORS

Soon after taking possession of the territory along the Baltic in 1702, Peter started work on his new capital and "window to the west," St. Petersburg. For the site he chose the islands and marshes near the mouth of the river Neva. Far removed from the heart of Russia, the location had many disadvantages and little to recommend it. The Tsar could have made a better choice, but

---

[1] By the settlements that followed the Revolution of 1917, Russia lost much of the territory Peter acquired by the treaty of Nystad. It managed, however, to reannex the territory in 1940.

he did not stop to consider the disadvantages or to listen to the
objections and complaints of his people. He thought only of completing the building of the city during his lifetime. Tens of thousands of soldiers and peasants were recruited for the work. At
first even ordinary tools were lacking, and there were neither adequate living quarters nor sufficient food for the workers. These
poor conditions, in addition to the severity of the climate, the un-
healthfulness of the pestilential swamps, and the hard labor,
killed thousands of workers. Estimates of the number of lives that
were sacrificed in the construction of the city run as high as one
hundred thousand. Lest the city be razed by fire and the capital
removed to Moscow, Peter decreed that stone be used wherever
possible in constructing the buildings. Finally, near the close of
his reign, he moved his government to the new city, which was
still little more than a prospect. Yet it was destined to remain the
capital of Russia until 1919. Known as Petrograd after Russia's
entry into the World War, since 1924 the city has borne the name
of Leningrad.

Peter did not long survive his triumph over Sweden and the
removal of the capital. Though not yet fifty-three, he was an old
man, his iron constitution undermined by decades of hard labor
and careless living. But he continued his vigorous work to the last.
Late in the year 1724 he was severely chilled in rescuing some
drowning sailors, became seriously ill, and died in January, 1725.
Although Peter did not succeed in transforming Russia, he did
accelerate its westernization. He also made Russia an important
factor in the international politics of Europe and gained a Baltic
port which served as a gateway for the entrance into Russia of
both the goods and the civilization of Europe. Finally he gave
Russia a westernized army of 200,000 men and also built a small
navy. All this he did at a frightful cost of human life, human suffering, and money. When he died, his death came as a relief to
most of his people, for it spelled the end of the sacrilegious attempts
to eradicate many time-honored customs and cherished ideas of
Old Russia. Considering the ill-will and the determined opposition which Peter's reforms aroused, it is remarkable that any of
them endured after his death.

Peter's death left the question of the succession undecided. In
1721 he had issued a ukase which decreed that the Tsar had the
right to nominate his successor, but had himself failed to exercise

the right. At the last he had laboriously scrawled on a piece of paper a message of which only the two words, "Forgive everything," could be deciphered. The issue was soon decided, however, by the Palace Guards when they raised Peter's wife to the throne as Catherine I despite the fact that she had no legitimate claim to it and little ability to rule. She was the first of a series of mediocre rulers, a number of whom, like herself, were placed on the throne by palace revolutions. So frequently did this occur in the eighteenth century that a contemporary diplomatist was moved to say: "The Russian throne is neither hereditary nor elective; it is seized." After an interval of about fifteen years Elizabeth Petrovna (1741–1762), a daughter of Peter, turned again to the program of her father. During her reign French thought and culture began to claim the interest of many at the Russian court. Under Elizabeth, Russia also played an important part in the Seven Years' War (1756–1763), thus showing its altered position in Europe. But it was not until the advent of Catherine II (1762–1796) that the process of Europeanizing Russia, expanding its territories, and magnifying its position in international politics was resumed with vigor.

CHAPTER EIGHTEEN

The Age of Louis XIV

LOUIS XIV, THE MAN AND THE KING

THE reign of Louis XIV, which covered the period from 1643 to 1715, is one of the most conspicuous in the history of monarchy. Such monarchs as Charles V and Philip II may have ruled over wider dominions, but they never attained the prestige and power that Louis XIV enjoyed. He was the "Grand Monarch," the "Sun King," the "First Gentleman of Europe." About him gathered a group of notable figures, including Corneille, Racine, Molière, La Fontaine, Colbert, Louvois, Vauban, Condé, and Turenne, whose achievements threw a brilliant luster over the king, the court, and the reign. Well could Pepys write: "All the princes of Europe have their eyes on him." He was the most famous prince of his time, which has ever since been known as the Age of Louis XIV. His court set a standard of magnificence which contemporary and later rulers endeavored to imitate but did not hope to equal. For the nobles of most European countries the language, taste, spirit, and art of Versailles became obligatory. "Society" everywhere was French, remaining so until the nineteenth century. Most other countries, except England, even built palaces in the style of those of Louis XIV.

In the history of France the reign of Louis XIV was the culmination of the system of absolute monarchy which had been developing since the Hundred Years' War. Before his advent the royal absolutism had been opposed by factions within the state, and after his death the monarchy showed symptoms of decay; but during his reign there was little opposition to the royal will. Whether or not he uttered it, the saying *L'état c'est moi* (I am the state) represents the actual situation under Louis. All potential threats to the royal power were carefully held in check. The Estates-General, which might have offered some opposition, was not convoked. Many of the provincial estates were suppressed, and those that survived were convened only to carry out the decrees of the king. Even the right of many cities to elect their mayors was abolished, the mayoralties being made hereditary and sold by the king to the highest bidders. Truly, Louis XIV was the state.

No king ever held a more exalted view of his office. Not only did Louis regard the kingship as of divine origin, but he believed himself to be God's vicar. All his decisions, he was convinced, were made under the special guidance and inspiration of the Almighty and were therefore characterized by a sort of divine infallibility. This idea had been instilled in him by his tutors. A royal catechism composed especially for his religious instruction stated that a king is "the vicegerent of God" and "the visible image of God on earth." One sentence read: "Your Majesty should always remember that you are a Vice-God." When he ascended the throne Louis was accorded almost divine honors by those about him. Extravagant flattery and bombastic praise became the sole means by which he could be approached. After his consecration as king, the rector of the University of Paris addressed him in the following words: "We are so dazzled by the new splendor which surrounds Your Majesty that we are not ashamed to appear dumbfounded in the presence of a light so brilliant and so extraordinary." Little wonder that Louis recognized no limits to his authority beyond those imposed by conscience and religion; that he believed himself the greatest of men; that he took as his emblem the sun, sole source of light and life; and that his pride grew until he felt that his subjects should willingly give their possessions, even their lives, to gratify his whims.

What sort of person was this Grand Monarch who had such exalted ideas of himself and his kingship? He was of medium height, and his face, with its large features and its pockmarks, was not handsome. But he had a commanding appearance and considerable personal charm. The ambassador of Brandenburg wrote in 1690: "The attractions of his person are his figure, his carriage, air, and fine bearing, an exterior full of grandeur and majesty." There was much kindness and generosity in his nature. The latter quality, however, was a weakness rather than a virtue, because it tended to impoverish the state and to increase the tax burdens of the French people. Vigorous of physique, he was fond of such strenuous sports as riding and hunting. He drank very little, but was a voracious eater. Says Saint-Simon: "He ate so prodigiously and so solidly morning and evening that no one could get accustomed to seeing it." [1] But despite his gormandizing and the stomach trouble from which he suffered, Louis lived until his seventy-seventh year. Throughout this long period he was in public always the Grand Monarch, dignified, calm, and courteous. His greatest weaknesses were his inordinate thirst for flattery and his unbounded selfishness. Of the latter quality Saint-Simon wrote: "The king loves and cares for himself alone and is himself his only object in life."

Of Louis XIV's mental ability it is more difficult to form a judgment. Badly educated in his youth, Louis had learned little of the subjects that would have best fitted him to be king. He acquired little geography, little history, and almost no knowledge of the social and economic conditions of the country over which he was to rule. To quote Saint-Simon, he "remained so ignorant that the most familiar historical and other facts were utterly unknown to him. He fell accordingly, and sometimes even in public, into the grossest absurdities." Louis himself realized his shortcomings in this respect. "It is bitterly humiliating," he wrote, "to be ignorant of things which everyone else knows." It may well have been the consciousness of his deficient education and a fear of appearing foolish which made him a king of few words. Although this lack of information obliged him to base his policies on knowledge supplied by others, Louis possessed real intelligence of a sort. He did not have the quick, spontaneous mind of his grandfather, Henry IV; yet he was capable of forming sound judgments. During the early part of his reign he exhibited con-

[1] Regarding the quantity of food he consumed the duchess of Orléans wrote: "I have often seen the king eat four platefuls of various kinds of soup, a whole pheasant, a partridge, a large dish of salad, stewed mutton with garlic, two large slices of ham, a plate of pastry, and then fruit and sweetmeats."

siderable skill in diplomacy. Later, when years of exposure to the adulation of his courtiers had distorted his judgment, he made some serious mistakes. In dealing with the social, economic, and religious problems of his kingdom Louis did not manifest the intelligence he had shown in diplomacy. His was definitely not a creative mind, for nothing that he accomplished bears the stamp of originality. On the other hand, he was patient, methodical, and diligent. Compared with his weak-willed and dreary predecessor (Louis XIII) and his debauched successor (Louis XV), Louis XIV stands as a ruler of considerable ability.

Although Louis had reached his majority in 1651, he had left the direction of affairs in the hands of Mazarin, giving no indication of a desire to rule. Great, therefore, was the astonishment when the young king of twenty-three declared, after the death of Mazarin, that he would be his own prime minister. It is reported that his mother, Anne of Austria, had difficulty in restraining herself from laughing aloud when she heard of the announcement. To Louis it was no laughing matter. He had determined that the proverb coined during the administration of his predecessor, "The king and the ruler are two different persons," was not to apply to him. For fifty-four years, until his death in 1715, he adhered conscientiously to his resolve, seldom deviating from the routine he drew up for himself on the day of Mazarin's death. So methodically did he labor that Saint-Simon was moved to write: "With an almanac and a watch you could tell exactly what the king was doing though you were three hundred leagues away." How seriously Louis took "the business of being king," as he called it, is indicated in his *Memoirs*, in which he admonishes the dauphin "not to forget that it is by work one reigns; to rule without working is ungrateful and defiant toward God, unjust and tyrannical toward men." Six to eight hours a day, exclusive of court ceremonies, he labored over the affairs of the state. "I request you," he told the secretaries of state in 1661, "to seal nothing without my order and to sign nothing without my consent." Yet he was unable to carry out his resolve to supervise everything. The task of ruling France was too great.

The ministers, appointed by Louis himself, were grouped in various councils. The most important of these was the Council of State (*Conseil d'État*), an advisory body composed of only four or five members who met with the king to consider such supreme

matters as international treaties and war. All members of this
council could participate in the discussions, but the king made
the final decisions. On exceptional occasions he might invite non-
members to attend a meeting for the purpose of giving him their
counsel. A second body was the Council of Dispatches (*Conseil des
Dépêches*), which considered questions of interior administration,
and included the secretaries of state who headed the various departments of administration. A third group, the Council of Finance (*Conseil des Finances*), dealt with questions of taxation. Both
the Council of Dispatches and the Council of Finance, like the
Council of State, met in the royal apartments and were presided
over by the king. But he did not preside over the fourth body,
the Privy Council (*Conseil Privé*). This was the highest judicial
court in France, with an authority that was somewhat vague.
There was no systematic division of affairs among the various
councils and consequently much confusion. Nevertheless, the
furthermost parts of the country were closely linked to the central
government through the thirty-four intendants, one for each of
the administrative districts into which France was divided.

THE ECONOMIC POLICIES OF COLBERT

It was the rare good fortune of Louis to have as one of his
ministers during the early part of his reign Jean-Baptiste Colbert
(1619–1683). Of bourgeois origin, Colbert was a dour individual,
gruff in manner and unsocial, but he had a clear mind and an
enormous capacity for work. He had been trained in the school
of Mazarin and upon the cardinal's death in 1661 was appointed
superintendent of finance by Louis XIV. Thereafter for more
than twenty years he served the king faithfully, often toiling sixteen hours a day. As he rose in the king's favor, Colbert gradually
exerted a larger influence upon the direction of affairs. Some idea
of his voluminous tasks may be gained from the fact that besides
the finances he also at various times supervised industry, commerce, agriculture, education, public works, the colonies, the
navy, the postal service, and to some extent even foreign affairs.
Thus the direction of most of the important branches of the administration was in his hands. His first great object was the establishment of some semblance of order in financial affairs, which
had steadily become more chaotic since Sully's death. The tax
farmers were again pocketing the bulk of the revenues, the na-

tional debt had grown until it was absorbing nearly half of the state income, money-lenders were charging the state exorbitant rates of interest, and the clergy and nobility were still claiming exemption from the taille and other taxes.

In reorganizing the national finances Colbert made no radical changes. Like Sully, he was unable to reform the deplorable system of taxation, but he minimized the frauds in the collection of revenues. Tax farmers who had accumulated large fortunes were required to show that they had gained their wealth honestly or to disgorge their gains. They were also forced to accept new contracts and thenceforth to render accurate account. With respect to the tax exemptions of the clergy and nobility, Colbert, like Sully and Richelieu, did not dare to make any drastic changes. He succeeded only in reducing the number to whom this exemption was permitted. All titles of nobility were subjected to a vigorous examination, and the large number who had secured exemptions on the basis of spurious titles were put back on the tax rolls. Colbert also reduced the national debt by repudiating some of the loans made by his predecessor at rates of twenty-five per cent or more, and by reducing the interest on the remainder. These measures largely increased the receipts of the treasury, and greatly curtailed expenditures. As early as 1667 Colbert had a surplus in the treasury. But it proved only temporary. The king's penchant for spending was soon to empty the treasury and increase the national debt.

In his industrial and commercial policies Colbert was the great exponent of mercantilism. Certain phases of mercantilist practice, particularly government regulation and subsidization of industry, and an extreme system of tariff protection, are still known as Colbertism. He was not, however, a theorist who was primarily interested in the mere application of mercantilist theories. He was intensely practical. His aim was to create a strong, self-sufficient France, and because mercantilist principles appeared to him the best means of achieving his end he adopted them. To make France self-sufficient he encouraged the old industries and also started many new ones. That most of the luxury businesses established by Henry IV had died out did not deter Colbert from reëstablishing them. Almost every year from 1663 to 1672 saw the revival of an old industry or the founding of a new one for the manufacture of such commodities as silks, carpets, lace, tapestries, brocades, pottery, glass, mosaics, and fine furniture. In an effort to rival the English and Dutch textiles, Colbert also set up royal industries for the manufacture of woolen goods. These budding industries were not only aided by state subsidies but were protected against foreign competition by high tariffs. In 1667 tariff rates were raised until they amounted almost to a general exclusion of imports. This policy led to tariff wars between Holland, England, and France, but it protected the new industries.

To keep French capital in France by making the country self-sufficient was only a part of Colbert's program; he wished also to draw capital into France from abroad. The best means of achieving this, he believed, was through the manufacture of quality products. Accordingly the manufacture of French goods was regulated in the minutest detail. Textiles, for example, had to have so many threads to the warp and the woof, and be of a specified width and length. A small army of inspectors went about to enforce these rules, and severe penalties were imposed for transgressing them. The system prohibited any innovation or alteration in the process of manufacture, but by giving standard qualities to French products it gained for them a great reputation abroad. When after Colbert's death the regulations threatened to throttle French industry, they were gradually relaxed. Colbert also invited foreign artisans to bring their skill and trade secrets to France, and insisted that every able-bodied man in France work. His opposition to idleness even moved him to condemn monks and nuns as unproductive. Denouncing the celibacy of the clergy, he encouraged early marriages and proclaimed tax remissions for families of ten children or over if none of them was a monk or a nun. He further sought to increase the output of labor by reducing the number of religious holidays, but was successful in abolishing only seventeen, thirty-eight others remaining on the calendar.

In another field, the development of French commerce, Colbert was equally active. His plan to aid internal trade by abolishing the local customs duties was only partially successful. He succeeded in establishing in the center of France a district known as the *Cinq Grosses Fermes* (Five Great Farms), in which goods could be transported freely from province to province, but in the remainder of the country the old multiplicity of duties remained. For oversea trade he took the Dutch as his model. Impressed by the success of their commercial companies, he decided to organize similar agencies which would dispute with them the trade both of the East and of the West. Accordingly, he founded in 1664 an East India Company and a West India Company. Unfortunately, both of these and a number of others established for trade in other parts of the globe failed before Colbert's death in 1683. Nor was Colbert's colonial policy much more successful. Despite all his efforts to encourage the settlement of French colonies in America, in the West Indies, in Madagascar, and in India, few Frenchmen voluntarily left for the French colonies. To the Huguenots, the only group that would have been glad to leave France, the colonies were closed; hence the first colonial empire of France was little more than a name.

Since his interests were centered in industry and commerce, Colbert failed to realize that in a country still predominantly agricultural the prosperity of the peasants was of basic importance. He did encourage horse-breeding and reclaim marshes, but the good wrought by such services was nullified by the bad effects of other policies. Because he feared that France might become dependent on other countries for its food, he imposed such heavy export duties on corn in 1664 that shipments virtually ceased. As a result the price of wheat was so low in years of good harvests that the peasants prayed for poor crops so that the prices would be higher. Moreover, Colbert's policy of protection reacted unfavorably upon French agriculture. In retaliation for the exclusion of their products, other countries put heavy taxes upon the agricultural exports of France, notably upon wine and spirits.

In 1683 Colbert went to the grave broken-hearted over the realization that much of his labor had been in vain. Though he had increased the national income, he had not succeeded in curbing the prodigality of the king or in preventing his ruinous wars. The royal expenditures and the cost of the wars emptied the treasury faster than he could fill it. However carefully the taxes were collected, it was still necessary to resort to other expedients for obtaining money. In the second place, his commercial policies had brought only mediocre results. Finally, even the outlook for his industrial policies was not bright. The religious persecution which culminated in the revocation of the Edict of Nantes was already driving the Huguenots out of France and thereby undermining many of the industries he had founded. Furthermore, the wars of Louis XIV decreased consumption at home and interfered with foreign trade. Such businesses as cloth-weaving, lace-making, silk-weaving, hat-making, tapestry-weaving, and paper-making declined greatly. Only those industries continued to prosper which produced the necessities of war, including clothing and shoes for the troops, and arms and ammunition. Thus Colbert's vision of a prosperous France, second to none in industry and commerce, was already blighted before he closed his eyes, and by the end of Louis's reign there was little left of his improvement.

THE PAGEANT OF VERSAILLES

Since his youth Louis had disliked Paris, for centuries the seat of the French monarchy. He hated the turbulent crowds and the narrow streets, on one of which a dagger had been plunged into the heart of Henry IV. He could not forget the unpleasant experiences of the Fronde when he had been at the mercy of the Parisian mob. Nor was the Louvre, which had served his predecessors as a royal residence and which Colbert styled "the most superb palace in the world," to his liking. He therefore decided to build outside of Paris a palace worthy of himself, one which would impress the popular imagination with its splendor. His choice was fixed upon a site near the village of Versailles, eleven miles southwest of Paris. It was a district of sandy wastes and desolate marshes, but for Louis, who during his youth had spent considerable time there in the royal hunting lodge, the place had attractions. The palace, begun in 1669, was not completed until 1701, although the court moved into it in 1682. For its construction and decoration the best talent of France was engaged. More than thirty-five thousand people worked at one time on the palace, the grounds, and the canal which was designed to supply water for the many fountains of the park. The cost of the undertaking was so immense that Louis destroyed the accounts before his death. Great also was the cost in human lives, for the fever-ridden marshes quickly decimated the ranks of the laborers, making it necessary to gather new recruits constantly. But as it was all "for the glory of the king," the work was pushed relentlessly.

The finished palace amazed the contemporary world. Its magnificent halls, the crimson and gold Salon of Diana, the green and gold Salon of Mars, the Salon of Mercury with its flawless marble, the Salon of Venus with its beautiful mosaics, and the Salon of Apollo or throne room with its solid silver throne, were

dazzling in their splendor. Most famous of them all is the Grand
Hall of Mirrors, two hundred forty feet in length, with its seventeen large windows, matched by as many framed Venetian mirrors, and its ceiling covered by Lebrun's paintings representing
incidents from the wars waged by Louis against Spain, Holland,
and Germany. At night thousands of candles set in immense chan-
deliers or in massive candlesticks lighted the grand rooms of the
structure. Outside, it was surrounded by a vast park studded with
fountains, ponds, and innumerable bronze vases and marble
statues of nymphs, dryads, and dancing fauns. Whole groves of
trees were collected from the finest forests of France, and terraces,
waterfalls, great lawns, and long promenades were laid out in
geometric forms with mathematical precision. In its monotonous
uniformity, oppressive magnificence, and decorative profusion
the palace breathes the spirit of the age and is symbolic of Louis
XIV and his monarchy. In the words of Saint-Armand: "The idol
is worthy of the temple, the temple of the idol."

To Versailles Louis moved his court, his ministers, and all officials in his service (1682). There he also gathered about him all
the great nobles of France, who by this time were cured of their
rebellious and independent habits. Richelieu had razed their
fortresses and supplanted them with intendants; Mazarin had
frustrated their efforts to regain their former position; and now
Louis XIV converted them into satellites and parasites. Every
member of the higher nobility was encouraged to leave his domains and migrate to Versailles to become a puppet of the king.
For those who desired favors from the monarch it was almost
compulsory to reside in Versailles. Thus the court of the Sun King
became the playground of the nobility. By day there were promenades in the park, drives, or hunting and hawking expeditions;
at night there were balls, masquerades, ballets, and concerts.
Often the comedies of Molière or the tragedies of Racine were
presented. But the principal diversions were card-playing, games
of chance, and billiards. At cards the stakes were on occasion exceedingly high, with the king paying the losses of certain favorites.
Each of these amusements had its own regulations and its own
etiquette. Indeed, everything at Versailles—birth and death, love
and marriage, pain and pleasure—was subject to the inexorable
laws of etiquette. To transgress these laws was the one unpardonable sin.

The central figure of the pageant was, of course, Louis himself. He was the sun around which revolved the whole planetary system of the court. To accentuate and enhance his grandeur was the chief function of the nobles. From the moment he arose in the morning until he retired at night they attended him—dressing him, praying with him, watching him eat and take his medicine, and finally undressing him at night. Every act of the king had its ritual, even those for which moderns desire the utmost privacy. The routine of etiquette began with the *lever*. Before the stroke of eight, at which time the king arose, no less than one hundred fifty nobles would gather in the anteroom of the king's chamber to participate in the royal lever, each having had his own lever previously. To hand the king his shirt or to assist him into the royal breeches was a coveted honor accorded only to princes of the blood and nobles of the highest rank. The lesser nobles had to content themselves with watching him wash his face and choose his wig for the day. During his meals, which the king usually ate alone, the nobles would again look on while a privileged few handed him the food that had been brought from the kitchens with elaborate ceremony, officers along the way eating portions of it as a test for poison. The last resplendent function of the day was the *coucher* or going-to-bed of the king, at which the ceremonies of the lever were reversed. No one submitted more patiently to all the rigidity of etiquette and formalism than Louis himself; he seemed actually to enjoy it.

Glittering and glamorous as the court may appear at a distance, it was not always thrilling to the participants. Lively at first, the life at Versailles soon became artificial and stilted, and during the last years of the king's life, when he "became religious," it was insufferably dull. Madame de Maintenon wrote to a friend: "If I could only make clear to you the hideous ennui that devours all of us." To escape from this tedium many of the courtiers interested themselves in the private affairs of others until the court became one of the worst hotbeds of gossip history has known. Others steeped themselves in licentiousness and immorality. In this respect even Louis XIV did not remain unblemished. He could truthfully say, as he often did, "Mais, Madame, après tout je ne suis pas un ange (But, madam, after all I am not an angel)." The queen, Marie Thérèse, who was ardently devoted to her husband and bore him six children, had to submit to the indignity of seeing installed in the royal palace such mistresses *en titre* as the Duchesse de La Vallière, the Marquise de Montespan, Mlle. de Fontanges, and Mme. de Maintenon. The last, the widow of the poet Scarron, became Louis's wife by a secret marriage in 1684, the year after the death of Marie Thérèse, but she was never recognized as queen. In brief, the refinement of the court was external and artificial, and the court life was shallow and insipid; behind the outward refinement there was little delicacy of sentiment, expression, or conduct.

Neither was the palace of Versailles as habitable as one might imagine. The huge structure was quite comfortless and lacked sanitary conveniences. Saint-Simon describes the apartment of the king as "inconvenient to the last degree, dull, stuffy, and stinking." Others also complained of the stench which pervaded the palace. Vile smells mingled with the odor of strong perfumes used by the nobility in lieu of a bath, for baths were usually taken only when they were prescribed by a physician as a cure for some illness. In the winter the immense rooms were bitterly cold despite the numerous fireplaces. Madame de Maintenon wrote: "The king's apartment is so cold that if I live there long I shall become a paralytic; not a door or a window will shut, and the wind recalls American hurricanes." Often it was so cold in the king's bedroom that the drinking water froze. Furthermore, the distance from the royal kitchens to the dining rooms was so great and the preliminary ritual of the meals so long that the food was quite cold when served. It was hardly food "fit to be served to a king," but Louis did not complain. One advantage he did have over the members of his court: he was the only one to use a fork, the others eating as best they could with a knife and their fingers.

THE RELIGIOUS HISTORY OF LOUIS XIV'S REIGN

Brought up by an ardent Catholic mother, Louis was punctilious in the observance of all outward forms of the Catholic religion throughout life. Only once in his life, it was said, did he miss hearing daily mass. But beyond the outward formalism and a hatred of heretics religion meant little to the French monarch. It was to him a matter of the heart, not of the mind, for he had little knowledge and less understanding of the dogmas of the Church. Saint-Simon says, "He was devout with the grossest ignorance," a verdict which is confirmed by other contemporaries.

Despite his devoutness and the fact that he took pride in the title "Eldest Son of the Church," there was almost perpetual friction between Louis and the pope over the question of papal authority in the French Church. The Grand Monarch was willing to let the pope decide questions of doctrine, but in other matters he desired his power to be as absolute over the Church as it was over the state. The pope, on the other hand, was just as firm in insisting upon his own authority over the French Church. The long quarrel which resulted from the conflicting claims came to a head in 1682 when the question was referred to the assembly of the French clergy. At this meeting Bossuet, bishop of Meaux, the leading spirit of the assembly and the spokesman of the king, drew up a statement known as the Declaration of Gallican Liberties, which declared that the authority of the pope in France does not go beyond matters of doctrine and that even in this respect he is subject to the decisions of a general council. The pope protested vigorously but in vain. Later Louis moderated his insistence upon the declaration, after he came increasingly under the influence of Madame de Maintenon, but it was never officially repealed.

The king's passion for absolutism and unity demanded that his subjects agree with him even in religion. He could not believe that a person who worshiped God in a different way could be a good subject. Such views were not unique, for they were shared by the Catholic clergy and approved by public opinion. Moreover, religious unity was still regarded as essential to political unity in most states. This was true in England and in other Protestant countries as well as in such Catholic lands as Spain, Italy, and France. The great obstacle to the achievement of religious unity in France was the Huguenots. Numbering perhaps a million and a half out of a population of about nineteen millions, the Huguenots, since the revocation of the political privileges by Richelieu, had been living quietly and working industriously, enjoying their religious freedom. Their proselyting zeal having cooled, they were no longer a menace to the Church. To the state they were an asset, for they showed great vigor in many lines of activity, particularly in the skilled handicrafts. But their presence in France irritated Louis. Not only did he regard the existence of heresy as a sin for which he was personally responsible, but he also considered that it would be a brilliant triumph for himself and for the Church if he could induce the Huguenots to renounce their Protestantism. Moreover, the extirpation of heresy in France, Louis believed, would go far toward atoning for the scandals of his private life.

The Edict of Nantes continued in force for many years after Louis became king, but it was interpreted so narrowly that the Huguenots were deprived of some of the liberties they had formerly enjoyed. Gradually more and more pressure was brought to bear upon them in an effort to "convert" them to Catholicism. Many of their schools were closed and more than a hundred churches were demolished. Next the government offered money bribes and special privileges. When these methods failed to induce the Huguenots to abjure their religion the Jesuit confessors of Louis and some of his ministers spurred the king on to greater severity against the heretics. Finally in 1681 violent methods were openly adopted. Dragoons were quartered in the homes of those Huguenots who steadfastly refused to yield. Louvois, the minister of war, wrote to the commander of the dragoons: "It is His Majesty's wish that the last severities should be inflicted on those who refuse to adopt his religion. Those who would have the stupid honor of being the last must be pushed to the last extremity. . . . The soldiers are to be allowed to live licentiously." Such measures were excused on the ground that "God makes use of every means" to save souls from damnation. So great was the fear inspired by the *dragonnades*, as the quartering of dragoons in the homes of the Huguenots was called, that entire communities announced their "conversion" at the news that the dragoons were coming. Finally in 1685 the king formally revoked the Edict of Nantes after he was told by his ministers that it was no longer needed because there were no longer any Huguenots.

The king's action received general approval. The universities, the academies, the courts of justice, the municipalities, all hailed the revocation as a great achievement. Medals were struck to honor the occasion, and statues were erected to Louis XIV. "It is the finest thing that was ever imagined or executed," said Madame de Sévigné. "Let us publish," said Bossuet, "the miracle of our time. . . . Let us say to the new Constantine, this new Theodosius, this new Marcian, this new Charlemagne: 'Through you heresy exists no more. God alone could achieve this marvel.'" What appeared to be a marvel and a "visible miracle" to many was in reality a serious blow to the prosperity of France. Though emigration was forbidden under the severest penalties, large numbers of Huguenots managed to flee across the borders. France thereby lost perhaps as many as two hundred thousand of its most industrious and energetic citizens—a loss which well-nigh destroyed some of its industries. The Huguenots fled to England, to Brandenburg, to Holland, and to America, carrying with them their wealth, skill, and spirit of enterprise.

Louis also took a definite stand against the religious movement called Jansenism, which arose within the Church. Cornelius Jansen (d.1638), bishop of Ypres, had provided the ideas for it in his book entitled *Augustinus*. The history and theology of the movement are too complex to be expounded here. Suffice it to say that the Jansenists advocated a puritanical mode of life, though they were in no way connected with Calvinism and had no desire to leave the Catholic Church. In their theology they proposed to restore the simpler Christianity of St. Augustine, an aim which involved the rejection of the theological developments of the Middle Ages. The center of the movement was the convent of Port Royal des Champs, near Versailles, and a community of men nearby who worked assiduously and also spent much time in prayer, meditation, and spiritual exercises. The schools attached to these communities soon became famous. Among the notable pupils who attended them was the future dramatist Racine.

Despite the fact that the Jansenists were faithful members of the Church, they were obnoxious to the king and the Jesuits. Louis XIV was ill-disposed toward them for various reasons. In the first place, he regarded them as a threat to the royal absolutism because they were ready to oppose the officials of the state if they believed that these officials were acting contrary to "the true faith." Secondly, Louis was irritated that, in an age of submission, the Jansenists had the audacity to show a spirit of independence and self-reliance. But the chief reason for the king's hostility was that the Jansenists were guilty of the "unpardonable sin" of having associated with the Frondeurs. As for the Jesuits, they feared the increasing influence of the Jansenists among the people and envied the success of the schools at Port Royal. They accused the Jansenists of being Calvinists in disguise. In 1656, however, no less a person than Blaise Pascal (1623–1662), noted mathematician and philosopher, launched a scathing counter-attack in his *Provincial Letters*. So skilfully did he expose the principles advocated by certain Jesuit casuists that the Jesuits could offer only a weak defense. But the Jesuits had the king on their side. In 1709, after having tried vainly for some decades to suppress the Jansenists, Louis decreed the razing of the convent at Port Royal and ordered the inmates to be dispersed among other institutions. However, the spirit of Jansenism refused to die. In a last effort to suppress it, Louis in 1713 procured from an obliging pope the bull *Unigenitus*, which condemned many Jansenist teachings as heresy. All this notwithstanding, Jansenism continued to be an important influence in France.

THE WARS OF LOUIS XIV

When Louis took over the reins of government in 1661 Europe, generally speaking, was at peace. He himself says in his *Memoirs:* "Everything was quiet everywhere. . . . Peace was established with my neighbors probably for as long a time as I should myself desire." But like most despots in history Louis thirsted for glory. Regarding his passion for it the Prussian envoy wrote: "It is his great weakness and fatal to the peace of Europe." Louis himself later confessed this weakness in the words: "Ambition and glory are always excusable in a prince and especially in a prince as young and as highly favored by fortune as I was." Beyond personal glory the Grand Monarch's aim was to win for France what he regarded as its natural boundaries. It is therefore not surprising that Louis was almost continuously at war for over half a century.

Louis had a strong army. He also had two able commanders in Condé and Turenne, and two invaluable military aides in Vauban and Louvois. Vauban, one of the great military engineers in history, did much to revolutionize the methods both of attacking and of defending fortified positions. It was said that to Vauban no fortress was impregnable. He also, it appears, invented the socket which permits a gun to be fired while the bayonet is attached to it. To prevent an invasion of France, Vauban built a line of primary and secondary fortresses along the exposed frontiers. At the same time Louvois, the energetic minister of war, gradually increased the size of the army until by 1678 it reached a total of 279,000. But size was not the only consideration. Louvois also saw to it that the army was well equipped. He replaced the pike with the gun and the bayonet, improved the artillery, introduced the use of copper pontoons for crossing rivers, established magazines for military supplies and food, and built military hospitals. Furthermore, he enforced a better discipline. One of the drillmasters of the time was General Martinet, whose name is still a byword for strict discipline. Not all of these reforms were introduced in the first decade of Louis's reign; nevertheless, in 1667 he had an army that was strong enough to take advantage of the weakness of the other European powers.

A pretext for war was soon found. According to an old local custom called the law of devolution, in a few provinces of the Spanish Netherlands the property of a man who married a second time went to the children of the first marriage, to the exclusion of those of the second. The queen of France, Marie Thérèse, was the eldest daughter of Philip IV of Spain by Philip's first marriage. Louis therefore contended that the Spanish Netherlands rightfully belonged to her. In the marriage contract Marie Thérèse had renounced all claims to the succession and to the Spanish territories. But this renunciation, Louis now declared, had been made on the condition that the queen's dowry be paid in full; and since it had not been paid, the renunciation was invalid. Actually the law of devolution had nothing whatsoever to do with the question of the royal succession, for it was a custom applicable only to private property. But it did serve as a necessary excuse for Louis's aggression. When Spain refused to recognize his claims, the French king decided in 1667 to occupy the Spanish Netherlands. In order not to arouse the fears of other European nations, he referred to his invasion as a "journey" he was taking for the purpose of claiming his wife's rightful inheritance. The campaign itself, known as the War of Devolution, was short and uneventful. Meeting with little resistance, the French army speedily overran the southern part of the Spanish Netherlands.

The very speed of the French monarch's success alarmed the other nations of Europe. Holland, in particular, feared that if Louis succeeded in adding the Spanish Netherlands to France his next step would be an attempt to annex the Dutch provinces. Both the Dutch and the English quickly smothered their mutual antagonism and joined with Sweden in 1668 to form the Triple Alliance against the pretensions of France. This alliance appeared so formidable to Louis that rather than risk a war with it he accepted the terms offered him in the treaty of Aix-la-Chapelle (1668). Louis was forced to renounce his claims to the Spanish Netherlands as a whole and to Franche-Comté, but he was permitted to keep about a dozen of the towns he had taken in Flanders.

The necessity of returning some of the territory he had overrun wounded Louis's pride severely. He therefore resolved that the Dutch Republic, which had taken the lead in frustrating his plans, should feel his vengeance. The Dutch themselves figuratively rubbed salt into the wounds of the Sun King by striking a medal which represented Joshua stopping the sun in its course. Cut to the quick by what he styled "Dutch insolence," Louis took steps to isolate Holland diplomatically. First England and then Sweden were successfully detached from the Triple Alliance. Charles II of England even signed the secret treaty of Dover (1670) whereby he agreed, in return for financial assistance, to aid Louis in the war against the Dutch and also to declare himself a Catholic at the first favorable opportunity. In the spring of 1672 when everything was ready, Louis ordered the invasion of Holland without the formality of declaring war. The large and well-equipped French army under the command of Condé and Turenne took town after town in quick succession. It appeared that the conquest of the United Provinces would be an easy matter. Condé urged a rapid march on Amsterdam for the purpose of overthrowing the Dutch government, but Louis, intoxicated by his success, refused to be hurried. While he was wasting time, the Dutch in a last desperate effort to save their capital opened the sluices and cut the dikes, turning the country around Amsterdam into a vast lagoon which the French could not cross.

While Louis, baffled by the waters, was retreating to Saint-Germain, resolute William III of Orange organized an imposing alliance against France which included Austria, Spain, Brandenburg, and Denmark, besides Holland. Moreover, the English Parliament compelled Charles II to detach himself from Louis. Thus, only Sweden remained the ally of France. Yet the war dragged on a few more years. During this period Louis lost his great general Turenne in battle. Furthermore, the cost of the war was causing financial difficulties in France. Finally the French ruler announced his willingness to conclude peace if he could add to his possessions. Again Spain was chosen to make the sacrifice, Holland retaining every inch of its territory. By the treaty of Nimwegen, ratified in 1678, Spain relinquished Franche-Comté and a number of Flemish towns to France. Louis was at the height of his glory. In two wars he had gained considerable territory and his army had demonstrated that it was the best in Europe. But the decline was near at hand.

The war with the Dutch, far from satisfying Louis's craving for glory and for territory, only increased his vanity and stimulated his ambition. No sooner was it ended than he began to cast about for further acquisitions. Recent treaties, including those of Westphalia, Aix-la-Chapelle, and Nimwegen, had been loosely phrased, giving to France certain areas "with their dependencies." In this vague and elastic expression Louis saw an opportunity to gain more territory. He now instituted certain tribunals called Chambers of Reunion (1679) to search out those lands which had formerly been dependencies of the territories he had acquired. After examining the records, the tribunals pronounced all Alsace and other districts to be the property of France, and Louis immediately sent French troops to take possession. The great city of Strasbourg offered resistance, but bribery and intimidation did their work, and in 1681 it too was "reunited."

Again the other nations of Europe became alarmed over Louis's aggressions, and a new coalition, known as the League of Augsburg, was formed to curb the Sun King's ambition. The members of this league were Spain, Holland, Savoy, Austria, and most of the lesser states of Germany. England also joined in 1688 after William III of Orange succeeded James II to the English throne. Thus France stood alone against nearly all the rest of Europe. Not that Louis believed himself and his resources unequal to the task. To show that he regarded himself as a match for the rest of Europe he had a medal struck bearing the inscription: *Nec pluribus impar* (Not unequal to many).

It is unnecessary to dwell upon the details of the war which began in 1688. The states of Europe were so loosely united that it seemed at first as if Louis would triumph. On land Vauban's chain of fortresses protected the French against an invasion of their country while their army was winning victories outside of France. But as the war progressed it became increasingly evident that the French navy was no match for the combined forces of the English and the Dutch. Moreover, the cost of the war was so tremendous that, after nine years of fighting, Louis was almost forced to accept the proposals for peace proferred him by the other war-weary nations. By the peace of Ryswick (1697) he surrendered all the territory he had taken during the war except Strasbourg, acknowledged William III of Orange as king of England, and granted a favorable commercial treaty to the Dutch.

Within a few years Louis plunged his country into a new war, fought on an even larger scale. Its cause was the disputed succession to the Spanish throne; hence it is known as the War of the Spanish Succession. For years it had been evident that idiotic Charles II of Spain, the last male representative of the Spanish Habsburgs, would have no children. The nearest heirs were the descendants of Louis XIV and of Emperor Leopold of Austria, both of whom had married a Spanish infanta. By descent the dauphin of France and his three sons had the strongest claim, but their way to the throne was barred by the renunciation Marie Thérèse had made in the treaty of the Pyrenees (1659). This renunciation Louis again declared invalid because Marie Thérèse had not received her dowry. The Emperor Leopold, on the other hand, aspiring to make Archduke Charles, his second son, king of Spain, held that the renunciation was valid. Accordingly, while Charles II was still clinging tenaciously to life, diplomatic negotiations for the possession of the throne were set on foot. In the end the efforts of the French ambassador triumphed; Charles made a will shortly before his death (1700), which designated as his successor Philip, duke of Anjou, second son of the dauphin of France.

When Charles II died about a month later, Louis openly accepted the will by presenting his grandson to the French court as the king of Spain. The duke of Anjou took the title of Philip V and immediately departed for Madrid, where he was received with wild acclaim by the Spaniards, who deluded themselves with the thought that the unity of the Spanish dominions had been preserved. Had Louis given assurance that Philip V would under no circumstance inherit the French crown—in other words, that France and Spain would never be united under one ruler—war might have been averted. But Louis was of no mind to do this. His attitude is well expressed by the phrase, "The Pyrenees exist no longer," even if he did not utter it. Such a union of France and Spain would have given France a preponderance not only in

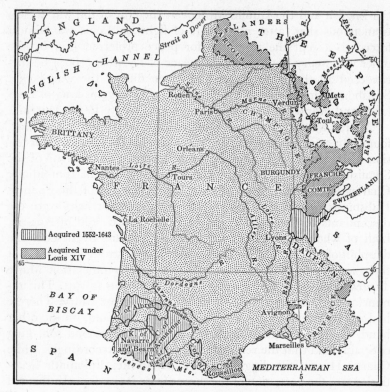

Growth of France, 1552–1715

Europe but also in the New World. To prevent this a coalition
consisting of England, Holland, Austria, and Brandenburg was
formed. Later Portugal, also, joined it. Louis's most important
ally was Bavaria, for Spain had by this time declined so far that
it had few soldiers and no ships worthy of mention.

The war which followed was fought in such scattered localities
as Germany, Italy, the Netherlands, Spain, Asia, and North
America. While the allied forces had two of the great generals of
history in the duke of Marlborough and Prince Eugene of Savoy,
the French had only generals of mediocre ability to oppose them,
though Louis's army was superior in numbers. Successful at first,
the French soon met a series of reverses. At Blenheim, a village
on the Danube, Marlborough and Prince Eugene defeated the
Franco-Bavarian army so decisively that the Bavarians sued for

peace and the French withdrew from Germany. Marlborough next invaded the Spanish Netherlands, where he won three notable victories: Ramillies (1706), Oudenarde (1708), and Malplaquet (1709). By 1709 the French were everywhere on the defensive and Louis was chastened to the extent of requesting peace. But the allies countered with such severe proposals that the war continued. In the subsequent period events turned somewhat in Louis's favor. The Spaniards, who had been of little help early in the war, recovered sufficiently to expel the enemy from their country, excepting Gibraltar and Barcelona. Moreover, they made it plain that they would not accept the Austrian archduke as their king. On the other hand, the enemies of Louis realized that Philip V was unlikely to submit to the dictation of France. Finally in 1711, after the Tories replaced the Whigs as the dominant party, England opened negotiations for peace. Though all parties were willing to end the war, the negotiations dragged on until 1713, when treaties were signed at Utrecht between England, Holland, Portugal, Savoy, and France. The next year peace was concluded between Austria and France by the treaty of Rastatt.

The treaties made the following settlement: (1) Philip V was recognized as king of Spain and of the Spanish possessions in America on the condition that the crowns of France and Spain should never be joined together. (2) In place of the Spanish throne Archduke Charles, who was now emperor, received Naples, Milan, Sardinia, and the Spanish Netherlands (hereafter called Austrian Netherlands). (3) England received Newfoundland, Nova Scotia (Acadia), and the Hudson's Bay territory from France; also Gibraltar and the island of Minorca (in the Mediterranean) from Spain. Furthermore, the English obtained a contract or asiento granting them limited rights of trade with the Spanish colonies. (4) France was permitted to retain Alsace, including Strasbourg, and in return acknowledged the succession of the house of Hanover to the English throne. (5) The duke of Savoy received Sicily and also the title of king. (6) The elector of Brandenburg was recognized as "king in Prussia" and permitted to add Spanish Guelderland to his domains.

Thus ended the last of the four wars of Louis XIV. In these wars the Grand Monarch had gained Franche-Comté, Strasbourg, and much of Flanders, and had established the boundaries of France practically as they remain today. But the territory he acquired was dearly bought with the blood of many subjects and at the cost of the impoverishment of France.

THE SETTING OF THE ROYAL SUN

The year in which Colbert died (1683) may be regarded as the zenith of the reign of Louis XIV. Thereafter its glory gradually departed. The prodigality of the king, the extravagance of the court, the all-devouring wars, the blundering of the administration, all joined in bringing on financial exhaustion and the ruin of commerce and industry. During the early part of the reign Colbert had exerted a salutary influence over the king's mind, but after Colbert's death Louis came under the influence of Louvois, Madame de Maintenon, and the Jesuits, whose advice often lacked discernment. Colbert frequently tried to curb the reckless expenditures of the Grand Monarch. As early as 1675 he had written to Louis: "I entreat Your Majesty to permit me to tell you that neither in war nor in peace have you ever consulted your finances to determine your expenditures, which are so extraordinary that they are certainly without example." In subsequent years he chided the king again and again for his extravagance. "All letters that come from the provinces, whether from the intendants, the receivers-general or even from the bishops, speak of it." But after Colbert's death Louis's advisers permitted him to follow his inclinations unrestrained. In some directions they even urged him on. Thus Louvois, like an "evil genius," encouraged the king in the war policy which proved so ruinous to the finances of France. In other respects Louis needed no encouragement. His penchant for constructing new palaces or rebuilding old ones developed into a veritable passion with the passing of the years. Besides Versailles, he erected the Trianon and a palace at Marly; he also rebuilt the palace of Saint-Germain entirely and altered the Louvre. Furthermore, his gifts and pensions to the court nobility continued to deplete the treasury. More and more the noble families at court were living in luxury entirely on money they received from the king.

The revenues which Louis spent so freely were being squeezed out of an impoverished nation by ruthless tax collectors. Probably at no other time in the history of France was there so much unnecessary suffering among the masses. It is a melancholy picture which Vauban paints in his *Projet de Dîme Royale* (Plan for a

Royal Tithe). "The highroads of the country," he says, "and the streets of the towns and cities are full of beggars whom nakedness and famine have driven forth. . . . One tenth of the population are actually beggars; five tenths do not absolutely beg, but are on the verge of starvation." In the fall of 1708 the intendant of Bordeaux wrote: "Most of the inhabitants have not wherewithal to sow their land." Most terrible was the winter of 1709, during which a shortage of food was accompanied by severe cold, resulting in famine and disease. In Paris, Rouen, and other cities food riots broke out, with mobs breaking into and pillaging bakeries. Of all this the king certainly had the fullest knowledge. When he visited Paris mobs surrounded his carriage crying "Bread! Bread!" "The king himself from his windows," Saint-Simon states, "heard the people crying aloud in the streets. . . . They uttered complaints, sharp and but little measured against the government and even against the king." Vauban, to whom Louis owed much, tried unavailingly to awaken in the king's heart some sympathy for the people. "I feel myself obliged in honor and conscience," he wrote, "to represent to Your Majesty that it seems to me that at all times there has not been in France sufficient consideration for the common people, and that far too little thought has been given to their interests. It is the most ruined and miserable class in the kingdom; it is, nevertheless, the most important, both in virtue of its numbers and the real and effective service which it renders to the state. For it bears all the burdens, and always has suffered, and still suffers the most." When Vauban dared to publish his report of the miseries of the people in 1707, the book was immediately suppressed by royal command.

At no time did the suffering of the people stir in the king's heart a lasting impulse to improve their lot or to abate his expenditures. If he had heard the maxim *Salus populi suprema lex* (The welfare of the people is the supreme law) it had little meaning for him. Not once did he endeavor to relieve the weak at the expense of the strong and wealthy. The national finances, already impaired during the last years of Colbert's ministry, fell into hopeless disorder in the period that followed. As the ordinary revenues were no longer sufficient to meet the cost of his wars and his court, his ministers were forced to resort to such other expedients as the sale of offices, forced loans, lotteries, and debasement of the coinage. When these also proved insufficient, new taxes were imposed—

first the capitation (1699), a poll tax in name but actually a second taille, and then the dixième, an income tax. Both should have fallen on all Frenchmen, but many members of the privileged classes managed to elude them, while peasants were imprisoned for non-payment of taxes in hitherto unheard of numbers. Yet the national debt continued to increase. Whereas the income from the ordinary revenues, including the new taxes, averaged seventy-five million francs per year during the last seven years of Louis's reign, the expenditures of the government averaged two hundred and nineteen millions per year. That part of the deficit which could not be made up by extraordinary means was simply added to the growing debt of the treasury. Thus Louis continued up to his end to lead France into ever deeper ruin.

The last years of his reign were years of personal sadness and grief for the aged monarch. Earlier it had appeared that the house of Bourbon was firmly established. The king, it is true, had only one son, but there were three grandsons. In 1711, however, the dauphin died and within the next three years two of Louis's grandsons followed their father to the grave. The third grandson was the former duke of Anjou who was now Philip V, king of Spain, and therefore barred from the succession to the French throne. This left the great-grandson of Louis, a sickly child who afterward became Louis XV, as the direct heir to the throne. In the summer of 1715 the Grand Monarch, whose health had been slowly declining, became mortally ill. As he saw death approaching, he began to have scruples about his reign. He summoned his great-grandson, then only five, to his bedside and solemnly said: "My child, you will soon be the king of a great realm. Never forget your obligations toward God; remember that you owe him all that you are. Try to preserve peace with your neighbors. I have been too fond of war. Do not imitate me in that, nor in the too great expenditures I have made. Lighten the burdens of your people as soon as you can, and do that which I have had the misfortune not to accomplish myself." Touching words that were to have no effect on his young successor. A few days later, on September 1, 1715, the king passed away in the seventy-seventh year of his life, serene and dignified to the end. His reign of seventy-two years is the longest in the history of France. Its legacy to the French people was a huge debt and an empty treasury.

It is reported that the court preacher Massillon opened the

funeral oration for Louis with the words: "God alone is great, my brethren." To the masses of France this was no revelation, for they had long ceased to believe in the greatness of their king; in fact, they regarded him as being primarily responsible for the tax burden under which they were staggering. Hence the death of Louis was for them an occasion for rejoicing rather than for sorrow. Many years later the duc de Richelieu wrote: "I cannot recall without horror the disgraceful conduct of the people of Paris on the day of the funeral of their sovereign. The death of the most odious tyrant could not have afforded more pleasure." But the eclipse of the Sun King was not permanent. His glory was to shine again for posterity. To this end Voltaire, resolute opponent of absolute monarchy that he was, contributed greatly by writing *The Century of Louis XIV*. Today "Louis the Magnificent" and the glitter and glamour of his court are still a source of romance for conversation, for books, and for the theater.

THE LITERATURE OF THE REIGN OF LOUIS XIV

In the sphere of literature the reign of Louis XIV was a golden age. No previous period had produced masterpieces in such profusion. It has been called the classical or Augustan age of French literature, since the writers who dominated it drew much of their inspiration from the Greek and Roman classics. The literary works of Louis's reign breathe the spirit of his court—its preoccupation with rules, order, and harmony, its love of grandeur, and its worship of absolutism. It was not an emotional literature, but one characterized by decorum, reserve, and dignity. Realizing the value of literature as a means both of enhancing his glory and of controlling public opinion and taste, Louis admitted almost all of the important writers at some time or other to court and gave pensions to a number of literary men, including Corneille and Racine. The writers, in turn, repaid him by giving a certain brilliance to his court and reign. Their favorite theme was not nature but man; more specifically, the men and women of the aristocracy, for whose delectation they wrote. Superficial in many respects, they reached a depth of psychological penetration into the inner life of man which has seldom been surpassed. The age produced little lyric poetry, despite the fact that two of its greatest figures, Racine and La Fontaine, were poets. The highest excellence was attained in the field of drama.

Of the many writers who made the period notable only a few can be considered here. The first in point of time was Corneille (1606–1684), who wrote his greatest works before Louis XIV began his personal reign, but continued to write until his death in 1684. A lawyer by profession, Corneille turned as a young man to the writing of plays. The first expression of his mature genius was the *Cid*, a tragedy which appeared in 1636. This play may be regarded as opening the Augustan or classical age, for it is the first great work to deal with the struggle of man against himself. Upon its appearance the *Cid* was widely and enthusiastically acclaimed. "It is as beautiful as the *Cid*" became a current saying. Certain critics, however, attacked the play so vigorously that Corneille became discouraged and wrote nothing further for four years. Then followed the period of his highest achievement. During the years from 1640 to 1644 he wrote among other plays the three which, together with the *Cid*, are probably his greatest works: *Horace*, *Cinna*, and *Polyeucte*. They are sublime in thought and eloquent in expression. The defects of some of the discourses—bombast, pomposity, and affectation—are those of the age. As a tragedian Corneille is not the equal of Shakespeare or the Greeks, but he does rank immediately below them. He excels particularly in portraying virtue, honor, and other great qualities of the human character.

The second great dramatist of the Augustan age is Racine (1639–1699). His first triumph was *Andromaque* (1667), which was followed in quick succession by a number of other plays, the most noteworthy being *Bajazet* (1672) and *Phèdre* (1677). In 1677 Racine withdrew from the theater because of religious scruples, married, and settled down to a life of peaceful simplicity. Twelve years later Madame de Maintenon, who had founded the school of St. Cyr, requested him to write a play for the young ladies of that institution. Racine responded with the graceful elegy *Esther* (1689), based on the biblical story. In 1691 he wrote a second biblical play, entitled *Athalie*, which many critics consider his masterpiece. Much of Racine's work is characterized by dramatic force and exquisite beauty of language, but he is, above all, a master in skilful dramatic construction and in the analysis of human passions. Few dramatists have equaled him in the delicate portrayal of love and jealousy. Voltaire, when asked to write a commentary on the works of Racine, said: "There is no commentary needed in this case. All that I could do would be to put at the bottom of each page the words 'beautiful, harmonious, admirable, pathetic, sublime.'"

The last of the great trio of dramatists of the age of Louis XIV was Molière (1622–1673). Whereas Corneille and Racine are distinguished for their tragedies, Molière is famous for his comedies. As a young man Molière traveled about France with a company of players for twelve years, writing many pieces that were performed by his company. But his first great comedy was not written until he set up a theater in Paris in 1658. It was a satire in one act, entitled *Les Précieuses Ridicules*, which ridiculed the bombastic language, the exaggerated manners, and the affectation of the age. Many other plays followed. Noteworthy among them are *Tartuffe* (1664), a daring attack on religious superstition and clerical hypocrisy, and *Don Juan ou le Festin de Pierre* (1665), a romantic comedy. His masterpiece is *Le Misanthrope* (1666), in which he gives vent to his indignation over the hard lot of the upright man in a frivolous and false society. It is considered by many critics to be the most subtle and most poetic of French dramas. As the greatest of French comedies it has no rival. Molière's works satirize the follies and faults of men and women of all classes, exposing to ridicule self-conceit, pedantry, sordid avarice, vanity, jealousy, or impudence wherever found. On the other hand, he exalted honor, sincerity, resolution. His chief claim to immortality rests on the universal types he created. His social-climbers, misers, misanthropes, and hypocrites existed not only in his time; they are with us today.

Another great literary figure of the age is La Fontaine (1621–1695), who also wrote for the stage but is today remembered for his *Fables*. La Fontaine published his first collection in 1668 and thereafter six others. It is not the plots of his *Fables*, which he borrowed from other fabulists as far back as Aesop, but the exquisite manner in which he treated them that sets La Fontaine apart. Full of keen observations, penetrating humor, and sage reflections, in a narrow sense the *Fables* are satires on all the members of contemporary society from the Grand Monarch down to the lowest lackey; in a wider sense, they are a burning commentary on the weaknesses and vices of the entire human race. In them, animals play the part of men. For example:

> Two cocks in friendship lived; a hen arrived
> And straightway war began.

Each fable points a moral. To those who regard themselves as being above reproach he says in the fable of *The Wallet:*

> With lynx's eyes we others see, ourselves with moles';
> All is excusable in us; in others, naught.
> One standard we employ to judge our brother,
> But try ourselves by quite another.
> A kind Creator has this lesson taught,
> That we are travelers; having each one sack
> To carry on the breast, another on the back.
> Our own defects in that behind we store,
> Our neighbors' faults we bear in that before.

The age of Louis XIV is remarkable not only for its dramas and for the *Fables* of La Fontaine but also for its letters and memoirs. It has been said that in the letters of Mme. de Sévigné (1626–1696) the epistolary art reached its highest perfection. More than fifteen hundred in number, most of them were written to a daughter who after her marriage had gone to live in a distant province. Besides recording the incidents of her own life, their author touches upon many aspects of the life of Paris and Versailles. She writes about the trifles of everyday life, the balls, gossips, and scandals of the court, the plays presented in the theater, the sermons that were preached, the current questions of religion and philosophy, her own domestic problems, her literary interests, and many other subjects. All the letters are vivid and picturesque, full of wit and epigram, and written in an easy and graceful style. To the student of history they are an invaluable collection of documents pertaining to the life of seventeenth century France.

No other work affords such an insight into the life of the court of Louis XIV as Saint-Simon's *Memoirs*, covering the period from 1691 to 1723 and presenting a lively picture of many contemporary events and characters. Unlike many other personal records, those of Saint-Simon were not an afterthought of old age, but were written, for the most part, soon after the events they describe had taken place. From 1694 until his death the writing of his *Memoirs* was the great interest of his life. As Chateaubriand put it: "He wrote like the devil for posterity." When he died a series of lawsuits over the ownership of the *Memoirs* prevented their publication. It was not until 1829 that they were issued in full, in an edition of forty volumes.

MOLIÈRE BREAKFASTING WITH
LOUIS XIV

LOUIS XIV

COLBERT

FREDERICK THE GREAT RECEIVES A
PETITION

FAUST AND MEPHISTOPHELES

GOETHE AND SCHILLER
MONUMENT AT WEIMAR

CHAPTER NINETEEN

Germany in the Eighteenth Century and the Rise of Prussia

GERMANY AT THE OPENING OF THE EIGHTEENTH CENTURY

GERMANY at the opening of the eighteenth century was a masterpiece of partition, entanglement, and confusion, with all possibilities of national growth checked by a horde of virtually independent princes ruling over states which were often mere pinpoints in the picture. The Holy Roman Empire still existed in name, and at its head there was still an emperor. In theory, the emperor had considerable power; actually, however, he retained only the shadow of an authority whose substance had largely been absorbed by the local nobility. Such power as he exercised was based not so much upon the imperial title as upon his hereditary possessions. With the rulers of the various states practically independent of the empire, little excuse or opportunity was afforded for the intervention of the emperor or for the functioning of any machinery of government set up by the empire. Only in some of the smaller and weaker states was it at times necessary for imperial officials to lend their support in matters of law and justice.

Besides the emperor, there were still an imperial diet, an imperial court, and a so-called imperial army; but they were little more than high-sounding names of institutions whose power had passed away. The imperial diet which convened at Regensburg (Ratisbon) could theoretically make laws for the empire, declare war, and conclude treaties. But the unanimous decisions which were necessary could be obtained only on rare occasions, and then the diet had no efficient means of enforcing them. Consequently the sessions had degenerated into senseless disputes over the vainest formalities. Such questions as the sequence in which toasts were to be drunk to the health of envoys, or whether certain envoys should sit on chairs upholstered in red or in green, often occupied the assembly for long periods. Not inaptly did Frederick the Great compare the members in their bickerings with dogs baying at the moon. Conditions were little better in the imperial court (*Reichskammergericht*) which continued to meet, first at Speyer, later at Wetzlar, to dispense justice to the estates of the empire. Because of official red tape, cases seldom came up for trial, and when they did were endlessly protracted. In the seventies of the eighteenth century more than sixty thousand cases were awaiting trial, a number which had not decreased when the court became defunct in 1806. The imperial army, a motley assemblage of small contingents from the various petty states, was of little value. Small in size, it was composed of the lowest type of recruits, equipped with diverse weapons and wholly lacking in *esprit de corps*.

Conditions in general were such that Friedrich Jacobi, a contemporary German author, was moved to write: "Common sense is disappearing from our political organization and all its arrangements are becoming so senseless, so absurd, so ludicrous that one would gladly take leave with a 'Lord, permit us to pass into the swine.'" Weak at home and without prestige abroad, the Holy Roman Empire was—as Voltaire put it—neither holy, nor Roman, nor an empire. Having failed both to assert its claim to universal rule and to unite the German people, it was tottering to its fall. That it had not collapsed was surprising to many who lived in the eighteenth century. Thus Goethe, in the earliest version of *Faust (Urfaust)*, makes one of the students in the drinking scene in Auerbach's Keller exclaim:

> The dear old holy Roman realm,
> How does it hold together?

Economically Germany was as much disunited as it was politically. Though the peace of Westphalia had theoretically abolished all internal customs, each petty ruler raised tariff barriers at his pleasure. The tariff frontiers which resulted not only netted the land but even cut up the rivers. On the Rhine between Strasbourg and the frontier of Holland alone there were no fewer than thirty customs stations. Trade was further hampered by the lack of common monetary standards. Efforts to establish monetary unity in the empire in 1660 and again in 1738 failed because of the emperor's lack of power. The confusion in the currency continued. The number of men possessing the right of coinage was prodigious. The Lower Rhenish circle alone (one of the ten circles of the empire) had more than sixty mints, a state of affairs which multiplied opportunities for fraud and sharp practice. The so-called Kippers (those who clipped coins) and Wippers (those who bought coins of high quality and reminted them after adding baser metals) profited exceedingly. In some parts of Germany the monetary confusion reached a stage at which the value of a coin depended upon the reputation of the man who offered it. Besides the tariff barriers and the monetary tangle, state and gild monopolies of the manufacture and sale of certain wares handicapped commerce and industry. In short, the prevailing economic conditions prevented both the free development of trade and industry and the growth of economic unity.

In social life, French customs, manners, etiquette, and standards of taste continued to hold sway during most of the eighteenth century. This Gallomania, as it was called by patriotic Germans, had first penetrated the life and culture of the upper classes, and then had spread to the wealthy bourgeoisie in the towns and cities. Whatever was not French—in other words, not *à la mode*—was regarded as coarse and barbaric. Accordingly, a knowledge of the French language was essential to anyone who wished to appear refined, German being relegated to the common people as vulgar. Only French governesses and French tutors could teach the children of the upper classes, only French maids could wait on noble dames, and only French cooks could prepare the viands of the nobility. At most of the German courts Louis XIV became the great exemplar to be imitated in all respects. Though the spirit at Frederick the Great's court was anything but German, he commented ironically on this tendency. "There is not a younger son of a side line," he stated, "who does not imagine himself to be something like Louis XIV. He builds his Versailles, has his mistresses, and maintains his armies." Many of the German princelings held a *lever*, even though only the steward and the master of the stables were present for it.

Thus the political, economic, and social condition of Germany in the eighteenth century seemed to preclude any hope of national regeneration. The individual states were everything, the empire was nothing. In all the empire only two states, Austria and Prussia, possessed importance in the general affairs of Europe. The former was under the rule of the house of Habsburg, while the latter, new but rapidly acquiring a vigorous reputation, was ruled by the Hohenzollern. At the opening of the eighteenth century the possessions of the Habsburgs comprised, in the main, Austria, Hungary, Bohemia, Silesia, Moravia, Styria, Carinthia, and the Tyrol. By the treaty of Utrecht (1715) they obtained the Spanish Netherlands and considerable additions to their territories in Italy, which now included Naples, Sardinia, the Tuscan ports, and most of Lombardy (the duchy of Mantua and part of the duchy of Milan). Inhabited by such diverse peoples, besides the Germans, as the Czechs of Bohemia, the Magyars of Hungary, the Flemings of the Netherlands, and the Italians in the various provinces of Italy, these territories were not united by a common language, race, history, or tradition. The sole bond which held the jumble together was loyalty to the reigning house. Each province had considerable autonomy, but there was a common administration of financial and commercial questions, centering in the Aulic Chamber (*Hofkammer*) at Vienna in Austria. Since Austria was the first of the Habsburg possessions and the center of the Habsburg government, the term *Austria* is used to designate the Habsburg power as a whole.

THE RISE OF PRUSSIA

The phenomenal advance of Prussia and the Hohenzollern was the outstanding fact in the political life of Germany during the period from the Thirty Years' War to the end of the eighteenth century. Because of their vast possessions the Habsburgs still held the dominant position among the German states at the opening of the eighteenth century, but before its close the Hohenzollern rose to a level with them. The cradle of Hohenzollern power was Brandenburg. On April 16, 1417, the Emperor Sigismund in return for various services had invested Frederick of Hohenzollern, then burgrave of Nuremberg, with the sovereignty of the mark of Brandenburg, together with the electoral dignity attached to it. As the name *mark* or *march* indicates, Brandenburg was a border province established as a buffer against the invasion of the Slavs. It encompassed about ten thousand square miles in the northeastern part of Germany, between the Elbe and the Oder, with Berlin near the center. To this nucleus the Hohenzollern had gradually added other domains. At the beginning of the seventeenth century they made two notable additions when in 1609 they gained by inheritance the principalities of Cleves, Mark, and Ravensburg, and in 1618 the valuable duchy of East Prussia. The last was still a fief of the Polish crown. In the thirteenth century the Teutonic Knights, one of the three great military-religious orders of the Crusades, had turned their attention from the heathen Moslems of Palestine to the heathen Slavs in Prussia; but after making themselves masters of East Prussia they had been forced to recognize the feudal sovereignty of the king of Poland. During the Reformation, Luther's doctrines made such inroads that the order was dissolved and the duchy of East Prussia was secularized under the rule of Albert of Hohenzollern. In 1618, when the line became extinct, the Brandenburg Hohenzollern fell heir to the duchy. It was an important acquisition indeed, for it almost doubled the territories of the electors.

Under Frederick William, the Great Elector, Brandenburg-Prussia took its place among the powers of northern Europe. When he ascended the throne, the Thirty Years' War was still raging. The domains of Brandenburg-Prussia during the preceding years had been repeatedly plundered and laid waste by both friend and foe, and their inhabitants had suffered much. Acting with the prompt determination which won for him the title of "the Great Elector," he decided at once to build an army which would be adequate to protect his territories from the depredations of the warring powers. Accordingly he concluded a truce with the Swedes, disbanded the few disorderly mercenaries which he found on his accession, and began the development of a new, well-disciplined standing army. Reëntering the war shortly before its end, he contrived to obtain considerable territory when peace was concluded. By the terms of the treaty of Westphalia he received Eastern Pomerania, the bishoprics of Halberstadt, Minden, and Camin, and the greater part of the bishopric of Magdeburg.

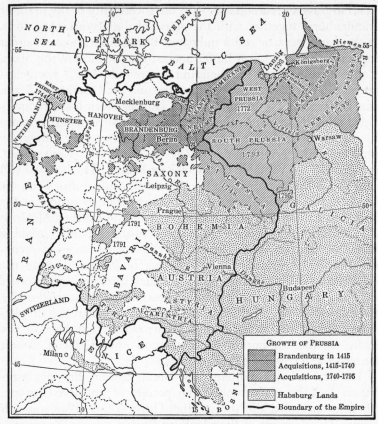

Growth of Prussia, 1648–1795

After the war he continued enlarging his army so that by 1651 he had a force of 16,000 highly trained and sternly disciplined soldiers—a number which was gradually increased until it reached 27,000 by the end of his reign. For the size of Frederick William's territories this was a considerable force, which made Brandenburg-Prussia, next to Austria, the strongest power in Germany.

Because he had a strong bargaining weapon in his army, the Great Elector was able to detach the duchy of East Prussia from the yoke of Polish sovereignty. When war broke out between Poland and Sweden in 1655 over the succession to the Polish throne, Frederick William intervened. By unscrupulous diplomacy—he did not hesitate to change sides at critical times—he finally induced the Polish king to renounce his suzerainty over East Prussia in return for the military support of Brandenburg-Prussia. The treaty of Oliva (1660), which concluded the war, confirmed the agreement, and Frederick William was thenceforth the independent sovereign of East Prussia. It was an achievement of far-reaching historical significance.

To enable his people to bear the cost of his large army, the Great Elector worked assiduously to promote the material prosperity of his domains. He sought to protect native industries by a high tariff and to encourage their expansion by subsidies and monopolies. As aids to internal trade and communication he constructed roads, established a system of mails, and built the Friedrich Wilhelm canal connecting the Oder with the Spree. Agriculture was fostered by the draining of marshes and the reclaiming of waste lands. To attract colonists to sparsely populated Prussia Frederick William offered free land, religious freedom, exemption from taxes for a given period, and financial assistance. In response, large numbers of settlers came from Holland, Silesia, Austria, and Poland. When Louis XIV revoked the Edict of Nantes in 1685, Frederick William, himself a Calvinist, offered special welcome to the persecuted Huguenots of France. These brought with them new skill and industries which gave Brandenburg-Prussia increased economic strength. In short, the Great Elector cultivated the resources of his territories with such success that the people prospered despite heavy taxes. But he did nothing to raise the peasantry from their low position.

While he was fostering agriculture, industry, and commerce, Frederick William was also engaged in centralizing the government and in making his power absolute. Hitherto self-government had prevailed in the widely scattered territories over which he ruled. Each province not only had its own administration but was opposed to any move which would deprive it of its separate constitution. Hence the centralization was achieved only after a considerable struggle with the proponents of separatism. The Great Elector's share in this work, which was not completed until the reign of Frederick the Great, was to lay the framework around which Prussian bureaucracy was built. Using force unhesitatingly where cunning and milder measures proved ineffectual, he went far toward supplanting the various decentralized agencies of government by a central administration. As a result the territories of

Brandenburg-Prussia were well on their way to becoming a united and powerful state when the Great Elector died in 1688.

Frederick III, son and successor of the Great Elector, lacked the statesmanship, the talent for rigid economy, and the tireless energy which had characterized his father. Physically deformed and of delicate health, he devoted much of his time to etiquette in an effort to rival the pomp and splendor of the court of Louis XIV. Meanwhile the government was entrusted to ministers who were not always distinguished for their scruples. Hence the reign of Frederick III shows a retrogression in certain respects. Nevertheless, Frederick made one major contribution to the rise of the Hohenzollern: he gained prestige for his house by obtaining the title of king. With his love of titles and pomp, Frederick had long desired to assume the royal dignity. Since he was a vassal of the emperor, however, he could not do so without the latter's permission. His opportunity came in 1700, just before the War of the Spanish Succession, when Emperor Leopold I found himself in need of military support and asked Frederick III for aid. The elector offered it, but at the price of the kingship. As no other help was to be had, the emperor was obliged to consent, and in 1701 Elector Frederick III became King Frederick I. According to a stipulation made by the emperor the title was not to apply to the territories within the empire, but only to the duchy of East Prussia. Moreover, to save the feelings of Poland, which still held West Prussia, the title read "Frederick I, king in Prussia." Later, when Frederick the Great added West Prussia to his domains, the title was changed to "king of Prussia."

The next ruler, Frederick William I, who became king in 1713, was one of the most eccentric monarchs who ever occupied a throne. He was a man of unattractive personality, coarse, choleric, despotic, and frugal to the point of miserliness. Having little feeling for the finer things of life, he regarded such pursuits as philosophy and literature with supreme contempt. So limited was his appreciation that beyond the affairs of state, particularly military affairs, he found little pleasure in anything but beer, tobacco, and coarse humor. Thoroughly despotic, he would fly into high dudgeon at the least opposition. As he saw it, there was only one side to a question, and that was his own. Nevertheless, Prussia made great progress under his rule. Believing that he reigned by divine right, Frederick William sought above all else to perform well the work with which God had entrusted him. He was a veritable dynamo, endeavoring to do everything, to supervise everything. "Salvation," he wrote, "is of the Lord, but everything else is my affair." Indolence he thought one of the worst of sins, and he would personally cane idlers, whether of high or low estate, when he came upon them. His achievements as king made possible the successes of Frederick the Great.

Building on the foundations laid by the Great Elector, Frederick William I continued the work of centralizing the Prussian state. In place of the former administrative colleges, he established soon after his accession the General Directory, a supreme board to which all provincial authorities were subordinated. He also did much to encourage the development of commerce and industry in Prussia by measures that were typically mercantilist, such as high import duties on foreign goods, the prohibition of the export of raw materials, and the establishment of new industries for the purpose of rendering Prussia independent of foreign manufactures. He further filled the royal treasury by strict economy in most matters, and by exploiting every possible source of revenue. But the central focus of all his efforts was the creation of a large army. Everything else was subsidiary to this object. Though he was frugal to the point of miserliness, no expenditure for military purposes was too great. The army at his accession numbered 38,000 men; by the time of his death he had raised it to 83,000, making Prussia, which was thirteenth among the European states in population, fourth in the size of its military forces. To supply the necessary recruits, voluntary enlistment was replaced by a system of universal liability to military service, with liberal exemptions. Under the new arrangement the country was divided into military cantons, each of which was required to furnish recruits for a certain regiment—a method which continued to be the basis of the Prussian military system until 1806. So stern a training was imposed that the Prussian troops became the best-drilled and best-disciplined in Europe. Hence it might be stated with ample justification that Frederick William, the "Royal Drill Sergeant," was the father of the so-called Prussian militarism.

In developing the Prussian army Frederick William I displayed a mania for tall soldiers. Agents were sent to all parts of the western world to collect tall men for the Potsdam Regiment of Giants. At the time of the king's death this regiment numbered

2500 grenadiers, many of them over seven feet tall. Yet, zealous as he was in building up his army, Frederick William made little use of it for conquest or aggrandizement. At times he would threaten, and even wave the sword wildly, but whenever war was in the offing he would become a pacifist. He could not, it seems, bring himself to sacrifice the lives of his beloved soldiers. His son, Frederick the Great, however, went far with this highly trained force, amply provided with "the sinews of war" by the systematic and rigorous economies of his father.

Few princes have spent a childhood and youth more unfortunate than that of Frederick II, better known as Frederick the Great, who had inclinations entirely dissimilar from those of his father. Very early young Frederick developed a decided taste for literature, art, music, and philosophy. The French tutor to whom his education was confided instilled in him a definite predilection for the French language and literature. Voltaire, the dominant French literary figure of the eighteenth century, was the hero of this Prussian crown prince in youth and later one of his principal correspondents and intimates. In the hope that he might become a second Voltaire, young Frederick began at an early age to write French verses. The things which his father regarded as natural manly pleasures—smoking coarse tobacco, consuming great quantities of beer, and slaying innumerable stags and boars in the chase—the son detested. He also abhorred military drills and military affairs in general, and often called his uniform a shroud. To the king the intellectual interests of his son were indubitable signs of effeminacy. The thought that Frederick with his interest in literature and music and his loathing for military affairs might one day ruin the Prussian state goaded Frederick William to fury. He decided that the future ruler of Prussia must be brought to his senses, and therefore missed no opportunity to reproach and taunt him with his "effeminate habits." If he found his son playing the flute or reading French books, the king would break the flute or burn the books, driving home such advice as he might give by a sound caning. On occasion young Frederick was even caned in the presence of the army.

The tyranny of his father gradually became so intolerable that Frederick decided to escape from the country. His companion in the flight was to be a young officer, Lieutenant von Katte, who for some years had been his bosom friend. But the plans of the two young men were disclosed to the king before they could be executed. In a paroxysm of rage, Frederick William ordered both his son and Katte committed to prison. When a court-martial dealt leniently with Katte, the king ordered the sentence annulled and condemned his son's companion to death. Worse than that, the sentence of decapitation was carried out in front of the prison window behind which Frederick was confined, and he was compelled to witness it. Not until he promised to obey his father in everything was he released. Then he was made clerk in the Chamber of War and Domains, so that he might familiarize himself with the administrative affairs of the kingdom. Simulating submission to the paternal will in order to avoid further clashes, Frederick soon became genuinely interested in the Prussian system of administration and in the Prussian military system, gaining knowledge which was to be invaluable to him later. Thenceforth relations between father and son grew so satisfactory that the father is reported to have said shortly before he died in 1740: "O my God, I die content, since I have so worthy a son and successor."

THE WARS OF FREDERICK THE GREAT

Frederick William's harsh methods bore fruit at the price of hardening and souring his son's gentle nature. No sooner did Frederick become king than he, too, began to burn the fires of war. By the time his reign was half over he had made his small state one of the great military powers of Europe and had proved himself one of the great military commanders of history. Some of his first measures were for the purpose of strengthening the Prussian army. He dismissed the useless regiment of giants, added more than ten thousand men to his forces, and increased his stock of war munitions. Having a well-filled treasury and an army ready to act, Frederick felt that he must put both to some use. He did not wait long for the decisive event. Only five months after he became king the Habsburg emperor, Charles VI, died. For many years Charles, who had no son, had striven to insure to his daughter Maria Theresa the succession to his hereditary domains. He had managed to obtain the signatures of all the states of Europe except Bavaria to a document called the Pragmatic Sanction, guaranteeing her succession to the Habsburg claims. Few, however, intended to keep their pledge. His old marshal, Prince Eugene of Savoy, had repeatedly endeavored to impress upon the emperor that a strong army and a full treasury would be the best insurance for the inviolability of his daughter's inheritance, and events proved the correctness of his view. Hardly had the funeral bells ceased tolling for Charles VI when the claims of the various states became articulate.

Frederick was the first claimant to strike out boldly. The Hohenzollern had long advanced claims to Silesia and the Habsburgs had, of course, rejected them as unjustified. Now Frederick saw the way open for the conquest of this coveted province. "All is provided for, all is in readiness," he wrote soon after the death of Charles VI; "consequently it remains only to put into execution plans which I have long had in mind." Figuratively tearing up the Pragmatic Sanction, the young Prussian king marched into Silesia in the dead of winter, without a declaration of war and before anyone was aware of his object. Much has been written either to defend Frederick's seizure of Silesia or to show that he had no right whatsoever to it. The Prussian king probably did not concern himself seriously with the question of right or wrong; at no time did he permit any scruples to interfere with his ambition. In his *Memoirs* he states that he was impelled to invade Silesia by a desire for glory and the wish to strengthen his state. To his friend Jordan he wrote shortly before his march into Silesia: "The satisfaction of seeing my name in the gazettes and, later, in history has seduced me. But for this cursed desire for glory, I assure you I should think only of my ease. What are fatigue, illness, and dangers in comparison with glory?"

Maria Theresa was wholly unprepared for the action. Frederick himself depicted her situation in the following words: "The court of Vienna was, after the death of the emperor, in an untoward situation. The finances were in disorder, the army broken up and disheartened by the ill success of the war with Turkey, the ministers were at variance with one another, and the throne was occupied by a young and inexperienced princess who had to defend a disputed succession." The few Austrian troops that were quartered in Silesia were soon routed, and most of the duchy was in Frederick's possession before the Austrian queen could do much for its defense. Thus Frederick added to Prussia nearly fourteen thousand square miles of territory and nearly a million and a half subjects. Silesia had been easy to seize, but it was difficult to

hold. Before Frederick gained undisputed possession of it he had
to fight two long wars and pay with the blood of his subjects for
every foot of Silesian ground.

Frederick's invasion was the first move in what was destined
to be the long and bloody War of the Austrian Succession (1741–
1748). France, Spain, Bavaria, Sweden, and Saxony soon joined
in the project of dismembering Austria. Great Britain, which had
important interests in Germany since its king was elector of Hanover, supported Austria. Colonial jealousy of France was also a
factor in Britain's decision. Thus the war had two main issues:
the destiny of Prussia, and the question of colonial supremacy.
Frederick, having achieved his object of seizing Silesia and not
wishing to crush Austria, withdrew from the war in 1742. But
when the subjects of Maria Theresa rallied about her and the
armies of Austria were successful against France, he began to
fear that Austria might try to regain Silesia after having defeated
France. Consequently he reëntered the struggle but, after winning a series of victories, again deserted his allies in 1745. Since
all parties were weary and exhausted, the peace of Aix-la-Chapelle
was finally concluded in 1748. It recognized Maria Theresa as
the ruler of the Habsburg dominions and confirmed Frederick in
the possession of Upper and Lower Silesia, but restored all other
conquests.

Satisfactory to neither Austria nor France, the treaty proved
to be but a truce. Maria Theresa could not reconcile herself to
the loss of Silesia. It is said that she shed tears whenever the name
of her lost province was mentioned. In France the treaty was exceedingly unpopular because it had given the French nothing for
their part in the war. The question of maritime and colonial supremacy also remained unsettled. Everything presaged another
war. It did not break out, however, for eight years. In the meantime all countries actively closed new alliances. So radical were
the realignments that they are summed up in the name "Diplomatic Revolution." Austria and France buried their age-long
enmity and concluded an alliance against Frederick; in this agreement they were also joined by Russia, Sweden, Saxony, and a
number of German states. Only England supported Frederick,
because of her colonial rivalry with France. Without England as
his ally to aid him with subsidies and to launch campaigns against
France in Asia and America, Frederick must have failed. As it

was, the coalition against him was so certain of victory that it had already begun to make a division of the Prussian territories. Of his possessions, Frederick was to be permitted to retain only Brandenburg, the cradle of Hohenzollern power.

In India (1751) and North America (1754) the war between the French and the English broke out before the Diplomatic Revolution was completed. In Europe the so-called Seven Years' War began when Frederick, unwilling to wait until his opponents were ready, unsheathed the sword by overrunning Saxony in 1756. The history of the conflict is too replete with incidents to be related here in any detail. After occupying Saxony the king of Prussia invaded Bohemia, but was forced to retire. In the next year (1757) he turned about and by the generalship which has earned for him the title of "the Great" won a series of brilliant victories. His first and probably most famous success was at Rossbach, not far from Leipzig. In a struggle that lasted less than two hours Frederick defeated a French and Austrian force almost three times the size of his own, capturing 16,000 prisoners. In the same year he also won a notable battle with the Austrians at Leuthen. Napoleon Bonaparte said of this victory: "It was a masterpiece in the way of evolutions, maneuvers, and determination, and would alone have sufficed to make Frederick immortal, and to rank him among the greatest generals."

Gradually, however, the odds threatened to overwhelm him. In 1759 he suffered a crushing defeat at the hands of the Austrians and Russians at Kunersdorf; only a fraction of the Prussian army survived. It was but the first of a series of disasters. Time and again Frederick rallied, but as the war continued his fortunes sank lower and lower. The heavy losses his army suffered began to exhaust the man power of Prussia; likewise his economic resources were drying up. Finally even England discontinued its subsidy. Repeatedly Frederick uttered words such as the following: "Every misfortune has befallen me! What is going to become of us next year? What will become of my people? What will happen to my army? I see no way of escape open to me; yet I shall do everything I can. We must conquer or perish." There were times when he was so depressed that he wished for death in battle or was at the point of ending his life with the box of poison he perpetually carried with him. Only the hope that some stroke of fortune would turn the tide in his favor impelled him to go on.

He did not hope in vain. The death of the Tsarina Elizabeth in 1762 changed the whole situation. Peter III, who succeeded her to the Russian throne, not only made peace with Prussia but also sent some of his troops to aid the Prussian ruler. Frederick could now write: "Heaven still stands by us and everything will turn out well." Thenceforth he managed to hold his own until his enemies were ready to make peace. The treaty signed at Hubertusburg in February, 1763, restored matters in Europe as they had been before the war. Frederick retained Silesia, but was forced to relinquish Saxony. The war between Great Britain, on the one side, and France and Spain, on the other, was terminated by the treaty of Paris, which established Great Britain as the dominant power in America and in India.[1]

The Seven Years' War was the last real war of Frederick's reign. Though he gained no new territory as a result of it, he did increase the prestige of Prussia immeasurably, winning for it the right to be considered the equal of France, Austria, and Spain in the councils of Europe. In 1772, together with Catherine II of Russia and Maria Theresa of Austria, Frederick partially dismembered Poland, receiving as his share the territory of West Prussia which filled the gap between Brandenburg and East Prussia. This addition not only increased the size of the Prussian state but also made it territorially more compact. That the seizure of Polish territory was an act of brigandage Frederick would have been the last to deny. In fact, he put the following question to D'Alembert: "Catherine and I are two brigands; but that pious Empress-Queen, how does she settle it with her confessor?" Yet few of his contemporaries denounced the division of Poland. Many even applauded it, regarding Poland as a center of political strife, religious bigotry, and aristocratic tyranny. Of the three partitions of Poland, only the first was made during Frederick's lifetime. The others took place during the reign of his successor.[2]

FREDERICK THE ENLIGHTENED DESPOT

As a ruler Frederick was representative of a certain group of statesmen who were called "enlightened despots" because they came more or less under the influence of ideas espoused by the French *philosophes*, particularly by Voltaire, Rousseau, Montes-

[1] See p. 598.   [2] See pp. 542–545.

quieu, Diderot, and D'Alembert.[1] The philosophes gave new vigor to the spirit of reform by assailing in their writings certain social evils and administrative abuses that were prevalent in the eighteenth century. They demanded efficiency of administration, religious toleration, abolition of privilege, freedom of discussion, and equality of all before the law. These demands were so tremendous, however, that they could be achieved only by an autocratic monarch. He alone could raze the citadels of abuse, privilege, and prejudice. Hence the philosophes turned to certain despots of the time—notably Frederick the Great, Catherine II, Joseph II, Pombal of Portugal, and Leopold of Tuscany—as the most likely instruments for realizing their ideals. To win the support of these rulers was relatively easy compared with the task of enlightening a whole nation, particularly when the former had already read their books and even offered them pensions. Though the results of this alliance between the philosophes and the philosophic despots were substantial it was not in the power of the despots to translate all the precepts of the philosophes into practice. Furthermore, some of the despots did not really desire to introduce certain of the reforms, fearing to jeopardize their rules.

Frederick the Great was one of the most eminent of the enlightened despots. His principle of government as he repeatedly stated it was: "The people are not here for the sake of the rulers, but the rulers for the sake of the people." To Voltaire, his spiritual father, he wrote: "My chief occupation is to fight the ignorance and the prejudices in this country. . . . I must enlighten my people, cultivate their manners and morals, and make them as happy as human beings can be; as happy as the means at my disposal permit me to make them." Yet it is easy to overstate the influence of the philosophes upon Frederick the king. Before their writings appeared he had already inaugurated a number of his reforms, and later he tried to carry out only those which fitted into his scheme of government. In the end Frederick's success as a ruler was due not so much to the influence of Voltaire and his associates as to his own political sagacity.

During the twenty-three years of his reign which followed the Seven Years' War Frederick devoted himself to giving Prussia the best possible administration. He worked hard at the business of being king, endeavoring to personify the maxim that "the king

[1] For a discussion of the philosophes see pp. 632–644.

is the first servant of the state." Rising at four in the summer and five in the winter, he labored long and strenuously at his desk. "You are right," he wrote to his friend Jordan, "in supposing that I work hard; I do so in order to live, for nothing has more resemblance to death than idleness." His government was not "of the people and by the people," but "everything for the people, nothing by the people." All the powers of the government were concentrated in himself. He personally read the plethora of letters, reports, complaints, and appeals sent in by his officials and subjects. As far as possible, he watched over every official, punishing any act of disobedience or negligence with Draconian severity. "In a state such as Prussia," he wrote, "it is absolutely necessary for the king to attend to his own affairs." Even the highest officials were but his clerks. This system worked well while Frederick ruled, but when his guiding genius was removed the Prussian administration soon lost its efficiency.

Frederick's policies for the improvement of commerce and industry were essentially those of his predecessors and remained within the lines of mercantilism. "The basic rule to follow in connection with all trade and manufacture," he wrote, "is to prevent money from flowing permanently out of the country. . . . The exodus of money can best be prevented by producing in Prussia all kinds of goods which were formerly imported." To achieve this end he levied prohibitive duties on foreign imports, established new industries, and drew up a series of regulations for both trade and industry. Not all of his projects were successful, however. For example, since the people did not relish the high duty he put on coffee in the hope that they would use beer-soup instead, smuggling became widespread, with the result that Frederick found it necessary to make a considerable reduction in the duty. Nevertheless, it may be said that, on the whole, industry flourished during his reign.

Frederick also gave much attention to the rehabilitation of agriculture after the Seven Years' War. He distributed seeds to the peasants who had suffered from hostile invasions, gave them cattle to restock their holdings and horses to plow their fields, rebuilt many houses and barns with funds from the state treasury, and temporarily reduced the taxes of those who had suffered most severely. Following the example of his predecessors, he invited colonists from other countries to settle in Prussia. The number of those who responded to his invitations has been estimated as high as 300,000. But whatever benefits Frederick's policies conferred on his subjects were counterbalanced in large part by the heavy taxes necessary for the upkeep of the army, which toward the end of the reign numbered almost 200,000 men. Moreover, Frederick, who prided himself on his enlightenment, did nothing to free the peasants from the bonds of serfdom. He considered the problem early in his reign, but the only result was a decree which stated that peasants living on the crown lands were to render not more than four days of statute service each week. The labor of the serfs who lived on the lands of the nobility remained virtually unlimited.

The most notable features of Frederick's reign were his reorganization of the administration of justice and his policy of religious toleration. In remodeling the judicial system Frederick abolished the use of torture except in special instances, made provisions for the disbarment of incompetent or dishonest lawyers, established uniform legal fees throughout his kingdom, and expedited the settling of lawsuits by decreeing that all cases must be cleared from the docket within a year. In short, he established a lawful administration of justice for his subjects. In religious affairs he was the most tolerant ruler in Europe. "All religions shall be tolerated in my states," Frederick said; "here everyone may seek salvation in his own way." Throughout his long reign he never deviated from that principle. When the pope suppressed the Jesuits, Frederick refused to allow the bull to be published in Prussia, thus opening the country as a refuge to the members of the order after they had been driven out of such Catholic countries as Portugal, Spain, and France.[1] Religious fanaticism, however, he repressed severely. "Whoever destroys fanaticism," he stated, "dries up the most pernicious source of feuds and enmities." He also granted his subjects considerable freedom of speech and freedom of the press. "Newspapers must not be interfered with if they are to be interesting," he said. Nevertheless, the freedom of speech and the freedom of the press were definitely circumscribed, as Voltaire discovered on his visit to Potsdam. "Pray do not tell

[1] The basic motive of Frederick's refusal to suppress the Jesuit order was probably the fact that the Jesuits were useful to the state as educators. Since so much was being spent on the upkeep of the army, Frederick could not afford to hire teachers to replace the Jesuits.

me," Lessing stated, "about your Berlin liberty of thought and writing; it merely consists in the liberty of circulating as many witticisms as you like against religion."

That Frederick's tolerance had definite limits is shown by his treatment of the Jews. Though they were granted religious freedom, they were denied most of the civil liberties. By an edict issued in 1750 Frederick restricted their rights and activities still further than they had been restricted by his father in 1730. Thereafter foreign Jews were barred from settling in Prussia, except on the payment of an exorbitant sum. Prussian Jews were excluded from all civil functions and forbidden to practice most trades, nor could they enter the professions or engage in agriculture. Limits were also set to their activities in commerce. "The more the Jews are excluded from commerce, the better it will be," the king stated. On the other hand, to further his mercantilist aims he encouraged wealthy Jews to invest their money in industry. He even went so far as to pay them subsidies, particularly for the manufacture of silk and other cloths. On every hand the Jews were heavily taxed. Besides paying the crown for their personal protection, they were burdened with other heavy taxes—for example those for marriages and for the election of elders in their community. In 1769 it was enacted that every Jew on the marriage of his son must buy from the royal manufacturies, for export, porcelain to the value of 300 Reichstaler. Where a poor Jew, to whom most of the avenues of economic income were closed, was to get so large a sum, Frederick did not stipulate.

As regards education Frederick was scarcely as philosophic in practice as in theory and conversation. "The education of youth," he stated, "must be considered as one of the principal objects of a government; it has an influence on everything." To D'Alembert he wrote: "The more one advances in age, the more one is convinced of the harm done to society by the neglected education of youth." Nevertheless, under him no essential changes took place in the Prussian system of education. Such improvements as he made were few and unimportant. His schoolmasters were most often handicraftsmen or invalid soldiers who thus earned their pensions. So little of the revenue was allocated for public instruction that professors at Halle, the most important of the Prussian universities, were barely able to live. In the words of one, they "worked like donkeys, but were fed like canaries." Frederick did, however, restore to vigorous life the Berlin Academy of Science, which during the reign of his father had fallen into contempt.

During the many years he was king, Frederick devoted his spare moments to philosophical studies, to correspondence with the philosophes, and to the writing of his numerous works, which fill thirty volumes. One of his principal recreations was listening to music or playing the flute, on which he was an accomplished performer. Often he would spend his evenings with the group of literary men he gathered about him. Discussions of literary and religious matters were free and lively. But as Frederick grew older he became more autocratic, even in discussions with his intimates, heaping bitter sarcasm on those who dared to contradict him. Like Voltaire, he was a deist, not an atheist. "Atheism," he wrote to his sister, "is a dogma to which one can adhere only when one's brain has become addled." As to the nature of God, Frederick said: "The finite cannot comprehend the infinite; consequently we are not capable of forming any precise idea of the Deity."

Frederick was of medium height and well proportioned. He had light brown hair and a rather long nose. His sparkling eyes were an index to his ever active mind. He was a capital horseman and generally appeared in public on horseback. After the War of the Austrian Succession he became as indifferent about his appearance as he had been meticulous before. He seldom shaved or washed even his hands and face. Usually he wore a uniform that was threadbare and spotted by snuff, which he used in prodigious quantities, or soiled by the paws of the greyhounds he had always about him. He lived simply, one of his principal extravagances being snuffboxes. When he died he left one hundred thirty, some of them richly ornamented with diamonds. Women he regarded as being "either vain or coquettes." Though he married Elizabeth of Brunswick-Bevern in 1732 to placate his father, he left her as soon as his father died. Thereafter he eschewed the company of women whenever he could.

When Frederick the Great died in 1786 after a reign of forty-six years, he left Prussia vastly larger in size and with a population that had increased from a little over two millions at the time of his accession to more than four millions. In everything he did his first and last concern was the state of Prussia. The interests of Germany as a whole found no place in his thoughts or plans. In his cultural tastes he was strongly prejudiced in favor of the

French. He read French works almost exclusively, spoke and wrote chiefly in French, and associated by preference with French men of learning. When he reorganized the Berlin Academy of Sciences which his grandfather had founded, he chose as its president the French scientist Maupertuis. By his express orders all papers read before it were to be written in French, for he considered the language of his countrymen as "diffuse, unmanageable, and lacking in grace." His knowledge of German literature was meager, and his interest in it negligible. As late as 1780, despite the fact that Lessing, Klopstock, Herder, Kant, and Goethe had produced immortal works, Frederick wrote to D'Alembert: "We have no good writers whatever." Goethe's *Goetz von Berlichingen* he styled a "detestable imitation" of the "abominable plays of Shakespeare," "those ridiculous farces which are fit only for the savages of Canada." Yet Frederick stirred the thought and imagination of the German people as no other German ruler since Frederick Barbarossa. His deeds inspired German writers, and Frederick himself was celebrated in song and story as a national hero.

THE REFORMS OF JOSEPH II

Though Frederick set the example for other "enlightened despots," Joseph II is the ruler who best represents this spirit. On the death of his father, Francis I, in 1765, Joseph became emperor of the moribund Holy Roman Empire and also co-regent with his mother in Austria. As emperor he had but little power, and in Austria the final authority remained in the hands of his mother, whose ideas of monarchical rule differed basically from his own. Maria Theresa stood for the old feudal and provincial system of government while her son wished to sweep away this medieval system and establish a new state which would embody the ideas he had culled from the writings of the philosophes. As soon as the death of Maria Theresa in 1780 gave him a free hand, Joseph released a veritable deluge of reforms. "I have made Philosophy the lawmaker of my empire," he wrote; "her logical applications are going to transform Austria." Edict followed edict until at the end of ten years there were six thousand decrees and more than eleven thousand new laws. The keynote of his political reforms was his desire to centralize the administration of his varied provinces. This necessitated the suppression of the old feudal governments and the creation of new administrative districts called circles—a system which was in essence that of pre-Revolutionary France—with an intendant as the administrator of each circle. Furthermore, in an effort to achieve unity of language, Joseph decreed that German was to be the official language of his state, which included such diverse nationalities as the Magyars, the Czechs, the Poles, and the Croats. German was also made com-. pulsory in all schools. Even in the universities all lectures and examinations, except those in theology, were to be given in German.

His economic and social reforms centered largely around the ideal of securing the equality, welfare, and happiness of his subjects. He issued a new penal code which put an end to much that was barbarous in the judicial systems of his provinces. It abolished the death penalty and the most brutal forms of punishment. "A death sentence," Joseph wrote, "has never the same effect as a lasting heavy punishment carries with it; for the first is quickly over and forgotten, but the other is long before the public eye." In extreme cases the criminals were to be sent to the galleys. All criminals, whether noblemen or peasants, were to be regarded as equal before the law and to receive the same punishments. "I owe justice to all without respect of persons," Joseph said. Marriage between Christians and non-Christians, witchcraft, and apostasy were removed from the list of crimes.

Two of the most enlightened of Joseph's reforms were the abolition of serfdom in 1781 and the edict of toleration issued in the same year. The former piece of legislation freed the peasants from the soil and gave them the right to own land, to marry whom they pleased, and to change their domiciles at will. All freedmen were put under the protection of the state and could no longer be fined or punished by the landowners. The edict of toleration granted the rights of citizenship and the free exercise of their religion to Protestants and to the members of the Greek Orthodox Church. Previously Roman Catholicism had been the official religion. It was in accordance with Joseph's principle that "prejudice, fanaticism, bondage of mind must disappear, and each of my subjects must be reinstated in the possession of his natural rights." Likewise most of the disabilities of the Jews were removed. Under Maria Theresa, who was equally opposed to Jews and Protestants, Jewish subjects seem to have been almost without civil rights, for they were forbidden to own real estate, to hold office, or to practice crafts. Joseph not only granted them toleration but also abolished the requirement that they wear yellow patches as distinguishing marks; he repealed the so-called body tax levied on all Jews, granted them full commercial and industrial freedom, gave them the right to practice all the arts and crafts, and opened all schools to the children of Jewish parents. Since the Jewish subjects were given the rights of citizenship, they were required, like all other subjects, to serve in the army. It is probably the first instance in history of compulsory service by Jews in a Christian army. Curiously enough, the orthodox Jews opposed Joseph's reforms, fearing that attendance at secular schools and serving in the army would undermine the orthodoxy of their children.

Joseph's ecclesiastical reforms were chiefly concerned with the nationalization of the Roman Catholic Church and its subordination to the state. In many respects his program paralleled the Gallicanism of the French kings. One step toward the establishment of an Austrian national church which would be controlled by the ruler of Austria rather than by the pope was the decree which stated that no papal bulls or regulations were to be published in Austria without the express permission of the government. All bishops were required at their installation to take an oath of obedience and loyalty to the government, marriage was made a purely civil contract, and education was freed from the control of the Church. Even the education of priests was put under state supervision. As Joseph thought the number of monasteries in his dominions excessive, he closed many. Of the 2163 monasteries in the Austrian lands more than seven hundred were dissolved and the number of monks and nuns was reduced from 65,000 to 27,000. The wealth confiscated from the monasteries was used to found hospitals, schools, and charitable institutions. Being himself a Catholic in a broader sense of the word, Joseph did not attack the basic doctrines of the Roman Catholic Church, though he did try to simplify its faith by purging it of pilgrimages, religious processions, the use of relics, and other practices that he regarded as superstitious. All the ecclesiastical reforms except the abolition of "superstitious practices" created little disturbance among the people; they excited the violent opposition of the pope, however, particularly since they attacked his authority. Pius VI even journeyed to Vienna in the hope that he might change the emperor's mind. But the long journey was fruitless, for Joseph received the pope with a marked coldness and conceded nothing.

In the promulgation of his reforms Joseph was undoubtedly actuated by the welfare of his subjects. To make them happy he labored from early morning until far into the night. So great was his application to his work that he shortened his life by his excessive labors. "I shall not cease," he said, "to labor with what physical and moral strength I may possess to do that which the service and welfare of my fatherland require of me." He was, however, lacking in tact, patience, and knowledge of men. Convinced that his reforms were for the good of the people, he rode roughshod over their cherished traditions and ingrained prejudices, permitting nothing to stand in his way. He did not realize that changes must be introduced gradually. As Frederick the Great put it, he "always takes the second step before the first." Proceeding with feverish energy, he often alienated the loyalty of the very people he was trying to help. The changes came so fast that they were bewildering. Hence his subjects viewed even beneficial results with suspicion and in many places with hostility. In two of Joseph's possessions, the Austrian Netherlands (Belgium) and Hungary, revolts broke out.

In the Austrian Netherlands Joseph had introduced much the same reforms as in Austria. He had suppressed certain monasteries, introduced religious toleration, and then had proceeded to modernize the administration. The local provincial Estates were abolished, the old provincial divisions were wiped out, and the country was divided into nine circles each under an intendant. Accustomed as they were to self-government and to the feudal organization of their government, the Belgians resisted the changes, regarding them as violations of age-old rights. Finally leaders of the opposition incited the people to revolt. In January, 1790, representatives of the rebel provinces met in Brussels, drew up a scheme of federation, and proclaimed the independence of their country as the United States of Belgium.[1]

In Hungary, also, the reforms met with a determined opposition. The Hungarians were offended at Joseph's efforts to make German their official language and to reduce their country to the status of an Austrian province. The edict decreeing the abolition of serfdom provoked even greater resentment. Not only did the

---

[1] The establishment of an independent republic was followed by internal dissensions which enabled Emperor Leopold II to reëstablish the Austrian ascendancy before the end of 1790.

nobles, indignant over the reduction of their privileges, refuse to carry it out, but they incited a revolt of the very peasants Joseph was trying to aid. The uprising was so successful that in January, 1790, Joseph was forced to rescind most of his reform decrees.

The realization that most of his reforms were failures saddened Joseph's last days. He was stricken with a fever and died on February 20, 1790, in his forty-ninth year. His health had already been undermined by his titanic labors. The epitaph he wrote for himself reads: "Here lies a prince whose intentions were pure; but who had the misfortune to see all his plans miscarry." Yet his efforts bore fruit in many fields. He did suppress much that was obsolete in the government of Austria; he did establish a measure of tolerance; and, most important of all, he did set high ideals for those who came after him. It was later acknowledged that his work saved Austria from the revolution which had broken out in France the year before his death. His decree abolishing serfdom voiced the principles which were applied in France, and from that center spread throughout Europe. His brother, Leopold II, succeeded him.

LITERATURE AND MUSIC

The great figure in the intellectual life of Germany at the turn of the seventeenth century was Gottfried Wilhelm Leibnitz (1656–1716), who shares with Isaac Newton the honor of having invented the calculus. Leibnitz wrote on many subjects, but the circle of his readers was small, for he wrote in Latin though he advocated the use of German as the literary language.

Not only was Latin still the language of learned writings, but until almost the end of the seventeeth century it was also the exclusive language of the university classroom. In 1687 Christian Thomasius of Leipzig shocked staid professors by boldly announcing a course to be given in German. To most university teachers his proposal seemed preposterous. The myth was even circulated that Thomasius lectured in German because he knew no Latin. However, his example was followed by some of his colleagues and also by teachers in other schools; and by the end of the next century Latin lectures in the universities were the exception, at least in Protestant universities. Besides introducing German into the lecture-room, Thomasius published the first German monthly journal (*Monatsschrift*) in 1688 and thereby became, in a sense, the father of German journalism. He also excited no small indignation by writing philosophical works in German. One of his books was returned by the College of Censors with the notation that it was "impossible to pronounce judgment on a work treating of philosophical matters in the German tongue." In spite of such rebuffs the movement started by Thomasius in the seventeenth century slowly developed, and in the eighteenth century German displaced Latin as the language of learning.

German literature in the early eighteenth century was largely a poor imitation of French and English models. In the middle decades, however, a number of figures appeared on the scene to usher in Germany's most brilliant literary period. This epoch is characterized by such variety that no one convenient label can be applied to the whole. The elements of three types—classicism, romanticism, and realism—are present. Each dominated the scene for a time; at no time was any one the sole trend or entirely absent.

The period may be said to begin with Gotthold Ephraim Lessing (1729–1781). As a critic, Lessing cleared the way for the new era by his attacks on the prevailing practice of copying French models. As a writer, he developed a lucid and vigorous style which served as a model for those who came after him. Herder said of him: "Since Luther no one has understood our language so well, nor used it in so masterly a fashion." As a dramatist, he created the first great exemplars of German literature. *Minna von Barnhelm* (1767) gave to Germany its first masterpiece of comedy, a drama which had the peculiar merit of being concerned with the events and ideas of the time and which placed German men and women on the stage. Goethe said of it: "It was like a glittering meteor. It taught us to perceive a higher state of things, of which the weak literary productions of that time gave no idea." Lessing's best known drama is probably *Nathan the Wise* (1779), which sets forth his ideas of religious tolerance and brotherhood. It is based on the story of the three rings, taken from Boccaccio's *Decameron*. The three rings symbolize the three religions, Christianity, Judaism, and Mohammedanism. All three, Lessing would say, are equally good; none may claim to be the only true one. This play is the outstanding literary expression of the German Enlightenment.

The second important figure of the golden age of German literature is Johann Gottfried Herder (1744–1803). Mediocre as a poet, Herder surpassed all his contemporaries in the breadth, and most of them in the depth, of his interests. These included science, philosophy, ecclesiastical and secular history, art, poetry, drama, religion, criticism, ethnology, esthetic theory, education, literature and language. But, varied and numerous as his writings on these subjects are, not one of them can be styled a finished masterpiece. Even his chief work, *Ideas toward a Philosophy of the History of Humanity*, was never completed. Nevertheless, Herder's writings have a stimulating and suggestive quality which made him the greatest inspirational force in Germany during the second half of the eighteenth century. Therein lies his claim to greatness. The key to his life and ideas is to be found in his conception of national life as an organic growth. He portrayed the history of mankind in terms of a series of national organisms, each developing its characteristic society, language, religion, literature, and art; yet each by its own development enriching mankind as a whole. "Every nationality," he wrote, "bears in itself the standard of its perfection, totally independent of all comparison with that of others." Accordingly Herder exhorted the German people to cultivate their national characteristics and denounced imitation of the ancients or of other nationalities as fatal to genuine progress. As his accentuation of the spontaneous and the original was an important factor in the rise of the *Sturm und Drang* (Storm and Stress) movement in German literature, so his exaltation of the native and the national stamped him as the prophet and precursor of the Romantic movement. His collection of folk songs (1778–1779), gathered from all over the globe, aroused interest in folk songs generally and also opened the way for a comparative study of literatures. Apart from his writings, Herder earned for himself a place in the history of German literature through his influence on Goethe.

Johann Wolfgang Goethe (1749–1832) is not only the first figure in the history of German literature but also one of the great figures in the literature of all time. He is to German what Shakespeare is to English and Homer is to Greek literature. Because of his many-sided interests, Goethe has been styled "the last of the encyclopaedic thinkers." His writings deal with most subjects of contemporary interest and comprise 132 volumes in the standard Weimar edition. The period of his literary activity was long, covering the last quarter of the eighteenth century and the first three decades of the nineteenth. *Goetz von Berlichingen*, his first important work, appeared in 1773 and at once established his literary fame. It was truly German in that it was founded upon the story of a German robber-knight of the sixteenth century. The following year saw the appearance of *The Sorrows of Werther*, a sentimental romance about a morbidly introspective egoist who, unable to adjust himself to his environment, finally commits suicide. It was an expression of the general sentimentality of the Storm and Stress period in German literature. Despite much adverse criticism, it was translated into many languages and Goethe became famous over Europe. In 1787 he completed his poetic dramas, *Iphigenie in Tauris* and *Egmont*. The former, based on a story from Euripides, ranks among the best dramatic poems in world literature. The latter is an historical play on a phase of the revolt of the Netherlands against Spain. Goethe's most ambitious effort in fiction was his *Wilhelm Meister*, the first part of which was published in 1796 under the title *Wilhelm Meister's Apprenticeship* and the second in 1829 as *Wilhelm Meister's Wanderings*. Though this novel is replete with the wisdom of Goethe, its diffuseness repels modern readers.

Faust is Goethe's greatest drama. It is one of the few poetic works which possess immortal vitality, and as such must be classed with Shakespeare's *Hamlet*, Homer's *Iliad*, and Dante's *Divine Comedy*. Five centuries had passed since the appearance of the *Divine Comedy* in which Dante measured the height of Heaven and fathomed the depths of Hell. Now Goethe in his *Faust* presented to the world the "divine comedy" of human life, showing to what heights man may rise and to what depths he may fall. He began work on it as early as 1774, publishing the first part in 1808. Not until 1831 did he complete the second part, which, by his command, was not given to the public until after his death. The drama is based on the legend of Dr. Faustus that Marlowe had used as the plot for his drama. The learned Dr. Faustus, having acquired all possible knowledge, is still dissatisfied. His desire to penetrate to the very essence of things and to taste the ultimate of worldly pleasures impels him to request from Mephistopheles the necessary power to do so. Satan promises to fulfill his wishes on condition that he receive Faust's soul at the expiration of a stated time. After Faust attains to the profoundest secrets of nature and exhausts all forms of human enjoyment, Mephistopheles collects his due at the appointed hour. Many critics believe that Faust is Goethe himself. He is modern man as well—modern man in search of pleasure and of the answer to the riddle of the universe.

Like Heinrich Heine at a later time, Goethe is also famous for his exquisite lyrics, not a small number of which have become the common property of the world through translations. No poet except Shakespeare has inspired so many composers. Among those who have set his poems to music are Beethoven, Mozart, Schubert, Schumann, Mendelssohn, Brahms, and Tchaikowski. Richard Wagner wrote an overture to *Faust*, Liszt a *Faustsymphonie*, and Schumann a choral work on the subject of *Faust*. Poems which have each had more than fifty musical settings are *Erlkönig, Der König in Thule, Heidenröslein*, and *Kennst Du das Land*, while his *Wandrers Nachtlied* has had more than a hundred.

Though he ranks below Goethe in influence on succeeding generations and in literary achievement, the works of Johann Christoph Friedrich Schiller (1759–1805) were probably dearer to the German people. His poetry was simple and idealistic, seeking to inculcate such sentiments as love of the fatherland and of honor, freedom, justice, and truth. He died at the early age of forty-five, but during his short life accomplished much. His first drama, *The Robbers*, which belongs to the Storm and Stress period, has been styled the work of a "fermenting genius." When this drama appeared, it excited great enthusiasm not only in Germany but throughout Europe; soon it was translated into the principal European languages. Schiller's genuine dramatic power was first evinced in *Don Carlos*, an historical drama concerned with the unfortunate son of Philip II of Spain. In the writing of such plays Schiller stands preëminent. His *Wallenstein*, based on the last period of the life of the picturesque general of the Thirty Years' War, appeared in 1800. Choosing the subject for his next drama from Scottish history, he published *Maria Stuart* in 1801. This play deals with the imprisonment and death of Mary Queen of Scots in England. *The Maid of Orleans* appeared in the same year; in it Schiller defends the character of Jeanne d'Arc against the satire of Voltaire in *La Pucelle*. His last, and probably his greatest, drama was his *Wilhelm Tell*, which glorifies the struggle of the Swiss for their independence. Its romantic interest is concentrated in the figure of Tell, who shoots the apple from the head of his child and later sends an arrow through the tyrant Gessler.

In addition to its outstanding literary figures, Germany also produced in the eighteenth century a number of musicians of the highest rank. There were, of course, great composers in other countries, but their achievements pale beside those of such masters as Bach, Handel, Haydn, Mozart, and Beethoven. These great figures, though German by birth, were not nationalistic. Like the poets and dramatists of eighteenth century Germany they firmly believed in the brotherhood of man. Addressed to all mankind, their work has become the common property of all.

The first two composers were so preëminent that in the history of music the early part of the eighteenth century is known as the age of Bach and Handel. Both were born in the same year (1685), only a month apart, but the paths they traveled differed as widely as their natures. They had this in common, however: both were supreme as composers of music inspired by and consecrated to the service of religion. Johann Sebastian Bach was born into a family whose hereditary profession was music. Since the middle of the sixteenth century the Thuringian Bachs had become increasingly notable in that field. In fact, the number of musicians in the Bach family was so large that in some parts of Germany the word *Bach* became almost synonymous with *musician*. Most of the musical Bachs devoted themselves to sacred music, although the secular forms were by no means neglected. The family retained its musical preëminence through the Thirty Years' War, producing musicians who ranked among the greatest in Europe.

All the talents of the Bach family culminated in Johann Sebastian. One of the consummate geniuses of musical history, he is to be classed as a creator with Michelangelo, Shakespeare, and Goethe. His sphere of activity included all types of composition then customary except opera—fugues, cantatas, masses, concertos, sonatas, and passion music. Every great organist and pianist since his time has found inspiration in his clavichord and organ compositions. His orchestral suites and concertos constitute some of the most beautiful music of their type. His two Passions, the *Passion according to St. John* and the *Passion according to St. Matthew*, are regarded by many as the loftiest musical expression of the Protestant faith. The primary inspiration of all of Bach's compositions was religious, for he regarded music as a "harmonious euphony to the glory of God." His place in the development of the Protestant choral may be compared with that of Palestrina in the history of the Gregorian chant. During his lifetime but few of his works were published. His contemporaries considered him principally an accomplished organist and a brilliant improvisor. At his death in 1750 his manuscript works were divided among his sons, and it was not until early in the nineteenth century, largely through the efforts of Felix Mendelssohn, that the world began to gain a better knowledge of his compositions. Although much of his work had been irretrievably lost by that time, enough has been recovered to fill fifty-nine large volumes.

Whereas Bach remained in Germany all his life as a pious, hard-working citizen and the father of twenty children, George Frederick Handel (as he anglicized his name), a confirmed bachelor, traveled widely. After receiving his earlier musical education in Germany, he spent a number of years improving his knowledge in Italy. Finally he went to England, where he became a naturalized Englishman. There, over a period of about twenty-five years, he wrote and produced a series of operas which included the well-known compositions, the "Largo" from *Xerxes* and the "March" from *Scipio*. Toward the end of his life he composed the oratorios which are his greatest achievement. His masterpiece, *The Messiah*, is known wherever classical music is heard. Its simple melodic expressiveness, grandeur of style, and lofty power make it a work of surpassing beauty. Handel wrote this oratorio in the short period of twenty-four days during his visit to Dublin in 1741 and it was immediately performed there. While engaged upon it he became so inspired by his subject that when he came to the Hallelujah chorus it seemed as if "all Heaven and Earth were lying open to his gaze." Eight years before his death Handel lost his sight, but continued his work without complaint. In all he wrote forty-three operas, ninety-four cantatas, and twenty-one oratorios, besides innumerable anthems and much instrumental music. When he died in 1759, he was laid to rest in Westminster Abbey with appropriate ceremonies. Nine years earlier his great contemporary Bach had been hurriedly buried in an unknown grave.

Soon after the middle of the eighteenth century musical life flourished in Austria, particularly in Vienna, the musical capital of Europe. Among the musicians associated with the Vienna circle were Christoph Willibald Gluck (1714–1787), Franz Joseph Haydn (1732–1809), and Wolfgang Amadeus Mozart (1756–1791). Gluck, famous for his operas, was of German birth, but spent considerable time in Paris, becoming like Handel an international figure. He was for a time singing teacher to Marie Antoinette, and it was through her influence that he was able to produce his opera

Iphigenia in Aulis in Paris (1774). He also wrote two other important operas, *Armide* and *Iphigenia in Tauris*. While Gluck was working in the vocal field, Haydn, the first great instrumental composer since Bach, was composing orchestral and chamber music. Most of the symphonies for which he is famous were written during the thirty years when he was leader of Count Esterhazy's orchestra. He also brought the string quartet into prominence by writing more than eighty compositions for it. Besides his many instrumental works Haydn composed two oratorios, *The Creation* and *The Seasons*, which are widely known. He has a further claim to fame as the teacher of Mozart. "It was from Haydn," Mozart said, "that I first learned the true way to compose quartets." But the pupil was soon to outstrip his teacher.

Mozart was probably more highly gifted by nature than any other figure in musical history. Music was to him as natural a means of expression as language is to most human beings. His genius was universal. He excelled in every form of musical composition known to his time, including symphonies, quartets, and quintets; piano concertos, sonatas, and church music; tragic, romantic, and comic operas. A child-prodigy, he composed little pieces at the age of five, a clavier concerto at six, and an opera when he was twelve. He died at the early age of thirty-five after a life of poverty. In his short existence Mozart wrote a prodigious quantity of music, leaving more than six hundred compositions in all. It is interesting to speculate on what he might have achieved had he lived beyond his youth. Among his works his operas are outstanding. It has been said of them that they ushered in the modern operatic era. The greatest include *The Wedding of Figaro*, *Don Giovanni*, and *The Magic Flute*. When this matchless genius died in 1791 his body, like that of Bach, was buried in an unmarked grave.

The year after Mozart's death Ludwig von Beethoven (1770–1827) came into the musical atmosphere of Vienna prepared for him by Haydn, Gluck, and Mozart. Some years earlier, Mozart, hearing young Beethoven play, said: "Mark that young man; he will make a name for himself in the world." It was no idle prophecy, for today Beethoven's music is probably better known than that of any other great composer. Since he wrote slowly and frequently revised his compositions, he did not produce so much as some of his predecessors, but this fact has given greater importance, to his individual compositions. His personal life was in one respect tragic. Hardly had he become established in Vienna, artistically, economically, and socially, when his sense of hearing began to fail (1798). Thenceforth his deafness slowly increased until by 1814 it was total. His condition moved him to state: "I can say with truth that my life is wretched. . . . In any other profession this might be more tolerable, but in mine such a condition is truly frightful." Yet this personal tragedy may have increased his powers of composition. In shutting out the sounds of the outside world, his deafness impelled him to express his personal feelings in music. The result was a series of compositions in which the emotional, the tragic, and the dramatic attained a height of expression which has probably never been surpassed. Though he wrote some vocal music—one opera, two masses, one oratorio, and two cantatas—the major part of his writing consisted of instrumental compositions too varied to be listed here. Of particular importance are his eleven overtures, nine symphonies, and scores of sonatas. Beethoven not only stands at the head of the classical school of composers but he is also in a sense the father of the romantic school. His works contain the germs of many trends which Schubert, Mendelssohn, and Schumann later developed.

CHAPTER TWENTY

Catherine II, Russia, and Poland

CATHERINE AND PETER III

CATHERINE II, often called Catherine the Great, who for thirty-four years ruled Russia with an iron hand, was not a Russian, but a German. She was born in 1729 in the little German principality of Anhalt-Zerbst, of a lineage that was neither particularly ancient nor illustrious. Her father was Prince Christian of Anhalt-Zerbst, one of the scores of minor princes of the Germany of that time. In baptism she received the name Sophia Augusta Frederica, but was called Fieckchen (diminutive of Sophia) by her parents and friends. A normal, healthy, intelligent child, Fieckchen was educated after the manner of her age. As she later said, she was brought up "to marry one or the other of the neighboring princelings." The turning point in her life came when, at the age of fifteen, she was invited to become the wife of the heir to the Russian throne. The Empress Elizabeth of Russia, soon after she was raised to the throne, had summoned her nephew Peter, the only son of her sister Anna and of Charles Frederick, duke of Holstein-Gottorp, to Russia; then she nominated him grand duke and heir to the imperial throne. Wishing to insure the succession of the house of Romanov, for she was childless, Elizabeth decided to provide a wife for her nephew. After looking about for a likely candidate for some time, she consulted Frederick the Great. Frederick proposed Sophia of Anhalt, hoping to cement a closer friendship between Russia and Prussia by the marriage alliance. His proposal met with the approval of Elizabeth, and soon the little German girl was on her way to Moscow.

Upon arriving in Russia, Sophia played her new rôle with enthusiasm. She was not content to remain a foreigner, but decided to identify herself completely with the Russian people. With this intention foremost in her mind, she lost no time in applying herself to the task of mastering the Russian language and in exchanging her Lutheran faith for that of the Orthodox Church. On the occasion of her admittance into the Russian Church she put off her old name and became Catherine Alexeievna. Soon after this the Fieckchen of yesterday also became the Grand Duchess of Russia. Her husband, Peter of Holstein-Gottorp (afterwards Peter III), had the vices but not the good qualities of the Romanovs. Though of good stature, he was ugly in appearance because of his pock-marked face. As a child he had been in feeble health, and consequently his education had been neglected. His tastes remained so puerile throughout his life that even after marriage he continued to play with dolls and toy soldiers. From early youth his interests had centered in the affairs of the barracks, the parade ground, and the minutiae of military life. While acquiring a taste for soldiering he also contracted the boorish manners and low habits of the barracks.

At first Catherine tried to win her husband's love, but she was unsuccessful. Estrangement followed, giving rise to a mutual antipathy which grew stronger with the passing of the years. Peter, for his part, sought congenial company for his low pastimes, while Catherine spent much of her time in reading. She started with fashionable French romances, but soon put them aside for more serious works. After reading Plutarch and Tacitus she turned to Montesquieu, Voltaire, and the Encyclopedists. Thus Catherine, before she succumbed to the unbridled immorality that surrounded her, laid the foundations for a broad education. At a court which was, generally speaking, sunk in sloth and ignorance she was indeed an anomaly.

In December, 1761, Elizabeth died, freeing Peter from the galling restraint under which he had been held so far as matters of state were concerned. He could now order things to suit himself. But his reign was destined to be short. Though some of the measures he promulgated soon after his accession were beneficent, such as the abolition of the torture chamber and of corporal punishment for military officers, he was so wholly unfitted to rule Russia that the task overwhelmed him. He manifested the greatest contempt for his subjects, regarded himself as a stranger in Russia, and continued to find his greatest joy in drilling his regiment of Holsteiners. His deficiency in judgment and lack of tact soon lost him the support of the greater part of the Russian people, particularly of the army and the Church, the two chief supports of the Russian throne. In the army Peter's German sympathies excited bitter antagonism. His hero was Frederick the Great, of whom he publicly spoke as "the king, my master." The fact that Russia, since the beginning of the Seven Years' War, had been fighting against Frederick, at great cost of men and money, meant little to him. Immediately upon his accession Peter abandoned not only Russia's confederates but also its conquests, and sent a large part of the Russian army to aid Frederick. He even spoke of going to Prussia to offer Russia to Frederick as a vassal state. Beyond this he offended the army by introducing the Prussian discipline and uniform, and by giving to his Holstein regiment preference over the Russian troops.

Peter also scandalized the faithful both by his gross conduct and by his attitude toward the Church. Regarding himself a Lutheran, he neglected the rites of the Orthodox Church and on one occasion openly showed contempt for them. The act by which he completely forfeited the support of the Church was the seizure of its vast possessions. In a ukase published on this occasion he expressed a wish to free the clergy from the burden of worldly cares, so that they could apply their entire attention to the task of saving souls. Accordingly he decreed that the extensive estates of the Church should henceforth be managed by his officers, and that the clergy should receive an annual pension in accordance with their various positions. The surplus income was to be devoted to the founding of hospitals, the endowment of colleges, and the general purposes of the state. Finally, Peter's uncouth behavior toward Catherine antagonized many Russians. No sooner did he think himself firmly seated on the throne than his aversion to Catherine flared into open hostility. He missed no opportunity to hurl the grossest insults at her and to humiliate her in public. At times he went so far as to speak of divorcing her. His idol,

Frederick the Great, warned him a number of times, counseling him to respect the feelings of his people and to remain on good terms with his wife, but the warnings went unheeded.

While Peter was alienating the loyalty of his subjects, Catherine left nothing undone to win their favor. To achieve her purpose she did not hesitate to resort to dissimulation, in which art she later became a past mistress. Though she was now a skeptic through reading the works of the French philosophes, she meticulously observed the rites of the Orthodox Church, made frequent pilgrimages to the churches of St. Petersburg, and prayed in public with all the semblance of sincere devotion. She openly disapproved of Peter's Prussian militarism and also proclaimed against the presence of Peter's regiment of Holsteiners in Russia. Her words, uttered at propitious moments and addressed to select persons, were calculated to reach the ears of the Russian soldiers, who, overlooking her Germanic origin, hailed her as a true Russian patriot. Early in June, 1762, the English ambassador could write that Catherine "is loved and respected by all, even as the Tsar is detested." While Peter was turning over in his mind the idea of divorcing her, Catherine quietly formed a party devoted to her interests and worked assiduously to strengthen it. She had no intention of permitting herself to be immured in a convent for the rest of her life. The goal which she set for herself was nothing less than that of overthrowing the Tsar and making herself ruler of Russia.

The *coup d'état* was no sooner planned than it was carried out. At the head of the group engaged in the conspiracy against Peter were the two Orlov brothers, Alexei and Gregory. When Peter foolishly retired to Oranienbaum with his regiment of Holsteiners, these two young officers of the Guard precipitated the revolution on June 28, 1762, by boldly taking Catherine to St. Petersburg, where the troops proclaimed her empress and took the oath of allegiance to her. Peter, when advised of Catherine's coup, could not make up his mind to offer resistance. Always irresolute, always pusillanimous, he finally settled the question by humbly abdicating without conditions. By order of Catherine he was arrested and sent in the care of Alexei Orlov to the Ropsha estate. There he died four days later under mysterious circumstances. If Catherine did not plot her husband's death she did connive at it by trying to conceal it. Upon receiving news of it she dined in public with her usual tranquil air. Not until the following day did she announce the Tsar's demise in the words: "We have received the information to our great sorrow and affliction that it was God's will to end the life of the former Tsar Peter III by a severe attack of haemorrhoidal colic." At no time did she make an effort to punish the perpetrators of the deed.

CATHERINE THE ENLIGHTENED DESPOT

Despite the fact that two direct heirs to the throne were living, Catherine was now empress of Russia, sovereign of the largest and most unwieldy state in Europe. She reveled in the power of an autocrat and immediately took the management of state affairs into her own hands. To the task of ruling Russia she brought a number of good qualities. She possessed political cunning in a high degree, a certain firmness of purpose, and a sound judgment of men. Voltaire, in admiration of her qualities, spoke of her as "that great man whose name is Catherine." After the narrow despotic rule of her predecessors, her rule was comparatively lenient until the outbreak of the French Revolution. She was tolerant in religious matters even to the extent of permitting the suppressed Jesuits to come to Russia. In the administration of her government she chose men for their ability regardless of their nationality or persuasions, generously rewarding those who rendered her faithful service. Her private life was the scandal of Europe. During her reign she lavished upon her favorites, principally young officers of the Russian army, nearly one hundred million rubles. Of them all, however, only Potemkin attained to any ascendancy in state affairs.

As to her person, all writers are agreed that Catherine was possessed of considerable charm at the time of her accession to power. Her features were regular, though somewhat masculine; her expression was intelligent and her manner vivacious. "She has a good color," a contemporary Englishman wrote, "and nevertheless endeavors to improve it with rouge, after the manner of all the women of this country." Catherine herself, after enduring the fulsome flattery of her courtiers for a number of decades, said: "I have never fancied myself extremely beautiful, but I had the gift of pleasing and that, I think, was my greatest gift." In size she was "under the middle height" with a tendency to grow stout. Toward the end of her life she became so portly below the waist as to appear almost deformed. Her health was, on the whole, excellent despite the strain of her incessant activity, for Catherine worked hard at the task of ruling Russia. She usually arose at six, and after a quick breakfast would immediately turn to matters of state, often devoting twelve or more hours to them.

Catherine found time, however, to keep up a regular correspondence with a number of learned men of Europe, particularly with Voltaire and Diderot. In the tournament of sparkling wit and subtle repartee between these men and the empress of Russia, the latter not only showed herself their equal but often outdid them. With Voltaire she carried on a correspondence from 1763 until his death in 1778, discussing many of her projected reforms and receiving many suggestions. To her invitations to come to Russia, however, the philosopher of Ferney remained cold. But Diderot succumbed to her urging and journeyed to St. Petersburg. During his stay he engaged in daily discussions of politics, legislation, and philosophy with the empress. These discussions were so free of formalities that Diderot, carried away by his enthusiasm, is said to have hit Her Majesty on the knee occasionally with the back of his hand. When Diderot was in financial straits Catherine purchased his library on condition that he retain it until his death. She also gave him an annual pension for acting as her librarian, an act which won her great applause from the liberals of Europe. After the publication of the Encyclopedia she asked d'Alembert, Diderot's colleague, to become the tutor of her grandchildren, but he refused and Catherine turned to the Swiss La Harpe, a confessed republican.

As a disciple of the French philosophes Catherine derived much pleasure from contemplating their reform ideas. She delighted in their flattery, in being called "Minerva," "the Semiramis of the North," "a candlestick bearing the light of the world," and in being hailed by them as a liberal. At all times she set much store by what the literary world of France thought of her. But though she styled herself "one of the champions of liberty and equality," she could not quite bring herself to translate into practice the ideas she had culled from the works of the philosophes. All her liberal declarations were destined to remain mere phrases. During most of her reign she was at the point of introducing reforms, but always stopped short of their execution. A liberal in theory, she remained the autocrat in her government. When Diderot pointed out to her the paradox of her liberal ideas and her autocratic methods, she replied: "You philosophers are fortunate people. You write on patient paper, whereas I, poor empress, am forced to write on the sensitive skin of human beings." She believed that because of the backwardness of the Russian people and the vastness of her empire only an autocratic form of government could function properly.

She did, however, make one noteworthy gesture in the direction of reform. In 1766 she summoned to Moscow a legislative commission to draft a new code of Russian laws and to consider many questions regarding social reforms, including the condition of serfdom. The commission, composed of six hundred fifty deputies, represented all classes and nationalities of the Russian Empire except the serfs. For its guidance Catherine had drawn up *Instructions* based mainly on Montesquieu's *Spirit of Laws* and Beccaria's *Crimes and Punishments*. Copies of these *Instructions*, printed in four languages, Russian, French, German, and Latin, were scattered through Europe, exciting the admiration of the liberals and the disgust and anger of the conservatives. In the summer of 1767 the sessions of the commission were opened with great solemnity. For a year and a half the members continued their deliberations, and at the end of that time were sent home. The commission, Catherine said, had given her "valuable hints for all the empire," but very little came of the work besides a reorganization of local government.

The humanitarian tone of the *Instructions* notwithstanding, Catherine did nothing for the peasants who constituted nearly ninety-five per cent of the population; in fact, during her reign their lot became harder. More than half were serfs and as such their condition was on the whole worse than that of the serfs in western Europe during the Middle Ages. While the peasants who lived on the lands owned by the state enjoyed certain privileges, the serfs on the private estates were subject to landlords whose authority over them was practically absolute. A landlord could increase or decrease the holdings of his serfs at his pleasure, he could transfer them from the soil to domestic service or to work in the factories and mines, he could order or forbid their marriage, and he could sell them singly or in families, either with the land or without. He also exercised wide judicial powers over them. Though such major crimes as brigandage and murder were tried in the public courts, all other crimes and offenses were tried and punished by the landowner. He could have a serf beaten or chained up, could send him into military service, and after 1765 could exile him to hard labor in Siberia. It is true the landlord was forbidden in theory to treat his serfs cruelly, but actually there was no redress against the arbitrary will of the master. The extent of legal protection is indicated by the fact that there was in the Russian code no definite punishment for a landlord who tortured his serf to death. For their holdings the manorial or agricultural peasants paid the landlord either in forced labor or in cash. The amount of labor or the size of the payments a serf owed his lord was in many cases regulated on the ability of the individual serf to render service or to make payments, with each lord squeezing out as much as possible. Thus during Catherine's reign the obligations of those who paid in money were greatly increased, and in some cases probably doubled. For those who paid in labor the usual requirement was three days' labor in each week by the adults of both sexes, but there were estates on which the serfs were compelled to work as much as six days a week. At seed or harvest time serfs were often required to work continuously for the lord, with little opportunity for attending to their own seeding or harvesting.

Nor was serfdom limited to agriculture. In the industries which had grown up since the accession of Peter the Great many of the workers were serfs who were either lent to an industry by the state or owned by the manager of the industry. The famous Stroganovs, for example, owned more than eighty thousand workers in their industrial establishments. Especially numerous were the serfs who labored in the mines of the Ural regions. Conditions here were most primitive, so that the mortality rate was high; but what did it matter so long as there were always other serfs to replace those who died? In general, the condition of the serfs was so hopeless that they were filled with a smoldering hatred for their masters.

On a number of occasions during Catherine's reign the peasants revolted. The most widespread of the peasant uprisings was that instigated in 1773 by Pugachev, an illiterate Don Cossack who posed as Peter III, though he did not bear even a remote resemblance to the dead Tsar. Within a short time after he sounded the call to arms in September, 1773, Pugachev managed to collect a force of about 25,000 men composed of agricultural serfs, miners, and other discontented elements. With these troops he marched down the Volga valley, inciting the peasants to rebellion, burning the mansions of the landed nobility, and hanging nobles, bailiffs, and government officials in cold blood. When Catherine realized the seriousness of the situation, she sent a large detachment which defeated and scattered the rebel forces, but Pugachev himself escaped and was soon at work raising a new army. In 1774 the revolt became so widespread that Catherine recalled a large force from the Turkish front to crush it. This force not only routed and dispersed Pugachev's army but also captured the leader, who was taken to Moscow in an iron cage and publicly executed in 1775.

The Pugachev rebellion had important results. First, it definitely ended any plans Catherine may have had for improving the lot of the peasants. Instead of removing some of the grievances which had caused many peasants to join the rebel forces, Catherine ruthlessly and unsparingly punished those who had participated in the revolt. Thousands were executed and other thousands were sent to Siberia or flogged, among the latter many women and children. To prevent similar uprisings in the future, Catherine formed a new alliance between the government and the landed nobles—an alliance which was to continue until the collapse of Tsarism in 1917. Whereas Peter I had attempted to fuse the classes, Catherine II again separated them sharply. This resulted, on the one hand, in increased privileges for the nobles and, on the other, in a more complete subjection of the peasants. In 1765 Catherine had already extended the authority of the nobles by permitting them to sentence their serfs to hard labor in Siberia. Two years later she had given new force to an old law which forbade peasants to make complaints against their landlords (except in certain cases) by decreeing that those who disobeyed this law were to be punished with the knout. After the Pugachev rebellion her government deliberately became blind to almost all cruelties that landlords might inflict on their peasants. Moreover, the theoretically liberal empress who had written, "O Liberty, the soul of all things, without thee were all things dead," increased the number of serfs in 1783 by a ukase which deprived the Ukrainian peasants of their freedom.[1]

[1] This decree was not so revolutionary as it may appear. Most peasants of the Ukraine were virtually, if not legally, serfs when the ukase was issued.

Though Russia remained predominantly an agricultural country, some progress in the establishment of new industries was made during Catherine's reign. Many factories were opened in various parts of Russia, some of them employing as many as a thousand workers. At the end of her rule St. Petersburg alone had more than a hundred factories. But as the workers in the factories were largely serfs who worked without machinery the technical level of the Russian industries was low. Not only were many of them owned by the state, but the articles they produced, including arms, ammunition, shoes, clothing, canvas, and cordage, were largely used by the state for the army and the navy. Besides factories there were also domestic or home industries in Russia. Merchants distributed raw materials to peasants and purchased the finished product at their own prices. Though the payment was low, the home worker had the advantage that he received at least some compensation for his work, whereas the factory serfs often received no wages. In time the home industries spread over a large part of northern and central Russia, especially among the free peasants and the serfs who made payments to their landowners in cash. Though factories which employed only free labor were opened at the beginning of the nineteenth century, the first modern machinery for use in the textile industries was not imported into Russia until 1840.

During Catherine's reign the foreign trade as well as the industries of Russia expanded greatly. Commercial treaties were concluded with various European countries, but the bulk of the trade was in the hands of the English. The imports were chiefly articles of luxury for the rich, such as toilet articles, wines, furniture, and fine textiles. Among the important exports were homespun linen cloth, furs, flax, hemp, wax, tallow, ship timber, and pig iron.

Being of western birth, Catherine naturally sympathized with the policy of introducing western civilization into Russia. She wished to make the society of her court as cultured as the society of Paris and Berlin. French fashions, clothes, and manners were readily adopted by the upper classes, and French became the fashionable language at the court. French tutors were imported to teach the children of the nobles, and Russian youths went in increasing numbers to study at foreign universities. Beneficial though it was, the French influence was limited to the upper classes. Moreover, it often changed only the externals of behavior without greatly affecting character. The educated Russian with his superficial veneer of French culture still remained fundamentally barbarian. Besides encouraging the pursuit of French culture, Catherine was active in bringing to Russia from western Europe some knowledge of science. In an effort to curb the ravages of smallpox, from which a million people are said to have perished in one epidemic year, she prevailed upon the English physician, Thomas Dimsdale, to come to Russia for the purpose of introducing inoculations against the disease. The empress herself set an example for her subjects by being one of the first to submit to inoculation. Catherine also made some small contributions to the spread of education. She contended that the education of women was as important as that of men, and in 1764 founded the Smolny Institute or "Society for the Training of the Daughters of the Nobility." Later in her reign she also made a feeble attempt to establish the Austrian system of normal schools in Russia, founding a number of such schools in St. Petersburg and Moscow. But these gestures were not the national system of education according to Locke and Rousseau which the empress had planned and which was to regenerate her country. Intellectually and spiritually the masses of the Russian people made little advance during her reign. So low was the general educational level that when Catherine died there were not more than three hundred lay schools for a population of twenty-six millions.

Of the greatest significance for the history of Russia, and for that of Europe generally, was Catherine's foreign policy. Her purpose was to add as much territory as possible to the Russian Empire, and she was very successful. No other sovereign since Ivan the Terrible aided Russia's expansion so much. By the end of her reign its frontiers touched the Black Sea, the Caspian, and the Baltic. First of all, with the aid of Frederick the Great and Maria Theresa she succeeded in utterly destroying Poland and annexing much of its territory. This deed, which has been posterity's greatest grievance against Catherine, was to ardent Russian patriots the crowning achievement of a glorious reign. It meant the recovery of provinces which had been separated from Russia during the Middle Ages. In defense of Catherine's acts Russian historians have pointed out that the provinces which Russia gained by the partitions of Poland were populated largely by Russians (Ukrainians and White Russians); that besides the Russians, the population consisted of Lithuanians and Letts, with only a small minority of Poles. It was not until after the Napoleonic wars that territory actually Polish from an ethnic point of view was joined to Russia.

More important economically than the annexation of Polish territory was the fact that Russia gained access to the Black Sea. Had it been possible for her to do so, Catherine would have dismembered Turkey much as she did Poland. In this case, however, the problem was more difficult. The Turk, already on the way to becoming the "Sick Man" of Europe, time and again displayed an extraordinary vigor which frustrated Catherine's plans. Having reached its greatest extent in Europe with the annexation of Crete and Podolia in the second half of the seventeenth century, the Turkish Empire had been forced by the treaty of Carlowitz (1699) to yield some of its territory to Hungary, to return Podolia to Poland, and to cede Azov to Russia. Hence this treaty has been styled "the first dismemberment of the Ottoman Empire." For Peter I the annexation of Azov meant the achievement of the first step toward gaining a "window" on the Black Sea, but in 1711 he was forced to restore Azov to Turkey. At her accession Catherine II revived Peter's plans for an outlet to the south in their entirety. By deliberate measures, such as fomenting rebellion in the dependencies of the sultan, the empress succeeded in goading the Turks to declare war in 1768. The most dramatic operation of the war was the progress of a Russian fleet under the command of Alexei Orlov from the Baltic through the North Sea, the English Channel, and the Atlantic to the Mediterranean. Sent to excite the Greeks to rise against the Turks, the expedition achieved little in this respect, but it won what is probably the most famous naval victory in Russian history when, on July 7, 1770, it destroyed the Turkish fleet off Tchesmé on the western coast of Asia Minor. Thereafter the war dragged on until peace was concluded in 1774.

The treaty, signed at the Bulgarian village of Kuchuk-Kainarji, gave Russia free access to the Black Sea, from which other nations were still excluded. The Crimea was made independent of Turkey, and Russia received the city of Azov and a number of strongholds north of the Black Sea. Of special importance for the future of Turkey were several vaguely worded clauses relating to its Christian subjects. One of these read: "The Sublime Porte promises to protect constantly the Christian religion and churches and allow the ministers of Russia at Constantinople to make representation on their behalf." On the basis of this and other clauses Russia later claimed a kind of protectorate of all the Christian subjects of the sultan, a claim which served as a pretext for repeated interference in the internal affairs of Turkey.

Catherine was far from satisfied with her gains. The success of her first venture seems to have suggested the plan of expelling the Turks from Europe entirely, and of establishing a new Byzantine Empire with Constantinople as its capital. In anticipation of her second grandson's rule over this empire she had named him Constantine and engaged a Greek nurse and a Greek servant for him so that he could learn the Greek language. Since she needed help for the execution of her scheme, Catherine turned to Joseph II of Austria, who was not averse to enlarging the borders of his territories on the southeast. The two sovereigns entered into an agreement to make common cause against the Ottoman Empire, going so far as to divide on paper the Turkish possessions in Europe. Then Catherine sent a Russian army into the Crimea, annexing it to Russia. When the sultan in 1787 demanded its restoration, Catherine refused and war began. But the Russians did not fare too well in the war. In the first place the Turks demonstrated with their reorganized army and navy that their strength was far from exhausted. Secondly, Russia could not use its entire military and naval forces against Turkey because it was attacked by Sweden, which sought to recover the territories it had previously lost to Russia. The Austrians moved against the Turks with a large army in 1788, but they at first achieved little. Later, when the tide turned, Joseph II was hampered in prosecuting the war by uprisings against his reforms in Hungary and in Belgium. In the midst of it all, Joseph died in 1790 and Leopold, who succeeded him, withdrew from the war, restoring to the Turks all the territory the Austrians had taken. Catherine, having made peace with Sweden, continued the struggle until the next year. By this time both parties were ready for peace, with the Turks dispirited and Catherine eager to give her entire attention to Polish affairs.

The treaty signed at Jassy in 1792 sanctioned Russia's annexation of the Crimea, confirmed it in the possession of the territories it had gained by the treaty of Kuchuk-Kainarji, and moved its western boundary to the river Dniester. The treaty did not, however, effect a partition of Turkey as Catherine had planned. Nor was she to resume her plan of driving the Turks from

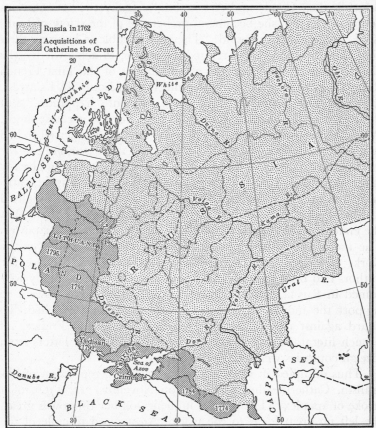

Territories Acquired by Catherine the Great

Europe. Thereafter her energies were absorbed by the French Revolution. It remained for her successors to revive the "On to Byzantium" policy and thereby add, in the nineteenth century, four more Russo-Turkish wars to the roster of those which had previously been fought.

When the French Revolution broke out in 1789, Catherine adopted an attitude of bitter and unrelenting antagonism toward it, regarding it as a definite threat to her throne. Anxiously she followed the course of events in France from day to day. Regarding the conditions there she said, *"Le pourquoi est le roi!* (The king is the cause). Everyone directs the king as he pleases: first Breteuil, then Condé and Artois, finally Lafayette." As early as September, 1789, she became apprehensive of the safety of Louis XVI. Prophetically she said: "They are capable of hanging their king. It is frightful!" She refused, of course, to acknowledge the Constitution of 1791 and the establishment of the First French Republic in the next year. When informed of Louis XVI's arrest, she wrote to a friend: "I have not a moment's happiness." But the report of the execution of Louis gave her the greatest shock. When the news reached the royal palace she betook herself to bed in a fever, bitterly exclaiming: *"L'égalité est un monstre, qui veut être roi* (Equality is a monster that wishes to be king)." Having already taken steps to prevent the spread of liberal ideas in Russia, Catherine now became a confirmed reactionary. She who had delighted in liberal ideas conceived such a fanatical hatred for them that she endeavored to eradicate them by all the means in her power. The use of the word *citizen* was strictly forbidden, and even the works of Cicero and Demosthenes were censored because the authors had been republicans. French *émigrés* were cordially welcomed in Russia, but all French subjects who did not swear to support the monarchic principle were summarily expelled. To guard against the infiltration of liberal ideas from France, all French literature was prohibited in Russia, and all letters from foreign countries were opened and read.

Thus occupied in vigorous and unrelenting repression of liberalism, Catherine died suddenly on November 17, 1796, of a stroke of apoplexy. Though her influence on her times was great, she left no great ideas to the world. An avowed disciple of the French Enlightenment, she was not so liberal or so "enlightened" as she pretended to be. If the introduction of sweeping reforms is an essential qualification of an "enlightened despot," Catherine can hardly be so classified. She projected many reforms, but actually achieved little that benefited her people. Her outstanding accomplishment consisted in making Russia a factor of the first magnitude in the affairs of Europe. She also left it far greater in extent than she found it. She could well say: "I came to Russia a poor girl. Russia has dowered me richly, but I have paid her back with Azov, the Crimea, and Poland." It must be remembered, however, that her annexations were far from being unmixed blessings. Much of the territory she added was a constant source of friction, giving rise to the Polish Question and the Eastern Question.

POLAND IN THE EIGHTEENTH CENTURY

At the beginning of the eighteenth century Poland was the third largest country of Europe, only Russia and Sweden being greater in size. With an area of about 280,000 square miles, it stretched from the Baltic almost to the Black Sea, and from the eastern borders of Germany to the western boundaries of Russia. The vast extent of the country was due to the union of Poland proper with Lithuania, which originally had been an independent state. The two were joined in 1386 when Ladislas Jagello, the reigning duke of Lithuania, married the daughter and heir of the last Polish king, thereby becoming king of Poland, but Lithuania was not incorporated into the government of Poland until 1560. In number of inhabitants Poland at the opening of the eighteenth century was the fourth largest country of Europe, with an estimated population of about eleven and one-half millions. The predominant religion was Roman Catholicism, a fact which accounts for the definite western cast of its literature, art, philosophy, and science.

The influence of Poland in European affairs had been most important, and its prosperity greatest, during the sixteenth century; after that the kingdom had declined. Its last great ruler was John Sobieski (1674–1696), who is remembered chiefly because he marched to the relief of Vienna when it was besieged by the Turks in 1683. The period after his death was one of continuous decadence until the final extinction of Poland in 1795. Among the causes which contributed to this decline were the weakness of the monarchy, the chaotic constitution with its pernicious *liberum veto*, the self-aggrandizement of the nobility, the decline of the middle class, the oppression of the peasantry, religious dissension and racial antipathies, and the lack of natural boundaries and a strong army. Of these the political causes were the most powerful. The others were weaknesses or destructive tendencies which hastened the decline, but which a strong government could have overcome or at least have curbed.

As a political state Poland was unique in Europe. Nominally a republic, it was ruled by a king chosen by the nobles, each of whom had the right to attend the election and participate in it. Although the principle that the monarchy was elective had been recognized as early as the second quarter of the fifteenth century, the crown had retained a considerable measure of independence until the Jagellonian dynasty died out in 1572. Prior to that time election had meant the choice of the natural successor by birth. Thereafter, however, no hereditary claims were admitted. Each succeeding king had to swear to certain stipulations, known as *pacta conventa*, by which he agreed not to name his successor, and to exercise only such powers as had been expressly conferred upon him. Thus, while the rulers of most of the other countries of Europe were freeing themselves from the last vestiges of control by a feudal nobility, the king of Poland was becoming more and more a crowned figurehead. At each election his power was diminished until he lost even the right of bestowing the patent of nobility. By the opening of the eighteenth century the principal prerogative which the king could still exercise was the appointment of civil and ecclesiastical officers. But since the appointments were for life, and the officials could not be dismissed unless the diet, sitting as a court of justice, had established guilt, the king lost all control over his officials once he had appointed them.

Inversely, as the king lost power, the nobles acquired it, until they became practically the sole possessors of all authority within the state. Although the Poles of noble extraction constituted only about eight per cent of the population, they were able effectively to exclude the other classes from all share in the government of the country. The power of making laws, of levying taxes, of declaring war and concluding peace, was vested in a diet composed of members of the nobility. True, the rights of the towns to send deputies to the diet had never been formally abolished, but after the beginning of the sixteenth century they had ceased to exercise this right because of the opposition of the nobles to the presence of delegates from the towns. Yet the situation would not have been so disastrous if the nobility had organized an efficient government. This, however, they did not do. Their primary aim was not efficient government but the maintenance of their own prerogatives.

So intent was the diet upon protecting the rights and privileges of the individual nobleman that the power which had been wrested from the crown was divided among the members until it virtually disappeared. Politically all nobles were regarded as equals, the higher titles commanding no preference. This principle of equality was carried so far that the will of one individual outweighed that of the rest of the diet. It gave rise to the rule that every measure must be passed by unanimous vote to become a law. A single member, by the use of his veto power (the liberum veto), could not only prevent the passing of a certain resolution but could dissolve the diet and render void all the previous decisions of that specific assembly. Although the liberum veto was founded on no written law, it had become an established constitutional practice after 1652, the year in which a deputy, by using it, succeeded in "exploding" the diet—that is, in dissolving it and nullifying all its decisions. It was possible under extraordinary conditions to suspend the liberum veto in order to give a majority the power to enact laws, but this expedient was seldom resorted to.

Because of this destructive veto, it was impossible to pass the much needed reforms. Rare indeed was the reform or resolution, no matter how conducive to the welfare of the country or how widely supported, to which not one deputy objected. Since the principal concern of the diet was the maintenance of a monopoly of power over the crown and the other classes alike, such laws as it passed were usually to the advantage of the nobility and at the expense of the other classes. Frequently the deputies from the provincial assemblies, or dietines, were instructed to dissolve the diet if it did not comply with certain specified local demands. Some dietines even went so far as to order their deputies to effect a dissolution for no other reason than to show their importance and to keep alive the right of "exploding" a diet. Between 1695 and 1762 no less than twelve diets were dissolved before a marshal could be elected to preside over the meetings. Of all the diets held between 1652 and 1764, only seven sessions lasted the normal time; almost one-third were dissolved by the veto of a single deputy. Since the diet met only once in two years and the sessions were limited to six weeks, the use of the liberum veto effectively paralyzed the functions of the only body that might have given Poland an orderly and efficient government. Agents of foreign countries were not backward in offering bribes to the members of the diet in order to prevent the passing of legislation prejudicial to their own interests. In 1697, for example, the representative of Brandenburg in Poland advised his master to send money for bribery "because everyone is now more concerned with his private interest than with the public welfare." Thus neighboring countries found the liberum veto a ready means of rendering Poland more impotent, and of paving the way for its final extinction.

With such power in their hands, the nobles in time became virtually the sole possessors of all rights and privileges. Their single duty was compulsory military service in case of war. The only restriction to which they submitted was the rule that they might not be merchants or artisans. Any nobleman who engaged in trade or became a craftsman thereby forfeited his rights to nobility. On the other hand, the nobles paid only such taxes as they levied upon themselves; they monopolized all political offices and also the higher offices in the Church; and they alone had the right to own land outside the cities—a right which they jealously guarded.

Since the nobility exercised all power and possessed all privileges, it might well be supposed that this class would be in a sound financial condition. This, however, was far from being the fact. Although all noblemen were politically equal and were forced to address one another as "brother," they were divided into a number of sharply differentiated social groups. At the top of the scale stood a few great families who possessed immense riches, owned vast estates, and maintained courts far surpassing that of the king in brilliancy. Below them were the middle-class nobles who devoted themselves primarily to the supervision of their landed estates. But the majority of the so-called nobility owned little or no land. Thousands attached themselves to one of the great families, serving as men-at-arms, supervisors of estates, or in some lesser capacity. Many lived in abject poverty. Nevertheless, the most poverty-stricken noble did not renounce a single claim because of his poverty. The condition of the gentry as a whole spoke eloquently of their failure to establish a utopia even for themselves.

There was in Poland no strong native middle class. The townsmen, comprising only about fifteen per cent of the population, were in large part Jews or foreigners. In the Middle Ages many towns had become prosperous from the transit trade which passed through Poland from the Black Sea. But as a result of the occupation of the territories around the Black Sea by the Turks in the fifteenth century and the shifting of the center of commerce from the Mediterranean to the Atlantic, the overland trade through Poland declined and with it the prosperity of the Polish towns. Thereafter the ruin of the towns was gradually completed by the restrictive legislation of the diet, which aimed to prevent the growth of a middle class that would be strong enough to challenge the supremacy of the nobility or to aid the king in changing the existing order. In 1565, for example, the diet forbade native merchants to import or export goods. Later it enacted a law (1643) which limited the maximum profit of native merchants to seven per cent. Thus, while the governments of all other nations of Europe were zealously fostering commerce and industry, the selfish policy of the Polish gentry was successfully stifling them. Such commerce and industry as existed at the opening of the eighteenth century was mainly in the hands of the Jews, who were not recognized as citizens, or of foreigners who had no care for the interests of Poland. The towns which had once flourished presented a sorrowful aspect. Most of them were collections of wooden houses in which a few artisans and trading Jews eked out a precarious existence, the majority of the inhabitants being dependent on agriculture for a living. Not one Polish city had as many as fifty thousand inhabitants, and only seven had a population of more than ten thousand.

The condition of the peasants, who made up more than seventy per cent of the population, was deplorable. During the sixteenth century—by which time the peasants of most of western Europe had freed or were gradually freeing themselves from the impositions of villenage—the Polish masses had been degraded into hopeless serfdom by a series of laws passed by the diet. At the opening of the eighteenth century five-sixths of the peasants were still serfs, and their condition was probably worse than that of similar groups in any other country of Europe. Even in Russia the state exercised some protection over the serfs, but in Poland they were wholly under the jurisdiction of the landlords. In judicial matters they had no appeal from the judgment of the lord's court. The lord's authority was so great that he could even determine their religion. So cheaply was the life of a serf regarded that a lord who killed one was subject only to a fine. Furthermore, the lord prescribed the amount of labor which each peasant owed him, sometimes as much as five or six days a week; he also required peasants to sell their crops and to buy the necessities of life through him. Ground down by taxes and by forced labor, often treated with incredible cruelty, and bereft of all hope of betterment, the Polish peasants continued to sink deeper into poverty and despair.

In addition to political anarchy and social disunion, Poland was robbed of its strength by racial and religious dissensions. The population was heterogeneous, only about half of it consisting of Poles. There were Lithuanians and Russians in Lithuania, Russians in the Ukraine and in Volhynia, Germans in West Prussia, and about a million Jews scattered over the land. All these groups were separated to a greater or lesser extent by national feelings which, in turn, were intensified by religious differences. Although the Roman Catholic Church was the state church of Poland, the non-Polish groups were largely dissenters. The Russians and some of the Lithuanians belonged to the Orthodox Church and had the support of Russia, while the Germans were mainly Protestants who looked to Prussia and Sweden for support. At first Protestantism made considerable progress in Poland, but the Jesuits, as previously stated, stopped its advance and regained much of the lost ground, introducing into Poland a militant spirit which aggravated the religious antagonisms. Thenceforward the Poles, who earlier had been one of the most tolerant of European nations, assumed a less friendly attitude toward non-Roman Catholics. During the last part of the seventeenth century and the first part of the eighteenth, both the Protestants and the members of the Greek Orthodox Church, known collectively as the "Dissidents," were limited in the exercise of their religion. In 1717 the building of new Dissident churches was interdicted by the diet. Later the laws of 1733 and 1736 deprived the Dissidents of their political and even of many of their civil rights. This religious intolerance afforded the neighbors of Poland an opportunity for creating further difficulties by intervening in Polish affairs in the name of toleration.

Torn by dissension and internal strife, Poland likewise had no natural defenses to aid in repelling the attacks of ambitious neighbors. Its extensive frontiers were not protected by mountains, nor were rivers its boundaries. Except for the protection of the Carpathian Mountains on the south, it lay exposed to the attack of its enemies on every side. This lack of natural boundaries might have been offset by a powerful army, but in this respect, also, Poland was weak. The diet, fearing that a large army might aid the king to strengthen his position, limited its size in 1717 to 24,000 men—an act which was equivalent to disarming Poland. Actually the standing army seldom reached more than half the stipulated strength, and was composed chiefly of cavalry, with little infantry and less artillery.

Not all the Polish people were as insensible to the growing impotence of the nation as were the nobles. There were some who saw that the constitution, with its attendant anarchy, and the country's military weakness were leading to destruction. Among these were several of the monarchs. King Jan Casimir, for example, told the diet in 1667 that unless drastic reforms were introduced the neighboring states would certainly tear Poland into shreds and stuff it into their pockets. His warnings were echoed by succeeding kings, but the nobles refused to read the handwriting on the wall. Interested above all in maintaining the status quo, they opposed all attempts at reform.

While Poland was declining, the neighboring states of Russia and Prussia were growing in size and military strength. Determined one day to dismember Poland, they resolved to prevent any reforms which might strengthen it and enable it to preserve its independence. Peter the Great had already established the policy of maintaining in Poland a state of chaos which would facilitate the absorption of Polish territory. Soon after Catherine II became empress of Russia, Peter's policy of posing as the defender of the rights of the Polish nobles against the absolutism of kings offered her an excuse for interfering in the affairs of the land. When King Augustus III of Poland died in 1763, Catherine moved troops into that country and without much difficulty secured the vacant throne for one of her favorites, the Polish nobleman Stanislaus Poniatowski. Thereafter Polish affairs were largely conducted from St. Petersburg. The year in which Stanislaus became king of Poland also saw the conclusion of an agreement between Catherine and Frederick the Great regarding the domestic affairs of Poland. They agreed that the old constitution with its elective kingship and liberum veto must be preserved at all costs. In other words, Poland must be prevented from setting its house in order. It was the first step toward final destruction of the Polish state.

THE PARTITIONS OF POLAND

Once their influence was established in Poland, the allies could no longer restrain their greed, and discussions leading to a partition of Polish territory were soon opened. But Catherine and Frederick the Great did not carry out the partition alone. Fearing the opposition of Austria, they decided to give Maria Theresa a share of the spoils. Maria Theresa at first shrank from the idea of robbing Poland. She could not forget that John Sobieski had saved Vienna in 1683. Yet the prospect of acquiring a large slice of territory was tempting. In the end she consented, with copious tears, to participate in the spoliation. As Frederick the Great expressed it: "The more she wept for Poland, the more she took of it." Under the pretext that the state of Polish anarchy was a standing menace to all neighbors, the three nations signed the first treaty of partition in 1772. The idea of dismembering Poland was not new. It had been suggested as early as the sixteenth century by the Emperor Maximilian II, and since that time had been discussed by various other rulers. In 1772 it became an accomplished fact. Prussia gained all of West Prussia except the cities of Danzig and Thorn; Austria secured Galicia and some adjoining territory; while Russia annexed White Russia and other territory from the eastern side of Poland.

The two decades following the first partition were in many respects a period of Polish intellectual and economic revival. The universities at Cracow and Vilna were revived and a renewed interest in the study of Polish literature, Polish history, and the Polish language was manifest, together with an interest in the literature of the French Enlightenment. Trade and commerce improved despite the loss of access to the Baltic. New industries sprang up, new banks were opened, and a system of canals was started. Even agricultural conditions improved with the freeing of many serfs by the great landowners. But the period was, above all, one of constitutional reform. The demands which had previously been articulated by only a few individuals now became more general. After the humiliating experiences of the first partition the more intelligent part of the nation realized that drastic reform of the constitution was the only possible means of saving Poland. King Stanislaus, who refused to be any longer the puppet of Russia, became the leader of the movement to give the country a workable constitution. The program included curtailment of the power of the nobility, establishment of an hereditary monarchy with the house of Saxony as heirs to Poniatowski, abolition of the liberum veto, election of a diet which could pass laws, representation of the burghers in the diet, and improvement of the conditions of the peasants. These and other reforms were finally incorporated in the memorable constitution of 1791. In May of that

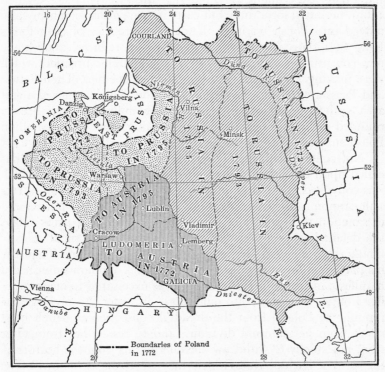

Partitions of Poland, 1772, 1793, 1795

year the constitution was adopted amid popular enthusiasm; it seemed as if a new era had dawned for Poland. Actually, however, the constitution, admirable as it was in itself, brought only fresh troubles.

The neighbors of Poland were not pleased to see their victim taking a new lease on life. Catherine, having twice guaranteed the old constitution, immediately declared against the new one.

The Russian minister at Warsaw announced that the empress "would, in virtue of her guarantee, march an army into Poland to restore the liberties of the Republic." Being at war with Turkey, she hastened to make peace in order to have a free hand for the affairs in Poland (Treaty of Jassy, January 8, 1792). At her command a large Russian army composed of 80,000 regulars and 20,000 Cossacks marched into Poland in 1792. The king of Prussia, Frederick William II (Frederick the Great having died in 1786), hesitated for a time, but early in 1793 a Prussian army also moved into Polish territory. Under the pressure of both forces King Stanislaus was forced to disavow all reforms, abolish the new constitution, and reëstablish all the anarchic practices which were making Poland an easy prey for her enemies. Then Russia and Prussia agreed to the second partition. Russia annexed a vast area with a population of about three millions, while Prussia rounded out its former acquisitions, taking more than a million Polish subjects. Austria did not share in the division.

Not content with merely seizing the territory, both countries called upon the Polish diet to sanction the deed. The diet which was convoked at Grodno under the mouths of Russian and Prussian cannon ratified the cession of territory to Russia, but refused to sanction the transfer of territory to Prussia. For twenty days the defenseless assembly remained adamant in its silent refusal; finally the prolonged silence was interpreted as consent. To justify his participation in the dissection, Frederick William published a manifesto in which he stated that it was necessary "to incorporate her frontier provinces into our states" in order "to preserve the republic of Poland from the dreadful consequences which must result from her internal divisions, and to rescue her from utter ruin, but chiefly to withdraw her inhabitants from the horrors of the destructive doctrines which they are bent to follow." The empress of Russia informed the world, in a declaration, that the only means of restraining the revolutionary tendencies of Poland was "by confining it within more narrow bounds, and by giving it proportions which better suited an intermediate power."

After the second partition the Polish people made a last desperate effort to save their state from total extinction by organizing an armed resistance. The leader of the resistance was Thaddeus Kosciusko, a man of considerable military experience. When the American colonies revolted against England, he had sailed to

FREDERICK THE GREAT

MARIA THERESA

CATHERINE THE GREAT

THADDEUS KOSCIUSKO

GEORGE III   *by Reynolds*

JOHN WESLEY

JAMES WATT

ADAM SMITH

Philadelphia and enlisted as a volunteer in the American army, distinguishing himself at Saratoga and Yellow Springs, and later serving as governor of West Point. At the end of the war Kosciusko returned to Poland, where he soon rose to the rank of major-general in the army. Sincerely devoted to the interests of his native country, he raised the standard of insurrection after the second partition and rallied his countrymen around it. For the first time in the history of Poland, peasants were permitted to bear arms in the defense of their country. They flocked to the colors of Kosciusko in large numbers, many of them armed only with scythes. In the beginning the Polish army won several victories against insuperable odds, but in a longer struggle the poorly equipped Poles were no match for the mighty forces of the three partitioning powers. On October 10, 1794, Kosciusko was severely wounded and taken prisoner by the Russians. Minus its leader, the insurrection collapsed.

After the king was compelled to abdicate, Warsaw and the territory as far as the Niemen was apportioned to Prussia; Austria received as its share Cracow and territory to the southeast; and Russia took Courland and the rest of Lithuania. Thus the name of Poland was erased from the list of nations. In the three divisions Russia received the lion's share, getting nearly twice the combined shares of Austria and Prussia.

CHAPTER TWENTY-ONE

England in the Eighteenth Century

THE ESTABLISHMENT OF THE HANOVERIAN DYNASTY

IN 1701 Parliament passed the Act of Settlement which made
Sophia of Hanover, a granddaughter of James I, the heir to
the English throne. But Sophia did not live to become queen,
for she died in 1713. Her son, George Lewis, elector of Hanover,
succeeded Queen Anne in the following year. Although Anne's
health had been failing, her death came so suddenly that the
Stuart sympathizers were completely unprepared for action, and
the accession of George was therefore accomplished peacefully. At
once and without opposition, on the very day of Anne's death
(August 1, 1714), he was proclaimed king of Great Britain and
Ireland as George I. Even Scotland and Ireland did not dissent.

Already fifty-four years of age, the new king possessed few
personal attractions. He was stolid in appearance, mediocre in
ability, narrow in his interests, uncouth in his ways, and common
in his tastes. The English throne was to him chiefly a means of
strengthening his position in Germany. His real home, to which
he returned whenever he could, was Hanover. Having spent all
his life in Germany, he was ignorant of the English language and
of English ways, and so great was his indifference to England that
he did not even try to learn English or to understand the English
character. On the other hand, he was just in his dealings and
possessed considerable common sense. That he, a foreigner with

but little knowledge of the English system, did not interfere much in governmental affairs was indeed a boon for England.

As the new king believed that the Tories were committed to the Stuarts, he chose his ministers from the Whig party. The Tories were still in power at the accession of George, but the first parliamentary election gave the Whigs a majority; thenceforth for nearly fifty years they managed to retain their supremacy. A noteworthy feature of this period is the beginning of the trend which culminated in "cabinet government" or the exercise by a group of ministers of the authority in government which had formerly been wielded by the king. Previously the principal ministers had been the king's servants. They were chosen or dismissed by him without concern for the approval of Parliament and were responsible only to him. But during the reigns of the first two Hanoverians the power of selecting the ministers with complete freedom and of determining policies was beginning to slip from the king's hands. Both William and Anne had seen the necessity of choosing ministers who could command the support of the House of Commons; nevertheless both rulers still considered themselves—and were assumed to be—responsible for the day-to-day conduct of the government and even for its broader administrative policies. They regularly presided over the meetings of an inner group of ministers called "the cabinet" in which questions of policy were discussed, took an important part in cabinet deliberations, and on occasions acted without consulting their advisers. George I and George II, however, attended cabinet meetings only on rare occasions. Absorbed in part by his position as ruler of Hanover, George I was willing to leave much of the responsibility for formulating policies to the cabinet, contenting himself with accepting or rejecting the proposals.[1]

The absence of the king from the cabinet meetings opened the

---

[1] The history of the cabinet in the eighteenth century is still controversial in many respects. It is frequently stated, for example, that George I seldom attended cabinet meetings because he was unable to speak English. Wolfgang Michael (*The Beginnings of the Hanoverian Dynasty*, vol. 1 [1936], p. 99), a distinguished authority on the period, states that this was not the reason, since the king's French was adequate and he could also converse with Walpole in Latin. "It was the general trend of constitutional development," he writes, "and not the king's ignorance of the English language which gradually made the work of government center in ministerial meetings held in his absence." For a summary of recent scholarship on the question of cabinet government see Trevor Williams, "The Cabinet in the Eighteenth Century," *History*, N.S., vol. 22 (1937–38), pp. 240–252.

way for some member to take a directing part and act as inter-
mediary between the king and the cabinet. This person gradually
came to be considered the "principal" or "prime" minister. Such
a minister was Sir Robert Walpole, who sat in the cabinet as First
Lord of the Treasury. Walpole was not only the confidant of the
king and the leading minister in the cabinet but also the most influential member of the Whig party in the House of Commons.
A coarse, bluff, good-humored, hard-drinking country squire, he
was also a person of considerable political sagacity. He held his
office for twenty years after assuming it in 1721. His principal aim
was to build up the prosperity of the country by encouraging
trade and industry. As a means to this end England must have
peace both at home and abroad. Hence he tried to allay political
and ecclesiastical strife and to avoid foreign entanglements. On
the whole, he was remarkably successful. Not only was the country
prosperous, but by a careful handling of the finances he managed
to reduce both the national debt and the land tax. Most of the
twenty years of his incumbency were years of peace. Well could
he say in 1735: "Fifty thousand men killed in Europe this year
and not a single Englishman." When war did break out in 1739,
it was only because Walpole could not prevent it.

In 1727 George I died while he was on his way to Hanover,
and was succeeded by his son, George II. The new king had a
better knowledge of the English language and of English affairs
than his father; yet he was still German in his tastes. Though
honest and well-meaning, George II was a man of few talents,
obstinate, quick-tempered, and shallow-minded. His best quality
was his personal courage; on the battlefield no one displayed
greater bravery than he. In affairs of state he was largely swayed
by Queen Caroline, whose ability was superior to her husband's.
Upon her advice he retained Walpole in office, and together the
queen and the prime minister cleverly managed the king. It was
a task requiring consummate tact. Since the king insisted that his
will must prevail, it became necessary for the prime minister to
direct the royal will into the proper channels. This he accomplished by confiding his policies to the queen, who skilfully
instilled them in the king's mind. George II then presented them
to Walpole as his own, and the prime minister obediently carried
them out. Thus the king was beguiled into believing that he was
the originator of Walpole's policies.

The death of the queen made the position of Walpole more vulnerable, but it was the war against Spain over the question of trade with the Spanish colonies that finally brought about his fall. As a convinced pacifist Walpole strove with all his power to prevent the war, taking for his motto the words which have since become famous: "Any peace is preferable even to successful war"; but to no avail. His opponents in Parliament, among them a fiery, eloquent young man named William Pitt, carried the day, forcing Walpole to consent to the war with Spain, which soon involved one with France.[1] He did not resign, however, until 1742, when his majority in Parliament became so small that it threatened to disappear entirely. Lecky, the great historian of eighteenth century England, has summed up Walpole's accomplishments in these words: "Finding England with a disputed succession and an unpopular sovereign, with a corrupt and factious Parliament, and an intolerant, ignorant and warlike people, he succeeded in giving it twenty years of unbroken peace and uniform prosperity, in establishing on an impregnable basis a dynasty which seemed tottering to its fall, in rendering the House of Commons the most powerful body in the State, in moderating permanently the ferocity of the political factions and the intolerance of ecclesiastical legislation."

In 1757 William Pitt, who had been an important factor in the overthrow of Walpole, became the leading spirit in the English government. It will be recalled that the War of the Austrian Succession was indecisive. No sooner had peace been concluded than Austria began to make preparations for war against Prussia. This time the British sided with Prussia, and France with Austria.[2] When the Seven Years' War broke out in 1756, however, the British were not prepared. Since the fall of Walpole the prime ministers had been second-rate statesmen who, though they saw that war was imminent, had done little to strengthen the English forces. The navy was in fair condition, but it could hardly be said that the British had an army. Their few regiments were poorly equipped, poorly disciplined, and poorly led. Indeed, the situation was so bad that Hanoverian and Hessian mercenaries had to be imported to defend England. From all sides came re-

---

[1] This war, which started as the War of Jenkins' Ear, was later merged in the War of the Austrian Succession. See p. 591.

[2] See pp. 499–501.

ports of defeats and disasters. It was even feared that Great Britain itself would be invaded. In this extremity the government was forced to turn to William Pitt as the only man who might save the situation. Pitt, later known as the earl of Chatham from the peerage he accepted in 1766, was a man of eloquence, unselfish devotion, and high ideals. He had been working tirelessly to rid the government of corruption ever since he became a member of Parliament in 1735. Up to 1757 George II's dislike and his own arrogance, aloofness, and irritability had prevented him from attaining to the leadership in the government. Now necessity left the king no choice. Despite his antipathy toward "the Great Commoner," as Pitt was called, he was forced to turn to him. This was the first instance of a king being compelled to take as a principal minister a man whom he both disliked and distrusted.

Though the duke of Newcastle remained in name the head of the government, it was Pitt who directed the conduct of the war. Undiscouraged by the state of affairs, he at once set to work with that characteristic vigor which moved Frederick the Great to remark that England had finally brought forth a man. So confident was Pitt of his own abilities that he said: "I am sure that I can save the country, and I am sure that no one else can." He infused some of his own ardor into the English people, particularly into those connected with the conduct of the war. He organized a militia for home defense, made plans to oust the French from both Canada and India, and fitted out expeditions to watch the French ports so that the French government would find it difficult to send supplies and reinforcements to its forces overseas. At the same time he saw that the French must be defeated in Europe if the war was not to drag on interminably. Hence he sent large subsidies to Frederick the Great, who was opposing a coalition which included France, Austria, and Russia. In short, Pitt's vigorous measures turned the war which had started so disastrously into the most successful war of the century for England.

THE REIGN OF GEORGE III

In the midst of the English successes George II died suddenly, October 25, 1760, at the age of seventy-seven. As his son Frederick had died in 1751, he was succeeded by his eldest grandson, George III. Only twenty-two years old when he ascended the throne, the new king could rightfully boast that he was "born and bred a Briton." He was conscientious, well-meaning, hard-working, and religious. His private life was exemplary—a novelty after the openly immoral lives of the two preceding kings. He lived simply and thriftily, devoting considerable time to agriculture and thereby earning for himself the nickname "Farmer George." On the other hand, he was narrow-minded and decidedly obstinate. He could not appreciate the views of others, and was harsh in his condemnation of all who did not agree with him. His mother, who had supervised his upbringing, had implanted in his mind exaggerated ideas of the royal prerogative. He accordingly resolved to be every inch a king. George III did not, however, attack the sovereignty of Parliament, for he was not aiming at absolute power. What he desired was the reëstablishment of the royal control over the administration of affairs which had been lost during the reigns of his two Hanoverian predecessors. He wished to hold in his own hands the determination of government policy and to make the ministers responsible to him instead of to the House of Commons.

Conditions were, by and large, favorable to the strivings of "Farmer George." Having fattened on the spoils of office and grown lazy, the Whigs had ceased to stand for any definite principles. Moreover, they had split into a number of factions which were now quarreling with one another. They had also lost much popular support because the people were tiring of the corrupt means the Whigs used to retain power. The Tories, on the other hand, convinced that the cause of the Stuarts was hopeless, were rallying round George III, who warmly welcomed their support. With their aid he was resolved to break the power of the Whig oligarchy and to make himself master in his own kingdom. His first move was to force the resignation of Pitt by refusing to support his plan for declaring war on Spain. Frederick the Great was so disappointed over this forced resignation that for the rest of his life he refused to trust the English. But the enemies of England were jubilant. "His dismissal is a greater gain to us than the winning of two battles," said the French philosopher Diderot. To George III it mattered little that England had lost such energetic leadership. For him the retirement of Pitt was a step toward the restoration of the royal authority. Though George now worked for peace, it was not until 1763 that the war was concluded. By the peace of Paris[1] England gained much, but might have gained considerably more had the king supported the audacious plans of the minister he deposed.

After the resignation of Pitt, George III devoted himself to strengthening a party in Parliament known as the "King's Friends." In supporting this party he spent much of the royal revenue for the purpose of buying votes or even seats in the House of Commons. Despite such measures, it was not easy for him to gain control of the direction of affairs. In the decade between 1760 and 1770 ministers and cabinets followed each other in quick succession. Finally, in 1770, Lord North became prime minister. During the period of North's ministry, which lasted until 1782, George III exercised the personal power for which he had striven, for Lord North represented the policy of the king rather than that of any party. Cabinet, Parliament, and government policy were under the king's control. At last his mother could rightly say, "Now, indeed, my son is king." For England the personal rule of the king brought disaster. George III's policy resulted in the loss of the American colonies and in a tremendous increase of the national debt. Toward the end of Lord North's ministry Parliament became alarmed over the king's power. In 1780 a resolution was passed which stated that "the influence of the crown has increased, is increasing, and ought not to be increased." The situation might have become serious had not the king in 1783 offered the position of prime minister to the younger William Pitt who, being equally popular with king and people, prevented a conflict between the two factions.

William Pitt the younger, second son of the Great Commoner, had been elected to Parliament at the age of twenty-two. An accomplished orator, he instantly made his mark in the House of Commons. After listening to his first speech Edmund Burke said in admiration: "He is not a chip off the old block, he is the old block itself." The next year young Pitt was made chancellor of the exchequer, and the year 1783 saw him become the youngest prime minister in English history. Many at first ridiculed the idea of a man of twenty-four heading the administration. The following rime illustrates the widespread feeling:

> A sight to make surrounding nations stare:
> A kingdom trusted to a schoolboy's care.

[1] For the terms of the peace see p. 598.

Few believed he would remain prime minister long, but he held his office for the remainder of his life (d. 1806) except for the period from 1801 to 1804. In person Pitt the younger was tall and dignified, though somewhat prim and unbending in public, with a somewhat Olympian aloofness. As a statesman he was devoted to the public welfare, superbly self-confident, scrupulously honest, and incorruptible. Under his leadership the re-created Tory party regained control of the government and continued to hold it for more than forty years.

But Pitt the younger was not, like Lord North, the mere mouthpiece of the king. He was as much the directing figure as Walpole had been. During the first part of his ministry he devoted himself to the task of putting the national finances on a sound footing. He cut down the expenditures of the government wherever possible, organized a system of auditing the national accounts, and introduced order into the chaos of the national finances. To check the widespread smuggling of his time, he reduced the customs duties on a number of articles, particularly on tea. With the duty on that product reduced from 119 to $12\frac{1}{2}$ per cent it was no longer profitable to engage in illicit trading. But Pitt's greatest achievement was his commercial treaty with France, concluded in 1787. This treaty, which was in a large measure the result of Adam Smith's teachings that two nations will benefit from a free exchange of goods,[1] abolished the duties on most of the staple products of Great Britain and France. Both nations profited from it through the importation of French wines and silks into England, and of English manufactures, especially hardware, into France. Pitt also advocated the abolition of the slave trade, parliamentary reform, and the removal of restrictions on Roman Catholics. For the first two he could not gain sufficient support. As for the Romanists, he succeeded only in opening the army and the bar to them.

Another important measure of Pitt's administration was the Act of Union (1800) which merged the parliaments of Great Britain and Ireland. As the eighteenth century progressed the dissatisfaction of the Irish with their government had become more and more patent. Though the great majority of the Irish were Roman Catholics, a Roman Catholic could not sit in the Irish parliament. He could not, in fact, even vote in a parliamentary election. Moreover, Poynings' Law[2] made the Irish

[1] See p. 574.   [2] See p. 248.

parliament a mere instrument of English interests. When the American colonies rebelled, the Irish were not slow to realize that the grievances of the American colonists were also theirs; that they were being ruled by a parliament in which they had no representation. The consequence was a widespread movement for a revision of the relations between Ireland and Great Britain. Since the English government was in no position to resist the Irish demands, Poynings' Law was repealed in 1782, and the Irish parliament was made an entirely independent body. The two countries were now connected only by a common executive. While the Irish desired complete independence, many English statesmen, and particularly Pitt the younger, sought to incorporate the Irish into the British government. During the French Revolution the Irish began to look to the French for aid in setting up an independent republic, but the ringleaders of the movement were arrested before the promised aid arrived.[1] When the Irish peasants tried to carry out the rebellion by themselves, they were punished with a savagery that was not soon forgotten. In an effort to end the strife between the two countries Pitt had a Union Bill put before the Irish House of Commons in 1799, but it was rejected by a large majority, much to the delight of the Irish people. In the following year, however, the articles of union were carried, the way having been cleared by bribery and intimidation, and were then passed by the English parliament and signed by the king. The Act of Union (1800) abolished the separate parliament of Ireland and made provisions for Irish representation in the British parliament. Four Irish bishops and twenty-eight Irish temporal lords were to sit in the House of Lords, while one hundred Irish members were given seats in the House of Commons. The name chosen for the two nations was "The United Kingdom of Great Britain and Ireland." On January 22, 1801, the first parliament representing Great Britain and Ireland met at Westminster, but the long-awaited emancipation of the Irish Catholics for which Pitt had worked did not take place. King George III declared it to be contrary to the oath he had taken to maintain the privileges of the Anglican Church. Hence the relations between the Irish and the British were anything but friendly.

During the last years of his first ministry William Pitt the

---

[1] Two small French expeditions arrived after the rebellion was over, only to be captured by the English.

younger spent most of his energy in preventing the French revolutionary spirit from spreading in England. When the French Revolution broke out in 1789 Pitt tried for a time to take a stand somewhere between its supporters and its opponents. But after he received the news of the massacres and the proclamation of the French republic, his attitude changed. Haunted by the fear of a similar revolution in England, the man who had been a proponent of liberal reform during the preceding decade became a reactionary, an advocate of coercion and repression. He suspended the Habeas Corpus Act, suppressed the two small clubs founded for the propagation of revolutionary doctrines, restricted the right of free meeting, and adopted other repressive measures.

There was little cause for such measures. Certain individuals had agreed with Charles James Fox, the Whig leader, when he said of the fall of the Bastille: "How much the greatest event it is that ever happened in the world, and how much the best!" but most Englishmen remained dispassionate spectators of that event. Certainly there were but few people who either contemplated or desired the overthrow of the existing system in England. In 1790 Edmund Burke had launched his crusade against the French Revolution by publishing his *Reflections on the Revolution in France,* one of the most powerful and influential pamphlets ever written. So immediate was its popularity that no less than seven thousand copies were sold in six days. In his treatise Burke styled the Revolution a "strange chaos of levity and ferocity, and of all sorts of crimes jumbled together with all sorts of follies." Though it provoked thirty-eight replies, among them Thomas Paine's *Rights of Man* (1791), the pamphlet nevertheless inspired panic in the propertied classes and generally won the upper and middle classes to a militant conservatism. More than this, it set the tone for English public opinion. Hence Pitt, supported by the king and by popular sympathy, found it easy to prevent the ideas of the French Revolution from taking root in British soil. Still, it has been said that the French Revolution was "the most important event in English history." That great upheaval did, it is true, release forces which were ultimately decisive factors in the establishment of democratic government in Great Britain, but for more than a generation it checked the progress of British liberal reform, despite the fact that the need for reform had become urgent because of a series of industrial changes summed up in the term "Industrial Revolution."

THE BEGINNINGS OF THE INDUSTRIAL REVOLUTION

At the beginning of the eighteenth century England was still chiefly an agricultural country, with more than three-fourths of the population living in the rural districts. The cities, except London, were small. Bristol, the second largest city in the kingdom, could boast a population of only thirty thousand. Such industry as existed was mostly domestic; that is, it was carried on in the cottages of the workers, whose main employment was agriculture. In the making of cloth, the most important industry, the whole family often participated; the wife and children carded the wool and spun the yarn while the weaver wove the cloth. Moreover, most products were still made by hand. For the work of spinning and weaving, the domestic workers used the old-fashioned spinning-wheel and the hand loom, just as they had been used centuries before. But great changes were to take place in the eighteenth and nineteenth centuries. The end of the eighteenth century saw human power being fast supplanted by machine power in the processes of manufacture; the domestic system was giving way to the factory system; and a substantial part of the population had already congregated in towns and cities to devote itself to purely industrial work. In short, at the end of the eighteenth century England was well on the way toward becoming the workshop of the world.

These great industrial changes which took place during the eighteenth and the first half of the nineteenth centuries are commonly summed up in the term "Industrial Revolution." The term must not, however, be interpreted too literally. There was no revolution in the sense of a sudden overturn of established practices. The changes came about slowly, without any sharp break in the course of historical development. Old ideas were modified and new ideas gradually took shape. Certainly the old conception of an industrial revolution which began in 1760 and ended in 1825 is, in the face of recent scholarship, no longer tenable.[1] The period must be extended in time, both backward and forward. The starting point must be moved nearer the beginning of the century—perhaps as far back as 1709, the year in which a method for smelt-

---

[1] This conception, as well as the term "Industrial Revolution," became current as the result of the publication in 1884 of Arnold Toynbee's *Lectures on the Industrial Revolution of the Eighteenth Century in England.*

ing iron with coal and lime was discovered; or at least to 1718, when a silk factory equipped with power machinery was opened near Derby. By 1760 the industrial changes were already far advanced in many of their phases. As the technical changes of the Industrial Revolution were not complete in a single British industry before 1830, the period must also be extended forward at least to the middle of the nineteenth century. Thus the process of change was gradual and long. Every step in it added another link to the chain of an industrial evolution which, in its effects, amounted to a "revolution."

The heart of the Industrial Revolution was the invention of machinery and its application to the processes of manufacture. This does not mean, however, that machines were not used in manufactures before this time. As early as the fourteenth century certain silk manufacturers at Bologna and Lucca in Italy seem to have used machines driven by both horse and water power. Toward the end of the sixteenth century an Englishman invented a machine with which woolen stockings could be knitted a hundred times faster than by hand. Later this machine was adapted to the knitting of caps and gloves, and also of cotton and silk hosiery. Regarding the last, John Evelyn wrote in his diary on May 3, 1661: "I went to see the wonderful engine for weaving silk stockings." There was also the ribbon loom for the weaving of ribbons, tapes, and braids; a machine which in its improved form embodied the essential principles of automatic weaving. Thus the use of machinery was not new. But, whereas machines had hitherto been a minor or subordinate factor in industry, they became the paramount factor during the period of the Industrial Revolution.

That the changes which are summed up in the term "Industrial Revolution" took place in England much sooner than in the continental countries was due to a combination of causes. First of all, the oversea expansion of England had opened markets which were ready to absorb more goods. Secondly, England had a tremendous advantage in that it had vast deposits of coal and iron, both of which were essential in the manufacture of machinery. Thirdly, the English inventors outstripped those of other countries. One must be careful, however, not to overemphasize the rôle of the inventors in the Industrial Revolution. The inventors were the servants and not the masters of the economic forces. They invented machines to satisfy the demands for more and cheaper goods for markets which had previously been opened by British oversea expansion. In India, for example, there was an almost unlimited market for cotton goods—in fact, for cheap goods of all kinds. To make the most of such markets it became necessary to increase the output and to reduce the prices. For this machinery was necessary. So pressing was the need for certain types of machines to accelerate production that the Royal Society of Arts offered premiums for their invention. The result was that machine after machine was invented, until the manufacturing processes were dominated by machinery. The social character of the inventions is shown by the fact that many minds were often engaged in working on the same problems, similar inventions frequently appearing at about the same time.

The textile industry took the lead in the application of machinery to the processes of manufacture. In 1718 Thomas Lombe opened near Derby a large factory equipped with complicated silk-spinning machinery driven by water power, the plans for which had been secretly obtained in Italy. This factory, which employed about three hundred men, was such a success that a second one was opened at Sheffield with about half as many employees. When Lombe's patent expired in 1732, others began to experiment with his machines, and other factories were started. Before 1760 there were silk factories in a number of English towns. At Macclesfield alone the silk factories employed more than two thousand workers, and at Stockport more than a thousand. These silk mills not only served as models for cotton factories but some of them were actually converted into cotton factories.

In the manufacture of cotton goods the first advance was made when Kay's flying shuttle, patented in 1733, came into use. This shuttle was used with the ordinary hand loom and could be jerked to and fro through the warp, enabling a single weaver not only to weave wider cloth but also to double his output. The subsequent invention of spinning machinery was not, as is frequently stated, the result of the invention of the flying shuttle, for inventors were already at work upon machines to hasten the process of spinning when Kay patented his shuttle. But the flying shuttle did stimulate the invention and use of spinning machinery. Used at first only by the wool weavers of certain districts, the flying shuttle came into use in the cotton-weaving factories about 1760, and caused a scarcity of yarns. In 1765 Hargreaves improved the method of spinning yarn with the old spinning wheel by constructing the spinning jenny, a spinning frame on which eight spindles—and ultimately more than a hundred—could be worked at once. Two years after the appearance of the spinning jenny Richard Arkwright produced the water-frame, which, by means of rollers revolving at different speeds, turned out finer and stronger yarn than could be made on the spinning jenny. With it a pure cotton yarn strong enough to be used for the warp was made for the first time in England and replaced the half-linen yarn formerly used. In 1779 Crompton combined the principles of the spinning jenny and the water-frame in his mule, which spun thread so strong and so fine that it could be used for the weaving of muslins, cambrics, and other sheer materials.

With their improved methods the spinners could now produce yarn faster than the weavers could use it. But in 1785 Edmund Cartwright invented a power loom which in time restored the balance. The power loom was a machine which could weave automatically, thus permitting a weaver to work with two or three machines at once. Somewhat clumsy at first, the power loom was gradually improved, and by 1815 was a really practical machine. Other inventions also helped to speed and increase the output of the textile industry. One such invention was the cylindrical press for printing calicoes, invented in 1783. Previously this work, done with wooden blocks, had been a slow and laborious task. With the new machine two men could print as much calico as a hundred could formerly. A new process of bleaching was also developed through the use of chlorine gas. Whereas cotton or linen had heretofore been soaked in sour milk and then exposed to the air for a period of six to eight months, textiles could now be bleached by the new method in a few days. Even the preparation of the raw material for the process of manufacture was speeded by a number of inventions. Various machines for combing and carding wool were invented in the eighteenth century, and in 1793 Eli Whitney, an American, invented the cotton gin, a machine which separates the seeds from the cotton fiber. All these inventions increased the output of textiles enormously. Some idea of the increase of cotton manufactures may be gained from the fact that the importation of raw cotton rose from a million and a half pounds in 1730 to more than a hundred million in 1815. In the manufacture of woolen goods machinery was adopted more slowly; yet seventeen million pounds of wool were imported in 1817 as compared with a million in 1766.

The bases of the mechanization of industry were coal and iron. At the opening of the eighteenth century, coal-mining was already an important industry in England, no less than two and one-half million tons being produced annually. Coal was used not only for heating purposes in the home but also in such industries as brewing, distilling, brickmaking, and the smelting of brass; but as yet no method had been invented for using coal in the smelting of iron. Until the eighteenth century all iron produced in England was smelted with charcoal, a process that was both expensive and so wasteful that wood had become scarce. This scarcity of wood necessitated the importation of much bar-iron from Russia and Sweden to supply the needs of English industry. Because of the high price of this imported iron many attempts—some as early as the reigns of James I and Charles I—were made to discover a process of smelting iron with coal. It was not until 1709, however, that the Darbys, ironmasters of Coalbrookdale, successfully worked out a method for smelting iron with coal and lime. The new method spread but slowly, because it was difficult to obtain a blast sufficiently powerful to smelt the iron with coal. Finally, about 1760, a man named Smeaton invented a blast furnace which could smelt iron both cheaply and quickly. Previously Benjamin Huntsman had invented a method for producing "cast" steel that was hard and flexible, suitable for knives, razors, and watchsprings. Other improvements followed. In 1783 Henry Cort patented a method of rolling iron into bars by means of rollers, instead of hammering it. Soon thereafter he also improved the quality of the iron by a process called "puddling," which burned out many impurities. A sufficient supply of good iron could now be obtained for many uses, and inventors were not slow in finding new uses for it. Not only were great quantities made into machinery, tools, and hardware but in 1779 the first cast-iron bridge was built across the Severn and in 1790 the first iron ship was launched.

The direct result of the application of machinery to the processes of manufacture was the rise of the factory system. There had been factories in England long before the Industrial Revolution. In the sixteenth century, for example, a certain Jack of Newbury had a clothing factory in which hundreds of workers were employed. But the factory system, which came with the invention of power machinery, was new. As the new machines were costly, the average worker did not have the capital to buy one or more of them. Even if he had been able to buy them and water-power had been available, such machines as Crompton's mule and Cartwright's power loom would have been too large for use in a cottage. Furthermore, the use of power made it more economical to concentrate many machines under one roof. This gradually spelled the doom of domestic industry, though hand workers were not entirely displaced. The average weaver, for example, with his spinning wheel and hand loom could not produce goods as cheaply as they could be made with power machinery. Hence it became necessary for the workers to flock to the factories. Yet the rapidity of the growth of the factory system can easily be exaggerated. In 1815 the number of domestic workers was still large, with the evils of the factory system affecting only a small part of the population. In fact, in the manufacture of woolen goods the factory system did not completely supersede the domestic system until the second half of the nineteenth century.

To drive the machinery in the new factories power was necessary. This was at first supplied by horses, oxen, and water mills. Of these the last was most generally used, necessitating the building of the factories near mill ponds or along streams. But during the eighteenth century steam power, a far greater force, was harnessed by a line of inventors. The steam engine or heat engine is not the product of one inventor. Like all great inventions, it is the result of a process of evolution in which the labors of one inventor stand as the natural sequel to those of his predecessors. Since the earliest times philosophers and scientists have speculated about the use of steam power. Hero of Alexandria, who lived in the second century before Christ, wrote in his *Pneumatics* of a "rotary engine driven by the reaction of steam issuing from the orifices in revolving arms." Though the apparatus was merely a toy, it shows that the ancients were acquainted with the expansive force of steam. During the many centuries between Hero's death and the period of the Industrial Revolution many contrivances for the use of steam power were constructed. In fact, by the opening of the eighteenth century all the essential details for the steam engine had been invented. All that was wanting was a mechanic who could combine them in a practical engine.

Such a mechanic appeared in Thomas Newcomen, who in

1712 built the first steam engine of the modern type, embodying a cylinder and a piston. All modern engines, whether used to supply power in factories or applied in the locomotive and in the steamship, are the direct descendants of Newcomen's engine. The only problem Newcomen was trying to solve was how to pump water from the mines of Great Britain. There had long been a pressing need for a contrivance which could clear the mine shafts of vast quantities of water, in order that the miners might go deeper in search of metals or coal. This need was in a sense met by Newcomen's steam pump. His engine was solely a pumping engine. It consumed a prodigious amount of coal, but this drawback did not prevent its being used for coal mines, because the lowest grade of coal could be burned in the engine, and at the mines this type of fuel was cheap. For mines which did not have a cheap supply of fuel at hand, the transportation of sufficient coal was expensive indeed. Hence the use of Newcomen's engine was restricted largely to coal mines.

From time to time various improvements were added to Newcomen's engine, but it remained for James Watt to make the first basic alterations. Watt, a maker and repairer of scientific instruments, became interested in the problem of steam power when he was asked to repair a Newcomen engine belonging to the University of Glasgow. Struck by the waste of steam caused by the alternate heating and chilling of the cylinder, he began the experiments which led to the invention of the separate condenser, patented by him in 1769. Watt's condenser vastly improved the engine, causing it to consume much less fuel and also make faster strokes. But even in its improved form it could be used only for pumping. The next problem was to adapt it for general industrial use. After many years of experimentation Watt obtained patents for a new engine in 1781 and 1782. The new engine embodied the principle of rotary motion and was double-acting, the steam working alternately on each side of the piston. The steam engine was now ready to supply the power to drive the machines in the factories. To manufacturers it offered the advantage of a continuous supply of power, whereas water power was largely dependent on the amount of water in the rivers and mill ponds. Moreover, steam power permitted the building of factories wherever sufficient coal could be procured. Consequently there was a demand for the new engines. To supply this demand Watt organized a firm in partnership with Matthew Boulton for the manufacture and sale of the improved engines. Despite difficulties regarding patent rights, the firm was extraordinarily successful. The common size of the engines sold was twenty horsepower, though some as large as eighty horsepower were produced.

With the new machines manufacturers could increase their output tremendously, but without better means of transportation they would have been unable to collect the raw materials or to distribute the finished products. The existing roads were in such a state of disrepair that heavy goods could be transported over them only in dry periods or when the ground was solidly frozen. Also the modes of transportation were primitive, the most common being by pack-horse trains. This method was so expensive that the charge for carrying coal from Liverpool to Manchester, a distance of about thirty miles, was commonly thirty pounds a ton. In the second half of the eighteenth century the problem was partly solved by the building of better roads. Between 1760 and 1774 Parliament passed no less than 524 acts dealing with the construction and maintenance of roads. In consequence transportation by means of wagons began to supersede the pack-horse trains. But even the new roads were badly constructed. It was not until near the turn of the century that Telford and Macadam, two Scottish engineers, introduced the modern science of road-building. Macadam's method was to lay a foundation of larger stones, put a second layer of smaller stones over the first, and then finish with a covering of crushed stones which was rolled smooth. These macadamized roads were so durable that they were soon built in all parts of Great Britain.

The need for better transportation also led to the improvement of a number of rivers before the middle of the century, but the first modern canal, extending from the coal mines at Worsley to Manchester, a distance of seven miles, was completed in 1761. When this canal proved its worth, many others were planned and completed. So great was the demand for them that in the four years after 1790 Parliament passed eighty-nine canal acts. It has been estimated that by 1803 there were already almost three thousand miles of canals in Great Britain, and canal-building was still going on at a rapid pace.

Hardly had Great Britain been covered with networks of roads and canals when Watt's improved steam engine was adapted to transportation. As early as 1802 a steamboat equipped with a Watt engine which turned a paddle-wheel was used for towing in the Forth and Clyde Canal, but was abandoned after a short time. Five years later Robert Fulton made steam navigation a commercial success on the Hudson in America with a steamboat for which Watt and Boulton had designed the engine. In Great Britain the first regular steamboat service was inaugurated on the Clyde in 1812. While the steamboat was being developed there was also much experimentation with locomotives. William Murdock, an associate of the Watt-Boulton firm, had already constructed a model locomotive in 1784 that ran eight miles an hour. In 1802 Richard Trevithick designed and built a large locomotive engine which was exhibited in London. Eleven years later William Hedley patented his "Puffing Billy," which could draw eight coal wagons at a speed of almost five miles per hour, and in the next year George Stephenson built his first locomotive. By 1815 Great Britain and the whole civilized world were on the eve of great changes in transportation.

Better transportation in addition to the application of machinery to the processes of manufacture meant wider markets and, therefore, more profits. It was not the workers, however, who pocketed the profits, but the employer or capitalist. As shown in a previous chapter, the use of capital on a large scale in commerce and industry dates back to the Middle Ages. In the English textile trade capitalism had been an important factor since the sixteenth century. By the early decades of the eighteenth century many of the textile workers were really wage-earners, though they still worked at home. Capitalists provided them with the raw materials, paid them wages, and sold the finished product. In some cases even the hand machines and tools the workers used were owned by their employers. In other industries there was a definite wage-earning class—for example, the potters, the brewers, and the miners. Of the iron industry one historian writes: "From the earliest period of which we have exact information iron-making in this country has been conducted on capitalistic lines—capitalistic not only in that the workers are dependent upon an employer for their raw material and market, but also in that they are brought together in a works, paid wages, and perform their duties under conditions not dissimilar to those of almost any large industry of modern times."[1] During the Industrial Revolution this condition

[1] T. S. Ashton, *Iron and Steel in the Industrial Revolution* (1924), p. 1.

became general. Capitalists gained control not only of the means of production but also of the supply of raw materials and the disposal of the finished products. Under this system the worker was now entirely at the mercy of the factory owners, for without machinery he could not work, even if he had been able to obtain a supply of raw materials. All he could sell was his labor, at terms prescribed by his employer. Thus in 1815 the capitalist was much more important than he had been in 1700, and the gulf which separated the worker from the employer was much wider.

The changes which have been listed were not introduced without opposition. From the very beginning the hand-workers, fearing that they would be deprived of a living, tried to prevent the use of machines in every possible way. Thus the weavers at first refused to use Kay's flying shuttle, even threatening its inventor with violence. When Hargreaves made his first spinning jenny, a mob broke into his house and destroyed the machine. Later, anti-machine riots took place in many localities, with gangs of desperate men attacking factories, smashing machines, and seeking to harm the inventors. But these struggles were vain, for machinery had come to stay.

AGRICULTURAL CHANGES

While the application of machinery was transforming industrial society, widespread changes were also taking place in the rural districts—changes which some historians have summed up under the term "Agrarian Revolution." Better methods of tillage were introduced, larger areas were put under cultivation, cattle were improved by selective breeding, and land was enclosed with unprecedented speed. The necessary stimulus for these changes was provided by the high prices which made improved farming profitable, the rise in the standard of living which increased the demand for food per head, the improvement of roads and the construction of canals which made markets more accessible, and the rapidly growing population which necessitated the production of more food.[1] Another factor in the improvement of agriculture was the interest of the prosperous merchants who bought country estates and began to infuse into agriculture the same spirit of enterprise that prevailed in commerce. One must be careful,

---

[1] The English population, estimated at five and one-half millions in 1688, increased so rapidly in the eighteenth century, particularly in the second half, that it almost doubled by the end of the century.

however, not to exaggerate the rapidity of the changes. Actually progress was very slow, and the changes were largely localized. At the end of the eighteenth century Arthur Young found that the agricultural methods were still quite primitive in many parts of the country.

In the first half of the eighteenth century a number of agriculturists advocated more scientific methods of agriculture as a means of increasing the productivity of the soil. The outstanding pioneer in this movement was Jethro Tull (1674-1740). Impressed during his travels in southern France by the methods employed in the cultivation of vineyards, Tull tried some of them on his own farm, and also advocated them to others in his *Horse-Hoeing Husbandry*, published in 1733. He informed the farmers of England that plants can gain the maximum of nourishment only when the surface of the ground is repeatedly broken into small particles. To facilitate this hoeing he devised the horse-hoe, a horse-drawn implement with three to six hoe-like blades. He also invented a drilling machine which deposited the seeds in the ground in parallel rows, thereby making the use of the horse-hoe possible. After Tull had pointed the way, other new implements were invented and the old ones were improved. The cumbrous plows in general use up to that time were made lighter and also improved in form; horse-drawn rakes and harrows came into wider use; also primitive machines for threshing began to make their appearance toward the end of the eighteenth century.

One of the great problems of earlier times had been the feeding of cattle during the winter. The number of cattle a farmer could keep during the winter months depended on his harvest of hay, straw, and oats. The rest were slaughtered in the fall and the meat was salted down for winter use. In the eighteenth century the serious difficulty of feeding cattle during the winter was removed by the cultivation of turnips, clover, and other root crops and artificial grasses. The raising of clover meant not only better pastures in the summer but more hay during the winter, while turnips were a great aid in keeping cattle in condition during the winter.[1] More

---

[1] The cultivation of artificial grasses—so called because they were raised from deliberately sown seeds whereas natural grass grows wild—also abolished the necessity for fallow, thereby increasing the arable land by one-third. As the grasses derive much of their nourishment from the air, they made but little demand on the soil. Moreover, their roots, which were allowed to decay in the soil, enriched it with elements essential to plant growth.

cattle could now be kept, and by spring the farmer had a larger supply of manure to fertilize his fields. Turnips were grown in England as early as the seventeenth century, but it was Lord Townshend (1676–1738) who first proved their value by cultivating them according to the methods prescribed by Tull, thereby earning for himself the nickname "Turnip" Townshend. Lord Townshend further demonstrated that the fertility of the soil could be increased immensely by mixing marl, a soft earth found some distance under the surface, with the top soil. He and his successors also gave greater attention to the use of such fertilizers as lime and bone, and to the rotation of crops in such a way that the soil could regain much of its fertility. It was "Turnip" Townshend who initiated the so-called Norfolk system of rotation which prescribed the sowing of turnips, barley or oats, clover, and wheat successively.

The improvements did not stop with the introduction of new crops and new methods of tillage. An increased demand for butcher's meat in the industrial centers led also to improvement of livestock by selective breeding. The great pioneer in this line was Robert Bakewell (1725–1794), whose aim was to breed animals in which the valuable joints would be well developed, and which would mature early. He was most successful with sheep. Previously sheep had been raised chiefly for their wool. The type most favored was small in frame, long-legged, and hardy enough to live on the scantiest food. Bakewell's experiments produced a breed of sheep, known as the New Leicesters, which had large bodies and fine-grained flesh, and which matured in two years as compared with three or four years for other breeds. He also improved the breed of horses by producing a smaller but stronger and hardier animal than the large draught horse of England. Bakewell's example was quickly followed, particularly in the breeding of cattle. Instead of wool and hides, quantity and quality of meat became the first consideration. Some idea of the improvements effected during the eighteenth century may be gained from the difference in the average size of cattle sold in Smithfield market in 1710 and 1795. Beeves increased in size from 370 to 800 pounds, calves from 50 to 148 pounds, sheep from 28 to 80 pounds, and lambs from 18 to 50 pounds. Breeding experiments were also conducted to increase the production of milk. At the beginning of the century the best dairy cows gave four gallons a day; at its close, the yield had increased to six and in some cases to as much as nine gallons.

The various improvements in agriculture and stock-breeding doomed the old agricultural system which allotted to the small peasant cultivators scattered strips in large open fields. This open-field system did not admit of the introduction of such new crops as turnips and clover unless all landholders agreed on the change. Neither did the narrow strips permit cross-harrowing or cross-plowing. Furthermore, so long as the cattle were herded promiscuously on the stubble fields or on the village commons, breeding experiments were impossible. Since the middle of the fifteenth century much land had been enclosed for sheep-farming, but when the existing demand for wool was met the process of enclosure slackened, although it did not stop. Much land remained that was not enclosed. At the end of the seventeenth century about half the arable land was still cultivated in open fields. But during the eighteenth century the process of enclosure was greatly accelerated, especially when it became evident that immense profits could be gained from the improved methods of agriculture and stock-breeding. It has been calculated that during the four decades from 1761 to 1801 almost two and one-half million acres of arable land were enclosed. Along with the movement for the enclosure of arable fields went a movement to enclose wastes and common pastures. In this way much land was added to the cultivated area.

Although the enclosures put under cultivation much land which had heretofore been of little value, and also made possible a wider adoption of improved methods of tillage, the system caused great suffering to the small peasant cultivators. In the end it was the influential squires and the larger tenants who benefited, with the small farmers coming off badly. In some parishes, it is true, the rights of the poor were carefully protected, but in others the effects of the enclosures were disastrous for them. Arthur Young, an ardent advocate of improved farming, said: "The fact is that by nineteen enclosure bills in twenty they [the poor] are injured." Some small farmers were tempted by the offers of their landlords and sold their land. In most cases the money they received was quickly spent; then these former landowners, having no means of subsistence, became destitute. Others lost their holdings because they lacked expert advice to prove their legal rights to them. Still others, unable to make a living because they could no longer pasture their cows and geese in the commons[1] or gather wood and turf in the wastes, were compelled to sell their land. Thus enclosures most often resulted in the absorption of the small holdings into the estates of the great landlords. It is estimated that from 1740 to 1788 alone forty thousand farms were absorbed by the great proprietors. While a few of the former small farmers were fortunate enough to rise to the position of capitalist tenant farmers, the rest either sank to the status of agricultural laborers or left the rural districts entirely. Most of the latter migrated to British oversea possessions or sought employment in the industrial towns.

Like industry, agriculture was becoming capitalistic. Previously a small farmer had made the rude implements he needed to cultivate the soil; now a small farmer who was unable to buy machinery, livestock, and fertilizers could not hope to compete with the capitalist farmers. Moreover, whereas formerly the small farmer had been able to supplement his income by spinning, weaving, lace-making, or some other form of manufacture, he was now deprived of that income because manufacturing was centering in the cities. Such conditions gradually caused the virtual disappearance of yeomen or small farmers in England. From the great upheaval caused by the agricultural and industrial changes three distinct agricultural classes were to emerge in the nineteenth century: the great landed proprietors who leased their lands for high rentals, the large farmers who rented the lands and carried on agriculture on a capitalistic, profit-making basis, and the laborer who worked for wages.

LIFE, THOUGHT, AND CULTURE

Although a reaction against the profligacy of the Restoration did set in, and although polite society did pride itself on its refinement, the early eighteenth century, beneath its surface refinement, was still an age of ignorance, brutality, and drunkenness. The masses of the population were untouched by what is today known as popular or primary education, and were therefore largely illiterate. The living conditions and poverty of the poorer classes in the cities—particularly London—cannot be exaggerated. Higher ed-

---

[1] As a current verse had it:

> "The law locks up the man or woman
> Who steals the goose from off the common;
> But leaves the greater villain loose
> Who steals the common from the goose."

ucation reached only a few. In 1750 only three hundred seventeen freshmen matriculated in the whole of England. Women were too often illiterate, and their position was still so low that they had few rights before the law. The brutality of the age is seen in the popular amusements, such as bear-baiting, bull-baiting, and cockfighting, and in the general contempt for human suffering. A modern is shocked by the severity of a criminal code which condemned women to be flogged publicly and even to be burned at the stake; which made it possible for debtors to be imprisoned for life; and which punished with death no less than one hundred sixty offenses. To the callous crowds of London, executions became occasions for merriment. Criminals on the way to the gallows were cheered, plentifully furnished with brandy, and even given a certain immortality in songs and poems. The insane were confined in Bethlehem Hospital, better known as Bedlam, where they were chained, beaten, and generally mistreated. Londoners went to see the unfortunate insane for amusement, much as one goes to see the animals in a zoo today.

In some respects the tone of society grew worse during the first half of the eighteenth century. Political practices became more venal, and offices and votes were bought and sold openly. Moreover, drunkenness increased to such an extent that it came to be regarded as the national vice. No section of society was free from it. It was a habit among men occupying the highest positions in the state, among fine gentlemen, and among the lowest classes. French wines had been the favorite drink of the aristocracy until the Methuen treaty of 1703 reduced by one-third the duty on Portuguese wines. Thereafter the heavier wines of Portugal, particularly port, became the beverage of the aristocracy. The consumption of prodigious quantities of port, in addition to excessive eating (styled "carnivoracity" by contemporary wits), made gout a common ailment among the upper classes. Charlatans who advertised sure cures for this affliction reaped a rich harvest. Some physicians recommended more drinking as a cure, even though the gout had in the first place been caused or at least aggravated by the consumption of alcohol. But if the upper classes suffered much from port, the lower classes suffered more from gin. Early in the eighteenth century more gin than beer was consumed. It is estimated that in 1736 every twenty-fifth house in London was a gin shop. Many of the shops boldly hung out signs which promised to make the customers "drunk for a penny, dead drunk for two-pence," and offered them clean straw to lie on while they were getting sober. Finally, in 1751, when the consumption of gin reached a total of eleven million gallons, the government took steps to curb the evil.

In matters of religion many Englishmen settled down into a state of apathy after the fierce theological disputes of the seventeenth century. The desire for civil tranquillity soon developed into a general desire for the reasonable, the rationally revealed. Irrational and undisciplined fancy was shunned. This championing of the reasonable engendered, in turn, contempt for any evidences of *enthusiasm*—a term which in the eighteenth century meant something very different from its present-day connotation. Derived from the Greek *en theos* (full of God), the word became associated with mystical delusions in religion. An enthusiast was characterized by an extravagant and fantastic devotion to an idea—a deluded person. The result of these delusions was a "fictitious piety" that "corrupts or petrifies the heart not less certainly than does a romantic sentimentality." Through the medium of these imaginings so devoid of reason, man "becomes a visionary, who lives on better terms with angels and with seraphs than with his children, servants, or neighbors; or he is one who, while he reverences the thrones, dominions, and powers of the invisible world, vents his spleen in railing at all dignities and powers of earth."[1] In general this religious outlook was regarded as a completely untrustworthy reliance on, and belief in, the validity of intuitive —hence emotional—processes and as an abdication of reason.

Lord Shaftesbury, in his famous *Letter concerning Enthusiasm*, describes enthusiasm as "a terrible distemper, almost as bad as the smallpox." As another contemporary put it: "A person wants good breeding, or is a very great enthusiast, who talks so much about religion." The Church of England, though it numbered among its members many devout and earnest souls, was marked by a lack of religious enthusiasm. Bishop Burnet wrote: "I must say the main body of our English clergy has always appeared dead and lifeless to me, and instead of animating one another they rather seem to lay one another to sleep." Their sermons, though often learned, were usually dry dissertations preached without gestures or elevation of voice. Among the Dissenters the conditions were

---

[1] Isaac Taylor, *The Natural History of Enthusiasm* (1830), p. 14.

much the same. The fervency which had characterized Puritanism in the seventeenth century had largely died out since the Act of Toleration had given legal standing to all Nonconformists. In polite society religion was regarded as a matter of the intellect rather than of the heart. Thus Archbishop Tillotson wrote: "Reason is the faculty whereby revelations are to be discerned."

The reaction against rational religion came in Wesleyanism or Methodism, which had its origin in the "Holy Club" formed by a group of students at Oxford in 1729 for the cultivation of personal piety and the performance of benevolent deeds. All the members of the group fasted regularly on Wednesdays and Fridays, received Holy Communion each week, instructed the children of the poor, and visited the sick and the inmates of prisons and almshouses. By their fellow students they were derisively dubbed "Methodists" because of the methodical regularity of their lives. The leader of the group was John Wesley, and two of its outstanding members were Charles Wesley, later to become famous as a hymn writer, and George Whitefield, who became a noted preacher. It was not one of the original designs of the group to found a new sect, for all were faithful members of the Established Church. All they desired was to keep the gospel alive in their own hearts and to preach it to such as had not heard it. In 1735 the two Wesleys left England for the newly founded colony of Georgia, to convert the Indians. But the undertaking was a pitiful failure and in 1738 the brothers returned to their native country.

The return of the Wesleys to England may be said to mark the beginning of the Methodist movement. Both John Wesley and George Whitefield now began to go about preaching "the glad tidings of salvation," as the former put it. Everywhere immense crowds were attracted by their sermons. Not that the doctrines they taught were in any sense new; the novelty lay in the fervent zeal with which these religious enthusiasts proclaimed them. Wesley's hearers were often overcome with convulsions, screaming and swooning, such manifestations being regarded as marks of divine inspiration or as miraculous proofs of a new birth. He himself wrote: "The power of God came so mightily among us that one, and another, and another, fell down as thunderstruck." To the clergy of the Anglican Church, however, Wesley and Whitefield appeared mad and their doctrines actually seditious. Gradually the pulpits were closed to them. Not to be discouraged, Whitefield began to preach to crowds in the open air. Though Wesley was at first shocked by this practice, regarding it as a breach of ecclesiastical order, he soon followed Whitefield's example. Even then Wesley was in many places treated as a disturber of the peace and on occasion was pelted with mud. Yet his dauntless courage never forsook him.

Wesleyanism was primarily a lower-class movement. Instead of taking into consideration the impassable gulf that separated the lower classes from the aristocracy, it went so far as to preach the universal brotherhood of man—not a heavenly brotherhood, but a brotherhood on earth. To the upper classes its doctrines were preposterous, unthinkable, and based on a social concept that went far beyond the limits of decorum. It was in this vein that the Duchess of Buckingham wrote to Lady Huntingdon when the latter invited her to hear Whitefield preach: "I thank Your Ladyship for the information concerning the *Methodist* preachers: their doctrines are most repulsive, strongly tinctured with Impertinence and Disrespect towards their Superiors, in perpetually endeavoring to level all ranks and do away with Distinctions. It is monstrous to be told that you have a heart as *sinful* as the Common Wretches that crawl the Earth. This is highly *offensive* and *insulting;* and I cannot but wonder that Your Ladyship should relish any sentiment so much at variance with High Rank and Good Breeding." Because of its emphasis on the belief that if man is to be ready for heaven his lot on this earth must be bettered in matters material as well as spiritual, Methodism became a factor in the Humanitarian movement.

Again and again Wesley pushed into the most hidden corners of England. For forty years he did not permit bad weather or bad roads to turn him from his course. It has been calculated that he journeyed on horseback some 225,000 miles to preach more than forty thousand sermons. At the age of eighty-three he wrote: "I am a wonder to myself. It is now twelve years since I have felt such a sensation as weariness. I am never tired either with writing, preaching, or traveling." Working to the last, he died in 1791 at the age of eighty-eight.

Whereas Whitefield was an eloquent preacher, Wesley was also an able organizer. He realized that if the effects of his preaching were to be made permanent there must be some kind of organization. Hence he established societies at various places. These societies gave to Methodism the appearance of an organized system. Some idea of the labor of Wesley and his associates may be gained from the fact that at the time of his death the Methodists in England numbered more than seventy-five thousand, with more than three hundred preachers, while in the United States two hundred preachers ministered to more than forty-three thousand Methodists. Yet Wesley disavowed to the last any intention of founding a new denomination. A year before his death he wrote in the *Arminian Magazine:* "I declare once more that I live and die a member of the Church of England; and that none who regard my judgment and advice will ever separate from it." Nevertheless, he had himself taken the first step toward secession by ordaining lay preachers when the Church of England refused to supply him with ministers. Not long after his death the movement broke away from the Established Church to form an independent denomination, which became an important factor in the national life of England. In Ireland and Scotland the movement exercised little influence, but in the United States the Methodists became the most numerous body of American Protestants. Today the influence of Methodism extends over both hemispheres, and its adherents number many millions of souls.

In 1776 a book was published which had as revolutionary effects in the realm of economic thought as had John Wesley's work on the religious life in England. Its title was *An Inquiry into the Nature and Causes of the Wealth of Nations*, and its author was Adam Smith. Born in Scotland in 1723, Smith became professor of moral philosophy in the University of Glasgow in 1752. This position he held until 1763, when he became tutor to the young duke of Buccleuch. On his travels with the duke, Smith spent about ten months in Paris, where he met various members of a group known as the Physiocrats. Though he had previously worked out the fundamental and characteristic principles of the system expounded in the *Wealth of Nations*, his discussions with such Physiocrats as Quesnay and Turgot developed his conceptions. Earlier Smith had absorbed from his friend Hume and from his teacher Hutcheson the idea of a beneficent law or order of nature which regulates human affairs. This concept he made the basis of his consideration of economic life. The pervasive mercantilist restrictions on trade and industry, he argued, are "unnatural" or contrary to the law of nature, and therefore defeat the very purpose for which they are designed. He declared that the maximum of wealth can be attained only through the unfettered action of individuals, for nature has arranged that each man in seeking his own welfare promotes the welfare of the nation. Smith attacked particularly the doctrine of the balance of trade, to which commercial orthodoxy still clung as if it were an unassailable dogma. Regarding it he wrote: "To attempt to increase the wealth of any country, either by introducing or by detaining in it an unnecessary quantity of gold and silver, is as absurd as it would be to attempt to increase the good cheer of private families by obliging them to keep an unnecessary number of kitchen utensils." He condemned as false the view that the prosperity of one nation must mean a loss to the others, stating that a prosperous neighbor offers a better market than an impoverished one. The doctrines expounded in the *Wealth of Nations* were not original. They had been stated before by Hume and others, but never so logically, so lucidly, and with such abundance of illustration. In the *Wealth of Nations*, a mass of uncoördinated ideas are for the first time arranged into a coherent system.

The *Wealth of Nations* had an immediate and far-reaching influence. When the book appeared it was instantly acclaimed, and before its author's death in 1790 it had passed through five editions. In France Napoleon Bonaparte was to adopt many of its suggestions, and in Germany Baron vom Stein was to proclaim some of its doctrines. To trace its influence in Great Britain would be tantamount to writing the story of free trade from 1776 to the close of the nineteenth century.[1] Smith's first and greatest disciple in England was William Pitt the younger, who immediately endeavored to put the master's teachings into practice. In his budget speech of 1792 Pitt stated that the writings of Adam Smith "will, I believe, furnish the best solution to every question connected with the history of commerce or with the systems of political economy." The *Wealth of Nations* profoundly influenced British colonial policy. Published in the same year in which the American colonies issued the Declaration of Independence, the book came too late to influence the settlement of that question; but by undermining the Mercantile System, which was largely responsible for the friction between the colonies and the mother country, it opened

---

[1] The final establishment of free trade in England was due, of course, not so much to the *Wealth of Nations* as to the fact that the interests of British industry were best served by a free-trade policy.

the way for a new British colonial policy which subsequently prevented similar contests. Adam Smith's position in the history of
economic thought has been compared with that of Charles Darwin
in the history of science. All economists since his time are to some
degree indebted to him, even as all natural scientists are to Darwin.

Besides being a fruitful age in the development of religion and
of economic thought, the eighteenth century was an important
period in the history of the arts, particularly of painting. Up to the
beginning of this century two kinds of paintings had been in vogue
in England: portraits and historical scenes. Of the two, portraits
had received the most attention. For the most part they were the
work of foreign painters who resided in England. Greatest among
these foreign artists were Hans Holbein, who painted many of the
personages at the court of Henry VIII; Van Dyke, who settled
in England during the reign of Charles I; and Rubens, who was
induced by the same Charles to spend some time at the English
court. At the beginning of the eighteenth century a number of
native English artists began to show skill and originality, but the
first to strike a distinctly national note was William Hogarth
(1697–1764). Both as a painter and as an engraver, Hogarth won a
unique place for himself through his vivid portrayals of contemporary life and manners. He was a pictorial chronicler, a
satirist who painted his essays instead of writing them, a humorist
whose comedies took the form of pictures. Charles Lamb said of
Hogarth's paintings that people "look at other pictures, but read
Hogarth's"; and commented further: "A set of severer satires
were never written upon paper or graven upon copper." With
unshrinking realism Hogarth portrayed the vices of the fashionable
circles, the follies of the aristocrats, and the drunkenness of the
lowly. Every picture had its moral. Thus, in *A Rake's Progress*
(1735) he warns the young aristocrats: "Waste your substance in
riotous living and you will end your days in Bedlam." In *Marriage
à la Mode* (1745) he would say: "See what comes of a marriage
that is contracted solely for money." Hogarth's practice of engraving his pictures for popular sale permitted him to reach a wide
public. While it still remained the privilege of the wealthy to own
original paintings, the price of Hogarth's prints was so low that
people in moderate circumstances were able to buy them.

No previous age in English history had witnessed such an interest in art as did the eighteenth century, especially the second

WILLIAM PITT
EARL OF CHATHAM
by Wedgwood

MARRIAGE À LA
MODE   *by Hogarth*

WEDGWOOD VASES

A RAKE'S PROGRESS
by Hogarth

JOSIAH WEDGWOOD
by Wedgwood

CAPTAIN JAMES COOK

LORD CORNWALLIS *by Gainsborough*

EAST INDIA HOUSE, LONDON

half. Not only do the exhibitions of paintings date from this century, but also the rise of art societies and academies for the encouragement of painting. In 1768 the Royal Academy was founded with Sir Joshua Reynolds (1723–1792), one of the greatest of English portrait painters, as its first president. Like Reynolds, Thomas Gainsborough (1727–1788), another important artist of the second half of the century, painted the portraits of the aristocrats but also produced a number of distinctly English scenes. Deserving of a prominent place in art as well as in industry is Josiah Wedgwood (1730–1795), who set a new standard of workmanship in the world of pottery. As works of art some of his finer wares are still unsurpassed. After improving the cream-colored earthenware, which became known as the Queen's Ware, for practical use, he turned to artistic pottery, producing with the help of an artist the well-known series of wares with Greek motives. Within a few years Wedgwood's wares became famous not only in England but throughout the continent. In 1774 he was commissioned by Catherine II of Russia to make a dinner service of 952 pieces. The plates and other dishes of this set were decorated with more than a thousand paintings of English castles and mansions, besides the normal rim decorations. As his epitaph states, he "converted a rude and inconsiderable manufactory into an elegant art and an important part of national commerce."

Another noteworthy event of the early eighteenth century was the publication in 1702 of the first English daily newspaper, the *Daily Courant*. As early as the reign of James I small printed sheets or packets of news had begun to appear from time to time without any set date for issuance. In 1622 there appeared the *Weekly Newes*, which is generally regarded as the first regularly published newspaper. It had many rivals and successors in the course of the seventeenth century. Printed on a single sheet of small size with poor type, these early papers sold for a penny or even less. So little capital was necessary that great numbers were started, but the life of the individual paper was generally short. To escape government censorship, many were printed in the obscurity of London alleys and were slipped into the coffee-houses (which were the centers of political and literary discussion in the eighteenth century), to be read with relish because they were forbidden. Already in 1643 the first illustrated sheet, called *Mercurius Civicus*, made its appearance. The first issue contained portraits of Charles I and Sir Thomas Fairfax, but the engraving was so poor that the pictures bore scarcely any likeness to their subjects. Two years after the appearance of the *Daily Courant*, a small news sheet printed on one side only, Daniel Defoe founded his weekly, the *Review*, which eventually was issued thrice weekly. Five years later Steele's *Tatler* appeared, and in 1711 the *Spectator* was published by Steele and Addison. Before the end of the eighteenth century two newspapers which still circulate, the *Morning Post* (1772) and the *London Times* (1788), came into existence.

In English literature as well as in religion the first half of the eighteenth century was an age of reason. Since the object of the poets and prose writers, with some exceptions, was to portray life as they perceived it through their intellects, the literature of the time, particularly the poetry, is singularly devoid of enthusiasm and romance. Whatever merits it has are due to its wit, its power of invention, and its spirit of satire. Probably never before or since has satire been so skilfully expressed. The literary models of the age were the Greek and Roman classics, in which many educated Englishmen found their "favorite ideas admirably expressed." Consequently this age has been called the Augustan or classical age of English literature. Most of the characteristics of the period are summed up in the work of Pope, who was the literary dictator in England from the death of Dryden in 1700 until his own death in 1744. For this reason the period is also called the Age of Pope. In his *Essay on Criticism* Pope, advocating excellence of style as the primary aim of the writer, sets up the ancients as models. His poem, *The Rape of the Lock*, satirized the foibles and weaknesses of his day, but his best work is probably his *Essay on Man*, an exposition of the ethical and religious ideas of his time. In general, his writings are characterized by perfection of form and polish of phrasing, but they lack depth, humor, and lofty imagination.

Important prose writers of the period were Joseph Addison (1672–1719), Richard Steele (1672–1729), and Jonathan Swift (1667–1745). Though both Addison and Steele wrote other works, their fame rests upon their essays. In 1709 Steele started a tri-weekly sheet called the *Tatler*, which contained a short essay besides some scraps of news. Addison contributed to this leaf only occasionally, but was a regular contributor to the *Spectator*, a daily sheet which replaced the *Tatler* in 1711. After eighteen months the *Spectator* gave way to the *Guardian*. The essays which appeared in the three periodicals are noted for their literary power, their clarity of style, their genial humor, and their portrayal of life. Steele's style is vivacious, but less graceful than Addison's. As a writer of graceful prose, Addison has seldom, if ever, been surpassed. It has been said of the essays of Addison and Steele that they brought literature down to everyday life. Swift, a master of ironical humor, is chiefly remembered as the author of *Gulliver's Travels*, which became a favorite romance with the young. Though it is read today in its expurgated form as a burlesque of travel and adventure, the original is a scathing satire on the shortcomings of Swift's era and of the human race of all time.

Another important prose writer was Daniel Defoe (1660–1731). While Addison, Steele, and Swift wrote for the educated classes of England, Defoe was a journalist or hack writer who could be understood even by the uneducated. By some he is regarded as the founder of sensational or "yellow" journalism. He had no set principles, and would often write anonymously on any or every side of a subject if he thought his pamphlets would sell. From 1704 to 1713 he published the *Review*, initiating in it the periodical essay which is equivalent to the editorial essays in the newspapers of today. The *Review* was in this respect the forerunner of Steele's more famous *Tatler*. A prolific writer, Defoe is said to have produced more than two hundred fifty distinct publications. Of them all only *Robinson Crusoe*, a book of adventure written when its author was past fifty-five, has retained its popularity. It is one of the immortal books in the English language. Together with Swift's *Gulliver's Travels* it prepared the way for the coming of the modern English novel. The striking feature of Defoe's writings is his art of achieving verisimilitude by the accumulation of detail. Indeed, in ability to give to invention the appearance of reality he remains unsurpassed. *Robinson Crusoe*, on its publication, was thought to be a true narrative. Moreover, his *Journal of the Plague Year* (1722) was so utterly convincing that it was for long accepted as an authentic history of the Great Plague of 1666 by an eyewitness, whereas it is actually a species of historical novel.

The literary dictator in the second half of the century until his death in 1784 was Samuel Johnson (1709–1784), though today his works are little read. After years of laborious work Johnson in 1755 published his famous *Dictionary*, which despite its faulty etymologies was the first adequate catalogue of the English language. His best literary production is his *Lives of the Poets*, published after he was seventy years old. Johnson's style at times rises to remarkable beauty, but at other times its Latinic constructions sound cumbrous and pompous. It was the latter quality which moved Goldsmith to say that Johnson could make little fishes talk like whales. As a personality Johnson was great enough to inspire James Boswell to write what is generally regarded as the finest biography in the English language. For two decades Boswell studied his subject, keeping a diary of Johnson's words and deeds. On the basis of his first-hand knowledge he wrote *The Life of Samuel Johnson*, published in 1791, which is still widely read and admired. Among the great prose writers of Johnson's age were Edmund Burke (1730–1797) and Edward Gibbon (1737–1794). In the United States Burke's memorable *Speech on Conciliation with America* is still read in most schools. But his greatest literary work is his *Reflections on the French Revolution* (1790), a masterpiece of eloquence, written as a protest against the Revolution which was "bearing so terrible a harvest across the waves of the Channel." Gibbon, a humorous bachelor, devoted more than twenty years to the writing of his masterpiece, *The Decline and Fall of the Roman Empire*, which carries the story of the Roman Empire to the fall of Constantinople in 1453. Though many of its statements and conclusions have been undermined by modern scholarship, it still remains a great literary and historical monument.

In the field of drama there is little that deserves mention before the appearance of the two plays of Oliver Goldsmith (1728–1774) and those of Richard Brinsley Sheridan (1751–1816). Goldsmith's *She Stoops to Conquer* (1773) combines genuine humanity, rollicking humor, and literary grace. Sheridan's best play is *The School for Scandal* (1777). Of all the English plays written during the interval from Shakespeare to Bernard Shaw these two are outstanding among those that have retained popularity.

One of the most notable literary developments of the eighteenth century was the rise of the modern English novel. All the elements of modern fiction had existed much earlier, but in Richardson's *Pamela*, published in 1740, the world of ordinary human life and feelings first became the subject matter of English fiction. For that reason many literary critics call him the father of the English novel. Richardson followed *Pamela* with *Clarissa Harlowe* and *Sir Charles Grandison*. All achieved a tremendous popularity in their time, becoming, so to speak, the first "best sellers" of fiction. Today they appear wearisomely long and excessively sentimental. The sentimentality of *Pamela* caused Henry Fielding (1707–1754) to write the novel *Joseph Andrews* (1742) as an "antidote." Fielding also wrote other novels, among them his masterpiece, *Tom Jones* (1749). The next important novelist was Tobias Smollett (1721–1771), who employed a much greater variety of incident and character than did his predecessors. His best work is *The Expedition of Humphrey Clinker* (1771). Previously, during the years 1759 to 1767, there had appeared in nine volumes—it was still incomplete—*The Life and Opinions of Tristram Shandy* by Laurence Sterne. In a strict sense it was not a novel but rather a series of episodes. Many of Sterne's characters—for example, Uncle Toby and Corporal Trim—have become dear to posterity. The novel which today is probably more widely read than any other of that period is Oliver Goldsmith's *Vicar of Wakefield* (1766), which presents some excellent pictures of eighteenth century manners. Throughout the second half of the eighteenth century the English novel grew in popularity, becoming early in the nineteenth the most important form of English literature.

Although many leading writers of the second half of the eighteenth century continued to appeal to reason and emphasized form and polish in their works, there were signs of the approaching Romantic Revival, which was to prefer the sentimental to the rational, and the natural and spontaneous to the artificial. Some suggestions of this revival appear in the poetry of Thomas Gray (1716–1771), author of the *Elegy in a Country Churchyard*, in the forged *Poems of Ossian* (1762), and in Percy's *Reliques of Ancient English Poetry* (1765), but the movement did not flower until the early part of the nineteenth century.

CHAPTER TWENTY-TWO

The Founding of the British Empire

ENGLISH OVERSEA ACTIVITIES DURING THE SEVENTEENTH
CENTURY

AFTER Pope Alexander VI divided the unexplored and pagan world between Spain and Portugal in the last decade of the fifteenth century, these two countries held for a time a virtual monopoly of the trade with both the East and the West. That this monopoly should eventually be challenged by other nations was only natural. During the sixteenth century, France, torn by religious wars, did not offer Spain and Portugal much competition. Nor did Germany, which was so split up into small states that united action in any commercial or colonial venture was impossible. It remained for the Dutch and the English, after the middle of the century, to contest the commercial supremacy of the Iberian states. For some time after the defeat of the Spanish Armada it seemed that the English would become the great commercial nation of Europe, but the internal troubles of the early Stuart period prevented the government from giving the necessary attention to commercial and colonial affairs. Hence it was the Dutch who made the most of the opportunity granted by the declining power of Spain and Portugal to wrest commercial supremacy from these nations.

The success of Holland during the first half of the seventeenth century taught the English how much wealth and strength could be derived from a vigorous commercial policy. No sooner had order been restored after the anarchy of the Civil War than the English began to challenge the supremacy of the Dutch. In 1651 the Commonwealth government aimed a blow at the Hollanders by passing a Navigation Act which sharply restricted their trade both with England and with the English colonies. This act and other causes brought about the first Anglo-Dutch war (1652–1654) followed by two more during the reign of Charles II. By the end of the third war (1674), commercial supremacy had passed to the English.

In the meantime, many English colonies had been established during the seventeenth century. The unsettled political and religious conditions at home, far from discouraging colonization, were an important cause for the planting of oversea settlements. Large numbers of the early colonists were people who found life in England intolerable because their consciences did not permit them to conform to the practices of the Anglican Church. It has been said, indeed, that religious persecution was indirectly far more responsible for the establishment of colonies than the direct efforts of the government. Another motive for migration to America lay in the hope of finding gold. In its charter the Virginia Company was expressly granted permission to "dig, mine and search for all Manner of Mines of Gold, Silver and Copper." Furthermore, it was hoped that the founding of colonies in America would prove to be a step toward the discovery of a northwest passage to the East; and that these settlements would serve as markets for English goods and provide the mother country with raw materials. Some Englishmen also believed that the home country was overpopulated and that colonization was desirable to relieve the excess. The work of colonization was carried on not by the English crown itself but by chartered companies; therefore, the governments of the various colonies differed according to the specifications of the charters. During the seventeenth century most colonies were independent to the extent of making their own laws and electing their own officials. The rest had governors appointed by the crown, a system which was gradually extended after the accession of Charles II.

Though various abortive attempts had previously been made, it was not until 1607 that the first permanent English colony was founded in America. In that year the Virginia Company founded

Jamestown with 143 settlers, the object being avowedly commercial. The second colony was established for religious reasons. It was that of the Pilgrim Fathers, who set sail for America in the *Mayflower*, landing at Plymouth on Cape Cod in 1620. Before another decade had passed, the crown granted a charter (1629) to the Massachusetts Bay Company, which established its headquarters at Boston. So many Puritans sought a home and religious freedom in Massachusetts that its population rose to nearly twenty thousand by 1640. The emigration of such large numbers soon caused the settlement of Connecticut, which in 1638 became a separate colony. Towns were also founded in the territory which now comprises New Hampshire and Maine. In 1636 Roger Williams, banished from Massachusetts because of his religious beliefs, had started a settlement in Rhode Island which he called Providence. This was the first New England colony to allow complete freedom of worship. Four years earlier, Charles I had granted the territory of Maryland to Lord Baltimore, whose son, Leonard Calvert, planted a colony on Chesapeake Bay (1634) to provide an oversea home for Roman Catholics.

During the period of the Restoration further progress was made in the establishment of English colonies in America. The large district to the south of Virginia, called Carolina, was granted by Charles II to eight courtiers in 1663 for exploitation. The two distinct settlements which were founded, one in the northern and the other in the southern portion of the territory, eventually led to its division into North and South Carolina. Between the southern colonies and the northern or New England group was a large block of land extending from Connecticut to Maryland which the Dutch had occupied and called New Netherland. Though Cromwell had planned the conquest of this territory, nothing had come of his projects. In 1664 Charles II granted it to his brother, the duke of York, who immediately sent out an expedition to gain possession. As the Dutch defenses were weak, the territory was taken without much effort, and New Amsterdam, the principal Dutch settlement, was renamed New York. This territory, which gave the English an unbroken coastline from Maine to the Spanish colony of Florida, was later divided into New York, New Jersey, and Delaware. The unoccupied land behind New Jersey, beyond the Delaware River, soon became Pennsylvania. In 1681 William Penn, a Quaker, received proprietary rights over it in settlement of a claim owed him by Charles II, and in the next year the first group of settlers laid the foundations of the city of Philadelphia. The colony was begun as a home for English Quakers, but because of the religious toleration offered, it soon attracted settlers from various countries of Europe.

Though many years earlier English navigators in search of a northwest passage had penetrated the northern waters of the New World, the English had done little to exploit commercially the territories discovered by these dauntless explorers. In 1670, however, the Hudson's Bay Company was organized for the purpose of carrying on commerce with the northern part of North America. It received the exclusive right to trade on the shores of Hudson's Bay and to erect fortresses for the defense of its monopoly. Since the climate was unsuitable, no colonies like those along the Atlantic seaboard were established, the company contenting itself with the establishment of posts for its dealings with the Indians. In this trade, from which it reaped large profits, furs were the main attraction. Since the royal charter had set no definite limits to the company's territory, the English traders moved westward in quest of furs, coming into contact with Frenchmen who were also intent upon garnering the riches offered by this trade. The result was that clashes took place between the English and the French despite the friendly relations between the two countries in Europe.

The colonizing interest of the English was not restricted to the mainland of North America. A number of colonies had also been founded on the islands to the south. Though the Spaniards soon after the first voyage of Columbus had occupied the larger islands of the West Indies (Cuba, Puerto Rico, Haiti, and Jamaica), they had regarded the smaller ones as unimportant. To these lesser islands the English turned their attention in the seventeenth century. The colony founded in Barbados in 1624 prospered so well that a dozen years later its white population numbered six thousand. Other islands of the West Indies upon which the English settled were St. Kitt's, Antigua, St. Lucia, and Montserrat. In 1655 an English force, after failing to conquer Haiti, took from the Spaniards the island of Jamaica, the largest of the English possessions in the Caribbean. Considered of little worth at first, this became one of the most valuable of the English colonies. Altogether, the British West Indies were an important source of wealth to the mother country. The principal occupation of the settlers was the raising of sugar-cane and the production of sugar, molasses, and rum. As the plantations were worked by African slaves, slave traders did a profitable business. The English also colonized the Bermudas, which lie some distance to the north of the West Indies group. Upon their discovery in 1609 they were annexed by the Virginia Company; a little later a company was organized to exploit them; and finally in 1684 they were made a crown colony.

Meanwhile the English had also gained a firm footing in India. The East India Company, after receiving a monopoly of the eastern trade from Queen Elizabeth in 1600, had at first successfully sent a number of fleets to the Moluccas, making handsome profits on the cargoes of spices they brought back. However, after the Dutch concluded a truce with Spain in 1609 they began to force out the English traders. The Dutch East India Company, backed by the Dutch nation, was more than a match for the English East India Company, which received little support from the home government. Hence the English had to retreat step by step until the Dutch had a virtual monopoly of the trade with the Eastern Archipelago. Thereafter the English devoted themselves to the trade with the mainland of India, which had previously been subsidiary. In India the Portuguese were their chief opponents until the English, by a series of victories culminating in the capture of Ormuz (1622), forced them to open their harbors to English shipping.

The first English factory was established in 1609 at Surat, which long remained the headquarters of the company. Gradually trading posts were founded at other places along the Indian coast, one of the most important being Madras (1639). When Charles II married Catherine of Braganza, the English received as part of the queen's dowry the two Portuguese trading posts of Tangier and Bombay. The former was abandoned in 1683, but Bombay became one of the most valuable possessions of the company. Finally, during the years 1686–1690 the English established themselves at Calcutta. It was from these three main bases, Calcutta, Bombay, and Madras, that the British power in India was later to expand.

In short, though the British Empire was still nonexistent when the seventeenth century opened, by 1689 its development was already far advanced. In North America settlements had been founded in all but one of the colonies that later formed the thirteen revolting states. This one, Georgia, was colonized in 1732. It has been estimated that in 1700 the population of the American colonies was nearly two hundred thousand. In the upper part of North America the Hudson's Bay Company was active, while on the islands to the south a number of English settlements were flourishing. Furthermore, the foundations had been laid for British rule in India. Besides all this, the English had taken the island of St. Helena from the Dutch, and used it as a stopping place on the way to India. They also had fishing stations in Newfoundland and stations for the slave trade in West Africa. By the end of the seventeenth century the power of the Dutch was declining rapidly, and France was taking their place as England's chief commercial rival.

THE BEGINNING OF THE DUEL WITH FRANCE

The long duel with France which began after the accession of William III in 1689, and did not end until Napoleon was exiled to St. Helena, held tremendous significance for the development of the British Empire. The main cause of the first wars was Louis XIV's threat to dominate Europe, but as the duel continued, commercial and colonial questions, which had at first been relatively unimportant, became more and more prominent, until finally they overshadowed the other issues. Like the English, the French had established no permanent colonies in the New World until the early part of the seventeenth century, when Samuel de Champlain in 1608 founded Quebec. Subsequently trading posts were set up at other points, also, one of the most important being Montreal. From Quebec and Montreal the French explored the country now called Canada, establishing a trade which brought the manufactured articles of France to the Indians in exchange for furs. Frenchmen also settled in the peninsula of Acadia (Nova Scotia) and on the island of Cape Breton. Furthermore, during the seventeenth century the French fishermen shared with English the island of Newfoundland. Yet the number of Frenchmen who migrated to the New World was small in comparison with the number of English who had settled there. When the Company of New France collapsed in 1664 after an unprofitable existence of thirty-seven years there were no more than 2500 Frenchmen in its Canadian settlements.

During the reign of Louis XIV the French embarked on a more vigorous colonial program under the guidance of Colbert. Trade with Canada was developed on a wider scale, Jesuit missionaries went out in increased numbers to convert the Indians, and plans for the exploration of unknown parts of the new continent were pushed more rapidly. Explorers and fur-hunters penetrated the country north and south of the St. Lawrence, and also advanced westward to Lake Superior. While the intrepid La Salle was exploring the regions about Lake Erie, Lake Huron, and Lake Superior, the Jesuits Marquette and Joliet traversed the region about Lake Michigan until they reached the Wisconsin. Launching their canoes, they floated down this stream to the Mississippi, continuing onward to the mouth of the Arkansas before they turned back. Upon receiving news of the discovery of the Mississippi, the Comte de Frontenac, who was governor of Canada, sent La Salle to complete the exploration of that great river in the hope of finding a short route to the East Indies. In 1682 La Salle made his way down the Mississippi to the Gulf of Mexico, taking possession of its vast basin in the name of France and naming it Louisiana in honor of the French king.

The number of settlers in Canada increased considerably during Colbert's administration, but the French did not cross the ocean in large numbers. The main attractions of the country were still fur-trapping and fur-trading, though there were agricultural districts along the St. Lawrence and in the vicinity of fortified posts. That the number of Frenchmen in New France was not larger may be ascribed in a measure to the closing of the French colonies to all but Catholics. Whereas the English Dissenters found asylum in the colonies of their country, the French Huguenots were forbidden to enter New France. Consequently the white population of Canada numbered no more than twelve thousand by 1689. The Huguenots who migrated to the New World settled in the English colonies and helped to strengthen them.

French commercial and colonial efforts extended also to other parts of the globe besides North America. In 1635 the French had occupied Martinique and Guadeloupe, two islands of the West Indies, and about the middle of the century they had taken possession of the Isle of Bourbon and the Isle of France (now called respectively Reunion and Mauritius) in the Indian Ocean as stopping places on the way to India. Though a number of French companies were chartered earlier, French success in India began only with the company organized by Colbert in 1664. In the years 1668 and 1669 unfortified factories were established at Surat and Masulipatam; in 1674 a third depot was founded at Pondicherry; and several years later another was opened at Chandernagore in Bengal. These four stations were later to serve as bases for the wars with the English.

Thus the French were the rivals of the English in India, and in North America their possessions hemmed in the English colonies. The conflict between the two powers began when the War of the League of Augsburg broke out in Europe in 1689 and immediately spread to North America. The American phase is known as King William's War. In numbers the English colonists had a decided advantage, but the French tried to offset this by more vigorous tactics. Under the leadership of Governor Frontenac the French and their Indian allies carried the war into New Hampshire, Maine, and New York. At a number of places the Indians burned towns and villages and brutally massacred many of the English inhabitants. The English, for their part, were successful in taking Port Royal (1690), but failed to capture Quebec. By the peace of Ryswick (1697) all conquests in North America were restored.

The treaty produced only a temporary cessation of strife. After a brief interval war was resumed in Europe over the question of the Spanish succession, with England and France on opposite sides. When the news reached North America the French and English colonists again took up arms against each other. This inter-colonial conflict is called Queen Anne's War. Like the preceding struggle, it was characterized by a series of bloody massacres. The outstanding feat was the capture of Port Royal by the British colonists in 1710, and the conquest of the entire province of Acadia, which was added to the British colonies under the name of Nova Scotia. By the treaty of Utrecht (1713) France officially ceded Nova Scotia to the English and surrendered all claims to Newfoundland and the Hudson's Bay territory. At the same time the English obtained Gibraltar and the island of Minorca from Spain; also the contract to supply the Spanish colonies with slaves (asiento) and the right to send one ship a year to Spanish America for general trade.

Although peace had been concluded, there still remained numerous causes for dispute between the French and the English.

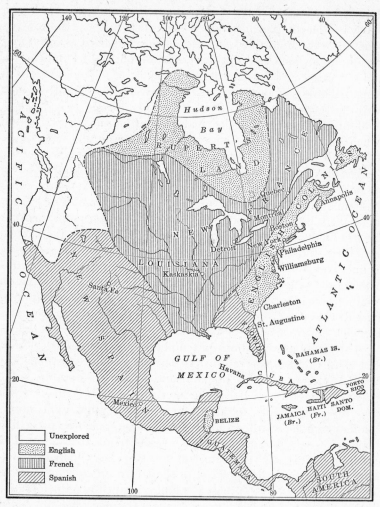

North America after the Treaty of Utrecht, 1713

The treaty had neither set a definite boundary for Nova Scotia nor settled the question of the control of the Mississippi valley. The hostility arising from these unsettled issues was aggravated by religious differences between the French and the English colonists. Furthermore, the loss of Acadia rankled in the minds of the French, its cession being regarded as by no means final. All this augured a renewal of the intercolonial war. But thanks to the efforts of Walpole and Cardinal Fleury, the two nations remained at peace for thirty years. During this period the French were busy strengthening their hold on their colonial possessions. To guard the mouth of the St. Lawrence they built on Cape Breton Island the fortress of Louisbourg, which soon became the strongest naval base in America, while a chain of forts was built to command the approaches to Canada from New York and New England. Plans were also laid to limit the English colonies to the narrow strip along the Atlantic coast through the construction of a line of forts from the St. Lawrence to New Orleans. Before the next war broke out in 1740 a number of these posts were actually erected.

The next conflict between the British and the French was preceded by the outbreak of war between Great Britain and Spain. Of all the European nations, Spain still possessed the greatest oversea empire, both in size and in potential wealth. Not only did the Spanish colonies still produce considerable quantities of precious metals, but they were also the source of other commodities for which there was a wide demand in Europe. Since the trade with its colonies was so lucrative, Spain preserved a monopoly despite the efforts of other nations to share in it. To gain a share had long been the object of the British. In the treaty of Utrecht Spain had finally consented to permit the sending of one British ship yearly for trade in Spanish America. It was not long, however, before the Spaniards accused the British of taking unfair advantage of their privilege by secretly reloading the one ship again and again from other ships. In an effort to stop this smuggling the Spanish authorities exercised their right of search, often with unnecessary cruelty. Tales of torture and abuse, mostly unfounded, soon roused a widespread indignation against the Spaniards in Great Britain. For a time Walpole was able to preserve peace, but the tale of Jenkins' ear made war inevitable. In 1738 an English sea captain named Jenkins appeared before the bar of the House of Commons with the story that Spanish coast-guards had boarded his ship, violently abused the crew, and finally hewn off his ear and thrown it in his face with an insulting message to the British ruler. To support his case Jenkins produced the ear neatly packed in wool. As Walpole could no longer resist the demands of the war party, war was declared against Spain in 1739. The issues of the War of Jenkins' Ear were soon merged in the War of the Austrian Succession, which broke out in the next year.

The intercolonial phase of the War of the Austrian Succession (1740–1748) is known as King George's War. It did not begin until March, 1744, when France opened hostilities on Great Britain. The outstanding event of the war in North America was the capture of Louisbourg by the British colonists after a siege of forty-eight days. When the conflict was concluded by the treaty of Aix-la-Chapelle in 1748, Louisbourg was restored in return for Madras, which the French had taken from the British in India.

THE COLONIAL PHASES OF THE SEVEN YEARS' WAR

Hitherto the intercolonial wars had been only the echoes of greater conflicts in Europe, and as such had been indecisive. In the next great struggle colonial and commercial questions were to be the chief issues between France and Great Britain. No sooner had the peace of Aix-la-Chapelle been signed than France immediately began preparations for the war both in Europe and in the colonies. The fortifications of Louisbourg were strengthened, and more links were constructed in the chain of forts from the St. Lawrence to New Orleans. Even though the two countries were officially at peace, hostilities between the French and English colonies had by no means ceased. The French continued to incite the Indians to attack English settlements and urged the people of Acadia to revolt. Unrest in Acadia finally became so widespread that the British found it necessary to deport the French settlers and scatter them through the colonies from Connecticut to Georgia. For the impending struggle the English colonies had the advantage of a larger population. The white settlers in New France numbered only about sixty thousand in 1750, while the colonial subjects of Great Britain, including Negro slaves, were reckoned at nearly a million and a half. But the French were united in their aims, whereas the British colonies were unable to agree on a common policy either of offense or of defense. Moreover, the British government at home had no clear conception of the issues involved in the colonial rivalry.

Though war was not officially declared in Europe until 1756, it really began in the preceding year in North America. Its immediate causes were conflicting claims to the Ohio valley. Soon after the treaty of Aix-la-Chapelle a group of London merchants and Virginia land speculators had formed the Ohio Land Company and had built a number of forts in the disputed territory.

Meanwhile the French were also busy establishing forts in other parts of the Ohio valley. Increasing tension between the British and the French resulted, culminating in the contest for the site at the point where the Monongahela and Alleghany rivers join to form the Ohio. Because it was the key position to the Ohio valley, both nations planned to erect a fort there. A young colonel named George Washington was sent with a small English force to occupy the site, but was obliged to relinquish it to the French, who built a fort which they called Fort Duquesne in honor of the governor of Canada.

Upon being informed of these events, the British government sent General Edward Braddock to America with two regiments of British infantry for the purpose of expelling the French from Fort Duquesne. The expedition ended in the disaster known as Braddock's defeat. The British, with their inelastic European methods of fighting, were no match for the French and Indians. Standing in the open in solid ranks, the British soldiers in their bright uniforms made excellent targets for the enemy hidden behind trees and logs. Of the 1500 men who had started out for Fort Duquesne, less than half straggled back to the English settlements in Virginia.

In general, things went badly for the British in North America during the early years of the war. Incompetent leadership, lack of enthusiasm, and want of concentrated effort caused the failure of most of their undertakings. Ignorant of the methods of warfare used by the French, the generals sent over from Great Britain were too proud to take advice from colonial officers. The French, on the other hand, had an able leader in General Montcalm, who employed his forces so judiciously that for two years the English were excluded from the disputed territory north of the Ohio. It seemed for a time that the French would triumph. But the turning point came soon after the accession of the elder Pitt to power in the home government (1757). With characteristic energy Pitt laid systematic plans for action, shelved the incompetent leaders, gave the commands to young men of ability, sent good troops to America, and supported them with naval forces. As a result, the British took a number of French strongholds. While the British fleet was blockading the harbors of Brest and Rochefort, so that the French could not send reinforcements to the colonies, a British force in America took Louisbourg (1758), thereby closing the front door to Canada. In the same year a second force blocked the southern road to Canada by the capture of Fort Duquesne, which was re-named Fort Pitt. Only at Fort Ticonderoga at the lower end of Lake Champlain were the British repulsed. The next year, how-ever, they took both Ticonderoga and Crown Point, closing also the middle way to Canada.

The most notable victory of the war was won by General James Wolfe at Quebec. Two expeditions were sent against this French stronghold, situated on a high rocky ridge above the St. Lawrence, protected by walls and batteries, and defended by 15,000 men under the command of Montcalm. The first, under General Jeffrey Amherst, went overland, while the second, under Wolfe, who had distinguished himself in the capture of Louisbourg, was trans-ported by a fleet under Admiral Saunders. Amherst took Fort Niagara, but was unable to get beyond Lake Champlain. Hence the second force was compelled to attack Quebec alone. As Wolfe had only 9000 men, the situation seemed hopeless. For three months he waited, constantly watching for any possible advantage that might be gained. Finally he resolved to make a desperate attempt to take the fort. On a dark night the English leader moved about 5000 of his men to the foot of the cliff above the city. Silently scaling the heights, he suddenly appeared with his men on the Plains of Abraham on the landward side of the fort, to the great astonishment of Montcalm. When the French came out to give battle, the British fought so furiously that victory was soon theirs. Both leaders were mortally wounded. Wolfe died happy in the knowledge that his army was victorious; Montcalm, when in-formed that his death was only a few hours away, exclaimed: "Thank God, I shall not live to see Quebec surrender." A few days later, on September 18, 1759, the fortress capitulated, mak-ing the collapse of the French power in Canada inevitable. The surrender of Montreal in the following year sealed the fate of French rule in Canada.

The British were equally successful in other ventures. In the West Indies, Guadeloupe, Martinique, and other islands were wrested from the French. An English squadron also took Senegal and Goree, the principal French stations on the West African coast. So successful were the British efforts against the French colonies that Horace Walpole wrote in good humor: "I really believe the French will come hither now, for they can be safe nowhere else." After Spain joined France in the war (1762), the British added also the city of Havana in Cuba and the Philippine Islands in the Far East to their conquests.

In India the French were defeated as decisively as in America. There the struggle was of more recent origin. While the mother countries were fighting on opposite sides in the War of the League of Augsburg and the War of the Spanish Succession, the two East India companies treated each other by mutual consent as if they were outside the quarrels in Europe. Devoting themselves exclusively to trade, they carefully avoided collisions and remained clear of entanglements in native politics. But in 1741 a Frenchman whose plans were to cause the two companies to engage in a struggle for supremacy in India became governor of Pondicherry, the headquarters of the French East India Company.

Possessed of a fertile imagination, François Dupleix dreamed of establishing a great French empire in India. As the first step, he wished to make the most of his opportunities to acquire an effective influence over the native princes; then he would use this influence to force the British out of India. Thereafter the French would have a virtual monopoly of the trade with India and would also be free to extend their political influence over the whole Indian Peninsula. Before Dupleix had proceeded far with his schemes, the War of the Austrian Succession broke out in Europe. After some desultory fighting the French directed a joint military and naval attack against Madras in the southern part of India. Since the British were entirely unprepared to resist, Madras was easily taken. It seemed, in fact, that the French would expel the English entirely from that part of India. But before this could be accomplished the war—to the chagrin of Dupleix—was ended by the treaty of Aix-la-Chapelle. His disappointment became more bitter when orders arrived from France to restore Madras to the English company.

Yet Dupleix did not discard his ambitious schemes. The peace between France and Great Britain prevented him from fighting openly against the rival English company, but he could continue to extend the French influence over the native governments. Political conditions in India were favorable to his plans. When the first Europeans arrived in India, they found most of the country under the sway of the Mogul emperor (the Great Mogul), whose capital was at Delhi and who ruled his vast territories by means of nawabs or nabobs (viceroys). This Mogul Empire had reached its zenith during the second half of the sixteenth century, after which it began to disintegrate. By the middle of the eighteenth century the authority of the Great Mogul had become shadowy. The nawabs still acknowledged the authority of the emperor when it suited their purpose; otherwise they were practically independent, much like the petty princes of the Holy Roman Empire. Since many of the nawabs were constantly in danger of being ousted by rivals, they were glad to put themselves under the protection of Dupleix, and therefore under his influence. In order to gain a larger military force Dupleix drilled companies of natives under the command of French officers. These men, called sepoys, fought in the European manner and were much superior to other Indian troops. By 1750 Dupleix's policy had so far succeeded that the nawabs of the whole of southeastern India were his allies.

Just when it seemed that the English power in India would be unable to survive, there came to the front a young British officer who was destined to dispel Dupleix's dream completely. Robert Clive had reached Madras some years before as a writer or junior clerk of the English East India Company. During the recent wars between the two companies he had exchanged the pen for the sword, distinguishing himself both by his exceptional courage and by his talents for leadership. His great opportunity to undermine the prestige of the French came in 1751 when the nawab of the Carnatic, one of their allies, attacked the English station at Trichinopoly. As a means of relieving the pressure, Clive conceived the idea of striking at Arcot, the capital of the Carnatic. Obtaining the consent of the governor of Madras, he set out with a force of only 200 Englishmen and 300 sepoys. To all appearances it was truly a foolhardy venture. But he moved so swiftly that the garrison fled in a panic without offering resistance. Having taken Arcot, Clive and his small force held it against the counter-attack of an army of 10,000 men. The capture and defense of Arcot was so dazzling an exploit that it greatly elevated the British in the estimation of the natives; and many chiefs who had formerly sided with the French now gave their support to the British. Nevertheless, Dupleix persisted in his schemes for two years longer, until in 1754 he was recalled to France. The directors of the French East India Company were more interested in immediate profits than in his project of establishing a great French empire in India.

During the Seven Years' War the struggle for supremacy in India was extended to include the province of Bengal in the northern part. The conflict began as a result of the tragedy of the Black Hole at Calcutta. Early in 1756 the old nawab of Bengal, a friend of the English, died and was succeeded by his grandson, Surajah Dowlah, a vicious and degenerate youth of twenty. The new nawab was determined to eject the English, for whom he cherished a violent hatred, from his territories. Collecting an army of 30,000 men, Surajah Dowlah suddenly attacked the English fort at Calcutta (Fort William). Many of the inhabitants of the fort promptly fled at the approach of the nawab's army, and the rest—146 in number—unable to offer effective resistance, surrendered. They were herded together for the night in a guardroom which has become known as the "Black Hole of Calcutta." In addition to being so small that the prisoners barely had room to stand, the room had only a few gratings for ventilation. The midsummer heat and the lack of air and water soon turned the tightly packed mass of human beings into a raving mob of despairing wretches who, in their frantic efforts to break down the door or to get near the gratings, trampled one another to death. Only 23 of 146 were alive in the morning.

Clive, upon being informed of the tragedy, immediately set forth with a small force, recovered Calcutta, and successfully held it against an attack by the nawab's troops. Surajah Dowlah, who had at first ridiculed the idea of an invasion of his territories, was now ready to come to terms. While the negotiations for a treaty were being carried on, Clive's men stormed Chandernagar, the French station in Bengal. By this move the nawab was deprived of French support, but he still vacillated, hoping for the arrival of a French force from the south. Finally Clive decided to strike a telling blow. He had only 3000 men, mainly sepoys, while Surajah Dowlah had an army of more than 50,000. The odds were overwhelming and failure would have meant expulsion of the British from Bengal, with the survivors exposed to the most hideous forms of torture the nawab could devise. For three days Clive hesitated; then he decided to attack at all costs. The battle soon turned into a rout of the nawab's army; his troops fled for their lives, trampling on the few Frenchmen who sought to stem the tide of retreat. Clive's victory at Plassey, achieved with the loss of only twenty-two men, firmly established British power in Bengal. Though a new nawab was chosen to replace Surajah Dowlah, he was only a tool. Clive was the real ruler of Bengal.

In the south the French made another attempt, under the leadership of the Comte de Lally, to establish their power at the expense of the English. Lally, who did not arrive in India until 1758, was a courageous soldier but so tactless and overbearing that he was on bad terms with his own men. He began by taking Fort St. David from the English, and then laid siege to Madras. There he failed. As he was about to storm the town after a siege of two months, a British fleet put in an appearance, forcing him to retire precipitately to Pondicherry. The end of the French power in India was at hand. In 1760 Lally was defeated in the battle of Wandewash, and in the next year Pondicherry itself surrendered to the British. The empire of the French in India had collapsed as completely as their empire in North America.

Peace was concluded at Paris on February 10, 1763. In India the British returned the trading stations that had been taken from the French, with the proviso that they were to be used only for trading purposes, and not as military establishments. In America France ceded Canada to Great Britain. It was also stipulated that all French territory east of the Mississippi, except New Orleans, should be British. As France, by a special treaty signed on the same day, gave Spain the town of New Orleans and the country west of the Mississippi known as Louisiana, the French flag no longer waved over any part of North America except the two small islands of St. Pierre and Miquelon in the Gulf of St. Lawrence. In Africa, Great Britain restored Goree to France; also Martinique and Guadeloupe in the West Indies. The British, however, took possession of St. Vincent's, Dominica, and Tobago, hitherto regarded as neutral islands. Spain, in return for Havana and Manila, ceded Florida to the British. Thus there was vested in the British crown the sovereignty over the whole eastern part of North America, from the Gulf of Mexico to the polar regions, and from the Atlantic to the Mississippi.

THE AMERICAN WAR OF INDEPENDENCE

The territorial gains of the British Empire during the Seven Years' War were partially offset by the loss of the thirteen Amer-

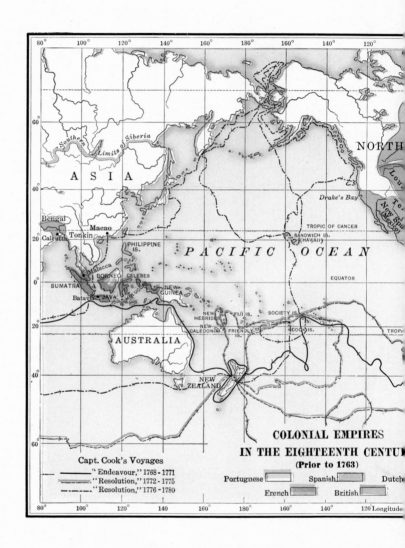

COLONIAL EMPIRES
IN THE EIGHTEENTH CENTU[RY]
(Prior to 1763)

Capt. Cook's Voyages

——— "Endeavour," 1768 - 1771
——— "Resolution," 1772 - 1775
—·—·— "Resolution," 1776 -1780

Portuguese   Spanish   Dutch
French   British

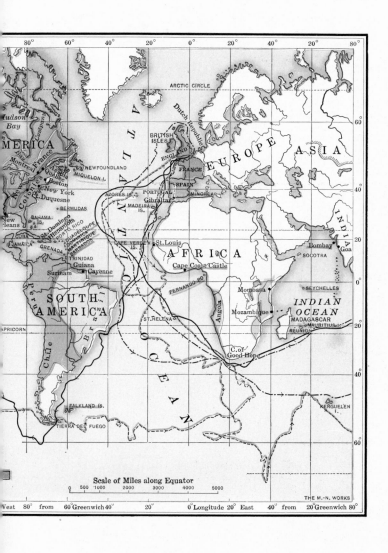

ican colonies, the most populous of the British oversea possessions, a few years later. A number of causes helped to bring about their revolt. In the first place, the restrictions of the Mercantile System contributed much toward making British rule in America unpopular. According to mercantilist theories the colonies were regarded primarily not as homes for a surplus population, but as dependencies held for their commercial value. They were supposed to provide the mother country with raw materials and also to serve as markets for her manufactured goods. In order to realize the ideal of a great self-sufficing commercial empire—an ideal by no means so selfish as it used to be pictured—progressive restrictions were placed on their industrial and commercial activities.

These restrictions were of three kinds. In the first group were the Navigation Acts, which were intended to protect British shipowners against foreign competition in the carrying trade. A second group of acts sought to give the English merchant a virtual monopoly of the trade with the colonies—with compensatory benefits to the colonists. Robert Walpole, for example, had endeavored to terminate the trade of the New England colonies with the French West Indies, to which the colonists sent cattle and other produce in exchange for sugar and molasses. To this end Parliament in 1733 passed the so-called Molasses Act, which imposed prohibitive duties on sugar and molasses imported from non-British colonies. A third class of acts was intended to prevent the rise in the colonies of any manufactures which might offer undue competition to the products of English industry. An act of 1699 prohibited the exportation of wool or woolen goods from the colonial area in which they were produced; another in 1732 forbade the exportation of beaver hats from the colony in which they were made; and an act of 1750 interdicted the manufacture of rolled iron or steel tools and weapons. The theory upon which this was based was that the empire should present a healthful balance between oversea districts producing raw materials and home districts devoted to manufacturing, with the carrying trade in the hands of its own people rather than of foreigners.

Though the British government passed many acts, it was able to enforce them only in part. On the one hand the British navy was still inadequate for its share of the task; and on the other, many colonial officials were easily bribed either with money or with a part of the smuggled cargo. Consequently smuggling was almost universal in the American colonies. New England merchants continued to carry on an illicit trade with the French West Indies even when Great Britain and France were officially at war. This smuggling was to become a source of friction between the colonies and the mother country when British officials decided to make the laws against it effective.

Secondly, many colonists had from the first regarded but lightly the ties which bound them to the mother country. This was particularly true of the Puritans, Quakers, and Roman Catholics, who had been forced to leave England in search of religious freedom. Such emigrants, though considering themselves loyal Englishmen and Englishwomen, could hardly be expected to cherish an ardent love for a government which had made life unpleasant for them. The British government, for its part, was so glad to rid itself of the religious dissenters that it gave them liberal charters to found colonies in North America. Connecticut and Rhode Island were granted the right to elect their own legislatures and governors, and to make their own laws without submitting them to the home government for approval. Massachusetts, until its charter was revised in 1685, elected its own governor, made its own laws, and even coined its own money. These were perhaps the freest democracies in the whole world. In the other colonies the crown or a proprietor under the crown (as in Pennsylvania and Maryland) appointed the governor. But the colonists elected the provincial assemblies which had control over legislation and taxation, and which also voted the salary of the governors out of the taxes collected. Though the governor had a veto over all its acts, the assembly prevailed because it could withhold the governor's salary until he approved the measures it passed. Thus the colonists developed the habit of doing as they pleased in matters of government. It was but natural that, being accustomed to such a large measure of autonomy, they should sooner or later demand that their independence be made complete. They gradually became confident that they could organize their affairs better than this was being done by a government three thousand miles away.

A third factor in the rise of a spirit of independence in the American colonies was the British conquest of Canada. In 1748 Peter Kalm, a Swedish botanist traveling in America, stated that the presence of the French in Canada was the only tie that bound the colonies to Great Britain; and at the end of the Seven Years' War there were British leaders who urged the retention of Guadaloupe and Martinique in place of Canada, which was to be returned to the French so that it might serve as a check to keep the colonies loyal. Vergennes declared: "I am persuaded England will ere long repent of having removed the only check that could keep her colonies in awe. They stand no longer in need of her protection. She will call on them towards supporting the burdens they have helped to bring on her, and they will answer by striking off all dependence." History soon proved the accuracy of Vergennes' prediction. So long as the French were in Canada the colonies needed the assistance of Great Britain. But when the perpetual menace of French invasion was removed through the annexation of Canada, they became more self-sufficient, and therefore more independent in spirit.

The differences between the colonists and the British government came into the open immediately after the Seven Years' War. George Grenville, who was made prime minister two months after the signing of the treaty of Paris, was determined to enforce the trade acts and stop the widespread smuggling. Moreover, he decided that the security of the colonies against the Indians and the Spaniards demanded the presence of a small standing army in America. As the war had saddled Great Britain with a war debt of unprecedented size, and as the colonies had received the principal gains from the conflict, Grenville believed it only reasonable that the colonists should defray in part the expense of maintaining this army. The cost of this force was estimated at about £300,000, no great sum. To this end the Stamp Act was passed in 1765, requiring that all newspapers, pamphlets, deeds, wills, and licenses in the American colonies be printed or written on stamped paper. But many colonists felt that they were well able to protect themselves, and regarded a standing army as a menace to their liberties. Above all, they refused to use the stamped paper, on the ground that Parliament had no right to impose direct taxes on them. Organizations called "Sons of Liberty" were formed throughout the colonies to oppose the efforts of the British government to enforce the act, a congress was called at New York, and colonial merchants formed agreements to boycott British goods. This threat to British manufactures, added to alarm over the disturbance in America, caused Parliament to repeal the act in 1766. Nevertheless, a so-called Declaratory Act was passed, asserting the right of Parliament to control the colonies "in all matters."

For a time quiet was restored, but in 1767 Charles Townshend, chancellor of the exchequer and leader in the House of Commons, took advantage of Pitt's illness to introduce new measures for the taxation of the colonists. Acts were passed which put direct taxes on glass, paint, paper, and tea. Since the proceeds were to be used to pay the salaries of judges and royal governors, the colonists saw in the Townshend Acts a further threat to their liberties, for they tended to remove the judges and governors from the control of the assemblies. The new taxes were opposed as resolutely as the Stamp Act had been. When it became plain that the laws could not be enforced, they were repealed in 1770. Only the tax on tea was retained, principally to show the colonists that the British government had the right to levy it. The Americans responded by refusing to buy tea from the English East India Company, smuggling it principally from Holland, though English shipments could be purchased for less. When the English East India Company nevertheless persisted in sending tea to America, the people of New York and Philadelphia would not permit the cargoes to be unloaded. In Charleston it was stored in damp cellars and left to rot. Three shiploads also arrived in Boston. There a group of about fifty men dressed as Indians boarded the ships and dumped the cargo into Boston harbor.

In England the news of the Boston Tea Party excited much indignation. George III and his prime minister, Lord North, decided that the spirit of violent insubordination in the colonies must be sharply rebuked. In this they had the support of the majority of the English people. Yet neither the king nor his subjects had any idea of the magnitude of such a task. "They will be lions," said General Gage, "while we are lambs; but if we take the resolute part, they will prove very meek, I promise you." At the behest of King George, the measures subsequently known as the Intolerable Acts were passed in 1774. They closed the port of Boston until that town should pay for the tea that had been destroyed, suspended the charter of Massachusetts, and put the colony under the rule of a military governor. Another act gave the governor of Massachusetts the right to send persons accused of murder while enforcing the laws to England or to another

colony for trial. At the same time Parliament passed the Quebec
Act, which sanctioned the exercise of the Roman Catholic religion in Canada, thereby winning the loyalty of the French
Canadians. It also extended the boundaries of Canada in the west
southward to the Ohio River, and gave immediate charge over
Indian affairs in this area to the government of Quebec. This was
not an illogical step in the administrative development of the
empire, and as a temporary measure offered many advantages.
But the colonists, fearing that it would block their movement
westward, drew exaggerated inferences from it.

Instead of submitting meekly, the Americans prepared to
resist measures which they deemed oppressive. On September 5,
1774, the first Continental Congress, composed of delegates from
all the colonies except Georgia, met in Philadelphia. This congress
drew up a statement of grievances against the British government,
formed an association to boycott British goods, and declared that
the other colonies would come to the support of Massachusetts
if the British government persisted in its efforts to force that
colony into submission. In England the elder Pitt and Edmund
Burke advocated a policy of conciliation, but Parliament and
the ministers of George III yielded to counsels of force. The first
armed conflict took place on April 19, 1775. A body of English
regulars, on their way from Boston to Concord for the purpose of
destroying military stores the colonists had illegally collected
there, came into conflict with a group of American "Minute
Men" drawn up on the village green of Lexington, with minor
casualties on both sides. After the British had destroyed what
military stores still remained at Concord, they were attacked by
the embattled farmers at Concord Bridge and forced to retreat.
As the news of Lexington and Concord spread through the
colonies, Minute Men from all parts of New England flocked to
Boston, where on June 17 the battle of Bunker Hill was fought.
Twice the colonial troops turned back the charge of the British,
but they had to give way before the third attack. At a tremendous
cost in human lives the British dislodged the Americans from their
positions. The moral victory, however, was on the side of the
Americans, for they had demonstrated that their raw militia
could stand up before the British regulars.

Meanwhile the second Continental Congress had met at
Philadelphia on May 10. It professed entire loyalty to the crown;

but in preparation for resistance to the new British measures it voted to raise a force of 20,000 men, the expenses to be defrayed by the united colonies. George Washington, who was made commander-in-chief of the Continental Army, immediately set to work preparing his forces to expel the British from Boston. In March, 1776, by throwing up entrenchments on Dorchester Heights to the south of Boston, he closed their exit on the land side. General Howe, realizing how difficult the task of dislodging Washington from his position would be, decided early in 1776 to evacuate Boston with his entire army and take possession of New York instead. Executive authority in the royal and proprietary provinces had now wholly collapsed. Washington's success in driving the British out of Boston so inspired the Americans with hope and courage that, despite the failure of an expedition against Quebec, the Continental Congress adopted on July 4, 1776, the Declaration of Independence, which Thomas Jefferson, taking the ideas of John Locke as a basis, had drawn up. It resolved that "these United Colonies are, and of right ought to be Free and Independent States; that they are absolved from all allegiance to the British Crown; and that all political connection between them and the State of Great Britain is and ought to be totally dissolved." This declaration, by transforming the British colonies into the United States of America, added a new name to the nations of the world. All over the thirteen states the action of the Congress was received with rejoicing: bells were rung, bonfires kindled, and guns fired as the news spread. But a long and bitter struggle lay ahead before the independence of the new nation was recognized by Great Britain.

The war began disastrously for the American states. Washington, after forcing the British to evacuate Boston, moved his army to Long Island. His aim was to thwart the British plan of severing New England from the rest of the colonies by obtaining control of the Hudson River. He fortified Brooklyn Heights, but was dislodged from this position by General Howe and his army, supported by a British fleet. Had Howe moved with energy, he could probably have terminated the war within a few months. As it was, Washington's army was forced to retreat from point to point before the British advance. Howe took New York, overran New Jersey, defeated Washington at Brandywine and Germantown, and occupied Philadelphia (1777). The outlook for

American independence was dark indeed. But the series of reverses was soon to be followed by an important victory. While Washington was engaging General Howe, a British force of 6000 men under General Burgoyne was marching southward from Canada. According to the British plan, Howe was to move up the Hudson from New York and join Burgoyne. This he failed to do. Though victorious at first, Burgoyne encountered greater difficulties as he advanced, for the opposing force under General Gates was daily growing larger. Finally, in October, 1777, Burgoyne was completely surrounded, and after some stubborn fighting was compelled to surrender with his entire army.

The surrender of Burgoyne at Saratoga was the turning point of the war. It dispelled the English hopes of an easy victory over the rebellious states. It gave the Americans a firm confidence in the ultimate success of their cause. Moreover, it moved the French, who had previously evinced a general sympathy with the Americans, to acknowledge openly the independence of the United States and to support the colonists in their struggle. When Lord North saw a war with France approaching, he signified his readiness to concede all the demands of the Americans except independence. But the concessions came too late. Congress would hear of nothing short of complete independence. In February, 1778, an alliance was concluded between France and the United States, both parties agreeing not to lay down their arms until the independence of the United States was won.

Since the Seven Years' War the French had been preparing to avenge the defeat they had suffered. While the British navy was being neglected, the French were rebuilding theirs. Now they were ready. With their fleet commanding the sea, they were able to send to America not only troops but also much needed supplies for Washington's ragged, half-starved, ill-equipped army. In 1779 Spain joined France, and the next year Holland became involved in the war against Great Britain, though it was to do little fighting because of internal conditions and the state of its army and navy. The navies of the two Bourbon powers soon combined in an attack on Gibraltar and Minorca. The latter succumbed, but Gibraltar was able to hold out against a siege lasting three years. The French and Spaniards also launched attacks upon the British West Indies, taking a number of the smaller islands.

In America the British engaged in no major offensive operations in the northern colonies after the surrender of Burgoyne. The principal scene of action shifted to the south. Without relinquishing his hold on New York, the British commander decided to send an army to Georgia and the Carolinas, where a large portion of the people were Loyalists. He hoped that with the aid of these Tories he would be able to detach the South from the Union. In December, 1778, a British army landed in Georgia, defeated the American forces stationed there, and captured Savannah. Early in 1780 the British attacked Charleston, the chief seaport of the South, and forced it to surrender. Again the prospects were anything but bright for the United States. Lord Cornwallis, who took command of the British forces in the South after the victory of Charleston, laid plans to gain control of the entire area. He won several victories, but his losses in men were so great that he finally gave up the plan of conquering the interior. Marching northward, he established his headquarters at Yorktown, where he could maintain contact with the British fleet. When Washington heard of Cornwallis's movements he secretly took the larger part of his troops into Virginia and joined Lafayette, who commanded an army there. This American and French land force, supported by a French fleet under Rochambeau, bombarded Yorktown both from the land and from the sea. Finding all avenues of escape closed, the British general raised the white flag on October 19, 1781, exactly four years after the surrender of Burgoyne. The capitulation of Cornwallis with his entire army virtually ended the fighting in America.

Outside the colonies the war was fought mainly on the sea. The only fighting which took place on European soil was at Gibraltar. In the maritime war, the combined fleets of France and Spain had been superior. Before peace was concluded, however, a British fleet was to gain a notable naval victory in the West Indies. The English Admiral Rodney defeated a French fleet under De Grasse in April, 1782, capturing five ships of the line. This victory in the Battle of the Saints, as it was called, saved the West Indies from further attacks by the French. In the same year the Bourbon powers abandoned the siege of Gibraltar after trying in vain for three years to take the fortress. All combatants were now ready for peace. The treaty between Great Britain and the United States was concluded in Paris on September 3, 1783. Great Britain acknowledged the independence of the thirteen states and agreed that the boundaries of the new nation should be the Great Lakes and Canada on the north, Florida on the south, and the Mississippi on the west. Great Britain's treaty with France and Spain, signed at Versailles in the same year, gave Florida and the island of Minorca to Spain, while France received several small islands in the West Indies, besides regaining Senegal, which Great Britain had taken during the Seven Years' War. The treaty between Great Britain and Holland was not signed until the following year. It gave to the British several Dutch stations in India and also the right to trade in the Moluccas.

THE NEW EMPIRE

The signing of the treaties which acknowledged the independence of the thirteen American states marks the end of the first period in the growth of the British Empire, or, as some historians have it, the end of the "old empire." British interest in colonies slackened for a time after the successful rebellion of the most populous of England's oversea possessions. The belief became widespread that other colonies would follow the example of the American states after the mother country had spent much money in developing and protecting them. Yet there was a small but powerful group which continued to urge the extension of the British oversea dominion. The result was that a new and greater empire slowly rose out of the ashes of the old one. Before the end of the century its foundations had been laid in America, India, and Australia. In reality this so-called "new empire" is but a continuation of the old, for it rests on earlier movements of expansion and on explorations undertaken before 1783.

After the loss of the thirteen colonies, Great Britain still had two groups of settlements in North America. First, there were the maritime colonies, including Newfoundland and Nova Scotia with its dependencies of Cape Breton Island and Prince Edward Island (Île de St. Jean). Since most of the French had been deported from Nova Scotia in 1755 and many colonists from Great Britain had settled there, the population of the maritime colonies was predominantly British. This was not the fact with the second group of settlements, situated along the St. Lawrence. In Quebec, the population of about sixty thousand was almost entirely French and Roman Catholic. It consisted largely of illiterate peasant farmers with a sprinkling of gentry, merchants, and priests.

Totally uninterested in politics, the French Canadians as yet cherished no desire for self-government. At first many Englishmen believed that the French Roman Catholics should be gradually forced to adopt Protestantism and English civil law, but in the end wiser counsel prevailed. The Quebec Act (1774) had granted the Roman Catholics religious freedom, confirmed the right of the priests to collect tithes, and permitted French law to remain in force in all civil matters. Although it irritated the Americans, the act bound the new French subjects so firmly to the British crown that all attempts to induce them to join the thirteen colonies in rebellion against the mother country proved vain.

A new era in the development of Canada was opened by the arrival of the United Empire Loyalists after the peace of 1783. The sentiment for revolt had been very far from universal in the thirteen colonies. When the war broke out a considerable minority took sides with George III. According to John Adams, one-third were loyal, one-third neutral, and one-third rebellious. It has been estimated that as many as fifty thousand colonists joined the British armies in America. All who did not join in the fight for independence were regarded after 1776 as traitors. In the heat of the war their property was confiscated and they were treated harshly. At the end of the conflict the French recommended a more clement treatment for the Loyalists, but the bitterness engendered was still so great that this recommendation went unheeded. About a hundred thousand United Empire Loyalists, as they delighted to call themselves, found it necessary to seek refuge outside the United States. Some returned to England, others settled in the West Indies and in Florida, and the remainder sought new homes in the northern possessions of Great Britain. Some thirty thousand chose Nova Scotia, so many migrating to the territory known as New Brunswick that it was separated from Nova Scotia in 1784. The rest of the refugee Loyalists, to the number of about ten thousand, found their way to the upper valley of the St. Lawrence, where they were given generous grants of land, with implements and animals, and laid the foundations of the rich province of Ontario.

In the maritime provinces the arrival of the Loyalists had created no special problems, for there the government and the laws had long been English, and representative government was already established. In Canada proper the situation was different. The Loyalists, steeped in English tradition, could hardly be expected to submit to the French civil law established by the Quebec Act. As there were by 1791 twenty thousand English-speaking people in Canada, it was time that some settlement of the question was made. After much debate Pitt's government passed the Canada Act in 1791. By it the country was divided into two provinces, Upper Canada or Ontario and Lower Canada or Quebec, with the Ottawa River forming part of the dividing line, though not down to its mouth. In the former province the population was largely British and Protestant, while in the latter it was predominantly French and Roman Catholic. Each province was to have a governor and a lieutenant-governor appointed by the British crown, a legislative council nominated for life by the governor, and a legislative assembly elected by the property-holders. Thus within a few years after the British had lost the thirteen colonies the basis had been established for six new states in North America (Ontario, Quebec, New Brunswick, Nova Scotia, Newfoundland, and Prince Edward Island).

During this period the English East India Company had been active in consolidating and extending its power. At the end of the Seven Years' War British ascendancy had been established only in the provinces of Bengal and Behar, and even there the dominion of the company was without legal status. It was the achievement of Clive during his second term as governor of Bengal to legalize the company's authority by entering into a formal agreement with the Mogul, who was still titular sovereign of India. This agreement gave the company the right to collect and administer the revenues of the provinces of Bengal, Behar, and Orissa in return for a fixed annual payment. Yet Clive was unable to establish a direct administration immediately, for he lacked men versed in the law, the languages, and the customs of the people. Consequently the collection of the revenues was left to natives under the loose supervision of the company's officials. Moreover, the administration of justice still remained in the hands of the nawab. Thus the government established by Clive was really a dual system which in practice was to prove cumbrous and unsatisfactory, but it did give the English East India Company a definite status as a territorial power. In the administration of the company itself Clive introduced a number of reforms. He forbade the taking of presents or bribes by servants of the company, wiped out other dishonest practices, and generally inaugurated a juster treatment of the natives. Worn out from the constant strain of his labors, and discouraged because his reforms had aroused so much opposition, Clive resigned his office and left India for the last time in January, 1767.

In England Parliament was disturbed by the fact that a trading company was exercising sovereign power in India. To put an end to this anomaly the Regulating Act was passed in 1773, despite the objections of the company's officials, who argued that their charter was being violated. This act, which may be regarded as the beginning of modern constitutional history in India, raised the governor of Bengal to the position of governor-general of all the company's possessions in India, making the governors of Madras and Bombay subordinate to him. In his work the governor-general was to be aided by four councilors who, like him, were to be nominated by the crown during the first five years. Furthermore, a Supreme Court of Judicature was to be established at Calcutta for the servants of the company, with a chief justice and three judges appointed by the crown. In short, the Regulating Act of 1773 definitely subjected the company to the control of the crown.

The first governor-general under the new act was Warren Hastings, who had been governor of Bengal since 1772. Hastings took further steps along the road to British political sovereignty in India by assuming direct responsibility for the government of Bengal. He replaced the native staff of revenue collectors with English officials and opened district courts of justice under English magistrates for the protection of the natives. In his relations with the other native states of India, Hastings' sole aim was to protect the territory already held by the company. Three powers —the French, the Mahrattas, and Hyder Ali, the ruler of Mysore —menaced the British possessions. That there should be difficulties with the French during an administration which covered the years from 1777 to 1783 was but natural. Soon after the news reached India that the French had taken sides with the American colonies, the French stations which had been restored in 1763 were again taken by the British. Thereafter the real threat came from the Mahrattas and the ruler of Mysore. The former were a Hindu people who, by developing their military strength, had gained

control of much of western and central India, while Hyder Ali was
a shrewd leader who had made the formerly insignificant state of
Mysore a great military power. Both the Mahrattas and Hyder
Ali aspired, with the help of the French, to expand their dominion

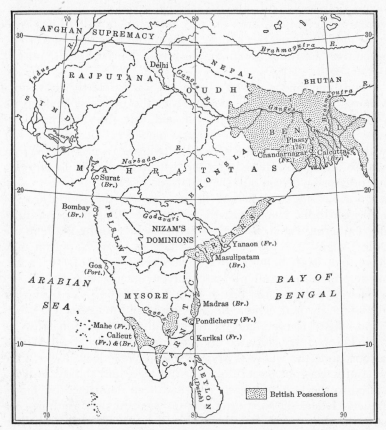

British and French Possessions in India in the Eighteenth Century

at the expense of the British. But Hastings frustrated all their plans
and ambitions by defeating them in rapid succession.

Throughout his tenure of office Hastings had been at strife with
the members of his council, who by four votes to one could over-
rule any plans he might project. By Pitt's India Act, passed in
1784, the governor-general was endowed with larger discretionary
powers. The new law virtually made the governor-general supreme

in his council. It also created in England a Board of Control, consisting of six commissioners, a secretary of state, and the chancellor of the exchequer, to which the political power exercised by the directors of the company was subordinated. In other words, this board, responsible directly to Parliament, was given direct supervision of the political and military affairs of British India. With some modifications, Pitt's India Act continued in force until 1858, when the East India Company was finally deprived of all political power.

For some time after Pitt's India Act was passed the East India Company still continued to adhere to the policy of making no further additions to the territory it held, though it became necessary in the cause of peace to annex a part of Mysore in 1792. But with the appointment of Richard Wellesley as governor-general in 1798, a man who believed that the British must either be supreme in India or be driven out, the expansion of British power became a conscious design. When Wellesley assumed the administration of British India, Napoleon was in Egypt weighing the possibilities of conquering India. Though Nelson's victory in the Battle of the Nile (August 1, 1798) shattered whatever plans Napoleon may have laid, Tipu Sultan, ruler of Mysore and son of Hyder Ali, made preparations, after a secret correspondence with the French Directory, to expel the British from India, failing to realize that the French would be able to give him but little assistance. When Tipu refused to repudiate the French alliance, a British army invaded his country, defeated his army, and took his capital. Within a short time the whole of Mysore was in Wellesley's power. One part of it was put under direct British rule, and the rest was restored to the Hindu dynasty that had been dethroned by Tipu's father, Hyder Ali. Next the Carnatic was added to Madras, constituting that presidency virtually as it has remained since; then the territory of Oudh, in northern India, was divided by a treaty so that one half came under direct British rule and the other was bound more firmly to the company; and finally the Mahrattas, who had been armed by the French, were decisively defeated and compelled to surrender a large part of their territory. By 1805, the year in which Wellesley was recalled to England, the British were well on the way toward gaining control of the entire Peninsula. They held a direct rule over a large part of India and exercised a controlling influence over most of the sovereigns who ruled the rest.

AUSTRALASIA

The second half of the eighteenth century also saw the beginnings of a great British expansion in Australasia. Just who was the first European to discover Australia it is impossible to say with certainty. Belief in the existence of a southern continent dates back to ancient times. A number of Greek astronomers had argued that, with Europe and Asia in the northern hemisphere, the balance and symmetry of the globe necessitated the existence of a continent in the southern hemisphere. In the sixteenth century this "unknown" continent (*Terra Australis incognita*) appeared on the globes of a number of cartographers. The East Indies, India, and America, however, absorbed the attention of European navigators to the extent that no attempts were made to find this continent. Early in the seventeenth century the Dutch took up the work of exploring that part of the globe. In 1616 a Dutch navigator touched the western coast of Australia and during the two succeeding decades other Dutchmen sighted or skirted parts of the northwestern and southwestern coast of the new continent.

Undoubtedly the most famous of the Dutch seamen who participated in the exploration of the South Seas was Abel Tasman, sent out in 1642 by Anthony van Diemen, the governor-general of the Dutch East Indies, to explore further the "great Southland." With his two small vessels Tasman sailed from Batavia to Mauritius, thence southward and eastward until he reached the land now called Tasmania, but which he named Van Diemen's Land in honor of the man who had sent him out. From there he sailed eastward, discovering New Zealand, the Friendly Islands, and other islands in the Pacific. Proceeding in a northwesterly direction, Tasman passed along the coast of New Guinea and returned to Batavia. Thus he accomplished the first circumnavigation of Australia without seeing any part of that continent. Toward the end of 1643 Tasman ventured forth from Batavia again with three ships. This time he surveyed the northern and northwestern coast of Australia, but failed to find the strait between New Guinea and Australia in quest of which he had been sent out. Though he took nominal possession of the new continent for the Netherlands, naming it New Holland, Tasman's report contained nothing to tempt the Dutch East India Company. Hence it did not follow up the discoveries.

The first Englishman to set foot on Australia was William Dampier, who visited the new continent twice, first in 1688 and again a decade later. On his second voyage he explored much of the western and northern coast, but his description of what he saw discouraged further interest in the country. "The land," he wrote, "was not very inviting, being but barren towards the sea, and affording me neither fresh water nor any great store of other refreshments."

It remained for Captain James Cook to gather the first real knowledge of Australia and New Zealand almost three-quarters of a century later. In 1768 Captain Cook, who had previously served as commander of a surveying vessel engaged in charting the St. Lawrence and the coasts of Nova Scotia and Newfoundland, was chosen by the British Admiralty to command a British expedition to the Pacific under the auspices of the Royal Society. He was to take the expedition to the island of Tahiti to observe the transit of the planet Venus across the face of the sun, and then sail southward in quest of the southern continent. Having fulfilled the first purpose, Cook sailed southward in his famous ship, the *Endeavour*, until he reached the north island of New Zealand in 1769. As he was eager to ascertain if the land he had found was part of the southern continent, he sailed around the two islands of New Zealand, spending six months in charting the coast. From New Zealand the expedition continued in a westerly direction to the eastern coast of Australia, which Cook named New South Wales, claiming it for Great Britain. One inlet along this coast was given the picturesque name of Botany Bay from the variety and abundance of flowers and plants along its shores, and plans were made to found an English colony there. Continuing northward from Botany Bay the expedition passed through Torres Strait and returned to England by the Cape of Good Hope.

Since British interest in the founding of new colonies was at ebb tide, the discoveries of Captain Cook might have been ignored if the English jails had not been overcrowded. Before the American Revolution it had been customary to transport convicts to the American colonies. Now, however, there was no outlet for the undesirables. To relieve the congestion in the English prisons, six transports, carrying 750 convicts (about 550 men and 200 women) together with a detachment of 200 marines as guards, were sent to Australia under the command of Captain Phillip, arriving there in 1788. Because of a lack of fresh water, Phillip did not found a settlement at Botany Bay, as Captain Cook had planned, but chose a site about eight miles to the north, on the shores of a magnificent harbor. Thus in 1788 the foundation of the Australian Commonwealth was laid at Sydney, as the first settlement was called. Gradually agriculture was established and the colony became self-supporting. The convicts worked mostly as agricultural laborers and upon the expiration of their sentences were given grants of land. The earliest free settlers were mainly discharged soldiers. Very early cattle and sheep were acclimatized. It was upon the latter that the future importance of Australia was to rest.

As reinforcements reached the colony other settlements were founded along the eastern coast. But during the quarter-century after the founding of Sydney the interior of Australia remained a land of mystery. A long wall of mountains (the Blue Mountains) down the whole eastern coast of Australia at some distance inland shut the colonists off from the interior. Since the flocks and herds were increasing fast, a need for more pasture land was soon felt. All the early attempts to find a passageway beyond the mountains ended in closed gorges or at the bottom of unscalable cliffs. Finally in 1813 a party of explorers found a way over the crest of the mountains, and discovered the fertile plains beyond. The opening of the vast pastoral districts marked the beginning of a new period in the development of New South Wales, for it assured the future of wool-growing which was to become the capital industry of Australia. Meanwhile the English population continued to increase until by 1820 it numbered about thirty thousand.

English interest in the antipodes was not, however, restricted to the continent of Australia. In 1804 a settlement had also been established in Tasmania, which in 1812 became a separate colony. By 1820 it had an English population of six thousand. New Zealand, though formally annexed in 1769 by Captain Cook, who believed it would provide a splendid field for colonization, was neglected for some decades. Lawless settlements of whalers and diverse adventurers sprang up at different places along the coast, and in 1814 missionaries came to work among the aborigines called Maoris, but the British government was to take no steps to assert its sovereignty over the two islands until 1835.

CHAPTER TWENTY-THREE

France on the Eve of the French Revolution

THE REIGN OF LOUIS XV

AFTER reaching its zenith during the reign of Louis XIV, the French monarchy declined rapidly under Louis XV and was abolished eighteen years after his death. The French governmental system as it had developed required a king who would closely supervise the work of his ministers; one who would take seriously, as did Louis XIV, the duties of his position. This Louis XV did not do. Hence the forces of disruption and dissolution gained strength, while those of order and progress grew steadily weaker. Moreover, Louis XIV had left the national finances in a state of confusion. His successor inherited not only an empty treasury, but a debt of more than three billion livres. It was a situation which called for drastic financial reforms and retrenchment. But Louis XV was interested neither in retrenchment nor in reform. Without any care for the final outcome, he continued to squander the money squeezed in taxes from an overburdened people. What was probably more fatal, France had little surcease from the wars which in the reign of Louis XIV had depleted the national exchequer. Under Louis XV a series of conflicts, particularly the War of the Austrian Succession and the Seven Years' War, tremendously increased the national debt and deprived

France of its high place both as a European power and as a leader in colonial affairs. In short, his reign was characterized by misrule, corruption, and administrative confusion; by a reckless squandering of money at home and exhausting wars abroad. All this served to undermine the monarchy and stimulate the forces of revolution.

As the successor to the throne was only five and one-half years old when Louis XIV died in 1715, it was necessary to appoint a regent. The Grand Monarch had made provision for a council of regency which was to exercise a restricted power, but, as he had predicted, his will was treated like so much waste paper. After his death the Parlement of Paris declared his nephew Philip, duke of Orleans, sole regent with full powers, a position which he held for eight years. Though he was well-meaning and had the necessary ability to grapple with the evils afflicting France, he lacked determination and had a strong distaste for work. Nevertheless, the beginning of his rule was promising. He reduced the cost of the armed forces of the nation, organized a special court to try cases of fraud and speculation among government officials, and forced corrupt officials to restore some of their ill-gotten gains. The policy of reform and retrenchment was soon discontinued, however, because he did not possess enough resolution to proceed in the face of opposition. Reaction set in. Thus the duke of Orleans, who might have been honored as initiator of the political and economic regeneration of his country, earned for himself only the reputation of being a weak-willed debauchee.

In 1723 Louis XV, having reached the age of thirteen, was declared ruler of France. He was the handsomest of the Bourbons and was later regarded as the best-looking man at the French court. He had a keen memory and great natural intelligence. Though his education had not been of the best, he possessed a good fund of general knowledge. The Prussian representative, who spent more than three decades in France, wrote: "The king of France, according to the testimony of all who know him, lacks neither intelligence nor knowledge." But he had on the whole been badly brought up. Permitted by his preceptors to do as he pleased, he became proud, stubborn, quick-tempered, and hard-hearted. Often he took a sadistic delight in hurting those who were about him. As a child he had found peculiar pleasure in strangling birds, and at the age of twelve had deliberately killed a tame deer which was wont to eat out of his hands. Secretive and taciturn, he spoke little except in the company of his intimates. At times he would say nothing for days, breaking his silence only to deliver a cutting remark. His principal pastime during early manhood was hunting, and later he became addicted to the pleasures of the table. All his life Louis was in the grip of an implacable boredom, from which he suffered as from an incurable disease. For brief moments he would free himself from it only to be overwhelmed again. Although he attended mass every day, his life was a parody on the doctrines of the Christian religion. Louis himself realized this. The consciousness of his sins caused him to be constantly haunted by a fear of hell, the devil, and death. The last was a favorite subject of conversation, and it is reported that he took special delight in asking the sick and aged where they would be buried.

The dominant trait of Louis as king was his indifference to affairs of state. At times he liked to talk about physics and astronomy or argue with prelates about liturgy, but for the business of the realm his aversion was perpetual. Consequently he did little beyond fulfilling the inescapable duty of attending council meetings at which great questions of state were decided, and even then he would yawn repeatedly and often doze. During the early part of his reign the king's indifference was not disastrous, for his preceptor, the Cardinal de Fleury, a man of integrity and considerable ability, ruled in his place. Fleury's régime (1723–1743) has been well called one of mealy-mouthed despotism. But though his ministry was hostile to reform it was, comparatively speaking, a period of prosperity, and for the most part one of quiet. While he was reducing the expenses of the government, the expanding commerce of France increased the annual income of the national treasury until in 1738 revenues equaled expenditures. It was the first time this had happened since the days of Colbert, and the last time it was to happen until the days of Napoleon. In his foreign policy Fleury's efforts were directed toward the avoidance of war. He believed that France needed, above all, a prolonged peace in order to build up its economic resources and consolidate its position in Europe. Hence, when Frederick II of Prussia invaded Silesia in 1740 Fleury urged that France take no part in the war. Like Walpole in England, however, he was forced to give way to the war party. France joined the league against Maria Theresa in a war that cost many human lives and much money, but brought the nation no gains. Fleury himself did not live to see its end. The added strain and worry proving too much for his health, he died in 1743 in his ninetieth year.

On the death of Fleury, Louis XV—now thirty-three—decided that he would no longer be a do-nothing king, and announced that he would henceforth be his own prime minister. For a time it seemed that he would adhere to this plan of personal government. Shortly after Fleury's death D'Argenson wrote: "The king is working hard." But Louis was incapable of sustained effort. Soon state affairs were left to the various ministers without the guiding hand of either a king or a prime minister. As the Duc de Richelieu wrote in his *Memoirs:* "The king was a sort of phantom. Each minister was more king than he." Since each minister had his own policy, confusion reigned supreme in the government. Louis presently decided to lead in person the French army that was ready to invade the Austrian Netherlands. Journeying to Metz, he was stricken there by a violent fever. For some time his life was despaired of. Quaking at the thought of hell, the king vowed to amend his evil ways and to take a greater interest in the public welfare if he should get well. The announcement of his recovery was greeted with outbursts of joy by the people, who still looked to the monarchy for their temporal salvation. *Te Deums* resounded in the churches, and Louis himself was given the title "Bien-Aimé" (Well-beloved). After witnessing the universal jubilation, the king himself was constrained to say: "What have I done that they love me so much?" Nevertheless, he did not long adhere to his resolutions. No sooner had he recovered than he went back to his old ways. In fact, he became more apathetic than ever toward the welfare of his subjects. Henceforth the deciding influence in the state was wielded by the successive mistresses of the king.

Louis at the age of fifteen had married Marie Leszczynski, daughter of the exiled King Stanislaus of Poland. She was seven years his senior, pious and good-natured, but neither clever nor attractive physically. In less than twelve years she bore him ten children, and during this period Louis was constant in his love for her. Whenever efforts were made to interest him in some other woman, he would say curtly: "I think the queen is more beautiful." But after the birth of the last child the king began to pay attention to other women at his court. Having once crossed the Rubicon of marital infidelity, he entered upon a series of amorous campaigns that were to occupy him until his death. Probably the most notorious of his mistresses was Antoinette Poisson, a young woman of bourgeois origin from whom he removed the plebeian stain by bestowing on her the title of Marquise de Pompadour. She is described by contemporaries as not only beautiful and vivacious, but as possessing considerable accomplishments. She was a skilful dancer, had some talent as an actress, and was interested in art and literature. By the nobility this wanton beauty was regarded as an upstart. High-born ladies and gentlemen frowned upon her not because of her misconduct, but because she had risen from the bourgeoisie. Her low birth was regarded as degrading to the monarchy. Had she been of the aristocracy, they would have found nothing amiss.

Once she had conquered the king, Madame Pompadour held her ascendancy over him for twenty years, until her death in 1764. Though her power in state affairs was not as absolute as her opponents stated, she was nevertheless the most influential person in France. Her favor was the surest road to preferment in the government, the army, and the Church, and in her boudoir many of the most important questions of national policy were decided. With a smattering of knowledge about foreign affairs, she was able to convince the king that she was a diplomatist of no mean ability. But her foreign policy brought only disaster and financial exhaustion to France. In her relations with the king she was more intent upon retaining her preponderant influence in state affairs than upon exciting in him a sense of his responsibilities. What little vigor Louis had previously shown died away completely under her sway. Soon it became her greatest problem to lift him from the depths of ennui into which he repeatedly sank. In an effort to amuse him she organized lavish fêtes and theatrical performances, while the troops of the French army often went unpaid. She also inspired the bored king with a mania for building which put on the national treasury an added strain it could ill endure. The condition of the national finances was such that only strict economy could ease the tax burdens of the people and decrease the enormous debt accruing from the wars. So long as Pompadour retained her influence this was impossible, as a number of ministers found out. Her interference in the government was fatal to any reform of the finances, any vigorous foreign policy, or any thoroughgoing reorganization of the government.

For a time Louis mourned the death of Madame Pompadour,

and also that of his wife in 1766. But soon Jeanne Bécu, better known as Madame du Barry, stepped into the place Madame Pompadour had occupied. She and her minions controlled the king during the last years of his life. Long before this his early popularity had vanished. When he passed along the streets few of his subjects still cried, "Vive le roi!" More and more he was regarded as an enemy of the people. D'Argenson, minister of foreign affairs from 1744 to 1747 and advocate of reform, wrote about the middle of the century: "The opinion gains ground everywhere that absolute monarchy is the worst conceivable form of government." Songs, satires, and attacks on the king appeared in profusion despite all the government could do to suppress them. In Paris the people were so hostile that a special road, significantly called "the road of revolt," was built to obviate the necessity of his passing through Paris when he traveled from Versailles to Compiègne. Louis himself said: "Why should I show myself to this low rabble who call me a Herod?"

Conditions were such that even Louis could not fail to read the handwriting on the wall. In the words of D'Argenson, there were "revolts at Toulouse, revolts for bread which give rise to the worst fears. In Guienne and other parts of the kingdom there is a riot at each market. The state of Paris is very disgusting, and the lieutenant of police is at his wit's end for a remedy. . . . Things are going from bad to worse; the finances are at the last gasp; the treasury is dry, always dry." Whether the old profligate uttered the oft-repeated statement, "Après nous le déluge," is questionable, but it is certain that he was apathetic regarding the plight of his successor. M. de Gontaud quotes Louis as saying: "Things will last my time at any rate." Beyond that he had no concern. It is therefore easy to understand why the king's death from smallpox in 1774 was not an occasion for mourning. A contemporary wrote: "I heard no remark, but it was easy to see the satisfaction expressed by every face." How low Louis had fallen in the popular estimation is evident from the fact that in Paris only four masses were said for his recovery during his last illness, whereas in 1744 there had been more than eighteen hundred. His reign had brought France to the very brink of revolution. Montesquieu read the signs of the times correctly when he wrote: "All that I have ever encountered in history of the symptoms that presage great revolutions exists and is increasing from day to day in France."

THE OLD RÉGIME

To understand the French Revolution it is necessary to know the chief features of the political, social, and economic order of eighteenth century France—in other words, of the Old Régime (*Ancien Régime*). The central feature of the government was the absolute monarchy, which during the reign of Louis XIV had assumed the form it was to retain until the Revolution. It was based on the idea of divine right and not on the consent of the people. As Louis XV expressed it: "A king is accountable for his conduct only to God." Theoretically, all the powers and functions of the government centered in the king. He appointed all the high officials, including the ambassadors, ministers, judges, and generals. All questions of foreign policy were ultimately decided by him. He made alliances, declared war, and concluded peace. Most of the actual work of administration was, of course, done by the king's councils. The councils, however, were only advisory; every important matter was submitted to the king for a final decision. Furthermore, the king was the source of all law. France had no legislative body like that of England. The royal decrees, usually drafted by the councils, became laws when they were registered in the law books by the Parlement of Paris.[1] This parlement had the right, before registering a decree, to make "remonstrances" which the king might heed or not, according to his desires. If the Parlement of Paris exercised its right of remonstrance, the king could assert himself by appearing in person to command it to register the decree in question, a ceremony which was called *lit de justice*.[2]

Moreover, the monarch was also the supreme judge. As such he could try any case or override the decision of any court in the land. By means of *lettres de cachet* [3] the king could imprison without trial whomsoever he pleased, and for as long a time as he desired, without giving any reason. Though its misuse has been exaggerated, this practice lent itself to injustice and abuse. A Frenchman

---

[1] The Parlement of Paris was the most important of the thirteen parlements or supreme courts of appeal for both civil and criminal cases. As the magistrates of the parlements either inherited or bought their offices, they could not be removed by the king without just cause.

[2] *Lit de justice* was literally the bed or divan upon which the king sat when he attended a session of the parlement.

[3] Orders contained in letters closed with the king's cachet or seal.

might find himself incarcerated in the Bastille, in Vincennes, or in some other prison if his enemies were powerful enough to secure a lettre de cachet from the king. And there was no legal means by which he could secure his release. Two illustrious persons confined in prison by this means were Voltaire and Mirabeau—the former because of a squabble with a ranking nobleman, and the latter at the request of his father, who hoped thereby to wean him from his debaucheries.

Finally, the king was the recipient of all government revenues. Whatever taxes were collected were put into the royal treasury, from which the king took whatever he needed for the expenses of the government and his court. He gave no account of his expenditures; in fact, no one but a few treasury officials knew the amounts that were spent. He could also impose new taxes at will. Thus there was theoretically no restriction on the king's power. As Louis XIV wrote in his *Memoirs:* "Kings are absolute masters and as such have a natural right to dispose of everything belonging to their subjects." In practice, however, there were many things the king could not do. On all sides his power was limited by customs, privileges, and traditions. He did not dare, for example, to disregard special rights granted to classes, cities, and corporations.

Though the government was centralized in theory, there was no real unity in France. The kingdom as a whole was little more than an aggregation of peoples and provinces. The various provinces had been added piece by piece since the time of Hugh Capet, and each had been permitted to retain certain ancient rights, laws, and practices. Those that had been joined to the kingdom more recently, the *pays d'état*, had even retained certain rights of self-government. Many provinces were separated from the others by customs barriers and by distinctive codes of law. Another factor making for separation was the weights and measures, which not only had different names but also different values in the various provinces. For purposes of administration the provinces were no longer important, except as military units. A royal governor was still at the head of each province, but he wielded little power. Since the time of Richelieu, as stated in an earlier chapter, the intendancies, thirty-four in number, had been the units of civil administration. At first the intendants who administered these divisions had been chosen exclusively from the middle class, but in the reign of Louis XVI they were all nobles. As the local representatives of the king, their power was nearly absolute, except in the pays d'état, where it was limited by the rights of the local assemblies. But besides the intendants there were others who laid claim to administrative rights. Many feudal seigneurs still had some rights of jurisdiction and police powers, and towns and cities had municipal constitutions which gave them certain rights of self-government. Altogether, the bewildering variety of divisions and subdivisions made the machinery of government complex and cumbersome. There were multitudes of officials with conflicting claims, there was much overlapping of functions, and there was much confusion.

The confusion was perhaps most evident in judicial affairs. First of all, there were the many royal courts which had been superimposed upon the courts that had grown up in France during the Middle Ages. Since the royal courts had been established without any well-organized system and the jurisdiction of the various courts had not been sharply defined, disputes over conflicting claims were not infrequent. Furthermore, although the royal courts had absorbed the most important functions of the old feudal and municipal courts, the latter had not been suppressed. The nobles still retained a remnant of jurisdiction over the peasants on their estates, and many cities and towns exercised jurisdiction over their citizens. The Roman Catholic Church, also, still possessed the right to try certain cases in which the higher clergy were involved. Thus, despite the theory that all justice emanated from the king, justice was still being administered in the name of the Church, of the feudal seigneurs, and of certain communes. The confusion caused by this multiplicity of courts—and their number was prodigious—was greatly aggravated by the diversity of laws. There was no general code for the whole of France. In the south the laws were based largely on Roman law, while in the north they derived principally from feudal custom and Frankish law. Within these larger regions were many differing codes. Voltaire said that a person traveling in France changed laws as often as he changed post horses. It has been calculated that on the eve of the Revolution there were more than three hundred distinct codes of law in force.

Far more important as a cause of discontent was the prevalence of inequality and privilege. The society of eighteenth century France was still divided, after the feudal manner, into three classes or estates: the clergy, the nobility, and the Third Estate. The first two, constituting about two per cent of the nation, were the privileged classes. Since the affairs of God were regarded as higher than the affairs of man, the clergy of the Roman Catholic Church held the highest ranking in the social order. Their estate included the higher clergy (archbishops, bishops, and abbots), the regular clergy (monks and nuns), and the parish priests and their assistants. One source of the income of this estate was the lands of the Church, amounting to about six per cent of the area of France. This ecclesiastical land was exempt from taxation, but every few years the general assembly of the clergy would vote a "gratuitous gift" to the state. A second source of income was the tithe, a tax collected on agricultural products including grain, straw, fruits, hemp, flax, beans, wool, lambs, and pigs. Nominally a tenth, the tithe varied in the different parts of France, averaging probably about a thirteenth. Thus the total income of the Church was considerable. The revenues were not distributed equally among the clergy. So much of the income from the land and the tithe went into the pockets of the higher clergy that some had incomes rivaling those of the wealthy noblemen. These prelates were themselves nobles and were appointed by the king. It was practically impossible for a low-born monk or priest to attain to the higher dignities, even though he excelled in piety, learning, or practical ability. Thus, of the more than one hundred thirty bishops of France in 1789, only one was a commoner. While most of the higher clergy remained with their flocks, some found life in their dioceses or abbeys boring, and therefore spent much or all of their time in Paris or at court, where they lived much like the noble courtiers.

Relatively distinct from their superiors both in social status and in mode of living were the parish priests and their assistants, who were of the same stratum as the people among whom they worked. Often regarded with disdain by the higher clergy, they were generally revered by the lower classes. Many were reduced to the barest necessities of life since they received but miserable stipends. Naturally this state of affairs which accorded to them a mere pittance while the higher clergy lived in luxury was not much to their liking, and at the time of the Revolution they demonstrated their sympathies by making common cause with the Third Estate.

The second privileged class was the nobles. They were exempt from the most burdensome of the direct taxes and from billeting troops, and the rich ecclesiastical benefices, the prelacies, and the high military offices were reserved for them. If they committed a crime, they could be tried only by the parlements; and if the death sentence was imposed, it was death by decapitation and not by hanging, as with the lower classes. Within the nobility were several groups; they did not form a homogeneous class. At the top were the so-called court nobility, or those who had been officially presented to the king. Since the time of Louis XIV most of the higher nobility spent much or all of their time at the royal court, where both sexes lived in luxury, pomp, and idleness. Their highest aim was to outdo one another in wearing costly garments and in giving ostentatious receptions and sumptuous feasts. To meet the expenses of living at court many received royal pensions in addition to their income from landed property. The nobles who, either by preference or from necessity, remained on their estates were known as the provincial nobility. Whereas some of these had considerable incomes, others lived in straitened circumstances. Yet even the poorest still regarded themselves as a class apart. Besides the court nobility and the provincial nobles, there was still another category, known as *noblesse de la robe*, which included the magistrates of the parlements and the other sovereign courts. Some of these had inherited their offices and titles, while others had purchased offices which conferred upon them the title of nobility. According to a statement by Necker, nearly half of the nobility as it existed on the eve of the Revolution was composed of families ennobled within two centuries by the purchase of offices. This class of newer nobility insisted even more arrogantly than the old upon their privileges and exemptions.

All those who were not clergymen or nobles belonged to the Third Estate. Since the privileged classes managed to evade paying most of the taxes, the main burden of the vast expenses of the administration, of the court, and of the frequent and prolonged wars fell upon this class. Like the nobility, the Third Estate also was comprised of a number of distinct groups. It included the high bourgeoisie, merchants and tradesmen, artisans and laborers, and the peasants. The upper stratum of the Third Estate was formed by professional men, officeholders, great merchants and financiers. Thus it included the best educated element of the nation and the leaders of commerce and industry. Despite such restrictions as the internal tolls and the diversity of weights and measures the internal trade of France had grown tremendously in the eighteenth century and the foreign trade had increased until it was second only to that of Great Britain. The immense riches which flowed into the country from this trade were garnered largely by the upper middle class, for the prejudices of the nobles kept most of them from engaging in trade. It was the members of this upper middle class who led the way to the Revolution. Regarding themselves as the equals of the two premier orders in wealth, education, and culture, they demanded that the social, legal, and political privileges of the clergy and the nobility be abolished. Moreover, they demanded a curb on the expenditures of the king and a general reform of the national finances. Thus it was not the "have nots" but the "haves" who were the leaders in the attack upon the old order.

The prosperity of the upper bourgeoisie, however, was not shared by the petty craftsmen, small shopkeepers, and journeymen or workers. These led lives which were, on the whole, penurious. While the merchants and factory directors were becoming more important, the artisans were losing their independence and sinking to the level of mere wage-earners. It is true that small-scale industry still predominated in France on the eve of the Revolution, but large-scale production had already been established in a number of industries, particularly in the manufacture of textiles. Rich merchants applied more and more of their capital to industry and large workshops in which a sharp division of labor was set up. After the middle of the century, machinery began to be used in certain manufactures. Either the French inventors, spurred on by the example of the English, produced inventions, or designs of machines were obtained from England and in some cases the machines themselves, despite the efforts of the English government to prevent their exportation. By 1789 there were, for example, some nine hundred spinning jennies in France. This nascent capitalist industry was gradually forcing upon the independent artisan the choice of rising above his class or becoming the employee of capitalist producers, and the choice was not always free. As for the journeymen who worked for the gild masters and the workers in the new capitalist industries, their lot was far from enviable. Usually both were required to work long hours for small wages, with little hope of betterment. In the silk industry at Lyons the usual working day was eighteen hours, and in numerous other industries the employees worked from fourteen to sixteen hours. Whenever a crisis occurred, large numbers of such workers were reduced to beggary. Desiring, above all, food and relief from unemployment and the fear of starvation, they became an active element in the popular gatherings of the Revolution.

The vast majority of the French people were peasants. The peasant class contained many different elements, including independent owners, tenant farmers, share-croppers (*métayers*), day laborers, and serfs. The economic condition of this class varied in the different parts of France. Where the soil was particularly fertile the peasant was prosperous, but in the other districts he was often destitute. The poorer peasants lived in thatch-covered mud huts that usually contained but one room. The room had no ceiling, and was furnished in a primitive manner. Frequently the family and the cattle lived under the same roof, separated only by a partition of boards or a screen of straw. Food was usually of the coarsest, consisting largely of buckwheat, barley, rye, oats, and milk; meat was a luxury reserved for unusual occasions. The most prosperous peasants were those who owned land. If the perpetual leaseholders—those who had the right to sell or bequeath their land—are regarded as owners, it may be said that the peasants owned a considerable part of France. The proportion varied in the different districts, but it was seldom less than two-fifths and sometimes more than half of the total area. Yet the average size of the holding of a peasant appears to have been small as a result of progressive parceling among heirs during the eighteenth century. Moreover, the methods of agriculture were still those that had been handed down from the Middle Ages. Most of the land was cultivated on the system of alternate crop and fallow, so that a large part of the arable land lay uncultivated each year. The rudimentary implements, the primitive methods of agriculture, the poor quality of the seed, and the lack of fertilizers kept down the size of the crops. Consequently, many of the proprietors were unable to support their families from their small plots. To supplement their income such peasants often leased land for short terms from the great lords or from the Church, or they practiced a trade on the side. Infinitely worse was the condition of those who did not own land. The lot of the share-croppers, many of whom had to give the lord half the crop in return for seed, livestock, and use of the land, was miserable indeed. Few were ever out of debt. As for the farm laborers, they worked only during the busy season, subsisting by whatever means they could during the rest of the year. When they were unable to find work, many turned to smuggling or brigandage.

Despite the fertility of the soil of France, the peasant population stood in perpetual fear of famine. In good years all would have enough to eat; but when the harvest was poor, want, famine, and attendant epidemics were widespread. Hardly a year passed in which there was not a serious shortage of grain in some part of France. Thus the vicar of a parish in Brittany wrote in 1772: "In my parish there are 2200 souls of whom at least 1800 beg for bread which they cannot find, and most of them live on the boiled stalks of cabbage or, failing that, on grass." When such famines occurred in one district, the innumerable tolls, the condition of the roads, and the multiplicity of weights and measures made the importation of grain from other districts difficult.

There were many among the upper classes who saw that the perennial scarcity could be relieved only by improved production. They therefore advocated the introduction of better methods of cultivation. After 1750, agricultural societies were organized in all the provinces for the purpose of stimulating an interest in scientific agriculture. These societies, and also the intendants and the provincial estates, recommended the raising of artificial grasses (clover, etc.), oil seed, and root crops (turnips, etc.) to the peasants, as a means both of improving the soil and of providing winter fodder for the cattle. But the results, on the whole, were meager. A number of large landowners, it is true, were moved by rising prices to adopt more scientific methods of agriculture on their estates, but the peasants opposed the much needed improvements because they involved not only the creation of large farms of the English type but also the enclosure of wastes and commons. While the former limited the opportunity of the peasant to obtain more land, the latter made it more difficult for him to gain a livelihood. Without the wastes and commons which furnished the peasants with pasturage for cattle, with fuel in the form of turf and wood, and with materials for making implements and repairing their houses, many small holdings were of little use. Despite the opposition of the peasants, some lords exercised their right to enclose a third or even two-thirds of the waste, and others simply dispossessed the users of the commons. The result was that the peasant who could no longer collect wood in the waste or pasture his cow or goat on the commons grew bitter against the government which supported the movement for improved methods of agriculture as well as against the landlord who had deprived him of his rights.

What the peasant wanted was not improved methods of agriculture, but freedom from the vexatious feudal dues. Though the state had largely taken over the duty of giving protection to the peasants, the lords still continued to collect feudal dues in money, in kind, and in various forms of compulsory labor. Even those who owned their land were not exempt from the feudal dues. The difference was this: whereas the owner paid only the dues, the tenant also paid rent. The dues required some peasants to help gather in the seigneur's harvest or to work on the roads gratuitously a certain number of days each year (*corvée*). When a peasant inherited land, he was obliged to make a payment which in some cases amounted to a year's rent; and when he sold his land, he had to give to the lord a share varying from one-sixteenth to one-fourth. One of the most resented of the feudal dues was the exclusive hunting rights of the nobles, which permitted them to pursue game over the cultivated fields of the peasants.[1] The banalities compelled the peasants to bake their bread in the lord's oven, to grind their grain in his mill, and to press their grapes in his winepress—for all of which services they made payments in kind. In addition to the feudal dues and services the peasant also had to pay taxes to the government and tithes to the Church. It has been estimated that about sixty per cent of a peasant's income was consumed by the seigniorial, royal, and ecclesiastical taxes. While the peasant paid only a small proportion of this total to the lord—perhaps not more than twelve per cent—he resented this payment most because he saw no justification for it.

If the condition of the French peasant was bad on the eve of the Revolution, it was better than that of the peasant of Germany, Italy, Russia, Poland, or Spain, and better than it had been in previous centuries in France. The decades since the beginning of the century had seen a growth of prosperity among large sections of the rural population. Important factors in this prosperity were the edicts of 1762 and 1765, which permitted the peasants to engage in industrial production as a by-employment. Within a short time after the acts were passed, peasants in nearly all parts of France were supplementing their income by the manufacture of

---

[1] Only a small percentage of the nobles possessed these hunting rights.

woolens, silks, linens, and laces. Conditions were also improving in other respects. Though it was not entirely eliminated until the Revolution, serfdom was fast disappearing in France, so that all peasants could look forward to personal freedom.[1] Yet a feeling of intense dissatisfaction was widespread among the French peasants—a dissatisfaction which offered a fertile ground for the seeds of revolution. This unrest was aggravated during the years immediately preceding 1789 by the efforts of the lords to increase the obligations of the peasants by reviving dues that had fallen into abeyance. Whereas some seigneurs were motivated simply by a desire to increase their incomes, others needed capital to introduce the new methods of agriculture. Furthermore, because of the rising prices rents increased greatly and in some cases were doubled during the quarter-century before 1789. All this prepared the peasants to follow any leader who would promise to abolish the hated system which burdened them with dues and hindered them in the full enjoyment of the rights of ownership.

A prolific source of discontent, both to the peasants and to the middle classes, was the government's system of taxation, to which reference has already been made. The taxes levied by the state were of two kinds, direct and indirect. Of the direct taxes the most burdensome for the Third Estate was the taille, a tax from which both the clergy and the nobility were exempt. The taille was not uniform throughout France. In some provinces it was a land tax, and in others a personal tax based upon the presumed income of an individual. It was arbitrarily assessed and often fell heaviest on those who could least afford it. Two other important taxes were the capitation and the vingtième. The former, a poll tax in name, was really a second taille, while the vingtième was an income tax, originally of five per cent, as the name implies, but in the reign of Louis XIV it amounted to about eleven per cent. Although all Frenchmen were supposed to pay both, the privileged classes largely managed to evade them.

Perhaps even more vicious and exasperating were the indirect taxes. They were mostly farmed out and included among others the customs duties and the gabelle or salt tax. Twelve of the provinces of central France (Cinque Grosses Fermes), as previously stated, formed a kind of tariff union within which merchandise

---

[1] The number of serfs in France in 1789 probably did not exceed a million and a half.

could be moved without the payment of customs duties, but in the rest of France they were still collected on goods transported from one province into another. In addition there were also many local tolls, all of which were indirectly paid by those who purchased the goods on which they were levied. But probably the most hated of all taxes was the gabelle. In France the sale of salt was a state monopoly, and in a large part of the country every citizen over eight years of age was required by law to purchase seven pounds of salt each year. If a citizen needed salt for any other purpose, as for cattle or for tanning, he had to purchase it separately. Conversely, salt bought for other purposes could not be used for cooking. To prevent this, poison was put into that sold for tanning processes, and gravel was mixed with that intended for cattle. However, the injustice lay not so much in the amount of salt each citizen was required to buy as in the variations among provinces; high taxes were imposed on salt in some provinces, whereas in others it was tax-free. Because of the tax the price might be twelve times as much in one province as in another; yet a citizen had to purchase his salt in the province in which he lived. The great difference in prices gave rise to much smuggling from one province into another. When smugglers were caught, they were punished severely. Calonne, one of the ministers of Louis XVI, said that because of the gabelle there were each year "four thousand attachments on houses, thirty-four hundred imprisonments, five hundred condemnations to the whipping-post, banishment or galleys."

THE CRITICS OF THE OLD RÉGIME

In the eighteenth century there arose a group of writers, known collectively as the *philosophes*,[1] who not only denounced the evils of the Old Régime but also propounded ideas which tended to subvert most of the theological, political, and social beliefs of the time. The outstanding figures among the philosophes were Voltaire, Montesquieu, Diderot, D'Alembert, and Rousseau, but they did not all belong to one school of thought. While the so-called Voltaireans or rationalists based their hopes of solving the problems of society on reason, Rousseau and his followers preached the authority of the feelings or natural impulses. Often both strains

---

[1] The word *philosophes* cannot properly be translated as "philosophers" because the writers whom it designates were reforming publicists and propagandists rather than speculative philosophers.

are to be found in the thought of one individual. However much the philosophes differed in other respects, all were at one in voicing a demand for widespread reforms. They demanded, among other things, civil freedom, religious toleration, abolition of the privileges of the aristocracy, a uniform and fair system of laws, equality of taxation, constitutional government, and the abolition of state monopolies. Their attack on the old abuses and old beliefs was relentless. It was an attack which neither the Church nor the state could restrain. Few of the ideas, however, which the philosophes used as weapons in their attack originated with them. They were mostly drawn from the writings of others. One of the principal sources was the writings of John Locke,[1] in which may be found the basic ideas upon which the political and social theories proclaimed by the philosophes rested. Thus the philosophes were popularizers rather than original thinkers.

The prevailing temper, at least until the publication of Rousseau's *New Heloise* in 1760, was that of rationalism. Because the rationalistic philosophes put such unbounded faith in the power of "reason" as a means of "enlightenment," the eighteenth century is often called the Age of Reason or the Age of Enlightenment. They taught that only through reason—in other words, through the use of his natural faculties—can man discover the secrets of nature and of his own being. Any knowledge gained from other sources—for example, revelation—was labeled spurious. All beliefs, customs, laws, and institutions, the rationalists declared, must be submitted to the test of reason, and whatever is not reasonable must be discarded summarily. Consequently, not only the venerated institutions were subjected to a searching criticism but also the very authority of the Church and of the state. Identifying the rational with the natural, they regarded natural laws as the rational order of things. Hence it became their great aim to discover natural laws and apply them to religion, society, and education. In politics their criteria led them to insist upon the rights of the individual. In religion they sought to eliminate all metaphysical speculation and revelation, all miracles and mysteries. Their tenets gave rise to a general scepticism regarding most dogmas of Christianity, and some of the philosophes gradually drifted toward atheism; but most of them remained deists—that is, they held to the belief in a benevolent deity.

[1] See pp. 431–432.

The man who gave most eloquent expression to the "philoso-phy" of rationalism was Voltaire. Born on November 22, 1694, the son of a notary, he was baptized François Marie Arouet. It was only when he began writing that he adopted the name Voltaire. By the age of seventeen his wit and ability had already gained him admittance into the leading circle of intellectuals of Paris. His fame as a satirical writer grew so quickly that there was hardly an anonymous lampoon that was not imputed to him. Indeed, he was thrown into the Bastille in 1717 by *lettre de cachet* because it was believed that he was the author of a caustic poem against the memory of the late Louis XIV. Soon after his release in 1718 his first tragedy, *Oedipe*, was produced and within a few years he was a famous dramatist. But in 1726 he found himself in the Bastille a second time as the result of a caustic retort to the Chevalier de Rohan, a member of one of the highest families of France. Set at liberty after a fortnight on condition that he leave the country, Voltaire went to England, where he remained for nearly three years. What he saw and learned there made a lasting impression on his mind. He studied the institutions, the philosophy, the science, and the literature of England; above all, he steeped him-self in the writings of Isaac Newton and John Locke. Locke's ideas were to have a decisive influence on Voltaire's thought. They be-came a kind of gospel which he preached during the rest of his life. Some years after his return to France Voltaire published his *Let-tres Philosophiques* (1734),[1] in which his English observations are made to serve, directly and indirectly, as the means of an attack upon the structure of French society.

When the Parlement of Paris condemned his *Lettres Philo-sophiques* to be burned by the common hangman, Voltaire, fearing that he would be placed under arrest, retired to Cirey, which was so near the border of Lorraine that he could flee to safety at a moment's notice. There, at the château of Madame du Chatelet, one of the most accomplished women of the time, he remained for fifteen years, until the death of his "divine Emilie" in 1749. Among the multitude of works he wrote during this period were

---

[1] As Voltaire was unable to get permission to publish the essays in France, they were published in Amsterdam. An English edition had been published some months earlier under the title *Letters concerning the English Nation*. The philosophes repeatedly evaded the censorship by having their books printed in Holland, Belgium, or the Netherlands, or by printing them secretly in France and purporting that they had been printed in a foreign city.

his *Elements of the Philosophy of Newton, Essay on Universal History,* and *Zadig.* After the death of Madame du Chatelet, Voltaire finally accepted the oft-repeated invitation of Frederick the Great to establish his permanent residence at the Prussian court. From afar the friendship between the two, based on an exchange of flatteries, had prospered exceedingly, but when they got together there were continual squabbles. Voltaire soon wearied of improving the French poems Frederick wrote—or, as he put it, "of washing the king's dirty linen." On the other hand, the Prussian king was angered by Voltaire's fondness for forbidden speculations and shady transactions. Finally in 1753 relations between the two became so strained that Voltaire left Prussia. Since the French government did not desire his presence in France, he spent some time in Geneva, and then settled at nearby Ferney, combining the rôles of country gentleman and man of letters. At the age of eighty-four he yielded to the requests of his many admirers to pay a visit to Paris, which he had not seen for twenty-eight years. Here he was received with such demonstrations of enthusiasm as few writers have enjoyed. He was literally overwhelmed with homage and attention. In the midst of this frenzy of admiration, the Sage of Ferney became ill and died in May, 1778. His relatives, fearing that the clergy of Paris would refuse him a Christian burial, had his body removed to Scellieres, where it was interred with the full rites of the Church. During the Revolution his remains were carried to the Pantheon.

Voltaire's life was one of prodigious intellectual activity. Constitutionally feeble and suffering from many ills, he worked all his life as if he were racing with death. The writings which flowed from his pen in an almost continuous stream are notable for their clearness and wit rather than for their originality. The ideas he expounded were largely borrowed from others, but he presented them in such a way that the average educated man could understand them. The range of subjects on which he wrote was wide— so wide, in fact, that he sacrificed depth to breadth. He was distinguished in his time as a wit, playwright, poet, essayist, novelist, student of science, historian, and pamphleteer. He wrote comedies, tragedies, lyric and epic verses, biographies, histories, and treatises on science, religion, philosophy, and other subjects. His lighter productions—tales, satires, epigrams, and poetry—are almost numberless. Timely, lively, and popular, his works were read by most Frenchmen who took an interest in literature. The pamphlets with which he inundated France were probably read more eagerly than the gazettes of the time. They were also widely circulated in other countries, making Voltaire in a sense the intellectual ruler of Europe. Among his disciples were such eminent figures as Catherine II of Russia, Frederick II of Prussia, Joseph II of Austria, Gustavus III of Sweden, Christian VII of Denmark, and Stanislaus of Poland. Today his plays seem stilted and most of his writings dull. He who would appreciate the abiding greatness of Voltaire must regard him as a man of action, a critic of the Old Régime, a social crusader. His life was an unceasing battle against the evils of his age. From the appearance of his *Lettres Philosophiques* to the end of his life he did not tire of attacking privilege, prejudice, superstition, torture, intolerance, serfdom, unjust laws, venality in the administration of justice, and arbitrary government. These he made his target again and again, often repeating his previous statements. "Yes, I say things over and over again," he said. "That's the privilege of my age and I'll say them over and over again until my countrymen are cured of their folly."

In his attacks on the evils of his age, Voltaire turned the sharpest edge of his sword against religious bigotry and persecution. Every person who suffered on account of his religious beliefs found in him an eloquent and tireless defender. That all religions but Roman Catholicism were outlawed in France was to Voltaire intolerable. "I shall never cease to preach tolerance from the house-tops, despite the groans of your clergy," he wrote, "until persecution is no more." *Écrasez l'infâme* (Crush the infamous thing) became the battle cry of Voltaire and his party. Translated freely it would read: "Fanatical intolerance and its offspring, the persecuting spirit, must be wiped out." Though Voltaire was bitter in his denunciation of all dogmatic and authoritative religions, the Church of Rome was the special target of his attacks. Again and again in innumerable lampoons, pamphlets, and letters he inveighed in the name of reason against those doctrines and practices of the Church which he regarded as gross superstitions and absurdities. "Men will continue to commit atrocities," he wrote, "so long as they believe absurdities." Of the immense force of idealism in Christianity he had no appreciation whatever. In his personal religion Voltaire was a deist. "I shall always," he wrote, "be of the opinion that a clock proves a clock-maker, and that the universe proves a God." This argument, which he regarded as incontrovertible, was the basis of his opposition to atheism. But the Supreme Being was to him little more than a theory. "My reason tells me," he wrote to Frederick the Great, "that God exists; but it also tells me that I cannot know what He is."

With all his faith in humanity Voltaire was no crusader for democracy. His political ideas, such as they were, offer consider-able justification for the remark that he was "a conservative in everything except religion." He demanded religious freedom and equality before the law for the masses; also that their tax burdens be made lighter. But he did not advocate government by the people. He had no desire to uproot the existing order by a violent revolution. It was his opinion that the evils afflicting the body politic could be eradicated peacefully and bloodlessly by an appeal to reason and enlightened common sense. His experience in England had left with him a profound admiration for the constitutional monarchy he found there. Such a monarchy prob-ably remained his ideal to the end of his life.

In many respects Voltaire the man did not measure up to Voltaire the writer who warred against persecution and injustice. There were times when he lost sight of his high purpose com-pletely, showing himself vain, egotistical, deceitful, quarrelsome, and vindictive. Rousseau characterized him as "that fine genius and base soul." Frederick the Great expressed the same opinion when he said: "If this man's heart only corresponded to his fine genius, what a man, my dear sir! He would obscure everything that exists." Voltaire's defenders have argued that the treachery of the system he attacked justified his deception and unscrupu-lousness; also that his continual bad health was one cause of his irascibility. Yet the fact remains that he at times engaged in endless petty quarrels, pursuing with a merciless hostility those who had the misfortune of incurring his displeasure. Moreover, he bitterly assailed all who in any way threatened to rival his glory and popularity. Diderot said, "He has a grudge against every pedestal." But if the homely savant with the wrinkled skin, long nose, and sparkling eyes was not a great character, he was, nevertheless, a stout champion of the oppressed. The Parisian masses of the Revolution, overlooking all his weaknesses and fail-ings, inscribed on his sarcophagus the words: "Poet, historian, philosopher, he trained the human mind to lofty flights and prepared us for freedom."

Among the most powerful allies of Voltaire were the Encyclopedists, a group of scholars and men of letters who collaborated in publishing the great French *Encyclopedia*, the central work of the rationalistic movement. The two leaders of this group were Denis Diderot (1713–1784), a stimulating writer and man of wide ability, and Jean D'Alembert (1717–1783), probably the most distinguished mathematician of the age. The project of the *Encyclopedia* was launched when a Parisian publisher requested Diderot to edit a translation of Chambers' *Cyclopedia or Dictionary of the Arts and Sciences*, first published in 1728. Diderot, regarding the English encyclopedia as unsatisfactory, conceived the idea of a larger and more comprehensive work. He discussed the plan with D'Alembert, and the two decided to put it into execution. Most of the prominent writers of the time were enlisted as collaborators, Voltaire himself writing several articles. Others who lent their aid were Rousseau, Montesquieu, Turgot, Quesnay, and Buffon. The publication of the *Encyclopedia* was spread over two decades. Soon after the first two volumes appeared (1751 and 1752) they were suppressed by the government. Other difficulties arose, but the editors continued their work until the last of the seventeen volumes was delivered to the subscribers in 1765. Later supplementary volumes of plates and text were added. The general aim of the editors was, on the one hand, to found all knowledge on science and reason and, on the other, to combat the older systems of thought based on authority and tradition. The thousands of sets published in France, and also the many editions issued in other parts of Europe, made the *Encyclopedia* a most successful means of spreading the ideas of the philosophes.

The man who may be said to have launched the attack on the evils of the Old Régime was the Baron de Montesquieu (1689–1755), an aristocrat with scholarly tastes and sufficient money and leisure to indulge them. In 1721 he had published his *Persian Letters*, a light but penetrating satire on the foibles and customs of French society. Purporting to be the comments of a Persian on what he observed while traveling in France, the letters deal, among other things, with such questions as religious toleration, taxation, codification of the laws, and crime and punishment.

Their trenchant satire and irresistible wit produced an immediate sensation in Paris and made Montesquieu one of the leading literary figures of the time. In 1748 Montesquieu published his masterpiece, *The Spirit of Laws,* on which he had worked for twenty years. The central theme of this great work is the relativity of laws and institutions. Its author concluded that the laws and institutions of a particular society are the products of historical conditions and of the physical environment. Therefore, they are not to be judged as good or bad in the abstract, but must be considered in relation to their antecedents and surroundings. Like Voltaire, Montesquieu held up the English government, which he had studied during a visit of seventeen months, as a model, praising its parliamentary system, its jury system, and the control of the finances by the legislature. He particularly recommended to the French the separation of the legislative, executive, and judicial powers, which he regarded as one of the basic principles of the English government. *The Spirit of Laws* enjoyed an immediate and tremendous popularity, no less than twenty-two editions being issued within the short period of eighteen months.

If the eighteenth century was the Age of Reason, it was also the age of emerging Romanticism. The high priest of the new movement and the philosophe whose influence was greatest in the last decades of the century was Jean Jacques Rousseau (1712–1778). Of French Huguenot stock, Rousseau was born in Geneva on June 28, 1712, the son of a watch-maker. His mother having died at his birth, the child was left in the care of an irresponsible father who allowed him to grow up without a semblance of discipline and with little regular education. Never having acquired the habit of self-control, Rousseau was impatient of any discipline or restraint throughout life, a fact which is the key not only to his character but also to his thought and writings. His early surroundings, the beautiful mountains and valleys of Switzerland, fostered in him a love of nature which never left him and which he later expressed in his writings. As a boy he was for a time a clerk's assistant in the office of a notary and was then apprenticed to an engraver. But a settled and regular life had no attractions for this romantic and undisciplined youth; so at the age of sixteen he ran away to begin an aimless career of vagabondage which was to last for twenty years. During these years he worked at this and that, as lackey, tutor, copyist, secretary, music teacher, and clerk, without remaining long at any occupation. Finally he arrived in Paris, where Diderot gave him some work to do for the *Encyclopedia*. Besides writing a few articles for the *Encyclopedia*, he also composed comedy, poetry, and light music. This was the sum of his labors up to the age of thirty-seven.

He was soon to become famous, however. One hot afternoon in 1749 as he was resting under a tree along the roadside, he read the announcement of a prize offered by the Academy of Dijon for the best essay on the subject: "Has the Progress of the Sciences and the Arts Contributed to Corrupt or Purify Morals?" Realizing that it was an opportunity to give vent to his sense of personal wrongs and to his opinions of social injustice, he penned his indictment of civilization. Men, he maintained, were worse for civilization because it had corrupted their natural goodness; they had deteriorated as the sciences and the arts progressed. The essay won the prize and immediately gave Rousseau a prominent rank among contemporary men of letters. Four years later he wrote a second essay, entitled "On the Origin of Inequality among Men," in which he further developed his general thesis by trying to show that the inequality and injustice of his time did not exist in primitive life. The gist of both essays is summed up in these words of their author: "Men are bad; my own sad experience furnishes the proof; yet man is naturally good, as I think I have shown. What then can so have degenerated him except the changes in his condition, the progress he has made, and the knowledge he has acquired?"

But Rousseau's fame rests on four subsequent works: the *New Heloise* (1760), *Émile* (1762), the *Social Contract* (1762), and his *Confessions*, published posthumously. The first is a romantic novel written as letters, a form probably borrowed from Richardson's *Pamela* and *Clarissa Harlowe*, both of which had been translated into French. In it Rousseau describes in eloquent language the beauties of nature and paints idyllic pictures of pastoral delights. In other words, it is a plea for the simple pleasures of country life against the artificiality of urban society. The novel appealed immediately to every class of French society, particularly to the feminine element. The presses could not turn out copies of the book fast enough. Women of rank stood in line before book shops to rent a copy at twelve sous an hour. To live the simple life of the characters in the *New Heloise* became a new affectation. Even

Marie Antoinette and her court were later to play at it. Thus the "back to nature" movement was launched.

In literature Rousseau's romantic enthusiasm for nature and his appeal to the emotions and sensibilities opened the way for a new age of poetical literature, known as the Romantic Revival. In consequence he has been styled "the father of the Romantic movement." His ideas stimulated or inspired, among others, Wordsworth, Byron, and Coleridge in England, Chateaubriand in France, and Herder, Schiller, Goethe, Tieck, and Schleiermacher in Germany.

In his *Émile* Rousseau attempts to reform the prevailing principles of education. Like his other writings it is an appeal from the artificial to the natural. It expounds the words of the heroine of the *New Heloise:* "Our children are not to be shaped by us into an external and artificial form; they are to develop according to their own nature." In other words, in *Émile* Rousseau prescribed a form of education which he believed would develop the natural and individual endowments of a child and preserve its natural goodness, for "everything is good as it comes from the hands of the Author of nature; but everything degenerates in the hands of man." It was an epoch-making book in the history of education. In emphasizing individualism and natural growth it became the starting point for new investigations and new advances. From it the educators who laid the broad foundations of modern elementary education, among them Basedow, Pestalozzi, and Froebel, drew much of their inspiration.

In the same year in which the *Émile* appeared Rousseau also published his *Social Contract*, a treatise on politics. After opening with the striking sentence, "Man is born free, but is everywhere in chains," he goes on to examine the foundations of civil authority. As the title indicates, Rousseau contends that all civil societies exist by virtue of a "social contract" or an agreement, either tacit or explicit, whereby the members surrender their individual rights to the "general will." Hence sovereignty rests with the people, and whatever government exists derives its authority from the people. This sovereignty of the people, as Rousseau tries to prove with ingenious sophistry, means the absolute freedom of the individual. Its corollary is evident. Since men are everywhere in chains, the sovereignty of the people has been usurped by the rulers; therefore the people have the right to depose the ruler or change the government for the purpose of restoring the freedom of the individual. The whole theory is founded on unreal hypotheses and is full of flaws in logic; nevertheless, the *Social Contract* is one of the most influential political treatises of all time. Hardly a measure was framed in the early part of the French Revolution which does not bear the mark of this "Bible of democratic government," as it has been styled. In fact, the very watchwords of the Revolution, "Liberty, Equality, Fraternity," were taken from it, and later Robespierre was to make a deliberate attempt to translate its theories into practice. Since that time the *Social Contract* has supplied slogans for many political movements. Because of the contradictory elements it contains, it has served both individualists and collectivists as a basis for their theories.

The *New Heloise*, *Émile*, and the *Social Contract*, all written within a short period, brought Rousseau great popularity but they also raised a storm of protest. The archbishop of Paris and others of the clergy denounced his *Émile* as subversive of religion, and he was forced into exile to escape imprisonment. It was the beginning of another series of wanderings which were to take him to Switzerland, to England, and, finally, back to France. He was to find little peace. The opposition which rose up against him on all sides made him suspicious and misanthropic. His sensitiveness was aggravated to such an extent that he suffered much from imaginary as well as from real attacks. In the hope that he might justify himself to posterity, Rousseau wrote his autobiography or *Confessions*. "I am going to show my fellow creatures," he wrote, "a man in all the integrity of nature." With all frankness he endeavored to present the facts of his life, even to the details of his love affairs. Yet what he wrote was colored by his vivid imagination and unconsciously molded to the pattern of the present. Nevertheless, the *Confessions* are not only indispensable for an understanding of their author but also remain an outstanding example of candor in autobiography. Mentally depressed during the last years of his life, Rousseau died in 1778 at Ermenonville and was interred there. In 1794 his remains were transported to the Pantheon by order of the National Convention, but in 1814 his tomb was opened and his bones, together with those of Voltaire, were disposed of in some unknown way.

The ideas propounded by Rousseau were collected from many

sources—from Locke, Shaftesbury, Hobbes, Montaigne, Montesquieu, Diderot, the Physiocrats, and others. But Rousseau transmuted the borrowed doctrines with his poetic imagination and touched them with his eloquence, so that they appealed to men with an unusual attractiveness. The central theme of his philosophy is the idea of a "return to nature"—an idea which is not to be taken literally. Rousseau himself repudiated a return to a primitive state as "unthinkable and absurd." The idea of a "return to nature" was rather a counterpoise to the artificiality of his age. Rousseau was convinced that society had departed too far from nature; that the misery, injustice, and inequality he saw about him were the result of man-made laws and man-made institutions. These laws and institutions he would change, to eliminate the social inequality and the oppression of the many by the few. This was his purpose in holding up before his contemporaries pictures of a social state in which the evils from which they were suffering did not exist. Although Rousseau's postulate that nature is always benevolent and virtuous was a product of his imagination, his "back to nature" gospel was, nevertheless, the most powerful regenerative force of the late eighteenth century, and of the nineteenth—one which turned the thought of Europe into new channels. There are few men in the history of modern times who have influenced the mind of the world as profoundly as did Rousseau. Politics, education, religion, aesthetics, morals, and literature all bear the impress of the ideas he proclaimed.

While the philosophes were striving for liberty of thought, a group of economists known as the Physiocrats were demanding economic freedom. The leading figures of the physiocratic school were Quesnay, physician to Louis XV and Madame Pompadour, and Turgot, the minister of Louis XVI. The *Tableau Économique* (1758) of the former and the *Reflections on the Formation and Distribution of Riches* (1770) of the latter contain the basic teachings of the Physiocrats. Their central doctrine was the idea that society like the physical world is subject to natural laws which are the work of a beneficent Supreme Being. These laws regulate also the economic life of a nation and must be permitted to assert themselves if men are to attain to the highest material well-being. That the natural laws may operate to their fullest extent the individual should have absolute freedom to buy and sell, to produce and transport, to labor or employ labor, and to borrow or lend capital. In a word, there must be complete freedom of trade and industry. Thus Physiocracy was, in a broader sense, a revolt against mercantilistic regulation of commerce and industry. To the state the Physiocrats said, "Laissez faire (Let things alone)." Not only did they advocate that the state cease to make further regulations but they also urged that the existing commercial and industrial regulations be abolished. Particularly objectionable to them were the internal customs duties which hampered the free transportation and sale of agricultural products, for they regarded agriculture as the principal source of a nation's wealth. The ideas of the Physiocrats did not exercise much popular influence, but Turgot put some of them into practice as intendant of Limoges and as finance minister of Louis XVI, and later they were to guide in some degree the policy of the National Constituent Assembly.

SUMMARY OF THE FORCES MAKING FOR CHANGE

The Old Régime represented absolutism in government, confusion and incompetence in administration, privilege in society, injustice in taxation, favoritism before the law, regulation in industry and commerce, and exploitation of the peasantry. Ranged against this order were the Third Estate and the lower secular clergy. The movement making for change was, broadly speaking, twofold. On the one hand there were the purely economic demands of the peasants, and on the other the broader demands of the middle class. The peasants resented the inequitable system of taxation which permitted the privileged classes to evade most of the taxes, but more than anything else they resented the seigniorial dues they were required to pay and for which they saw no justification. The members of the middle class, particularly the prosperous merchants and the professional men, demanded social equality; an order which would give them a voice in public affairs; an equal opportunity to obtain the higher offices in the Church, the army, and the navy; a reform of the entire fiscal system and equal taxation for all; a curb on government expenditures which, in undermining the credit of the state, were threatening the security of their loans and investments; and, finally, greater freedom for the individual, including freedom of thought and economic freedom.

The extent to which the philosophes were responsible for the Revolution is still a debatable question. This much can be said with certainty, however: the evils and abuses of the Old Régime, not the philosophes, were the primary causes of the great upheaval. These evils and abuses were so evident that they needed no philosophes to make them known. Furthermore, the philosophes did not advocate violent revolution. They hoped to accomplish their reforms by "enlightenment" or, in other words, by the diffusion of knowledge. An enlightened public opinion, they believed, would compel governments to eliminate the evils without resort to force. Nor did the philosophes preach democracy. Excepting Rousseau, most of the philosophes looked either to "enlightened" despotism or to a constitutional monarchy like that of England as the best form of government to carry out their policies. Hence, one cannot seriously assert that without the philosophes there would have been no revolution. However, the philosophes made the evils stand out more glaringly. Furthermore, they undermined the respect for the existing institutions by their determined attacks on authority and tradition. More than this, their doctrines of civil liberty and constitutional government provided the principles for the reorganization of society. Thus the least that may be said of the influence of the philosophes is that without them the Revolution would not have been the same.

A further influence upon the public mind was the American Revolution. From the very first this struggle of the colonies for independence stirred the imagination of the French people. The followers of the philosophes were enthusiastic over the Declaration of Independence, particularly over its assertion of the natural rights of man. Even to the high society of Paris and Versailles Benjamin Franklin, with his plain clothes and simple manners, appeared as the incarnation of Rousseau's "natural man." After the successful conclusion of the struggle the French soldiers who had aided the colonies returned as disciples of freedom and critics of the existing régime. As Madame Campan put it: "Our youth flew to the wars waged in the New World for liberty and against the rights of thrones. Liberty prevailed; they returned triumphant to France, and brought with them the seeds of independence."[1] So great was the enthusiasm for the Americans that Arthur Young was moved to write: "The American Revolution has laid the foundation for another in France, if the government does not take care of itself." The Chevalier de Parny, a contemporary poet and an attendant

[1] *Memoirs of Madame Campan*, ed. by J. H. Rose, vol. 2 (1917), p. 333.

at court, published an epistle to the citizens of Boston in which are found the lines:

> You, happy people, freed from kings and queens,
> Dance to the rattling of the chains that bind
> In servile shame the rest of humankind.

Similar sentiments were also expressed on the stage. In the play *La Vallée de Shénandoah en Virginie* a colonist of Virginia welcomes immigrants who had fled from oppression in Europe and also treats his slaves as friends. Then the whole cast sings:

> Here there reigns equality,
> Here man to man is brother,
> And in this land reigns no false pride
> Adored in every other.[1]

In a more practical way the coming of the Revolution was hastened by the participation of France in the American War of Independence. The French national debt which was already large was increased by the cost of the war to a point where bankruptcy could be prevented only by drastic reforms. Had the government been able to surmount its financial difficulties the Revolution might have been avoided or at least postponed. As it was, the insolvency of the government necessitated the calling of the Estates-General which gave the Third Estate the opportunity to bring its grievances out into the open. Thus the financial embarrassment of the government was the most immediate cause of the Revolution.

[1] Cited in B. Faÿ, *The Revolutionary Spirit in France and America* (1927), p. 259.

CHAPTER TWENTY-FOUR

The Beginning of the French Revolution

THE LAST YEARS OF THE OLD RÉGIME

IF EVER France had need of a great king, it was at the death of Louis XV. The machinery of government was in such a state of disrepair that only a monarch possessing the highest powers of statesmanship could make it function smoothly. The king who was called to govern France at this most critical period was a plain-featured youth of twenty, large of person, with an inclination to corpulence. He had many good qualities. He was simple, honest, kind, and gentle; religious without fanatical intolerance, economical in his personal expenses, and untouched by the immorality of the French court. As the Princesse de Lamballe wrote in her *Memoirs:* "After the long and corrupt reign of an old debauched Prince, whose vices were degrading to himself and to a nation groaning under the lash . . . , the most cheering changes were expected from the known exemplariness of his successor." His knowledge was by no means as limited as it has often been depicted. He had learned several languages besides French, read much history, and shown an aptitude for geography. His intentions also were of the best. Probably no man ever had the good of his people more at heart. Loyal to the monarchy still, the same populace which had hurled imprecations at the coffin of Louis XV enthusiastically hailed his grandson in the hope that he would sweep away the accumulations of abuse. They called the young monarch Louis the Desired, and even the philosophes rejoiced at his accession. D'Alembert, for example, wrote to Frederick the Great: "He is just what we ought to desire as our king, if a propitious fate had not given him to us." In many windows the portrait of the new king was placed between those of Louis XII and Henry IV with the words: "XII and IV make XVI." One Parisian even wrote "Resurrexit (He is resurrected)" on the base of the statue of Henry IV on the Pont Neuf. But Louis was to blast the hopes of his people. He was not a resurrected Henry IV. Before many years passed, it became clear that he was wholly unfitted to lead his country to better things.

Unfortunately, Louis XVI was wanting in the qualities of a king. Naturally timid and reserved, he lacked the regal bearing which had distinguished his predecessor. His heaviness of mind made him slow in comprehending, though he could judge clearly when he understood. Initiative and curiosity he had none. Instead of striving to gain an adequate knowledge of French affairs as an aid in making decisions, he spent much time in locksmithing and hunting. Often he would be so exhausted from the hunt that he would sleep through the council meetings in which important matters were decided. His greatest weakness, however, was his lack of self-confidence. This is the key to his character and conduct. He could not bring himself to form a definite opinion and then adhere to it. If his views clashed with those of another, he quickly changed them lest he expose himself to censure. Consequently his opinions were usually the echo of the last person with whom he had conversed. As the queen wrote in 1791: "At the time when one believes him to be convinced, a word, an argument, makes him change irrevocably; that is the reason why a thousand things are not to be undertaken." Any emergency would find him bewildered and floundering.

Marie Antoinette, the queen, possessed many qualities that Louis did not have, but she was for other reasons unsuited to her position. The youngest daughter of Maria Theresa, she had been married to Louis in 1770 in order to strengthen the alliance between France and Austria which had proved so disastrous in the Seven Years' War. With her slim figure, regular features, beautiful blond hair, and striking white complexion, she was personally attractive. Moreover, she was affectionate, lively, gracious, and eager to please. On the other hand, she was wilful and impetuous,

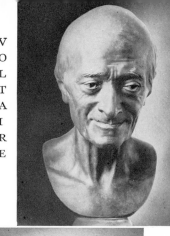

RIE ANTOINETTE AND HER CHILDREN

THE LAST OF THE GIRONDISTS

THE JACOBIN CLUB

ROBESPIERRE

DANTON
by David

THE BASTILLE AS IT
LOOKED IN THE
EIGHTEENTH CENTURY

and often haughty toward those whom she disliked. Above all, she lacked depth, tact, and stability. She could not for any length of time interest herself in a serious occupation. As a child she had been so flighty that her tutor wrote: "I cannot accustom her to investigate any subject thoroughly, although I feel that she is quite capable of it." Consequently her education had been super-ficial. In truth, she possessed but few accomplishments. Such was the girl who at fourteen became the dauphiness and at nineteen the queen of France. Beloved at first by the French people, she soon became the object of an intense hatred. In part this was due to the fact that, as her brother said, "she was young and thought-less." The stilted atmosphere of the court was so boring that she sought relief in frivolities not unusual to one of her age, but un-becoming to a queen. Mostly harmless in themselves, such diver-sions and adventures as attendance at public masked balls or riding unescorted in a cab in Paris shocked the people and compro-mised her dignity. Her enemies and the scandalmongers were only too ready to put the worst possible interpretation on her acts and to turn everything into calumny. Soon libel after libel appeared, until the most stupid lies and the coarsest scandals found ready acceptance with the Parisian populace.

More reprehensible than her escapades was Marie Antoinette's interference in governmental affairs. After Louis became king his wife gained a lifelong influence over him. This influence she used at times to find offices for her favorites or to remove ministers whom she disliked. When the news of her meddling reached Austria, both her mother and her brother, the Emperor Joseph II, chided her. "What business have you to interfere with the placing of ministers, to get such a department given to this one and such to that?" her brother wrote. "You behave more like a Pompadour or a Du Barry than a great Princess," Maria Theresa told her. It was to no avail. Her intervention continued, and since she saw things only from her point of view it wrought much harm. The queen also gave much offense by her extravagance. As dauphiness she had spent little on dress and jewelry, and even as queen she at first avoided all useless expenses. It was not long, however, before her love of fine clothes and adornments asserted itself. In addition to buying large quantities of feathers and fripperies with which to bedeck herself, Marie Antoinette spent vast sums for jewels when the royal treasury could ill support such expenditures. Next came gambling for high stakes, at which she sometimes lost large sums. Little wonder that the people who were in need of bread called her "Madame Deficit" and denounced her as the cause of their poverty.

At the beginning of his reign Louis raised sanguine expectations of reform by renouncing the grant of money which it had been customary to give to the king at his accession and by promising economy in public expenditures. Moreover, he chose as controller-general of finances the economist Turgot, whose very name was a pledge of reform. As intendant of Limoges for thirteen years Turgot had shown what might be done for France as a whole. The principles which were to guide his policy were set down by the new minister in a letter to the king. They were: no bankruptcy, no new taxes, no loans. There was only one way of solving the financial problem, he told the king, and that was by limiting expenditures to income. That it would be a difficult task Turgot realized only too well. "I shall be feared, hated perhaps by the great majority of the court, by all those who solicit favors," he wrote. Throwing himself into the work with great energy, he curtailed the extravagance of the royal household, abolished thousands of useless offices, and reformed the collection of the taxes in such a way as to increase the revenues. Within a short time he managed to reduce greatly the indebtedness of the government and to reëstablish its credit. He also encouraged agricultural production by establishing free trade in grain, a reform which Voltaire greeted with the words: "It seems that new heavens and a new earth have made their appearance." Turgot converted the corvées into money payments to be levied on all landowners, with no exemptions for the privileged classes, and relieved industry of its hampering restrictions by suppressing the trade gilds. He even entertained ideas of commuting the feudal dues and of abolishing the inequalities of taxation. But before he could seriously take up these changes he was forced out of office.

In carrying out his reforms Turgot, as he foresaw, excited much opposition. The court party opposed him because he was trying to reduce the expenses of the royal household, the nobles resented the substitution of a general land tax for the corvées which had previously been borne only by the peasants, the parlements were incensed over his attacks on privilege, the artisans hated him for dissolving the gilds, others were opposed to his tax reforms, and some of his colleagues were envious of his influence over the king. Marie Antoinette, who had said when he was appointed, "M. Turgot is a very honest man, which is most essential for the finances," became openly hostile because he had ended the political career of one of her favorites and disapproved of her extravagance. In short, all who had profited from the evils and abuses began to demand his dismissal. For a time the king resisted the demands. He honestly favored the reform policy of Turgot and was heard to exclaim: "It is only Turgot and I who love the people." Turgot himself wrote several letters to Louis counseling him to stand firmly for reform. In one he went so far as to say: "It was weakness, Sire, which laid the head of Charles I on the block—it was weakness that caused all the misfortunes of the last reign." But the words had little effect. After a time Louis gave way before the persistent clamors, particularly of the queen and her party, and on May 12, 1776, dismissed his faithful minister. Within a few months after Turgot's fall most of his reforms were undone. Thus Louis doomed any hope of eradicating even the most flagrant evils and abuses.

After a short interval Jacques Necker, a foreign-born Protestant who had won distinction as a banker, took over the task of regulating the finances. Warned by the fate of Turgot, he decided to introduce reforms more slowly and meanwhile to borrow money to meet the deficit. When he found it necessary in 1778 to borrow large sums to finance French participation in the American War of Independence, the deficit grew so large that he was forced to cut down the pensions to courtiers and to discharge many officials of the king's household. In an effort to justify his administration he took the unprecedented step in 1781 of publishing a statement of revenue and expenditure, called *Compte rendu*. The statement was deceptive, for Necker had juggled the figures to make it appear that there was a surplus in the treasury. Nevertheless, the people learned for the first time how much money was collected by the government and how it was spent. They realized particularly how much was consumed by the court in the form of pensions and gifts. The courtiers were furious. They decided that because Necker had made their incomes a matter of common knowledge he must go the way of Turgot. Necker settled the issue by resigning in 1781, leaving the finances in a worse condition than when he took office.[1]

---

[1] It is noteworthy that Necker was instrumental in freeing the last serfs on the royal domains and in abolishing the practice of torturing prisoners before their trials.

In 1783 Calonne was made minister of finance. His administration was based on the idea that the government must create the appearance of prosperity by spending freely if it would restore its credit. Accordingly he borrowed large sums from the bankers and spent or distributed them on all sides with a lavish hand. For the courtiers it was the golden age of plenty; and even the poor benefited from the construction of public works. By 1786, however, he borrowed so much that the bankers were unwilling to lend the government more. Then in despair Calonne advised the king to summon the Assembly of Notables for the purpose of discussing new taxes. But the 144 members of the privileged classes who met at Versailles in 1787 were not interested in new taxes. The remedy they suggested was the dismissal of Calonne—a suggestion which Louis carried out but which left unsolved the problem of an empty treasury and a huge deficit. After trying vainly with the help of another finance minister to stave off bankruptcy, Louis found himself in 1788 reduced to the necessity of recalling Necker, who promptly demanded that the Estates-General be convoked.

THE MEETING OF THE ESTATES-GENERAL

The announcement that the Estates-General was to be called precipitated a warm discussion as to how the deputies should be elected, and the number of representatives each order should have. The "Patriots" demanded that the Third Estate, since it far outnumbered the nobility and the clergy, should have as many representatives as those two orders together. After a period of indecision the government finally announced that the Third Estate was to have "double representation," but it failed to specify whether the representatives of each order were to meet separately and vote by order or whether all the deputies were to deliberate together and vote as individuals. While the representatives of the nobility were elected by direct vote, those of the clergy were chosen in some instances by direct and in others by indirect vote. It was of great importance that the parish priests were allowed to vote. Being so much more numerous than the higher clergy, they were able to elect a majority of the delegates representing the clergy. For the election of the deputies of the Third Estate a complex method was prescribed. Every male member of the Third Estate who had reached the age of twenty-five and was registered on the tax rolls was given the right to vote for electors who then met in district conventions to choose delegates to the Estates-General. The deputies chosen to represent the Third Estate were elected almost entirely from its own ranks, excepting the Abbé Siéyès and a few priests, and Mirabeau and a few other noblemen. Almost half of the commoners were lawyers, the rest being drawn mostly from the other professions. Less than a score belonged to the lower classes of the Third Estate. Thus the representatives of the Third Estate were men who had absorbed the teachings of Voltaire, Rousseau, and Montesquieu, and were convinced that the government must be reformed.

The years immediately preceding the elections were a period of widespread economic distress. Beginning in 1785 there had been a series of bad harvests caused by floods, drought, or hailstorms in large parts of France. Bread became so scarce that famine prices were demanded for it, and the suffering among the poor peasants was severe. Equally serious was the industrial crisis, which came largely, though not entirely, as the result of the commercial treaty concluded with England in 1786. By this treaty the duties in both countries were reduced to twelve or even to ten per cent of the value of the goods. The tariff on cottons, woolens, and hosiery, for example, was set at twelve per cent, while English hardware was admitted into France on the payment of a duty of ten per cent. Though the treaty increased the total amount of the trade between the two countries, it was disastrous to certain French industries, particularly those producing textiles and hardware. No sooner was the agreement put in force in May, 1787, than the French markets were flooded with textiles and hardware that sold for less than the corresponding French goods. Consequently many factories that were unable to dispose of their goods were forced to close down, and large numbers of workmen lost their employment. On top of this came one of the coldest winters France had known—so cold that in Paris bonfires were lighted throughout the city to keep the poor from freezing to death.

Yet the prospect of a meeting of the Estates-General gave the people hope. From one end to the other France was humming with excitement; everywhere the meeting was being discussed orally and in print. The censorship notwithstanding, no fewer than 150 different pamphlets dealing with the political situation were widely circulated. The most famous was that of Abbé Siéyès, entitled

What Is the Third Estate? It opened with the following lines: "What is the Third Estate? Everything. What has it been in the political order up to the present? Nothing. What does it ask? To become something." According to traditional custom, the government invited the various assemblies of the three classes to draw up *cahiers* or "notebooks of grievances" for the consideration of the Estates-General. These cahiers show that the people of France were not opposed to the idea of monarchy in itself. What they did demand was a constitution to limit and regulate the power of the monarch. The power of making laws and of voting taxes, they specified, should be vested in an assembly representing the nation and meeting at stated times. Some cahiers went so far as to request the deputies not to vote taxes until the government had acceded to their demand for a constitution. Many cahiers of the nobility as well as of the Third Estate condemned the lettres de cachet, demanded freedom of speech and of the press, and requested trial by jury. The demand for equal taxation voiced so widely by the Third Estate was also included in some cahiers of the privileged orders. On the other hand, the nobility emphatically rejected equality of rights and also insisted upon the old method of voting by order. Since most of the statements of the Third Estate were drawn up by members of the middle class, such demands of the peasants as the abolition of the feudal dues and the regulation of the rights of pasturage on waste lands were kept somewhat in the background.

Toward the end of April, 1789, deputies began to arrive at Versailles, and on May 5 the meeting of the Estates-General was formally opened. Louis read a brief speech and Necker a long, boring one. However, neither the king nor his minister presented a program of reform or laid down a course of action, both contenting themselves with a declaration that the finances must be put in order. Nor was the question whether the new body should vote by order or by member settled. The Third Estate took matters into its own hands by refusing to verify credentials until the three orders should meet in a body and vote by head. For six weeks the orders debated the question, with the Third Estate holding firmly to its demands. Finally, after a number of parish priests came over from the clergy, the commoners and curates declared themselves on June 17 the National Assembly. It was the first great act of the French Revolution. On June 20, when the deputies arrived at the

Europe in 1789

Boundary of the Empire

Scale of Miles
0   50 100   200   300

ATLANTIC OCEAN

PORTUGAL

Lisbon
Douro
Tagus
Guadiana
Guadalquivir
Sevilla
Gibraltar Br.
Ceuta

MADRID
SPAIN
Saragossa
NAVARRE
CATALONIA
Barcelona
Tortosa
IVISA
Valencia
MAJORCA
MINORCA

MEDITERRANEAN SEA

AFRICA

Biscay
Bay of Biscay
Brest
Nantes
Loire
Bordeaux
Bayonne
Garonne
FRANCE
Seine
Havre
Valmy
Paris
Verdun
Metz
Orange
Rhône
Marseilles
Toulon
Nice
Genoa
PIEDMONT
Florence
SAVOY
SWITZERLAND
Berne
TYROL
Munich

ENGLAND
London
Ostend
Brussels
NETHERLANDS
The Hague
Amsterdam
UNITED NETHERLANDS
Bremen
Cassel
Cologne
Mainz
WÜRTEM-BERG
EMPIRE
BOHEMIA
Prague
SAXONY
Dresden
Berlin
PRUSSIA
BRANDENBURG

SCOTLAND
Edinburgh
IRELAND
Dublin
WALES
NORTH SEA
JUTLAND
DENMARK
Copenhagen
SWEDEN
GOTLAND
BORNHOLM
RÜGEN
S. POMERANIA
Königsberg
BALTIC SEA

RIVER
To Russia 1772
To Russia 1793
To Prussia 1772
To Austria 1772
To Prussia 1793
To Austria 1795
Cracow
Lemberg
WARSAW
To Prussia 1795

RUSSIA

SARDINIA
Cagliari
CORSICA
STATES OF THE CHURCH
ROME
TUSCANY
PARMA
MODENA
Venice
ADRIATIC SEA
ISTRIA
STYRIA
AUSTRIA
Vienna
Presburg
MORAVIA
ILLYRIA
CARNIOLA
CARINTHIA

NAPLES
KINGDOM OF THE TWO SICILIES
CALABRIA
ALBANIA
Scutari
Janina

Naples

HUNGARY
Agram
CROATIA
BOSNIA
Theiss
Danube
Belgrade
SERVIA
MONTENEGRO

GREECE
CRETE
Smyrna
Brusa

OTTOMAN EMPIRE
TRANSYLVANIA
WALLACHIA
Bukharest
BULGARIA
Sofia
Varna
Adrianople
Constantinople
Salonika

MOLDAVIA
Jassy
Pruth
Dniester
Bug
Dnieper

BLACK SEA

Salle des Menus Plaisirs for their session, they found the doors locked against them. Placards announced that the hall was being prepared for the royal sitting to be held two days hence. The deputies feared it was a move to force them to vote by order. Therefore, instead of dispersing, they repaired to a large building near by, in which the princes sometimes played tennis; and there, under the leadership of the astronomer Bailly, they solemnly swore not to separate "until the constitution of the kingdom shall be established and consolidated on firm foundations."[1] This oath, known to history as the Tennis Court Oath, was really an assertion that sovereignty did not reside in the house of Bourbon, but in the people.

In the royal session on June 23 a clerk first read a declaration in which the king annulled the resolutions on June 17 and ordered the three estates to meet separately, except when he should permit them to meet together. The declaration also promised such reforms as equal taxation and the levying of new taxes only with the consent of the Estates-General. Then Louis himself made a short speech, ending it with the words: "I order you, gentlemen, to separate immediately, and to go tomorrow morning, each to the chamber allotted to your order, to take up again your sessions." Having concluded his speech, the king withdrew, followed by the nobility and the clergy. But the Third Estate remained seated in the center of the hall. "Gentlemen," cried De Brézé, the master of ceremonies, "you know the king's wishes." Thereupon the nobleman Mirabeau, who represented the Third Estate, is reported to have said in a thundering voice: "Go and tell those who sent you that we are here by the will of the people, and that we will go only if we are driven out by bayonets!" De Brézé, awestruck by the unexpected reply, left the hall. The Assembly immediately passed a declaration stating that any attempt to arrest a deputy for anything said or done in the Estates-General was treason. But for the moment the king had no intention of using force. When the master of ceremonies reported the refusal of the Third Estate to leave, Louis replied, with a weary gesture: "They mean to stay! . . . Well then, damn it! let them stay!" It was another striking display of Louis XVI's weakness. For the Third

---

[1] Because of its work of drawing up a constitution the National Assembly is also called the National Constituent Assembly or simply the Constituent Assembly, the former being the official name adopted by the assembly itself.

Estate it was a great triumph. The next day a majority of the clergy joined the National Assembly, followed the day after by a group of noblemen. Finally, on June 27, the king himself ordered the clergy and the nobility to unite with the Third Estate.

THE FALL OF THE BASTILLE

The king had surrendered to the demands of the Third Estate, but soon various rumors had it that he was planning to reverse his decision. Early in July troops, mostly Swiss and German mercenaries, began to arrive in the vicinity of Versailles and Paris, so that by the 13th some 18,000 were concentrated in that region. Though the king avowed that the disorders and outbreaks in or near the capital necessitated their presence, it was widely believed that they had been collected for the purpose of dissolving the National Assembly. The Assembly, apprehensive of its safety, requested without effect that the regiments be withdrawn. Instead of withdrawing them, the king took the further step on July 11 of dismissing Necker, whom the people regarded as a champion of reform. In Paris, where there had been wild excitement for days over the presence of the troops, pandemonium broke loose. Mobs surged through the streets, breaking into gunsmith shops in search of arms and looting taverns and bakeries. The French soldiers, instead of repressing the disorders, mutinied and joined the mobs. On the morning of July 14 the populace seized many muskets and some cannon at the Hôtel des Invalides. Then the cry was sounded, "To the Bastille!"

The Bastille was a castle-like fortress which had been built centuries earlier to guard the Saint-Antoine gate of the old city. After the city expanded beyond its original limits the fortress had become a prison. Among the famous personages who had been confined there by means of lettres de cachet were Voltaire and Mirabeau. In 1789 it held seven prisoners (four counterfeiters, two lunatics, and a debauchee) and only one of them was incarcerated for political reasons. But the people chose to believe otherwise. Stories were circulated of deep underground dungeons in which innocent men had been immured for many years without seeing the light of the sun. Rumors were also current that vast quantities of powder and muskets were stored there. There is no evidence that the mob at first entertained the idea of storming the Bastille. Its sole intention seems to have been to procure arms. The deputation sent for that purpose was graciously received by De Launay, commander of a garrison numbering a few more than a hundred, but he refused their request. When the drawbridge was lowered for the exit of the deputation, part of the mob swarmed across it into the courtyard. De Launay could still have held out, for the fortress itself had not been forced. The defenders did fire on the crowd in the courtyard, so that the drawbridge could be raised again; but when a detachment of the Garde Française arrived with cannon, the morale of the garrison broke down and De Launay capitulated on the promise of the self-appointed leaders that no harm should come to him and his men. However, when the gates were opened the crowd rushed in and, in revenge for about one hundred attackers who had been killed, literally hacked the commander in pieces. Several other officers and a number of their men were also murdered by the mob. The Bastille, emblem of the absolute power of the Bourbons, was leveled to the ground. The anniversary of its fall is still celebrated as the birthday of French liberty.

When Louis heard the news he exclaimed to the messenger: "This is a revolt!" "No, Sire," was the answer; "it is a revolution." Once more the king decided to make concessions. He not only recalled Necker but also appeared before the Assembly in person to announce that he would withdraw the troops. The news calmed the wrought-up passions of Paris, and some semblance of order was restored by the National Guard, which had been organized by the bourgeoisie of Paris several weeks before, and of which Lafayette was now made commander. Furthermore, a new city government was formed and Bailly was chosen mayor of Paris. On July 17 Louis himself visited Paris to strengthen the feeling in his favor. He was met at the gates by the mayor, who presented him with the keys of the city. "Henry IV," Bailly said, "reconquered his people; now the people have reconquered their king!" At the Hôtel de Ville the king appeared before the crowd wearing the new tricolor cockade (red, white, and blue), the symbol of the revolutionary government, and was heartily cheered. The sovereign, it seemed, was about to be reconciled with his people. To the court party the storming of the Bastille was an omen of worse things to come. Consequently a number of high noblemen, including the count of Artois, the king's brother, decided to seek safety in flight. It was the beginning of a great royalist emigration.

The queen did not flee with the nobles. Had she done so, the fate of Louis XVI might well have been different.

The disorders of July were by no means confined to Paris. During the weeks preceding the fall of the Bastille there had been a number of local uprisings among the peasantry, caused by a scarcity of food. During the weeks after July 14 the people were gripped by the Great Fear. This widespread apprehension was not a single movement, but a series of waves emanating from various centers. One important cause was the belief that the "aristocrats" were plotting to destroy the Revolution. In many districts the fear expressed itself in the words, "The brigands are coming." Whence they were coming no one knew, but it was believed that they had been sent out by the aristocrats to butcher those who were sponsoring the Revolution. Both townspeople and peasants armed themselves and made frantic preparations to resist attack. When the brigands did not arrive the townspeople returned to their normal duties, but in the country many of the armed bands of peasants struck at the feudal nobility. Their purpose was to obtain the manor rolls on which the feudal dues were recorded, for they believed that if these were destroyed the lords could no longer require them to pay the dues. If the seigneur refused to surrender the rolls voluntarily, force was employed. In a number of instances châteaux and manor houses were burned. Murders, however, were rare.

THE WORK OF THE NATIONAL CONSTITUENT ASSEMBLY

When a report of the uprisings reached the Assembly its members seemed at a loss for a remedy. But at eight o'clock on the evening of August 4, as it was ready to adjourn for the day, the Vicomte de Noailles in an impassioned speech proposed the redemption of certain feudal dues in money and the abolition of the others as a means of ending the plundering in the provinces. His suggestions were greeted with vigorous applause by the Third Estate and soon the nobles, reassured by the promise of compensation, joined in the enthusiasm. For the rest of the night they vied with one another and with the clergy in abrogating their rights and privileges. When the session ended at dawn, many feudal dues had been abolished without compensation, and the rest had been declared redeemable for money.[1] Serfdom, tithes, the seigniorial

---

[1] As the peasants were either unable or unwilling to pay the lords any compensation, the feudal dues were completely abolished in 1793.

corvées, the exclusive right of the nobles to hunt and fish, and the manorial courts were all abolished. Furthermore, the principle of equal taxation was proclaimed, the sale of judicial and municipal offices was discontinued, and all citizens, without distinction, were declared eligible to any office, whether civil, military, or ecclesiastical. Finally the Assembly closed the session by proclaiming Louis XVI "the restorer of French liberty." It had been a night of hysteria. Nevertheless, the reforms that were thus begun form the most enduring contribution of the French Revolution.

As the rights of all Frenchmen had been made equal, it became necessary to define these rights. For this purpose the Assembly drew up the Declaration of the Rights of Man, the most famous document of the early period of the Revolution. Its provisions had as their aim the suppression of specific abuses listed in the cahiers. The declaration contained, among others, the following statements: "Men are born and remain free and equal in rights. . . . The aim of every political association is the preservation of the natural and imprescriptible rights of man. These rights are liberty, property, security, and resistance to oppression. . . . The source of all sovereignty is essentially in the nation; no body, no individual can exercise authority that does not proceed from it in plain terms. . . . Liberty consists in the power to do anything that does not injure others. . . . Law is the expression of the general will. . . . No man can be accused, arrested, or detained except in the cases determined by the law and according to the forms it had prescribed. . . . No one should be disturbed on account of his opinions, even religious, provided their manifestation does not derange the public order established by law. . . . The free communication of ideas and opinions is one of the most precious of the rights of man; every citizen then can freely speak, write, and print, subject to responsibility for the abuse of this freedom in the cases determined by law."[1]

While the Assembly was at work drawing up the constitution of which the Declaration of Rights was to be a part, disturbing rumors reached Paris from Versailles. Weeks had passed and still the king had ratified neither the decrees of the memorable session of August 4 nor the early articles of the constitution. Suspicion again ran high that the king, under the urgings of the queen, was

---

[1] Complete text in Anderson, *The Constitutions and Other Select Documents Illustrative of the History of France* (1908), pp. 59–61.

planning to undo the work of the Revolution. This suspicion was strengthened by the arrival, toward the end of September, of the Regiment of Flanders at Versailles. At a banquet given it by the royal bodyguard on October 1 there were enthusiastic demonstrations in favor of the royal family. A number of wine-exhilarated men tore off their tricolor cockades, shouted denunciations of the Assembly, and pledged their loyalty to the king. When highly embellished reports of the banquet reached Paris they caused another famous incident of the Revolution. At the time the situation in the capital was desperate. The uncertainties of the Revolution had proved so harmful to business that thousands of artisans and workingmen had been thrown out of work. Bread was so scarce that it could be obtained only at exorbitant prices. The threat of starvation alarmed many. Radical journals which had been established since the fall of the Bastille—among them one soon to be called *L'Ami du peuple*, of which Jean Paul Marat was the editor—were fanning the embers of discontent. Time and again they attacked the Assembly because it was not carrying out practical reforms fast enough. They also stated that if the king and the Assembly were moved to Paris, the price of bread would drop and the Assembly would speed its reforms.

This discontent finally culminated in the incident known as "The March of the Women to Versailles." Just how the march started is somewhat obscure. It seems that on the morning of October 5 a crowd of women assembled before the Hôtel de Ville to demand bread from the municipal government. When the officials were unable to produce bread, the crowd became unruly. To save the "city hall" from being ransacked by the women, one Maillard who had played a prominent part in the capture of the Bastille seized a drum and shouted, "To Versailles!" Along the way others joined the crowd until it numbered thousands.[1] Later in the day Lafayette and his National Guards also set off for Versailles to prevent the mob from committing acts of violence. When the women arrived they surrounded the hall in which the Assembly was in session and sent in a deputation to demand that the price of bread be lowered by law. The Assembly appointed a delegation to go with the women to the king. After much hesitation Louis finally promised measures to provide Paris with bread,

[1] Seven or eight thousand according to Madelin, *The French Revolution* (1916), p. 104.

and about midnight Lafayette arrived to restore order. Toward morning, however, after Lafayette had retired for a little rest, a small group tried to force their way into the apartment of the queen, whom they regarded as a primary cause of their troubles. Two members of the royal bodyguard who tried to block the way were killed, but the queen escaped to the king's apartment. The next morning, when Lafayette and the royal family appeared on a balcony they were cheered; nevertheless, the crowd insisted that the royal family accompany it to Paris. Several hours later the procession started for Paris, with the crowd surrounding the royal carriage, gleefully shouting: "We have the baker, and the baker's wife, and the baker's little boy. Now we shall have bread." That night the royal family was installed in the Tuileries. Little did either Louis or Marie Antoinette realize that they were never to see Versailles again.

Within ten days the Assembly by its own vote also moved to Paris, where it finally took up its quarters in a spacious riding academy that had been built near the Tuileries by Louis XV. Thenceforth it was to be dominated in large measure by the mobs of Paris. In the three large galleries of the hall in which it met, the citizens gathered to listen to the proceedings and applaud or hiss. On days when more important issues were debated large crowds collected outside to cheer or denounce. All this encouraged certain orators of the Assembly to make more revolutionary speeches and more radical suggestions.

In Paris the Assembly continued the work of drawing up the constitution. What it actually did was to vote a series of reforms, many of which were put in force immediately. Later they were all incorporated in a single document known as the Constitution of 1791. Under this constitution a hereditary monarchy was preserved, but the power of the sovereign was strictly limited according to the formula of "the separation of powers" which Montesquieu had so strongly recommended. Not only was the legislative power vested in a Legislative Assembly of one house, but the king was deprived of the right to appoint judges. Though he was still to direct the diplomacy of the nation, he could not declare war or sign treaties without permission of the Legislative Assembly. In legislative matters he was granted a suspensive veto; that is, he could temporarily stop all measures passed by the Legislative Assembly, except those that were constitutional or fiscal. Measures passed by three successive legislatures were to become laws without the monarch's assent. In addition to the legislative power, the Legislative Assembly was given control of both the assessment of taxes and the expenditure of the national revenues. No longer could the king spend as much as he wished or contract debts for which the nation was responsible. Henceforth he was allotted a civil list with twenty-five million francs as the maximum. The Legislative Assembly, which under the new constitution became the supreme power in the state, was composed of 745 deputies elected for a period of two years. Despite the Declaration of the Rights of Man the right of suffrage was granted only to "active citizens" or, in other words, to those who annually paid taxes to the amount of three days' wages. Those who paid less or no taxes at all were designated "passive citizens" and were given no voice in the government.[1] Only those who paid taxes equivalent to a silver mark (about fifty francs) were eligible for election to the Assembly. Thus the control of the government was placed in the hands of the moneyed classes.

The Constituent Assembly also voted numerous other reforms which were incorporated in the constitution. The chaotic system of administrative divisions, which included provinces, generalities, and bailiwicks, was replaced by a system of divisions and subdivisions that was both simple and uniform. France was divided into eighty-three departments which were subdivided into districts, cantons, and communes—a system which has remained the basis of French administration to the present day. Each department was administered by officials elected by the voters of that department, and was therefore a kind of little republic. The reorganization of the judiciary proceeded along much the same lines, the complex system of courts giving way to a simplified judicial system. The judges, who had hitherto purchased their offices, were henceforth to be elected for a period of six years. In criminal cases the jury, unknown in France up to this time, was established, and punishments were made less cruel by the abolition of torture, branding, and the pillory. Attempts by Robespierre to outlaw the death penalty were unsuccessful, but it was decided that the death penalty be inflicted by decapitation, a mode of execution hitherto reserved for the nobility, and in

---

[1] Camille Desmoulins pointed out that both Corneille and Rousseau would have been listed as "passive citizens."

1792 the guillotine[1] was made the official instrument of execution. Furthermore, reforms of the military organization abolished the sale of offices, opened the commissions to all, and raised the pay of the common soldiers. The gilds and trading companies were also suppressed, and every Frenchman was given the right to follow any occupation or engage in any trade. Finally, to symbolize the inauguration of a new order, the tricolor was adopted as the national flag.

However, the principal purpose for which the Estates-General had been summoned originally was to suggest means of solving the financial problem of the government. During the first months the National Assembly was in session the financial crisis grew steadily worse. The former taxes (taille, gabelle, etc.) were abolished, but the new taxes (the land tax and the tax on the profits of trade and industry) returned very little to the treasury owing to the existing confusion. On the other hand, the expenses of the government had increased. Because of the scarcity of wheat in France, the government had to buy much abroad to feed the people. No less than seventeen million livres' worth of wheat was purchased in two months for the working people of Paris. Though loans had twice been voted by the National Assembly, the public was unwilling to lend money to the state. As a solution of the crisis Talleyrand, bishop of Autun, proposed the confiscation and sale of the church lands in October, 1789—a solution previously suggested by Calonne and also in a number of cahiers. After much debate the proposal was finally adopted and in December, 1789, the Assembly decided to issue a series of treasury bills or *assignats* redeemable in land instead of in cash. This was followed in the spring of 1790 by an issue of assignats to the value of four hundred million francs in the form of legal tender. The assignats might have retained a high value if no more had been issued. But again and again, as the treasury needed money, more were put into circulation until they finally depreciated to the point of worthlessness. As it was, they maintained a reasonably high value until near the end of the year 1794. During this period, in which the other sources of revenue produced little, the assignats gave the government a means of meeting the current obligations.

[1] The mechanical axe was not, as is often stated, invented by the man whose name it bears. In medieval Germany it was well known by the name of "French trap" and there are also instances of its use in early modern times. During the period of the French Revolution it came to be called guillotine because Dr. Ramon Guillotin suggested its use for the numerous executions.

As the Assembly had seized the lands of the Church and abolished the tithes, it became necessary to make provision for the maintenance of the secular clergy and for the continuation of worship. The Assembly also undertook to reorganize the whole ecclesiastical system. Having previously dissolved most of the monasteries and forbidden the taking of perpetual vows, it now drew up the Civil Constitution of the Clergy, which established a new order for bishops and priests. This civil constitution provided that, instead of about 140 bishops, there were henceforth to be only 83, the bishoprics having been reorganized so that they corresponded with the new departments into which France had been divided. Both bishops and parish priests were to be elected in the same manner as other government officials, and were also to receive their salary from the government. In other words, the clergy practically became officials of the state. It was further decreed that all clergymen who refused to swear fidelity to the constitution were to be dismissed. Thus the Catholic Church in France became a national institution entirely separate from papal jurisdiction, though the spiritual supremacy of the pope was still recognized. The new arrangement eliminated many abuses, but on the whole it was a grave mistake. The attempt by the government to enforce the Civil Constitution of the Clergy was to evoke much opposition and alienate the support of many who had previously favored the Revolution. Later it was to give rise to rebellion and civil war. Less than half of the clergy swore to support the constitution. The rest, known as the non-juring clergy, became staunch opponents of the Assembly and its endeavors to regenerate France. In 1791 the pope issued a bull which declared the constitution based on heretical principles. This turned the sympathies of the great majority of pious Catholics against the new ecclesiastical order.

Louis XVI put his signature to the constitution only after much hesitation. Later, when he saw how widespread the opposition to the new arrangement was, he regretted having signed it, feeling that it had imperiled his own salvation and that of his subjects. Gradually he began to consider the idea of repudiating this and other reforms, and of fleeing from it all. The thought seems to have become a resolve at Eastertime, when a crowd of Parisians prevented the royal family from going to St. Cloud to hear mass by a non-juring priest. Unfortunately Mirabeau, the one man who might have dissuaded Louis from taking such an injudicious step, had died in April, 1791, worn out as much from dissipation as from hard work. Thereafter Louis came entirely under the influence of the queen. Together their Majesties laid plans for the escape. A carriage was obtained and on the night of June 20, 1791, the royal family secretly started for the frontier, the queen disguised as a Russian lady and the king as her valet. But the attempt to reach the border miscarried. Not only was much time lost in starting, but the progress of the royal party was so slow that the convoys which were to meet it did not await its arrival. Moreover, the king, having left Paris some distance behind, became so elated over his escape that he forgot the need of concealment and was recognized. At Varennes, a village near the frontier, the royal party was detained by the authorities to await the arrival of orders from Paris. The orders arrived the next morning, directing that the royal family be brought back to the Tuileries. On the return journey crowds assembled along the roads to hurl taunts, jeers, and insults at the royal pair, the queen being the special target, for she was regarded as the instigator of the flight. In Paris, where the king and his family arrived on June 24, they were received in gloomy silence by the large crowd which had turned out to see them.

Hitherto the Assembly had been able to count on the acquiescence if not on the hearty approval of the king. But his attempted flight and the declaration criticizing the new constitution which he had left behind convinced them that Louis was an unwilling collaborator in the reforms. The radical journals now began to demand a republic in no uncertain terms. But the Assembly, though it had suspended the king, was not yet ready to proclaim a republic. Hence, when the king showed himself in a penitent mood, he was reinstated. Then Louis formally accepted the new constitution and on September 30, 1791, the weary deputies dissolved the National Constituent Assembly.

Within a short period the National Assembly had wrought tremendous changes in France. (1) It had limited the royal authority and placed the political power of the nation in the hands of an elected assembly. (2) It had decreed the abolition of all personal feudal dues and the redemption of the land dues for money. (3) It had swept away all privileges, suppressed the hodgepodge of taxes, and demolished all barriers to the free circulation of goods in France. (4) It had replaced the complicated overlapping territorial divisions with a system that was not only simple but also uniform for all parts of France. (5) It had reorganized and simplified the administration of justice, provided for the election of judges, and instituted the jury for criminal cases. (6) It had effected a partial reorganization of the army and established liberty of work by dissolving the medieval gilds. (7) It had stripped the Church of its special privileges and of its wealth, and had made the clergy officials of the state. On the day before the National Assembly was dissolved, Robespierre had announced, "The Revolution is finished," an opinion which many shared with him. But the future was to show that this optimism was unfounded.

THE LEGISLATIVE ASSEMBLY

The Legislative Assembly met on October 1, 1791. It had been elected for a period of two years, but was to sit less than a year. As the National Assembly, in a spirit of self-denial, had decreed that none of its members were to be eligible for election to the Legislative Assembly, the new body was composed of men entirely without legislative experience. This inexperience was not, however, a major factor in the failure of the experiment with a limited monarchy. The constitution already stood condemned in the eyes of many when it was put in force. Of a total number of about 745 deputies only 264 registered with the Right, the group avowedly in favor of a constitutional monarchy. The so-called Left was composed of deputies who desired to overthrow the constitution and continue the Revolution. Though numerically small—it had but 136 members—it was an aggressive group. The rest of the deputies, about 345 in number, comprised the Center. This group adhered to no fixed policy and voted with either the Right or the Left according to the impulse of the moment. In general it may be said that the sentiment in the Legislative Assembly was at first in favor of a constitutional monarchy, though there was no agreement as to the form of the constitution. However, while the "Constitutionals" were weakening themselves by dissensions, the power of the Left was growing. Soon it dominated the Center so completely that this group ceased to identify itself with more moderate measures.

Outside the Legislative Assembly the constitutional monarchy was menaced on the one hand by those who believed that the Revolution had gone too far, and on the other by those who demanded further reforms. Among the former were the non-juring priests. Opposed to the religious arrangement of the new order because it conflicted with their convictions, they excited the people by telling them that the sacraments administered by the priests who had taken the oath were null and void. As a result there were disorders and uprisings in various parts of France, particularly in the Vendée, where a great popular insurrection took place against the new government. Besides the non-juring clergy, the émigrés or nobles who had emigrated from France also constituted a danger to the constitutional settlement. Since the fall of the Bastille increasing numbers of nobles, including the officers of the army, had been leaving France, where their lives were in constant danger. These émigrés, embittered by their experiences and eager to regain the privileges they had enjoyed before 1789, worked ceaselessly for the downfall of the constitutional monarchy. While some sought to stir up opposition by inflammatory pamphlets and newspapers which were smuggled into France, others contemplated the use of force to overthrow the new order. For this purpose military organizations were formed both at Worms and at Coblentz. Moreover, the émigrés urged foreign powers, particularly Austria and Prussia, to intervene in French affairs for the purpose of restoring the absolute monarchy.

The appeal of the émigrés did not fall on deaf ears. The absolute rulers, fearing that their own subjects might at any moment be seized with the desire to emulate the French people, had their own reasons for desiring to see absolute monarchy restored in France. Most eager of all was Leopold II of Austria. As an absolute monarch he was hostile to liberalism; as the brother of Marie Antoinette he was interested in the fate of the French royal family; and as the ruler of Austria he desired a French government which would continue the Franco-Austrian alliance. Nevertheless, Leopold did not desire war, and therefore refused the request of the émigrés for military assistance against France. But he did meet with Frederick William II in August, 1791, to issue the famous Declaration of Pillnitz which declared that the reëstablishment of order and absolute monarchy in France was the concern of all the rulers of Europe.

Upon the French radicals the declaration had the opposite effect of that desired by the rulers of Austria and Prussia. Instead of intimidating them, it spurred them on to greater efforts to achieve the dethronement of the king. After a temporary improvement in trade and industry, stimulated by the issue of assignats, the common people were again facing starvation because of high prices and a lack of grain. The millennium which they had fondly imagined the Estates-General would usher in had not arrived. There was much talk of the Revolution being over, but the masses had gained nothing. When the assignats began to decline in value, stagnation set in again in many industries, and large numbers were deprived of their employment. Artisans and workers loudly decried the general depression, demanding that something be done to ease their lot; that the theories of absolute equality which had been mouthed so glibly by members of the National Constituent Assembly be carried out.

Influential centers of the agitation against the government were the political clubs, which had gradually become more and more revolutionary. The most important of these was organized by the Breton deputies to the Estates-General for the purpose of discussing in advance all questions that were to be decided in the National Assembly. When the Assembly moved to Paris the club secured as a meeting place the convent of the Jacobin Friars, where it met under the name of "Society of the Friends of the Constitution Meeting at the Jacobins in Paris." This was abbreviated by the enemies of the group to Jacobins, the name by which the club has since been known. In addition to deputies the Jacobin Club also admitted other members, largely from the upper middle class, for even in its most radical stages it was never proletarian in its membership. While the Legislative Assembly was in session the members of the Jacobin Club gathered night after night to debate national questions or to discuss means of hastening the overthrow of the monarchy. The group at Paris was but the mother society. Affiliated clubs sprang up in other centers until France was covered by a network of Jacobin societies. How widespread the influence of the Jacobins was is shown by the fact that during the first week after the Legislative Assembly convened no less than 136 deputies inscribed their names in the register of the mother society. When it was first founded, the Jacobin Club was composed of men whose views were moderate.

Gradually, however, it had become a center of revolutionary ideas and the moderate members had withdrawn, leaving the leadership to such figures as Marat, Danton, and Robespierre.

Jean Paul Marat (1743–1793), a Swiss by birth, had been a physician, student of science, and writer of tracts on medical, scientific, and political subjects during the period preceding the Revolution. When the Revolution broke out he was moved to take up the cudgels in behalf of the masses by a profound pity for the downtrodden and oppressed, a burning desire for fame, and a violent hatred of all who were in authority, engendered by his failure to achieve recognition as a great scientist. At first he went about in person to denounce those who were in power and to urge the poor to demand their rights, but after the fall of the Bastille, in which he claimed a share, he began to issue a journal called *L'Ami du peuple*, so that his ideas would have a wider circulation. His public consisted chiefly of artisans, laborers, and the unemployed poor of Paris, to whom he endeared himself by his audacity and apparent sincerity in condemning social injustice. Vehement from the start in his denunciations of "the foes of the people," he soon reached a point where he approved any and every form of violence as a means of freeing the people from the chains of slavery and oppression. His favorite remedy for social injustice was the guillotine. Asking at first for five hundred heads, he gradually increased his demands, declaring finally that France could be saved only if 270,000 heads were cut off. Actually, however, Marat was not so bloodthirsty as his words. He himself stated that the sufferings of the poor were so great that gross invective and dire threats were necessary to frighten the authorities into relieving them. In his political program he was at first in favor of a limited monarchy. It was only after the king's attempted flight that he became convinced that Louis was "the greatest enemy of the Revolution." Thereafter he repeatedly advocated the establishment of a dictatorship, probably in the hope that he would be chosen dictator. When the republic was established in 1792, he renamed his journal *Journal de la République française*.

The greatest orator and demagogue of the trio was George Jacques Danton (1759–1794), who was not only a leading member of the Jacobin Club but also one of the founders of the Cordelier Club. His powerful physique, massive head, pock-marked face, bull's neck, thick hair, broad brow, and piercing eyes gave him an appearance which in itself overawed the people before he started speaking. By his contemporaries he was called "Hercules," "Atlas," and "Cyclops." As an orator he moved his listeners with his impetuous speech, sonorous voice, and dramatic gestures. Before the Revolution he had achieved considerable success as lawyer to the king's council, an office he had purchased. This office gave him an excellent opportunity to observe the abuses in the government, and when the Revolution broke out he was ready for the part he was to play. He was not a political theorist but rather an opportunist and man of action. Since the reforms of the National Assembly were not sufficiently thoroughgoing to please him, Danton in his thundering voice demanded further reforms. Of a kindly nature, he could become ruthless when the country was in danger or when the reforms that had been established were threatened, but he was not so bloodthirsty as some of the other leaders of the Revolution. His following was drawn largely from the better element of the Parisian populace as Marat's was from the lower.

Maximilien Robespierre (1758–1794), destined to become the outstanding figure of the second phase of the Revolution, was a lawyer by profession. After being admitted to the practice of law, he was appointed judge of the criminal court in the diocese of Arras but, because all human life was at that time sacred to him, resigned his office rather than pronounce a death sentence. His spiritual father was Rousseau. Essentially of a religious temperament, Robespierre adopted the *Social Contract* as his Bible. As a result of rereading it time and again, he became deeply imbued with the theory of democratic government. The realization of this theory in the form of "a Republic of Virtue and Justice" became the great aim of his life. As a member of the National Assembly he championed democracy and universal suffrage against the conservatives and impressed the other deputies by his sincerity. "He'll go far," Mirabeau stated, "because he believes everything he says." Robespierre was so sure that his gospel according to Rousseau was the panacea for all the ills afflicting society that he missed no opportunity to proclaim it. It was his narrowness of vision that finally won power for him. He recited his creed again and again, patiently and persistently, until the people put faith in his words and looked to him for "salvation." As the months passed, Robespierre slowly arrived at the conviction that his ideal republic could be established only by state intervention. Then he began to uphold as means for achieving his end those things that he had previously condemned, including force, the death penalty, war, and despotism. The weak and corrupt men who did not desire "a Republic of Virtue and Justice" he came to regard as unworthy of gentleness. This new Robespierre, the apostle of terror, was a far cry from the lawyer of Arras to whom all human life was sacred. In the Jacobin Club it was his oratorical ability that made him a preëminent figure. Later this ability enabled him to dominate the Convention through many crises. Because he scorned wealth and insisted that a servant of the people must be distinguished for "virtue," he won for himself the epithet "the Incorruptible."

As Danton, Marat, and Robespierre had no seats in the Legislative Assembly, the leadership of the Left within the Assembly fell to an aggressive group of young orators who drew their inspiration from the classical writers of antiquity and from Rousseau. Because its leaders came from the Gironde, this group was soon called the Girondists. The aim of the Girondists was the abolition of the monarchy and the establishment of a republic. Of the science of government they knew little, but they were able to impart their enthusiasm for the republican idea to others. The most notable members of this group were Brissot, a talented journalist; Vergniaud, who was probably the greatest orator the Revolution produced; and Condorcet, one of the last of the philosophes. The leading spirit of the Girondists outside the Legislative Assembly was Madame Roland, the wife of a government official. As a girl she was, in her own words, "transported to delirium" by the reading of ancient history and was "miserable not to have been born a Spartan or a Roman." Later she discovered "the divine Rousseau," whom she called "the friend of humanity, its benefactor and mine," and whose writings excited in her a desire for an ideal republic. For royalty she conceived such a dislike that "it seemed to her the height of absurdity." Moreover, she nursed a violent hatred for Marie Antoinette and had set her heart on the downfall of the queen. Such was the inspirer and adviser of the Girondists. In the words of Aulard: "Mme. Roland was for the Girondists a religion which united them. . . . They loved one another through her."[1] The Girondists

[1] Aulard, *French Revolution*, transl. by Miall, vol. 3 (1910), p. 38.

met in her apartment to discuss their plans and methods of procedure and it was she who drew up many of their manifestoes, documents, and papers.

With the Girondists taking the initiative, the Legislative Assembly passed a measure on October 30, 1791, which decreed that the count of Provence, the eldest of the brothers of Louis XVI, should forfeit his rights to the throne if he did not return to France within two months. On November 9 the Assembly ordered the émigrés to return before January 1, 1792, or incur the penalty of death and the confiscation of their property. Twenty days later the non-juring priests were attacked. They were called upon to take the civic oath or to forfeit their pensions and also be regarded as rebels. When the decrees were sent to the king, he accepted the one against his brother but vetoed the other two as contrary to the Declaration of Rights and the constitution. This further increased his unpopularity in Paris and started a new crisis. Both the Girondists and the Jacobins eagerly seized the opportunity to demand that Louis be dethroned. Then came the war which was to hasten the overthrow of the monarchy.

FOREIGN WAR AND THE END OF THE MONARCHY

Ever since the Declaration of Pillnitz, France had gradually been drifting toward war with Austria. Francis II, the new emperor who had ascended the imperial throne after the death of Leopold on March 1, 1792, was more inclined toward war than his father had been. In addition to his concern over the safety of Marie Antoinette and Louis XVI, Francis had several grievances against France. First, the Austrian government demanded that the pope be indemnified for the loss of the territory of Avignon which the National Assembly had annexed in September, 1791, with the consent of the inhabitants but without the permission of the Roman pontiff. Secondly, the imperial government sought compensation from France for those German nobles who had lost their feudal rights in Alsace by the decrees of August 4, 1789. In the main, however, the question of war or peace was decided by the French. Not only did they have a great grievance against the emperor because he refused to disperse the émigrés who had collected armed forces in the German Empire near the borders of France, but beyond this the parties in the Assembly eagerly desired war as a means of achieving their respective aims.

The members of the Right (also called Feuillants from their connection with the Feuillant Club) favored it because they hoped it would give the king an opportunity to regain his lost authority; the members of the Left wanted it because they regarded it as the best means of overthrowing the monarchy and establishing a republic. Only Robespierre and a group of his followers were opposed to it, because they feared that a successful war would strengthen the authority of the king.

On April 20, 1792, Louis, accompanied by his ministers, appeared before the Assembly for the purpose of formally proposing war. The vote in favor of it was almost unanimous, only seven deputies voting against it. Thus began a war which with short intervals of peace was to last more than twenty years. In an attempt to separate the interests of Austria from those of Prussia, war had been declared against Francis II as "king of Hungary and Bohemia," not as emperor. But before long Frederick William II, regarding the declaration of war as directed also against him, decided to join Francis II. From the very outset the French army, which was poorly equipped, poorly drilled, and without able leaders, met with a series of reverses. Had the Austrians and Prussians been ready to make the most of the unpreparedness of France, they might have taken Paris within a short time. The rulers of both states, however, were occupied with the affairs which were soon to lead to the Second and Third Partitions of Poland. Moreover, they did not see the need for haste, being certain that France was steadily growing weaker. Meanwhile in Paris the news of the military reverses and the discovery that the country had been unprepared for war excited a widespread anger which vented itself in attacks on the king. When Louis dismissed his Girondist ministry and chose one that was more conservative, a mob went to the Assembly on June 20, the anniversary of the Tennis Court Oath, with a petition demanding that the monarch recall the dismissed ministers. Afterwards the mob forced its way into the Tuileries and for hours crowded around the king, threatening and insulting him. The monarchy survived that day, but its fate was soon to be sealed by the so-called Brunswick Manifesto.

On June 27 the duke of Brunswick, commander of the joint military forces of Austria and Prussia, issued under his name a proclamation which was, it appears, largely the work of the émigrés. It stated in part: "Convinced that the sound part of the

French nation abhors the excesses of a faction which dominates it, and that the greatest number of the inhabitants look forward with impatience to the moment of relief to declare themselves against the odious enterprises of their oppressors, His Majesty the Emperor and His Majesty the King of Prussia, call upon them and invite them to return without delay to the ways of reason, justice, order and peace." [1] Moreover, it threatened with summary punishment all who should try to resist the advance of the allied army, and declared that Paris would be totally destroyed if "the Tuileries be entered by force or attacked, if the least violence or outrage be offered to their Majesties, the king, queen and royal family." If the authors of the proclamation sought to terrify the people of Paris into submission, they failed to achieve their purpose, for the proclamation had the contrary effect; it only served to arouse a more determined opposition. To many the proclamation was a proof of their suspicions that the king was in treasonable correspondence with the enemy. Though Louis disavowed all connection with the manifesto, he was unable to save his throne. In many quarters the demand was now voiced for the dethronement of the king. "So long as we do not demand the dethronement of Louis XVI," said a speaker before the Jacobin Club, "we do nothing for liberty."

During the days after the publication of the Brunswick Manifesto Jacobin leaders, particularly Danton and Desmoulins, applied themselves diligently to the task of organizing a popular uprising for the purpose of overthrowing the monarchy. The result was the insurrection of August 10, 1792. This time the mob was not composed solely of Parisians. The municipality of Marseilles had sent a band of 500 men who marched into Paris singing the verses of the new song, known as the *Marseillaise*, which was to become the battle hymn of the French republic. About eight o'clock on the morning of August 10 the insurrectionists advanced against the Tuileries shouting, "Down with M. Veto!" Though the Tuileries were guarded by 950 Swiss and about 4000 National Guards, the latter could not be trusted. Hence the royal family sought refuge in the hall of the Legislative Assembly. After the National Guards had either joined the mob or dispersed, a lively battle was waged between the insurrectionists and the Swiss Guards for about forty-five minutes. Then Louis, wishing to avoid

[1] Full text of the manifesto in Anderson, *op. cit.*, pp. 118–122.

further bloodshed, ordered the Guards to cease firing and to withdraw. The order was promptly obeyed. But as the Swiss retreated
through the Tuileries garden one column was attacked and cut
down almost to a man. The rest reached the hall of the Assembly,
though several were later butchered on their way to prison. Not
satisfied with this carnage, the insurgents rushed through the
palace, smashing the furniture and mirrors—everything, in fact,
that reminded them of royalty. Meanwhile the Legislative Assembly, fearful of the mob, hastily suspended the king from his
functions and sent him with Marie Antoinette and the dauphin as
prisoners to the ancient tower of the Temple. It was also decided
that a National Convention be summoned to meet without delay
for the purpose of drawing up a new constitution. Thus ended the
monarchy of the Bourbons.

The period from August 10 to the meeting of the National Convention late in September was full of excitement. Having suspended the king, the Legislative Assembly appointed a provisional
government. Danton was the first minister chosen. Officially minister of justice, he practically became the executive itself. His aim
was to save the Revolution, which seemed in danger. The peasants in the Vendée district had risen against the government and
the enemy was steadily advancing toward Paris. On September 2 a
messenger brought the news to Paris that the allies had laid siege
to Verdun and that the fortress could hold out no longer than two
days. Frantically the Paris Commune and the provisional government worked to gather recruits. Volunteers ready to leave for the
front were troubled, however, by rumors that the non-juring
priests and the aristocrats who filled the prisons of Paris to capacity
had made plans to break out with the aid of help from the outside
and to massacre the families of the Patriots. As the court set up to
try the suspects worked too slowly, the people decided to settle
matters by themselves, and resolutions were passed by various
sections of the Commune that all priests and suspicious persons
who were then in prison be put to death. The result was the so-
called September Massacres, which started on September 2 and
continued until September 7. The actual slaughter was carried
out by a small group. It began on the afternoon of the same day
when a wagon which was taking a number of priests to one of the
prisons was stopped and the priests were murdered. At the prison
of the Abbaye a group of self-appointed judges organized a court

with Maillard, who had led the march to Versailles, as chief judge. One after the other the prisoners were tried before this court and if acquitted were released but if found guilty were executed on the spot. During the succeeding days similar courts were set up at the other prisons of Paris. "The murderers became so intoxicated with slaughter that common-law and political prisoners, women and children, were slain indiscriminately. . . . There are different estimates of the numbers of the slain, varying from eleven hundred to fourteen hundred."[1] As the reports of the massacres spread all over Europe, they did much to discredit the French Revolution.

[1] A. Mathiez, *The French Revolution*, transl. by C. H. Phillips (1928), p. 181.

CHAPTER TWENTY-FIVE

The First French Republic

THE ESTABLISHMENT OF THE REPUBLIC

THE National Convention met on September 20, 1792, an auspicious time for its opening, for that same day the advance of the allied army was checked by the French artillery at Valmy. The engagement was indecisive, but it convinced the duke of Brunswick that his demoralized army was not strong enough to penetrate to Paris, and he withdrew from French territory. This retreat left the Convention free to devote itself to other matters. As a body it was not without experience, for most of its members had sat either in the National Assembly or in the Legislative Assembly. The Right was formed by the Girondists; the Center (called the Plain or the Marsh) was again without a definite policy; while the Left (called the Mountain and its members Montagnards because this group occupied the highest seats in the amphitheater) was dominated by the Jacobins. All the leading Jacobins had seats, including Danton, Marat, Robespierre, Saint-Just, and Camille Desmoulins. As in the Legislative Assembly, the members of the Convention had no common aim. Aggressive minorities were again to write the history of France. On one question, however, the members were agreed. At the end of the first regular session on September 21 they abolished royalty in France. This was done without much enthusiasm and without mention of a republic. Not until the next day, and then only indirectly, was

France declared a republic in the statement that "all public documents shall henceforth bear the date of the first year of the French Republic." In the words of M. Aulard: "It seems that the French Republic was introduced furtively into history, as if the Convention were saying to the nation, 'There is no other course possible.'"

The monarchy having been abolished, there remained the problem of the fate of Louis XVI or, as he was now called, Louis Capet. All parties in the Convention were agreed that the king could not be set free, but there unanimity stopped. Whereas the Girondists wished to hold him a prisoner until the end of the war and then banish him from France, the Jacobins were resolved on his death. They were convinced, as Saint-Just remarked, that it was a crime in itself to be a king. Furthermore, they believed the republic to be in danger so long as the king was alive. The discovery of a secret compartment in the Tuileries containing letters and documents which proved that the king was hostile to the Revolution and had been guilty of treasonable relations with the émigrés silenced all objections to his trial, which began on December 11 before the Convention. Louis answered all the questions put to him, but in an effort to save his life made the mistake of denying every article of the indictment, even those which had been proved. When the question "Is Louis guilty?" was finally put to the members of the Convention on January 14, 1793, they cast an almost unanimous affirmative. Even yet, the Girondists hoped to save the king from the guillotine. But after many hours of debate and disorder, he was condemned to death by a small majority.

While the opponents of the death penalty tried to postpone the execution, the Jacobins demanded that the sentence be carried out immediately, Marat declaring emphatically that "the Republic is only a house of cards until the head of the tyrant falls under the axe of the law." In the end the Jacobins prevailed. On January 20 the execution was set for the following day, and next morning Louis was driven to the Plâce de la Révolution. On the scaffold he tried to address the people, but the roll of drums drowned his voice. The executioners quickly pushed him under the guillotine and in a moment his head dropped into the basket, with a great shout of "Vive la Nation!" from the assembled crowds. In the face of death Louis evinced a courage which he had failed to show in the ordinary affairs of life.

The execution of Louis had a striking effect upon the attitude of most European countries toward France. In England the news excited such indignation that the French minister was summarily expelled and Pitt hastened preparations for war. There were also other reasons which reconciled Pitt, who previously had desired peace, to the prospect of hostilities. One was the proclamation of December 15, 1792, by which the Convention declared that the French armies would establish the sovereignty of the people in every country they occupied, thereby throwing down the gauntlet to all monarchical governments of Europe. Other causes of friction were the opening of the Scheldt by the French and the acceptance of the doctrine of natural boundaries (Rhine, Atlantic, Pyrenees, Mediterranean, and Alps) by the Convention, involving the annexation of both Holland and Belgium. Rather than permit the French to seize these territories Pitt was ready to face anything. After the report of the execution of Louis reached England the people in the streets began to shout "War with France!" But it was the Convention which declared war against England (February 1, 1793), expecting the English people to rise up and overthrow the monarchy rather than fight the French. In its enthusiasm for republican ideas, the Convention failed to realize how widespread was the fear of revolutionary doctrines in England. On the same day war was also declared against Holland. Hostilities with other nations followed, so that by the spring of 1793 the coalition against France consisted of Austria, Prussia, Spain, Portugal, and Naples, in addition to England and Holland. Russia did not join because Catharine II was intent on prosecuting her schemes in Poland.

France was threatened not only by foreign enemies but by internal disturbances as well. Within its borders the Catholic peasants in the Vendée were in rebellion. Moreover, there were bread riots in Paris and uprisings elsewhere. The situation called for united action on the part of the Convention. All differences should have been buried for the sake of France. But the members were incapable of this. A struggle for power broke out between the Girondists and the Jacobins, growing more and more bitter as the weeks passed. Its underlying causes are somewhat involved. In the first place, while the Jacobins or Montagnards drew their immediate support from Paris, the Girondists, most of whom came from the provinces, were opposed to what they styled "the dictatorship of Paris." They believed that power should be distributed equally among all the provinces of France and that Paris, being only one of eighty-three provinces, should exercise only one eighty-third of the authority. Moreover, they began to advocate the removal of the Convention to a city where it would be less exposed to the threats of the populace. The Jacobins, in turn, asserted the need of the "moral leadership" of Paris and accused the Girondists of "federalism"—that is, of trying to split France into eighty-three small republics.

But the differences between the Girondists and the Jacobins were more deep-rooted than the mere question of the "dictatorship of Paris." The two groups were also at odds in their social program. Politically all were revolutionists who professed their adherence to the principles of "Liberty, Equality, Fraternity," and almost all had at one time been members of the Jacobin Club. Gradually, however, they had divided into two groups accepting different social aims. The Girondist deputies tended more and more to represent the interests of the upper bourgeoisie, while the Jacobins increasingly became the champions of the working classes. Most of the Girondist leaders had been members of the Legislative Assembly; in other words, they had been able to meet high property qualifications. Hence their natural interests were those of the propertied and commercial classes. They desired a state which would uphold the sanctity of private property and establish commercial and industrial liberty (laissez faire). Since their desires were fulfilled in the republic as it was then organized, they wished the Revolution to stop. Any further revolutionary measures, they believed, would endanger the security of private property and restrict the economic freedom of the individual. In particular they opposed the remedies advocated by the Jacobins, including control of prices, regulation of wages, requisitions on the rich, and economic centralization. The Jacobins, like the Girondists, were also of the middle class. But they had risen to power through the support of the working classes, and therefore sponsored the popular demands, either from sympathy with these demands or from motives of political expediency.

Accusations and counter-accusations were hurled back and forth, becoming constantly more acrimonious until each group regarded the other as guilty of treason. Danton, whose first concern was the fate of France, pleaded with the deputies to forget their quarrels. "Let us beat the enemy," he said, "and dispute afterwards." But the battle between the factions continued. The Jacobins had the advantage of being able to organize and act, while the Girondists did little more than orate and threaten. Finally, the Commune of Paris intervened. On May 31, 1793, a large body of National Guards and armed ruffians surrounded the Tuileries, where the Convention now held its sessions, and demanded that the leading Girondists be expelled. Under such pressure the Convention gave way, suspending twenty-two of the Girondist leaders on June 2. This left the Jacobin leaders predominant.

The first move of the Jacobins was an attempt to conciliate public opinion in the departments by drawing up a constitution. The draft was completed in a few days and on June 24 accepted by the Convention. More than any other constitution of the revolutionary period, it embodied the theory of direct popular control of the government. There were to be no property qualifications either for voters or for candidates. Every male citizen who had reached twenty-one was given the right to vote in the election of deputies for the single assembly in which the sole power of making laws was vested. The executive power was to be entrusted to a committee of twenty-four selected by the Assembly from a list drawn up by electors chosen by the voters. After the constitution had been approved by the Convention, it was submitted to the primary assemblies throughout the country for ratification. Its acceptance was announced on August 10, but no attempt was made to put it into effect.

The government inaugurated earlier by the Convention remained in force. At its head stood an executive committee or Committee of Public Safety, the creation of which had been largely the work of Danton, though he did not long remain a member. This committee, first chosen in April, 1793, was composed of nine members—later of twelve. From September, 1793, to July, 1794, it wielded an authority that was almost dictatorial, and the Convention, in which the chief authority in the state was nominally vested, was little more than its tool. It disposed of all matters, domestic and foreign. It appointed and dismissed ministers, administered the finances, organized the armies, selected the generals, planned the military operations, and sought to sustain law and order within France. It also appointed representatives called "deputies on mission" to supervise the conduct of military operations and conduct negotiations with foreign powers. Its members were elected by the Convention for a month, but could be, and were, reëlected again and again. Two of its most conspicuous members were Robespierre and Saint-Just. Subordinate to the Committee of Public Safety were the Committee of General Security, which had been organized for the purpose of exercising a general police control over France, and the Revolutionary Tribunal, an extraordinary court instituted to try those who were guilty of counter-revolutionary activities. From the sentence of this court there was no appeal.

THE POLICY OF TERROR

The situation confronting the Committee of Public Safety after the fall of the Girondists became desperate. A number of the Girondists who had been expelled from the Convention managed to escape to the provinces, where they preached rebellion. Bordeaux, Marseilles, and Lyons, three of the four largest provincial cities of France, were soon controlled by the rebels. In the Vendée the insurgents were proving a match for the government troops, and the Austrians and Prussians had again invaded France in a second attempt to reach Paris. In the capital and other towns food was scarce and the financial crisis acute. To save both the republic and the Revolution, the Jacobin leaders, supported by the Paris Commune, decided on a policy of terror. Robespierre wrote in his notebook: "What we need is a single will." The means adopted to achieve this "single will" was a series of decrees for the arrest of all those suspected of conspiring or wishing to conspire against the republic. The most important of these was the Law of Suspects, which the Convention passed on September 17, 1793, and which ordered the arrest of all who showed themselves in favor of the monarchy or who had "not constantly manifested their attachment to the Revolution." It was so vague that it left room for abuses of every sort. Furthermore, the Revolutionary Tribunal, the great instrument of the Terror, was reorganized to try cases with greater speed. Thus was inaugurated the Terror, which was to claim the lives of thousands of insurgents of every rank.

Month by month the prisons grew more crowded. So many suspects were arrested that it became necessary to use as prisons such buildings as monasteries, convents, churches, warehouses, town halls, and private dwellings. The total number of persons arrested from the spring of 1793 to August, 1794, is estimated at half a million. The number executed was not as large as many writers of the past have stated. In most courts the imposition of the death penalty was the exception rather than the rule, such other penalties as fines, deportation, imprisonment, the pillory, and the galleys being imposed whenever possible. On the average only three to four per cent of those arrested suffered the death penalty. Nevertheless, the number was considerable. In Paris it became the custom to send batches of condemned prisoners to the guillotine each week. Though small at first, the number of victims which the tumbrils carted to the Plâce de la Révolution grew larger as the weeks passed. It is estimated that 2639 persons were guillotined in Paris alone during the Terror. From Paris the deputies on mission carried the Terror to the departments. They were responsible for the most barbarous practices. To clear the congested prisons at Nantes, boats loaded with prisoners were sunk in the Loire on three or four occasions. Suspects were also shot in batches, and their bodies thrown into the Loire. A recent study sets the total number of persons executed in all France during the Terror at 16,594.[1] To this number must be added those who died from disease and undernourishment in insanitary and congested prisons; also those who were executed without trial, particularly in the Vendée. Thus it is probable that between thirty-five and forty thousand persons lost their lives.

Among those who appeared before the Revolutionary Tribunal was Charlotte Corday, a young woman of twenty-four who, on July 13, 1793, had stabbed Marat to death. Having been told by the Girondists that Marat was an enemy of freedom and the cause of many of the woes of France, she resolved to kill him. She gained entrance to his residence on the pretext that she had important news which must be conveyed to him in person. As Marat, who was in his bath seeking relief from his skin disease, started to write down the "information," she plunged into his heart a large kitchen knife she had bought for two francs. At her trial Charlotte Corday offered no defense, going to her death

[1] D. Greer, *The Incidence of the Terror* (1935), p. 25 sq. As the author points out, the Terror was much less sanguinary than a number of other repressions in history, including the Sepoy Mutiny in India and the Red Terror in Russia.

cheerfully under the delusion that she had saved France. The
following October Marie Antoinette, now called "the Widow
Capet," was brought to trial for treason. Though she was clearly
guilty of treason, certain leaders of the Paris Commune made the
unfounded additional charges that she had corrupted the morals
of her son. After an unnecessarily extended trial, she went to the
scaffold with a courage that partly redeemed her former conduct.
A week after her death twenty-one of the Girondist leaders who
had been expelled from the Convention were carted to the guillotine, and a short time later Madame Roland went the same road.
Others executed were Madame du Barry, the last favorite of
Louis XV; Bailly, former mayor of Paris and president of the
National Assembly; and the duke of Orléans (Philippe Égalité),
a prince of the royal house who had voted for the death of
Louis XVI.

In Paris the Terror put an end to riots and established an
outward obedience to the Republic. It must not be supposed,
however, that a gloom hung over the city during this time. Men
and women were careful not to express unorthodox political
opinions lest some informer denounce them, but otherwise life
went on as before. Only a minority of the people were interested
in politics. For the majority the primary consideration was the
problem of obtaining the necessaries of existence and a little
amusement. During the Terror life in Paris was, if anything, more
gay than usual. All the theaters were open, and both they and
the cafés were crowded to capacity. Even in the jails life was
not so somber as might be expected. Many of the prisoners of
both sexes were permitted to associate freely with each other, and
those who had money could purchase good food and wine. There
were parties, dances, and amusements of various kinds. Though
prisoners were forbidden to communicate with relatives and
friends outside, there were means of circumventing even this
restriction. Yet when all allowances are made, conditions in the
old prisons with their small dark cells and lack of sanitation were
often appalling. There was little gaiety and liveliness of heart in the
Conciergerie, which housed the prisoners soon to appear before
the Revolutionary Tribunal and those who had been condemned
to death.[1]

---

[1] The condemned were usually sent to the guillotine within twenty-four hours
after the sentence had been pronounced.

During this period there was a tendency both in the Convention and without to discard everything that smacked of royalty or "superstition." Instead of knee breeches, which were regarded as a symbol of aristocracy, men wore trousers—hence the expression *sans culottes* or "without short breeches," which became the slogan of the more radical revolutionists. Among the women it became the fashion to imitate the dress of ancient Greece and Rome. Stiffened skirts and narrow bodices gave way to loose robes, and high-heeled shoes to sandals; the hair was permitted to flow loosely upon the shoulders. Men also exchanged their given names for names taken from the classics. "Monsieur" and "Madame" as well as the titles of nobility were abolished, "Citizen" and "Citizeness" becoming the proper mode of address. The effort to eradicate every reference to royalty is seen in the revolutionary playing cards, on which Liberties, Equalities, and Fraternities were substituted for Kings, Queens, and Jacks. A more important change was the abolition by the Convention of the Gregorian calendar, with its saints' days and religious festivals.

The new revolutionary calendar designated September 22, 1792, as the first day of the Year One, although it was not put in force until November 28, 1793. It divided the year into twelve equal months of thirty days, the names of the new months being taken from the characteristics of the seasons.[1] Each month was divided into three decades or periods of ten days, with every tenth day a day of rest. The five or six days necessary to complete the year at the end of twelve months were called Sans-Culottides and were set aside as national holidays. The new calendar, however, was never popular with the masses of the French people. There were a number of reasons for this. First, many were offended by the complete absence of any trace of religion in it, and particularly because it abolished Sunday. Secondly, the new order gave the people only three holidays each month instead of four. Thirdly, the new calendar caused much inconvenience because it necessitated dating events twice—once to comply with the

---

[1] The names of the autumn months were Vendémiaire (vintage month), Brumaire (fog month), and Frimaire (frost month); of the winter months, Nivôse (snow month), Pluviôse (rain month), and Ventôse (wind month); of the spring months, Germinal (sprouting month), Floréal (flower month), and Prairial (meadow month); of the summer months, Messidor (harvest month), Thermidor (heat month), and Fructidor (fruit month).

law, and again to make times intelligible to the outside world. Officially, this calendar was used to the entire exclusion of the old calendar until 1801, and was not finally abandoned until January 1, 1806.

In the same spirit a movement was launched to dechristianize France. On November 10, 1793, a number of deputies wearing red liberty caps marched to the cathedral of Notre Dame to consecrate it to the worship of reason and to enthrone an actress as the goddess of reason. A short time later the Commune closed all the churches of Paris, an example which was followed in other parts of France. It is estimated that within twenty days no fewer than 2436 French churches were closed or converted into temples of reason. But neither the Convention as a whole nor the people of France approved such a radical change. Later Robespierre, to whom as a follower of Rousseau the worship of reason was abhorrent because it bred atheism, and the Committee of Public Safety replaced the worship of reason with the worship of the Supreme Being, a vague deism hardly less revolutionary than the former.

Attempts were also made by the government to relieve the financial situation and the acute distress of the poor. Despite the fact that there was a good harvest in 1793, bread was dear because of the depreciation of the assignats. In some localities it was eight sous a pound, whereas the average wage of a workingman in France was twenty sous a day. In general, the prices had risen as the assignats declined, and by August, 1793, they had fallen to twenty-two per cent of their face value. The government tried to stop the depreciation by issuing a decree which threatened with harsh penalties, and later with death, those who differentiated between coin and assignats in a business transaction or who refused to accept payment in assignats. For a time the emergency measures were effective and the circulating value of the assignats rose to forty-eight per cent of their face value in December, 1793. To curb the rise in prices the government, in the preceding May, had passed the Law of the Maximum which decreed that each commune should fix a maximum price for grain and flour. When difficulties arose because the price varied in the different communes a decree of September made the "maximum" uniform for the whole republic. Next the principle of the maximum was extended to all necessaries, including meat, vegetables, sugar, cloth, leather, wood, and fuel. But as the government had no means of controlling commerce the decrees failed to achieve the desired results. Many farmers and dealers refused to sell their goods at the legal prices, even though the government tried to intimidate them by summoning a few before the Revolutionary Tribunal. Finally in December, 1794, the Law of the Maximum was repealed. Other decrees of the Convention abolished all feudal rights without compensation (July, 1793) and put up for sale the lands of the émigrés which the Legislative Assembly had confiscated. For the most part these lands were sold in plots of two or three acres and peasants were permitted to pay for them in small annual instalments.

Meanwhile the tide of the war had turned in favor of the French. Through the energetic efforts of the Committee of Public Safety—and particularly those of Lazare Carnot—the ill-disciplined and ill-equipped French troops had been transformed into efficient armies. On becoming a member of the Committee in August, 1793, Carnot was given almost complete authority over the army and at once began the task of reorganizing the military forces of France, a task which he carried out so successfully that he was given the title "Organizer of Victory." The Convention lent him its support by ordering the *levée en masse* (August 23, 1793), which called on every man, woman, and child of France to assist against the enemy. All unmarried men from eighteen to twenty-five were summoned for duty at the front, and the rest of the nation was to aid in transport, garrison, munitions, and hospital work. The levée en masse furnished Carnot with a plentiful supply of recruits which were then carefully drilled and thoroughly disciplined under his supervision. He also put at the head of the armies such commanders as Hoche, Pichegru, and Jourdan, who not only restored discipline but also adopted new strategy and new tactics. The result of these changes was that the year 1793 ended with a series of victories. The enemy was driven back near the borders of France; Toulon, which had rebelled against the republican government, was retaken; and the insurrection in the Vendée was suppressed. In the spring of 1794 the French armies took the offensive and invaded neighboring countries, carrying with them the principles of the Revolution and introducing social and legal changes which were for the most part to remain permanent.

So long as France and the republic were in danger there was some excuse for the policy of terror, but this was changed by the victories of 1793 and 1794. With the enemy expelled from France and the French armies overrunning the Netherlands, the claim that the Terror was a political necessity became ridiculous. Consequently a strong reaction began to set in against it. Among those who favored a more moderate policy were Danton and Camille Desmoulins. The former, sickened by the bloodshed, was moved to exclaim: "I shall break that damned guillotine before long or I shall fall under it." He probably expected to break it, but he fell under it instead. Robespierre, who no longer had any use for Danton or his party, was determined to annihilate both, a task which was facilitated by the fact that other members of the Committee of Public Safety hated Danton because he had attacked their policy. It is reported that at his last meeting with Robespierre, Danton pleaded: "Let us forget our private resentments and think only of the country, its needs and its dangers." But Robespierre was cold to the suggestion. A few days later Danton stood before the Revolutionary Tribunal. He defended himself with such eloquence that he was not permitted to finish his speech. On April 4, 1794, he and fifteen others, including Desmoulins, were condemned to death; and the next afternoon the prisoners were carried to the scaffold in three tumbrils. Only once did Danton falter, and that was when he bade his wife farewell. But he immediately checked himself with "No weakness, Danton." After witnessing the execution of his friends, Danton was guillotined. His last words, addressed to the executioner, were: "Show my head to the people; it is worth it." Thus died the once dreaded Titan of the Jacobins.

Robespierre was now the most conspicuous figure in France. Yet his power was by no means so absolute as it has often been depicted. He was the spokesman of the Committee of Public Safety both in the Convention and in the Jacobin Club, but the policy of the Committee was a joint policy, even though individual phases of it, such as the worship of the Supreme Being, may have been suggested by him. In other words, he was the interpreter and defender rather than the dictator of the policy of the Committee of Public Safety. Robespierre, however, had a burning desire to establish an ideal republic in which he would play the leading rôle. It was this ambition that proved his undoing. Danton showed himself an able prophet when he said on the way to the guillotine: "Robespierre will follow me." Less than four months later the prophecy was fulfilled. The immediate cause of Robespierre's downfall was the Law of 22 Prairial (June 10, 1794) which he had drafted with his own hand. The law divided the Revolutionary Tribunal into four parts so that it could act more quickly against the "enemies of the people"; permitted the use of any kind of testimony, whether material, moral, verbal, or written against a suspect; and denied the accused the right of counsel. But the clause which doomed Robespierre was the one which gave the Committee of Public Safety the right to send any member of the Convention before the Revolutionary Tribunal. Although the Convention voted the decree, it revolted the next day and struck out the clause affecting the members of the Convention. Nevertheless, the members opposed to Robespierre no longer felt safe. From that time on they combined against him. When Robespierre appeared before the Convention on July 26 (8 Thermidor) to demand a final purification, he was accused of trying to establish a dictatorship. "What paralyses the republic," said one of the deputies, "is the man who has just spoken." Robespierre, realizing that he had lost his majority support in the Convention, mumbled to himself, "I am a lost man." He tried to rally the Parisian populace to his support, but even that effort failed. When a detachment of troops sent by the Convention to arrest him forced its way into the room in which he was deliberating with his colleagues, it found him with his jaw shattered by a pistol shot. While some believe that the wound was self-inflicted in an attempt at suicide, others hold that he was shot by a gendarme. In his maimed condition Robespierre was taken to the Conciergerie and guillotined, on July 28 (10 Thermidor), together with twenty-one of his followers.

THE THERMIDOREAN REACTION

The men who brought about the overthrow of Robespierre did not purpose to discard the policy of terror. They were intent primarily on saving their own heads by cutting off that of Robespierre. But they dared not continue the Terror because the tide of public opinion was running in favor of moderation. The change which followed is summed up in the term "Thermidorean Reaction." The Law of 22 Prairial was repealed, many thousands of imprisoned suspects were set free, and the Paris Commune was automatically dissolved when the administration of the city was put into the hands of executive committees appointed by the Convention. Trials and condemnations still continued for some months, but the number of those executed was comparatively small. Before the end of 1794 even the Law of Suspects was repealed. In the government the Convention regained the dominant power from the Committee of Public Safety, which was then remodeled. To prevent any one faction from dominating the Committee, it was decreed that one-fourth of its members should be renewed every month and that at least one month must pass before a former member was eligible for reëlection. The Revolutionary Tribunal, which was to be dissolved entirely in 1795, was reorganized to provide a legal defense for the accused.

A widespread reaction against Jacobin ideals set in, and the bourgeoisie resumed control both within the Convention and outside. Everywhere the Jacobins became objects of suspicion. In Paris groups of young men (Muscadins) armed with clubs went about attacking Jacobins, and in the provinces a veritable "White Terror" was inaugurated against them by organized groups. The Jacobin Club of Paris was first ordered by the Convention to expel all the friends of Robespierre and to sever all connections with the provincial clubs; then, on November 12, 1794, it was closed. All the leading Jacobins who had played a part in establishing the Terror were punished. Carrier, who was responsible for the mass executions at Nantes during the Terror, and Fouquier-Tinville, the public prosecutor, were sent to the guillotine. Marat's remains were removed from the Panthéon and buried in an obscure grave. In December the seventy-three Girondist deputies who had been imprisoned for protesting the expulsion of their leaders were not only freed but also reinstated in their seats in the Convention. The reaction is seen also in the realm of religion. When the Convention early in 1795 permitted freedom of worship, many Catholic churches were reopened and large numbers of non-juring priests returned to France. Finally, in June, even the official use of the word *revolutionary* was discontinued. In short, conservatism became the order of the day.

The reaction against the Jacobin ideals was, in fact, so great that many Frenchmen favored a restoration of the Bourbon monarchy. To forestall such a restoration and to insure the continuance of middle-class rule the Convention drew up a new constitution, known as the Constitution of the Year III. Although it theoretically recognized suffrage as the right of every citizen, only those who paid direct taxes or had served their country at the front were permitted to vote or hold office. There were to be two legislative councils: the Council of Elders (Anciens), composed of two hundred fifty men who were at least forty and either married or widowers; and the Council of Five Hundred, composed of five hundred men who were at least thirty. The former body was to propose laws, while the latter was to revise the bills and vote on their acceptance. The executive power was vested in a Directory of five members who were at least forty years of age. They were to be chosen for a term of five years by the Elders from a list drawn up by the Five Hundred, with one Director retiring each year. When the constitution was submitted to the voters, it was accepted by a large majority, but the Convention did not stop there. Mindful of how the work of the National Assembly had been undone by its successor and fearful that a return of royalism might result in their being tried as regicides, the members passed two decrees which required the electors to choose two-thirds of the new legislators from the membership of the Convention. Although the decrees were accepted by the voters, the opposition was more pronounced. Paris was overwhelmingly against them.

The Parisians did not let matters rest with a hostile vote. So intense was their opposition that the royalists were able to organize an insurrection which aimed to force the Convention to repeal the decrees. Of the forty-eight sections of Paris, forty-four supported the revolt and by 12 Vendémiaire (October 4, 1795) some thirty thousand Parisians were ready for the attack on the Convention scheduled for the next day. Had the insurrectionists marched against the Convention immediately, they might have been successful. Instead they spent the night from the 12th to the 13th in shouting and torchlight processions. Meanwhile desperate measures were being taken for the defense of the Convention. Barras, to whom the task had been entrusted, called to his assistance Napoleon Bonaparte, a young lieutenant of artillery who had distinguished himself at the siege of Toulon and was now in Paris waiting for something to turn up. During the night Napoleon had some artillery brought from a military camp near Paris, set it up around the Tuileries, and posted between five and six thousand men in readiness for the attack. On the afternoon of 13 Vendémiaire, when the insurrectionists marched on the Tuileries, Napoleon was ready. As they advanced he greeted them with a charge of grapeshot which tore great gaps in their ranks. After a vain attempt to reorganize, the attackers broke ranks and fled, leaving the streets covered with dead and wounded. The Convention was saved. It was not the Convention, however, but the army, that had triumphed.

Three weeks later, on 4 Brumaire (October 26, 1795), the president of the Convention announced: "The National Convention declares that its mission is fulfilled, and its session terminated." Thus the National Convention was dissolved after having been in session since September, 1792. Though it left reminiscences of bloodshed and terror, it also left entries on the credit side of the ledger. Not only did it save the country from invasion but it also made France the dominant power of Europe. Moreover, it rendered notable services to the future of France by completing the destruction of the feudal régime, by establishing a uniform system of weights and measures (metric system) which was later adopted by other countries, and by starting the work of preparing a uniform code of law for France—a task which Napoleon was to finish and for which he was to garner the credit. Other creations of the Convention were the National Archives, the Museum of the Louvre, and the National Library. The Convention also devoted some attention to the question of education. It sought to diminish the need for normal schools by opening the École Normale of Paris, and to promote technical instruction by founding the Polytechnic School.[1] On the day before its dissolution it passed a law providing for the opening of one or more schools in each canton, thereby laying the foundation for the public school system which had been outlined earlier by Condorcet. It was left to the Directory, however, to carry out this law.

THE DIRECTORY

The Directory, as the government under the Constitution of the Year III is called, lasted four years, from November, 1795, to November, 1799. It inherited most of the problems which had vexed the National Convention. Because the Directors were unable to solve these problems entirely, they have frequently been characterized as mediocre. The fact is that most of them were men of wide

---

[1] It also founded three schools of medicine in which carefully selected students were given thorough instruction, organized a National Conservatory of Arts and Industries to promote the advancement of industry, and reorganized the Jardin du roi into the Museum of Natural History, voting funds to enable outstanding scientists to conduct researches in its laboratories.

experience and of more than average ability, some possessing special aptitudes for their particular work. With the exception of Barras, who was notoriously corrupt, they were an honest, hard-working group—men who worked zealously and courageously to establish order and quiet in France. In some instances, it is true, their policy lacked wisdom and in others their efforts were fore-doomed to failure, but on the whole they achieved a considerable degree of success. The oft-repeated statement that France was in a state of chaos, both politically and financially, until Napoleon es-tablished some semblance of order is not in accordance with the facts. Many of the reforms that were achieved under the Consulate which succeeded the Directory were possible only because the Directors had done the preliminary work.

One of the great tasks confronting the Directory was that of restoring order in France. Tired of revolutionary agitations and upheavals, the majority of Frenchmen wanted quiet. The peas-ants desired it in order to enjoy the advantages they had gained from the Revolution; the working classes in the cities wanted it in the hope that it would bring them steady employment and relief from the threat of starvation; and the business interests needed it if they were to make the most of the freedom of trade that had been established in France. A particular cause of unrest in the provinces was the armed bands of criminals, unemployed, and malcontents of all kinds which terrorized the countryside and which the Con-vention had failed to suppress. Then the revolt in the Vendée had flared up again. The Directory established tolerable order and obedience, though it probably achieved less in this respect than in others. Some progress was made in suppressing brigandage; and General Hoche, to whom the task was entrusted, succeeded in gaining control of the insurrection in the Vendée. There was also improvement in other respects. "Political morality," writes M. Aulard, "improved under the Directory, especially in the sense that a spirit of obedience to the laws became popularized. If there were *coups d'état* they were not the work of the people in the street, but of the government, or the legislative body, in the form of laws and without bloody encounters."[1]

The greatest threats to the stability of the political settlement came from the royalists and from the radicals. The danger from the former was more critical because they were the more numerous

[1] *Modern France*, ed. by A. Tilley (1922), p. 135.

and they attempted to incite insurrection in various parts of the country. Though some peasants were sympathetic to the royalist cause, most of them were decidedly anti-royalist, for they feared that the return of the monarchy might mean the restoration of feudal dues. The radicals, on the other hand, lacked the necessary leadership for an organized movement, most of the leaders having perished on the scaffold.

One noteworthy conspiracy against the government was that of a group led by François Noël Babeuf, who called himself "Gracchus" Babeuf. The principal source of all the calamities afflicting society, Babeuf said, is private property; hence he aimed at establishing a communistic society in which private property would be unknown. As the first step he demanded that the Constitution of 1793[1] be put in operation. By his preachings in *Le Tribun du peuple*, a journal which he edited, Babeuf attracted a large number of adherents, particularly from among those who had formerly been associated with the Jacobins. Most of Babeuf's followers did not share his radical opinions, but they were at one with him in their opposition to the government. In the spring of 1796 the Babouvists, as the followers of Babeuf are known, plotted an insurrection against the Directory. But before they could be carried out, the plans were betrayed to the Directors, who immediately arrested the leaders of the conspiracy. Babeuf was tried and guillotined, and with his death the movement collapsed. In the nineteenth century, however, Babouvist ideas were to crop up again and again. The historical importance of Babeuf lies in the fact that he preached doctrines in many respects identical with those of the later so-called "Scientific Socialism."

A second task awaiting the Directors was the restoration of the finances. Not only was the treasury empty, but the troops were in need of provisions and clothes. The whole economic system, in fact, was breaking down as a result of the sudden depreciation of the assignats after the repeal of the maximum in December, 1794. By April, 1795, they had dropped to twenty per cent of their face value and by November to one per cent. Nevertheless, the government found it necessary to issue still more, for the income from public revenues covered only a fraction of the government expenses. Finally in February, 1796, by which time the value of the assignats was less than the cost of the printing, the government

[1] See p. 681.

authorized the destruction of the engraved plates and the printing presses used in printing them. But before financial order could be restored it was necessary to retire at least a considerable part of the thirty billion francs in assignats. For this purpose the Directory issued a new paper currency in the form of land notes (*mandats territoriaux*) which, it was hoped, would retain a high value. But they, too, depreciated rapidly and in February, 1797, the government issued a decree which virtually demonetized them. Thereafter France gradually returned to a metallic currency. In 1797 the Directory also made an attempt to balance the budget by reducing expenditures and reorganizing the national debt. Two-thirds of the debt was liquidated with drafts on which the government paid no interest; the rest, known as the "Consolidated Third," was redeemed with bonds bearing interest at five per cent. In effect the transaction was tantamount to a repudiation of two-thirds of the debt, for the drafts soon declined to three per cent of their nominal value and during the Consulate were called in at a price slightly above their market value. Thus the Directory reduced the financial obligations of the state, but in doing so forfeited the support of those who held the drafts.

A third task of the Directory was the conclusion of a general European peace. The prospects for this were not unfavorable. The French armies had gained control of both the Austrian and the Dutch Netherlands. While the former were annexed to France, the latter were transformed into the Batavian Republic, which became a dependency. Furthermore, the coalition against France was dissolving. In February, 1795, the grand duke of Tuscany had revoked his adhesion to it and in the following April the king of Prussia, originally the most ardent advocate of the war against France, deserted it. By the treaty signed at Basel, Prussia gave France a free hand on the left bank of the Rhine in return for a promise that the French would not penetrate into Germany beyond a certain line of demarcation. Several months later peace was also concluded between Spain and France. Thus, when the Directory was inaugurated, only two formidable members remained in the coalition—Austria and England. At the beginning of 1796 plans were made to strike at Vienna from three directions. One army was to approach it through the valley of the Danube, a second through the valley of the Main, and a third by way of Italy. The first two armies were not to fare so well, but the Army of Italy was to win signal triumphs under the command of General Napoleon Bonaparte, who later made himself the supreme master of France.

THE RISE OF NAPOLEON BONAPARTE

Napoleon Bonaparte or Buonaparte (as he spelled it until 1796) was born August 15, 1769,[1] in Ajaccio on the island of Corsica, which had shortly before come under French rule. He was the second son of Carlo Buonaparte, an impecunious lawyer belonging to the lower nobility, and Letizia Ramolino, a woman of great energy and beauty. Both parents were descendants of Italian families. When young Napoleon was nine years old his father obtained for him a scholarship in the military school at Brienne in northeastern France, where the scions of the French nobility were prepared for a military career. In some respects the years he spent there were not happy. His schoolmates taunted him about Corsica, his Italian ancestry, and his poverty. A proud and sensitive young boy, he became so embittered that he withdrew from the society of the others, spending his time in reading and dreaming of the day when he would liberate Corsica from French rule. In the classroom he displayed neither extraordinary gifts nor unusual industry, taking an interest only in mathematics, geography, and history. To quote his own words: "It was the general opinion that I was fit for nothing except geometry." Yet he passed his examinations and was graduated. On the official certificate he received at the time, he is characterized as "inordinately self-centered and ambitious, with aspirations that stop at nothing." Certainly in these respects the boy was the father of the man.

After leaving the school at Brienne, Napoleon spent a year at the Military College in Paris and was then given a commission as second lieutenant of artillery (September 1, 1785). The young officer, for he was only sixteen when he received his commission, found garrison life tedious. To relieve his boredom he resumed his reading, which included Corneille, Racine, Voltaire, Montaigne, Montesquieu, and Raynal; Plutarch, Plato, Livy, and Tacitus in French translations; and also Adam Smith's *Wealth of Nations* and Necker's *Compte rendu*. But his favorite author was Rousseau; and, strange to say, the work of Rousseau that interested him most was

---

[1] This date is the one most generally accepted as authentic. There are some historians, however, who believe that Napoleon was born in 1768. For a discussion of this question see W. M. Sloane's *Life of Napoleon Bonaparte*, vol. 1 (1915), p. 36 sq.

the *Social Contract*. He further read treatises on military affairs and from them garnered the basic ideas of his later military strategy.

After the French Revolution broke out, Napoleon went to Corsica three times to start a revolution against French rule. His final visit in 1793 and his failure to launch a successful movement for independence completely shattered his dream of Corsican freedom. Thereafter he turned his entire attention toward a career in France. His rise was rapid. As a commander of artillery during the siege of Toulon in 1793 he so distinguished himself that he was raised to the rank of brigadier-general of artillery by the Committee of Public Safety. During the months that followed he became attached to the party of Robespierre; and when that party was overthrown on 9 Thermidor, he lost his commission as general and was imprisoned as a suspect. It was only by an avowal of his attachment to the Revolution in a letter to the Convention that he saved himself. The spring of 1795 saw Napoleon in Paris without a command and without money, but with a firm faith in his own destiny. His opportunity came when Barras called on him to assist in the defense of the Convention. It was the turning point in his career. As a reward for his services on 13 Vendémiaire he was made commander-in-chief of the Army of the Interior after Barras resigned that command to become a member of the Directory. Thus Napoleon found himself almost overnight a person of importance. Yet he was not satisfied. Being familiar with the Italian front, he felt that he could best put his ideas of warfare into practice there. Hence he remained in Paris for the purpose of wringing from the Directors the command of the French army in Italy. A plan of campaign against Austria which he drew up convinced the Directors of his fitness for the command and on March 2, 1796, he was appointed commander-in-chief of the Army of Italy by a unanimous vote.

Before Napoleon departed to assume the command of the Army of Italy he was married to Josephine Beauharnais, a young widow who had a son and a daughter, Eugene and Hortense. Born and reared in the French West Indies, Josephine had come to France as a young girl and had married a young noble, Count Alexandre de Beauharnais. But only three days before the fall of Robespierre the Terror claimed Beauharnais, who had previously been a general in the French army, as a victim. The penniless widow was befriended by Barras, and it was probably through the latter that Napoleon met her. Six years older than Napoleon, she was hardly a beauty, but she possessed considerable charm and a certain Creole allurement, despite her bad teeth and lack of education. Before long the young general fell passionately in love with her and fervently proposed marriage. "My sword is at my side," he told her, "and with it I shall go far." Though Josephine did not lose her heart to him, she accepted the proposal because she regarded him as a young man of promise. On March 9, 1796, they were married by a civil ceremony.

After a honeymoon of only two days Napoleon left his bride to assume the command of the Army of Italy. When he arrived at Nice, the headquarters of the army, his youth (for he was not yet twenty-seven), his small stature, and his sickly appearance made an unfavorable impression upon the generals of his staff.[1] A number of them, seasoned veterans who had rendered important services, received him with bad grace, ascribing his appointment to political favoritism. But he quickly gained the respect of his subordinates. His pointed questions regarding the position and spirit of the troops soon demonstrated his knowledge and experience. Masséna, on leaving the first council, was heard to remark to Augereau: "We have found our master." One of Napoleon's aides later wrote: "From the moment when Bonaparte took over the command, his personality imposed itself on all. Though somewhat lacking in dignity, and decidedly awkward in attitude and movements, he had something imperious in his bearing, his glance and his manner of speaking, so that one felt compelled to listen." The new commander-in-chief found his troops both demoralized and lacking proper supplies and equipment. So critical was the lack of supplies that it had been necessary for them to resort to looting in order to escape starvation. With characteristic vigor Napoleon addressed himself to the task of procuring supplies and inspiring his men with a new confidence. During his exile on St. Helena he dictated to a companion the words he supposedly addressed to the soldiers upon his arrival at Nice. They read in part: "Soldiers, you are ill-fed and almost naked; the government owes you much, it can give you nothing. ... I will lead you into the world's most fertile plains. Rich provinces, great towns, will be in your power. There you shall

---

[1] It was his frail, unwarlike appearance that earned for him the title "The Little Corporal," which was to contribute much to his popularity in France.

find honor, glory, and riches." What he dictated was probably a romanticized version of the speech he actually made. This much, however, is true: Napoleon did infuse a new spirit in his troops.

On April 9 the new general launched his offensive against the combined Austrian and Sardinian forces and after a series of battles succeeded in separating them. Leaving a small detachment to watch the Austrians, he next dealt the Sardinian army such a smashing blow that the king of Sardinia sued for an armistice in order to save Turin, his capital. The treaty of peace between Sardinia and France which followed a short time later left Napoleon free to proceed with his principal task, that of driving the Austrians from Italy. On May 10 the French troops in a surprise move appeared at Lodi, where they crossed the river Adda in the face of a murderous fire and drove the Austrians to flight. The immediate result of this victory was the retreat of the Austrians to Mantua, and on May 16 Napoleon triumphantly entered Milan. Soon the dukes of Parma, Modena, and Tuscany submitted to the conqueror, and after he threatened to march on Rome the pope sent an ambassador to conclude an armistice. From these states Napoleon collected large requisitions of money which he remitted to France. In addition, he confiscated some of the finest works of Italian art and sent them to Paris. But great as his success had been, his work was far from finished. There still remained the task of driving the Austrians from Italy. While Napoleon was at Milan the Austrians were reorganizing their forces. Large reinforcements were brought in from Germany, so that in a short time an army of about 70,000 was ready under the command of Marshal Wurmser to oppose Napoleon's 40,000 troops.

Long months of fighting followed before the issue was decided. To complete the conquest of northern Italy it was necessary for Napoleon to take the strongly fortified town of Mantua. After he laid siege to it, the Austrians sent an army across the Alps four times to relieve the beleaguered fortress. Each time he defeated the relieving army. Since his troops were inferior in numbers, Bonaparte had to rely on surprise attacks after forced marches. These daring tactics proved effective against the old methodical type of strategy which the Austrian commanders employed, and finally enabled him to triumph in decisive fashion. In February, 1797, Wurmser was forced to surrender Mantua together with some 20,000 men. Forcing the Austrians steadily back, Napoleon crossed the Alps with his army and advanced to within eighty miles of Vienna before the Austrians opened negotiations for peace. The preliminaries were signed at Leoben in April, and in the following October a definitive treaty was concluded at Campo Formio. It sanctioned the annexation of the Austrian Netherlands (Belgium) to France, recognized the Rhine as the eastern frontier of France, and gave Austria most of the Venetian territories in return for Milan, which was then joined to territory taken from Venice and from the pope to form the Cisalpine Republic. Thus his First Italian Campaign—one of the most startling and successful in military history—eliminated Austria from the First Coalition. Only England and Portugal were left in arms.

After an absence of twenty-one months Napoleon returned to Paris, his star definitely in the ascendant. The victories in Italy and Germany had made him a famous and important figure whose name was on the lips of most Frenchmen. In Paris he was received as a war hero and was cheered by the populace whenever he appeared in public. Even the Directory received him with a certain cordiality. Everything seemed to be working in his favor. Undoubtedly Bonaparte already entertained the idea of seizing power in France. On the way to Paris he had said to Miot de Mélito: "I have tasted supremacy and I can no longer renounce it." But, as he himself observed, the time was not ripe. His popularity was not yet so great that he could rely upon it in a contest with the Directors. He must wait for a more favorable opportunity and meanwhile enhance or, at least, preserve his popularity. At first he accepted the command of an expedition that was being prepared for an invasion of England, but after a tour along the northern coast he reported that such an invasion was impracticable so long as the British retained the mastery of the seas. Instead of a direct attack on England, he proposed "an expedition to the Levant which would menace England's trade with India." The East had long fascinated him. As he had said to Bourienne: "This little Europe has not enough to offer. The Orient is the place to go. All great reputations have been made there." His specific aim was the conquest of Egypt. From Milan he had already written to the Directory: "The time is not distant when we shall perceive that really to destroy England we must seize on Egypt." The Directors, apprehensive of his being a Caesar, decided in favor of the expedition to Egypt.

In May, 1798, the expedition set sail from Toulon. It consisted of thirteen men-of-war, nine frigates, and more than two hundred transports to convey the 28,000 picked troops. In addition there was a staff of savants, experts in archeology, geography, geometry, mechanics, mineralogy, botany, and zoology, who were to study the artistic and literary treasures of Egypt and Mesopotamia. On the way to Egypt the fleet seized the island of Malta and proclaimed it a French possession. Then the expedition headed for Alexandria, which was taken in a few hours with the loss of about fifty men. Proclaiming himself the liberator of the Arabs from the Mamelukes, a military-feudal aristocracy, Napoleon pushed on toward Cairo, the second largest city of Egypt. It was a march that entailed great hardships. The equipment of the French soldiers, their uniforms of thick cloth and their heavy arms, was unsuited to the hot climate. More than this, there was a great scarcity of water, for the villagers along the line of march had either poisoned or polluted the wells before abandoning their homes. According to the report of a clerk of the staff, five or six hundred men perished from thirst during the first week. Nevertheless, Napoleon pressed on. After a number of skirmishes, the French met the Mameluke army within sight of the Pyramids and completely routed it. The moral effect of the victory upon the people of Cairo was so great that the city surrendered without resistance when the French appeared before it. Thus within three weeks Napoleon had made himself master of Egypt.

But on the sea disaster awaited the French. On August 1 Admiral Nelson, who had been sent out by the English, found the French ships anchored in the Bay of Aboukir and immediately started action. The contest began at sunset and continued throughout the night. When the smoke of battle cleared next morning, it was found that of the thirteen French men-of-war nine had been captured by the English and two had been destroyed.

The destruction or capture of the French ships in the Battle of the Nile cut Napoleon and his army off from the rest of the world. Upon hearing the news he is reported to have said: "We must either die or emerge great, like the ancients." For the time being he devoted himself to the task of pacifying Egypt and organizing an independent Egyptian government. Meanwhile the sultan of Turkey, far from reconciled to the loss of one of his provinces, was collecting an army to drive out the French. Determined to meet this army before it reached Egypt, Napoleon at once advanced into Syria. City after city surrendered to him, and he even succeeded in taking Jaffa, though with some difficulty. But when he laid siege to Acre the garrison, assisted by Captain Sidney Smith of the British navy, offered such a gallant defense that after two months he was forced to abandon the siege and retreat to Egypt. Even there the situation was critical. In his absence the Mamelukes had reoccupied Cairo and a Turkish army had been landed at Aboukir by the English fleet. After quickly reëstablishing his power at Cairo, Napoleon mustered every available man for an attack on the Turkish forces. The result was a signal triumph for him. Almost all of the 15,000 Turkish soldiers that had been landed by the English were slain in the battle, which was Napoleon's finale in Egypt. News regarding the political situation in France made him decide to return home immediately thereafter. Leaving his army in Egypt,[1] he embarked 500 of his most trustworthy soldiers in four vessels and secretly set sail for France. Several times the vessels narrowly escaped capture, but finally they reached the bay of Frejus after a voyage of forty-seven days.

While Napoleon was in Egypt, a second coalition of European powers had been formed against the French. Its primary purpose was to curb the aggressive foreign policy of France, which had expressed itself in the establishment of a circle of affiliated republics. Not satisfied with changing Holland into the Batavian Republic, and establishing the Cisalpine Republic in northern Italy and the Ligurian Republic in Genoa, the Directory had turned the Papal States into the Roman Republic, sent an army into Switzerland to set up the Helvetic Republic, and transformed the kingdom of Naples into the Parthenopean Republic. This policy of "republicanization" not only alarmed Austria but also excited the fears of Tsar Paul of Russia, who had succeeded his mother, Catherine II, at her death in 1796. Hence England was able to enlist the aid of both countries in the war against France. Moreover, the sultan of Turkey also made common cause with

---

[1] The army Napoleon left in Egypt was not evacuated until 1801. By that time it was so decimated by disease that it numbered scarcely 6000 men.

the coalition. In the war which began in March, 1799, the French were at first defeated at almost every point. In Germany they were compelled to retreat to the Rhine, and in Italy an Austro-Russian army had not only forced them to abandon Milan, Rome, and Naples but had also put an end to the Italian republics. It was the news of these French reverses which had decided Napoleon to return.

Before Napoleon reached France Masséna had restored the prestige of the French arms by defeating the Austro-Russian army which had crossed the Alps into Switzerland; yet the French people were weary of war. They longed for a general who could terminate the seemingly perpetual conflict by an honorable peace; and Bonaparte, whose military reputation was enhanced by the news of the victory of Aboukir, was regarded by many as that general. Also such other factors as the financial difficulties of the Directory and the desire for a more stable police order in France favored the ambitions of Napoleon, who was now determined to depose the Directory. It is easy, however, to exaggerate the factors in his favor. The success of his plans was not, as is often stated, inevitable. The victory of Masséna had relieved the military situation, and the Directory might well have been able to adjust the other difficulties.

Once back in Paris, Napoleon carefully surveyed the political field and then joined hands with Siéyès, who had recently been made a Director. Together the two men quickly laid a plot for the overthrow of the Directory. It was agreed between them that a stronger executive must be established in the form of a committee of three. This triumvirate was to be composed of Napoleon, Siéyès, and Ducos, who, like Siéyès, was also a Director. The change was to be introduced not by a popular uprising but by a vote of the legislative bodies. In the Council of the Elders a majority was won for the plan, and in the Council of the Five Hundred Lucien Bonaparte, who had been elected president of that body, would, it was expected, command a majority. Nevertheless, the plot almost miscarried.

The date set for the coup d'état was 18 Brumaire (November 9, 1799). On the pretext that a Jacobin plot against the government had been discovered in Paris, the Council of the Elders was to be convoked at an early hour on that day, but those deputies who could not be counted on to coöperate were not to be summoned.

In the meeting the Elders were to vote the transfer of the sessions of both councils to St. Cloud, ostensibly to remove them from the menace of the Jacobin plot but actually to prevent the mobs of Paris from interfering with the execution of the coup d'état. Besides adjourning the sessions to St. Cloud, the Elders were also to invest Napoleon with the command of the troops in Paris. This accomplished, Siéyès, Ducos, and Barras were to resign from the Directory, thus making the establishment of a new executive power necessary. Up to this point the plans were carried out smoothly. The Elders decreed that the Councils were to meet at St. Cloud on the following day, Napoleon was made commander of the Paris troops, the three Directors resigned, and the other two were taken into custody. But on the next day the Council of the Five Hundred almost frustrated the execution of the plot. When the session of the Councils opened at St. Cloud, Napoleon first addressed the Elders, telling them that the country was in danger and requesting permission to refashion the government. By the time he reached the hall in which the Five Hundred were assembled, the latter already had been informed of Napoleon's demands. At his entrance the deputies arose in a burst of indignation with cries of "Down with the tyrant! Down with the dictator! Outlaw him!" Some of the irate deputies even rushed at Napoleon and would have mobbed him if his guards had not stepped in. The excitement was such that Napoleon collapsed in a faint and was carried out by the soldiers.

For the moment all seemed lost. As soon as Bonaparte was revived, he began to harangue the soldiers but failed to evoke any enthusiasm for his cause. Finally his brother Lucien stepped in to save the day. Addressing the troops as the president of the Five Hundred, he accused certain deputies of interfering with the deliberations of the Council for their own private ends and called upon the soldiers to liberate the majority of the Council from their influence. Convinced that the act was entirely legal, one division went to clear the hall. Many of the deputies became terror-stricken at the advance of the grenadiers and fled through the doors and windows; those who remained were expelled from the hall at the point of bayonets. That evening the Elders voted the abolition of the Directory, entrusting the provisional government to Napoleon, Siéyès, and Ducos. Similar action was taken the same night by a remnant of about thirty members of the Five

Hundred. Thus was accomplished the coup d'état which put an end to the First French Republic in everything but name.

LITERATURE AND ART

The Revolution was not a great period in the history of French literature. There was no dearth of literary products, but they were mostly mediocre, for the attention of the better minds was absorbed by political matters. In the theater, plays were presented as usual before packed houses. It has been estimated that during the decade of the Revolution (1789–1799) more than a thousand different plays were produced. Their literary value, however, was not great since they were largely political propaganda in the guise of art, their purpose being to denounce the Old Régime and to indoctrinate the audience with liberal or radical ideas. Perhaps the most representative playwright was Joseph Chénier (1764–1811). A disciple of Voltaire, Chénier used the stage to present his ideas to the public. Thus in his *Charles IX* one may read such lines as these:

> Vain rights of the nobility
> Which in other days force extorted from weakness.

In the same manner he scored privilege, absolute government, and religious fanaticism in his other plays.

Another noteworthy figure of the revolutionary period is André Chénier (1762–1794), poet and brother of the dramatist. An ardent advocate of liberty, Chénier enthusiastically welcomed the Revolution, but his enthusiasm was soon cooled by the excesses of the revolutionary party. While continuing to proclaim his theories of liberty, he did not hesitate to denounce the policies employed by the revolutionaries, particularly the rule of terror. His courage cost him his life. In 1794 he was arrested and after spending some months in prison was condemned to the guillotine on the flimsy charge of being a party to a plot to break prison. With twenty-five others he was executed on the 7 Thermidor, just two days before Robespierre met the same fate and the Terror came to an end. Only thirty-two, André Chénier, like Keats, died just as his poetic gift was ripening. Since he had published hardly anything, his poems were known only to an intimate circle of friends. It was not until 1819 that the first complete edition of them appeared. His poetry was essentially classical,

though critics have discovered romantic elements in it. Among his
most celebrated poems is the ode *Le Jeu de Paume* (The Tennis
Court), which he wrote during the early part of the Revolution.
While he was in prison he produced the *Iambes*, a series of political
satires which rank among the best of all time. During the same
months he also composed one of the most beautiful and most
touching of his poems, *Le Jeune Captive* (The Young Captive)
which was probably inspired by the imprisonment of the beautiful young duchess of Fleury. One stanza in particular he might
have written for himself:

> O Death, canst thou not wait? Depart from me, and go
> To comfort those sad hearts whom pale despair, and woe,
> And shame, perchance have wrung.
> For me the woods still offer verdant ways,
> The Loves their kisses, and the Muses praise:
> I would not die so young!

If literature did not flourish during the revolutionary period,
journalism did. In fact, the power of political journalism in
France may be dated from the Revolution. Previously the
periodicals had discussed literature, science, and social affairs,
but political affairs had occupied only a small space in them.
During the Revolution, particularly after the Declaration of the
Rights of Man provided for liberty of the press, political journals
of every shade of opinion appeared in large numbers. It is estimated that within five years more than a thousand such newspapers were published. Most of them were shortlived, poorly
written, poorly printed, and abusive in content. Only two survived the Revolution; and only one, *Le Journal des Débats*, is still
published.

But journalism was not the only means of communication.
The revolutionary period was also a great age of oratory. Not
only did the members of the various political assemblies vie with
one another in trying to sway the sympathies of their fellow members but even the reports of committees were presented in oratorical fashion. Incomparably the greatest speaker of the National
Assembly was Mirabeau, who has been called the "French
Demosthenes." During a period of twenty months he delivered
no fewer than one hundred fifty speeches before that body. His
massive appearance, apparent earnestness, and his fiery manner
gave his speeches an unparalleled effect in the National Assembly.

In the National Convention oratorical duels were an almost daily occurrence. Among the gifted orators of this body were Danton, Robespierre, Saint-Just, Vergniaud, and Condorcet. Of them all, however, only Danton spoke extemporaneously, the others delivering set speeches which had been carefully prepared. With Napoleon's rise to power political oratory ceased. Thereafter his was the only voice heard. Political journalism of a non-official nature also disappeared, for freedom of the press did not fit into his scheme of things. The strict government censorship was fatal not only to journalism but to all forms of literary expression. Consequently the France of the Napoleonic period produced only two writers of importance, Madame de Staël (1766–1817) and Chateaubriand (1768–1848). Whereas the official literature of the time was in the decaying classical or neo-classical tradition, Mme. de Staël and Chateaubriand were pioneers of the Romantic movement, and their importance lies therein.

Madame de Staël, daughter of the famous financier Jacques Necker, grew up in an environment permeated by the ideas of Rousseau. After publishing her first work, *Letters concerning Jean-Jacques Rousseau*, at the age of twenty-two, she wrote a number of political pamphlets during the revolutionary period. Because of her bold opposition to Napoleon's government, her life during the decade after 1803 was largely one of exile and travel. The enmity between Madame de Staël and Napoleon was a clash of two antagonistic philosophies. As a disciple of Rousseau, she firmly believed in liberty as the first condition of human progress, while he personified reaction against Rousseauism. The idea of individual liberty was contrary to his ambition for absolute power; hence he feared to allow any protagonist of this idea within forty leagues of Paris. Making her headquarters at Coppet (an estate near Geneva) during the years of her exile, Mme. de Staël wrote her two most important works, *Corinne* (1807), a novel inspired by a visit to Italy, and *De l'Allemagne* (1810), a lively but rose-colored picture of Germany. The significance of the latter lies in the fact that it disclosed to the French the world of German literary and philosophical ideas. Though the French censor sanctioned the publication of the book, the government immediately seized all copies when it was published because it contained certain thinly veiled protests against Napoleon's military despotism. Republished after Bonaparte's fall, the book exercised a marked influence on French thought. Briefly, Mme. de Staël's importance as a forerunner of romanticism lies in the fact that she sounded a personal note in her writings and also expressed enthusiasm for the "romantic" poetry of the age of chivalry.

More important as a pioneer of romanticism was François Auguste, Viscount de Chateaubriand. Of him Gautier says: "Chateaubriand may be regarded as the grandfather or, if you prefer it, as the sachem of romanticism in France." After serving as an officer in the French army for some years, young Chateaubriand resigned in 1791 and embarked for America, ostensibly to discover a northwest passage to the East. He did not discover the passage, but he did find enough literary material to last him through a long life. Returning to Europe, he joined the army of the émigrés at Coblenz, was wounded, and retired to England, where he spent the years until 1800 in dire poverty. Soon after the Consulate was established he reëntered France and in 1801 published *Atala*, the work which established his literary reputation. *Atala* is a story of an American Indian girl who falls in love with a prisoner her father has brought into camp. She sets him free and flees with him, but as she has promised her Christian mother that she will never marry, she commits suicide rather than break her vow. Because of its sentimentality and its glowing descriptions of primitive nature, it influenced both the form and the sentiment of later romantic fiction. As an idealized picture of the American Indian it was the precursor of James Fenimore Cooper's *Leatherstocking Tales*. Two other romantic imaginative tales of Chateaubriand are *René* and *Les Natchez*. In all three the author describes the wonders and beauties of the New World in lyric prose, extolling the life of the "noble savage" after the manner of Rousseau.

In 1802 Chateaubriand published his *Génie du Christianisme* (Genius of Christianity), the work upon which his reputation chiefly rests. His purpose in writing it was to show that Christianity is superior to other religions in a poetic and aesthetic sense. He recommended it not so much because it is true, but because it is beautiful. In other words, Christianity was to him a matter of sentiment rather than of reason. Though not a profound work, Chateaubriand's *Genius of Christianity* is distinguished by its beauty of language, its passionate eloquence, and its magnificent de-

THE DUKE OF WELLINGTON
By permission of the Huntington Art Gallery

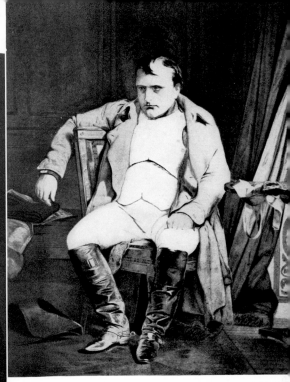

NAPOLEON AT FONTAINEBLEAU

US VII

by David

MADAME DE STAËL

OF WHAT MALADY WILL
HE DIE? *by Goya*

TOILETTE OF THE DEMONS
by Goya

THE CORONATION OF NAPOLEON AND JOSEPHINE *by David*

scriptions. Its welcome in France was great and immediate, the first edition being exhausted in less than a week. Appearing as it did shortly after Napoleon had concluded his Concordat (1801) with the pope, it was not only influential in reëstablishing the popularity of Roman Catholicism in France but was also, so to speak, the justification and glorification of the Concordat. Bonaparte, who was not slow to see its effect, rewarded the author by making him secretary of the legation at Rome, but after the execution of the Duc d'Enghien, Chateaubriand resigned, refusing to be associated in any way with the author of so great a crime. The activity of his last years is beyond the scope of this work.

While classicism was declining in French literature, it was being revived in French art. The return to the practice and ideas of the ancients is seen in architecture and in sculpture, but it was in painting that the classical influence was deepest and most lasting. Though symptoms of the classical strain may be detected in French painting as far back as the middle of the eighteenth century, it was in the work of Jacques Louis David (1748–1825) that classicism reached its culmination. After studying for some years under the French painter Vien, who had classical leanings, David went to Rome, where during a stay of five years he developed a deep veneration for the art of Greece and Rome. Adopting a rigidly classical style he returned to France in 1780 to become "the high priest of classicism." Soon after his return he was commissioned by Louis XVI to paint *The Oath of the Horatii*, a subject suggested by a scene in Corneille's tragedy *Les Horaces*. This and the paintings that followed soon after, including *The Death of Socrates*, were received so enthusiastically that David rose to the position of recognized leader of French art. When the National Assembly decided to commemorate the Oath of the Tennis Court in painting, David was chosen to execute the picture. He never completed it, but he made a sketch for it which still exists. Later the National Convention, of which David was a member, set up under his direction the equivalent of a Ministry of Fine Arts. Thus he became, so to speak, the art dictator of the Revolution. When Marat fell a victim to Charlotte Corday's knife (July 13, 1793), David painted his *Death of Marat* and several months later made a famous sketch of Marie Antoinette on her way to the guillotine. A zealous Jacobin and a great admirer of

Robespierre, David barely escaped the guillotine himself during the Thermidorean Reaction, being released from prison only when a general amnesty was issued by the Convention.

During the Consulate the former Jacobin came under the influence of the First Consul to the extent of making his style of painting less severe to please the new ruler of France. Napoleon, recognizing the possibilities for propaganda in David's art, culti- vated his friendship and after the establishment of the empire made him "first painter to the Imperial Court." The fruit of the association of painter and emperor was the series of paintings celebrating great moments in the life of Bonaparte, including *Bonaparte Crossing Mount St. Bernard, The Distribution of the Eagles,* and *The Coronation of Napoleon and Josephine.* The last, which depicts the moment of the coronation when Napoleon is about to place the crown on the head of Josephine, is regarded by many critics as David's masterpiece. The original, now in the Louvre, is 21 feet high and 33 feet long; it contains more than two hundred figures. Before the painting was unveiled to the public Napoleon himself went to the artist's studio to see it, and after viewing it for half an hour from various angles was so delighted with it that he bestowed the medal of the Legion of Honor on David. After his return from the Second Italian Campaign Napoleon requested his court painter to paint his portrait. When the emperor refused to sit for the picture, the painter decided to do an ideal portrait. The result was *Bonaparte Crossing Mount St. Bernard.* The symbolical significance of the picture is evident. It represents Napoleon as riding a fiery steed, whereas he actually crossed Mount St. Bernard on a mule, led by a peasant. After Waterloo David fled to Brussels, where he died in 1825 at the age of seventy-seven. He was prob- ably at his best as a portrait painter. Among his celebrated por- traits are those of Mme. Récamier and of Pope Pius VII. His general style can best be described as "sculpturesque." The influence he established was continued in various modified forms by his pupils and by others.

The same period which saw David establishing classicism in French art found Francisco Goya y Lucientes (1746–1828) pro- ducing in Spain, after an age of barrenness which had set in with the passing of Velasquez and Murillo, an art that is thor- oughly representative of the Spanish people. Spanish life in all its picturesque diversity is the subject of his work. Though he portrayed also its bright side, Goya had a special love for the bizarre and the grotesque, the brutal and the bloody. Thus a series of his early paintings includes *A Bull Fight*, *The Flagellants*, *Meeting of the Court of the Inquisition*, and *The Interior of a Madhouse*. His works comprise sketches, paintings, water colors, portraits, genre pictures, caricatures, and etchings. To understand them one must keep in mind that he was a revolutionist. By means of his art he declaimed against the Inquisition, hypocrisy, cruelty, tyranny, and religious fanaticism no less than did the philosophes of France in their books. Hence he has been called "the Spanish expression of the French Revolution." His *Caprices*, a collection of etchings, are almost unrivaled as merciless exposures of existing political and social evils.

As a painter Goya's art is based on the natural, but he painted in so many styles that his works have been compared with those of Velasquez, Rembrandt, Reynolds, and others. His pictures always tell a definite story, for he recorded in them what he saw. Often he worked in a condition approaching frenzy. At such times he did not even stop to pick up his brush, using instead a knife, a rag, a stick, or simply his fingers to put the pigment on the canvas. Seizing what he regarded as essential, he would express it in the fewest possible strokes and then declare the picture finished. His religious pictures are not a measure of his power, being mostly commonplace and utterly devoid of religious feeling. Some of his best work is seen in his portraits. Here he displayed the remarkable gift of being able to present the character of his subject. Among his notable portraits are those of Charles III, Charles IV, Queen Maria Louisa, Manuel Godoy, Joseph Bonaparte, and Ferdinand VII. In 1799 Goya reached the highest place in his profession when he was appointed first painter to the Spanish court. When Napoleon tricked Charles IV and Ferdinand VII into resigning the Spanish crown and King Joseph Bonaparte came to Spain, Goya remained "painter to the king." During the period of the French invasions he made the series of etchings called *The Horrors of War*, which depict rapine, murder, terror, famine, and desolation in their stark reality. Upon the return of Ferdinand VII to Spain in 1814 Goya quickly regained the royal favor. He died in 1828 at Bordeaux in France, where he had spent the last years of his life.

CHAPTER TWENTY-SIX

The Napoleonic Era

THE PRELUDE TO THE EMPIRE

ON DECEMBER 13, 1799, a little more than a month after
the coup d'état of Brumaire, the new Constitution of the
Year VIII was ready. Though republican in name, it did
not in practice recognize the sovereignty of the people or safe-
guard public and parliamentary liberties. The executive power was
nominally vested in a committee of three Consuls, but the actual
authority was concentrated in the First Consul, the other two
serving largely as a blind. He was given the right to appoint and
dismiss most officials, including the heads of the various administrative departments, all military and naval officials, and all ambassadors and agents of the government. He also signed treaties
of peace and declarations of war, subject to ratification by the
legislature. The function of the voters was limited to choosing a
list of candidates from which the Senate, a body appointed in the
first instance by the Consuls,[1] was to select the members of the
bicameral legislature. The legislature was to consist of the Tribu-
nate of a hundred members, who were to discuss legislation, and
of the Legislative Body of three hundred, who were to vote on proposed laws without discussion. The power of initiating legislation
was reserved for the Council of State, a body chosen by the First
Consul. When the constitution was submitted to the French people,

[1] Subsequent vacancies were to be filled by the Senate itself.

they accepted it by an overwhelming vote. Siéyès and Ducos were then retired and Cambacérès and Lebrun chosen as colleagues of First Consul Bonaparte. Neither of the new Consuls ever did anything to prevent the First Consul from making his supremacy complete.

The man who assumed the duties of First Consul on December 25, 1799, and who subsequently became Emperor of the French, was about five feet six inches tall, with well-formed limbs and a deep chest. His hair was dark brown; his eyes were bluish gray, and his teeth good but irregular. Though his habits were on the whole simple, he lived energetically. He ate very quickly, usually spending only from seven to twelve minutes over a meal. In his relationship with others he could be kind, generous, and affectionate, but in his later years he became stern and unbending. At all times he was somewhat nervous and irritable; and on a few occasions he lost control of himself to the extent of beating or kicking his ministers or attendants. His strong body was such a dynamo of energy that in his prime he hardly knew the meaning of fatigue. Whether at one subject or many, he could work for fourteen hours without being exhausted. "I am conscious," he said, "of no limit to the work I can get through."

In this strong body was lodged a mind both imaginative and practical. Napoleon could not only conceive great plans but carry them out. His mathematical intellect was aided by a marvelous memory which enabled him to utilize his detailed knowledge, and by a force of will that impelled him to strive toward his goal with unwearying persistence. As he put it: "When I come to a resolution everything is forgotten except that which may lead to its attainment." His mind was ceaselessly active. In 1809 he said to his confidant, Count Roederer: "As for me, I am always working. I do a great deal of thinking. If I seem always ready to meet any difficulty, to face any emergency, it is because before undertaking any enterprise I have spent a long time thinking it out, and seeing what might happen. It is not a genius that reveals to me suddenly in secret what to say or do in circumstances unexpected by others; it is my reflection, my thinking things out. I am always at work— at dinner, at the theater; in the night I get up to work."

One of Napoleon's first concerns after he took up the duties of his office was to put an end to rebellion, strife, and disorder in France before launching his campaign against the Second Coalition. Two major problems were the suppression of brigandage and the pacification of the west, where rebellion had flared up again among the Vendéeans in the summer of 1799. In many parts of the country, particularly in the southern and central portions, bands of outlaws had become so bold that they not only robbed travelers and terrorized villages but made occasional raids on some of the larger towns, attempting "to create the impression that they were avenging the fate of the dethroned royalty and the Catholic altar."[1] Against these bands Bonaparte adopted severe measures. Military detachments, sent out with orders to deal summarily with all brigands and their accomplices, did their work well. By the spring of 1800 they had succeeded in wiping out many of the bands that were the scourge of France. In dealing with the Vendéeans the First Consul adopted more conciliatory tactics. He proclaimed an amnesty for all rebels who would submit within a specified time, gave assurances that he would grant Catholics freedom of worship, permitted many non-juring priests to return to France, and even went so far as to give the impression that he was not averse to a return of the Bourbons. Most of the leading rebels submitted peacefully and the rest were forced to lay down their arms. Thus Napoleon terminated the civil wars which had intermittently vexed the revolutionary governments over a period of seven years.

Having made his government respected at home, the First Consul turned his attention to the war against the Second Coalition. He gave command of the Army of the Rhine to Moreau, and himself prepared to lead an army into Italy for the purpose of recovering control and striking a decisive blow at Austria. Though the First Consul was forbidden by the constitution to command an army in person, he circumvented this prohibition by giving the nominal leadership of the Army of Italy to Berthier. All plans for the Second Italian Campaign were laid with the utmost secrecy. At a time when his enemies thought him occupied with the multifarious duties of government, the First Consul was on his way to Geneva. From there he took most of his army over the hazardous route through the Great St. Bernard Pass. It was a picturesque achievement, but has been overpraised since Napoleon himself did not cross until only the rear guard remained. Arriving unexpectedly in Italy at the rear of the Austrian army, he took posses-

[1] Tarlé, *Bonaparte*, transl. by J. Cournos (1937), p. 94.

sion of Milan, after which he advanced against the Austrian army. The decisive battle was fought at Marengo. At first defeat seemed certain, for he had greatly weakened his army by sending a number of divisions under Desaix to prevent the Austrians from escaping either to the north or the south. But Desaix was recalled just in time to help win an overwhelming victory. The Austrian army was completely routed, with the loss of thousands of prisoners and half of their artillery. With retreat cut off, the Austrians were compelled to arrange an armistice which gave Napoleon control of most of Italy. Still they refused to conclude a final peace. But when Moreau opened the road to Vienna by his victory at Hohenlinden in Bavaria (December, 1800), they had to sue for terms. The treaty was signed at Lunéville in February, 1801. Though it was in the main a renewal of the treaty of Campo Formio, its terms were more severe.

Having eliminated Austria from the Second Coalition, Napoleon proceeded to detach Tsar Paul of Russia by ordering the release, without ransom, of 6000 Russian prisoners the French had taken in 1799; by proposing the restoration of Malta to the Knights of St. John, of whom the Tsar was Grand Master; and by skilfully flattering the Tsar. Paul completely turned against England, joining with Napoleon in an alliance that purposed to secure for France and Russia a predominance in the affairs of Europe. This left only England in arms against France, and even the English were ready for peace. Despite the fact that they had added French and Dutch colonies to their possessions, their commerce had suffered from the closing of many European markets to English goods and from the attacks of French privateers. In England high prices were causing much disaffection, and the people began to shout for "Bread and peace!" As for Napoleon, he not only desired peace for the purpose of organizing the internal affairs of France and consolidating his rule, but he also saw the futility of trying to force it on England, particularly after Tsar Paul was assassinated (March, 1801) and his successor, Alexander I, made overtures of friendship to England. Negotiations were therefore opened in 1801 and the treaty was signed at Amiens in March, 1802. By its terms the English restored all conquests except Spanish Trinidad and Dutch Ceylon. The island of Malta, taken from the French in 1800, was to be given to the Knights of St. John, and the Cape of Good Hope returned to the Dutch. The French pledged themselves to withdraw their forces from southern Italy, and both the French and the English agreed to restore Egypt to the Ottoman Empire. Although the British prime minister declared the peace to be "a genuine reconciliation between the two first nations of the world," it was to last only a short time.

THE REORGANIZATION OF FRANCE

In the interval between wars Napoleon demonstrated that he was no less able as an administrator than as a soldier. His first achievement was the settlement of the religious question which had been such a prolific source of division in France ever since the Civil Constitution of the Clergy was promulgated in 1790. Napoleon himself opened the negotiations with Pope Pius VII. The agreement finally signed, known as the Concordat of 1801, recognized the Roman Catholic religion as that of the majority of French citizens and accorded to all French Catholics freedom of worship so long as they observed the police regulations. The First Consul was given the right to nominate all bishops, whereupon the pope was to confer upon them the usual canonical institution. The lower clerics were to be appointed by the bishops, subject to ratification by the state. All ecclesiastics were to promise fidelity to the government, which was to pay them a suitable salary. Finally, the pope promised that neither he nor his successor would ever molest the holders of the alienated church property.

The clause regarding "police regulations" gave Napoleon the opportunity to circumscribe sharply the activities of the Church. After the pope had published the bulls connected with the Concordat, Napoleon drew up a list of regulations known as the "Organic Articles" and added them to the Concordat in such a way as to make it appear that they had been part of the original agreement. The Organic Articles asserted the supremacy of the state over the Church in emphatic words. They forbade the publication of bulls or the decrees of general councils without the express permission of the government, provided that one liturgy and one catechism[1] be used throughout France, and, in general, minutely regulated the relations between church and state. They also made

[1] This catechism which was later provided by the state contained such statements as the following: "We owe to our Emperor Napoleon I love, respect, obedience, fidelity, military service, tributes decreed for the defense of the Empire and of his throne; we owe to him also fervent prayers for his safety and for the prosperity of the state, both spiritual and material."

provisions for paying the salaries of the Protestant ministers from the state treasury.

Although there was much dissatisfaction with the Concordat in military circles, among the intellectuals, and on the part of many Catholics, it nevertheless did much to appease religious discord in France and strengthen Napoleon's government. And this was undoubtedly the First Consul's purpose. He himself had little sympathy with religious doctrines and observances, but he appreciated the influence of the Church upon the people and the importance of having this influence on his side. Hence he wrote to his chief agent in the negotiations with the pope: "Treat the pope as if he had 200,000 men." At St. Helena he frankly laid bare his motives. "With the aid of Catholicism," he said, "I should more easily attain all my great results. Abroad, Catholicism would keep the pope on my side; and with my influence and our forces in Italy, I did not despair of having, sooner or later, by one means or another, the direction of this pope. And thenceforth, what an influence! What a lever of opinion for the rest of the world!"

Probably the most celebrated of Napoleon's achievements was the Civil Code or Code Napoléon, which brought order out of the legal chaos in France. The idea of gathering up the confused parts of French law and codifying them was not original with the First Consul. Ever since the fifteenth century it had occupied the minds of many eminent Frenchmen. At the beginning of the Revolution the National Assembly had voted a resolution for a general code, but had done nothing further about it. Later the Convention appointed a committee which actually drew up a code; however, the draft was discarded as being too complex. It remained for Napoleon to take up the work in his energetic way and carry it to completion. In 1800 he appointed a commission of four eminent lawyers to prepare a civil code, and when the draft was ready he submitted it to the Council of State for discussion and amendment. The final draft is notable for its precision, its lucid order, and its clearness of detail. Since its promulgation in March, 1804, the Civil Code has been substantially amended and modified, but its general outline has been preserved. Napoleon himself regarded it as his most enduring contribution. At St. Helena he said: "My true glory is not that I have gained forty battles. Waterloo will efface the memory of those victories. But that which nothing can efface, which will live forever, is my Civil Code."

There has been considerable debate among historians over Napoleon's share in the work of completing the Civil Code. His supporters have exaggerated his participation and his opponents have minimized it. This much is certain: Napoleon displayed more than a perfunctory interest in the work. While the first draft was being discussed by the Council of State, he frequently presided over the sessions, taking an active part in the discussions. He himself, it appears, formulated the laws dealing with marriage, divorce, and property. Thus he gave much more than the title to the code which bears his name. Thibeaudeau, an eyewitness of the work, wrote: "On some points his influence may seem to have been unfortunate. But how small a price for the rest. His all-powerful will was the lever removing all obstacles. His energy and his ambition were the instruments to which we owe the achievement of the great task, a task which had been unfulfilled for centuries, and, but for him, might still in our own day have remained undone."

The Civil Code was only the first of a number of codes. It was followed by the Code of Civil Procedure (1806), the Code of Commerce (1807), the Code of Criminal Procedure (1808), and the Penal Code (1810). The later codes became increasingly reactionary; in other words, they tended more and more to support the growing despotism of Napoleon. Even the Civil Code was at bottom undemocratic. Though it made the law the same for the whole of France, it did not establish the equality of all before the law. Illegitimate children, for example, were denied the rights accorded to those who were legitimate, and wives were put under the authority of their husbands. In general, the codes favored the property-owning middle class. Thus the Criminal Code, while carefully protecting the interests of the employer, forbade unions and strikes, the only weapons of the workingman against exploitation. These codes served as models for many codes drawn up in the nineteenth century both in Europe and in Latin America. By some nations the Civil Code was adopted with only slight modifications.

Another achievement of Napoleon was the creation of the Bank of France. During the last years of the monarchy various financiers had voiced the need for a central credit establishment on the plan of the Bank of England. But the Revolution supervened and the question received no further consideration until

1796, when a group of bankers drew up plans for a bank. Nothing more was done, however, until Napoleon took up the question of finances after 18 Brumaire. Since the existing banks had no confidence in the government and were therefore unwilling to discount government obligations, the First Consul consulted with some of the men who had drawn up the project in 1796 and then decided to found a bank that would serve the interests of the government and also give the necessary accommodations to commerce. Accordingly he created the Bank of France with a capital of 30,000,000 francs, to be raised by the sale of 30,000 shares of stock. The new bank paid the government annuities, had charge of the government lotteries, and financed certain undertakings of the government. To give the bank a broader basis its capital was raised to 45,000,000 francs in 1803. At the same time it was also given the exclusive privilege of issuing banknotes in Paris. After 1803 it gradually extended its influence over the whole of France, through its branches, and has remained the most powerful financial institution in the country.

The government of the Consulate also continued the work of restoring order in the national finances. National debts were consolidated by the redemption, at a proportion of their nominal value, of all the extant securities, drafts, vouchers, exchequer bills, and warrants for arrears of interest, of which there were more than sixty kinds, all more or less depreciated. Furthermore, the apportionment and collection of taxes was entrusted to agents appointed by the central government, a change which resulted in the elimination of much corruption, a fairer apportionment of taxes, and a more certain income to the government. This reorganization of the tax system and the practice of strict economy in government expenditures made possible the balancing of the national budget of the Year X (1801–1802). But neither these nor the other financial reforms of the Consulate made for a high degree of financial stability. Business interests never felt complete confidence in the policy of the government because Napoleon did not present his proposals "in a strictly legal and candid fashion."[1] Hence the market value of the government bonds averaged only a little more than half their face amounts.

The centralization of the tax system was but a prelude to the centralization of the entire administration. The administrative

[1] *Cambridge Modern History*, vol. 9 (1918), p. 27.

divisions which had previously been set up were retained, but a law of February 16, 1800, substituted government by the central authorities for local self-government. The prefect, appointed by the central government, was henceforth to be the chief administrative officer of the department. The subdivisions of the department, now called arrondissements instead of districts, were put under the supervision of the subprefect, also appointed by the central government. Even the mayors of the communes, who had formerly been elected, were henceforth to be appointed. Thus the machinery was ready for the centralized despotism of Napoleon.

In 1802 Napoleon also created the Legion of Honor. Although all decorations and marks of distinction had been abolished during the Revolution, the revolutionists gave such rewards as inscribed swords, muskets, drums, or drumsticks to those who performed extraordinary feats of bravery. Napoleon, who realized that men love distinctions, had also rewarded meritorious service with swords of honor during the period of the Directory. After he became First Consul he pondered the idea of founding an institution which would reward civil as well as military merit. Thibeaudeau quotes him as saying: "I don't think that the French love liberty and equality: the French are not at all changed by ten years of revolution. . . . They have one feeling—honor. We must nourish that feeling." The practical result of his deliberations was the founding of the Legion of Honor, of which those upon whom "arms of honor" were conferred automatically became members. This institution not only bound both the soldiers and the civil servants closer to the person of Napoleon, but in creating an aristocracy of merit it also gave a certain luster to his rule. How highly it was regarded in France is shown by the fact that it survived both the fall of Napoleon and the various revolutions of the nineteenth century. Even today its awards of merit and honor are still greatly coveted.

Education, too, occupied Napoleon's attention. In 1802 a law was passed which provided for a general reorganization of the higher schools. It was carried out only in part. For secondary education twenty-nine lycées were founded, and for higher education a number of schools of medicine, law, and design were established. Napoleon's most important reform was the creation of the Imperial University (1808), a teaching corporation which was given exclusive charge of education in France. "No school," the decree stated, "can be established outside the University and without the authorization of its head." At the head of the University stood the grand master, who may be regarded as the forerunner of the later minister of national education. Thus education, which under the Old Régime had been in the hands of the Church, was put under the control of the state. Napoleon's aim was not enlightenment, but the production of good soldiers and of citizens who would be loyal to him. He himself said: "My aim in establishing a teaching body is to have a means of directing personal and moral opinions." Primary education found but a small place in Napoleon's scheme. The decree of 1808 makes mention of elementary schools, but little was done to establish them. Nor did Napoleon give much attention to the education of women. He did, however, draw up a curriculum for the school at Ecouen in which the orphaned daughters of his soldiers were to be instructed. In his educational scheme for girls religion was given the first place. Thus he wrote:

What shall be taught to the young ladies who are to be educated at Ecouen? First, religion in all its severity. . . . You must bring up women who believe and not women who argue. The feebleness of the female brain, the instability of their ideas, their destination in the social order, the necessity on their part of constant and perpetual resignation and of a sort of prompt and indulgent charity—all this can be obtained only through religion, through a religion that is both kind and charitable.[1]

Though he was successful in many other respects, Napoleon failed in his attempts to restore the French colonial empire in the New World. Successful in obtaining Louisiana from Spain, he failed in the attempt to reëstablish French rule in San Domingo. When the white planters had refused to recognize the equality of Negroes and whites, as it was proclaimed by the revolutionists in France, the Negro slaves and mulattoes of San Domingo had risen in revolt, driven out the planters, and desolated a large part of the colony. After a time Toussaint l'Ouverture, a Negro leader of remarkable gifts, had restored order and organized a government which was nominally under French suzerainty. This government freed the slaves and also released commerce from its former restrictions, with the result that the people of San Domingo became prosperous. All this, however, was contrary to the plans and principles of Napoleon. He therefore sent an expedition of 20,000 men

---

[1] Cited by W. F. Paris, *Napoleon's Legion* (1928), p. 135.

under the command of his brother-in-law, General Leclerc, to reëstablish the direct rule of France, restore the exiled white planters, and revive slavery. It was an act which Napoleon later regarded as the greatest folly of his life. After overcoming the stouthearted resistance of the natives, the French expedition sent Toussaint to France, where he died in 1803. Despite this success, disaster overwhelmed the expedition. Yellow fever wrought such havoc among the soldiers that after seven months the expedition had shrunk to 8000. Though reinforcements arrived from France, disease and the opposition of the natives finally obliged the French to abandon the island. The attempt to establish French domination in Louisiana also came to nothing. When Napoleon's plans became known, they aroused such resentment along the western border of the United States that the cry for war against France was sounded. The prospect of armed conflict with the United States and the fact that a renewal of war with England was inevitable moved Napoleon to abandon his plans in 1803 and to sell Louisiana to the United States for sixty million francs ($11,250,000).

Already popular in the army because of his Italian victories, Napoleon became popular among all classes as a result of his reforms. When this popularity was further increased by the discovery of a plot against his life, the First Consul made the most of it by putting before the people the proposal that he be made consul for life (May, 1802). The response in favor of it was overwhelming, three and one-half million Frenchmen voting in the affirmative and only eight thousand declaring against it. A modification of the constitution made him practically absolute, but Napoleon was still not satisfied. He desired his power to be embellished with the pomp and trappings of hereditary monarchy. This desire was fulfilled in 1804 when the French people voted him the title of "Emperor of the French," only some twenty-five hundred negative votes being cast. He assumed the title in May, and was crowned in the cathedral of Notre Dame on December 2, 1804, with imposing ceremonies. To give a religious significance to the coronation, Pope Pius VII was invited to attend. Napoleon did not, however, permit the pope to crown him. Taking the crown from the hands of the supreme pontiff, the new emperor placed it on the altar, then took it and crowned himself. In the spring of 1805 he also exchanged the title of "President of the Italian (Cisalpine) Republic" for that of "King of Italy." Journeying to Italy, he placed upon his own head the iron crown of Lombardy which had been worn by Charlemagne. "God gave it to me," Napoleon said. "Beware who dares to touch it." It was a challenge that was soon to be accepted.

THE WAR AGAINST THE THIRD COALITION

In May, 1803, a little more than a year after the signing of the treaty of Amiens, war had broken out anew between France and England. Napoleon had never regarded the peace as more than a breathing space in his efforts to destroy the commerce and colonial empire of England—a breathing space which he needed to consolidate his power. Even while negotiations for peace were going on he was upsetting the balance of power by having himself declared president of the Cisalpine Republic, which was thereafter called the Italian Republic. Other acts which aroused the fears and hostility of the English were the annexation of Piedmont, the reorganization of Switzerland, the attempt to revive the French colonial empire, and the high protective tariff, amounting almost to exclusion, which the French government put on English goods. So marked did the anti-French feeling become that the English refused to carry out the stipulation of the treaty of Amiens which provided for the evacuation of Malta. When Napoleon raged and stormed, declaring the retention of Malta by England to be an outrage against Europe, the English responded with a declaration of war. Military operations began when Napoleon sent one French army into Hanover, of which George III was ruler, and another to the mouth of the Elbe to cut off British trade with the interior of Germany. Meanwhile England was trying to form a new coalition against France. Though Russia and Austria hesitated for a time, the Third Coalition gradually became a reality after the return of Pitt to power in the spring of 1804. Early in 1805 a treaty was signed between England and Russia, and soon thereafter the alliance was also joined by Sweden and Austria, with Prussia remaining apart for the time being. Among the allies the opinion was general that Napoleon was not prepared for war—an illusion, indeed, as the future was to demonstrate. Not only was the army of Napoleon ready, but he had also worked out his plan of campaign with careful minuteness.

Soon after the renewal of war between England and France,

Bonaparte had laid plans for an invasion of England. Whether he actually intended to carry out the project or whether he was only trying to arouse the fears of the English is still a moot question.[1] If he intended an actual invasion the scheme was extremely rash. An army was concentrated at Boulogne, large enough, it was believed, to overwhelm any English force that might oppose it. Flatboats were collected to transport this army across the Channel, and the troops were trained to embark and disembark quickly. Whatever their purpose may have been, these preparations spread alarm in England. Every possible precaution was taken against invasion. Large volunteer forces were organized in readiness for a march to the coast at a moment's notice, the coast itself was fortified, and a part of the English fleet remained in the Channel to frustrate any attempted crossing. For two years the English people anxiously awaited the lighting of the beacons that were to announce the invasion. But Napoleon seemed unable to solve the problem of transporting troops across the Channel. When his plans for luring the English fleet from the Channel miscarried in the summer of 1805, he quickly marched the army he had collected at Boulogne into Bavaria, where the Austrian army under General Mack had taken a position at Ulm. Before the Austrian leader was aware of the real intentions of Bonaparte, he found himself surrounded. It was necessary for him either to strike desperately at the ring encircling him or to capitulate. He chose the latter, surrendering on October 20, 1805, with most of his force.

The French triumph at Ulm was offset on October 21 by a crushing naval defeat in the battle of Trafalgar. On that day the English fleet sighted the combined fleet of France and Spain which it had long been seeking. Admiral Nelson, who had only twenty-seven ships of the line to thirty-three of the opposition, nevertheless advanced to the attack. His carefully planned scheme of battle forced one enemy ship after the other to haul down its flag until eighteen ships were taken, while the rest fled in disorder toward Cadiz. It was the greatest naval victory of modern times, but it was a costly triumph, for it ended the brilliant career of Nelson. Mortally wounded early in the battle, he lived just

---

[1] Those authorities who still believe that Napoleon did not intend to execute the plans are in the minority. The entire question is ably discussed by Harold C. Deutsch in his *Genesis of Napoleonic Imperialism* (1938), pp. 173–183.

long enough to know that his fleet had achieved a transcendent success. For the navies of France and Spain the battle of Trafalgar was a shattering blow from which they did not recover before the end of the war. After Trafalgar Napoleon did not try again to contest the English naval supremacy.

The destruction of the French fleet definitely put an end to Napoleon's hopes of invading England, but it did not interfere with his campaign in Germany, where his victory at Ulm had opened the way to Vienna. Advancing into Austria without delay, he occupied the capital from which the Habsburgs had fled, and then marched northward toward Moravia, where a large Austro-Russian force was assembling. So desirous were Tsar Alexander I and Emperor Francis II of earning glory by defeating Napoleon that they advanced to meet him. It was exactly what the French emperor had hoped for but had not expected. Affecting an inde- cision which completely deceived the Austro-Russian command- ers, he fell back to take a position near Austerlitz. There the allied army walked into his trap. On December 2, 1805, the first anni- versary of his coronation as emperor, Napoleon won what is probably his most celebrated victory, routing the Austro-Russian forces so completely that they retreated with a loss of more than 20,000 men. Addressing his victorious army he said: "Soldiers, I am satisfied with you! In the battle of Austerlitz you have justified all my expectations of your bravery; you have adorned your eagles with immortal glory, and it will be enough for any one of you to say, 'I was at the battle of Austerlitz,' to draw forth the reply, 'Here is a brave man.'" The defeat of the allies was so crushing that the Emperor Francis II sued for peace, while the Tsar withdrew with his army to his own country. The treaty between France and Austria, signed at Pressburg in December, 1805, stipulated that the latter cede Venetia to Napoleon's king- dom of Italy, the Tyrol to Bavaria, and territory in western Germany to Baden and Würtemberg. The emperor further re- nounced all feudal rights over Bavaria, Würtemberg, and Baden and recognized the rulers of the first two states as kings.

After the treaty of Pressburg Napoleon considered himself strong enough to establish a series of vassal states as props for his throne. His first step in this direction was to depose the Bourbon rulers of Naples, Ferdinand IV and Queen Caroline. Despite their promise to remain neutral in the war, these two rulers had opened their country to both Russian and British forces. But when the Russians met defeat at Austerlitz the Tsar recalled his troops and the British likewise departed, leaving the country at the mercy of Napoleon. Early in 1806 Joseph Bonaparte, older brother of Napoleon and a man of considerable common sense, led an army into Naples, took possession of its capital, and was proclaimed king of Naples and Sicily by his brother. All of Italy excepting the Papal States was now subject to Napoleon's will, and even the Papal States were not entirely independent despite the resolute stand of the pope. The next objective of Napoleon was Holland, the government of which had already undergone a number of changes. This time the government was transformed into a constitutional monarchy with Louis Bonaparte, a younger brother of Napoleon, as king (June, 1806). Louis, a mild character, was soon to identify himself with the interests of his subjects rather than with those of his brother, much to the chagrin of the latter.

THE REARRANGEMENT OF GERMANY

Having added two names to the list of European kings, Napoleon proceeded to reconstitute Germany and make it tributary. Already in 1803 he had greatly reduced the number of German states by suppressing forty-five of the Free Imperial Cities and all but one of the ecclesiastical states, most of the territory being added to such secondary states as Baden, Bavaria, and Würtemberg. In July, 1806, he introduced further changes by forming the Confederation of the Rhine, composed of the kings of Bavaria and Würtemberg, the grand duke of Baden, and thirteen lesser princes. While each state was to retain full sovereignty and independence in domestic affairs, their common interests were to be regulated by a diet at Frankfort. Napoleon was declared Protector of the Confederation, and it was bound to France by an alliance that was both defensive and offensive. Its army was to be drilled under French officers, and its foreign policy was to be dictated by France. In short, for purposes of war and foreign policy it became a part of France. On August 1, when the sixteen states announced their withdrawal from the Holy Roman Empire at the Diet of Ratisbon, Napoleon's envoy declared that his master no longer recognized the empire's existence. A few days later Emperor Francis II officially released the states from their allegiance and abdicated, retaining only the title of Francis I, Emperor of Austria, which he had assumed two years before. Thus the Holy Roman Empire, with its history of more than a thousand years, finally collapsed.

About this time the Prussian government, which had persisted in remaining neutral when its assistance would have been of the greatest service to the coalition, began to adopt a hostile attitude toward Napoleon. Its growing enmity was stimulated by the fact that Napoleon had offered to restore Hanover to England after having granted it to Prussia. The Prussians felt that they could place no faith in the promises of the French emperor. During the summer of 1806 they increased the size of their army, called out all the reserves, and frantically made preparations for war. Recalling the achievements of the Prussian army in the Seven Years' War, they confidently believed that they had the best army and the ablest commanders in Europe. As one Prussian officer put it: "His Majesty's army could produce several generals equal to M. Bonaparte." Actually the Prussian army had deteriorated since the days of Frederick the Great, while the Grand Army of Napoleon was at the highest pitch of efficiency. It was therefore a rash act for the Prussians to oppose the French without waiting for help from England or Russia. When they advanced early in October, Napoleon used against them the very manoeuvres which had been so successful against the Austrians at Ulm. He completely surrounded the Prussian army, isolating it from its resources. Thereupon his opponents divided their forces into two masses to make a breach in the French line. While the first section of the Prussian army was being defeated by Davout at Auerstadt, Napoleon himself engaged the second near Jena. For a time the battle at Jena was hotly contested, but a cavalry charge broke the Prussian army so that it fled in panic. In the two battles (October 14, 1806) no fewer than 20,000 Prussians were killed or captured, and the duke of Brunswick, commander-in-chief of the Prussian forces, was mortally wounded. The hero of the day was Marshal Davout, who had defeated a Prussian force nearly twice the size of his own; yet his name was barely mentioned in the bulletin issued by Napoleon.

After the battle the French pursued and captured most of the fleeing Prussians. This left Berlin defenseless. Within a fortnight the French army occupied the Prussian capital, and

Napoleon himself entered it in triumph, after having stopped at Potsdam to pay homage at the grave of Frederick the Great, whom he had long admired. So complete was the military collapse of Prussia that fortress after fortress surrendered without offering resistance. In less than six weeks after the opening of the war, Napoleon was master of nearly the whole of the Prussian kingdom with its population of about nine millions. When the king sued for an armistice, Napoleon made his demands so severe that even the timorous Frederick William III rejected them. With the help the Russians had promised him, he was determined to offer further resistance. In consequence it became the immediate problem of Napoleon to stop the Russian army advancing to aid the Prussians. Leaving Berlin, he transferred the seat of the war to Prussian Poland, where his arrival was hailed with great enthusiasm by the Poles. Napoleon had no intention of exciting the enmity of Austria by the restoration of Polish independence; on the other hand, he did not discourage the hopes of the Poles, for he wished to enlist as many as possible to strengthen his army for the contest with the Russians.

With his army fortified by the addition of Polish volunteers, Napoleon turned against the Russian army, which, under the command of Benningsen, had taken a stand at the village of Eylau, near Koenigsberg. The battle, fought in a blinding snowstorm, was one of the bloodiest of Napoleon's career. Both sides doggedly refused to give way, and when darkness forced a cessation of the fighting the field was covered with 30,000 dead. For the first time in his military career Napoleon had failed to win; in fact, he even considered retreating, but was spared the ignominy when the Russians withdrew. Though he at once laid claim to victory because of the Russian retreat, his prestige suffered as a result of the battle. Before renewing hostilities he spent the rest of the winter and the spring of 1807 filling the gaps which had been torn in the ranks of his army by death and desertion, calling upon every part of his empire for recruits. By June he had an army that outnumbered the Russians nearly two to one. All this time the Russians had done nothing to follow up the check they had administered to Bonaparte at Eylau. It was only after the French took Danzig, the last fortress besides Koenigsberg that Prussia still held, that Benningsen bestirred himself. Then he blundered much as the Russians had blundered at Austerlitz. The result was the defeat at Friedland (June 14, 1807), in which the Russians lost more than 15,000 men, killed or wounded. The Tsar asked for an armistice. Frederick William III, deserted by his ally and deprived of the last Prussian towns by the French, could only submit.

The treaties of peace were signed at Tilsit in July, 1807. In the hope that he might influence Napoleon, Tsar Alexander I came to conduct the negotiations himself. The interview between the two monarchs took place on a raft moored in the middle of the river Niemen where they would have complete privacy. Napoleon, bent on getting Alexander to aid him against England and to watch central Europe so that he could devote himself to the conquest of Spain, was most gracious. Instead of imposing severe terms, he asked for little more than the Ionian Islands and gave Russia a slice of Prussian Poland in return. The Tsar recognized the various changes Napoleon had made in Europe, including the establishment of the Confederation of the Rhine and of the kingdoms of Italy, Naples, Holland, and Westphalia. To gain his support, the Emperor of the French led him to believe that he could have a free hand in the East.[1] Though Napoleon actually had no intention of making such liberal concessions, he beguiled Alexander to such good effect that the latter was completely won over. Secret conventions for future joint action on the part of the two monarchs followed. Alexander was to mediate between France and England, and if the English refused to come to terms was to join Napoleon in the war against them. Napoleon, for his part, was to mediate between Russia and the Turks, and if the latter proved obstinate both were to join in liberating the European provinces, except Constantinople, from them. When the two sovereigns parted each believed he had won support for his own purposes.

The Prussian king was treated more harshly, being forced to make great sacrifices. Though the beautiful Queen Louisa of Prussia journeyed to Tilsit in an effort to soften the heart of the Corsican, she failed to gain any concessions. The principal provisions of the treaty were: (1) Prussia was to pay a large indemnity and permit French garrisons to occupy its fortresses until the indemnity was paid. (2) Prussia was to join the coalition against

---

[1] The one definite exception Napoleon made, it appears, was Constantinople. At St. Helena he said: "Alexander wanted Constantinople, which would have destroyed the equilibrium of power in Europe."

England. (3) Prussia was to give up all territory west of the Elbe, together with the territory that had been taken from Poland in the second and third partitions. The latter, excepting the part given to Russia, was transformed into the duchy of Warsaw and put under the rule of the king of Saxony. The Prussian territories west of the Elbe were added to the principalities of Hesse-Cassel and Brunswick to form the Kingdom of Westphalia, of which Napoleon's brother Jerome was made king. Altogether Prussia lost nearly half of its territory and population.

THE CONTINENTAL SYSTEM

There still remained to be achieved Napoleon's great object of crushing England. Since his lack of a navy precluded any attempt to invade that nation, he decided to ruin it through its trade; in other words, by means of a commercial war. The principles upon which his plan rested were essentially mercantilistic and had previously been applied in a lesser degree. The plan itself, known as the Continental System, was formally launched by the so-called Berlin Decree (issued on November 21, 1806, while Napoleon was in Berlin), the purpose of which was to prevent English wares from entering continental markets. The decree forbade all commerce and correspondence with the British and declared all British property on the continent confiscated and all vessels that had only touched at a British port subject to seizure. The British retaliated in 1807 with the Orders in Council which enjoined that all colonial goods—for example, cotton, sugar, and coffee—should be transported to the European continent only by British shippers or by neutral ships which had paid duty on the wares at an English port. In other words, no neutral ship was to be allowed to enter a continental port without first having stopped at an English port to pay a duty on its cargo of colonial goods. Napoleon, who was in Italy when he was informed of the Orders in Council, replied with the Milan Decree, which declared subject to seizure all neutral vessels that complied with the British orders. Neutral shipping, particularly that of the United States, suffered greatly from the trade restrictions. American ships trading with France were liable to seizure by the English if they did not stop to pay a tax, and by the French if they did. While Napoleon greatly modified his decrees in 1810, he never rescinded them entirely.[1] The Orders in

---

[1] The system was abolished after his fall.

Council were modified at various times to make them less severe on neutral shipping and in 1812 were annulled, but not soon enough to avert war with the United States.

In the end Napoleon's plan proved futile. Among the obstacles to its success were the desire of the people under his rule for British and especially colonial goods and by his inability to stop the widespread smuggling of the forbidden goods into continental countries. But at first Napoleon was certain that he could ruin England if he could enlist the other continental states on his side. Although he had gained the support of many of them, he was still faced with the task of winning Sweden, Denmark, Portugal, and Austria for his plan. Upon the first, Russia was to exert pressure. Accordingly, when Sweden refused to withdraw from its alliance with Great Britain, Alexander I sent an army to occupy Finland, but it was not until a year later that the Swedish government agreed to enter the Continental System. Meanwhile the English, fearing that Napoleon would seize the Danish fleet as he had earlier taken that of the Dutch, sent out an expedition (July, 1807) which bombarded Copenhagen, confiscated the military stores, and took the fleet, which was then convoyed to England. The result was that the Danes joined whole-heartedly in closing their ports to British trade. While the English were acting against Denmark, Napoleon was trying to secure the support of Portugal for his Continental System. He ordered Prince John, the regent of Portugal, to close all ports against English commerce and to confiscate all English property. As the prince and his ministers were afraid to offend either France or England, they adopted a middle course by declaring themselves ready to close the Portuguese ports to English trade but refusing to confiscate all English property. Napoleon was so displeased with this policy that in October, 1807, he sent a French army of 20,000 men under Marshal Junot into Portugal with orders to march on Lisbon. The news of the advance of the French terrified the Portuguese court. The regent declared his willingness to carry out the demands of Napoleon unconditionally, but it was too late, for the latter had already announced the dethronement of the house of Braganza. This left the royal family the choice of being taken prisoners by the French army or seeking refuge in the Portuguese colony of Brazil. It chose the latter. On the same day on which the royal family set sail, Junot and his army entered Lisbon without resistance.

THE ATTACK ON SPAIN

Having realized his desires with respect to Portugal, Napoleon turned his attention in the direction of Spain. Although Spain since 1795 had been a lukewarm ally of France, there were indications that the Spanish government would seize any favorable opportunity to free itself from the overlordship of the French emperor. This determined him to overthrow the ruling house of Spain in favor of a ruler upon whose support he could rely, for he had need of the entire naval resources of Spain for his attempt to enforce the blockade against England, and of the Spanish ports to enforce the self-blockade of the continent. Napoleon believed that he could gain control of Spain with as little effort as he had occupied Portugal. The government of Spain was, indeed, extraordinarily weak. The dull-minded, pleasure-loving Charles IV was nominally the ruler, but the actual administration of the government was in the hands of Queen Maria Luisa and Manuel Godoy, her lover. Equally contemptible was the insipid Ferdinand, prince of Asturias and heir to the throne. When in March, 1808, Ferdinand revolted against his father and had himself proclaimed king as Ferdinand VII, Napoleon invited the members of the royal family to Bayonne, offering to act as mediator between them. There he succeeded by threats and cajolery in obtaining the abdication of both Charles IV and Ferdinand VII. With Spain seemingly his, he gave the Spanish throne to his brother Joseph and made Murat, his brother-in-law, king of Naples.

But Bonaparte had reckoned without the people of Spain. The masses who had not been consulted would have no part of.French rule. Regarding Joseph Bonaparte as a foreign despot, the people everywhere took up arms against him. At first the French troops advancing into Spain were able to drive back the bands of Spaniards who attacked them, but the resistance gradually stiffened. Finally on July 22, the very day on which Joseph entered Madrid, a French army of about 17,000 men under General Dupont was forced to surrender at Baylen. It was the most decisive check that an imperial force had met. Ten days later the new king and the French troops retreated from Madrid to the region beyond the Ebro. Not long afterwards disaster also befell the French in Portugal when a British force of 10,000 men under the command of Sir Arthur Wellesley—later duke of Wellington—defeated the army of

Junot near Lisbon. The next day Junot signed an agreement which provided that the French evacuate Portugal.

Napoleon saw that if he would save his prestige, which had been greatly weakened by the reverses, he must put down the Spanish uprising by force and retrieve his brother's throne. Hence he resolved to lead an army across the Pyrenees in person. As both Prussia and Austria were becoming restive, he held an interview with the Tsar at Erfurt for the purpose of securing his power in eastern Europe, and then set out for Spain. His army numbered more than 200,000 men, including some of his best troops—troops that had helped him win his great victories. Moreover, with these troops went the best marshals of France, leaders of wide experience. As for the Spaniards, their victories over the French had made them so confident that many looked forward not only to the deliverance of Spain but also to the conquest of France as a retaliatory measure. Instead of making preparations to stop the invading army, they spent the time celebrating their victories. In comparison with those of Napoleon, the Spanish troops were poorly drilled, poorly equipped, and without able leaders. In short, they were no match for the crack French regiments, and after a few engagements in which the Spanish troops were easily forced back, Napoleon entered Madrid.

Once in Madrid, Napoleon promulgated a series of revolutionary changes. The Inquisition was abolished, all feudal rights were annulled, the provincial customs were suppressed, and the monasteries were reduced to one-third of their former number. The emperor then issued a proclamation in which he asked the Spanish people to accept the constitutional government of Joseph, telling them that if they would not, "I shall myself assume the crown of Spain and I shall find means of making those who are refractory respect it, for God has given me both the power and the will to overcome all obstacles." A minority accepted the new king, but the majority declined. To most Spaniards he was still a usurper. Even the reforms, wholesome as they were, appeared hateful because they had been proclaimed by a foreign monarch. All this, however, was not patent to Napoleon. Regarding the issue in Spain as settled, he prepared to complete the conquest of the Iberian Peninsula by advancing against the English forces which, under Sir John Moore, had invaded northwestern Spain. But the English retreated. Before Napoleon could overtake them he received news that Austria was preparing for war. This and vague rumors that a plot was being formed against him at home decided him to relinquish the pursuit of the English to Marshal Soult and to return to Paris immediately.

NAPOLEON AT HIS ZENITH

The treaty of Pressburg (1805), by which Napoleon deprived Austria of much territory, had excited widespread indignation. Since that time the Austrian government had been busy strengthening its army and making preparations for a war which seemed inevitable. The belief was general in Austria that Napoleon would sooner or later demand more territory, and men also feared that he might dethrone the Habsburgs as he had the Spanish Bourbons. Since a large part of his army was engaged in Spain, the time appeared propitious for a war against him. Hence in April, 1809, Austria issued a declaration of war, the Archduke Charles declaring that it was "in behalf of the liberty and national honor of Germany" and calling on all Germans to rise against the oppressor. But the attempt to free Germany from the Napoleonic yoke was premature. After the declaration of war Napoleon immediately left Paris and within three weeks succeeded, by a series of brilliant manoeuvres, in reaching Vienna, which made but a weak attempt at resistance. Nevertheless, the Austrians did not, as he had hoped, sue for peace. A short time later, as he was trying to cross the Danube, he was attacked at Aspern and forced to fall back to the island of Lobau. In July, however, he redeemed his reputation for invincibility by defeating the Austrian army in a bloody battle at Wagram. It was a decisive blow. For several weeks the Austrian government waited in vain for help from England or Prussia and then signed the treaty of Vienna in October, 1809. Besides ceding nearly fifty thousand square miles of territory with a population of more than three million inhabitants to various states of Napoleon's empire, Austria had to pay a large indemnity, reduce its standing army to 150,000 men, and promise to import no English goods.

Not many months after the treaty of Vienna, Napoleon was able to fulfill his desire to marry into one of the ancient dynasties of Europe. For years the idea of divorcing Josephine because she had borne him no heir had been in his mind. As early as 1807 a list of the marriageable princesses of Europe had been drawn up for him. It was not, however, until his return from Austria that divorce proceedings were instituted. Josephine, who had become deeply attached to her husband, sobbingly gave her consent and in December, 1809, the divorce was granted. At first Napoleon considered asking the hand of one of the sisters of Tsar Alexander I, but abandoned the idea when he was certain that the Dowager Empress, who hated him, would decide against such a marriage. The choice finally fell on Marie Louise, daughter of Francis I of Austria. Though there was little enthusiasm in Austria for the marriage, Francis was persuaded by Metternich to give his daughter to Napoleon in the interests of peace. The marriage, celebrated in April, 1810, was for some years quite amicable. In March, 1811, the new empress gave birth to a boy upon whom the proud Napoleon bestowed the title of "King of Rome."

After his marriage to Marie Louise Napoleon made further additions to his empire. Previously, in May, 1809, he had annexed the Papal States over the protest of Pope Pius VII; now (July, 1810) he incorporated Holland in the French Empire. For some time Napoleon had been dissatisfied with his brother because Louis, as king of Holland, had honestly endeavored to work for the benefit of his subjects, even trying to lighten the burden the Emperor of the French had imposed upon them. When Louis neglected to enforce orders regarding the exclusion of English goods, Napoleon lost patience and sent troops and customs officers into Holland. As the troops approached Amsterdam, the king abdicated in favor of his son and fled to Germany, happy to be free from the cares of royalty. A few days later the annexation of Holland was proclaimed. With further annexation of a part of northern Germany, including the ports of Hamburg, Bremen, and Lübeck, for the purpose of preventing English goods from entering the Elbe and Weser, Napoleon's empire reached its widest extent. Moreover, Napoleon himself appeared to be at the height of his power. Not only was he the ruler of a France which extended from the North Sea to the Bay of Naples and eastward to the Adriatic; he was also the king of Italy and the protector of the Confederation of the Rhine. Austria and Prussia, the two states of Germany that were not members of the confederation, were tributary to him. His brother Joseph was king of Spain, his brother Jerome was king of Westphalia, and his brother-in-law Murat was king of Naples. In a word, most of continental Europe seemed to be at his feet.

Despite its apparent strength, the Napoleonic Empire was a flimsy structure. It was held together by military force, and any diminution of this support would correspondingly endanger its cohesion. The army was, in fact, no longer the powerful instrument it had been. The great battles, such as Austerlitz, Jena, Eylau, and Friedland, had thinned the ranks of the veterans who had been trained in the wars of the Revolution. More and more the emperor was being compelled to depend on foreign contingents of whose loyalty he could not be certain, and upon youthful inexperienced French conscripts called to arms before they had reached the regular age. Not only was the quality of his troops deteriorating but Napoleon himself was not so alert as he had been earlier in his career. Overwhelmed by work and difficulties, and overconfident by reason of his past victories, he was no longer planning his campaigns so minutely as formerly. What was worse, he was permitting his unbounded ambition to betray him into schemes and plans which his saner judgment would have told him were unsound and dangerous. While he was losing touch with reality and the strength of his army was being impaired, he was meeting with a more determined opposition. In a number of the vassal states a sense of nationality was awakening, and the people were increasingly resenting the domination of a foreign power, the monetary exactions, and the levies of recruits. Moreover, Napoleon's attempt to enforce the Continental System was ruining their commerce and causing widespread economic suffering. This suffering, however, did not seem to disturb the emperor. So determined was he to bring England to its knees that he treated those whose hands touched British goods with great severity. All this roused much hatred against him, causing him to be regarded outside France, Italy, and Belgium as a selfish, insensate tyrant. In short, on all sides the forces were gathering for that great popular insurrection of Europe which was to result in the collapse of Napoleon's colossal empire and in his dethronement.

One country in particular was making ready to free itself from the Napoleonic yoke—Germany. The practical leader of the movement was Prussia. Crushed and humiliated by the treaty of Tilsit, and with much of its territory occupied by French garrisons, Prussia nevertheless began quietly to rebuild its strength. While some leaders were strengthening the Prussian state, others were endeavoring to rouse a feeling of German patriotism. Among the latter was Johann Gottlieb Fichte (1762–1814), who during the winter of 1807–1808 delivered in Berlin his celebrated *Addresses to the German Nation* in which he prophesied a glorious future for the German people. Another prominent figure was the poet Ernst Moritz Arndt (1769–1860), whose fiery hatred of Napoleon impelled him to work unceasingly to awaken a national spirit. Deploring the inertia of the German people, he wrote many stirring poems on the duty of hating Frenchmen and of fighting for the fatherland. One of the most famous of his poems is *What Is the German Fatherland?* In answering the question he said:

> The whole of Germany it must be,
> As far as the German mother-tongue sounds.

In 1809 Frederick William III founded the University of Berlin, which soon became the chief center for the cultivation of German patriotism. Patriotic societies sprang up with branches in many parts of the country. Such a society was the Tugendbund or League of Virtue which, though founded ostensibly for the "revival of morality, religion, serious taste and public spirit," had as its ultimate aim the deliverance not of Prussia alone but of the whole of Germany from the ascendancy of Napoleon. Though this league was dissolved at the bidding of the Emperor of the French on December 31, 1810, its members continued individually to excite the patriotic zeal of the people.

Simultaneously a group of men were busy inaugurating social, political, and military reforms. The leader of this group was Baron vom Stein, whom Frederick William III made his chief minister in October, 1807. Only five days after his appointment Stein submitted for the king's signature the celebrated Emancipation Edict, often called the Prussian Magna Carta, which had previously been drawn up by a reform commission. The purpose of the act was threefold. First, it decreed that "from Martinmas, 1810," all serfs were to be free. Second, it removed the restrictions on the sale of land which hitherto had made it illegal for a nobleman to buy citizen or peasant land and, conversely, for a citizen or peasant to buy noble land. Third, it granted to every citizen a free choice of occupation, thus opening to all the careers which had previously been restricted to certain classes. Another important measure which Baron vom Stein introduced

(November 19, 1808) virtually gave to the townspeople the control of the local government previously exercised by narrow oligarchies or by royal officials appointed without regard to their fitness. But Stein's ministry suddenly came to an end a little more than a year after he had been appointed. A letter containing evidence of his efforts to excite revolt against Napoleon was intercepted by the French police. He therefore resigned rather than bring the vengeance of the "terrible Corsican" on Prussia. A short time later Napoleon proscribed him as a fomenter of disorder in Germany and as an enemy of France, ordering his arrest and the confiscation of his property. Before he could be seized, however, the former Prussian minister found refuge in Austria. His work in Prussia was carried on by his successor, Prince von Hardenberg.

While Stein was introducing his social and political reforms, Scharnhorst was reorganizing the Prussian army. The fundamental idea of his military measures was to make the Prussian army a truly national force. Foreign mercenaries, of which there had long been large numbers in the Prussian army, were dismissed and the universal liability to military service was enforced. This principle had already been established in Prussia by Frederick William I, but the exemptions were so numerous and the foreign enlistments so large that the law was really a dead letter. Now it was decided that national defense was the duty of every able-bodied man. As Marshal Blücher, who was to play a leading part in the overthrow of Napoleon, put it: "No one must be exempted; it must be a disgrace to a man not to have served." To prevent the development of a hostile force Napoleon had decreed that the Prussian army must not be larger than 42,000 men. This restriction was circumvented by replacing the 42,000 with an equal number of new recruits as soon as they had been sufficiently drilled, while the drilling of those who had been dismissed to their homes was continued in secret by sergeants sent out for that purpose. In this way a force three times as large as that permitted by Napoleon was made ready for the inevitable struggle.

THE TURN OF THE TIDE

The event that undermined Napoleon's power was the disastrous Russian campaign of 1812 after his break with Alexander I. For a time after they had concluded the alliance at Tilsit the two emperors worked together in outward harmony. Gradually, however, friction developed from various causes. Napoleon had permitted the Tsar to annex certain areas, but these acquisitions did not slake Alexander's thirst for land. He wanted Constantinople and resented the fact that Napoleon had refused him permission at Tilsit to take it. The incipient breach between the two was widened when Napoleon added territory to the duchy of Warsaw. Having deplored the existence of this duchy from the first, Alexander saw in its enlargement a step toward the restoration of Poland and a menace to his tenure of Polish lands. A third grievance was Napoleon's marriage to Marie Louise of Austria. Since France and Austria were now united by a marriage alliance, the Tsar concluded that he would no longer be permitted to extend his frontiers at the expense of Austria. But the chief cause of the break between the two emperors was the Continental System, the enforcement of which was proving ruinous to the economic interests of Russia. Though still willing to exclude British ships from trading with Russia, the Tsar refused to sacrifice the wealth of his subjects any longer by excluding the ships of neutral countries. Hence at the end of the year 1810 he issued a proclamation which opened the harbors of Russia to all ships sailing under a neutral flag. Moreover, he imposed duties on many French products.

Napoleon, who had already expressed his dissatisfaction over the lukewarm support the Russians had given him in the last war against Austria, now became greatly incensed over the Tsar's virtual abandonment of the Continental System and resolved to reduce Russia to a state of complete submission. Nevertheless, in order to gain time for adequate preparations, he continued to carry on negotiations with the Russians. It was his aim to collect the largest army the world had ever seen. To this end he not only conscripted every possible recruit in France but he also collected auxiliary troops from his empire until he had an army of more than 400,000. Besides the main army there was a secondary force of about 130,000 which was to support the army of invasion and also guard against an uprising in Germany. Numbers are not, however, an accurate indication of the strength of Napoleon's army. Less than half of the total number of troops were French. The rest were auxiliaries who, having been collected from other nations, were often secret enemies of the French. On the other hand, it was a well-equipped army. Napoleon had seen to it that the equipment was complete down to the smallest detail. When all was ready, the vast army was set in motion. At the last moment some of his marshals still tried to dissuade him from undertaking what they regarded as a foolhardy campaign, but their arguments fell on deaf ears.

In June, 1812, the Grand Army crossed the river Niemen, at that time the frontier of Russia. But the Russians did not offer battle. It was their plan to retreat before Napoleon's army and thereby entice it into a desolate country where famine, fatigue, and winter would rob it of whatever advantages it possessed. The plan worked well. Napoleon, eager to overtake the retreating Russians and force them to give battle, pursued them with all possible speed into a country which had been systematically denuded of all supplies. Finally the Russians made a stand at Borodino, about two days' journey from Moscow. By this time the number of men in Napoleon's army had already been decreased by 150,000 through sickness, starvation, desertion, or capture by the Russians. These losses Napoleon hoped to overshadow by a great victory. "Soldiers," he said to his troops, "here is the battle you have so much desired. Victory depends on you. We need one, in order to have abundance, good quarters, and a speedy return to France. Conduct yourselves as at Austerlitz and Friedland." In a stubbornly fought battle Napoleon gained an advantage but neglected to make the most of it, permitting the Russians to retreat in good order. The victory, such as it was, cost Napoleon 30,000 men, while the losses of the Russian army reached nearly 50,000. Thereafter the Russians continued to retreat without venturing another battle and on September 14, 1812, the Grand Army entered Moscow. It found the city abandoned by most of its inhabitants, but there appeared to be a considerable supply of food. Taking possession of the deserted houses, the soldiers hoped at last to enjoy some rest after the terrible march across Russia. But even this was denied them. A fire, probably started by the departing citizens of Moscow, spread until three-fourths of the city together with its stores became prey to the flames. Thus, instead of food and rest, the Grand Army found only flames, famine, and desolation.

Napoleon still nourished one last illusion. Confident that with Moscow in his possession he would be able to conclude an advantageous treaty, he sent flattering letters to the Tsar, expecting overtures for peace in return. September passed into October and still the expected answer did not arrive. With each passing day it was becoming more difficult for the troops to sustain themselves, and then only by foraging in a wider circle. Moreover, the approach of winter was becoming constantly more menacing. At last, after waiting five weeks, Napoleon realized that Alexander had no intention of concluding a treaty. From the first the Tsar had resolved not to make peace so long as a French soldier who was not a prisoner remained on Russian soil. "I would let my beard grow," Alexander is reported to have said, "and go to eat potatoes with the last of my peasants rather than sign the shame of my country and of my beloved people whose sacrifices I know how to prize. Napoleon or I—I or he; for he and I can no longer reign together. I have learned to know him; he will no longer deceive me." This left Napoleon no other choice but to retreat. In an attempt to disguise his failure he decided to return by a southern route. But even this plan was frustrated when the Russian commander, anticipating such a move, sent his army to occupy the road to the south. As the remnants of Napoleon's army started back over the route by which the Grand Army had reached Moscow, the Russians followed in its wake or hung upon its flank, cutting down stragglers and harassing the famished troops in every possible way. To add immeasurably to the hardships of the retreating army, winter set in. The temperature dropped below zero, and every morning would see the stiff forms of soldiers who had frozen to death about their scanty camp fires. Only one thought was in the mind of the survivors; to get out of Russia as quickly as possible. Most of the plunder the soldiers had collected at Moscow and the heavy guns were soon abandoned; and even the sick, wounded, and weary—in short, all those who slowed the progress of the retreating army—were left behind without pity. About the middle of December a disorganized mob of about 20,000 soldiers staggered across the Russian border. It was all that remained of the mighty Grand Army. The rest had deserted or perished, or were prisoners in Russia.

Napoleon himself had left the wreck of his army on December 5 to return to Paris. Traveling night and day, he reached Paris on December 18, and at once threw himself with his old vigor into the task of putting the machinery of government into perfect working order and of reviving the ardor for his cause which had flagged during his absence. His primary concern, as always, was the army. He did not doubt for a moment, it seems, that he could build another army to replace the one that had been destroyed in Russia; in fact he had already announced that he would be back on the Niemen with a force of 300,000 men in the spring. As the ordinary conscription of 1813 yielded only 140,000 men, many who had formerly been exempted were called and also the conscripts of 1814. By May 1 Napoleon again had an army of more than 300,000 in Germany, but it was composed largely of unseasoned recruits, many of them being mere lads of seventeen. Though not lacking in bravery, these young recruits were inferior to their predecessors in solidity and endurance.

THE WAR OF LIBERATION

While Napoleon was working feverishly to raise a new army, developments of the greatest importance were taking place outside France. Alexander I, having attained his purpose of driving Napoleon's army out of Russia, decided to liberate Europe from the Napoleonic yoke. He soon found an ally in Prussia. In February, 1813, the two nations signed a treaty in which they promised not to lay down their arms until "the independence of Europe" had been achieved. The next month Prussia officially declared the war which is called the War of Liberation because Prussia had been so long under the domination of Napoleon. All the other German princes were urged to join the alliance against France on the threat of being deprived of their states. The Confederation of the Rhine was declared dissolved and a general uprising was organized in some of the states that had belonged to it. Austria, however, still remained neutral, waiting to see the results of the first battles before deciding whether to join with Napoleon or with the allies.

The military operations of the war began after Napoleon joined his army on the Elbe toward the end of April for the immediate purpose of taking Leipzig. To prevent this the allied army marched against him, the two forces meeting in battle on May 2 at Lützen, near the historic field on which Gustavus Adolphus had met his death. Inspired by the words and the presence of their emperor, the untried troops of Napoleon fought so bravely that they remained masters of the field. Yet the

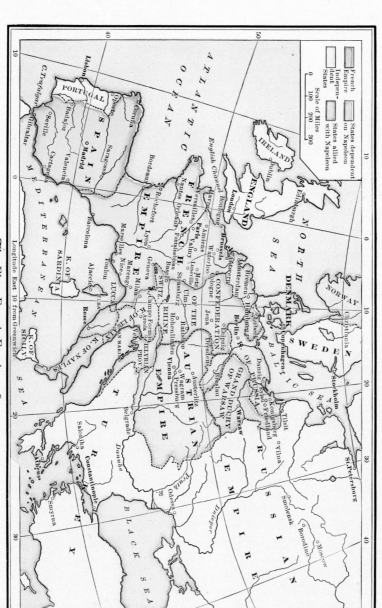

The First French Empire, 1812

victory was as expensive as it was indecisive, for it cost Napoleon
12,000 men. Three weeks later a second battle was fought at
Bautzen, with the French troops again forcing the allies to retreat.
But the opposition was growing stronger. In August, 1813,
Napoleon's father-in-law, the Emperor Francis, cast his lot
with the allies after Napoleon had rejected the peace terms
presented to him by the Austrian minister Metternich. Bonaparte
was now menaced from three sides by armies whose movements
were directed by two generals who had formerly served under
him: Bernadotte, now the "crown prince" of Sweden, and
Moreau, who had been exiled from France for participating in a
plot against the government. Before the allied forces closed in
on him, Napoleon managed to win another victory at Dresden,
but at Leipzig (October 16–19) it was another story. In this
battle, sometimes called the "Battle of the Nations," which lasted
three days, he lost the best part of his army. At nightfall on the
third day the "invincible" Corsican ordered a retreat which
turned into a rout the next day. The remnant of the army retreated across Germany and, after defeating the Bavarians who
were trying to check the retreat, sought safety beyond the Rhine.

During the months after the battle of Leipzig the vast empire
Napoleon had built collapsed completely. While the Prussians
were forcing the French garrisons to surrender the fortresses they
held in Prussia, the other states of Germany followed the example
of Bavaria which had earlier deserted Napoleon to join the allies.
Soon Jerome Bonaparte was forced to leave Westphalia, and
Germany was entirely free of French rule. In November the
Dutch openly rebelled against Napoleon, recalled the prince of
Orange, and with the help of the English recovered the fortresses
held by the French. Also most of Italy was soon free of the domination of Napoleon. In the north the Austrians defeated the
French army and drove it back to the Adige; in the Papal States
the pope, whom Napoleon had released after a long period of
strict surveillance, resumed the rule; and in Naples King Murat
deserted Napoleon's cause in an effort to save his throne. Meanwhile in Spain Wellington had taken Pampeluna and forced the
French army to retire beyond the Pyrenees. So widespread was
the change that Napoleon himself exclaimed: "The continent
marched with France last year; this year the continent is marching with England." Not much more than the France of Louis XVI

remained of the vast empire. And in France itself discontent was beginning to manifest itself in several provinces.

Though his empire had collapsed, Napoleon still had the opportunity to save for himself a larger France than that over which the Bourbons had ruled. The victory of Leipzig had brought the allies to the Rhine, but they hesitated to advance into France, for even after Leipzig the military reputation of Napoleon still inspired respect. The allies also feared that a great national uprising such as had taken place in 1793 might result if France were invaded. Furthermore, neither Austria nor England desired to exalt Russia unduly by weakening France. Hence Metternich, with the support of the representatives of England and Prussia, notified the French ambassador that the powers would regard Napoleon's acceptance of the natural boundaries of France (the Rhine, the Alps, and the Pyrenees) a basis for peace. Despite the fact that he was threatened with complete ruin on all sides, Bonaparte did not send a forthright answer to the proposal. He still trusted that some turn of fortune would permit him to make larger demands. It was a vain hope. When the proposal was not promptly accepted, the allies decided to continue the war. The opening of the year 1814 saw Blücher cross the Rhine with a Prussian army, while an army of Russians and Austrians under the command of Schwarzenberg entered France through Switzerland. To stem the tide of invasion Napoleon had at most a force of about 80,000, hardly a third as large as the force of the allies. But the difference did not lie only in numbers. Napoleon's troops were also inferior in quality and equipment.

Yet with his conscripted boys Napoleon fought one of his most brilliant campaigns in a desperate effort to avert ultimate disaster. Time and again he turned back the invaders or held his own against superior numbers. In February he won ten battles in twenty days, but defeat was inevitable. His best efforts were not sufficient to stop the advance of the allies on Paris. Early on March 30 the combined forces of Schwarzenberg and Blücher attacked the capital. After a resistance of only a few hours the city capitulated and on the next day the Tsar and the king of Prussia triumphantly entered the city at the head of their troops. The reception which the people of Paris gave them was on the whole friendly. As the monarchs rode along the boulevards they were hailed by many with shouts of "Vive Alexander!" and "Vive le Roi de Prusse!"

Mingled with these greetings were cries of "Vive le roi!" and "Vivent les Bourbons!"[1] All this encouraged the allied rulers to issue a declaration which stated that they would not treat with Napoleon or with any member of his family. Meanwhile Bonaparte himself was at Fontainebleau making plans to drive the allies out of Paris. He did not regard his situation as hopeless so long as the army remained faithful to him. But his marshals, who saw the futility of trying to continue the fighting with a handful of raw troops, persuaded him to sign an abdication. A week later Napoleon set his signature to the settlement which gave him sovereign rights over the island of Elba, while Marie Louise received the Italian duchy of Parma. As the fallen emperor traveled southward through France to embark for Elba the most vile insults, and even threats of physical harm, were hurled at him. The former idol of the people had become the "Corsican Ogre."

THE RESTORATION OF THE BOURBONS

Four days after the dethronement of Napoleon the Bourbons were recalled. The little Louis XVII, as the son of Louis XVI was styled by the royalists, having succumbed in prison, the succession passed to the count of Provence, who called himself Louis XVIII. But the Bourbons did not return as monarchs by divine right. In the statement which recalled them it was carefully stated that "the French people voluntarily calls to the throne of France, Louis Stanislas Xavier, brother of the last king, and, after him, the members of the house of Bourbon." On May 2, 1814, the new king entered Paris after having issued an edict on the previous day in which he promised to give the country a constitution. His appearance would not evoke admiration. An infirm old man of sixty with heavy features and a sharp expression, he was so unwieldy in size and so crippled by gout that he could hardly move without assistance. Mentally, however, he was a man of considerable intelligence and scholarly tastes, and in so far as he had any principles, they were moderate. But a series of measures dictated by the reactionary party soon alienated public opinion from his government. For one thing, the substitution of the white flag for the tricolor irritated both the peasants and the soldiers; the former associated all the evils of the Old Régime, such as tithes and seigno-

---

[1] This display of enthusiasm, it appears, was largely stage-managed by a coterie of royalists under the leadership of Talleyrand to insure the restoration of the Bourbons.

, rial rights, with the white flag, and the soldiers disliked the change because they had carried the tricolor into battle for more than two decades.

A second grievance of the army against the government was the fact that soon after fourteen thousand officers had been retired on half pay for economic reasons, a multitude of returned émigrés, many of whom had fought against France, were given high positions in the army and in the navy. This return of the émigrés to their place at the court, as if there had been no Revolution, was widely resented, particularly when they began to clamor for the restitution of their confiscated estates. Soon the hundreds of thousands of peasants who had purchased these lands from the state, began to regret the restoration of the Bourbons. To be sure, the constitution promulgated on June 4, 1814, guaranteed the possession of all lands that had been purchased from the state; and it also provided for individual liberty and gave to the people a larger share in legislation than Napoleon had granted them. But the acts of the king made his subjects suspicious of the sincerity of his promises to uphold the constitution. Moreover, Louis was tactless enough to refer to himself as king "by the grace of God," thereby giving sustenance to the rumors that absolute monarchy and feudalism would soon be reëstablished.

While the government of Louis XVIII was making large sections of the population regret the restoration of the Bourbons, the allies were wrangling at Vienna over the division of Europe. The great powers were so divided in their aims and desires that there was little agreement on anything. Alexander I had come to the Congress with the avowed purpose of securing the whole of Poland, intending to set it up as a separate state with himself as king. Prussia, at first opposed to the Tsar's project, was won over by Alexander's proposal to hand over to Frederick William the whole of Saxony. To thwart the plans of these two nations soon became the primary purpose of the other powers. Whereas England worked against a preponderance of Russia, Austria looked with alarm on the growing power of both Russia and Prussia. Talleyrand, who represented France, immediately aligned himself with Austria and England against the Russo-Prussian combination. Matters went so far that the representatives of France, England, and Austria signed an agreement to resort to war, if necessary, in defense of their principles. Upon hearing of this secret treaty the Tsar became

more moderate in his demands, but just as the spirit of compromise
was beginning to prevail the Congress was startled by the news
that Napoleon had left Elba.

THE HUNDRED DAYS

Ever since his abdication the former Emperor of the French
had cherished the project of regaining his throne. From Elba he
had carefully watched events in Europe, waiting for the propitious
hour. He knew of the growing unpopularity of the Bourbon rule in
France and he was also informed of the dissensions among the
powers at Vienna. The latest report led him to believe that the differences between the great nations were such as to prevent a peaceful settlement. Carefully weighing all the factors for and against
the success of an attempt to regain the throne, he concluded that
his chances were good. With his guard of about eleven hundred
men he embarked on a flotilla of seven ships and on March 1
reached the shores of France near Cannes.

Next day the little band of invaders started on the celebrated
march to Paris. Instead of passing through Toulon and Marseilles,
which he knew to be fiercely royalist, Napoleon went northward
toward Lyons. At first he was received coldly, but as the march
progressed there was more and more enthusiasm in his behalf.
Regiment after regiment of French soldiers joined him, so that he
was soon at the head of a considerable force. At Grenoble he announced that he had "come to save France from the outrages of
the returning nobles; to secure to the peasant the possession of his
land; to uphold the rights won in 1789 against a minority which is
seeking to reëstablish the privileges of caste and the feudal burdens
of the last century." The proclamation proved effective in that it
won both the peasants and the workingmen for his cause. Before
he reached Lyons he declared the Bourbons deposed and then
formally resumed the functions of emperor. As Napoleon approached Paris Louis XVIII, realizing the hopelessness of his
cause, departed for the frontier. The next evening Bonaparte
entered the Tuileries. He had, as he later boasted, regained the
throne without shedding a drop of blood.

At the news of the return of Napoleon to France all the discord
between the powers at Vienna ceased and a proclamation was
issued which outlawed him as "a common enemy and disturber
of the peace of the world." This declaration was followed by a

renewal of the treaty of Chaumont concluded in March, 1814, whereby the four nations (Russia, England, Austria, and Prussia) had pledged themselves not to lay down their arms, except by common consent, until the object of the war was attained. Each nation promised to furnish 150,000 men and it was decided that Wellington and Blücher, the commanders respectively of the English and Prussian armies, were to invade France through the Netherlands, while the Tsar and Schwarzenberg with the Russian and Austrian troops were to advance from the middle and upper Rhine. All were firm in the resolve not to treat with Napoleon. They refused even to listen to his offer to observe the treaties they had made with the Bourbons and to his avowals that he desired only peace.

In France the restored emperor was exerting the most strenuous efforts to prepare for the war. He believed that the allies would be unable to open the campaign before the middle of July, but early in June the armies of Blücher and Wellington were approaching the frontier through Belgium. Hence Bonaparte was compelled to start the war before his own preparations were completed. His plan was to attack and defeat the Prussian and British armies separately before they could unite. With his army of about 130,000 he succeeded in winning two indecisive victories over the Prussians; then came Waterloo. Wellington, who had fallen back to Waterloo to await Napoleon's attack, received a message from Blücher that he would join the English general for the battle. Napoleon, having neglected to watch carefully the movements of Blücher, was unaware of his exact whereabouts; hence he made the grievous error of assuming that the Prussians were too far away to join the British.

When the battle began on Sunday, June 18, Wellington adopted defensive tactics while waiting for Blücher's arrival, throwing back the French attacks time and again. All day the British squares stood like an irresistible wall. Then, with the arrival of Blücher late in the afternoon, the Anglo-Prussian forces took the offensive. So determined was their onslaught that the French gave way, taking to their heels with the allies hard in pursuit. Failing to rally his forces, Napoleon hastened to Paris, arriving on June 21. He was still hopeful, but when he saw that he had lost control of the government, he abdicated the next day in favor of his son. On the approach of the British and Prussian armies, he went to Rochefort, there, if possible, to board a ship for the United States. Instead, finding it impossible to evade the vigilance of the British cruisers that were blockading the port, he surrendered to the captain of the English man-of-war *Bellerophon*. It was well for him that he did so. In France his life would not have been safe, and had he fallen into the hands of the Prussians they might have carried out Blücher's threat to execute him.

ST. HELENA AND AFTER

This time the allies decided to put him where he could not again return to cause further wars and bloodshed. The place chosen for his custody was the island of St. Helena, approximately 1200 miles off the west coast of Africa. There Napoleon lived until his death on May 5, 1821, of cancer of the stomach. In his will the ex-emperor had written: "I desire that my ashes repose on the banks of the Seine in the midst of the French people whom I have loved so dearly." This wish remained unfulfilled for nineteen years, when his remains were conveyed to Paris and laid to rest in the vault of the Invalides.

Though Napoleon the man was dead, Napoleon the demi-god was being born. The captivity and death of the "Little Corporal" formed the starting point of the Napoleonic legend which presented an ideal Napoleon who had unselfishly striven for the good of his subjects and of mankind. After the reports, largely fictitious, of the petty persecutions he suffered at the hands of the English governor of St. Helena had begun to evoke sympathy for the exile on the tiny ocean-girdled island, popular song and story lent their aid in weaving about him the halo of martyrdom. Hatred of the self-seeking tyrant soon gave way to pity for the "Prometheus chained to the rock"—a pity that effaced the memory of the long years of war and bloodshed which had been caused by Napoleon's insane ambition. Napoleon himself made the most of his captivity to prepare his own apotheosis. In a conscious effort to influence posterity he not only presented a glorified account of his campaigns in his conversations, which were daily recorded, and in the memoirs he dictated, but he also represented himself as the unselfish friend of peace, liberty, and national rights. Had he not, he asked, saved the Revolution and maintained its principles? "I sowed liberty with both hands," he said, "wherever I instituted the Civil Code." In his efforts to idealize himself he did not even hesitate to compare himself with the crucified Christ. Consequently St. Helena became a sort of Golgotha for those upon whom the Napoleonic legend cast its spell. After the exile's death the gospel of Napoleon "the friend and savior of the people" was carried into many lands, winning numberless converts. In France, where the people were dissatisfied with the government, it was so widely accepted that Napoleon's nephew found it possible to resurrect the French Empire and ascend the imperial throne as Napoleon III.

Today, more than a century after his death, the "great Corsican" still fascinates the imagination of mankind. He spoke the truth when he said: "What a romance my life has been!" His rise to power, his precipitous fall, and his "romantic" end are still subjects of unfailing interest. Because of the wide interest in his personality and career there has been a constant stream of literature dealing with his life. Probably more books have been written about him than about any other figure of modern times. But despite the light that has been projected on him he still remains something of a mystery. Not one biographer has succeeded in solving completely "the riddle of Napoleon." Most of them agree, however, that he was a man of extraordinary talents; that in him were concentrated diversity of practical abilities, force of will, intensity of ambition, keenness of vision, and tireless energy in such a degree as in few other individuals of history. By the unsparing use of his natural gifts he developed an efficiency that was adequate, up to a certain point, for the needs of the time. More than this, by his peculiar ability to stir the imagination of men he was able to attract to himself the enthusiasm and devotion the Revolution had evoked. These two factors, supported by good fortune, furnish the key to Napoleon's success. They made it possible for him to take the Revolution at flood tide and turn it to his own account.

It was his efficiency and his ability to command the devotion of his troops that made possible his unrivaled military career. Thus his knowledge of how Toulon might be taken attracted attention to him, and his "efficiency" in defending the Convention opened the way for his attainment of the command of the Army of Italy. The most remarkable feature of his military strategy was not its originality, for most of his favorite manoeuvres can be found in the military writings of the eighteenth century, but the manner of its execution. Besides a prodigious knowledge of detail Napoleon brought to his military tasks the ability to think clearly, to arrive at a decision quickly, and to carry out the decision with equal rapidity. Marshal Foch, avowed pupil of Napoleon, said: "General-in-chief at the age of twenty-seven, he already knew everything that had been written and done before him in the military art. Having sought out its principles with the help of his rare natural talent, he did more than learn, he understood events and grasped what had to be done under new conditions."[1] Napoleon was to his troops, with whom he shared the dangers and toils of war, nothing less than a god. Their affection and devotion contributed much toward making it possible for him to achieve results which at times bordered on the miraculous. In a "Eulogy" delivered at the Invalides on the centenary of Napoleon's death (May 5, 1921) Marshal Foch declared: "He remains the Great Captain, superior to all others by his prodigious genius." Regarding the fall of Napoleon, Foch said that he "succumbed, not for lack of genius but for having essayed the impossible, for having undertaken, with a France exhausted in every fiber, to bend to his will a Europe which had already learned from misfortune and was soon to stand together in arms against him."

The abilities he demonstrated as a general also characterize Napoleon the administrator. In the words of Lord Rosebery: "He controlled every wheel and spring, large or small, of his vast machinery of government. It was, as it were, his plaything. He was his own War Office, his own Foreign Office, his own Admiralty, his own ministry of every kind. . . . His financial management by which he sustained a vast empire with power and splendor, but with rigid economy, and without a debt, is a marvel and a mystery. In all the offices of state he knew everything, guided everything, inspired everything."[2]

Napoleon's character as a man was not equal, however, to his ability as a general or a statesman. He was not above petty deceits, deep-seated hatreds, and outbursts of brutality. At no time after his rise to power did he permit himself to be bound by a moral code. To one who dared remonstrate with him he said:

---

[1] Cited by Wickham Steed in "Foch and Napoleon: Pupil and Master," *Review of Reviews*, vol. 78 (1929), p. 280.

[2] *Napoleon, the Last Phase*, p. 251. To Lord Rosebery's statement one might add the remark that the expenses of Napoleon's government and of his wars were paid to a large extent by the countries he occupied.

"I am no ordinary man, and the laws of propriety and morals are not applicable to me." Most frequently he regarded the good of others in the light of his own goal—a goal that can largely be summed up in the word "self-aggrandizement." For the satisfaction of his selfish ambitions he carried on wars that caused untold sufferings and cost millions of lives. Though in his youth he was nauseated by the sight of blood, later he became so callous that he could regard the battlefield at Borodino, covered with wounded, dying, and dead, as the finest sight he had seen. Great as were his potentialities for the progress of civilization, they came to little because he was unable to curb his insane ambitions. His most permanent direct contribution was the Code. Most of his other achievements vanished with his fall. His vast empire, which carried the frontiers of France to Hamburg and Trieste, collapsed even before his fall. Of all the territorial changes he made only two were permanent: the annexation of the Swiss district of the Valteline to the Cisalpine (Italian) Republic (1797), and the sale of Louisiana to the United States (1803). Thus Napoleon falls short when the test of creativeness is applied to him. On the whole, he destroyed more than he created. Yet his destruction was not an unmixed evil, for among the things he swept away were class barriers and feudal vexations. He also prepared the way for the unification of both Germany and Italy. In Germany he amalgamated so many of the little states that the settlement of 1815 saw only thirty-nine sovereign princes and free cities in place of the old Holy Roman Empire with its three hundred fifty states. In Italy he exercised a direct influence on the growth of a national spirit by telling the people that they must rise from local to national feelings. After all has been said, there is perhaps no better short characterization of Napoleon than that of de Tocqueville: "He was as great as a man can be without virtue."

Appendix

SELECT BIBLIOGRAPHY

RULERS OF EUROPEAN STATES

Select Bibliography

Aids to the study of history. An excellent introductory volume to the study of history is Allan Nevins' *Gateway to history* (1938), which brings out the richer meanings of history and explains its objects and difficulties. Other useful volumes are Allen Johnson's *The historian and historical evidence* (1926), F. J. Teggart's *Theory of history* (1925), H. E. Barnes' *The new history and the social studies* (1925), and Lucy M. Salmon's *Historical material* (1933). Concise accurate outlines of European history may be found in K. J. Ploetz's *Manual of universal history*, translated and enlarged by W. H. Tillinghast, revised under the editorship of H. E. Barnes, with the collaboration of A. H. Imlah, T. P. Peardon, and J. H. Wuorinen (1925).

Bibliographical aids. Invaluable for the general student is *A guide to historical literature* (1931), edited by G. M. Dutcher, H. R. Shipman, S. B. Fay, and others, which contains a selected and classified bibliography of the whole field of history, with critical notes by specialists. For materials on German history there is the classic *Quellenkunde der deutschen Geschichte* (9th ed., 1931) of F. C. Dahlmann and G. Waitz, which lists both sources and secondary works. For British history there are the two excellent volumes of the *Bibliography of British history: Tudor period, 1485–1603*, edited by Conyers Read (1933), and *Stuart period, 1603–1714*, edited by Godfrey Davies (1928). A third important volume is Clyde L. Grose's *Select bibliography of British history, 1660–1760* (1939), which also contains many helpful critical notes. An equally useful work is Judith B. Williams' *Guide to the printed materials for English social and economic history, 1750–1850* (2 vols., 1927). For the history of France there are H. Hauser's *Sources de l'histoire de France, 1494–1610* (4 vols., 1906–15) and E. Bourgeois and L. André's *Sources de l'histoire de France, 1610–1715* (5 vols., 1913–26). Other aids include (for Spain) B. Sánchez Alonso's *Fuentes de la historia española e hispanoamericana* (2nd rev. ed., 1927), R. Ballester y Castell's *Bibliografía de la historia de España* (1921), and S. Aguado Bleye's *Manual de historia de España* (2 vols., 1927–28); (for Italy) E. Calvi's *Biblioteca di bibliografia storica italiana* (1903–07);

(for Slavic history) R. J. Kerner's *Slavic Europe: a selected bibliography in the western European languages, comprising history, languages and literatures* (1918); (for Sweden) Samuel E. Bring's *Bibliografisk Handbok till Sveriges Historia* (1934).

For periodical literature. The two most useful indexes for periodicals in English and for a select list of foreign periodicals are the *Readers' guide to periodical literature* (1900 ff.) and the *International index to periodicals* (1907 ff.). Invaluable for nineteenth century periodicals is *Poole's index to periodical literature* (1899 ff.). A comprehensive index for German periodicals is the *Bibliographie der deutschen Zeitschriftenliteratur* (1897 ff.). There is a French periodical index covering the years 1897–99, entitled *Répertoire bibliographique des principales revues françaises* (3 vols., 1898–1900), which was unfortunately discontinued. For the fine arts and education see the *Art index: a cumulative author and subject index to a selected list of the fine arts* (1929 ff.) and the *Education index: a cumulative author and subject index to a selected list of educational periodicals, books and pamphlets* (1929 ff.).

Historical atlases. William R. Shepherd's *Historical atlas* (7th ed., 1929) is a good atlas for both school and home use. Ramsay Muir and George Philip's *Historical atlas* (10th ed., 1929) and C. Grant Robertson and J. G. Bartholomew's *Historical atlas of modern Europe* (2nd rev. ed., 1924) have accompanying text passages which explain the maps. Another useful work is the *Cambridge modern history atlas* (2nd ed., 1925), edited by A. W. Ward and G. W. Prothero (*Cambridge modern history*, vol. 14).

Encyclopedias. The most authoritative reference work for the social sciences is the *Encyclopedia of the social sciences* (15 vols., 1929–35), a monumental work which includes articles by outstanding scholars from all parts of the world. Noteworthy among the standard general encyclopedias in English are the *Encyclopaedia Britannica* (14th ed., 25 vols., 1929, supplemented annually by a bulletin called *The world of today;* less modern but more extensive and detailed is the 11th ed., 29 vols., 1910–11), the *Encyclopedia Americana* (30 vols., 1932), and the *New international encyclopedia* (2nd ed., 23 vols., 1926–27). In addition to the encyclopedias in English there are others in all the major languages of Europe. Useful for the history of religion are the *Encyclopedia of religion and ethics* (12 vols., 1922), the *Catholic encyclopedia* (17 vols., 1928), the *Jewish encyclopedia* (12 vols., 1901–06), and *The new Schaff-Herzog encyclopedia of religious knowledge* (30 vols., 1908–14). Monroe's *Cyclopedia of education* (5 vols., 1911–13) is out of date in many respects but still useful for the history of education. For biography the *Dictionary of national biography* (21 vols., 1885–1922, with supplementary volumes for the period to 1930) and the *Allgemeine deutsche Biographie* (56 vols., 1875–1912) are valuable and in some instances indispensable for England and Germany respectively. A French dictionary of national biography which promises to be more extensive than the foregoing is the new *Dictionnaire de biographie française,* of which vols. 1 and 2 and part of vol. 3 have appeared (1933–39). An older work which, as the title indicates, is not limited to France is Michaud's *Biographie universelle* (45 vols., 1843–65).

General works. Among the longer works which cover the period from the Renaissance to 1815 there is the *Cambridge modern history,* planned by Lord

Acton, edited by A. W. Ward, G. W. Prothero, and S. Leathes (14 vols., 1902–12), with extensive bibliographies; still an authoritative survey. *The rise of modern Europe*, edited by W. L. Langer (of which vols. 1, 12–14, and 16 have appeared, 1932–38), will when completed offer a scholarly up-to-date survey of modern history. H. A. L. Fisher's *History of Europe* (3 vols., 1935) is illuminating, swift-moving, and well-written. *European civilization: its origin and development* (6 vols., 1934–37), edited by Edward Eyre, contains some excellent studies but lacks cohesion; its general viewpoint is Catholic. *Periods of European history* (9 vols., 1927–32), edited by A. Hassall, is a good survey of the political history of the continental states from 476 to 1920. In French there is the sound, objective, and readable longer survey, *Histoire générale du 4ᵉ siècle à nos jours* (12 vols., 1893–1904), edited by E. Lavisse and A. Rambaud. In German there is the comprehensive and scholarly series, *Allgemeine Geschichte in Einzeldarstellungen* (50 vols., 1879–93), edited by Wilhelm Oncken.

General works on cultural history. J. H. Randall's *Making of the modern mind* (1926) is an interesting, well-written, provocative survey. Lynn Thorndike's *Short history of civilization* (1926) offers a sound and compact sketch of the broader aspects of civilization from primitive to modern times. Preserved Smith's *History of modern culture:* vol. 1, *The great renewal, 1543–1687* (1930); vol. 2, *The enlightenment, 1687–1776* (1934) is judicious and well-balanced; a mine of solid information. Egon Friedell's *Cultural history of the modern age*, translated from the German by C. F. Atkinson (3 vols., 1930–32), is often vivid and penetrating, often superficial and diffuse; it stresses the unity of periods rather than the continuity of history, and is popular rather than scholarly. Harry E. Barnes' *Intellectual and cultural history of the western world* (1937) contains a wealth of facts but lacks integration. In the field of art Helen Gardner's *Art through the ages* (1926) is a standard handbook. A second good survey is Solomon Reinach's *Apollo*, translated by F. Simmonds (new ed., 1924); it is profusely illustrated. J. Pijoan's *History of art*, translated by R. L. Roys (3 vols., 1927), offers a more comprehensive and more detailed survey.

General works on economic history. *Economic history of Europe*, part 2 (1928), by M. M. Knight, H. E. Barnes, and F. Flügel, and *Economic development of modern Europe*, by F. A. Ogg and W. R. Sharp (1926), offer good brief surveys of the economic history of the period from the Renaissance to 1815. W. Cunningham's *Essay on western civilization in its economic aspects* (2 vols., 1898–1900) sketches the history of the economic development of modern Europe along broad lines. Herbert Heaton's *Economic history of Europe* (1936) is a recent textbook, written in a vigorous style, which contains an excellent short account of the period from 1500 to 1815, and extensive reading lists. Clive Day's *History of commerce* (new ed., 1922) is a sound, comprehensive, and readable textbook. N. S. B. Gras's *History of agriculture in Europe and America* (1925) is a useful handbook. For the rise of the middle class there is Frederick C. Palm's interesting survey, *The middle classes: then and now* (1936).

Nationalism and nationality. Carlton J. H. Hayes' *Essays in nationalism* (1926) is a penetrating study of the factors which have contributed to the growth of the national idea and of nationalism. The different types of modern nationalism are subjected to a careful analysis in the same author's *Historical evolution of modern nationalism* (1931). An able survey in German of the development of the national idea is W. Mitscherlich's *Der Nationalismus Westeuropas* (1920). George C. Powers' *Nationalism at the council of Constance, 1414–1418* (1927) contains much useful information, but lacks integration. For further references see K. S. Pinson's excellent *Bibliographical introduction to nationalism* (1935), with brief discussions of the works listed.

CHAPTER ONE

The Rise of National States

General. E. P. Cheyney's *Dawn of a new era, 1250–1453* (1936; vol. 1 of *The rise of modern Europe*, edited by W. L. Langer) is a work of careful scholarship and literary excellence, with a critical bibliography. A. F. Pollard's *Factors in modern history* (new ed., 1926) is a readable and stimulating book which deals chiefly with England but is valuable for the early period in general. V. Marcu's *Birth of nations, from the unity of faith to the democracy of money*, translated by Eden and Cedar Paul (1932), fails to do justice to its subject; it is superficial, turgid, ill-balanced. The political history of the period is well presented in R. Lodge's *Close of the Middle Ages, 1273–1494* (1928) and A. H. Johnson's *Europe in the sixteenth century, 1494–1598* (1928; vols. 3 and 4 of *Periods of European history*, edited by A. Hassall). W. T. Waugh's *History of Europe, 1378–1494* (1932) and A. J. Grant's *History of Europe, 1494–1610* (1932; vols. 4 and 5 of Methuen's *History of medieval and modern Europe*) present fresh treatments of the period in a pleasant style, with considerable attention to non-political matters. The last volume (vol. 8, 1936) of the *Cambridge medieval history* is devoted mainly to the fifteenth century. J. Huizinga's *Waning of the Middle Ages* is an original and challenging study of the temper of the fifteenth century. J. W. Thompson's *Economic and social history in the later Middle Ages* (1931) contains some illuminating chapters on the fifteenth century. J. W. Allen's *History of political thought in the sixteenth century* (1928) is a stimulating book.

Spain. The standard authority in English on Spanish history to the death of Philip II is R. B. Merriman's *The rise of the Spanish empire in the old world and in the new* (4 vols., 1918–34), of which vol. 1 covers the Middle Ages and vol. 2 the reign of the "Catholic kings." Among the shorter general histories C. E. Chapman's *History of Spain* (1918) is one of the best. Other useful surveys are *The history of Spain* by L. Bertrand and Sir Charles Petrie (1934), *Spain, a short history of its politics, literature, and art from the earliest times to the present*, by H. D. Sedgwick (1925), and *The Spanish people, their origin, growth, and influence*, by M. A. S. Hume (1901). A useful handbook is E. A. Peers' *Spain, a companion to Spanish studies* (1929), with extensive bibliographies at the end of each chapter. For the history of Spanish civilization there is the volume by the eminent Spanish histo-

rian, Rafael Altamira, entitled *A history of Spanish civilization,* translated
by P. Volkov (1930). The civilization of both Spain and Portugal is the
subject of a brilliant essay by the Portuguese historian, Oliviera Martins,
translated by A. F. G. Bell under the title *A history of Iberian civilization*
(1930). Edward D. Salmon's *Imperial Spain* (1931; Berkshire series) contains a readable succinct survey of the reigns of Ferdinand and Isabella,
Charles V, and Philip II.

There is a good short survey of the reign of Ferdinand and Isabella in
the *Cambridge modern history,* vol. I (1912), pp. 347–383. W. H. Prescott's
History of the reign of Ferdinand and Isabella the Catholic, edited by W. H.
Munro (4 vols., 1904), still makes delightful reading but is antiquated in
its scholarship. J. H. Mariejol's *Espagne sous Ferdinand et Isabelle: le gouvernement, les institutions, et les moeurs* (1892) is the best survey of the period.
A clear and interesting study of the life and work of Isabella is Irene L.
Plunket's *Isabel of Castile and the making of the Spanish nation, 1451–1504*
(1919). W. T. Walsh's *Isabella of Spain, the last crusader* (1930) is uncritical.
Useful for a study of this period is M. A. S. Hume's *Spain, its greatness
and decay, 1479–1788* (3rd ed., revised by E. Armstrong, 1931). An invaluable
book for a knowledge of the religious and intellectual history of the period
is R. Merton's *Cardinal Ximenes and the making of Spain* (1935). The first
chapters of R. T. Davies' *The golden century of Spain, 1501–1621* (1937)
offer an interesting and readable account of the last years of the reign of
Ferdinand and Isabella. H. C. Lea's *History of the inquisition in Spain*
(4 vols., 1906–07) is a work of solid scholarship. F. D. Mocatta's *The Jews
of Spain and Portugal and the inquisition* (1928) is a good account of the
subject written by a Jewish historian. For a brief account of Jewish life in
Spain the student may consult Salo W. Baron's *Social and religious history
of the Jews* (3 vols., 1937); the best history of Jewish civilization through the
ages, a work of thorough scholarship. Valeriu Marcu's *Expulsion of the Jews
from Spain,* translated from the German by M. Firth (1935), is superficial. A
valuable collection of source materials has been published by Fritz Baer under
the title *Die Juden im christlichen Spanien: Urkunden und Regesten* (2 vols.,
1936). Books on the Moors are listed in the bibliography for Chapter Ten.

Portugal. Among the shorter histories of Portugal in English H. M.
Stephens' *Portugal* (4th ed., 1908), with a continuation by M. A. S. Hume,
is still the best. For Portuguese civilization there is the aforementioned *History of Iberian civilization* by Oliviera Martins (1930). Another excellent work
by the same author is *The golden age of Prince Henry the Navigator,* translated by J. J. Abraham and W. E. Reynolds (1914). G. Young's *Portugal old
and young* (1917) is marked by a strong anti-Spanish and anti-clerical bias.
For the Portuguese inquisition see A. Herculano's *History of the origin and
establishment of the inquisition in Portugal,* translated by J. C. Branner (1926).
For further references on Portugal see the bibliography for Chapter Four.

France. Good introductory volumes to the history of France are C. Seignobos' *The evolution of the French people,* translated from the French by
Catherine A. Phillips (1932), J. Bainville's *History of France,* translated
by A. and C. Gauss (1926), H. D. Sedgwick's *France, a short history of its
politics, literature and art from the earliest times to the present* (1929), and

P. Van Dyke's *Story of France* (1928). Arthur J. Grant's *French monarchy, 1483–1789* (2 vols., 4th ed., 1920) is a good readable survey of the political, military, and diplomatic history of the period. C. A. H. Guignebert's *Short history of the French people*, translated by F. G. Richmond (2 vols., 1930), is lively and up-to-date but marred by errors and inaccuracies and by a patriotic bias. A longer reliable, though somewhat dry, survey of French history is G. W. Kitchin's *History of France* (3 vols., 4th rev. ed., 1899–1903). More spirited but less accurate is J. R. M. MacDonald's *History of France* (3 vols., 1915). The standard longer history in French is the *Histoire de France depuis les origines jusqu'à la révolution*, a coöperative work edited by E. Lavisse (9 vols. in 18, 1900–11). A topical treatment of French history (literature, science, diplomacy, political history, etc.) may be found in the *Histoire de la nation française* by a group of eminent French historians, edited by G. Hanotaux (15 vols., 1920–24). An invaluable work for the early modern period is J. S. C. Bridge's *History of France from the death of Louis XI* (5 vols., 1921–36) covering the period from 1483 to 1515. A good biography of Louis XI in English is Pierre Champion's *Louis XI*, translated and adapted by Winifred S. Whale (1929). There is also a useful older biography (1907) by Christopher Hare (pseudonym for Marian Andrews).

England. Authoritative larger histories of England include W. Hunt and R. L. Poole's *Political history of England* (12 vols., 1906–13) and Oman's *History of England* (7 vols., 1904–13; various new editions). *Social England*, edited by H. D. Traill and J. S. Mann (6 vols., 1897–1904), contains a wealth of information on English social and economic life. Noteworthy among the shorter surveys of England are G. M. Trevelyan's *History of England* (new and enlarged ed., 1937), C. E. Robinson's *England, a history of British progress* (1928), F. C. Dietz's *Political and social history of England* (1927), and W. E. Lunt's *History of England* (1927). A. F. Pollard's *Evolution of parliament* (1926) is indispensable for the study of English constitutional history. R. B. Mowat's *Wars of the Roses, 1377–1471* (1914) is a useful study based on secondary materials. George B. Adams' *Constitutional history of England*, revised with continuation by Robert L. Schuyler (1934), is a good manual of English constitutional history. *Sources of English constitutional history*, edited by C. Stephenson and F. G. Marcham (1937), offers a selection of documents from the year 600 to the present with a general bibliography for English history. E. P. Cheyney's *Introduction to the industrial and social history of England* (rev. ed., 1920) is a good short survey of English economic history. There are two good biographies of Henry VII, one by Gladys Temperley (1918) and the other by James Gairdner (1892). Kenneth Pickthorn's *Early Tudor government* (2 vols., 1934) is a comprehensive summary of the latest scholarship on the subject. A. F. Pollard's *Reign of Henry VII from contemporary sources* (3 vols., 1913–14) is an invaluable collection of documents. For further references see the bibliography for Chapter Nine.

Germany. H. Pinnow's *History of Germany*, translated by Mabel B. Brailsford (1933), is a good introductory manual written from the viewpoint of a broad-minded liberalism. A careful brief analysis of the critical turning points that have determined the direction of German history can be found in Johannes Haller's *Epochs of German history*, translated by E. W. Dickes

(1930). Written with vigor and clarity, E. F. Henderson's *Short history of Germany* (rev. ed., 1916, 2 vols.) remains one of the best surveys of the political history, though it is in some respects outdated. Ernst Richard's *History of German civilization* (1910) contains some interesting materials, but is badly organized and not always sound. James Bryce's *Holy Roman Empire* (rev. ed., 1919) is still the most lucid and succinct account of the confused history of that empire. In German, B. Gebhardt's *Handbuch der deutschen Geschichte* (2 vols., 7th ed., 1930–31), revised by R. Holtzmann, is a reasonably accurate, well-organized survey of German history. G. Steinhausen's *Geschichte der deutschen Kultur* (1929) and C. Gebauer's *Deutsche Kulturgeschichte der Neuzeit* (1932) are two competent accounts of the history of German civilization. Johannes Janssen's *History of the German people at the close of the Middle Ages*, translated by A. M. Christie and M. A. Mitchell (17 vols., 1896–1925), contains a wealth of information not available elsewhere, but is markedly Catholic in its interpretation. P. Van Dyke's *Renascence portraits* (1905), pp. 259–375, contains a penetrating study of Maximilian I. R. W. Seton-Watson's *Maximilian I* (1902) is a popular but fairly sound biography. More readable but less sound is *Maximilian the dreamer* (1917) by C. Hare (pseudonym for Marian Andrews).

Italy. H. D. Sedgwick's *Short history of Italy, 476–1900* (1905), Janet P. Trevelyan's *Short history of the Italian people from the barbarian invasions to the attainment of unity* (1920), and *Italy, medieval and modern*, by E. M. Jamison and others (1919), are good simple readable surveys. O. Browning has written an interesting short history of Italy from 1409 to 1530 under the title *The age of the condottieri* (1895). H. P. Cotterill's *Italy from Dante to Tasso, 1300–1600* (1919) is a good account of the period viewed from the standpoint of the chief cities. *The life and times of Niccolo Machiavelli* by Pasquale Villari, translated from the Italian by L. Villari (rev. ed., 2 vols., 1898), is still one of the best accounts of the period in English. Ferdinand Schevill's *History of Florence from the founding of the city through the Renaissance* (1936) is scholarly and up-to-date. A useful older account is F. A. Hyett's *Florence, her history and art to the fall of the republic* (1903). G. F. Young's *The Medici* (various editions since 1909) is a reasonably good account of the Medici period. Cecilia M. Ady's *History of Milan under the Sforza* (1907) is scholarly and readable. The best longer history of Venice in English is W. C. Hazlitt's *History of the Venetian republic, her rise, her greatness, her civilization* (4th rev. ed., 2 vols., 1915). Horatio F. Brown has written a number of sound and attractive books on Venice, among them *Studies in the history of Venice* (2 vols., 1907) and *Venice, an historical sketch of the republic* (2nd rev. ed., 1895). There are excellent brief studies of Machiavelli and his philosophy in *Social and political ideas of some great thinkers of the Renaissance and the Reformation*, edited by F. J. C. Hearnshaw (1925), and in Paul Roeder's *Man of the Renaissance* (1933). Other useful studies are Ettore Janni's *Machiavelli*, translated by M. Enthoven (1930), L. Dyer's *Machiavelli and the modern state* (1904), and D. Erskine Muir's *Machiavelli and his times* (1936). The writings of Machiavelli have been issued in translation in various editions. For Machiavelli as he is revealed in his letters there is O. Ferrara's *Private correspondence of Nicolo Machiavelli* (1929).

CHAPTER TWO

The Renaissance

General. E. F. Jacob's *Renaissance* (1930) is a good short introductory booklet. A competent longer survey is H. S. Lucas' *The Renaissance and the Reformation* (1934). E. M. Hulme's *Renaissance, the Protestant revolution and the Catholic reformation in continental Europe* (rev. ed., 1917) contains a wealth of information but lacks organization and unity. Useful surveys of varying merit are W. H. Hudson's *Story of the Renaissance* (1912), Edith Sichel's *The Renaissance* (1914; Home university library), and J. D. Symon and S. L. Benusan's *The Renaissance and its makers* (1913). *The civilization of the Renaissance* by J. W. Thompson, G. Rowley, F. Schevill, and G. Sarton (1929) is an interesting little volume of lectures which present a number of new suggestions. L. Funck-Brentano's *Renaissance* (1936) is vivid and entertaining, but lacks integration; its sweeping generalizations are often misleading. M. Whitcomb's *Literary source-book of the Renaissance* (2nd ed., 1903) is a collection of sources to illustrate the literary and intellectual side of the Italian and German Renaissance. W. H. Woodward's *Studies in education during the age of the Renaissance* (1914) is a well-balanced survey of the rise of humanistic education. G. Voigt's *Wiederbelebung des klassischen Altertums* (3rd ed., 2 vols., 1893) and L. Geiger's *Renaissance und Humanismus in Italien und Deutschland* (1882) are scholarly but somewhat antiquated. J. E. Sandys' *History of classical scholarship* (3 vols., 1903–08) is an important pioneer work.

The Renaissance in Italy. H. Vaughan's *Studies in the Italian Renaissance* (1930) is a series of lively lectures which form a good introduction to the subject. Jakob Burckhardt's *Civilization of the period of the Renaissance in Italy* (many editions in English) is a readable account which identifies the Renaissance with humanism. The same may be said of Maud F. Jerrold's *Italy in the Renaissance* (1928). The standard longer account is still J. A. Symonds' *Renaissance in Italy* (7 vols.: 1. *Age of the despots*; 2. *Revival of learning*; 3. *Fine arts*; 4–5. *Italian literature*; 6–7. *Catholic reaction*; latest ed., 1927–29). There is also a *Short history of the Renaissance in Italy* by the same author, edited by A. Pearson (1894), which is a somewhat dull compendium of facts. J. B. Fletcher's *The literature of the Italian Renaissance* (1934) is urbane and informative. Rachel Taylor's *Aspects of the Italian Renaissance* (1923) is to be classed as belles-lettres rather than as history. The fullest life of Petrarch in English to 1347 is E. H. R. Tatham's *Francesco Petrarca, 1304–47* (2 vols., 1925–26). *Petrarch, the first modern scholar and man of letters*, by J. H. Robinson and H. W. Rolfe (2nd rev. ed., 1914), is a charming study of Petrarch's letters. H. C. Hollway-Calthrop's *Petrarch, his life and times* (1907) is a reasonably sound popular biography. Pierre de Nolhac's *Petrarch and the ancient world* (1907) is readable but not always sound. Edward Hutton's *Giovanni Boccaccio* (1910) is useful but not entirely trustworthy. A spirited discussion of Castiglione's *Courtier* may be found in

R. Roeder's *Man of the Renaissance* (1933). The standard English life of Castiglione is that of Julia Cartwright (2 vols., 1908). *The book of the courtier* has appeared in English in a number of translations.

Erasmus and Reuchlin. There are two first-rate short biographies of Erasmus in English: Preserved Smith's *Erasmus: a study of his life, ideals and place in history* (1923) and J. Huizinga's *Erasmus* (1934). J. Mangan's *Life, character and influence of Desiderius Erasmus* (2 vols., 1927) is a painstaking study that is somewhat hostile to its subject and not always convincing. There is a good life in German by E. Major (1926). P. S. Allen's *Erasmus: lectures and wayfaring sketches* (1934) is a series of charming essays by an acknowledged authority. A useful short study is Rachel Giese's "Erasmus and the fine arts," *Journal of modern history*, vol. 7 (1935), pp. 257–279. A. Hyma's *Youth of Erasmus* (1930) is a scholarly and revealing book. The same author has published a booklet of selections from the sources under the title *Erasmus and the humanists* (1930). F. M. Nichols' *Epistles of Erasmus from his earliest letters to his fifty-first year*, arranged in order of time (3 vols., 1901–18), makes the letters of Erasmus available in English in an excellent translation with full notes. An excellent English edition of *The praise of folly* is the translation by John Wilson with an introduction by Mrs. P. S. Allen (1913). Preserved Smith has written an interesting analysis of the *Colloquies* entitled *Key to the colloquies of Erasmus* (1927). For further bibliographical references the student may consult E. W. Nelson's "Recent literature concerning Erasmus," *Journal of modern history*, vol. 1 (1929), pp. 88–102. There is no life of Reuchlin in English. The standard German biography is L. Geiger's *Reuchlin, sein Leben und seine Werke* (1871).

England. L. Einstein's *Italian Renaissance in England* (1902) is a readable scholarly study. F. Seebohm's *Oxford reformers* (3rd rev. ed., 1914) is a penetrating analysis of certain thought-currents of the English Renaissance. T. M. Lindsay's "Englishmen and the classical renaissance," *Cambridge history of English literature*, vol. 3 (1918), pp. 1–24, is an excellent brief survey. E. M. G. Routh's *Sir Thomas More and his friends, 1477–1535* (1934) is really a study of the intellectual life of early sixteenth century England. R. W. Chambers' *Thomas More* (1935) is a first-rate biography. *More's Utopia and his social teachings*, by W. E. Campbell (1929), contains some illuminating reflections on More's writings. F. L. Baumann's "Sir Thomas More," *Journal of modern history*, vol. 4 (1932), pp. 604–615, offers a comprehensive and critical review of recent works on the author of the *Utopia*. "Recent literature of the English Renaissance," by Hardin Craig and others, is a bibliographical article which has appeared annually since 1926 (vol. 23) in *Studies in Philology* and includes the more important books, articles, and reviews which appear in the course of each year.

France. A. Tilley's *French Renaissance* (1919) is an excellent introductory booklet. The same author's *Dawn of the French Renaissance* (1918) is the standard work on the subject. Another work by the same author is *Studies in the French Renaissance* (1921), a series of penetrating studies. A valuable book for the history of France during the period of the Renaissance is L. Batiffol's *Century of the Renaissance*, translated from the French by Elsie F. Buckley (1916). The most sound and scholarly biography of Rabelais in English is Jean Plattard's *Life of Rabelais*, translated by L. B. Roche (1930), but it is dry and somewhat difficult for the average reader. A more readable life is A. J. Nock and C. R. Wilson's *Rabelais* (1929), a competent and careful study. Another useful life is that by S. Putnam (1929). Anatole France's *Rabelais*, translated by E. Boyd (1929), is a series of popular lectures; it is not always sound. For Montaigne there is A. Tilley's "French humanism and Montaigne," *Cambridge modern history*, vol. 3 (1904), pp. 53–72. Edith Sichel's *Montaigne* (new ed., 1911) is a simple readable life. A. Lamande's *Montaigne*, translated by A. van Duym (1928), is lively but rather sentimental. For the educational theories of Rabelais and Montaigne see K. A. Sarafian's *French educational theorists* (1933).

   Printing. The most scholarly and reliable account of the invention of printing in Asia is T. F. Carter's *Invention of printing in China and its spread westward* (new ed., 1931). A. H. Allen's *The beginnings of printing* (1923) is a good brief popular account. A longer popular account which contains much sound information is D. C. McMurtrie's *Golden book* (1927). The same author's *The book, the story of printing and bookmaking* (1937) is a competent up-to-date survey. J. C. Oswald's *History of printing, its development through five hundred years* (1928) is a popular account that is good for the earlier but inadequate for the later period. For Italy in particular there is G. Biagi's *The book in Italy during the fifteenth and sixteenth centuries*, with explanatory text by W. D. Orcutt (1928).

CHAPTER THREE

Renaissance Art

   General. Helen Gardner's *Art through the ages* (1926) is probably the best brief survey of the history of art in English. O. Hagen's *Art epochs and their leaders* (1927) is clear and concise. Another useful survey is S. Reinach's *Apollo* (rev. ed., 1922), profusely illustrated. For the Middle Ages, W. R. Lethaby's *Medieval art from the peace of the church to the eve of the Renaissance, 312–1350* (1913) is valuable. B. Berenson's *Studies in medieval painting* (1930) is a series of essays by an eminent art critic. T. Cox's *Renaissance in Europe, 1400–1600* (1933) is a useful little handbook on the various forms of Renaissance art. E. Faure's *History of art*, translated from the French by W. Pach (4 vols., 1923), has one volume on Renaissance art; interpretative, illuminating, and suggestive.

   Italy. O. P. Fairfield's *Italian Renaissance in art* (1928) is a survey which ranks high for its soundness, lucidity of presentation, and charm of style. An older survey by a distinguished art critic is H. Woelfflin's *The art of the Italian Renaissance*, translated by Sir Walter Armstrong (1913). The first chapters of C. J. Holmes' *Introduction to Italian painting* (1930) present a clear and simple account of Renaissance painting. Then there is the lucidly written and profusely illustrated *History of Italian painting* by F. J. Mather (1923). B. Berenson has published a series of acute and revealing studies of

Italian painting: *Venetian painters of the Renaissance* (3rd rev. ed., 1903); *North Italian painters of the Renaissance* (1907); *Central Italian painters of the Renaissance* (2nd rev. ed., 1909); *Florentine painters of the Renaissance* (3rd rev. ed., 1909). All these have been assembled in one volume under the title *The Italian painters of the Renaissance* (1930) to form an admirable survey. G. Vasari's *Lives of the most eminent painters, sculptors and architects*, translated from the Italian by G. du C. de Vere (10 vols., 1912–16), is a mine of information by an artist who lived from 1511 to 1574.

Special studies. Edward McCurdy has written two simple yet sound and scholarly studies of Leonardo, *The mind of Leonardo da Vinci* (1928), which reveals the scope of learning of the great genius of the Italian Renaissance, and *Leonardo da Vinci: the artist* (1933). The same author has also brought together and translated the reflections and speculations of Leonardo in *The notebooks of Leonardo da Vinci* (2 vols., 1938). Useful to the discriminating student is O. Siren's *Leonardo da Vinci, the artist and the man*, revised with the aid of W. Rankin and others (1916). D. L. Finlayson's *Michelangelo the man* (1936) is a popular biography which contains much excellent material. A longer scholarly biography is J. A. Symonds' *Life of Michelangelo Buonnarotti* (2 vols., 1911). J. A. Crowe and G. B. Cavalcaselle collaborated in writing *Raphael, his life and works* (2 vols., 1882–85) and *Titian, his life and times* (2 vols., 1877); both are works of solid information. S. L. Benusan's *Titian* (1909) is a sound, readable life.

Sculpture. G. H. Chase and C. R. Post's *History of sculpture* (1925) is a lucid, authoritative, and well-planned survey of the development of sculpture from the beginnings of civilization to the twentieth century. H. N. Fowler's *History of sculpture* (1916), which covers the same period, is also sound. W. G. Waters' *Italian sculptors* (2nd enlarged ed., 1926) is a comprehensive presentation of biographical facts and critical comments; valuable for reference. Two useful older works are D. A. Crawford's *Evolution of Italian sculpture* (1909) and L. Freeman's *Italian sculpture of the Renaissance* (1901).

Architecture. Geoffrey Scott's *Architecture of humanism* (2nd ed., 1924) is an excellent study of the subject. W. Anderson's *Architecture of the Renaissance in Italy* (5th ed., 1927), revised and enlarged by A. Stratton, is a popular but valuable study. Other useful volumes are G. Gromort's *Italian Renaissance architecture*, translated from the French by G. F. Waters (1922), and Dagobert Frey's *Architecture of the Renaissance from Brunelleschi to Michelangelo* (1925). C. H. Moore's *Character of Renaissance architecture* (1905) is outdated in some respects.

Flemish and German art. Max Rooses' *Art in Flanders* (1914) is a concise and readable little handbook, densely packed with information on the development of Flemish art from its beginnings to the nineteenth century. Sir Martin Conway's *The Van Eycks and their followers* (1922) is clear and authoritative, one of the best English accounts of early Flemish art. Roger E. Fry's *Flemish art* (1927) is a brief introduction, in lecture form, to Flemish art. F. Nüchter's *Albrecht Dürer*, translated from the German by L. D. Williams (1912), can be recommended as a simple introduction to German art. Helen A. Dickinson's *German masters of art* (1914) is an elaborate and scholarly history of the development of German painting. J. LaFarge's *Great* *masters* (1903) contains illuminating accounts of Rubens and Dürer. Hans Reinhardt's *Holbein*, translated by P. Montagu-Pollock (1938), gives a comprehensive and well-balanced view of Holbein's art.

CHAPTER FOUR

The Age of Exploration

General. James A. Williamson's *Europe overseas* (1925) and James E. Gillespie's *History of geographical discovery* (1933; Berkshire series) are two concise and simple introductory booklets. For the background of the Age of Discovery the student may consult G. H. T. Kimble's *Geography in the Middle Ages* (1938), the best brief survey of the subject. A clear and concise survey of the evolution of geographical thought since the earliest times may be found in *The making of geography* (1933), by R. E. Dickinson and O. J. Howarth. J. N. L. Baker's *History of geographical discovery and exploration* (new ed., 1937) is scholarly, authoritative, and up-to-date. The best shorter account of the Age of Discovery is *The great age of discovery*, edited by A. P. Newton (1932), a series of essays by eminent English historians. L. Outhwaite's *Unrolling the map, the story of exploration* (1935) records the history of exploration and explorers from 3000 B.C. to the present; a thorough and interesting book. W. C. Abbott's *Expansion of Europe* (2 vols., 1919) is a comprehensive survey of European civilization in the sixteenth, seventeenth, and eighteenth centuries as well as of oversea activities. The first three volumes of Justin Winsor, ed., *Narrative and critical history of America* (1884–89) contain excellent monographs on all phases of exploration with a wide array of early maps and charts. Another useful work is E. P. Cheyney's *European background of American history, 1300–1600* (1904). J. B. Brebner's *The explorers of North America* (1933) is a vivid and comprehensive account of the explorations in North America to the end of the eighteenth century. John C. Beaglehole's *The exploration of the Pacific* (1934) is an excellent survey of the subject. For the early explorations in West Africa there is John W. Blake's *European beginnings in West Africa, 1454–1578* (1937), a scholarly book packed with details.

The Norsemen. An interesting up-to-date survey of explorations in the North Atlantic from the days of the Norsemen to the second half of the sixteenth century may be found in Vilhjalmur Stefansson's introduction to *The three voyages of Martin Frobisher* (2 vols., 1938). G. M. Gathorne-Hardy's *Norse discoverers of America, the Wineland sagas translated and discussed* (1921) pieces the Norse sagas together, with a competent discussion of the questions involved.

Portuguese discovery. E. Prestage's *Portuguese pioneers* (1933) is an excellent synthesis of modern scholarship on the history of the early Portuguese explorers and explorations. The best life of Prince Henry the Navigator in English is by C. R. Beazley (1895). J. P. Oliviera Martins' *Golden age of Prince Henry the Navigator*, translated by J. J. Abraham and W. E. Reynolds (1914), is brilliant but not always dependable. K. G. Jayne's *Vasco da Gama and his successors, 1460–1580* (1910) contains excellent short biographies of the builders of the Portuguese power in the East. R. S. Whiteway's *Rise of the Portuguese power in India, 1497–1550* (1899) is a brief sketch devoted largely to political affairs. F. C. Danvers' *The Portuguese in India* (2 vols., 1894) is a comprehensive and scholarly study. E. Prestage's *Albuquerque* (1929) is concise, scholarly, and readable. The older biography of Albuquerque by H. M. Stephens is still useful and generally sound. The question of the discovery of Brazil is ably treated by C. E. Nowell, "The discovery of Brazil—accidental or intentional?" *Hispanic American historical review*, vol. 16 (1936), pp. 311–338. R. G. Watson's *Spanish and Portuguese South America during the colonial period* (2 vols., 1884) is outdated in many respects but still useful.

Spain. For Spanish exploration and colonization the best general survey is R. B. Merriman's *Rise of the Spanish empire in the old world and in the new* (4 vols., 1919–34). E. G. Bourne's *Spain in America* (1904) is still the best concise work on the subject. I. B. Richman's *Spanish conquerors, a chronicle of the dawn of the Spanish empire overseas* (1918) is a sound and well-written summary. The early chapters of J. Fred Rippy's *Historical evolution of Hispanic America* (1932) contain an excellent short treatment of the colonial period of Spanish America. Bernard Moses' *Spanish dependencies in South America, an introduction to the history of their civilization* (2 vols., 1914), is a useful and interesting longer account. Charles Duff's *The truth about Columbus and the discovery of America* (1936) is an honest effort to present solid facts in so far as they are ascertainable; well-written and suggestive. For a selection of documents regarding Columbus the student may consult *Select documents illustrating the four voyages of Columbus*, translated and edited with introduction by Cecil Jane (2 vols., 1930–32). F. A. Kirkpatrick's *Spanish conquistadores* (1934) is a good account of the Spanish conquests in America during the sixteenth century, with the story centering around individuals. P. A. Means' *The Spanish main* (1935) is a well-documented and well-written book, written largely from the Spanish point of view. The same ground is covered by A. P. Newton's equally readable and authoritative *European nations in the West Indies, 1493–1688* (1933), written from the point of view of the enemies of Spain. C. H. Haring's *Trade and navigation between Spain and the Indies in the time of the Hapsburgs* (1918) is an excellent monograph. An able survey along broader lines of the early history of Hispanic America is to be found in Charles E. Chapman's *Colonial Hispanic America* (1933).

The papal line of demarcation. For the question of the papal line of demarcation see H. Vander Linden's "Alexander VI and the demarcation of the maritime and colonial domains of Spain and Portugal, 1493–94," *American historical review*, vol. 22 (1916), pp. 1–20, and E. G. Bourne's *Essays in historical criticism* (1901), pp. 193–217.

Mexico and Peru. The early chapters of Henry B. Parkes' *History of Mexico* (1938) form an excellent introduction to the Spanish conquest and rule of Mexico. H. D. Sedgwick's *Cortes the conqueror* (1927) is a readable and reasonably sound biography but is too favorable to Cortez. Bernal Diaz del Castillo, one of the conquerors, wrote an account of the conquest of Mexico which is available in a number of editions, one being *The discovery and conquest of Mexico*, translated with an introduction and notes by A. P. Maudslay (1928). There is a condensation by Kate Stephens under the title *The mastering of Mexico* (1916). The letters of Cortez to Charles V have been translated by F. A. MacNutt (2 vols., 1908). W. H. Prescott's *History of the conquest of Mexico* is still the best longer treatment but should be read in the more up-to-date editions with critical notes (4 vols., edited by W. H. Munro [1904] or, better, 2 vols., with an introduction by T. A. Joyce [1922]). The same author's *History of the conquest of Peru* is also a classic and has been edited by W. H. Munro (3 vols., 1904). P. A. Means' *Fall of the Inca empire and the Spanish rule in Peru, 1530–1780* (1932) is a concise, spirited, well-documented narrative. Frank Shay's *Incredible Pizarro* (1932) is an interesting and informative biography but not always accurate. The best treatment of the viceregal administration of the Spanish colonial period is Lillian E. Fisher's *Viceregal administration in the Spanish-American colonies* (1926). Donald E. Smith's *Viceroy of New Spain* (1913) is an older but still useful study. For further literature on the expansion of New Spain to the north see J. L. Mecham's "The northern expansion of New Spain, a selected descriptive bibliographical list," *Hispanic American historical review*, vol. 7 (1927), pp. 237–276.

Magellan. F. H. H. Guillemard's *Life of Ferdinand Magellan* (1890) is still the best biography of Magellan. A. S. Hildebrand's *Magellan* (1925) and E. F. Benson's *Magellan* (1929) are two clear and reasonably sound popular biographies. For a first-hand narrative of the first circumnavigation of the globe the student may consult *Magellan's voyage around the world*, by Antonio Pigafetta, who accompanied Magellan; translation with notes by J. A. Robertson (2 vols., with an index in a separate volume, 1906).

English. The most authoritative and readable account of the early English explorations and maritime activities is to be found in James A. Williamson's *Maritime enterprise, 1485–1558* (1913) and in his *Age of Drake* (1938). More general studies of English expansion by the same author include *Foundation and growth of the British empire* (3rd rev. ed., 1933) and *Short history of British expansion* (new ed., 2 vols., 1930). For the Cabots see the same author's *Voyages of the Cabots* (1929). J. A. Williamson has also written the best English life of Hawkins (1927). Another good life of Hawkins is that of Philip Gosse (1930). The original narratives of the various voyages of English seamen which Richard Hakluyt collected in the sixteenth century and which are invaluable for a first-hand knowledge have been republished by the Hakluyt Society in various editions. D. Bell's *Elizabethan seamen* (1936) is vigorous and well-balanced, a good introduction to the subject. The same author has also written an excellent short biography of Drake (1935). E. F. Benson's *Drake* (1927) is a sound and picturesque narrative, written with gusto. An important study of the rise of England as a maritime power is J. S. Corbett's *Drake and the Tudor navy* (2 vols., 1898). Sir William Foster's *England's quest of eastern trade* (2 vols., 1933) is a vivid and scholarly narrative of the English efforts to break the Portuguese and Spanish monopoly of the Far Eastern trade.

The search for a northwest and northeast passage. N. M. Crouse's *In quest of the western ocean* (1928) is an excellent comprehensive account of the search for a westward passage. L. J. Burpee's *Search for the western sea* (1908) is still valuable for its account of the history of geographical exploration in Canada. *The three voyages of Martin Frobisher*, edited by Vilhjalmur Stefansson with the collaboration of Eloise McCaskill (2 vols., 1938), offers first-hand accounts of attempts to find the northwest passage. There is a sound and interestingly written popular life of Frobisher by William McFee (1928).

French explorations. The early chapters of *Adventures of New France*, by William B. Munro and George M. Wrong (1918), are a good introduction to the subject; also the first three chapters of vol. 4 (1884) of *Narrative and critical history of America*, edited by Justin Winsor. For a fuller treatment there is Francis Parkman's *Pioneers of France in the new world* (1865), a readable work of sound scholarship. S. E. Dawson's *The Saint Lawrence, its basin and borderlands* (1905) relates the story of the discovery of the Saint Lawrence basin and adjacent territories; trustworthy and spirited. Other useful works are Hiram B. Stephens' *Jacques Cartier and his four voyages to Canada* (1890), Charles W. Colby's *Founder of New France, a chronicle of Champlain* (1915), and N. E. Dionne's *Champlain* (1926). For first-hand narratives of the French explorations see *The precursors of Jacques Cartier*, a collection of documents edited by H. P. Biggar (1911); *The voyages of Cartier*, published from the original with translation, notes, and appendices by H. P. Biggar (1924); and *The voyages of Samuel de Champlain*, translated and edited under the general editorship of H. P. Biggar (6 vols., 1922–36).

CHAPTER FIVE

Capitalism, Banking, and Mercantilism

Studies in economic history. Laurence B. Packard's *Commercial revolution* (1927; Berkshire series) is a lucid brief survey of the economic development of Europe from 1400 to 1700. The best one-volume account of the development of commerce is Clive Day's *History of commerce* (rev. and enlarged ed., 1922). The best longer account is William S. Lindsay's *History of merchant shipping and ancient commerce* (4 vols., 1874–76). W. Oakeshott's *Commerce and society: a short history of trade and its effects on civilization* (1936) contains a wealth of facts but frequently fails to point out their interrelationships. Miriam Beard's *History of the business man* (1938) is a comprehensive study written in a lively style; it covers the period from the Homeric age down to modern times. F. C. Lane's *Venetian ships and shipbuilders of the Renaissance* (1934) is a painstaking study of the economic history of Venice in the fifteenth and sixteenth centuries. *Florentine merchants in the age of the Medici*, edited by G. R. V. Richards (1932), contains a selection of letters and documents from the Selfridge collection of Medici manuscripts. There is a survey of the more recent literature on the Hanseatic League by Carl Brinckmann in the

Journal of economic and business history, vol. 2 (1930), pp. 585–602. David Hannay's *The great chartered companies* (1926) is the best general survey of the subject. A useful older work on the English commercial companies is George Cawston and A. H. Keane's *Early chartered companies, 1296–1858* (1896). W. R. Scott's *Constitution and finance of English, Scottish and Irish joint-stock companies to 1720* (3 vols., 1910–12) is a standard work. Cyrus H. Karraker's *Hispaniola treasure* (1934) presents a graphic account of one of the few successful companies that were founded in England during the period of speculative hysteria, 1680–1730. G. F. Renard's *Guilds in the Middle Ages*, translated by Dorothy Terry (1919), is the best brief survey of the subject in English. For the later period of English gild history there is Stella Kramer's scholarly *English craft gilds, studies in their progress and decline* (1927). Jonathan F. Scott's *Historical essays on apprenticeship* (1914) contains some interesting reflections on apprenticeship and its decline.

Capitalism. The best shorter survey of the historical development of modern capitalism is Henri E. Sée's *Modern capitalism, its origin and evolution*, translated by Homer B. Vanderblue and G. F. Doriot (1928). A sound and lucid treatment in French is H. Pirenne's *Les périodes de l'histoire sociale du capitalisme* (1914). Werner Sombart's *Der moderne Kapitalismus* (2nd ed., 4 vols., 1916–27) is the longer standard work in German, though some of its conclusions have been criticized. This work has been condensed in F. L. Nussbaum's *History of the economic institutions of modern Europe: an introduction to "Der moderne Kapitalismus" of Werner Sombart* (1933), the only longer study of capitalism in English. Other important works of Sombart for the advanced student are *The quintessence of capitalism; a study of the history and psychology of the modern business man*, translated by M. Epstein (1915); *The Jews and modern capitalism*, also translated by Epstein (1913); and *Krieg und Kapitalismus* (1913). For a discussion of both Sombart and Weber see Talcott Parsons' articles in the *Journal of political economy*, vol. 36 (1928), pp. 641–661, and vol. 37 (1929), pp. 31–51. For the sixteenth century there is Richard Ehrenberg's *Capital and finance in the age of the Renaissance, a study of the Fuggers and their connections*, translated from the German by H. M. Lucas (1928); scholarly and informative. Useful studies in German include J. Strieder's *Zur Genesis des modernen Kapitalismus* (2nd rev. ed., 1935); Fritz Gerlich's *Geschichte und Theorie des Kapitalismus* (1913); and Lujo Brentano's *Die Anfänge des modernen Kapitalismus* (1916). For capitalism and religion see R. H. Tawney's *Religion and the rise of capitalism* (1926) and A. Hyma's "Calvinism and capitalism in the Netherlands, 1555–1700," *Journal of modern history*, vol. 10 (1938), pp. 321–343. Earl J. Hamilton's "American treasure and the rise of capitalism," *Economica*, vol. 9 (1929), pp. 338–357, is an informative article. There are two excellent bibliographical studies on capitalism: M. Postan's "Medieval capitalism," *Economic history review*, vol. 4 (1934), pp. 212–227, and R. H. Tawney's "Modern capitalism," *ibid.*, pp. 336–356.

Slavery. On the question of forced native labor in the Spanish colonies, 1492–1550, see Lesley B. Simpson's *The encomienda in Spain* (1929), a well-documented work. H. A. Wyndham's *The Atlantic and slavery* (1935) contains much useful and illuminating information. Other informative books are

Sir Harry H. Johnston's *The negro in the new world* (1910), George F. Dow's *Slave ships and slaving* (1927), Ulrich B. Phillips' *American negro slavery* (1918), and C. M. MacInnes' *England and slavery* (1934). *Documents illustrative of the history of the slave trade to America*, edited by Elizabeth Donnan (4 vols., 1930–35), is a monumental collection of source materials. For slavery in Brazil see Percy A. Martin's "Slavery and abolition in Brazil," *Hispanic American historical review*, vol. 13 (1933), pp. 151–196. Francis A. MacNutt's *Bartholomew de Las Casas, his life, his apostolate, and his writings* (1909) is a valuable study of this important figure.

Banking. Noble F. Hoggson's *Banking through the ages* (1926) is a readable brief survey. A useful older work is J. W. Gilbart's *History, principles and practice of banking* (2 vols., 1907). A. V. Judges' "Money, finance and banking from the Renaissance to the eighteenth century" in *European civilization, its origin and development*, edited by Edward Eyre, vol. 5 (1937), pp. 401–499, is an able survey. Abbot P. Usher has written two illuminating articles on early banking: "Deposit banking in Barcelona, 1300–1700," *Journal of economic and business history*, vol. 4 (1932), pp. 121–155, and "The origins of banking: the primitive banks of deposit, 1200–1600," *Economic history review*, vol. 4 (1934), pp. 399–428. A. Andréadès' *History of the bank of England* (2nd ed., 1924) is a readable and compact survey. R. D. Richards' *Early history of banking in England* (1929) deals with the goldsmith bankers and the early years of the Bank of England. For insurance see C. F. Trenerry's *Origin and early history of insurance* (1926). For the development of coinage see George MacDonald's *Evolution of coinage* (1916), W. A. Shaw's *History of currency, 1252 to 1894* (1896), and W. Täuber's *Geld und Kredit im Mittelalter* (1933). Earl J. Hamilton's "Imports of American gold and silver into Spain, 1503–1660," *Quarterly journal of economics*, vol. 43 (1929), pp. 436–472, is an illuminating article.

Mercantilism. The best shorter treatment of mercantilism in English is John W. Horrocks' *Short history of mercantilism* (1925). A longer competent treatment in English is Eli F. Heckscher's *Mercantilism*, translated by Mendel Schapiro (2 vols., 1935), but it does not include Spanish and Portuguese mercantilism. An older well-known short account is Gustave F. Schmoller's *The mercantile system and its historical significance* (1910). Valuable for the study of Spanish mercantilism are Earl J. Hamilton's "Spanish mercantilism before 1700" in *Facts and factors in economic history* (articles by former students of E. F. Gay; 1932), pp. 214–239, and Andres V. Castillo's *Spanish mercantilism, Gerónimo de Uztáriz, economist* (1930). Charles W. Cole's *French mercantilist doctrines before Colbert* (1932) is an able study. For Colbert there is the same author's detailed and scholarly study, *Colbert and a century of French mercantilism* (2 vols., 1939). English mercantilism is competently treated in William Cunningham's *Growth of English industry and commerce in modern times* (5th ed., 3 vols., 1910–12). E. A. Johnson's *Predecessors of Adam Smith: the growth of British economic thought* (1937) offers a series of interesting studies of economists of the age of mercantilism. Bruno K. Suviranta's *Theory of the balance of trade in England* (Helsingfors, 1923) is a scholarly treatment of one phase of English mercantilism.

background of the age. For the preceding century there is Lynn Thorndike's *Science and thought in the fifteenth century* (1929). The best account of warfare in the sixteenth century is Sir Charles Oman's *History of the art of warfare in the sixteenth century* (1937). There is no good work in English on the social life of the sixteenth century. Vol. 2 of Max von Boehn's *Modes and manners*, translated by Joan Joshua (4 vols., 1932–35), contains a sketchy popular account which in some respects is highly misleading. For the social history of the period the students should consult special works on the various countries that are listed in other sections of this bibliography. Useful books which treat the penal methods of the sixteenth century include George Ives' *History of penal methods* (1914), Harry E. Barnes' *Story of punishment* (1930), Theodor Hampe's *Crime and punishment in Germany*, translated by Malcolm Letts (1929), and Werner Laurie's *History of corporal punishment* (1938). There is a plethora of books on witchcraft and the devil; among others: Nikolaus Paulus' *Hexenwahn und Hexenprozess, vornehmlich im sechzehnten Jahrhundert* (1910), Max Osborn's *Die Teufellitteratur des sechzehnten Jahrhunderts* (1893), Montague Sommers' *History of witchcraft and demonology* (1926), R. L. Thompson's *History of the devil* (1929), and Wallace Notestein's *History of witchcraft in England from 1558 to 1718* (1911). The story of the calendar is lucidly sketched in Alexander Philip's *The calendar: its history, structure and improvement* (1921), P. W. Wilson's *Romance of the calendar* (1937), and S. H. Hooke's *New Year's Day: the story of the calendar* (1928).

CHAPTER SEVEN

The Reformation

General. Preserved Smith's *Age of the Reformation* (1920) is the best one-volume account of the subject in English. A standard longer work is Thomas M. Lindsay's *History of the Reformation* (2 vols., 1928). C. Beard's *Hibbert lectures on the Reformation*, edited by E. Barker (1927), is still a good introductory sketch though it was written in 1883. W. Walker's *Reformation* (1900) is a shorter survey, conservative and moderately Protestant in tone. *The Renaissance and the Reformation*, by Henry S. Lucas (1934), is judicious and readable. R. H. Bainton has written a stimulating article entitled "Changing ideas and ideals in the sixteenth century," *Journal of modern history*, vol. 8 (1936), pp. 417–443. *The Reformation and the contemplative life*, by D. and G. Mathews (1934), shows the "interaction of two opposing attitudes toward life and society." B. J. Kidd's *Documents illustrative of the continental Reformation* (1911) is a useful collection of source materials. For the period before Luther there is George V. Jourdan's *Movement towards Catholic reform in the early sixteenth century* (1914) and J. Loserth's *Huss and Wyclif* (new ed., 1925).

Germany. Leopold von Ranke's *History of the German Reformation*, translated by Sarah Austin and edited by R. A. Johnson (new ed., 1914), is in many respects still the best treatment of the subject. Henry C. Vedder's *Reformation in Germany* (1914) interprets the religious struggle in terms of economics in a somewhat one-sided fashion. Roy Pascal's *Social basis of the German Reformation* (1933) is interesting and instructive. A good popular treatment in German is Friedrich von Bezold's *Geschichte der deutschen Reformation* (1890). G. A. H. von Below's *Ursachen der Reformation* (1917) is a suggestive study. Austin P. Evans' *An episode in the struggle for religious freedom* (1924) is a scholarly study of the sectaries of Nuremberg during the years 1524–28. For further references see K. Schottenleher's *Bibliographie zur deutschen Geschichte im Zeitalter der Glaubensspaltung, 1517–1585* (1936).

Luther. Preserved Smith's *Life and letters of Martin Luther* (2nd ed., 1914) is a fair-minded, accurate, and readable biography. Arthur C. McGiffert's *Martin Luther, the man and his work* (1911) is a popular biography, well-written and reasonably accurate. J. Koestlin's *Life of Luther*, translated from the German (new ed., 1913), is a standard biography, scholarly and detailed. The best longer work on Luther in English is J. Mackinnon's *Luther and the Reformation* (4 vols., 1925–30), up-to-date, well-documented, and readable. Heinrich Boehmer's *Luther and the Reformation in the light of recent research*, translated from the 5th German edition by E. S. G. Potter (1930), is sympathetic but not uncritical. F. Funck-Brentano's *Luther*, translated from the French by E. F. Buckley (1936), is a spirited and challenging popular treatment. A short summary of the life and work of Luther from the Catholic viewpoint may be found in Joseph Clayton's *Luther and his work* (1937). A longer Catholic biography is H. Grisar's *Luther*, authorized translation from the German by E. M. Lamond, edited by L. Cappadelta (6 vols., 1913–17). Edwin P. Booth's *Martin Luther, oak of Saxony* (1933) is a readable biography by an admirer of Luther. Robert H. Fife's *Young Luther: the intellectual and religious development of Martin Luther to 1518* (1928) contains an excellent account of the influences that molded Luther's early life. The more important letters of Luther have been translated by Preserved Smith and C. M. Jacobs under the title *Luther's correspondence and other contemporary letters* (2 vols., 1913–18). The more important early treatises of Luther are translated into English in *Luther's primary works*, by H. Wace and C. A. Buchheim (1896). Notable biographies of other German reformers are Hastings Eells' *Martin Bucer* (1931), Hajo Holborn's *Ulrich von Hutten and the German Reformation*, translated by Roland H. Bainton (1937), and J. W. Richard's *Melanchthon* (1898). Albert Hyma has published a booklet of source materials under the title *The theological development of Luther from Erfurt to Augsburg* (1928; Landmarks in History series, edited by B. E. Schmitt).

The Peasants' War. The causes of the Peasants' War are ably discussed in J. Salwyn Schapiro's *Social reform and the Reformation* (1909). E. B. Bax's *Peasants' War in Germany, 1525–1526* (1899) is a popular account marred by a socialistic bias. A more recent and useful work in German is Wilhelm Stolze's *Bauernkrieg und Reformation* (1926). For source materials see *Akten zur Geschichte des Bauernkrieges in Mitteldeutschland*, edited by O. Merx (2 vols., 1923–34).

Scandinavia. For Sweden see the histories of Sweden listed in the bibliography for Chapter Seventeen. For a more detailed treatment there is

Paul B. Watson's *Swedish revolution under Gustavus Vasa* (1889), written in a lively style from a definite Protestant standpoint. C. Bergendorff's *Olavius Petri and the ecclesiastical transformation in Sweden, 1521–1552* (1928) links the Swedish Reformation with that of Germany through Petri, a student of Luther. Two good books in German are H. Holmquist's *Schwedische Reformation* (1926) and O. Brandt's *Freiheitskampf Schwedens unter Gustavus Vasa*. For Denmark there is a brief sketch in J. Stefánsson's *Denmark and Sweden, with Finland and Iceland* (1917). For Norway and Iceland see Knut Gjerset's *History of the Norwegian people* (2 vols., 1915) and *History of Iceland* (1924).

Zwingli, Calvin and Knox. For Zwingli see the *Cambridge modern history*, vol. 2 (1903), pp. 305–341. The best biography of Zwingli in English is that of Samuel M. Jackson (1900). F. C. Palm's *Calvinism and the religious wars* (1932) is a good brief introductory account, with an extensive bibliography. Robert N. C. Hunt's *Calvin* (1933) is a short biography which makes the reformer's personality intelligible and explains why his doctrines were so attractive. Georgia Harkness' *John Calvin, the man and his ethics* (1931) is a fair-minded and penetrating study with carefully weighed verdicts. An older but still valuable biography is Williston Walker's *Calvin* (1906). Another readable and useful study is Hugh Y. Reyburn's *John Calvin, his life, letters and work* (1914). J. Mackinnon's *Calvin and the Reformation* (1936) is an up-to-date critical survey of the reformer's work and influence by a distinguished historian. Another useful study is B. B. Warfield's *Calvin and Calvinism*, edited by E. D. Warfield (1931). The monumental work on Calvin is Émile Doumerge's *Jean Calvin, les hommes et les choses de son temps* (7 vols., 1899–1927). The *Institutes* of Calvin have been published in numerous English translations. The letters of John Calvin have been collected by Jules Bonnet and translated into English by D. Constable (2 vols., 1855–57). For Servetus see Roland H. Bainton's bibliographical article, "The present state of Servetus studies," *Journal of modern history*, vol. 4 (1932), pp. 72–88. For Knox there is the biography by Andrew Lang (1905), written from the sources. There is also a brief readable biography in the Great Lives series by G. Pearce (1936). Edwin Muir's *John Knox: portrait of a Calvinist* (1929) is a well-written and well-informed attempt to interpret Knox psychologically. For further books on Scotland see the bibliography for Chapter Nine.

CHAPTER EIGHT

The Catholic Reformation

Catholic Reformation. The most recent account in English is B. J. Kidd's *Counter-reformation, 1550–1600* (1933), a condensed and scholarly survey. Useful older accounts include A. W. Ward's *Counter-reformation* (1888) and Arthur R. Pennington's *Counter-reformation in Europe* (1899). J. Broderick's *St. Peter Canisius* (1935) is valuable for the Catholic Reformation in Germany. W. Maurenbrecher's *Geschichte der katholischen Reformation* (vol. 1,

1880) is an account by a liberal Catholic. Then there is the readable survey *Geschichte der Gegenreformation,* by Gustav Droysen (1893). A more recent useful work is H. Gille's *Zeitalter der Gegenreformation* (1930). The best studies of the reform movement in Italy are G. K. Brown's *Italy and the Reformation to 1550* (1933) and Frederic C. Church's *Italian reformers, 1534-64* (1932). The latter has also written an excellent bibliographical article on the subject, "The literature of the Italian Reformation," *Journal of modern history,* vol. 3 (1931), pp. 457-473. For Poland there is Paul Fox's scholarly *Reformation in Poland, some social and economic aspects* (1924).

The Council of Trent. J. Waterworth's *History of the council of Trent, with the canons and decrees of the council* (1848) is a good account by a Catholic historian. A useful brief account is R. F. Littledale's *Short history of the council of Trent* (1888). Two other works in English are F. Burgener's *History of the council of Trent,* translated from the French by D. D. Scott (1853), and T. W. A. Buckley's *History of the council of Trent* (1852). In German there is a more recent work by Kurt Schmidt entitled *Studien zur Geschichte des Konzils von Trient* (1925).

The Index and the Inquisition. The fullest work on the Index in English is George H. Putnam's *Censorship of the church of Rome and its influence on the production and distribution of literature* (2 vols., 1906-07). This work is based to a large extent on Franz H. Reusch's *Index der verbotenen Bücher* (2 vols., 1883-85). There is a booklet written "for Catholic booklovers" by Francis S. Betten, entitled *The Roman index of forbidden books briefly explained* (1909; 2nd rev. ed., 1932). For the Inquisition see Henry C. Lea's *History of the inquisition of the Middle Ages* (3 vols., 1888), based on a study of the sources. J. Guiraud's *Medieval inquisition* (1929) is an apology which discusses the mechanics and not the morals of the system. For the Inquisition in Spain there is H. C. Lea's *History of the inquisition in Spain* (4 vols., 1906-07), a monumental work. The same author's *Chapters from the religious history of Spain connected with the inquisition* (1890) contains earlier studies on the same subject. F. Lucka's *Torquemada und die spanische Inquisition* (1926) relates the story with Torquemada as the central character. The most recent account is Cecil Roth's *Spanish inquisition* (1938). The Papal Inquisition is treated in G. Buschbell's *Reformation und Inquisition in Italien um die Mitte des sechzehnten Jahrhunderts* (1910).

The Jesuits. A good survey of the history of the society is to be found in Heinrich Boehmer's *The Jesuits,* translated from the 4th revised edition by P. Strodach (1928). Joseph McCabe's *Candid history of the Jesuits* (1913) is an account by a former Catholic. The most comprehensive account of the Jesuits in English is *The Jesuits, 1534-1921: a history of the Society of Jesus from its foundation to the present time* (2 vols., 1921), by Thomas J. Campbell, a member of the society. There is also an interesting and impartial study in English by René Fülop-Miller entitled *The power and secret of the Jesuits,* translated by F. S. Flint and D. F. Tait (1930).

CHAPTER NINE

England under the Tudors

General. Conyers Read's *The Tudors: personalities and practical politics in the sixteenth century* (1936) is a sound and well-written little book. Another short, readable, and up-to-date volume on the period is C. H. Williams' *Making of the Tudor despotism* (1935), with an excellent critical bibliography. *The great Tudors*, edited by Katharine Garvin (1936), contains an informative collection of fifty-two studies on the great figures of Tudor England, written largely by specialists. For the political history of the period there are two solid informative volumes in *The political history of England*, edited by W. Hunt and R. L. Poole: vol. 5, *From the accession of Henry VII to the death of Henry VIII, 1485-1547* (1906), by H. A. L. Fisher, and vol. 6, *From the accession of Edward VI to the death of Elizabeth, 1547-1603* (1910), by A. F. Pollard. Another sound survey of the period is A. D. Innes' *England under the Tudors* (1905; vol. 4 of Oman's *History of England*). J. A. Froude's *History of England from the fall of Wolsey to the defeat of the Spanish Armada* (new ed., 12 vols., 1899) is still unrivaled for its general picture of the period. A brief description of social and economic life may be found in L. F. Salzman's *England in Tudor times* (1926). L. B. Wright's *Middle-class culture in Elizabethan England* (1935) is a revealing volume. G. B. Salter has published an interesting compilation from the reports of the Venetian representatives, under the title *Tudor England through Venetian eyes* (1932). J. R. Tanner's *Tudor constitutional documents, 1485-1603* (1921) is a well-selected collection. The best general account of the economic history of the period is to be found in E. Lipson's *Economic history of England* (5th ed., 3 vols., 1929-31; 7th ed., vol. 1, rev. and enlarged, 1937). W. Cunningham's *Growth of English industry and commerce* (2 vols., rev. ed., 1903-05) is a useful volume. For the history of agriculture R. W. Prothero's (Lord Ernle) *English farming: past and present*, edited by Sir A. D. Hall (1936), and R. H. Tawney's *Agrarian problems in the sixteenth century* (1912) are valuable. R. H. Tawney and Eileen Power's *Tudor economic documents* (1924) touch upon every phase of economic history. A more general collection is A. E. Bland, P. A. Brown, and R. H. Tawney's *Select documents of economic history* (1914), covering England from the earliest times to 1832. The field of governmental finance is ably surveyed in the scholarly works of Frederick C. Dietz: *English government finance, 1485-1558* (1921) and *English public finance, 1558-1641* (1932). Other books on the Tudor period are listed in the bibliography for Chapter One. For further references see the *Bibliography of British history: Tudor period, 1485-1603*, edited by Conyers Read (1933), which lists the important books published on the Tudor period up to 1932 with explanatory and critical notes.

Biographies. The best biography of Henry VIII is A. F. Pollard's admirable study (first published in 1905). Invaluable for the study of the constitutional history of the reign of Henry VIII as well as of Wolsey himself is the same author's biography of Wolsey (1929). F. Hackett's *Henry the*

Eighth (1929) is a popular life which gives special attention to each of Henry's six wives. The best study of Edward VI is the introduction to his *Literary remains* (1857), by J. G. Nichols. J. M. Stone's *History of Mary I, queen of England* (1901) is the fullest account of Mary's life; it is written from the Catholic point of view. B. White's *Mary Tudor* (1935) is sympathetic but not uncritical.

The English Reformation. R. S. Arrowsmith's *Prelude to the Reformation* (1923) offers an account of English church life from the age of Wyclif to the breach with Rome. O. A. Marti's *Economic causes of the Reformation in England* (1929) is a useful study. A good survey of the Reformation is G. Constant's *Reformation in England:* vol. 1, *The English schism,* translated by R. E. Scantlebury (1934). Other useful studies include A. F. Pollard's *Thomas Cranmer and the English Reformation* (new ed., 1926), J. Gairdner's *English church in the sixteenth century* (1902), and G. G. Perry's *History of the Reformation in England* (1888). For the dissolution of the monasteries see G. Baskerville's painstaking study entitled *English monks and the suppression of the monasteries* (1937). Valuable for the economic aspects of the dissolution is A. Savine's *English monasteries on the eve of the dissolution* (1909). The standard Roman Catholic account is F. A. Gasquet's *Henry VIII and the English monasteries* (2 vols., 1906).

Elizabethan England. The most authoritative and up-to-date biography of the "Virgin queen" is J. E. Neale's *Elizabeth* (1934). Well-written and still valuable is M. Creighton's *Elizabeth* (1899). L. Strachey's *Elizabeth and Essex* (1928) is brilliant and colorful. Katharine Anthony's *Queen Elizabeth* (1929) and M. Waldman's *Elizabeth, queen of England* (1933) are two readable popular biographies. Indispensable for a more intimate knowledge are *The letters of Queen Elizabeth,* edited by G. B. Harrison (1935). J. B. Black's *Reign of Elizabeth* (1936) and A. Browning's *Age of Elizabeth* (1935) are clear, sound, and readable surveys. Valuable for the foreign policy of Elizabeth's reign is Conyers Read's *Mr. Secretary Walsingham and the policy of Queen Elizabeth* (3 vols., 1925), with a critical bibliography. E. P. Cheyney's *England from the Spanish Armada to the death of Elizabeth* (2 vols., 1914–26) is a work of distinction by an eminent American historian. M. St. C. Byrne's *Elizabethan life in town and country* (1925) is an interesting sketch of many phases of Elizabethan life. An invaluable longer and more comprehensive study is *Shakespeare's England,* edited by Sir Walter Raleigh and written by authorities in each field (2 vols., 1916). W. K. Jordan's *Development of religious toleration in England from the beginning of the Reformation to the death of Elizabeth* (1931) is the best study of the subject. For the history of Puritanism during the reign of Elizabeth there are three valuable works founded on a first-hand study of the sources: Christina H. Garrett's *Marian exiles: a study in the origins of Elizabethan Puritanism* (1938), M. M. Knappen's *Tudor Puritanism* (1939), and William Haller's *The rise of Puritanism* (1938).

Elizabethan literature. A good recent survey is Esther C. Dunn's *Literature of Shakespeare's England* (1936). An older work by a well-known authority is G. Saintsbury's *History of Elizabethan literature* (1903). Another competent survey is F. E. Schelling's *English literature during the lifetime of Shakespeare*

(1910). Hardin Craig's *The enchanted glass; the Elizabethan mind in literature* (1936) is a unique and illuminating study of Elizabethan thought as expressed in contemporary literature. G. R. Potter's *Elizabethan verse and prose* (1928) is a good anthology for non-dramatic literature. *The literature of England,* by G. B. Woods, H. A. Watt, and G. K. Anderson (2 vols., 1936), is a good general anthology. Outstanding books on Shakespeare are J. Q. Adams' *Life of William Shakespeare* (1923), E. K. Chambers' *William Shakespeare* (2 vols., 1930), W. A. Neilson and A. H. Thorndike's *Facts about Shakespeare* (1931), T. M. Parrott's *Shakespeare* (1934), and Sir Sidney Lee's *Life of William Shakespeare* (rev. ed., 1916).

Scotland and Ireland. R. L. Mackie's *History of Scotland* (1931) is a reliable survey written with vigor and clarity. Agnes M. Mackenzie's *Scotland of Queen Mary and the religious wars, 1513–1638* (1936) is a scholarly and spirited book of first-rate importance. Among the numerous biographies of Mary, that by Thomas F. Henderson (2 vols., 1905) is notable. The same author's *Casket letters* (2nd ed., 1890) probably presents best the case for the authenticity of the letters. M. A. S. Hume's *Love affairs of Mary, queen of Scots, a political history* (1903) is a useful volume. Notable among the more recent lives are Marjorie Bowen's (pseudonym for Mrs. G. M. V. Long) *Mary, queen of Scots* (1934), unsympathetic but often penetrating, and George A. Campbell's *Mary, queen of Scots* (1936), a sober piece of work. A. G. C. Gordon-Smith's *Babington plot* (1936) and R. F. Gore-Brown's *Lord Bothwell* (1937) are useful works. For Ireland there is Mary Hayden and G. A. Moonan's *Short history of the Irish people from the earliest times to 1920* (1921), which is moderately Irish in its viewpoint. A second survey is Robert Dunlop's *Ireland, from the earliest times to the present day* (1922); moderate and authentic. R. D. Edwards' *Church and state in Tudor Ireland* (1935) is a well-balanced and scholarly study written from the Irish point of view. For further books on Ireland the student may consult Constantia Maxwell's *Short bibliography of Irish history* (1923).

CHAPTER TEN

Spain under Philip II and Its Decline in the Seventeenth Century

Philip II and his reign. For a brief survey of Philip II's reign the student may consult one of the histories of Spain listed in the bibliography for Chapter One. There is a reasonably good survey by Martin Hume in the *Cambridge modern history,* vol. 3 (1918), pp. 475–525. The same author has also written a readable biography of Philip II (1897). There is also a readable short account of Philip II and his reign in R. T. Davies' *Golden century of Spain* (1937), pp. 115–226. An admirable fuller account of Philip and his reign is to be found in vol. 4 (1934) of R. B. Merriman's *Rise of the Spanish empire.* J. H. Mariejol's *Philip II, the first modern king,* translated from the French by W. B. Wells (1934), is a good biography despite its title. David Loth's

Philip II (1932) is a readable popular biography that is not always convincing. The most detailed biography of the Spanish king is Henri Forneron's *Histoire de Philippe II* (4 vols., 1881–82). W. H. Prescott's *History of the reign of Philip the Second* (3 vols., 1855–58) is more valuable as literature than as history. There is an excellent account of the battle of Lepanto in Sir Charles Oman's *Art of war in the sixteenth century* (1937). The preparations for the battle are interestingly described in E. von Normann-Friedenfels' *Don Juan de Austria und die Schlacht bei Lepanto* (1902). W. Stirling-Maxwell's *Don John of Austria* (2 vols., 1883) is still useful. For the Moriscos there is the scholarly work of Henry C. Lea, *The Moriscos of Spain, their conversion and expulsion* (1901). Another valuable work is Richard Dozy's *Spanish Islam: a history of the Moslems in Spain,* translated by F. G. Stokes (1913). The English side of the Armada campaign is stated in Julian Corbett's *Drake and the Tudor navy* (2 vols., 1899). The Spanish story is told in C. Fernández Duro's *La Armada invencible* (2 vols., 1884–85). A useful short account in English is John R. Hale's *Great Armada* (1913).

Decline of Spain. There is no good comprehensive account of the causes of Spain's decline. A suggestive short study is E. J. Hamilton's "The decline of Spain," *Economic history review,* vol. 8 (1938), pp. 168–179. A valuable study in German is Konrad Häbler's *Wirtschaftliche Blüte Spaniens im sechzehnten Jahrhundert und ihr Verfall* (1888). Useful and often penetrating comments may be found in M. A. S. Hume's *Spain, its greatness and decay* (3rd ed., 1931), J. Klein's *The mesta* (1920), R. T. Davies' *Golden century of Spain, 1501–1621* (1937), and Oliviera Martins' *History of Iberian civilization* (1930). There are short surveys by M. A. S. Hume of the reigns of Philip III and Philip IV in the *Cambridge modern history,* vol. 3 (1907), pp. 526–548, and vol. 4 (1907), pp. 623–665. The same author has also written a longer study on the reign of Philip IV entitled *Court of Philip IV, Spain in decadence* (1907). For a brief survey of Charles II and his reign see the *Cambridge modern history,* vol. 5 (1908), pp. 372–400, or one of the general histories of Spain. A longer detailed account is to be found in A. Alphonse's *Ende der Habsburger in Spanien* (2 vols., 1929).

Spanish culture. Havelock Ellis' *The soul of Spain* (1909; new ed., 1937) is a readable, penetrating study. Three of the best shorter histories of Spanish literature in English are J. Fitzmaurice-Kelly's *New history of Spanish literature* (1927), George T. Northup's *Introduction to Spanish literature* (1925), and E. Mérimée's *History of Spanish literature,* translated, revised, and enlarged by S. G. Morley (1931). George Ticknor's *History of Spanish literature* (3 vols., 4th ed., 1872) is a useful longer history. There are two good lives of Cervantes in English, one by Rudolph Schevill (1919) and the other by J. Fitzmaurice-Kelly (1892). Both have also written illuminating studies of Lope de Vega—the former under the title, *The dramatic art of Lope de Vega* (Publications in modern philology of the University of California, vol. 6 [1918]) and the latter a short work entitled *Lope de Vega and the Spanish drama* (1902). There is an excellent account of Spanish painting in A. Pijoan's *History of art* (3 vols., 1927–28). Other useful books are Charles H. Caffin's *Story of Spanish painting* (1917), E. Harris' *Spanish painting* (1938), M. Dieulafoy's *Art in Spain and Portugal* (1913), and Chandler R. Post's

History of Spanish painting (7 vols. in 10, 1930–38). Frank Rutter's *El Greco* (1930) is a moderately successful attempt to put El Greco in his place in the history of painting. For Murillo there is the readable life by A. F. Calvert (1907). Shorter studies of Velasquez and his art include Walter Armstrong's *Velasquez* (1897) and Robert A. M. Stevenson's *Velasquez* (1906). A fuller account is to be found in A. L. Baldry's *Velasquez* (1905).

CHAPTER ELEVEN

The Rise and Decline of the Dutch Republic

Political and economic. The standard history of the northern provinces in English is P. J. Blok's *History of the people of the Netherlands*, translated by O. A. Bierstadt and Ruth Putnam (5 vols., 1898–1912). For the southern provinces there is the monumental *Histoire de Belgique*, by Henri Pirenne (7 vols., 1902–32). G. Edmundson's *History of Holland* (1922) is a well-written and fairly accurate survey. Motley's *Rise of the Dutch republic*, which has appeared in numerous editions, is a work of literature rather than a sound history; warmly partisan to the Dutch and the Protestants. A good account of the revolt in English is P. Geyl's *Revolt of the Netherlands, 1555–1609* (1932). Equally authoritative for the succeeding period is the same author's *The Netherlands divided, 1609–1648* (1936). A useful history of the revolt as seen from Antwerp is J. Wegg's *Decline of Antwerp under Philip of Spain* (1924). Another phase is presented in *The siege and relief of Leyden, 1574*, by R. Fruin, translated by E. Trevelyan (1927). The most authoritative biography of William the Silent is P. J. Blok's *Willem de Eerste, prins van Oranje* (2 vols., 1919–20). There are two good biographies of the Dutch leader in English: Ruth Putnam's *William the Silent, prince of Orange, 1533–1584, and the revolt of the Netherlands* (1911) and F. Harrison's *William the Silent* (1924). The first part of E. Baasch's *Holländische Wirtschaftsgeschichte* (1927) offers a scholarly survey of the economic history of the Dutch Republic. The principal features of the decline and dissolution of the Dutch Republic are vividly sketched in H. W. Van Loon's *Fall of the Dutch republic* (2nd ed., 1924).

Maritime and colonial activities. H. W. Van Loon's *Golden book of the Dutch navigators* (1916) is a spirited account founded on a study of the sources. An informative short treatise in English on Dutch colonial policy is Clive Day's *The Dutch in Java* (1904). A. Vanderbosch's *Dutch East Indies* (1934) is a comprehensive and painstaking study. Another valuable account is J. S. Furnivall's *Netherlands India* (1939). More detailed is E. S. de Klerck's *History of the Netherlands East Indies* (2 vols., 1938); by a Dutch historian who carefully studied the sources. Valuable for the rise of Dutch power is H. E. Egerton's "The transference of colonial power to the United Provinces and England," *Cambridge modern history*, vol. 4 (1907), pp. 728–759. The conflicting economic interests of the Dutch and the English are ably presented in G. Edmundson's *Anglo-Dutch rivalry during the first half of the seventeenth century* (1911). William E. Griffis' *Story of New Netherland*

(1913) deals with the activities of the Dutch in America. Lucy M. Salmon's *The Dutch West India Company on the Hudson* (1915) is an informative short treatise. W. R. Shepherd's *Story of New Amsterdam* (1926) is a pleasantly written account of New York in the days of the Dutch West India Company.
Dutch civilization and culture. J. Huizinga's *Holländische Kultur des siebzehnten Jahrhunderts* (1933) is a series of essays on Dutch civilization in the seventeenth century by an eminent Dutch historian. Emil Lucka's *Die grosse Zeit der Niederländer* (1936) is an interesting study of the same period along somewhat broader lines. This writer knows of no history of Dutch literature in English. A useful survey in German is that by L. Schneider, entitled *Geschichte der niederländischen Literatur* (1887). There is an excellent life of Vondel in English by A. J. Barnouw (1925). Vondel's *Lucifer* has been translated into English by Leonard C. Van Noppen (1899; reprint, 1917). The relationship between Milton and Vondel is treated in George Edmundson's *Milton and Vondel: a curiosity in literature* (1885). There is a penetrating essay on Grotius in the *Social and political ideas of some great thinkers of the sixteenth and seventeenth centuries*, edited by F. J. C. Hearnshaw (1926). A longer study is W. S. M. Knight's *Life and works of Hugo Grotius* (1925), which takes a somewhat unfavorable view of Grotius' character. R. H. Wilenski's *Introduction to Dutch art* (1929) is an original and acute survey of Dutch art from 1580 to 1700. The evolution of Dutch painting is competently traced in Charles H. Caffin's *Story of Dutch painting* (1911). A valuable study of a more limited period is C. H. Collins Barker's *Dutch painting in the seventeenth century* (1926).

CHAPTER TWELVE

The Rise of Absolute Monarchy in France

Sixteenth century. For a list of histories of France see the bibliography for Chapter One. Louis Batiffol's *Century of the Renaissance*, translated from the French by Elsie F. Buckley (1916), is a lucid account of sixteenth century France. There is a good brief treatment of the Reformation in France in Preserved Smith's *Age of the Reformation* (1933); also in vol. 2 of Thomas M. Lindsay's *History of the Reformation* (1928). A somewhat fuller account of the period is to be found in vol. 1 of A. J. Grant's *French monarchy* (2 vols., 1900). A valuable book in French is Jean Viénot's *Histoire de la réforme française des origines à l'édit de Nantes* (1926). The social and cultural background of the movement is ably presented in Pierre Imbart de la Tour's *Les origines de la réforme* (3 vols., 1905–14). There is a good brief account of the French Wars of Religion in the *Cambridge modern history*, vol. 3 (1918), pp. 1–52. Another good brief account is A. Tilley's *French wars of religion* (1919). An excellent longer account in French is that of J. H. Mariéjol in vol. 6 of *Histoire de France*, edited by E. Lavisse. The political aspects are ably discussed in Edward Armstrong's *French wars of religion* (2nd ed., 1904). A more detailed and more comprehensive account of the Wars of Religion to 1576 is offered in James W. Thompson's *Wars of religion in France* (1909).

An older but still useful work on the period is Leopold von Ranke's *Civil wars and monarchy in France in the sixteenth and seventeenth centuries,* translated by M. A. Garvey (2 vols., 1852). The first chapters of Arthur J. Grant's *Huguenots* (1934; Home university library) contain a lucid brief survey of the early history of the Huguenots. H. M. Baird's *History of the rise of the Huguenots of France* (reprint, 2 vols., 1907) is readable but has strong Protestant leanings. The best English biography of Catherine de Médicis is that by Paul Van Dyke (2 vols., 1922). Henry D. Sedgwick's *House of Guise* (1938) is a good popular account. There is a competent account of the massacre of St. Bartholomew by Sylvia L. England (1938). A. W. Whitehead's *Gaspard de Coligny* (1904) is a good biography based on a study of the sources. An important study of one of the most influential figures of the period is Franklin C. Palm's *Politics and religion in sixteenth-century France, a study of the career of Henry of Montmorency-Damville* (1927). The same author has published a small collection of source materials with an historical introduction under the title, *The establishment of French absolutism, 1574–1610* (1928). Abbott P. Usher's *History of the grain trade in France, 1400–1700* (1913) is a valuable study. For the history of French commerce in general Henri Pigeonneau's *Histoire du commerce de la France* (2 vols., 1885–97) is useful. French civilization from the Renaissance through the Napoleonic period is ably and often brilliantly discussed in A. L. Guerard's *Life and death of an ideal; France in the classical age* (1928).

Henry IV. There are good brief surveys of Henry's reign in the *Cambridge modern history,* vol. 3 (1918), pp. 657–695, and Jacques Boulenger's *Seventeenth century* (*National history of France*), pp. 286–327. The best short life in English is P. F. Willert's *Henry of Navarre* (1902). Though not a work of original research, Quentin Hurst's *Henry of Navarre* (1938) is a well-organized, readable, and reasonably sound biography. The most detailed and comprehensive work on Henry and his reign is Auguste Poisson's *Histoire du règne de Henri IV* (3rd rev. ed., 4 vols., 1865–66). Adair G. Williams has written two scholarly and informative articles: "The abjuration of Henry of Navarre," *Journal of modern history,* vol. 5 (1933), pp. 143–171, and "The absolution of Henry of Navarre," *ibid.,* vol. 6 (1934), pp. 379–404. There is an excellent discussion of Sully's work in Eleanor C. Lodge's *Sully, Colbert and Turgot; a chapter in French economic history* (1931). There is a good biography of Sully in French by Henri Carré entitled *Sully: sa vie et son oeuvre, 1559–1641* (1932). Sully's *Memoirs* have appeared in a number of editions in English. For the question of the "Grand Design" see *Sully's Grand design of Henry IV,* with an introduction by David Ogg (1921). Henry's relations with the Huguenots are treated in Henry M. Baird's *The Huguenots and Henry of Navarre* (2 vols., 1886).

Richelieu and Mazarin. The history of France from the death of Henry IV to the death of Mazarin is covered in an interesting and scholarly manner in James B. Perkins' *France under Mazarin,* with a review of the administration of Richelieu (2 vols., 1886). There are good short surveys of the reigns of Richelieu and Mazarin in the *Cambridge modern history,* vol. 4 (1907), pp. 118–157 and 592–622, in David Ogg's *Europe in the seventeenth century* (1925), pp. 183–226, and in J. Boulenger's *Seventeenth century* (1920), pp. 30–112 and 136–171. J. B. Perkins' *Richelieu and the growth of the French power* (1900) is still one of the best accounts of the French minister's life. A more recent brief but excellent study is Auguste Bailly's *The cardinal dictator: a portrait of Richelieu*, translated from the French by Hamish Miles (1936). A useful older biography is R. Lodge's *Richelieu* (1896). There is a good biography of Mazarin in English by Arthur Hassall (reprint, 1934).

CHAPTER THIRTEEN ·

Germany and the Thirty Years' War

Germany before the Thirty Years' War. There is no up-to-date study in English of the history of Germany during the period from 1555 to 1618. Good accounts of the political conditions are A. W. Ward's "The empire under Ferdinand I and Maximilian II" and "The empire under Rudolf II," *Cambridge modern history*, vol. 3 (1918), pp. 140–181 and 696–735, respectively. An older but still useful political survey of the period is to be found in W. Stubbs' *Lectures on European history*, edited by A. Hassall (1904), pp. 144–180, 254–264. The political and religious background of the war is briefly summarized in E. F. Henderson's *History of Germany* (1908), part 1, pp. 422–449, and in Henry O. Wakeman's *Europe, 1598–1715* (1911), pp. 39–62. Chapters 8 and 9 of Georg Steinhausen's *Geschichte der deutschen Kultur* (3rd ed., 1929) offer a good general survey of the period. A standard older work on the period in German is M. Ritter's *Deutsche Geschichte im Zeitalter der Gegenreformation und des dreissigjährigen Krieges, 1555–1648* (3 vols., 1889–1908). Useful also is Leopold von Ranke's *Zur deutschen Geschichte: vom Religionsfrieden bis zum dreissigjährigen Kriege* (1874). For the economic decline of Germany after 1555 see E. Gothein's *Deutschland vor dem dreissigjährigen Krieg* (1908), R. Ehrenberg's *Hamburg und England: der Niedergang der deutschen Volkswirtschaft* (1896), *Die Kultur der Gegenwart*, by F. von Bezold and others (part 2, 1908), and Karl Lamprecht's *Deutsche Geschichte*, vol. 5, part 2 (1895), pp. 476–507.

Thirty Years' War. The best one-volume account in English is C. V. Wedgwood's *The Thirty Years' War* (1939), a scholarly and penetrating survey. Samuel R. Gardiner's *Thirty Years' War, 1618–1648* (1897) is a useful shorter survey. The longer work of Anton Gindeley entitled *History of the Thirty Years' War*, translated by A. Ten Brook (2 vols., 1884), is antiquated in many respects. There is a good short summary of the war in David Ogg's *Europe in the seventeenth century* (1925). A somewhat fuller survey is contained in the chapters by A. W. Ward (1, 3, 6, 7, 13, 14), in the *Cambridge modern history*, vol. 4 (1907). H. G. R. Reade's *Sidelights on the Thirty Years' War* (3 vols., 1925) contains valuable information but lacks critical notes. Gustav Freytag's vividly written but often fanciful *Bilder aus der deutschen Vergangenheit*, which has appeared in numerous editions since 1859 and also in an English translation, is to be classed as literature rather than as history. The same may be said of Friedrich Schiller's *Geschichte des dreissigjährigen Krieges*.

Special works. Francis Watson's *Wallenstein, soldier under Saturn* (1938) is a competent and painstaking study, closely packed with detail. Leopold von Ranke's *Geschichte Wallensteins*, first published in 1869, is still a good general account. *Caricatures of the "Winter King" of Bohemia*, with introduction, notes, and translations by E. A. Beller (1928), is an interesting and valuable contribution to the literature on the period. J. A. Gade has written an informative popular life of Christian IV (1928). There is a lively account of the military exploits of the Swedish king by Sir George F. McMunn, entitled *Gustavus Adolphus, the northern hurricane* (1930). C. R. L. Fletcher's *Gustavus Adolphus and the struggle of Protestantism for existence* (1892) is written from a definite Protestant viewpoint and is a political study rather than a biography. An older instructive work is John L. Stevens' *History of Gustavus Adolphus* (1884). There is an up-to-date scholarly account of the public career of Gustavus in German by Georg Wittrock (1930).

Effects of the war. See C. V. Wedgwood's *The Thirty Years' War* (1939). The best special study in English of the effects of the Thirty Years' War is A. W. Ward's "The effects of the Thirty Years' War," *Proceedings of the Royal Institute of Great Britain*, vol. 20 (1914), pp. 368–398, but it stands in need of revision regarding the decline of the population, which it estimates as having been one-half. Revisionist studies on the effects of the Thirty Years' War include B. Haendcke's *Deutsche Kultur im Zeitalter des dreissigjährigen Krieges* (1906); O. Redlich's "Der dreissigjährige Krieg und die deutsche Kultur," *Ausgewählte Schriften* (1925), pp. 23–38; D. Duerr's "Hat der dreissigjährige Krieg die deutsche Kultur vernichtet?" *Württembergische Vierteljahrshefte*, N. F. vol. 23 (1914), pp. 302–326; Ilse Hoffmann's *Deutschland im Zeitalter des dreissigjährigen Krieges: nach Berichten und Urteilen englischer Augenzeugen* (1927); and K. Beschorner's "Wiederaufbau der meisten im dreissigjährigen Kriege zerstörten Dörfer," *Studium Lipsiense* (1909), pp. 73–88. The most radical of the revisionists is R. Hoeniger ("Der dreissigjährige Krieg und die deutsche Kultur," *Preussische Jahrbücher*, vol. 138 [1909], pp. 402–450), who goes so far as to state without proof that the population of Germany did not decrease appreciably during the war. The war, he contends, consumed only the natural increase of the population, which he estimates at three millions. The pioneer revisionist was Bernhard Erdmannsdörffer (*Deutsche Geschichte, 1648-1740* [1892]). Some writers have used Grimmelshausen's *Simplicissimus* to support statements regarding the horrors and the destruction of the war despite the fact that it is avowedly a work of fiction.

CHAPTER FOURTEEN

The Beginnings of Modern Science

General. An excellent account of the development of modern science and its relation to society is to be found in *Science and civilization*, edited by Francis S. Marvin (1923). There is a thought-provoking lecture entitled "The history of science and the history of civilization" in George Sarton's

The history of science and the new humanism (1931). R. J. Harvey-Gibson's
Two thousand years of science (1929), W. T. Sedgwick and H. W. Tyler's
Short history of science (1921), W. C. Dampier-Whetham's *History of science*
(new ed., 1932), Dorothy M. Turner's *Book of scientific discovery* (1933),
Benjamin Ginzburg's *Adventure of science* (1930), and W. Libby's *Introduction to the history of science* (1917) are useful surveys of the history of science.
Abraham Wolf's *History of science, technology and philosophy in the sixteenth
and seventeenth centuries* (1935) and *History of science, technology and philosophy in the eighteenth century* (1939) offer a fuller and more comprehensive
account; they are sound and readable. The individual scientists are competently treated in Martin Gumpert's *Trail-blazers of science*, translated
from the German by E. L. Shuman (1936), Philip Lenard's *Great men of
science; a history of scientific progress*, translated from the German by H. S.
Hatfield (1933), Ivor B. Hart's *Makers of science, mathematics, physics,
astronomy* (1923), and R. J. Harvey-Gibson's *Master thinkers* (1928). For
the history of astronomy Arthur Berry's *Short history of astronomy* (1899;
reprint, 1910), George Forbes' *History of astronomy* (reprint, 1921), Henry S.
Williams' *The great astronomers* (1930), and Hector C. Macpherson's *Makers
of astronomy* (1933) are informative volumes. Good surveys of the history
of physics are offered in Carl T. Chase's *History of experimental physics*
(1932), H. Buckley's *Short history of physics* (1927), Henry Crew's *Rise of
modern physics* (2nd ed., 1935), and Ivor B. Hart's *The great physicists*
(1927). For the development of physical thought there is the excellent survey
by Albert Einstein and L. Infeld entitled *The evolution of physics; the growth
of ideas from early concepts to relativity and quanta* (1938).

    Beginnings of modern science. For the development of science during the
Middle Ages Lynn Thorndike's scholarly and detailed *History of magic and
experimental science* (4 vols., 1923-34) is invaluable. Equally important is
the same author's *Science and thought in the fifteenth century* (1929). Charles
Singer's *From magic to science; essays on the scientific twilight* (1928) is an
informative little volume by an authority on the history of science. A competent study of Leonardo is Edward McCurdy's *The mind of Leonardo da Vinci*
(1928). The same author has collected the reflections and speculations of
Leonardo in *The notebooks of Leonardo da Vinci* (2 vols., 1938). Other valuable
studies are Ivor B. Hart's *The mechanical investigations of Leonardo da Vinci*
(1925), J. P. McMurrich's *Leonardo da Vinci the anatomist* (1931), and
Franz M. Feldhaus' *Leonardo der Techniker und Erfinder* (1913). Dorothy
Stimson's *The gradual acceptance of the Copernican theory of the universe* (1917)
is the best account of the subject in English. The story of the acceptance
of the Copernican theory in England is ably treated in Francis R. Johnson's
*Astronomical thought in Renaissance England; a study of the English scientific
writings from 1500 to 1645* (1937). For Galileo there is Émile Namer's *Galileo,
searcher of the heavens*, translated and adapted from the French by Sibyl
Harris (1931), a work of painstaking research. Another good biography of
Galileo is that by John J. Fahie (1903). Lane Cooper's *Aristotle, Galileo and
the tower of Pisa* (1935) essays to show that the story regarding the dropping
of weights from the Tower of Pisa is a myth. There are a number of good
studies on Galileo in German, including Rudolph Laemmel's *Galileo Galilei*

im Licht des zwanzigsten Jahrhunderts (1927), Leonardo Olschki's *Galilei und seine Zeit* (1927), and *Galilei und sein Kampf für die copernicanische Lehre*, edited by E. Wohlwill (2 vols., 1909–26). The Italian historian Antonio Favaro has examined the life and writings of Galileo most minutely, but most of his writings have not been translated into English. A sample of his work in English is his introduction to Galileo's *Dialogues concerning two new sciences*, translated from the Italian and the Latin by Henry Crew and Alfonso de Salvio (1914). Louis T. More's *Isaac Newton* (1937) is "the most complete and most lucid examination of the Newtonian principles in terms of modern scientific language." A more compact life is that by J. W. N. Sullivan (1937), authoritatively and brilliantly written. Still more compact is S. Brodetsky's *Sir Isaac Newton* (1927). G. N. Clark's *Science and social welfare in the age of Newton* (1937) is an informative little volume. Useful as a corrective is Morris R. Cohen's "The myth about Bacon and the inductive method," *Scientific monthly*, vol. 23 (1926), pp. 504–508. For the scientific societies there is the excellent study by Martha (Ornstein) Bronfenbrenner, *The rôle of scientific societies in the seventeenth century* (1928). More limited is Harcourt Brown's *Scientific organizations in seventeenth-century France* (1934), a work of careful scholarship. Philip Schorr's *Science and superstition in the eighteenth century; a study of the treatment of science in two encyclopedias of 1725–1750* (1932) is an illuminating work.

Medicine, anatomy, and physiology. Victor Robinson's *Story of medicine* (1931) is a sound and readable survey covering the period from the dawn of civilization to the present. A short synopsis of the history of medicine is to be found in Bernard Dawson's *History of medicine* (1932). A. H. Buck's *Dawn of modern medicine* (1920) deals with the latter half of the eighteenth and the first part of the nineteenth century. Henry E. Siegrist's *Great doctors; a biographical history of medicine*, translated by Eden and Cedar Paul (1933), is a notable work by a distinguished student of medical history. The history of physiology is competently surveyed in Sir Michael Foster's *Lectures on the history of physiology during the sixteenth, seventeenth and eighteenth centuries* (reprint, 1924). Charles Singer's *Discovery of the circulation of blood* (1923) is a lucid and authoritative treatment of the subject. A valuable study is the same writer's *Evolution of anatomy* (1925). A noteworthy biography of Vesalius is that by James M. Ball (1910). For Harvey see *The works of William Harvey*, translated from the Latin, with a life of the author, by Robert Willis (1847).

Inventions. Abbott P. Usher's *History of mechanical inventions* (1929) is an excellent survey. Other useful volumes on the history of inventions include T. C. Bridges' *Book of invention* (1925), Bradley A. Fiske's *Invention, the master-key to progress* (1921), E. B. Barwick's *Man's genius; the story of famous inventions and their development* (1932), Archie F. Collins' *Bird's-eye view of invention* (1926), and Floyd L. Darrow's *Thinkers and doers* (1925). For the development of mathematics the student may consult J. W. N. Sullivan's *History of mathematics in Europe* (1925), Vera Sanford's *Short history of mathematics* (1930), or F. Cajori's *History of mathematics* (2nd rev. ed., 1919). Charles A. Ealand's *Romance of the microscope* (1921) and R. S. Clay and T. H. Court's *History of the microscope* (1932) contain lucid accounts

of the development of that instrument. For the thermometer there is Henry
C. Bolton's *Evolution of the thermometer, 1592–1743* (1900). There is a good
account of the invention and development of the telescope in Louis Bell's
The telescope (1922) and G. E. Pendray's *Men, mirrors, and stars* (1935).

Naturalists. Louis C. Miall's *The early naturalists; their lives and work,
1530–1789* (1912) is a sound and lucid survey. There are good short accounts
of the work of Malpighi, Swammerdam, Leeuwenhoek, Redi, Grew, Linnaeus, and others in Erik Nordenskiöld's *History of biology*, translated from
the Swedish by L. B. Eyre (1932); William A. Locy's *Biology and its makers*
(3rd ed., rev. 1928) and *Growth of biology* (1925); and Charles Singer's *The
story of living things* (1931). Clifford Dobell's *Antony van Leeuwenhoek and
his "little animals"* (1932) is an authoritative and entertaining life of the
father of protozoölogy and bacteriology. There is a readable and informative
chapter on Leeuwenhoek in Paul de Kruif's popular *Microbe hunters* (1926).

Chemistry. James E. Marsh's *The origins and growth of chemical science*
(1929), Forris J. Moore's *History of chemistry*, revised by W. T. Hall (1931),
Floyd L. Darrow's *Story of chemistry* (1927), and James C. Brown's *History
of chemistry from the earliest times* (1920) are useful general surveys. More
limited in scope is John M. Stillman's *Story of early chemistry* (1924). Other
useful books are Bernard Jaffe's *Crucibles, the lives and achievements of great
chemists* (1930), Eric J. Holmyard's *The great chemists* (1928), and Leonard A. Coles' *Book of chemical discovery* (1933). W. R. Aykroyd's *Three
philosophers* (1935) gives a vivid picture of Lavoisier, Priestley, and Cavendish, and of their work.

Electricity. There is a good short summary entitled "The foundations
of the electrical age" in Dorothy M. Turner's *Book of scientific discovery*
(1933), pp. 152–173. W. F. Shearcroft's *Story of electricity* (1925) and William A. Dugin's *Electricity; its history and development* (1912) are readable
brief sketches. A longer popular and reasonably sound account is Ernest
Greenwood's *Amber to amperes; the story of electricity* (1931). Park Benjamin's
History of electricity from antiquity to the days of Benjamin Franklin (1898)
is still one of the best accounts of the subject.

CHAPTER FIFTEEN

The Struggle for Constitutional Monarchy
in England

Early Stuart period. J. D. Mackie's *Cavalier and Puritan* (rev. ed., 1936)
is a lucid and interesting short introduction to the period. Godfrey Davies'
Early Stuarts, 1603–1660 (1937) contains a somewhat fuller sound and comprehensive survey of the period, presenting the latest findings of historical
scholarship. Another valuable study is G. M. Trevelyan's *England under
the Stuarts* (1904). F. C. Montague's *History of England from the accession
of James I to the Restoration, 1603–1660* (1907; vol. 7 of *Political history of
England,* edited by Hunt and Poole) is an authoritative survey of the political

history. The most extensive account of the period is Samuel R. Gardiner's *History of England, 1603–1642* (10 vols., 1895–99). The social history of the period is treated in vol. 4 of *Social England*, edited by H. D. Traill and J. S. Mann (1904). Mary Coate's *Social life in Stuart England* (1924) presents much varied information in popular form. A good brief summary of the basic issues involved in the constitutional struggle may be found in G. B. Adams' *Constitutional history of England*, revised with continuation by Robert L. Schuyler (1934). For a fuller account the student may consult J. R. Tanner's *English constitutional conflicts of the seventeenth century* (1928), J. A. R. Marriott's *Crisis of English liberty* (1930), or Idris D. Jones' *The English revolution* (1931). G. P. Gooch's *English democratic ideas in the seventeenth century* (2nd ed., 1927), with supplementary notes by H. J. Laski, is a valuable study of the period. Valuable, too, are the pertinent chapters of A. F. Pollard's *Evolution of parliament* (1926). Fourteen Parliamentary diaries are edited and analyzed in *Commons debates, 1621* by Wallace Notestein, Frances H. Relf, and Hartley Simpson (7 vols., 1936). A useful volume of source materials is G. W. Prothero's *Select statutes and other constitutional documents illustrative of the reigns of Elizabeth and James I* (4th ed., 1913). W. K. Jordan's *Development of religious toleration in England from the accession of James I to the convention of the Long Parliament, 1603–1640* (1936) is a continuation of the same author's rich study of the preceding period. For further references see *Bibliography of British history: Stuart period, 1603–1714*, edited by Godfrey Davies (1928) with critical comments.

James I and Charles I. A good short life of James I is that by H. R. Williamson (1936). A somewhat longer competent biography is Charles Williams' *James I* (1934). *James I of England* by Clara and Hardy Steeholm (1938) is an interesting popular biography which is concerned primarily with James as a human being. *The political works of James I*, edited with introduction and bibliography by C. H. McIlwain (1918), is valuable for the study of the political principles of the Stuarts. There are two sound and readable essays on James I and Charles I in Eva Scott's *Six Stuart sovereigns* (1935). A good brief life of Charles I is that by P. Pakenham (1936). F. M. G. Higham's *Charles I* (1932) is a well-balanced, competent biography. G. M. Young's able study, *Charles I and Cromwell* (1935), endeavors to trace the steps which led Charles I to the scaffold. Of Prince Rupert there is a full life by James Cleugh (1934). C. Wilkinson's *Prince Rupert the Cavalier* (1934) deals mainly with Prince Rupert the military commander in the civil wars. Other useful works are J. G. Muddiman's *Trial of King Charles I* (1928), A. S. Duncan-Jones' *Archbishop Laud* (1927), C. V. Wedgwood's *Strafford* (1935), H. D. Traill's *Strafford* (1889), H. R. Williamson's *John Hampden* (1933), C. E. Wade's *John Pym* (1912), and W. H. Holloway's *Story of Naseby* (2nd ed., 1923).

Commonwealth and Protectorate. A good brief introductory volume is A. S. Turberville's *Commonwealth and Restoration* (rev. ed., 1936). The standard longer work on the period is S. R. Gardiner's *History of the commonwealth and protectorate* (new ed., 4 vols., 1903). C. H. Firth's *Last years of the protectorate, 1656–58* (2 vols., 1909) continues the work of Gardiner; it is readable, accurate, impartial. S. R. Gardiner's *Oliver Cromwell* (1901) and

C. H. Firth's *Oliver Cromwell* (1935) are two scholarly works of the first importance. A more recent biography of Cromwell is that by John Buchan (1934); it is judicious, well-written, and good especially for the military history of the civil wars. John Drinkwater has written a good popular biography of Cromwell which is often brilliant in its analysis (1927). There is also a spirited biography by G. R. Stirling Taylor (1927) which "interprets Cromwell in the light of his belief that he was the chosen instrument of God." F. H. Hayward's *The unknown Cromwell* (1934) is a defense of the Protector which is not always convincing. For the economic history of the Protectorate there is a well-written volume by M. P. Ashley, *Financial and commercial policy under the Cromwellian protectorate* (1934). The religious history of the period is ably treated in G. B. Tatham's *Puritans in power, a study of the English church from 1640 to 1660* (1913) and in *History of the English church*, edited by W. R. W. Stephens and W. Hunt, vol. 6, *1625-1714*, by W. H. Hutton (1907). Good accounts of the history of Scotland and Ireland during this period are to be found in Andrew Lang's *History of Scotland*, vol. 3 (1905), and Richard Bagwell's *Ireland under the Stuarts and during the interregnum* (2 vols., 1909). For source materials see *The writings and speeches of Oliver Cromwell:* vol. 1, *1599-1649* (1937), edited by W. C. Abbott, with an introduction, notes and a sketch of Cromwell's life. An older work is that of Thomas Carlyle entitled *The letters and speeches of Oliver Cromwell*, edited with notes by S. C. Lomas and an introduction by C. H. Firth (3 vols., 1904). S. R. Gardiner's *Constitutional documents of the Puritan revolution, 1625-1660* (3rd ed., 1906) is a good collection with a valuable introduction. For further references see Wilbur C. Abbott's monumental *Bibliography of Cromwell* (1929), "a list of printed materials relating to Oliver Cromwell, together with a list of portraits and caricatures."

Cavalier and Puritan literature. The best account of Cavalier and Puritan literature is to be found in the *Cambridge history of English literature*, vol. 6 (1920). For shorter accounts the student may consult E. Legouis and L. Cazamian's *History of English literature*, vol. 2 (1927), C. C. Osgood's *Voice of England* (1935), John Buchan's *History of English literature* (1927), or any other good survey. Barrett Wendell's *Temper of the seventeenth century* (1904) and H. J. C. Grierson's *Cross currents in English literature in the seventeenth century* (1929) are informative special studies of the period. There is an interesting anthology entitled *Cavalier and Puritan ballads and broadsides, illustrating the period of the Great Rebellion, 1640-1660*, edited with an introduction by E. H. Rollins (1923). A good biography of Bunyan is that by W. H. Hutton (1928). Sound and readable biographies of Milton have been written by Mark Pattison (reprint, 1911), Sir Walter Raleigh (1900), and Rose Macaulay (1933). Another readable biography is that by Dora N. Raymond, entitled *Oliver's secretary: John Milton in an era of revolt* (1932), which emphasizes the years of his foreign secretaryship.

CHAPTER SIXTEEN

England from the Restoration to the Death of Queen Anne

Restoration. G. N. Clark's *The later Stuarts, 1660–1714* (1934) is a good up-to-date survey of the period. Arthur Bryant has written an excellent account of Restoration England under the title *England of Charles II* (1934). The same author's *King Charles II* (1931) is a spirited, sympathetic, and provocative study. A third book by the same author is *The postman's horn* (1936), an anthology of letters "illustrating every stage and aspect of life in Restoration England." A comprehensive account of the period is to be found in David Ogg's *England in the reign of Charles II* (2 vols., 1934). R. Lodge's *History of England from the Restoration to the death of William III* (1910; vol. 8 of *Political history of England*, edited by Hunt and Poole) is an authoritative account of the political history. On the foreign policy of the period there is Keith Feiling's illuminating and well-documented *British foreign policy, 1660–1672* (1930). Thora G. Stone's *England under the Restoration, 1660–1688* (1923) is a well-chosen collection of extracts from contemporary documents to illustrate the various phases of contemporary life. A reasonably good brief character study of Charles II may be found in John Hayward's *Charles II* (1933). W. B. Bell's *Great fire of London* (1920) and *Great plague of London in 1665* (1924) are sound, readable, and exhaustive, the best studies of the subjects. F. G. M. Higham's *King James the Second* (1934) is competent, readable, and free from partisanship. Thomas Babington Macaulay's classic *History of England from the accession of James II* (in various editions of from 5 to 10 vols., first printed 1849–61) cannot be recommended to uncritical readers. Two illuminating studies of the financial relations of Charles II and James II with Louis XIV are C. L. Grose, "Louis XIV's financial relations with Charles II and the English parliament," *Journal of modern history*, vol. 1 (1929), pp. 177–204, and R. H. George, "The financial relations of Louis XIV and James II," *ibid.*, vol. 3 (1931), pp. 392–413. G. M. Trevelyan's *English revolution, 1688–1689* (1939) is a short account by a distinguished historian.

William and Mary; Queen Anne. G. J. Renier's *William of Orange* (1933) is a readable, well-balanced, though somewhat unsympathetic brief life of William III. H. D. Traill's *William III* (1888; numerous reprints) is an older brief life by a distinguished English historian. Nellie M. Waterson has written a good personal portrait of Mary under the title *Mary II, queen of England* (1928). The standard work on the period of Queen Anne is G. M. Trevelyan's *England under Queen Anne* (3 vols., 1930–34). Keith Feiling's *History of the Tory party, 1640–1714* (1924) and W. T. Morgan's *English political parties and leaders in the reign of Queen Anne, 1702–1710* (1920) throw considerable light on the political history of the period. B. C. Brown's *Anne Stuart, queen of England* (1929) and M. R. Hopkinson's *Anne of England* (1934) are personal portraits which give only scant attention to the political, economic, and military affairs of the reign. A good, readable survey of Marlborough's life is H. J. and E. A. Edwards' *Short life of Marlborough* (1926). The definitive biography is Winston Churchill's *Marlborough: his life and times* (6 vols., 1933–38). Sir John Fortescue's *Marlborough* (1932) is a popular summary of Marlborough's military career. Marlborough's campaigns are treated in a scholarly manner in C. T. Atkinson's *Marlborough and the rise of the British army* (1921) and F. Taylor's *Wars of Marlborough* (2 vols., unfinished, 1921). For a list of pamphlets and memoirs of the reign of Queen Anne see W. T. Morgan's *Bibliography of British history, 1700–1715* (2 vols., 1935–37).

Literature. The literature of the period is treated in the *Cambridge history of English literature*, vol. 8 (1920). Students will also find some of the works listed in the bibliography for the preceding chapter useful for this period. There is a good short life of Dryden by George E. Saintsbury (1894; English Men of Letters series). There is also a more recent readable brief life by Christopher Hollis (1933). Mark Van Doren's *The poetry of John Dryden* (1920) is an illuminating study. A good study of Pepys is J. R. Tanner's *Mr. Pepys: an introduction to the diary together with a sketch of his later life* (1925). A. Ponsonby's *Samuel Pepys* (1928) and *John Evelyn* (1933) are two delightful books. There is a good brief summary of the political philosophy of Locke in H. J. Laski's *Political thought in England from Locke to Bentham* (1920). Henry R. F. Bourne's *Life of John Locke* (2 vols., 1876) is the most detailed biography of Locke. A good brief biography is that by Thomas Fowler (1890, reprints; English Men of Letters series). The best general analysis of Locke's thought this writer knows, is to be found in Richard I. Aaron's *John Locke* (1937). Sterling P. Lamprecht's *The moral and political philosophy of John Locke* (1918), Albert Hofstadter's *Locke and scepticism* (1935), and Kenneth MacLean's *John Locke and English literature of the eighteenth century* (1937) are useful special studies.

CHAPTER SEVENTEEN

Russia to the Death of Peter the Great

General works. The most detailed and also the most authentic account in English of Russian history from the earliest times to the death of Catherine II (with a brief survey to 1907) is Vasilii O. Kliuchevski's *History of Russia*, translated from the Russian by C. J. Hogarth (5 vols., 1911–31); translation poor. A longer work in French is *Histoire de Russie* by P. Milioukov, C. Seignobos, and L. Eisenmann (3 vols., 1932–33); lucid and modern in tone; treats cultural, social, and economic as well as political problems. In German there is Karl Stählin's sound and readable *Geschichte Russlands von den Anfängen bis zur Gegenwart* (3 vols., 1923–35). A. Rambaud's *Popular history of Russia from the earliest times to 1877* (2 vols., 1904) is a readable work but antiquated in many respects. Among the better short surveys may be listed Hans von Eckardt's *Russia*, translated by C. A. Phillips (1932),

George Vernadsky's *History of Russia* (1929), S. Platonov's *History of Russia*, translated by E. Aronsberg and edited by F. A. Golder (1929), Sir Bernard Pares' *History of Russia* (1926), and *Russia from the Varangians to the Bolsheviks*, by C. R. Beazley, N. Forbes, and G. A. Birkett (1918). George Vernadsky's *Political and diplomatic history of Russia* (1936) is a useful manual. For the social history of Russia, D. S. Mirsky's *Russia, a social history*, translated by C. G. Seligman (1931), is lucid and informative. M. N. Pokrovsky's *History of Russia from the earliest times to the rise of commercial capitalism*, translated by J. D. Clarkson and M. R. M. Griffiths (1931), is a brief Marxist survey. A more comprehensive work by the same author is his *Brief history of Russia*, translated by D. S. Mirsky (2 vols., 1933). The best general survey of the economic development is J. Mavor's *Economic history of Russia* (2 vols., 2nd rev. and enlarged ed., 1925). A notable work on the Russian peasantry is Geroid T. Robinson's scholarly and illuminating *Rural Russia under the old régime* (1932).

Works on the early period. Frank Nowak's *Medieval Slavdom and the rise of Russia* (1930; Berkshire series) is a lucid short introduction to early Russian history, with a good bibliography. A good brief summary of this period is to be found in G. Alexinsky's *Modern Russia*, translated by B. Miall (1913). There is a suggestive essay by Stuart R. Tompkins on "The Varangians in Russian history" in *Medieval and historiographical essays in honor of James W. Thompson* (1938), pp. 465-489. Samuel H. Cross's "Medieval Russian contacts with the west," *Speculum*, vol. 10 (1935), pp. 137-144, is an informative short study. *The chronicle of Novgorod*, translated and edited by Robert Mitchell and Nevill Forbes (1914), covers the period from 1016 to 1471 and gives a vivid picture of the great Russian trading center. A useful work on the Tartars is Jeremiah Curtin's *Mongols in Russia* (1908). In French there are two valuable studies by K. Waliszewski: *Les origines de la Russie moderne; la crise révolutionnaire, 1584-1614* (1906) and *Le berceau d'une dynastie; les premiers Romanov, 1613-1682* (1909); both are written in a spirited style from a study of the sources. F. A. Golder's *Russian expansion on the Pacific, 1641-1850* (1914) contains a useful account of the exploration and development of eastern Siberia. Robert N. Bain's *Slavonic Europe, a political history of Poland and Russia from 1447 to 1796* (1908) is useful for the struggle between Russia and Poland, though not always sound.

Biographical studies. K. Waliszewski's *Ivan the Terrible*, translated from the French by Lady Mary Loyd (1904), is an older work of painstaking scholarship. Stephen Graham has written a vivid popular portrait of Ivan which is reasonably sound (1933). The same author's *Boris Godunof* (1933) attempts with some success to delineate a complex personality. Among the biographies of Peter, E. Schuyler's *Peter the Great* (2 vols., 1884) is notable both for its scholarship and its readability. Another notable work is K. Waliszewski's *Peter the Great*, translated from the French by Lady Mary Loyd (2 vols., 1897). A valuable study in French is V. Kliuchevski's *Pierre le Grand et son oeuvre*, translated from the Russian by H. de Witte (1930). There is a readable popular biography of Peter by Stephen Graham (1929). G. Oudard's *Peter the Great*, translated by F. M. Atkinson (1929), is severe in its judgments of Peter and in some respects untrustworthy. A sound treatment of Peter's political aims is to be found in R. Stupperich's *Staats-gedanke und Religionspolitik Peters des Grossen* (1936). For the period after Peter's death there are two well-written and informative studies by K. Walis-zewski, *L'héritage de Pierre le Grand, règnes des femmes, gouvernement des favoris, 1725–1741* (1900) and *La dernière des Romanov, Elizabeth Ire, impéra-trice de Russie, 1741–1762* (1902). M. Kovalevski's *Russian political institu-tions* (1902) is important because there is so little on the subject in English, but it leaves much to be desired. The history of the Russian and Polish Jews is graphically narrated in S. M. Dubnov's *History of the Jews in Russia and Poland* (3 vols., 1916–20).

Sweden. A good short survey of the political, social, and cultural develop-ment of the Swedish people may be found in A. A. Stomberg's *History of Sweden* (1931) and in C. Hallendorff and A. Schück's *History of Sweden*, translated from the Swedish by Mrs. L. Yapp (1929). An older work which deals with the political history of the Scandinavian peninsula with particular emphasis on the sixteenth and seventeenth centuries is R. N. Bain's *Scan-dinavia, a political history of Denmark, Norway and Sweden from 1513 to 1900* (1905). Voltaire's biography of Charles XII is a literary classic but antiquated as a work of history. Probably the best biography of Charles XII in English is John A. Gade's *Charles the Twelfth* (1916). Still useful, though outdated in some respects, are O. Browning's *Charles XII of Sweden* (1899) and R. N. Bain's *Charles XII and the collapse of the Swedish empire* (1895). There is also a reasonably sound brief popular life by Eveline Godley (1928). A longer biography in Swedish which shows a careful and thorough study of the sources is F. G. Bengtsson's *Karl XII*, of which only the first volume has appeared. O. Haintz's *König Karl XII* (vol. 1, 1936) is a scholarly work in German.

CHAPTER EIGHTEEN
The Age of Louis XIV

Reign of Louis XIV. Laurence B. Packard's *Age of Louis XIV* (1929) is a good introductory booklet. There is a well-written review of Louis XIV's administration in J. B. Perkins' *France under the regency* (1892). Other good surveys of the reign are to be found in the *Cambridge modern history*, vol. 5 (1908), pp. 1–91, Jacques Boulenger's *Seventeenth century* (1920; *National history of France*), pp. 172–393, A. J. Grant's *French Monarchy*, vol. 2 (1914), pp. 1–151, and David Ogg's *Europe in the seventeenth century* (1925), pp. 281–364. A standard survey of the reign in French is that by Louis Madelin in *Histoire de la nation française*, edited by G. Hanotaux, vol. 7 (1924), pp. 285–388. An equally authoritative longer account is to be found in *Histoire de France*, edited by E. Lavisse, vol. 7 (1906), parts 1 and 2, and vol. 8 (1908), part 1. George N. Clark's *Seventeenth century* (1929) offers a general survey of European civilization during that century. The student may also consult the histories of France listed in the bibliography for Chapter One. The diplomacy of the period is competently treated in *La diplomatie française au temps de Louis XIV* (1930). Henri Sée's *Les idées politiques en France au XVIIe siècle* (1923) contains lucid summaries and criticisms of the principal works on political theory published during the century in France.

Biographical studies. Arthur Hassall's *Louis XIV and the zenith of the French monarchy* (1895; numerous reprints) is still one of the best English biographies of Louis. A more recent successful life is that by Karl Bartz, translated from the German by L. Marie Sieveking (1937); it is moderate in its point of view and is written in a vigorous style. David Ogg has written a good short biography of Louis XIV (1933; Home university library). Other useful biographies are C. S. Forester's *Louis XIV* (1928) and Louis Bertrand's *Louis XIV*, translated from the French by C. B. Chase (1929). The memoirs which Louis dictated for the instruction of the dauphin have been translated into English by H. Wilson under the title *A king's lessons in statecraft*, with an introduction and notes by Jean Longnon (1924); they are valuable as illustrating the king's political ideas.

Economic history. There is a readable short chapter entitled "Colbert and mercantilism" in L. B. Packard's *Commercial revolution* (1927; Berkshire series). Arthur J. Sargent's *Economic policy of Colbert* (1899) gives a short account of the work of Louis XIV's minister. A longer scholarly account is to be found in Charles W. Cole's *Colbert and a century of French mercantilism* (2 vols., 1939). Pierre Clément's scholarly *Histoire de Colbert et de son administration* (3rd ed., 2 vols., 1892) is still useful as a whole, though it has been superseded in some respects by special studies. Two other useful works in French are Germain Martin's *La grande industrie sous le règne de Louis XIV* (1899) and his *L'histoire du credit en France sous le règne de Louis XIV* (1913), but they are not always accurate. The best account of Colbert's colonial policy is S. L. Mims' *Colbert's West India policy* (1912).

Social history. The social history of the period is ably sketched in Cécile Hugon's *Social France in the seventeenth century* (1911). An interesting account of court life is to be found in Cecilia Hill's *Versailles; its life and history* (1925). James E. Farmer's *Versailles and the court under Louis XIV* (1905) contains much useful and interesting information but is rather too favorable to the Grand Monarque. *The royal ark*, by Saint-René Taillandier (1932), gives an interesting popular account of the court of Louis XIV. An invaluable commentary on the social life of the time is Saint-Simon's *Memoirs*, abridged translation by K. P. Wormley (4 vols., 1899); French edition (41 vols., 1879–1928).

Religious history. There is a lucid account of Gallicanism in Arthur Galton's *Church and state in France, 1300–1907* (1907). Arthur J. Grant's *The Huguenots* (1934; Home university library) contains a good brief account of the revocation of the edict of Nantes and its consequences (pp. 142–204). Abbé Joseph Dedieu's *Le rôle politique des protestants français, 1685–1715* (1920) emphasizes particularly the activities of the Huguenot refugees in the struggle against Louis XIV. *The Huguenots and the revocation of the edict of Nantes*, by Henry M. Baird (2 vols., 1895), is a readable work written from the Protestant point of view. One of the best studies of Jansenism is Nigel Abercrombie's *The origins of Jansenism* (1936). Notable studies of

Jansenism in French are A. Gazier's *Histoire générale du mouvement janséniste* (1922) and C. A. Sainte-Beuve's *Port Royal* (1882).

Literature. William A. Nitze and Edwin P. Dargan's *History of French literature* (rev. ed., 1927) and Charles H. C. Wright's *History of French literature* (new ed., 1925) are two good surveys. Good treatises on the literature of the period are H. Caudwell's *Introduction to French classicism* (1931) and Charles H. C. Wright's *French classicism* (1920). The developments leading to French classicism are ably treated in Arthur Tilley's *From Montaigne to Molière* (2nd rev. ed., 1923). Another important work by the same author is *The decline of the age of Louis XIV; or, French literature, 1687–1715* (1929). A. L. Guérard's *Life and death of an ideal: France in the classical age* (1928) surveys in a spirited fashion the life and culture of the Classical Age. Useful biographical studies in English of the leading literary figures of the age are Leon H. Vincent's *Corneille* (1901), Brander Matthews' *Molière* (1910, new ed., 1926), H. C. Chatfield-Taylor's *Molière* (1906), Mary Duclaux's *Racine* (1925), Frank Hamel's *Jean de la Fontaine* (1911), and Arthur Tilley's *Madame de Sévigné* (1936).

CHAPTER NINETEEN

Germany in the Eighteenth Century and the Rise of Prussia

General. A longer treatment in German is Karl Biedermann's *Deutschland im achtzehnten Jahrhundert* (2nd rev. ed., 4 vols., 1880); many of its viewpoints have been greatly modified by recent scholarship. A more recent reasonably sound work of a popular nature is Max von Boehn's *Deutschland im achtzehnten Jahrhundert* (2 vols., 1922). The best general account in English of the political and military history of the period is C. T. Atkinson's *History of Germany, 1715–1815* (1908). Walter H. Bruford's *Germany in the eighteenth century* (1935) gives a lucid account of the social life of the time, particularly as it affected the development of German literature. Bernhard Erdmannsdörffer's *Deutsche Geschichte, 1648–1740* (2 vols., 1892–93) is valuable for the first forty years of the century. See also the histories of Germany listed in the bibliography for Chapter One.

Rise of Prussia. Sidney B. Fay's *The rise of Brandenburg-Prussia to 1786* (1937; Berkshire series) is an excellent brief introductory survey. The first part of Ferdinand Schevill's *Making of modern Germany* (1916) gives a spirited summary of the rise of Prussia. *The evolution of Prussia*, by J. A. R. Marriott and C. G. Robertson (1915), is the best one-volume account of the subject; it is lucid and well-written. Herbert Tuttle's *History of Prussia* (4 vols., 1884–96) is antiquated in many respects but still useful for the development of Prussian institutions and for diplomatic history. A. D. Innes' *The Hohenzollerns* (1915) is a good brief sketch of the rise of that house. Leopold von Ranke's *Memoirs of the house of Brandenburg and history of*

Prussia during the seventeenth and eighteenth centuries, translated by Sir A. and Lady Duff-Gordon (3 vols., 1849), is one of the best works of a distinguished historian and admirer of the Hohenzollern. A useful introduction to the study of the life and achievements of the Great Elector is C. E. Maurice's *Life of Frederick William the Great Elector of Brandenburg* (1926). A good brief summary is A. W. Ward's "The Great Elector and the first Prussian king," *Cambridge modern history,* vol. 5 (1908), pp. 639–672. Excellent works in French on the early history of Prussia are Albert Waddington's *Histoire de Prusse* (2 vols., 1911–22) and *Le Grand Électeur, Frédéric Guillaume de Brandenbourg* (2 vols., 1905–08). There is a good brief survey of the reign of Frederick William I in the *Cambridge modern history,* vol. 6 (1918), pp. 205–227. Walter L. Dorn's scholarly study, "The Prussian bureaucracy in the eighteenth century," *Political science quarterly,* vol. 46 (1931), pp. 403–423, and vol. 47 (1932), pp. 75–94, shows how the machinery of the Prussian government functioned.

Enlightened despots. For the enlightened despots there is the readable brief survey by Geoffrey Bruun (1929; Berkshire series). A good longer account is Arthur H. Johnson's *Age of the enlightened despots, 1660–1789,* revised by C. T. Atkinson, with a preface by Sir Robert Johnson (1933). G. M. Dutcher has written two suggestive articles: "The enlightened despotism," *Annual report of the American historical association for 1920,* pp. 189–198, and "Further considerations on the origin and nature of the enlightened despotism," *Persecutions and liberty: essays in honor of George L. Burr* (1931), pp. 375–404. Leo Gershoy's *Enlightened despots (Rise of modern Europe,* vol. 11) is promised for early publication.

Frederick the Great. The most complete life of Frederick is Reinhold Koser's *König Friedrich der Grosse* (4 vols., 1912). There is a brief life in English by Margaret Goldsmith (1929) which is sober and well-written. A fuller life is William F. Reddaway's *Frederick the Great and the rise of Prussia* (1904); the best of the English biographies. Norwood Young's *Life of Frederick the Great* (1919) is marred by inaccuracies, but useful as an antidote to the hero-worship of Carlyle and other writers. F. J. P. Veale's *Frederick the Great* (1935) is of the nature of an apology for the Prussian king. Invaluable for the study of the early life of Frederick are two works by Ernest Lavisse, *The youth of Frederick the Great,* translated by M. B. Coleman (1892), and *Le grand Frédéric avant l'avènement* (1893). There is an excellent short essay on "Voltaire and Frederick the Great" in Lytton Strachey's *Books and characters* (1922). For a fuller account of the relationship between philosopher and king see Émile Henriot's *Voltaire et Frédéric II* (1927). *Letters of Voltaire and Frederick the Great* is a well-chosen selection, translated with an introduction by Richard Aldington (1927). A more intimate knowledge of the Prussian ruler can be gained from reading *Frederick the Great, memoirs of his reader, Henri de Catt, 1758–1760,* translated by F. S. Flint (2 vols., 1929).

Wars of Frederick the Great. There is a good short summary of the War of the Austrian Succession and of the Seven Years' War in the *Cambridge modern history,* vol. 6 (1918), pp. 228–300. A useful longer account of the latter is to be found in F. W. Longman's *Frederick the Great and the Seven Years' War* (1889). On the relationship of Prussia and Great Britain there is Sir Richard Lodge's *Great Britain and Prussia in the eighteenth century* (1923). Sir Ernest Satow's *Silesian loan and Frederick the Great* (1915) is an interesting study of Frederick's diplomatic methods. The diplomatic rivalry between Prussia and Austria during the years 1763–79 is the subject of an illuminating study entitled *Frederic the Great and Kaiser Joseph*, by Harold W. V. Temperley (1915).

Maria Theresa and Joseph II. James F. Bright's *Maria Theresa* (1897) is a good brief biography of the Austrian empress. Three popular biographies of Maria Theresa have appeared in recent years: Jabez A. Mahan's *Maria Theresa of Austria* (1932), Margaret Goldsmith's *Maria Theresa of Austria* (1936), and Constance L. Morris' *Maria Theresa, the last conservative* (1937); all are readable and reasonably sound but emphasize the personal side of her story. A good biography in German is Karl Tschuppik's *Maria Theresia* (1934). There is a good short account of Joseph's reign in the *Cambridge modern history*, vol. 6 (1918), pp. 626–656. Saul Padover's *The revolutionary emperor, Joseph the Second* (1934) is a competent and readable biography. A useful older biography is James F. Bright's *Joseph II* (1897). In German there is the scholarly volume *Kaiser Joseph II*, by Ernst Benedikt (1936), based on a first-hand study of the sources. Robert J. Kerner's *Bohemia in the eighteenth century: a study in political, economic and social history with special reference to the reign of Leopold II, 1790–1792* (1932) is a valuable study for the period preceding the wars of the French Revolution.

German literature in the eighteenth century. Kuno Francke's *History of German literature as determined by social forces* (1931) and John G. Robertson's *History of German literature* (rev. ed., 1931) are two of the better surveys of German literature. Wilhelm Scherer's *History of German literature*, translated by Mrs. F. C. Conybeare (2 vols., 1886), is readable but antiquated in many respects and often misleading. Jethro Bithell's *Germany, a companion to German studies* (1932) is readable and contains much useful information, but some of its interpretations are antiquated and its statements are not always sound. The best life of Lessing is by Erich Schmidt (2 vols., 4th ed., 1923). Henry B. Garland's *Lessing, the founder of modern German literature* (1937) is a brief study of the man and his work. There is an older biography of Lessing in English by James Sime (2 vols., 1877) which is still useful. The best life of Herder is that by R. Haym (2 vols., 1880–85). In English there is R. Ergang's *Herder and the foundations of German nationalism* (1931), with a short survey of Herder's life. There is no definitive biography of Goethe. Three German biographies of merit are those by K. Heinemann (2 vols., 3rd ed., 1903), F. Gundolf (1930), and G. Witkowski (1899). There is a reasonably good shorter biography in English by John G. Robertson, entitled *The life and work of Goethe* (1932). The older English biography of G. H. Lewes (1856), which enjoyed a wide circulation, leaves much to be desired. A work of considerable merit is A. Bielschowsky's *Goethe*, translated into English by W. A. Cooper (2 vols., 1905–08). Two of the better complete biographies of Schiller in German are those by Eugen Kühnemann (7th ed., 1927) and Karl Berger (new ed., 2 vols., 1924). There is a good one-volume life in English by Calvin Thomas (1901). K. S. Pinson's *Pietism as a factor in the rise of German nationalism* (1934) is a work of sound scholarship.

Music. Alfred Einstein's *Short history of music* (1936), Theodore M. Finney's *History of music* (1935), Cecil Gray's *History of music* (1928), and Karl Nef's *Outline of the history of music*, translated by C. F. Pfatteicher (1935), are good short surveys of the history of music. Somewhat fuller accounts are to be found in Charles Burney's *General history of music from the earliest times to 1789* (new ed., 2 vols., 1935) and Emil Naumann's *History of music* (new ed., 2 vols., 1900). An excellent longer work is the *Oxford history of music*, edited by Sir W. H. Hadow (8 vols., 1929–34). For reference there is the *Dictionary of music and musicians*, edited by Sir George Grove (3rd ed., 5 vols., 1927–28), with a supplementary volume edited by W. S. Pratt and C. N. Boyd (1928). Among the useful shorter works on the individual musicians are C. F. A. Williams' *Bach* (1934), C. S. Terry's *Bach* (1928) and *The music of Bach, an introduction* (1933), W. N. Flower's *Handel, his personality and his times* (1922), C. F. A. Williams' *Handel* (1935), J. C. Hadden's *Haydn* (1934), D. G. A. Fox's *Haydn, an introduction* (1928), H. Berlioz's *Gluck and his operas*, translated by E. Evans (1915), E. Newman's *Gluck and the opera* (1895), Eric Blom's *Mozart* (1935), E. J. Breakspeare's *Mozart* (1902), Paul Bekker's *Beethoven*, translated into English by M. M. Bozman (1925), Marion M. Scott's *Beethoven* (1934), and H. Grace's *Ludwig von Beethoven* (1927).

CHAPTER TWENTY

Russia under Catherine II and the Dismemberment of Poland

Reign of Catherine II. There is a good short survey of Catherine's reign in the *Cambridge modern history*, vol. 6 (1918), pp. 657–701. For other brief accounts see the Russian histories listed in the bibliography for Chapter Seventeen. Of the English biographies of Catherine II, K. Waliszewski's *Romance of an empress, Catherine II of Russia* (1894) is still outstanding. E. A. Hodgetts' *Life of Catherine the Great of Russia* (1914) is rather too favorable to the empress. Katharine Anthony's *Catherine the Great* (1926) and Gina Kaus' *Catherine the Great*, translated from the German by June Head (1935), are popular biographies dealing largely with the private life and the love affairs of the Russian empress. Catherine's correspondence with Voltaire has been edited by W. F. Reddaway under the title *Documents of Catherine the Great* (1931); it contains also the Instructions of 1767, all in the original French. Charles de Larivière's *Cathérine le grand d'après sa correspondance* (1895) is valuable for Catherine's attitude toward the French Revolution. See also the bibliography for Chapter Seventeen.

Poland. R. Dyboski's *Outlines of Polish history* (2nd ed., rev. and enlarged, 1933) is a lucid, impartial, and readable introductory survey of the political and cultural history of Poland. Older but clear and judicious is Julia S. Orvis' *Brief history of Poland* (1916). Useful for the constitutional and social development is G. E. Slocombe's *Poland* (1916). E. H. Lewinski-Corwin's *Political history of Poland* (1917) is based on a study of the sources, but suffers from a patriotic bias. K. Waliszewski's *Poland the unknown*, translated from the French (1919), interprets Polish history from the Polish viewpoint; it is not always convincing. E. C. Corsi's *Poland, land of the white eagle* (1933) is popular in the worst sense of the word, superficial, unreliable, akin to historical fiction. R. N. Bain's *Slavonic Europe, a political history of Poland and Russia from 1447 to 1796* (1908) is still useful as an account of the struggle between the two nations. R. Dyboski's *Periods of Polish literary history* (1923) is a lucid brief survey. On the religious history of Poland to 1573 there is the illuminating study by Paul Fox, entitled *The Reformation in Poland, some social and economic aspects* (1924). A complete account of the Protestant movement by a Protestant is W. Krasinski's *Historical sketch of the rise, progress, and decline of the Reformation in Poland* (2 vols., 1838–40). Of the first importance for a study of the partitions is R. H. Lord's *Second partition of Poland* (1915) with an introduction which presents the best summary of the conditions which led to the partitions. Monica M. Gardner's *Kosciuszko* is a pleasantly written, well-informed biography of the Polish hero. An informative study of King Stanislas and his times is R. N. Bain's *The last king of Poland and his contemporaries* (1909).

CHAPTER TWENTY-ONE

England in the Eighteenth Century

General. S. Maccoby's *Eighteenth-century England* (1931), R. B. Mowat's *England in the eighteenth century* (1932), and W. Selley's *England in the eighteenth century* (1934) are good surveys of the various phases of English life in the eighteenth century. The best longer work is William Lecky's *History of England in the eighteenth century* (7 vols., 1913); notable for its lucid comprehension of English political, social, and economic life. J. W. Jeudwine's *Religion, commerce, liberty, 1683–1793* (1925) is a useful and revealing book. The political thought of the period is ably sketched in Harold J. Laski's *Political thought in England from Locke to Bentham* (1920; Home university library). A learned presentation of the history of the cabinet in the eighteenth century is to be found in vol. 2 of E. R. Turner's *The cabinet council of England in the seventeenth and eighteenth centuries, 1622–1784,* edited by Gaudence Megaro, with an introduction by E. R. Adair (1932). W. T. Laprade's *Public opinion and politics in eighteenth century England to the fall of Walpole* (1936) is a good exposition of the political life of the period; it is illustrated by references to contemporary literature, but presupposes considerable knowledge of the period. For further references the student may consult the following excellent bibliographical articles: C. L. Grose's "Thirty years' study of a formerly neglected century of British history, 1660–1760," *Journal of modern history*, vol. 2 (1930), pp. 448–471, and W. T. Laprade's "The present state of the history of England in the

eighteenth century," *ibid.*, vol. 4 (1932), pp. 581–603. Judith B. Williams'
Guide to printed materials for English social and economic history, 1750–1850
(2 vols., 1926) is a monumental work of reference.

Special studies. Edith L. Elias' *In Georgian times* (1914) presents a series
of short character studies of the great figures of the period. The best work
on the reign of George I is W. Michael's *The beginnings of the Hanoverian
dynasty*, translated from the German (vol. 1, 1936). C. E. Vulliamy's *Royal
George; a study of King George III* (1935) is a lucid, sympathetic, and carefully considered study. J. D. Griffith Davies' *George the Third, a record of a
king's reign* (1936) is spirited but rather too sympathetic. Bonamy Dobrée
has edited a selection of George's letters under the title *The letters of King
George III* (1935). G. R. Stirling Taylor's *Walpole and his age* (1931) is a
solid biography, based on a mass of new materials. J. Morley's *Walpole*
(1889) is still useful for its skilful interpretation. A useful special study is
N. A. Brisco's *Economic policy of Robert Walpole* (1907). The most complete
biographies of Lord Chatham are A. von Ruville's *William Pitt* (3 vols.,
1907) and Basil Williams' *Life of William Pitt, earl of Chatham* (2 vols.,
1913). Reasonably good shorter lives of Chatham are those by A. S. Mc-
Dowall (1905), Frederic Harrison (1905), Lord Rosebery (1910), and Brian
Tunstall (1939). The best account of the life and activities of the younger
Pitt is to be found in the biography by John H. Rose (2 vols., 1911). A briefer
study which is in part supplementary to the longer work is the same author's
Short life of William Pitt (1925). P. W. Wilson's *Pitt the younger* (1930) is
a readable, reasonably sound popular biography. E. Lascelles' *Life of Charles
James Fox* is sound, informative, and charmingly written. John Morley's
Edmund Burke, a historical study (1867) and *Burke* (1879) are two well-
written studies, but rather too sympathetic. There is a useful, well-written
biography of Burke by B. Newman (1927). R. H. Murray's *Burke* (1931)
is a work of considerable scholarship but not always lucid. Valuable for the
period of the French Revolution are Philip A. Brown's *The French Revolution in English history* (1918) and W. T. Laprade's *England and the French
Revolution* (1909).

Beginnings of the Industrial Revolution. A standard work on the subject
is Paul Mantoux's *Industrial revolution of the eighteenth century*, translated
by M. Vernon (1927). Lillian Knowles' *The industrial and commercial revolutions in Great Britain* (1921) contains a mass of useful information, well-
arranged, clearly and forcefully stated. A. Toynbee's *Lectures on the industrial
revolution of the eighteenth century in England* (1884; new ed., 1908) was a
pioneer work on the subject but is now antiquated in many respects. Conditions in England during the early part of the Industrial Revolution are
vividly portrayed in M. Dorothy George's *England in transition* (1931).
Another informative volume is L. W. Moffitt's *England on the eve of the
industrial revolution* (1925). Witt Bowden's *Industrial society in England
toward the end of the eighteenth century* (1925) is a competent study of
the social effects of the industrial changes. The same author has published
a collection of source materials to illustrate the Industrial Revolution, under
the title *The industrial revolution* (1928). Valuable chapters on the early period
of the Industrial Revolution are to be found in H. de B. Gibbins' *Industrial*

history of England, revised and enlarged by J. F. Rees (1926), G. H. Perris'
Industrial history of modern England (1914), A. Redford's *Economic history
of England, 1760–1860* (1931), and J. L. and B. Hammond's *Rise of modern
industry* (5th rev. ed., 1937). The authors of the last work have written three
illuminating studies on the effects of the industrial changes on the working
classes: *The village labourer, 1760–1832* (1911), *The town labourer, 1760–
1832* (1917), and *The skilled labourer, 1760–1832* (1919). *The cotton trade
and industrial Lancashire, 1600–1780*, by A. P. Wadsworth and Julia Mann
(1931), is a thorough study of the subject. Another valuable special study
is Herbert Heaton's *The Yorkshire woollen and worsted industries* (1920). A
comprehensive survey of the cotton industry is to be found in G. W. Daniels'
The early English cotton industry (1920). *The coal industry of the eighteenth
century*, by T. S. Ashton and J. Sykes (1929), and J. U. Nef's *Rise of the
British coal industry* (2 vols., 1933) are two sound and revealing works.
J. H. Park and E. Glouberman's "The importance of chemical developments
in the textile industries during the industrial revolution," *Journal of chemical
education*, vol. 9 (1932), pp. 1143–1170, is an excellent brief account of the
subject. Brief sketches of the various inventions of the Industrial Revolution are given in Abbott P. Usher's *History of mechanical inventions* (1929).
T. S. Ashton's *Iron and steel in the industrial revolution* (1924) is a valuable
study. For the development of transportation and the steam engine there are
E. A. Pratt's *History of inland transport and communication in England*
(1912) and Sir James Ewing's *The steam-engine and other heat-engines* (1926).
H. Hamilton's *Industrial revolution in Scotland* (1932) presents a wealth of
knowledge regarding the industrial changes in that country.

   Agriculture. A lucid short account of the agricultural changes is to be
found in chapters 6, 7, and 8 of John Orr's *Short history of British agriculture*
(1922). R. E. Prothero's (Lord Ernle's) *English farming: past and present*,
edited by Sir A. D. Hall (1936), is a sound, simple, and readable survey.
The same author's *Pioneers and progress of English farming* (1888) is also
valuable. Other competent and useful works are M. E. Seebohm's *Evolution
of the English farm* (1927), G. Slater's *English peasantry and the enclosure
of common fields* (1907), and Naomi Riches' *Agricultural revolution in Norfolk* (1937). For a lively brief discussion of agricultural methods in the early
seventeenth century see G. E. Fussell's "Farming methods in the early
Stuart period," *Journal of modern history*, vol. 7 (1935), pp. 1–21, 129–140.

   Life and literature. *Johnson's England, 1709–1784*, edited by A. S. Turberville (2 vols., 1933), is a mine of information on the life and literature of
eighteenth century England. The main currents of English thought are
lucidly and authoritatively presented in Leslie Stephen's *History of English
thought in the eighteenth century* (3rd ed., 2 vols., 1902). An equally valuable
briefer study is the same author's *English literature and society in the eighteenth
century* (1907). R. Bayne-Powell's *Eighteenth-century London life* (1938) is
interesting but not very scholarly. A. S. Turberville has written a readable
and suggestive account of Georgian society under the title *English men and
manners in the eighteenth century* (1926). The effect of a century of oversea
expansion on English social life is ably portrayed in J. B. Botsford's *English
society in the eighteenth century as influenced from oversea* (1924). Stebelton H.

Nulle's *Thomas Pelham-Holles, duke of Newcastle* (1931) contains some excellent pen pictures of life in early eighteenth century England. A good biography of Samuel Johnson is that by S. C. Roberts (1935). Carl Van Doren has written a competent and readable life of Swift (1931).

Wesley and Methodism. The definitive life of John Wesley is that by John S. Simon (5 vols., 1923–34). Good short lives are W. H. Hutton's *John Wesley* (1927) and C. T. Winchester's *Life of John Wesley* (1906). Umphrey Lee's *Historical background of early Methodist enthusiasm* (1931) is a scholarly and lucid treatment of the subject. Noteworthy recent books on Wesley and Methodism are M. Edwards' *John Wesley and the eighteenth century* (1933), G. C. Cell's *The rediscovery of John Wesley* (1935), and M. Piette's *Wesley in the evolution of Protestantism*, translated by J. B. Howard (1937).

Art. John Rothenstein's *Introduction to English painting* (1933) and Charles Johnson's *English painting from the seventh century to the present day* (1932) are useful general surveys which contain brief accounts of the lives and work of Hogarth, Gainsborough, and Reynolds. There is a somewhat fuller account of these artists in Reginald H. Wilenski's *Masters of English painting* (1934). Marjorie Bowen's *Hogarth: the cockney's mirror* (1936) is a readable and informative popular biography, but somewhat highly colored. Useful older biographies of Hogarth are those by Austin Dobson (1902), G. Baldwin Brown (1905), and C. Lewis Hind (1910). Competent biographies of Gainsborough are those by W. T. Whitley (1915) and Sir Walter Armstrong (1898). The latter has also written a life of Sir Joshua Reynolds (1900). A more recent life of Reynolds is that by John Steegmann (1933); brief and informative. There is a good brief summary of the work of Josiah Wedgwood by Joseph H. Park in *Antiques*, vol. 26 (1934), pp. 64–66. William Burton's *Josiah Wedgwood and his pottery* (1922) is a useful short study. The most detailed and scholarly life of Wedgwood is that by Eliza Meteyard (2 vols., 1865–66).

Adam Smith. There is a reasonably good short life of Adam Smith by Francis W. Hirst (1904). Somewhat fuller is John Rae's *Life of Adam Smith* (1895). There is a good summary of Smith's life and works in Leslie Stephen's *English thought in the eighteenth century*, vol. 2 (1902), pp. 70–80 and 315–328, and in Charles Gide and Charles Rist's *History of economic doctrines*, translated by R. Richards (1915), pp. 50–117. Jan St. Lewiński's *Founders of political economy* (1922) and T. F. Kinloch's *Six English economists* (1928) contain informative studies of the man and his ideas. Adam Smith's teachings are subjected to a searching analysis in *The house of Adam Smith*, by Eli Ginzberg (1934). Another useful study is Glenn R. Morrow's *The ethical and economic theories of Adam Smith* (1923). *Adam Smith, 1776–1926, a series of lectures to commemorate the sesquicentennial of the publication of the "Wealth of Nations"* (1928) is rich in illuminating reflections. New light is shed on the early history of the man and the development of his thought in William R. Scott's *Adam Smith as student and professor* (1937; Glasgow university publication, no. 46). Edgar A. J. Johnson's *Predecessors of Adam Smith: the growth of British economic thought* (1937) is an interesting and clearly written survey of the writings of a select group of earlier English economists.

CHAPTER TWENTY-TWO

The Founding of the British Empire

General studies. The best general survey of British expansion along broader lines is James A. Williamson's *Short history of British expansion* (2 vols., 2nd ed., 1930). An excellent concise survey is the same author's *Foundation and growth of the British empire* (3rd rev. ed., 1933). Howard Robinson's *Development of the British empire* (rev. and enlarged ed., 1936) offers a swift-moving, well-organized, and clearly written survey of the history of the British Empire. Another good survey is Charles F. Mullett's *British Empire* (1939); scholarly, lucid, and well-written. Other useful shorter surveys are William H. Woodward's *Short history of the expansion of the British empire, 1500–1930* (1931), Charles P. Lucas' *Story of the empire* (1924; vol. 2 of *The British empire*, edited by Hugh Gunn), and C. S. Higham's *History of the British empire* (4th ed., 1931). An authoritative longer work on the British Empire is the *Cambridge history of the British empire*, edited by J. H. Rose, A. P. Newton, and others (of which vols. 1 and 4–8 have appeared, 1929–36). Another valuable longer work is *The British empire, a survey*, edited by Hugh Gunn (12 vols., 1924). H. E. Egerton's *Short history of British colonial policy* (9th ed., 1932) is a standard work on the subject. C. M. MacInnes' *Introduction to the economic history of the empire* (1936) and Lillian Knowles' *Economic development of the British overseas empire* (1924) are two first-rate works on the economic history of the empire. The best general survey of the period to 1783 is vol. 1 (1929) of the *Cambridge history of the British empire*. A readable shorter sketch is A. P. Newton's *British empire to 1783: its political, social and economic development* (1935). James T. Adams' *The building of the British empire* (1939) is a readable sketch covering the period from pre-Roman Britain to 1783. Excellent introductions to the history of the particular colonies are presented in the *Historical geography of the British colonies* (13 vols., 1887–1924), edited by Sir Charles Lucas, with an introductory volume by Hugh E. Egerton entitled *The origin and growth of Greater Britain* (new ed., 1924). An important study of a more limited period is Arthur D. Innes' *Maritime and colonial expansion of England under the Stuarts, 1603–1714* (1931). For further references see W. F. Craven's excellent bibliographical article, "Historical study of the British empire," *Journal of modern history*, vol. 6 (1934), pp. 40–69.

North American colonies. For English and French explorations see the bibliography for Chapter Four. A useful short treatment of English activities in America is L. G. Tyler's *England in America* (1904; vol. 4 of the American Nation series). For a longer study, with valuable illustrations, see *Narrative and critical history of America*, vols. 3, 4, and 5, edited by Justin Winsor (1884–89). The whole process of the colonization of North America is treated in Herbert E. Bolton and Thomas M. Marshall's *Colonization of North America, 1492–1783* (1920). The most detailed and comprehensive history of continental America is Herbert L. Osgood's *American colonies in the seventeenth century* (3 vols., 1904–07). *American colonies in the eighteenth*

century (4 vols., 1924–25) by the same author, published posthumously under
the editorship of Dixon R. Fox, carries the account to 1763. Another notable
work by a distinguished American scholar is Charles M. Andrews' *The colonial
period of American history* (3 vols., 1934–37). Invaluable though written
from the viewpoint of the British archives are the studies of British colonial
policy by George L. Beer: *Commercial policy of England toward the American
colonies* (1893), *Origins of the British colonial system, 1578–1660* (1908), *Old
colonial system, 1660–1754:* part 1, *Establishment of the system, 1660–1688*
(2 vols., 1912), and *British colonial policy, 1754–1765* (new ed., 1922). Other
important works are M. W. Jernegan's *The American colonies, 1492–1750*
(1929), H. I. Priestley's *Coming of the white man, 1492–1819* (1929), and T.
J. Wertenbaker's *First Americans, 1607–1690* (1927; vols. 1 and 2 of *History
of American life*, edited by Arthur M. Schlesinger and Dixon R. Fox).

West Indies. The early history of the English in the West Indies is ably
treated in Arthur P. Newton's *European nations in the West Indies, 1493–
1688* (1933). The succeeding period is competently treated in Frank W.
Pitman's *Development of the British West Indies, 1700–1763* (1917). *A guide
for the study of British Caribbean history, 1763–1834* (1932), by Lowell J.
Ragatz, is an invaluable aid to the student of British West Indian history.

Anglo-French struggle. A. G. Bradley's *Fight with France for North
America* (1900) is a sound, readable survey of the struggle. George M.
Wrong's *Rise and fall of New France* (2 vols., 1928) is a standard account of
the subject. *Adventurers of New France*, by William B. Munro and George M.
Wrong (1918; Chronicles of America series, vol. 3), is a lucid and well-
written account of the French colonies in America and of their conquest.
A good brief summary of the early history of Canada is to be found in the
first chapters of Carl Wittke's *History of Canada* (new ed., 1933). J. B.
Brebner's *New England's outpost: Acadia before the conquest of Canada*
(1927) is a sound and readable treatment of the early history of Nova Scotia
to 1758. Stanley Pargellis' "Braddock's defeat," *American historical review*,
vol. 41 (1936), pp. 253–269, presents a revaluation of the traditional inter-
pretation. The American phase of the Seven Years' War is ably treated in
A. G. Bradley's *Britain across the seas: America* (1911) and in R. G. Thwaite's
France in America, 1497–1763 (1905). W. T. Waugh's *Wolfe and North
America* (1929) is a competent study. The same author has also written a
good popular biography of Wolfe (1934). F. E. Whitton's *Wolfe and North
America* (1929) gives a good account of Wolfe's military activities. H. A.
Innis' *The fur trade in Canada, an introduction to Canadian economic history*
(1930) and H. P. Biggar's *The early trading companies of New France* (1901)
are two valuable studies on the early economic history of Canada.

American Revolution. Claude H. Van Tyne's *Causes of the war of independence, being the first volume of a history of the founding of the American
republic* (1922) and *The war of independence; American phase, being the
second volume of the founding of the American republic* (1929) set a high
standard of scholarship; they are clear, readable, and objective. G. M.
Trevelyan's older work, *The American Revolution* (6 vols., 1903–09), is despite its Whig bias a classic. The background of the Revolution is admirably
sketched in Arthur M. Schlesinger's *Colonial merchants and the American*

Revolution, 1763–1776 (1918), Hugh E. Egerton's *Causes and character of the American Revolution* (1923) and George E. Howard's *Preliminaries of the Revolution, 1763–1775* (1906; American Nation series, vol. 8). For the English side there are the useful summary by F. J. Hinkhouse, *The preliminaries of the American Revolution as seen in the English press, 1763–1775* (1926) and the valuable work by Dora M. Clark, *British opinion of the American Revolution* (1930). R. Coupland's *American Revolution and the British empire* (1930) is a series of provocative lectures which are not always convincing. An indispensable volume for the transition of the colonies to states is Allan Nevins' *American states during and after the Revolution, 1775–1789* (1924). On the military history of the Revolution there is H. Nickerson's *Turning point of the Revolution or Burgoyne in America* (1928), a detailed study based on the sources. Other useful works for the military history are Rupert Hughes' *George Washington*, vols. 2 and 3 (1927; 1930), T. G. Frothingham's *Washington, commander-in-chief* (1930), Sir John W. Fortescue's *History of the British army*, vol. 3 (1902), and E. E. Curtis' *The organization of the British army in the American Revolution* (1927). Louis Gottschalk's *Lafayette comes to America* (1935) and *Lafayette joins the American army* (1937) are two valuable studies. A useful older work is C. Tower's *Marquis de la Fayette in the American Revolution* (2 vols., 1894; reprint, 1926). Claude H. Van Tyne's *Loyalists in the American Revolution* (1902) is the only general work on the subject; it is concise and impartial. George M. Wrong's *Canada and the American Revolution; the disruption of the first British empire* (1935) is a careful and spirited account, controversial in some respects.

The East. *England's quest of eastern trade*, by Sir William Foster (1933), is a masterly account of the English efforts to break the Portuguese and Spanish monopolies of the Far Eastern trade during the period, 1497–1650. A. W. Tilby's *British India, 1600–1828* (2nd rev. ed., 1911) presents a well-written summary of the early period of British rule in India. Sir Alfred Lyall's *Rise and expansion of British power in India* (5th ed., 1910) is a competent study written from the British point of view. Hugh G. Rawlinson's *British beginnings in western India, 1579–1657* (1920) gives an account of British activities at Surat. Edward Thompson and G. T. Garratt's *Rise and fulfillment of British rule in India* (1934) is detailed, up-to-date, and impartial. The *Cambridge shorter history of India*, edited by J. Allan, Sir T. W. Haig, and H. H. Dodwell (1934), is compact and scholarly but is limited almost entirely to political history. The story of India under British rule is ably narrated in *A short history of India*, by W. H. Moreland and A. C. Chatterjee (1936), with some excellent chapters on the economic and cultural changes. A useful older work is Sir William W. Hunter's *History of British India* (2 vols., 1899–1900). Arthur D. Innis' *Short history of the British in India* (5th ed., 1910), Paul E. Roberts' *History of British India* (1923), and John A. R. Marriott's *The English in India* (1932) are useful shorter surveys. Arthur B. Keith's *Constitutional history of India, 1600–1935* (1936) sheds much light on the relationship between Britain and India. An excellent account of the Franco-British rivalry in India is to be found in Henry Dodwell's *Dupleix and Clive: the beginning of an empire* (1920). W. H. Dalgliesh's *Company of the Indies in the days of Dupleix* (1933) is a careful and informative work. Sir George Forrest's *Life of Lord Clive* (2 vols., 1918) is a work of sound scholarship but poorly organized. Ramsay Muir's *Making of British India, 1756–1858* (1915) is an extremely useful collection of dispatches, treaties, statutes, and other documents. A. M. Davies' *Strange destiny: a biography of Warren Hastings* (1935) is a thorough and well-written biography. P. E. Roberts' *India under Wellesley* (1929) offers an excellent survey of the principal events of Wellesley's rule.

The new empire. The early chapters of *The British empire since 1783*, by A. P. Newton and J. Ewing (1929), give a simple brief account of the empire to 1815. Helen T. Manning's *British colonial government after the American revolution, 1782–1820* (1933) is an admirably balanced and well-written account. Arthur P. Newton's *The old empire and the new*, with an introduction by Sir Charles Lucas (1917), is a series of interesting and instructive lectures. For a short summary of the history of Canada during and immediately after the American Revolution the student may consult Carl Wittke's *History of Canada* (rev. ed., 1933). For a longer account there is Sir Charles Lucas' *History of Canada, 1763–1812* (1909). Other useful works include W. P. M. Kennedy's *Constitution of Canada, 1534–1937* (2nd ed., 1938), R. Coupland's *Quebec act* (1925), and Hilda M. Neatby's *Administration of justice under the Quebec act* (1937). For further works on Canadian history the student may consult R. G. Trotter's *Canadian history, a syllabus and guide to reading* (rev. ed., 1934).

Australasia. George A. Wood's *Discovery of Australia* (1921) offers an authoritative account of the successive explorations of the Australasian seas from the thirteenth to the nineteenth century. The discovery of Australia and the exploration of the South Seas is also ably treated in Edward Heawood's *Geographical discovery in the seventeenth and eighteenth centuries* (1912). Arthur W. Jose's *History of Australasia from the earliest times to the present day* (15th ed., 1929); Edward Jenks' *History of the Australasian colonies* (rev. ed., 1912) and J. D. Rogers' *Australasia* (1907; vol. 6 of *Historical geography of the British colonies*, edited by Sir Charles Lucas) are three of the best histories of Australasia. R. T. Gould's *Captain Cook* (1935) is a brief but eminently sound biography. The journals of Captain Cook's voyages have been published in various editions. Ernest Scott's *Short history of Australia* (5th ed., 1927) is a good survey of Australian history. John B. Condliffe's *Short history of New Zealand* (5th ed., 1935) is a good handbook on the economic, political, and constitutional history of that country. The early settlements in New Zealand are treated in a sound scholarly manner in J. S. Marais' *Colonization of New Zealand* (1927).

CHAPTER TWENTY-THREE

France on the Eve of the Revolution

Reign of Louis XV. James B. Perkins' *France under Louis XV* (2 vols., 1897) is still the best survey of the reign of Louis XV in English. The period immediately after the death of Louis XIV is treated by the same author in another volume entitled *France under the regency* (1892). Pierre Gaxotte's *Louis the Fifteenth and his times*, translated by J. L. May (1934), is too favorable to Louis. Arthur M. Wilson's *Foreign policy during the administration of Cardinal Fleury, 1726–1743, a study in diplomacy and commercial development* (1936) is a sound, scholarly treatment of the subject. There is a competent treatment of the industrial development in G. Martin's *La grande industrie en France sous le règne de Louis XV* (1920). Marcelle Tinayre's *Madame de Pompadour*, translated by Ethel C. Mayne (1925), is an attempt to penetrate to the real woman. *The Du Barry*, by Karl von Schumacher, translated by Dorothy M. Richardson (1932), is a work of painstaking research.

Old régime. The first chapters of Leo Gershoy's *French Revolution and Napoleon* (1933) form an excellent brief survey of France in the Old Régime. The same may be said of the first chapters of Louis Gottschalk's *Era of the French Revolution, 1715–1815* (1929). Another brief survey is to be found in the *Cambridge modern history*, vol. 8 (1907), pp. 1–78. There are excellent longer accounts in *Histoire de France*, edited by E. Lavisse, vol. 8, part 2 (1909), and vol. 9, part 1 (1910), and in *Histoire générale*, edited by E. Lavisse and A. Rambaud, vols. 7 and 8 (1896). Casimir Stryienski's *The eighteenth century*, translated from the French by H. N. Dickinson (1916), is interesting but uncritical. Henri Sée's *Economic and social conditions in France during the eighteenth century*, translated by E. H. Zeydel (1927), is the best brief survey of the subject. Another valuable study by the same author is *L'évolution de la pensée politique en France au XVIIIᵉ siècle* (1925). A third important study by the same author is *L'évolution commerciale et industrielle de la France sous l'ancien régime* (1925). For a knowledge of labor conditions in the Old Régime, E. Levasseur's *Histoire des classes ouvrières avant 1789*, vol. 2 (1901), is invaluable. Indispensable for its picture of rural conditions is *L'état des classes agricoles en France à la veille de la révolution* by Ivan V. Luchitskii (Loutchisky) (1911). A first-hand account of the peasantry is to be found in Arthur Young's *Travels in France during the years 1787, 1788, 1789*, edited by Constantia Maxwell (1929; other editions of the same work). Louis Ducros' *French society in the eighteenth century*, translated by W. de Geijer (1926), gives a vivid picture of both urban and provincial life. Amusing and based on reasonably trustworthy sources is Lucienne Ercole's *Court life: France in the eighteenth century*, translated by G. Struve and H. Miles (1932). Constantia Maxwell's *The English traveller in France, 1698–1815* (1932) is a description of French conditions as seen through the eyes of various Englishmen. The impressions of foreign travelers in France during a somewhat longer period are recorded in Albert A. Babeau's *Les voyageurs en France depuis la renaissance jusqu'à la révolution* (1885). A. de Tocqueville's *The old régime and the French Revolution*, translated by John Bonner (1856), presents the most profound analysis of the causes of the French Revolution. Another valuable study of the forces which produced the French Revolution is E. J. Lowell's *Eve of the French Revolution* (1892; reprints). Felix Rocquain's *Revolutionary spirit preceding the French Revolution*, abridged translation by J. D. Hunting (1892), shows that the revolutionary spirit was growing before the philosophes began their attacks. Bernard

Faÿ's *The revolutionary spirit in France and America* (1927) is a competent treatment of the basic causes of the Revolution and of the relationship of the revolutionary ideas in France and America.

Age of Enlightenment. Kingsley Martin's *French liberal thought in the eighteenth century* (1929) is a stimulating survey, the best on the subject in English. A useful longer work is William E. H. Lecky's *History of the rise and influence of the spirit of rationalism* (rev. ed., 2 vols., 1914). The significant features of the philosophical thought of the age are competently treated in John G. Hibben's *Philosophy of the enlightenment* (1910), which includes England and Germany as well as France. There is an excellent brief summary of the ideas and aims of the philosophes in J. Salwyn Schapiro's *Condorcet and the rise of liberalism* (1934), pp. 23–65. The connection between French and English thought is traced in Harold J. Laski's brilliant study, *The rise of European liberalism* (1936). A series of stimulating essays on the individual philosophes are to be found in *The social and political ideas of some great French thinkers of the age of reason*, edited by F. J. C. Hearnshaw (1930), and in Émile Faguet's *Dix-huitième siècle; études littéraires* (1930). Carl Becker's *The heavenly city of the eighteenth century philosophers* (1932) contains four engaging and provocative lectures on the intellectual movement in the eighteenth century. The political philosophy of the leading philosophes is discussed in a lucid and succinct fashion in Thomas I. Cook's *History of political philosophy from Plato to Burke* (1936). Marius Roustan's *Pioneers of the French Revolution*, translated by F. Whyte (1926), is a lucid and lively account of the influence of the philosophes. Daniel Mornet's *Les origines intellectuelles de la révolution française, 1715–1787* (1933) is a vast mine of facts, but lacks integration and is not easy reading. A second important work by the same author is *French thought in the eighteenth century*, translated by L. M. Levin (1929), an able treatment of the rise and spread of liberal ideas. For further references the student may consult the excellent bibliographical article by Louis Gottschalk, "Studies since 1920 of French thought in the period of the enlightenment," *Journal of modern history*, vol. 4 (1932), pp. 242–260.

Voltaire. There is no definitive study of Voltaire. The most detailed biography is Gustave Desnoiresterres' *Voltaire et la société française au 18ᵉ siècle* (8 vols., 1867–76). A good shorter biography in French is that by Gustave Lanson (1910). In English there is a reasonably good life by S. G. Tallentyre (pseudonym of Evelyn B. Hall) (3rd ed., 1910). The same author has also translated a selection from the correspondence of Voltaire under the title *Voltaire in his letters* (1919). An admirable brief life of Voltaire is that by Henry N. Brailsford (1935; Home university library). André Maurois' brief life of Voltaire, translated from the French by H. Miles (1935), is informative and amusing. Norman L. Torrey's *The spirit of Voltaire* (1938) is a penetrating study. John Morley's *Voltaire* (1871; reprints) has been largely superseded. Useful for the formative period of his life is John C. Collins' *Voltaire, Montesquieu and Rousseau in England* (1908). Richard Aldington's *Voltaire* (1925) is an excellent guide to his writings. Alfred Noyes' *Voltaire* (1936) is an attempt "to popularize Voltaire's religiosity"; it does not carry conviction. A sound and scholarly study of Voltaire's religious ideas and their origins is Norman L. Torrey's *Voltaire and the English deists* (1930). The same author has also published a short book of selections from Voltaire's writings entitled *Voltaire and the enlightenment* (1931) to illustrate Voltaire's views on toleration. Margaret S. Libby's *The attitude of Voltaire to magic and the sciences* (1935) presents a detailed analysis of his ideas and writings on science. For further references the student may consult Mary M. H. Barr's *Bibliography of writings on Voltaire, 1825–1925* (1929). A supplement to this book is the same author's bibliographical article, "Bibliographical data on Voltaire from 1926 to 1930," *Modern language notes*, vol. 48 (1933), pp. 292–307. There is a more recent review article of literature on Voltaire by Raymond O. Rockwood, *Journal of modern history*, vol. 9 (1937), pp. 493–501.

Rousseau. The publication of the correspondence of Rousseau in twenty volumes, edited by T. Dufour and Pierre-Paul Plan (1924–34), more than doubled the number of Rousseau's letters easily available to scholars. Charles W. Hendel has translated a selection of these letters under the title *Citizen of Geneva; selections from the letters of Jean-Jacques Rousseau* (1937), with an introductory essay which presents a reappraisal of Rousseau on the basis of his correspondence. More recently Robert B. Mowat has published a longer study of the personality and life of the great philosophe, entitled *Jean-Jacques Rousseau* (1938), in the preparation of which he has used the correspondence to supplement and, what is more important, to correct the *Confessions*. From these two studies a Rousseau emerges who is less anomalous than the traditional Rousseau. In the light of them John Morley's *Rousseau* (2 vols., 1873; reprints) becomes so antiquated as to be almost valueless. A reasonably good account of the teachings of Rousseau is to be found in Matthew Josephson's *Rousseau* (1931). Ernest H. Wright has written an admirable little book entitled *The meaning of Rousseau* (1929), which attempts to discover Rousseau's real intentions. More comprehensive accounts of the development of Rousseau's thought are Charles W. Hendel's *Rousseau, moralist* (2 vols., 1934) and A. Schinz's *La pensée de J. J. Rousseau: essai d'interprétation nouvelle* (2 vols., 1929). Another revealing book is Harald Höffding's *Rousseau and his philosophy*, translated from the Danish by William Richards and Leo E. Saidla (1930). There are able discussions of Rousseau's political concepts in Thomas I. Cook's *History of political philosophy from Plato to Burke* (1936) and W. A. Dunning's *History of political theories from Rousseau to Spencer* (1920). An excellent English edition of the political writings of Rousseau is Charles E. Vaughan's *The political writings of Rousseau* (2 vols., 1915). Alfred Cobban has written a penetrating study entitled *Rousseau and the modern state* (1934). There is a handy edition of the *Social contract* in the Everyman series with an interpretive introduction by G. D. H. Cole. Translations of the other writings of Rousseau are also available. Thomas Davidson's *Rousseau and education according to nature* (1907) is a useful account of Rousseau's ideas on education. The idea of the natural man is treated in H. N. Fairchild's *The noble savage, a study in romantic idealism* (1928).

Other philosophes. There is an excellent short analysis of Montesquieu's thought in Kingsley Martin's *French liberal thought in the eighteenth century*

(1929), pp. 147–170, and in *The social and political ideas of some great French thinkers of the age of reason*, edited by F. J. C. Hearnshaw (1930). Montesquieu's political ideas are competently treated in Thomas I. Cook's *History of political philosophy* (1936), pp. 580–608, and Charles E. Vaughan's *Studies in the history of political philosophy*, edited by A. G. Little, vol. 1 (1925), pp. 253–302. Albert Sorel's *Montesquieu*, translated by M. B. and E. P. Anderson (1888), is an excellent longer analysis. John Morley's *Diderot and the encyclopaedists* (2 vols., 1886) is still useful. There are informative essays on Diderot and D'Alembert in S. G. Tallentyre's *The friends of Voltaire* (1907). Havelock Ellis wrote a readable and stimulating essay on Diderot which is to be found in *The new spirit* (4th ed., 1926; other editions). There are good biographies of Diderot and D'Alembert in French in the series *Les grands écrivains français*. J. Salwyn Schapiro's *Condorcet and the rise of liberalism* (1934) is a sound, penetrating, and well-written analysis of Condorcet's ideas and their influence. W. H. Wickwar's *Baron d'Holbach* (1935) treats in concise fashion a much neglected figure.

Physiocrats. There is a lucid brief discussion of the Physiocrats and their ideas in chapter one of Charles Gide and Charles Rist's *History of economic doctrines*, translated by R. Richards (1915). A useful longer account is Henry Higgs' *Physiocrats, six lectures on the French économistes of the eighteenth century* (1897). There are two valuable studies in French by G. Weulersse, *Le mouvement physiocratique en France de 1756 à 1770* (1910) and *Les physiocrates* (1931). Mario Einaudi's *The physiocratic doctrine of judicial control*, with an introduction by C. H. McIlwain (1938), is a valuable special study. Leon Say's *Turgot*, translated by M. B. Anderson (1888)—there is another translation by G. Masson (1888)—gives a good account of his administrative work as an expression of Physiocrat ideas.

CHAPTER TWENTY-FOUR

The Beginning of the French Revolution

General studies. Leo Gershoy's *French revolution, 1789–1799* (1935; Berkshire series) is a readable brief summary. The same author's *French revolution and Napoleon* (1933) is a clearly written, scholarly survey. Another good survey is Louis Gottschalk's *Era of the French revolution* (1929). Other useful volumes are H. E. Bourne's *The revolutionary period in Europe* (1914) and J. H. Rose's *The revolutionary and Napoleonic era* (7th ed., 1935). Crane Brinton's *A decade of revolution, 1789–1799* (1934; vol. 12 of *The rise of modern Europe*, edited by W. L. Langer) is judicious, readable, and up-to-date. Albert Mathiez' *French revolution* (1928) and *After Robespierre, the thermidorean reaction* (1931), both translated by Catherine A. Phillips, are two notable volumes by a distinguished scholar interpreting the Revolution in terms of a class struggle. L. Madelin's *French revolution*, translated from the French (1916), is well-written but disfigured by a Bonapartist party bias. Useful shorter accounts of the political history of the Revolution are E. D. Bradby's *French revolution* (1926) and S. Mathew's *French revolution* (rev. ed., 1923). A. Aulard's *French revolution, a political history*, translated from the French by B. Miall (4 vols., 1910), is a standard work. Charles D. Hazen's *French revolution* (2 vols., 1932) is a detailed, well-written account. An older work, Henry M. Stephens' *History of the French revolution* (2 vols., 1902), presents a detailed treatment of internal affairs to 1793, but is often uncritical in its conclusions. The classic *French revolution* by Thomas Carlyle, first published in 1837, still has a certain value despite its shortcomings, but should be read in the edition of J. H. Rose (3 vols., 1902) or in that of C. R. L. Fletcher (3 vols., 1902). Pierre Gaxotte's *French revolution*, translated by Catherine A. Phillips (1932), is a popular history with a strong leaning toward fiction. Valuable accounts of the French Revolution are to be found in such coöperative works as the *Cambridge modern history*, vol. 8 (1907), and *Histoire de France contemporaine*, edited by E. Lavisse, vols. 1 and 2 (1920). An authoritative up-to-date work in French for more advanced reading is *La révolution française*, by G. Lefebvre, R. Guyot, and P. Sagnac (1930; vol. 13 of *Peuples et civilisation*). For further references the student will find helpful H. E. Bourne's bibliographical article, "A decade of studies in the French revolution," *Journal of modern history*, vol. 1 (1929), pp. 256–279; also the *Guide to historical literature*, edited by W. H. Allison, S. B. Fay, A. H. Shearer, and H. R. Shipman. There are also excellent annotated bibliographies in L. Gershoy's *French revolution and Napoleon* and C. Brinton's *Decade of revolution*.

Source books and memoirs. E. L. Higgins' *The French revolution as told by contemporaries* (1938) is an excellent collection of documents and excerpts from the sources, all translated into English. Another valuable book is Frank M. Anderson's *The constitutions and other select documents illustrative of the history of France, 1789–1907* (2nd ed., 1908). A useful collection in the original French is L. G. W. Legg's *Select documents of the French revolution* (2 vols., 1905). H. M. Stephens' *Principal speeches of the statesmen and orators of the French revolution, 1789–1795* (2 vols., 1892) presents the speeches in the original French with an English introduction. Useful for the court life of the nobles are the *Memoirs of Madame Campan*, edited by J. H. Rose (2 vols., 1917). Gouverneur Morris' *Diary of the French revolution*, edited by B. C. Davenport (2 vols., 1939), presents a lively account covering the years 1789–1793. Other useful memoirs are those of Lafayette, Talleyrand, Bailly, Lally-Tollendal, and Barère.

Special studies. The attempts at reform during the first part of Louis XVI's reign are ably summarized in the early chapters of A. Mathiez' *French revolution*. There is a good account of the activities of Turgot in Eleanor Lodge's *Sully, Colbert and Turgot* (1931). Another useful work is *The life and writings of Turgot*, edited by W. W. Stephens (1895). A good brief summary of the question of finances is to be found in the *Cambridge modern history*, vol. 8 (1907), pp. 66–78. In the same volume (pp. 79–118) there is also a good brief survey of the attempts at reform. Saul K. Padover's *Life and death of Louis XVI* (1939) is a readable biography based on a considerable study of the sources. The two volumes by Nesta H. Webster, *Louis XVI and Marie Antoinette before the revolution* (1936) and *Louis XVI and Marie*

Antoinette during the revolution (1937) are an enthusiastic defense of Louis XVI
and Marie Antoinette based on the fantastic idea that "the French Revolution was due to the machinations of the Freemasons"—can hardly be classed
as serious history. Hilaire Belloc's *Marie Antoinette* (2nd ed., 1924) is a competent sympathetic study. Katharine Anthony's *Marie Antoinette* (1933) is a
readable popular life. J. B. Morton's *The dauphin* (1937) presents the recorded facts dealing with the son of Marie Antoinette. Fred M. Fling's
The youth of Mirabeau (1908) not only explains the development of Mirabeau's character but also contains much information on the provincial nobility. P. F. Willert's *Mirabeau* (1898) is a useful short life. An excellent
biography in French is L. Barthou's *Mirabeau* (1914). There is also a good
biography in German by Alfred Stern, entitled *Das Leben Mirabeaus* (2 vols.,
1889). On the early period of Lafayette's life there are the two scholarly
volumes by Louis Gottschalk, listed in the bibliography for Chapter Twenty-
two. The best full biography is É. Charavay's *Le général La Fayette, 1757–
1834* (1898). A number of popular biographies of Lafayette have appeared in
recent years, including those by H. D. Sedgwick (1928), Brand Whitlock
(2 vols., 1929), J. S. Penman (1929), M. de la Bedoyère (1933), and A. A.
Latzko (1936); of varying merit, they are all popular accounts, and contribute little that is new. There is an excellent review article of books on
Lafayette by Louis Gottschalk in *Journal of modern history*, vol. 2 (1930),
pp. 281–287. For a fuller bibliography there is *Lafayette, a bibliography*, compiled by Stuart W. Jackson (1930), which was published only in a limited
edition. G. G. van Deusen's *Sieyès: his life and his nationalism* (1933) is a
valuable scholarly study. The best life of Talleyrand is that by G. Lacour-
Gayet (4 vols., 1928–34)—in French. There is a readable brief life of Talleyrand in English by Duff Cooper (1933) which presents the French statesman
in too favorable a light. Crane Brinton's *The lives of Talleyrand* (1936) is
interesting. John M. S. Allison's *Malesherbes* (1938) presents the career of a
figure who is representative of the *noblesse de la robe*. J. M. Whitham's *Biographical history of the French revolution* (1931) and *Men and women of the
French revolution* (1933) contain some excellent pen pictures of the leading
figures. Other lively and informative works of the same nature are J. M.
Thompson's *Leaders of the French revolution* (1929), L. Madelin's *Figures of
the revolution*, translated by Richard Curtis (1929), and Henri Béraud's
Twelve portraits of the French revolution, translated by Madeleine Boyd
(1928). A useful older work is W. W. Stephens' *Women of the French revolution* (1912).

Estates-General and cahiers. Mitchell B. Garrett's *The estates general
of 1789: the problems of composition and organization* (1935) is an invaluable
study. There is an informative short study by George G. Andrews entitled
"Double representation and vote by head before the French revolution,"
in *South Atlantic quarterly*, vol. 26 (1927), pp. 373–391. Interesting sidelights
on the National Assembly are to be found in C. L. Benson's "How the
French deputies were paid in 1789–1791," *Journal of modern history*, vol. 5
(1933), pp. 19–33. Beatrice F. Hyslop's *Guide to the general cahiers of 1789*
(1936) and *French nationalism in 1789 according to the general cahiers* (1934)
are two valuable studies. An informative short study is Boyd C. Shafer's

"Bourgeois nationalism in the pamphlets on the eve of the French revolution," *Journal of modern history*, vol. 10 (1938), pp. 31–50.

Special studies. There is a good brief summary of the economic policies of the revolutionary period in Shepard B. Clough's *France: a history of national economics, 1789–1939* (1939), pp. 31–59. For a good short account of the assignats see Ralph H. Hawtrey's *Currency and credit* (3rd ed., 1928), pp. 297–319. The definitive longer account is S. E. Harris' *The assignats* (1930). A notable work on one phase of the economic conditions is Frederick L. Nussbaum's *Commercial policy in the French revolution: a study of the career of G. J. A. Ducher* (1923). The most valuable and comprehensive study of the peasants and their problems is Georges Lefebvre's *Les paysans du Nord pendant la révolution française* (2 vols., 1924). A good account of the events preceding August 4 is to be found in Sydney Herbert's *The fall of feudalism in France* (1921). G. Lefebvre's *La grande peur de 1789* (1932) is the best study on the subject; detailed and comprehensive. The subject is briefly treated by Louis Gottschalk in "The peasant in the French revolution," *Political science quarterly*, vol. 48 (1933), pp. 589–599. The best account of the September massacres is Pierre Caron's *Les massacres de septembre* (1935). For a brief account in English the student may consult L. Gershoy's *French revolution and Napoleon* or A. Mathiez' *French revolution*. W. M. Sloane's *The French revolution and religious reform* (1901) is a good account of the subject. In French there is A. Mathiez' *La révolution et l'église* (1910). H. B. Hill's "The constitutions of continental Europe: 1789–1813," *Journal of modern history*, vol. 8 (1936), pp. 82–94, is an excellent bibliographical article. The standard work on the military history of the French Revolution to 1793 is A. Chuquet's *Les guerres de la révolution* (11 vols., 1886–96). J. H. Clapham's *The causes of the war of 1792* (1899) is a lucid piece of work. L. B. Pfeiffer's *The uprising of June 20, 1792* (1913) is a competent study.

The Revolution outside France. There is a good brief survey of the effect of the revolutionary ideas on the mind of Europe in the *Cambridge modern history*, vol. 8 (1907), pp. 754–790. The same volume contains other valuable chapters on the various European countries. A good survey in French is to be found in vol. 8 (1896) of *Histoire générale*, edited by E. Lavisse and A. Rambaud. Two longer classic works are H. von Sybel's *Geschichte der Revolutionszeit* (10 vols., rev. ed., 1897–1900) and A. Sorel's *L'Europe et la révolution française* (8 vols., 1895–1904). The former has been translated into English by W. C. Perry under the title *History of the French revolution* (4 vols., 1867–79). H. M. Stephens' *Europe, 1789–1815* (1893) is crammed with facts but somewhat out-of-date. The gradual dissolution of feudalism throughout Europe is treated in Henri Doniol's *La révolution française et la féodalité* (2nd ed., 1876). For England and Russia see the bibliography for Chapters Twenty-one and Twenty. George P. Gooch's *Germany and the French revolution* (1920) traces the effect of the French Revolution on the thinkers and writers of Germany. A valuable study in German is Alfred Stern's *Der Einfluss der französischen Revolution auf das deutsche Geistesleben* (1928). For Holland there is L. Legrand's *La révolution française en Hollande* (1895). Valuable for the American reaction to the French Revolution is C. D. Hazen's *American opinion of the French revolution* (1897).

CHAPTER TWENTY-FIVE

The First French Republic

For general accounts of the period see the bibliography for the preceding chapter.

Special studies. Crane Brinton's *The Jacobins* (1930) is interesting and informative. Another lively account of the Jacobins is that by E. S. Scudder (1936). There is an excellent short discussion of Jacobin nationalism in C. J. H. Hayes' *Historical evolution of modern nationalism* (1931), pp. 43–83. George G. Andrews' "Making the revolutionary calendar," *American historical review*, vol. 36 (1931), pp. 515–532, is an informative short study. W. B. Kerr's *The reign of terror* (1927) is a competent account by a disciple of Mathiez. A notable shorter study is Donald Greer's *The incidence of the terror during the French revolution: a statistical interpretation* (1935). G. Lefebvre's *Les thermidoriens* (1937) is a clearly written brief account by a distinguished scholar. A. Goodwin's "The French executive directory: a revaluation," *History*, vol. 22 (1938), pp. 201–218, is a notable article. For the military history of the period there is the valuable series of studies by R. W. Phipps, *The armies of the first French republic and the rise of the marshals of Napoleon* (4 vols., 1926–35). A valuable study of a much neglected subject is A. T. Mahan's *Influence of sea power on the French revolution and empire, 1793–1812* (6th ed., 1895). Samuel Bernstein's "Babeuf and babouvism," *Science and society*, vol. 2 (1937), pp. 29–57, 166–194, is a spirited short account based on a first-hand study of the sources. Ernest B. Bax's *The last episode of the French revolution* (1911) is an older popular account of Babeuf and his movement written from a socialist viewpoint.

Biographical studies. Reginald S. Ward's *Robespierre* (1934) is one of the best of the many biographies of the revolutionary leader. A longer biography of Robespierre is that by J. M. Thompson (2 vols., 1935), written in the tradition of Mathiez. A useful one-volume study is that by H. Belloc (1901). The most readable life of Danton is that by L. Madelin (1914), but it is not altogether sound. A. Mathiez' studies of Danton are hostile to their subject. Useful older lives of Danton are those by H. Belloc (1899) and A. H. Beesly (1899). Louis Gottschalk's *Marat* (1927) is a penetrating analysis of the man and his ideas. There are two excellent biographies of Saint-Just, a shorter one by Geoffrey Bruun (1932) and a fuller one by Eugene N. Curtis (1936). C. Young's *A lady who loved herself* (1930) is a reasonably good study of Madame Roland. J. S. Schapiro's *Condorcet* (1934) has previously been cited.

Literature and art. For a general account of the literature of the period the student may consult the histories of literature listed in the bibliography for Chapter Eighteen. There is a good brief essay on Chénier the poet in John C. Bailey's *The claims of French poetry* (1909), pp. 147–173. A good biography of Chénier in French is that by E. Faguet (1902; *Grands écrivains français*). An excellent account of the beginnings of romanticism is M. B. Finch and E. A. Peers' *The origins of French romanticism* (1920). R. McNair

Wilson's *Germaine de Staël* (1931) is a spirited somewhat unsympathetic biography, based on a study of the sources. Margaret Goldsmith's *Madame de Staël* (1938) is a readable brief sketch of the part Madame de Staël played in the French Revolution and in the Napoleonic period. Another useful life is Andrew C. Haggard's *Madame de Staël, her trials and triumphs* (1922). There is also the older life by the eminent historian Albert Sorel, translated by Fanny H. Gardiner (1891). For an informative essay on Chateaubriand see Irving Babbitt's *Masters of modern French criticism* (1912), pp. 60–78. André Maurois' *Chateaubriand*, translated by Vera Fraser (1938), is an interestingly written popular biography. Two simple and readable handbooks on French painting are C. H. Caffin's *Story of French painting* (1911) and P. G. Konody and X. Latham's *Introduction to French painting* (1932). W. R. Valentiner's *David and the French revolution* (1929) is an illuminating short study. For general accounts of Spanish painting see the bibliography for Chapter Ten. Albert F. Calvert's *Goya* (1908) is a useful brief life, profusely illustrated. A fuller biography is that by Charles Poore (1938).

Early period of Napoleon's life. Oscar Browning's *Napoleon, the first phase 1769–1793* (1905), which appeared in a revised edition as *Boyhood and youth of Napoleon* (1906), is a readable and scholarly study. Bonaparte's life up to the capture of Toulon is related in a detailed and skilful manner in Arthur Chuquet's *La jeunesse de Napoléon* (3 vols., 1897–99). An authoritative account by an admirer of Napoleon is Albert Vandal's *L'avènement de Bonaparte* (2 vols., 1902–07). Norwood Young's *The growth of Napoleon* (1910) is an attempt to explain him on the basis of environment; interesting but not always sound. Spenser Wilkinson's *The rise of Napoleon Bonaparte* (1930) is a valuable study of Napoleon's military ideas and their sources. *Bonaparte's adventures in Egypt*, by P. G. Elgood (1931), is a competent account by a student of military affairs.

CHAPTER TWENTY-SIX

The Napoleonic Era

General studies. In addition to the general surveys cited in the bibliography for the preceding chapter the student will find brief summaries of the various movements and events of the period in the *Cambridge modern history*, vol. 9 (1918), the *Histoire générale*, vol. 9 (1897), and the *Histoire de France contemporaine*, edited by E. Lavisse, vol. 3 (1921). Notable among the better biographies of Napoleon are A. Fournier's *Napoleon the First*, translated by M. B. Corwin and A. D. Bissell and edited by E. G. Bourne (1903), and J. H. Rose's *Life of Napoleon the First* (2 vols. in one, 11th ed., 1934). The more recent brilliant life of Napoleon by Jacques Bainville, translated from the French by Hamish Miles (1932), seeks to explain rather than narrate the events of his life. F. M. Kircheisen's *Napoleon*, translated by Henry S. Lawrence (1931), is an admirably balanced account by an eminent specialist; one of the best biographies of Napoleon in English. An outstanding one-volume biography in French is Georges Lefebvre's *Napoléon* (1935). Eugene Tarlé's *Bonaparte*, translated from the Russian by John Cournos (1937), is a study by a Marxist historian, but good enough to find a place among the better English biographies of Napoleon. A longer popular work by an American historian is William M. Sloane's *Life of Napoleon Bonaparte* (4 vols., 4th rev. ed., 1915); also an edition with an introduction by H. W. Van Loon (2 vols., 1939). George G. Andrews' *Napoleon in review* (1939) presents a review of aspects and characteristics of the man; readable and suggestive. One of the most widely circulated popular biographies of Napoleon is that by Emil Ludwig, translated by Eden and Cedar Paul (1926), an attempt at a psychological interpretation; stimulating, but not always accurate. There are also useful brief accounts by R. M. Johnston (1904; reprints) and H. A. L. Fisher (1912; Home university library). R. M. Johnston's *The Corsican* (1910) presents "a diary of Napoleon's life in his own words." A similar work is F. M. Kircheisen's *Napoleon's autobiography, the personal memoirs of Bonaparte compiled from his own letters and diaries*, translated by F. Collins (1931). A. L. Guérard's *Reflections on the Napoleonic legend* (1923) is a good antidote for extravagant hero worship. Walter Geer's *Napoleon and his family* (3 vols., 1927-29) is an able treatment. The same author also wrote two painstaking and interesting volumes entitled *Napoleon and Josephine* (1925) and *Napoleon and Marie-Louise* (1925). There is a handy selection of 300 of Napoleon's letters entitled *Napoleon self-revealed*, translated and edited by J. M. Thompson (1934). Louis Madelin's *The consulate and the empire*, translated by E. F. Buckby (2 vols., 1934), is well-written but suffers from an excessive admiration of Napoleon. Hubert N. Richardson's *Dictionary of Napoleon and his times* (1921) is a useful one-volume reference work. For further references the student may consult the excellent review article by George M. Dutcher, "Napoleon and the Napoleonic period," *Journal of modern history*, vol. 4 (1932), pp. 446-462; also the *Guide to historical literature*, previously mentioned.

Special studies. Henry H. Walsh's *The concordat of 1801: a study of the problem of nationalism in the relations of church and state* (1933) is an illuminating study. The story of the Legion of Honor is interestingly told in *Napoleon's legion*, by W. F. Paris (1928). E. Gabory's *Napoléon et la Vendée* (1914) is a notable work. An excellent treatment of the military campaigns is to be found in J. H. Rose's biography of Napoleon. The best longer treatment in English is T. A. Dodge's *Napoleon, a history of the art of war, from the beginning of the French revolution to the battle of Waterloo* (4 vols., 1904-07). Sir Charles Oman's *Studies in Napoleonic wars* (1929) is illuminating. A. T. Mahan's *The influence of sea power upon the French revolution and the empire* (2 vols., 14th ed., 1919) is useful but overemphasizes the importance of sea power. Harold C. Deutsch's "Napoleonic policy and the project of a descent upon England," *Journal of modern history*, vol. 2 (1930), pp. 541-568, is a competent brief study of the subject.

Economic history. There is a good brief summary of Napoleon's economic policies in Shepard B. Clough's *France: a history of national economics, 1789-1939* (1939), pp. 60-90. E. Levasseur's *Histoire du commerce en France*, vol. 2 (1912), *Histoire des classes ouvrières et de l'industrie en France depuis*

1789 à 1870, vol. 1 (rev. ed., 1903), and *Histoire du commerce de la France*, vol. 2 (1912) are important studies covering the economic history of the period. The best account in English of the economic blockade is Eli F. Heckscher's *The continental system; an economic interpretation* (1922). Broader in its scope and equally useful is *Napoleon's navigation system*, by Frank E. Melvin (1919). E. Tarlé's *Le blocus continental et le royaume d'Italie* (new ed., 1931) traces the effect of the continental system on the commerce and industry of Italy.

Diplomacy, international relations, and imperialism. The currents of international politics are clearly described in Geoffrey Bruun's *Europe and the French imperium* (1938; vol. 13 of *The rise of modern Europe*, edited by W. L. Langer). R. B. Mowat's *The diplomacy of Napoleon* (1924) is a lucid, impartial, and comprehensive treatment of Napoleon's conduct of foreign affairs from Campo Formio to his second abdication. *The genesis of Napoleonic imperialism*, by Harold C. Deutsch (1938), is a sound and clearly written treatment of Napoleon's diplomacy during the period 1800–1805. H. Butterfield's *The peace treaties of Napoleon, 1806–1808* (1929) is a scholarly and penetrating monograph. Paul F. Shupp's *The European powers and the near eastern question, 1806–1807* (1931) is an able study of a difficult problem. On the colonial question there is Carl L. Lokke's excellent short article, "French dreams of colonial empire under the directory and the consulate," *Journal of modern history*, vol. 2 (1930), pp. 237–250. The same author's longer study, *France and the colonial question: a study of contemporary French opinion, 1763–1801* (1932) is an interesting account of French thought during those years. Useful and comprehensive is E. W. Lyon's *Louisiana in French diplomacy, 1759–1804* (1934). P. H. Giddens' "Contemporary American opinion of Napoleon," *Journal of American history*, vol. 26 (1932), pp. 189–204, is a notable short study. For Napoleon's relations with Switzerland the student may consult W. Oechsli's excellent *History of Switzerland, 1499–1914*, translated by Eden and Cedar Paul (1922). For the Dutch Netherlands there is a readable and scholarly account in P. J. Blok's *History of the people of the Netherlands*, vol. 5 (1912).

England. An excellent brief treatment of the relations between Napoleon and England is J. H. Rose's "The contest with Napoleon," *Cambridge history of British foreign policy*, vol. 1 (1922), pp. 309–391. A more comprehensive treatment is to be found in P. Coquelle's *Napoléon et l'Angleterre* (1904). For the last years of the period C. K. Webster's *British diplomacy, 1813–1815* (1921) is an indispensable guide. F. J. MacCunn's *The contemporary English view of Napoleon* (1914) is a useful volume. Valuable for the economic history of the period is A. Cunningham's *British credit in the last Napoleonic war* (1910). W. F. Galpin's *The grain supply of England during the Napoleonic period* (1925) attempts to show that Britain's supposed shortage of grain was relatively illusory. For further references see the bibliography for Chapter Twenty-one.

Italy. For a general survey see the histories of Italy listed in the bibliography for Chapter One. The first part of Pietro Orsi's *Modern Italy, 1748–1922* (3rd rev. ed., 1923) offers a popular account of the period. Robert M. Johnston's *The Napoleonic empire in southern Italy and the rise of the secret* *societies* (2 vols., 1904) is an interesting study of the Two Sicilies during this period. The extinction of the Venetian state by Napoleon is ably treated in George B. McClellan's *Venice and Bonaparte* (1931), with excellent chapters on the political, economic, and social life of Venice in the eighteenth century. A valuable work in French is Louis Madelin's *La Rome de Napoléon: la domination française à Rome de 1809 à 1814* (1906).

Reorganization of Germany. F. Meinecke's *Das Zeitalter der deutschen Erhebung, 1795–1815* (1913) is the best survey of the period. A good account in English of the extension of French ideas to Germany is H. A. L. Fisher's *Studies in Napoleonic statesmanship, Germany* (1903). Still useful, though outdated in many respects, is J. R. Seeley's *Life of Stein* (3 vols., 1879). Guy S. Ford's *Stein and the era of reform in Prussia, 1807–1815* (1922) contains a good account of the German minister and his work. Another valuable study by the same author is *Hanover and Prussia, 1795–1803; a study in neutrality* (1903). *Napoleon's nemesis; the life of Baron Stein* by Constantin de Grunwald, translated from the French by C. F. Atkinson (1936), is a good short biography based on a first-hand study of the sources. Reinhold Aris' *History of political thought in Germany from 1789 to 1815* (1936) is a comprehensive survey but lacks clarity and spirit. Valuable for the rise of a national spirit is Alfred G. Pundt's *Arndt and the nationalist awakening of Germany* (1936). For Austria there is Walter C. Langsam's scholarly monograph, *The Napoleonic wars and German nationalism in Austria* (1930). The end of the Holy Roman Empire is treated in H. von Srbik's scholarly account, *Das österreichische Kaisertum und das Ende des heiligen römischen Reiches, 1804–1806* (1927).

Spain. Brief surveys of the period are to be found in the histories of Spain listed in the bibliography for Chapter One. There is a useful account of the last years of the period in the first chapters of Robert Sencourt's *The Spanish crown, 1808–1931* (1932). For the war in Spain there is Sir Charles Oman's monumental *History of the Peninsular War* (7 vols., 1902–30). F. C. Beatson's *With Wellington in the Pyrenees* (1914) offers a shorter detailed account of military affairs. A good biography of Godoy is that by H. R. Madol, ably translated by G. D. H. Pidcock (1934). Two valuable works in French are A. Fugier's *Napoléon et l'Espagne* (2 vols., 1930) and G. de Grandmaison's *L'Espagne de Napoléon* (3 vols., 1908–31).

Russia. For a brief summary of Russian history during this period the student may consult the histories of Russia listed in the bibliography for Chapter Seventeen. There is a good brief summary of Russia under Alexander I and the invasion of 1812 in the *Cambridge modern history*, vol. 9 (1918), pp. 483–505. The period is also treated in A. A. Kornilov's interesting and lucid *Modern Russian history*, translated by Alexander S. Kaun, vol. 1 (1916). For economic history there is J. Mavor's *Economic history of Russia*, vol. 1 (2nd rev. ed., 1926). Two of K. Waliszewski's studies cover the period, *Paul the First of Russia*, translated from the French (1913), and *Le règne d'Alexandre Ier* (3 vols., 1923–25). There is a lively popular biography of Alexander I entitled *The enigmatic czar*, by Maurice Paleologue, translated by Edwin and Willa Muir (1938); informative but not always sound.

Last period of Napoleon's life. The military history is ably treated in the two works of Henri Houssaye, *Napoleon and the campaign of 1814*, translated by R. S. McClintock (1914), and *1815, Waterloo*, translated by A. E. Mann (1900); also by S. R. Willis (1905). John C. Ropes' *The campaign of Waterloo* (1892) is a reasonably sound popular account. A more recent study is A. F. Becke's *Napoleon and Waterloo, the emperor's campaign with the armée du nord, 1815* (1936); a competent account by an admirer of Napoleon. E. J. Knapton's "Some aspects of the Bourbon restoration of 1814," *Journal of modern history*, vol. 6 (1934), pp. 405–424, is an interesting and illuminating article. Franklin D. Scott's valuable study, *Bernadotte and the fall of Napoleon* (1936), traces the influence of Bernadotte on the fall of the emperor of the French. H. Houssaye's *The return of Napoleon*, translated by T. C. Macaulay (1934), is the work of a great military historian. Philip Guedalla's *The hundred days* (1934) is a lively account based on a study of the sources. *The fall of Napoleon*, by O. Browning (1907), is clearly written and authoritative. Philip Guedalla's *The duke* (1931) is a brilliant sketch of Wellington. Napoleon's exile at St. Helena and his place in history are brilliantly treated in Lord Rosebery's *Napoleon, the last phase* (1901). *Napoleon in captivity: the reports of Count Balmain*, translated and edited by Julian Park (1928), presents the impartial and well-written reports of the Russian commissioner to his government. There are a number of readable and informative biographies of Metternich in English including those by Arthur Herman (1932), Algernon Cecil (1933), and H. du Coudray (1935). Charles K. Webster's *Congress of Vienna, 1814–1815* (1920) is an authoritative and clearly written account of the congress and its work.

Rulers of European States

DENMARK

John, King, 1481–1513
Christian II, 1513–1523
Frederick I, 1523–1533
Christian III, 1533–1559
Frederick II, 1559–1588
Christian IV, 1588–1648
Frederick III, 1648–1670

Christian V, 1670–1699
Frederick IV, 1699–1730
Christian VI, 1730–1746
Frederick V, 1746–1766
Christian VII, 1766–1808
Frederick VI, 1808–1839

ENGLAND AND IRELAND

Henry VII, King, 1485–1509
Henry VIII, 1509–1547
Edward VI, 1547–1553

Mary I, 1553–1558
Elizabeth, 1558–1603

ENGLAND, IRELAND, AND SCOTLAND

James I (James VI of Scotland),
1603–1625
Charles I, 1625–1649
The Commonwealth, 1649–1660
(Oliver Cromwell)

Charles II, 1660–1685
James II (VII of Scotland), 1685–1688
William III and Mary II, 1689–1694
William III, 1694–1702

GREAT BRITAIN AND IRELAND

(after 1707)

Anne, 1702–1714
George I, 1714–1727

George II, 1727–1760
George III, 1760–1820

Appendix

FRANCE

Charles VII, King, 1422–1461
Louis XI, 1461–1483
Charles VIII, 1483–1498
Louis XII, 1498–1515
Francis I, 1515–1547
Henry II, 1547–1559
Francis II, 1559–1560
Charles IX, 1560–1574
Henry III, 1574–1589

Henry IV, 1589–1610
Louis XIII, 1610–1643
Louis XIV, 1643–1715
Louis XV, 1715–1774
Louis XVI, 1774–1792
First Republic, 1792–1804
Napoleon I, Emperor, 1804–1814
Louis XVIII, 1814–1824

HOLY ROMAN EMPIRE

Maximilian I, Emperor, 1493–1519
Charles V, 1519–1556
Ferdinand I, 1558–1564
Maximilian II, 1564–1576
Rudolph II, 1576–1612
Matthias, 1612–1619
Ferdinand II, 1619–1637
Ferdinand III, 1637–1657
Leopold I, 1658–1705

Joseph I, 1705–1711
Charles VI, 1711–1740
Charles VII, 1742–1745
Francis I, 1745–1765
Joseph II, 1765–1790
Leopold II, 1790–1792
Francis II, 1792–1806 (Francis I, Emperor of Austria, after 1804)

PAPACY

Pius II, Pope, 1458–1464
Paul II, 1464–1471
Sixtus IV, 1471–1484
Innocent VIII, 1484–1492
Alexander VI, 1492–1503
Pius III, 1503
Julius II, 1503–1513
Leo X, 1513–1521
Adrian VI, 1522–1523
Clement VII, 1523–1534
Paul III, 1534–1549
Julius III, 1550–1555
Marcellus II, 1555
Paul IV, 1555–1559
Pius IV, 1559–1565
Pius V, 1566–1572
Gregory XIII, 1572–1585
Sixtus V, 1585–1590
Urban VII, 1590
Gregory XIV, 1590–1591
Innocent IX, 1591

Clement VIII, 1592–1605
Leo XI, 1605
Paul V, 1605–1621
Gregory XV, 1621–1623
Urban VIII, 1623–1644
Innocent X, 1644–1655
Alexander VII, 1655–1667
Clement IX, 1667–1669
Clement X, 1670–1676
Innocent XI, 1676–1689
Alexander VIII, 1689–1691
Innocent XII, 1691–1700
Clement XI, 1700–1721
Innocent XIII, 1721–1724
Benedict XIII, 1724–1730
Clement XII, 1730–1740
Benedict XIV, 1740–1758
Clement XIII, 1758–1769
Clement XIV, 1769–1774
Pius VI, 1775–1799
Pius VII, 1800–1823

PORTUGAL

Emmanuel I, King, 1495–1521
John III, 1521–1557
Sebastian, 1557–1578
Henry, 1578–1580
Ruled from Spain, 1580–1640
John IV, 1640–1656

Alphonso VI, 1656–1667
Peter II, 1667–1706
John V, 1706–1750
Joseph, 1750–1777
Maria I and Peter III, 1777–1786
Maria I, 1786–1816

PRUSSIA

Frederick William, the Great Elector of Brandenburg, 1640–1688
Frederick III, of Brandenburg (Frederick I, King in Prussia, 1701–1713), 1688–1713

Frederick William I, King, 1713–1740
Frederick II (the Great), 1740–1786
Frederick William II, 1786–1797
Frederick William III, 1797–1840

RUSSIA

Ivan III, Tsar, 1462–1505
Basil IV, 1505–1533
Ivan IV (the Terrible), 1533–1584
Theodore I, 1584–1598
Boris Godunov, 1598–1605
Michael (Romanov), 1613–1645
Alexis, 1645–1676
Theodore II, 1676–1682
Ivan V and Peter I, 1682–1689
Peter I (the Great), 1689–1725

Catherine I, 1725–1727
Peter II, 1727–1730
Anna, 1730–1740
Ivan VI, 1740–1741
Elizabeth, 1741–1762
Peter III, 1762
Catherine II (the Great), 1762–1796
Paul, 1796–1801
Alexander I, 1801–1825

SPAIN

Ferdinand of Aragon, and Isabella of Castile, 1479–1504
Ferdinand, 1504–1516
Charles I (Emperor Charles V), 1516–1556
Philip II, 1556–1598
Philip III, 1598–1621
Philip IV, 1621–1665

Charles II, 1665–1700
Philip V (Philip of Anjou), 1700–1746
Ferdinand VI, 1746–1759
Charles III, 1759–1788
Charles IV, 1788–1808
Joseph Bonaparte, 1808–1813
Ferdinand VII, 1813–1833

SWEDEN

Gustavus I (Vasa), King, 1523–1560
Eric XIV, 1560–1568
John III, 1568–1592
Sigismund, 1592–1599 (King of Poland, 1587–1632)
Charles IX, 1599–1611
Gustavus II (Adolphus), 1611–1632
Christina, 1632–1654
Charles X, 1654–1660

Charles XI, 1660–1697
Charles XII, 1697–1718
Ulrica Eleonora, 1718–1720
Frederick I, 1720–1751
Adolphus Frederick, 1751–1771
Gustavus III, 1771–1792
Gustavus IV, 1792–1809
Charles XIII, 1809–1818

UNITED PROVINCES

William I (the Silent), Stadtholder, 1581–1584

Maurice, 1584–1625

Frederick Henry, 1625–1647

William II, 1647–1650

John DeWitt, Grand Pensionary, 1650–1672

William III, Stadtholder, 1672–1702

(King of England and Scotland, 1689–1702)

William IV, 1711–1751

William V, 1751–1795

Republic, 1795–1806

Louis Bonaparte, King, 1806–1810

Annexed to France, 1810–1813

William I, King, 1813–1840

Index

ICELAND

A T L A N T I C   O C E A N

FAROE
ISLAND

SHETLAND
ISLANDS

BRITISH ISLES

Central
Plain

Central
Plain

Loire R.

Seine R.

PLAIN OF FRANCE

Rhine R.

Danube R.

CARPATHIAN

Rhone R.

A L P S

Hungarian
Plain

Danube R.

Wallachian
Plain

PYRENEES

Douro R.

Sierra Morena

I B E R I A N

Tagus R.

PENINSULA

Sierra Nevada

BALEARIC IS.

CORSICA

A P E N N I N E S

ITALIAN PENINSULA

ADRIATIC SEA

BALKAN MTS.

BALKAN
PENINSULA

B

TAB
ASIA

SARDINIA

M E D I T E R R A N E A N

SICILY

AEGEAN SEA

ATLAS MTS.

ALGERIAN PLATEAUS

ALGERIAN SAHARA

S A H A R A

CRETE

S E A

LIBYAN DESERT

Tibesti Highlands

Physical Features of
EUROPE

Forests chiefly
of Conifers

Steppes, Scrub,
and Semi-Desert

Easily Cultivated Soils
with Mixed Woods

Desert

Scale of Miles

0   200   400   600   800